AUTHOR

Hilary Bradt's career as an occupational therapist ended when potential employers noticed that the time taken off for travel exceeded the periods of employment. With her husband George, she self-published her first guidebook in 1974 during an extended journey through South America. As well as running Bradt Travel Guides Hilary worked for 25 years as a tour leader in South America and Africa, and latterly in Madagascar which she has visited almost every year since 1982. Her in-depth knowledge of the country has brought her lecture engagements at the Royal Geographical Society, the Smithsonian Institution and on board expedition cruise ships, as well as numerous commissions for travel articles.

AUTHOR STORY

In 1975 I attended a slide show in Cape Town given by a zoo collector who had just returned from a country called Madagascar. By the end of the evening I knew I had to go there. It wasn't just the lemurs, it was the utter otherness of this little-known island that entranced me. So I went, and I fell in love, and I've been returning ever since.

Madagascar has brought me the best of times and the worst of times. I have exalted at the discovery of some of the strangest creatures in the world, laughed at the dancing sifakas and gushed over baby lemurs; I have snorkelled over multicoloured coral and watched a lobster make its cautious way over the seabed; I have made the only footprints on a deserted beach overhung with coconut palms and swum in the sand-warmed sea in the moonlight. I have also endured the misery of 14-hour taxi-brousse journeys, the exhausting heat of the lowlands and the unexpectedly cold nights in the highlands. And I have been lost in the rainforest for four days and eaten roasted insects. I have also been robbed several times. Yet all I remember are the good times. Even the insects – treehoppers belonging to the Fulgoridae family if you must know – were tasty! A few years ago someone wrote to me: 'I went for the lemurs, but in the end it's the people I'll remember.' Me too. This is one of the poorest countries in the world, yet the overriding impression is of joy and laughter.

I can hardly remember a time when I wasn't writing this biennial guide. Although the first edition was published in 1988, it was preceded in 1984 by a stapled booklet, A Glance at Madagascar, written for the handful of tour operators venturing to send visitors to this woefully haphazard country, then the No Frills Guide to Madagascar in 1986. It's a bit like my compost bin: layer is added to layer, the original material gets compressed but its goodness remains, and new matter is incorporated. The end product is, I hope, enriching, but it is never finished. There's always more to add.

Reprinted February 2008
Ninth edition July 2007   First published 1988
Bradt Travel Guides Ltd, 23 High Street, Chalfont St Peter, Bucks SL9 9QE, England.
www.bradtguides.com
Published in the USA by The Globe Pequot Press Inc, 246 Goose Lane,
PO Box 480, Guilford, Connecticut 06475-0480

ISBN-10: 1 84162 197 8   ISBN-13: 978 1 84162 197 5
British Library Cataloguing in Publication Data
A catalogue record for this book is available from the British Library

Photographs Daniel Austin (DA), Jim Bond (JB), Kate Booth (KB), Hilary Bradt (HB), Katie Fillion (KF), Nick Garbutt (NG), Gavin Hart (GH), Bill Love (BL), Dorothy Pooley (DP), Bryn Thomas (BT)
Front cover Coquerel's sifaka, Ankarafantsika (DA)
Back cover Parson's chameleon (NG), Malagasy child, Anakao (DA)
Title page Malagasy girls, Mahasoa (DA), Ring-tailed lemur (DA), Avenue of the Baobabs (DA)

Illustrations Janet Robinson, Carole Vincer (baobabs)
Maps Alan Whitaker
Typeset from the author's disc by Wakewing
Printed and bound in India by Nutech Photolithographer, New Delhi

FEEDBACK WANTED

One of the joys of publishing new editions of this guide is the chance to add readers' views on Madagascar as well as the all-important hard information on favourite hotels, restaurants, and travel off the beaten track. With the speed of change currently happening in Madagascar, this feedback is needed even more.

Whatever your experiences in Madagascar, irrespective of whether you travelled there independently or as part of an organised group, do write to tell me about it. Particularly welcome is hard information with accurately noted addresses and prices, and readers who include a map to show the location of their new find have me almost weeping with joy.

Whether you have loved Madagascar or hated it, I'd like to hear from you in time for the next edition which is scheduled for late 2009.

Happy travelling

Hilary Bradt

Bradt Travel Guides, 23 High Street, Chalfont St Peter, Bucks SL9 9QE, England;
✆ +44 (0)1753 893444; f +44 (0)1753 892333; www.bradtguides.com.

LEADING CONTRIBUTORS

DANIEL AUSTIN In 2006 I received 19 pages of impeccable update information along with six newly drawn maps from Daniel and his partner Kelly Green, following their six-month photographic expedition to Madagascar. A year and 1,720 emails later Daniel is my collaborator, editor, researcher and all-round quality-controller. His dedication to the job is demonstrated by one email that started 'Once more the arrival of the postman heralds the dawning of my bedtime'. Daniel is an accomplished photographer and a fanatic of all things Malagasy, especially the wildlife.

KELLY GREEN A zoologist with a special interest in the frogs of Madagascar, Kelly co-authored the new natural history chapter with Daniel. Marine zoology is one of her passions and she plans to explore Madagascar's reefs when she and Daniel return in 2008 to research the 10th edition of this guide.

UPDATERS

My thanks to **Ony Rakotoarivelo** and **Lorna Gillespie** for slogging round the hotels and – more pleasurably – the restaurants of Tana and Antsirabe. Also to **Mei-Ling McNamara** who did such a super job updating Taolagnaro that she has been commissioned to write the Bradt guide to Senegal. **Crystal Lynn Thompson** struggled with powercuts and unhelpful hoteliers to gather information on Toliara, and **Remi Doomernik** managed to tell me all the changes in Ambositra as well as helping to run a charity there. The same applies to **Kimberly Baldwin Radford**, who, with her husband Colin, runs the inspiring charity HELP in Toamasina; it's no coincidence that this section is one of the most detailed in the book. **Samantha Cameron** somehow fitted in the Fianarantsoa update in between her 24/7 job with Feedback Madagascar, and **Joanna Durbin** kept me abreast of changes in the protected areas despite an equally heavy workload for Durrell. A special thank you to various Peace Corps Volunteers for their valuable insiders' information; **Sheena Jones** laboriously texted me the news on Mananjary where she is posted, and **Sandra and Bobby O'Neil** did a terrific job on the Mahajanga area. Malagasy guide **Hery Andrianianfefana** stepped in with some badly-needed Ranomafana information, and finally, my old stalwart, **Derek Schuurman** of Rainbow Tours, kept up a constant flow of emails describing new tourism developments as well as writing boxes on his favourite subjects, birding and music.

EXPERT CONTRIBUTORS

I owe a huge debt to the specialists whose 'boxes' are found throughout this book. Most are conservationists, some are historians, others work in health care.

Well-known zoologists include **Alison Jolly**, **Nick Garbutt** (a big thank you to Nick for his mammals and lemurs sections), **Chris Birkinshaw**, **Jean Jacques Randriamanindry**, **Jonathan Ekstrom** (vasa parrots) and **Richard Jenkins** (bats). Specialists in invertebrates, **Jon Roff** and **Len de Beer** brought a new and fascinating dimension to the world of creepy crawlies, while botanists **Gavin Hart** and **Jim Bond** added their knowledge of succulents and baobabs. Travel medicine expert, **Jane Wilson Howarth**, updated her chapter on health, and **Gordon Rattray** added his tips on travel for people with disabilities. **Camilla Backhouse** wrote about hats and **Joseph Radaccia** enthused about lambas. **Jean Jacques Randriamanindry** wrote about the Antalaotra people, and once again historian **John Grehan** contributed his unique research into the role of Madagascar in World War Two.

Sometimes a reader writes in with such an unusual story, I ask him or her to describe the experience in a 'box'. My favourites are carried over from previous editions but new box-masters are **Marko Petrovic**, who continues to astonish me with his extraordinary adventures (if you can call nearly losing a leg an adventure) and following the theme tenuously, **Chris Howles** and **Peter Jourdier** describe their experiences as volunteers in Madagascar. Still on the adventure theme, there's **Kathryn Goodenough**'s achievement of accessing Anjanaharibe Sud 'the wrong way' and the tough bicycling trip of **Kailas Narendran** and **Katie Fillion** in the northeast. Another pair of cyclists, **Nina and Bill French**, provided loads of good cycling information as well as a description of the Fandrahasana sect. Then there are the gentle, heart-warming stories such as **Rupert Parker**'s anecdotes of eccentric Madagascar and **Lee Miller**'s evocative descriptions of favourite happenings during his holiday.

Thanks to all of you.

Travellers and residents of Madagascar have all played their part in updating this book. They wrote about their travels, their lucky finds and their occasional disasters. There was some wonderful information here, from letters or emails many pages long to a short snippet of vital information. I am always amazed that people are willing to take the time and trouble to write such letters; they make all the difference to the information I can provide.

Here are their names in alphabetical order: Ben Badgett, David Baum, Ann & Phil Bloor, David Bostock, James Brehaut, Catherine Brinkley, Jeremy Bullard, Udi Columbus, Robert Conway, Julian Cooke, Elisabeth Cox, Joeri de Bekker, Jan de la Barlaan, Irene Boswell, Sally Crook, Hilary Dennison, Mark Fenn, Karen Freeman, Pascal Girod, Anne Gray, Richard Hammond, Sarah Hammond, Rojosoa Harinala, Christian Herz, Alex Holroyd-Smith, Fabian Hymas, Simon Jackson, Paul Janssen, Gareth Kett, Nina Kolbe, Gary Lemmer, Kim Loohuis, Dylan Lossie, Manfred of Madagascar-on-bike.com, Eric Mathieu, Heather Merriam, Daniel Morgan, Roelf Mulder, David Nation, David Owen, Karen Paterson, Jilly Pollard, Antonio Quintero, Nivo Ravelojaona, Wybe Rood, Silke Rother, Jeremy Sabel, Roger Safford, Derek Antonio Serra, Andrew & Catherine Shimmin, Katie Slocombe, Bryn Thomas, Petra van der Bij, Miguel Vences, Greta Venema, Sil Westra, Mike Wilson and Gilli Wyer.

Back in Bucks my heartfelt thanks to Anna Moores, Janet Mears and Sally Brock for coping with so many last-minute corrections and changes.

PERSPECTIVES ON MADAGASCAR

THE 17TH CENTURY

[Madagascar is] the chiefest paradise this day upon earth.

Richard Boothby, 1630

I could not but endeavour to dissuade others from undergoing the miseries that will follow the persons of such as adventure themselves for Madagascar ... from which place, God divert the residence and adventures of all good men.

Powle Waldegrave, 1649

THE 21ST CENTURY

The beauty of the land I had expected, but the gentle openheartedness and hospitality of the people took me by storm. I have lived and travelled extensively in South America, Europe and Eastern Africa but I have never encountered such lovely people as the Malagasy!

My advice is to see Madagascar before the Malagasy finish with it.

Contents

France, Spain, Italy and the Indie ... must be ransackt to make sauce for our meat;
while we impoverish the land, air and water to enrich our private table ... Besides,
these happy people have no need of any foreign commodity, nature having sufficiently
supplied their necessities wherewith they remain contented. But it is we that are in
want, and are compelled like famished wolves to range the world about for our living,
to the hazards of both our souls and bodies, the one by the corruption of the air, the
other by the corruption of religion.

Walter Hamond, A Paradox Prooving that the Inhabitants of ... Madagascar ... are the
Happiest People in the World, *1640*

Introduction

Madagascar has changed more in the last three years than any other period in my 30-year acquaintance with the island. Why? Because the current president is committed to both development and conservation (the two don't have to be mutually antagonistic) and, ironically, because a cartoon film that had little to do with Madagascar, has made the island a household name.

Yes, the island has changed, but step away from the main tourist routes and it is utterly, unchangeably unique. Researching this edition I'm particularly struck by the number of visitors touring by bicycle, visiting tiny villages which seldom see foreigners. I'm reminded of an experience a couple of years ago when I was travelling with a small group of family and friends. We asked the driver if we could stop at a school – any school – along the road between Antsirabe and Fianarantsoa. The head teacher was delighted by our request and took us to the single classroom where the assorted boys and girls were crammed together on benches chanting their lessons. To say that our appearance created a diversion would be an understatement – the photos we took show facial expressions ranging from suspicion to radiant delight. However, three little children in the front row hid their faces on their arms. Their teacher explained: they were siblings who lived many kilometres away in the mountains and they had never seen white people at close quarters before. They were afraid. Yet this was on one of the most popular tourist routes in Madagascar.

Our next request, since it was Sunday, was to look in on a church service. We chose one of the many imposing Protestant churches near Fianar and again our driver and guide asked permission for us to sit at the back. But the priest was late (this was, after all, Madagascar) so after half-an-hour the congregation offered to sing a hymn especially for us. They sang beautifully, in seemingly effortless harmony. It was one of the most moving musical performances I have ever experienced and most of us were dabbing our eyes by the end.

This is what's so magical about Madagascar. In even the most visited areas you can experience something special, or guarantee it by venturing well off the beaten track. Or you can join other tourists in a fail-safe wildlife experience or luxuriate in one of the new fly-in beach resorts.

The choice is yours – lucky you!

Some day, when I am old and worn and there is nothing new to see, I shall go back to the palm-fringed lagoons, the sun-drenched, rolling moors, the pink villages, and the purple peaks of Madagascar.

E A Powell, Beyond the Utmost Purple Rim, 1925

LIST OF BOXES

Part One

GENERAL INFORMATION

GEOGRAPHY

Name Madagascar or The Malagasy Republic; *Repoblikan'i Madagasikara*
Location 400km off the east coast of Africa, south of the Equator
Size 587,040km². 2½ times the size of Great Britain; slightly smaller than Texas. The world's fourth largest island.
Capital Antananarivo (Tana; Tananarive)
Main towns Fianarantsoa, Antsirabe, Toliara (Tulear), Taolagnaro (Fort Dauphin), Toamasina (Tamatave), Mahajanga (Majunga), Antsiranana (Diego Suarez). The French colonial names in parentheses are still commonly used.
Highest point Mt Maromokotro (Tsaratanana massif) 2,876m (9,450ft)
Climate Tropical, with most rain falling between December and March

HUMAN STATISTICS

Population Approximately 18.6 million
Population growth per year 2.9%
Life expectancy Men 55, women 60.
Language Three official languages: Malagasy, French and English
Religion Mainly Christian, roughly divided between Protestants and Catholics. Some Muslims and Hindus, largely in the Asian communities.

POLITICS/ADMINISTRATION/ECONOMY

President Marc Ravalomanana
Prime minister Charles Rabemananjara
Main exports Prawns, vanilla
GDP growth 4.7% in 2006, 5.6% in 2007 (projected); GDP per capita: US$900 (PPP)
Flag White, green and red (white vertical band, green and red horizontal bands)
Public holidays 1 Jan, 29 Mar, 1 May, 26 Jun, 15 Aug, 1 Nov, 25 Dec, 30 Dec
Motto Fatherland, Liberty, Justice

NATURAL HISTORY

Fauna and flora Cut off from mainland Africa for millions of years, the island's flora and fauna has evolved into unique species. Of the estimated 200,000 forms of life on the island, 150,000 are found nowhere else in the world.
Protected areas Until 2003 only 3% of the island's vulnerable habitats were protected. In September of that year the new government pledged to increase this to 10% by 2008, and is on target to achieve this.

PRACTICAL DETAILS

Main international airport Ivato, Antananarivo
Time GMT+3
Electricity voltage 220V, plugs two-pin (continental style)
International telephone code 00 261
Currency Ariary (Ar)
Rate of exchange (June 2007) £1 = 4,087Ar, €1 = 2,771Ar, US$1 = 2,064Ar

IMPORTANT UPDATE (2008)

Email addresses Wanadoo has changed to moov; eg: boraha@wanadoo.mg is now boraha@moov.mg. This affects many of the email addresses in this book. Check the Bradt website (*www.bradtguides.com*) for other updates.

The Country

GEOGRAPHY

A chain of mountains runs like a spine down the east-centre of the island descending sharply to the Indian Ocean, leaving only a narrow coastal plain. These eastern mountain slopes bear the remains of the dense rainforest which once covered all of the eastern section of the island. The western plain is wider and the climate drier, supporting forests of deciduous trees and acres of savannah grassland. Madagascar's highest mountain is Maromokotro (9,450ft/2,876m), part of the Massif of Tsaratanana, in the north of the island. In the south is the 'spiny forest' also known as the 'spiny desert'.

CLIMATE

Madagascar has a tropical climate: November to March – summer (wet season), hot with variable rainfall; April to October – winter (dry season), mainly dry and mild. That said, climate change is affecting every country in the world and Madagascar is no exception. The once reliable weather pattern has gone. Rain can come early or late. You can be lucky or unlucky.

The normal pattern of weather is that southwest trade winds drop their moisture on the eastern mountain slopes and blow hot and dry in the west. North and northwest 'monsoon' air currents bring heavy rain in summer, decreasing southward so that the rainfall in Taolagnaro is half that of Toamasina. There are also considerable variations of temperature dictated by altitude and latitude. On the summer solstice of 22 December the sun is directly over the Tropic of Capricorn, and the weather is very warm. Conversely, June is the coolest month.

Average midday temperatures in the dry season are 77°F (25°C) in the highlands and 86°F (30°C) on the coast. These statistics are misleading, however, since in June the night-time temperature can drop to near freezing in the highlands and it

RAINFALL CHART

Region	Jan	Feb	Mar	Apr	May	Jun	Jul	Aug	Sep	Oct	Nov	Dec
West	●	●	●	●	✳	✳	✳	✳	✳	✳	✳	●
Highlands	●	●	●	●	✳	○	○	○	✳	✳	✳	●
East	●	●	●	●	●	●	●	✳	✳	✳	✳	✳
South	●	●	●	✳	○	○	○	○	✳	✳	✳	●
North	●	●	●	✳	✳	✳	✳	✳	✳	✳	✳	●
Northwest (Sambirano)	●	●	●	●	✳	✳	✳	✳	✳	✳	✳	●

● = rain   ✳ = driest months   ○ = fine but cool

3

Madagascar has always suffered from cyclones which generally receive scant attention from the English-speaking media. Between 1968 and 2000 the country experienced 25 severe cyclones which affected 6.2 million people, and kill 2,583. Half of that figure was accounted for in one year: 2000.

The year 2004 was a devastating one, with Elita killing 29 people and Gafilo adding a further 222; over 260,000 people were made homeless. Some meteorologists consider Gafilo to be Madagascar's most destructive cyclone ever.

The cyclone season of 2007 was underway as this book went to press. By March the island had been buffeted or threatened by cyclones Anita, Bondo, Clovis, Dora, Enok, Favio and Gamede. Then came the big one: Indlala. This has done extensive damage from Sambava to Toamasina, with Antalaha particularly badly hit, losing an estimated 90% of its vanilla crop.

The cyclone season is from January to April. Visit the east coast during those months at your own risk!

is cool in the south. The winter daytime temperatures are very pleasant, and the hot summer season is usually tempered by cool breezes on the coast.

The east of Madagascar frequently suffers from cyclones during February and March and these may brush other areas in the north or west.

The map and chart in this section give easy reference to the driest and wettest months and regions, but remember: even in the rainiest months there will be sunny intervals, and in the driest there may be heavy showers. For more advice on the best months to visit Madagascar see *When to visit, Chapter 4*.

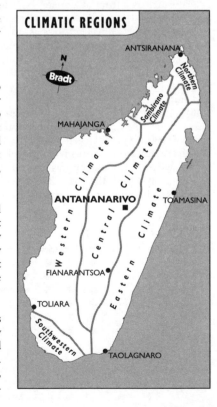

CLIMATIC REGIONS

West Rainfall decreases from north to south. Variation in day/night winter temperatures increases from north to south. Average number of dry months: seven or eight. Highest average annual rainfall within zone (major town): Mahajanga, 152cm. Lowest: Toliara, 36cm.

Central Both temperature and rainfall are influenced by altitude. Day/night temperatures in Antananarivo vary by 14°C. The major rainy season usually starts at the end of November. Highest average annual rainfall within zone (major town): Antsirabe, 140cm.

East In the northeast and central areas there are no months (or weeks) entirely without rain; but drier, more settled weather prevails in the southeast. Reasonably dry months: May, September, October, November.

Possible months for travel: April, December, January (but cyclone danger in January). Difficult months for travel (torrential rain and cyclones) are February, March. Highest annual rainfall in zone: Maroantsetra, 410cm. Lowest: Taolagnaro (Fort Dauphin), 152cm.

Southwest The driest part of Madagascar. The extreme west may receive only 5cm of rain a year, increasing to around 34cm in the east.

North This is similar to the east zone except for the dry climate of the Antsiranana (Diego Suarez) region, which gets only 92cm of rain per year, with a long and fairly reliable dry season.

Northwest (Sambirano) Dominated by the Massif of Tsaratanana, this region includes the island of Nosy Be and has a micro-climate with frequent heavy rain alternating with sunshine.

A BRIEF HISTORY

This is just a glance at Madagascar's fascinating history. For a full account read A History of Madagascar *by Sir Mervyn Brown. See page 458.*

THE FIRST EUROPEANS The first Europeans to sight Madagascar were the Portuguese in 1500, although there is evidence of earlier Arab settlements on the coast. There were unsuccessful attempts to establish French and British settlements during the next couple of centuries; these failed due to disease and hostile local people. Hence a remarkably homogeneous and united country was able to develop under its own rulers.

By the early 1700s, the island had become a haven for pirates and slave-traders, who both traded with and fought the local kings who ruled the clans of the east and west coast.

THE RISE OF THE MERINA KINGDOM The powerful Merina Kingdom was forged by Andrianampoinimerina (be thankful that this was a shortened version of his full name: Andrianampoinimerinandriantsimitoviaminandriampanjaka!).

Succeeding to the tiny kingdom of Ambohimanga in 1787, by 1808 he had united the various Merina kingdoms and conquered the other highland tribes. In many ways the Merina Kingdom at this time paralleled that of the Inca Empire in Peru: Andrianampoinimerina was considered to have almost divine powers and his obedient subjects were well provided for: each was given enough land for his family's rice needs, with some left over to pay a rice tribute to the king, and community projects such as the building of irrigation canals were imposed through forced labour (though with bonuses for the most productive worker). The burning of forests was forbidden.

Conquest was always foremost in the monarch's mind, however, and it was his son, King Radama I, who fulfilled his father's command to 'Take the sea as frontier to your kingdom'. This king had a friendly relationship with Britain, which in 1817 and 1820 signed treaties under which Madagascar was recognised as an independent state. Britain supplied arms and advisers to help Radama conquer most of the rest of the island.

THE LONDON MISSIONARY SOCIETY To further strengthen ties between the two countries, the British Governor of Mauritius, which had recently been seized from the French, encouraged King Radama I to invite the London Missionary Society to

The most intriguing insight into 18th-century Madagascar was provided by Robert Drury, who was shipwrecked off the island in 1701 and spent over 16 years there, much of the time as a slave to the Antandroy or Sakalava chiefs.

Drury was only 15 when his boat foundered off the southern tip of Madagascar (he had been permitted by his father to go to India with trade goods). The shipwreck survivors were treated well by the local king but kept prisoners for reasons of status. After a few days they made a bid for freedom by seizing the king and some of his courtiers as a hostage and marching east. They were followed by hundreds of warriors who watched for any relaxation in the guard; they were without water for three days as they crossed the burning hot desert and just as they came in sight of the River Mandrare (having released the hostages) they were attacked and many were speared to death.

For ten years Drury was a slave of the Antandroy royal family. He worked with cattle and eventually was appointed royal butcher, the task of slaughtering a cow for ritual purposes being supposedly that of someone of royal blood – and lighter skin. Drury was a useful substitute. He also acquired a wife.

Wars with the neighbouring Mahafaly gave him the opportunity to escape north across the desert to St Augustine's Bay, some 250 miles away. Here he hoped to find a ship to England, but his luck turned and he again became a slave, this time to the Sakalava. When a ship did come in, his master refused to consider selling him to the captain, and Drury's desperate effort to get word to the ship through a message written on a leaf came to nothing when the messenger lost the leaf and substituted another less meaningful one. Two more years of relative freedom followed, and he finally got away in 1717, nearly 17 years after his shipwreck.

Ever quick to put his experience to good use, he later returned to Madagascar as a slave trader!

See *Further Reading* for a book on Robert Drury.

send teachers. In 1818 a small group of Welsh missionaries arrived in Tamatave (now Toamasina). David Jones and Thomas Bevan brought their wives and children, but within a few weeks only Jones remained alive; the others had all died of fever. Jones retreated to Mauritius, but returned to Madagascar in 1820, along with equally dedicated missionary teachers and artisans, to devote the rest of his life to its people. The British influence was established and a written language introduced for the first time (apart from some ancient Arabic texts) using the Roman alphabet.

'THE WICKED QUEEN' AND HER SUCCESSORS Radama's widow and successor, Queen Ranavalona I, was determined to rid the land of Christianity and European influence, and reigned long enough (33 years) largely to achieve her aim. These were repressive times for Malagasy as well as foreigners. One way of dealing with people suspected of witchcraft or other evil practices was the 'Ordeal by Tangena' (see box opposite).

It was during Queen Ranavalona's reign that an extraordinary Frenchman arrived in Madagascar: Jean Laborde, who, building on the work of the British missionaries, introduced the island to many aspects of Western technology. He remained in the queen's favour until 1857 – much longer than the other Europeans (see box on page 181).

The queen drove the missionaries out of Madagascar and many Malagasy Christians were martyred. However, the missionaries and European influence returned in greater strength after the Queen's death and in 1869 Christianity became the official religion of the Merina Kingdom.

When James Hastie, royal tutor, arrived in Madagascar in 1817 he witnessed and described one of the more barbaric tortures that King Radama I was using on his subjects: the Ordeal of Tangena. *Tangena* is a Malagasy shrub with a poisonous kernel in its fruit. This poison was used to determine the guilt or innocence of a suspected criminal. A 'meal' consisting of three pieces of chicken skin, rice and the crushed tangena kernel was prepared. The suspect was then forced to drink large quantities of water to make him – or her – vomit. If all three pieces of chicken skin reappeared the person was innocent (but often died anyway as a result of the poison). If the skin remained in the stomach the unfortunate suspect was killed, usually after limbs, or bits of limbs and other extremities, had been lopped off first.

One of the successes of Hastie's influence on the king was that the monarch agreed that, although the Ordeal by Tangena should continue, dogs could stand in for the accused. This decision was ignored by Queen Ranavalona who used it freely on the Christian martyrs she persecuted with such enthusiasm. Sir Mervyn Brown (from whose book, *A History of Madagascar*, this information is extracted) estimates that several thousand Malagasy met their deaths through the tangena shrub during Queen Ranavalona's long reign. Even during this period of xenophobia the queen was reluctant to subject the Europeans under arrest to the ordeal because of the inevitable political repercussions. Prudently, the poison was administered to chickens; all but one promptly died (the 'innocent' chicken/European was a bit too useful to condemn).

The Ordeal by Tangena was finally abolished by Queen Ranavalona's son, King Radama II, in 1861.

After Queen Ranavalona I came King Radama II, a peace-loving and pro-European monarch who was assassinated after a two-year reign in 1863. There is a widely held belief, however, that he survived strangulation with a silk cord (it was taboo to shed royal blood) and lived in hiding in the northwest for many years (see box on page 404). There is also a belief (less widely held) that he was assassinated because he was the illegitimate son of Queen Ranavalona I and Jean Laborde.

After the death of Radama II, Queen Rasoherina came to the throne, but the monarchy was now in decline and power shifted to the prime minister who shrewdly married the queen. He was overthrown by a brother, Rainilaiarivony, who continued the tradition by marrying three successive queens and exercising all the power. During this period, 1863-96, the monarchs (in title only) were Queen Rasoherina, Queen Ranavalona II and lastly Queen Ranavalona III.

THE FRENCH CONQUEST Even during the period of British influence the French maintained a long-standing claim to Madagascar and in 1883 they attacked and occupied the main ports. The Franco-Malagasy War lasted thirty months, and was concluded by a harsh treaty making Madagascar a form of French protectorate. Prime Minister Rainilaiarivony, hoping for British support, managed to evade full acceptance of this status but the British government signed away its interest in the Convention of Zanzibar in 1890. The French finally imposed their rule by invasion in 1895. For a year the country was a full protectorate and in 1896 Madagascar became a French colony. A year later Queen Ranavalona III was exiled to Algeria and the monarchy abolished.

The first French Governor-General of Madagascar, Joseph Simon Gallieni, was an able and relatively benign administrator. He set out to break the power of the Merina aristocracy and remove the British influence by banning the teaching of English. French became the official language.

MADAGASCAR AND THE JEWS OF EUROPE

John Grehan

During the latter years of the 1930s, German Nazis, as well as many anti-Semites across Europe, wanted to rid the continent of all Jews. Their solution to the 'Jewish Question' was the wholesale deportation of European Jews to Madagascar. What became known as 'The Madagascar Plan' was first discussed as early as November 1938, a year before the outbreak of World War II. (As Madagascar was a French colony one can only wonder at what degree of collusion there was between the French and German governments over this proposal at that time.)

The annexation of Poland in 1939 brought yet more Jews under German administration. This led to a revival of The Madagascar Plan and prompted the President of the Academy of German Law – Hans Franc – to suggest that as many as three million Jews should be shipped to Madagascar. This would have meant the German occupation of the island and this was certainly discussed in 1940 within days of the fall of France. Indeed, Franz Rademacher of the German Foreign Office drew up firm arrangements for installing the Jews in Madagascar in September 1940, and he planned to visit the island to 'map out' the details.

It was intended that the island would be under the authority of Heinrich Himmler though largely administered by the Jews themselves. Franc, in a speech in July 1940, even claimed that Jewish leaders had accepted the Madagascar Plan. But the Jews had been deceived if they thought that Madagascar had been chosen as the place for a sustainable Jewish homeland. Madagascar was to be a vast 'reservation' in which, because of the poor climatic and agricultural conditions, the Jews would slowly die out. Some have gone even further and suggested that Madagascar was to be the place where the mass extermination of the Jews – with the gas chambers, ovens and all the associated paraphernalia of the death camps – would take place. Certainly the remoteness of Madagascar would have provided the Germans with the privacy they wanted for conducting such atrocities.

Until well into 1941 The Madagascar Plan was Germany's stated 'Final Solution'. It was only when such a policy became impractical, and it was the Royal Navy's mastery of the seas which made the plan impractical, that exportation gave way to extermination and another, and more terrible, Final Solution to the Jewish Problem took its place.

John Grehan is the author of The Forgotten Invasion, *see* Further Reading *on page 459.*

BRITISH MILITARY TRAINING AND THE TWO WORLD WARS Britain has played an important part in the military history of Madagascar. During the wars which preceded colonisation British mercenaries trained the Malagasy army to fight the French. During World War I 46,000 Malagasy were recruited for the allies and over 2,000 killed. In 1942, when Madagascar was under the control of the Vichy French, the British invaded Madagascar to forestall the possibility of the Japanese Navy making use of the great harbour of Diego Suarez (see box on pages 366–7).

In 1943 Madagascar was handed back to France under a Free French Government. An uprising by the Malagasy against the French in 1947 was bloodily repressed (some 80,000 are said to have died) but the spirit of nationalism lived on and in 1960 the country achieved full independence.

THE FIRST 30 YEARS OF INDEPENDENCE The first president, Philibert Tsiranana, was 'pro-France' but in 1972 he stepped down in the face of increasing unrest and student demonstrations against French neo-colonialism. An interim government headed by General Ramanantsoa ended France's special position and introduced a more nationalistic foreign and economic policy.

In 1975, after a period of turmoil, a military directorate handed power to a naval officer, Didier Ratsiraka, who had served as Foreign Minister under Ramanantsoa. Ratsiraka established the Second Republic, changing the country's name from The Malagasy Republic to The Democratic Republic of Madagascar. He introduced his own brand of 'Christian-Marxism' and his manifesto, set out in a 'little red book', was approved by referendum. Socialist policies such as the nationalisation of banks followed. Within a few years the economy had collapsed and has remained in severe difficulties ever since. Ratsiraka was nevertheless twice re-elected, though there were claims of ballot rigging and intimidation.

INTO THE 21ST CENTURY In 1991 a pro-democracy coalition called the Forces Vives, in which the churches played an important part, organised a series of strikes and daily demonstrations calling for Ratsiraka's resignation. Around 500,000 demonstrators marched on the president's palace. Though unarmed and orderly, they were fired on by the presidential guards and an estimated 100 died. This episode further weakened Ratsiraka and at the end of the year he relinquished executive power and agreed to a referendum which approved a new constitution and fresh elections in 1992/93. Albert Zafy won the election.

The Third Republic, born in 1993, soon ran into trouble. Albert Zafy refused to accept the limitations on his presidential role required by the new constitution and in 1995 won a referendum which gave him, rather than the Assembly, the right to appoint the prime minister. Zafy's continuing breaches of the constitution led to his impeachment by the National Assembly, and in the ensuing presidential election former president Ratsiraka emerged the winner. Ratsiraka then piloted through major amendments to the constitution which restored most of the dictatorial powers that he had formerly enjoyed.

The first round of presidential elections was held in December 2001. The official results showed the mayor of Antananarivo, Marc Ravalomanana, leading with 46% so that a second round would be necessary. However, results collected by various observer groups indicated that Ravalomanana was the outright winner with 52%.

'LA CRISE POLITIQUE' JANUARY–JULY 2002 Even in the sometimes bizarre politics of the developing world the spectacle of two 'presidents' in two 'capitals' with two set of 'ministers' was unusual. Friends of Madagascar watched appalled as the country unravelled itself to the indifference of the leaders of the industrialised world.

Every day the people marched peacefully, backed by the Protestant Church of which Ravalomanana is a prominent member. Ratsiraka declared Martial Law which was countered by Ravalomanana declaring himself president and installing his own ministers in government offices. Ratsiraka retreated with his government to his home town of Toamasina and was supported by the Governors of the other coastal provinces. All this was accomplished with the minimum of violence. But then Ratsiraka's supporters isolated the capital by blocking all roads leading to the city and by dynamiting the bridges. The people of Antananarivo faced a tenfold increase in the price of fuel, and basic staples such as rice, sugar and salt disappeared from the shops. Air Madagascar was grounded. The army was split behind the two leaders. As the months passed, the blockade caused malnutrition and death to the vulnerable in Tana and hardship to all. Many businesses faced bankruptcy.

In May, the balance of power started to shift. A court-monitored recount confirmed that Ravalomanana had won the election, and he was sworn in as president. Ratsiraka steadfastly refused to accept this and the blockades continued and the death toll, hitherto kept remarkably low, started to rise. As the army's support for Ratsiraka dwindled and switched to Ravalomanana, it became possible to use force to dismantle the barricades and to take Ratsiraka strongholds such as Mahajanga and Antsiranana. The USA, Norway and Switzerland were the first nations to recognise Ravalomanana as the rightful president. France, which had prolonged the crisis by delaying recognition because of its close links with Ratsiraka, was finally compelled to go along, followed by most European countries, which had been awaiting a lead from France. However most African presidents, who had supported Ratsiraka as a fellow member of their dictators' club, continued to reject Ravalomanana's legitimacy, and it was nearly a year before Madagascar was re-admitted into the African Union.

2003 ONWARD Once safely in power, Ravalomanana set about rebuilding the infrastructure, launching an ambitious road-building programme, and putting in motion his Durban Vision (see page 72) with the aim of conserving the environment by tripling the protected areas.

In the presidential elections of December 2006 Marc Ravalomanana won 54.8% of the vote, thus securing a second five-year term. In his acceptance speech he focused on the Madagascar Action Plan, saying:

> As President of the Republic of Madagascar, I publicly declare my commitment to providing the necessary leadership for the MAP to contribute to the rapid and sustainable development of Madagascar. We will succeed.

He suggested a shift in emphasis to developing a wider base, involving the regions and the heads of the 17,500 *Fokontany* (communities) in any activities. In April 2007 the MAP won 75% approval in a referendum.

The president promised more training and education and stressed the need to be competitive to attract further foreign investment. The new prime minister, General Charles Rabemananjara, set targets for economic growth of 5.6% and an inflation rate below 10%.

GOVERNMENT AND POLITICS

Madagascar is governed by a presidential system, but the powers of the president have varied under the different constitutions adopted over the last 40 years. At independence the constitution was based closely on the French, with the president head of the government as well as head of state. Under the 'socialist revolution' (1975–91) President Ratsiraka had virtually dictatorial powers, supported by large majorities for his party AREMA in the National Assembly. The strength of older left-wing parties prevented him from establishing a formal one-party state, but the constitution provided that only socialist parties could compete in elections. After his overthrow in 1991 the pendulum swung to a parliamentary constitution similar to the German or the British, with a largely ceremonial president and power vested in a prime minister elected by the National Assembly. But this was effectively destroyed by President Zafy's refusal to accept the constitutional limits on his power and when Ratsiraka subsequently returned to power he rewrote the constitution to restore nearly all his old powers; it is this rewritten constitution that is still in force.

Since colonial times the country has been divided for purposes of local government into six provinces, each consisting of hundreds of communes or municipalities with Governors and Prefects appointed by the central government but, in an effort to move towards decentralisation, other systems of local government are being considered.

An important factor in politics has been the coastal people's mistrust of the Merina who conquered them in the 19th century. The numerical superiority of the coastal people has ensured their dominance of parliament and government. When Ratsiraka was in trouble in 1991, and again in 2002, he stirred up coastal hostility to the Merina. However, the emergence of Marc Ravalomanana as the first Merina elected president indicates that the coastal/plateau divide is now much less significant, though some coastal politicians such as ex-President Zafy still try to exploit it.

Corruption was virtually unknown during the post-independence government of Tsiranana, but became firmly established during Ratsiraka's Second Republic. During his first term of office, President Ravalomanana launched a major campaign against corruption which is showing some success.

ECONOMY

Over the past 30 years Madagascar has declined from being modestly prosperous to becoming one of the poorest countries in the world. Under Tsiranana's post-independence government, a combination of careful management and political stability produced a steady growth in GNP and an improvement in living standards. However, from the late '70s Ratsiraka's unwise policies of nationalisation and centralisation, coupled with a worsening of the terms of trade following successive oil-price shocks, led to the collapse of the economy. For 25 years the average GNP growth was zero so that, with the population doubling, living standards were halved. Reluctant recourse to the IMF and its policies of austerity and liberalisation led to some improvement in the late '80s but the disruptions of successive political crises, notably those of 1991 and 2002, checked and sometimes reversed this recovery. In particular the blockading of the capital by Ratsiraka's forces in 2002 virtually halted external trade and seriously damaged the growing industrial sector which was largely dependent on exports.

Madagascar has always had an adverse balance of trade, but in the post-independence days the deficit was modest and covered by various payments from France. The economic collapse under the Second Republic greatly increased the deficit, and the country has since been dependent on massive support from the IMF, the World Bank, the European Union and various bilateral donors led by France, with the USA also playing an important role. The local currency, the *franc malgache*, was maintained in parity with the French franc long after its real value had declined. In 2003 the franc was replaced by the ariary. President Ravalomanana's abolition of a wide range of import taxes, designed to stimulate the economy, led in the short term to a rapid increase of imports without a corresponding rise in exports. The consequent increase in the trade gap caused a spectacular collapse of the currency in the first half of 2004, with the ariary losing over half its value.

The economy has always been based on agriculture, with rice by far the largest crop, providing enough to feed the population and leave some over for export. However, under the Second Republic the severe decline in the road infrastructure isolated many rice-growers from the markets, while the low official price paid to the growers discouraged them from growing a surplus for sale and led them to revert to a subsistence economy. Rice production accordingly failed to keep pace with the growing population so that the country now has to import some 30% of its needs, at considerable expense in foreign exchange. The main cash crops for export have been vanilla, of which Madagascar is the world's largest producer, and coffee; but while vanilla has remained a leading export earner, coffee production has declined and the sector seems unlikely to recover. In the last decade prawns, either fished or farmed in the inlets on the west coast, have become a major export item. Much hope has been invested in tourism, and with the doubling of visitor figures in seven years and an ambitious target of 700,000 by 2012, this continues to be one of the pillars of the economy.

The hitherto small mining sector (semi-precious stones, mica and chromite) has recently expanded with the discovery of large deposits of sapphire but, partly because of government corruption, nearly all the gems have been exported illegally so that the economy has not benefited. QMM, a Canadian subsidiary of the British mining firm Rio Tinto, has begun exploiting the substantial deposits of ilmenite on the southeast coast (see pages 270–1). This is on such a scale that it could in due course add as much as 10% to the country's export earnings. In 2007 a Canadian/Japanese/South Korean consortium will start work on an even bigger nickel project that will bring $100 million a year to the economy. Alcan is studying a potential bauxite mine in the southeast of the country and other firms are planning to exploit deposits of copper, nickel, platinum and gold. There are known to be substantial reserves of oil and gas, which were hitherto uneconomic to extract when the oil price was low. The spectacular rise in the price in 2005-6 caused a revival of interest and a number of oil companies, including six British firms, are now engaged in exploration.

A delegation of the International Monetary Fund (IMF) that visited the country in October 2006 expressed their approval of the country's achievements in economic growth and success in controlling inflation.

In 2006 the GDP growth was estimated to be 4.7% with a prediction of 5.6% for 2007.

FOREIGN AID In 2007 the International Monetary Fund completed a positive first review of Madagascar's economic performance under the US$81million three-year Poverty Reduction and Growth Facility arrangement agreed in July 2006. Madagascar can now draw a further amount equivalent to US$11.8m, on which the annual interest rate is only 0.5%.

In 2006 the European Union confirmed its commitment of €462 million under the tenth FED programme, and pledged €12.1 million to 13 NGOs to help reduce poverty in Madagascar and in February 2007 granted €10 million for the second phase of its aid for rural development. Japan offered $10.7 million between 2007 and 2010, primarily to support small businesses, and $2.8 million to help regulate rice prices during shortages, as well as a gift of 8,800 tonnes of rice. Russia is considering the cancellation of some $100 million of debt.

TOURISM STATISTICS There were 311,000 foreign visitors to Madagascar in 2006, a 14% increase over the 277,000 in 2005 with the number helped by a marketing campaign in France. The figure for 2000 was 138,000. In 2007 the Ministry of Tourism hopes to boost the number of tourists from Italy, currently second after the French and generally higher spenders, and to persuade them to visit more than just Nosy Be. The government target is for 700,000 visitors by 2012.

2

People and Culture

ORIGINS

Archaeologists believe that the first people arrived in Madagascar from Indonesia/Malaya about 2,000 years ago. A journey in a reconstructed boat of those times has proved that the direct crossing of the Indian Ocean – 6,400km – was possible, though most experts agree that it is much more likely that the immigrants came in their outrigger canoes via Southern India and East Africa, where they established small Indonesian colonies. The strong African element in the coastal populations probably derived from later migrations from these colonies since their language is also essentially Malayo-Polynesian with only slightly more Bantu-Swahili words than elsewhere in the island. The Merina people of the highlands retain remarkably Indonesian characteristics and may have arrived as recently as 500–600 years ago.

Later arrivals, mainly on the east coast, from Arabia and elsewhere in the Indian Ocean, were also absorbed into the Malagasy-speaking population, while leaving their mark in certain local customs clearly derived from Islam. The two-continent origin of the Malagasy is easily observed, from the highland tribes who most resemble Indonesians, to the African type characterised by the Bara or Makoa in the south. In between are the elements of both races which make the Malagasy so varied and attractive in appearance. Thus there is racial diversity but cultural uniformity.

BELIEFS AND CUSTOMS

The Afro-Asian origin of the Malagasy has produced a people with complicated and fascinating beliefs and customs. Despite the various tribes or clans, the country shares not only a common language but a belief in the power of dead ancestors (*razana*). This cult of the dead, far from being a morbid preoccupation, is a celebration of life since the dead ancestors are considered to be potent forces that continue to share in family life. If the *razana* are remembered by the living, the Malagasy believe, they thrive in the spirit world and can be relied on to look after their descendants in a host of different ways. These ancestors wield considerable power, their 'wishes' dictating the behaviour of the family or community. Their

DID YOU KNOW?

- Earthquakes mean that whales are bathing their children.
- If a woman maintains a bending posture when arranging eggs in a nest, the chickens will have crooked necks.
- If the walls of a house incline towards the south, the wife will be the stronger one; if they incline towards the north it will be the husband.
- Burning a knot on a piece of string causes the knees to grow big.

property is respected, so a great-grandfather's field may not be sold or changed to a different crop. Calamities are usually blamed on the anger of *razana*, and a zebu bull may be sacrificed in appeasement. Large herds of zebu cattle are kept as a 'bank' of potential sacrificial offerings.

Belief in tradition, in the accumulated wisdom of the ancestors, has shaped the Malagasy culture. Respect for their elders and courtesy to all fellow humans is part of the tradition. But so is resistance to change.

SPIRITUAL BELIEFS At the beginning of time the Creator was Zanahary or Andriananahary. Now the Malagasy worship one god, Andriamanitra, who is neither male nor female. (Andriamanitra is also a word for silk, the fabric of burial shrouds.)

Many rural people believe in 'secondary gods' or nature spirits, which may be male or female, and which inhabit certain trees, rocks (which are known as *ody*) or rivers. People seeking help from the spirit world may visit one of these sites for prayer. Spirits are also thought to possess humans who fall into a trance-like state, called *tromba* by the Sakalava and *bilo* by the Antandroy. Some clans or communities believe that spirits can also possess animals, particularly crocodiles.

The Malagasy equivalent of the soul is *ambiroa*. When a person is in a dream state it can temporarily separate from the body, and at death it becomes an immortal *razana*. Death, therefore, is merely a change and not an end. A special ceremony usually marks this rite of passage, with feasting and the sacrifice of zebu. The mood of the participants alternates between sorrow and joy.

Fady The dictates of the *razana* are obeyed in a complicated network of *fady*. Although *fady* (the plural is also *fady*) is usually translated as 'taboo' this does not truly convey the meaning: these are beliefs related to actions, food, or days of the week when it is 'dangerous to…'. *Fady* vary from family to family and community to community, and even from person to person.

The following are some examples related to actions and food among the Merina: it may be *fady* to sing while you are eating (violators will develop elongated teeth); it is also *fady* to hand an egg directly to another person – it must first be put on the ground; for the people of Andranoro it is *fady* to ask for salt directly, so one has to request 'that which flavours the food'. A *fady* connected with objects is that the spade used to dig a grave should have a loose handle since it is dangerous to have too firm a connection between the living and the dead.

Social *fady*, like *vintana* (see below), often involve the days of the week. For example, among the Merina it is *fady* to hold a funeral on a Tuesday, or there will be another death. Among the Tsimihety, and some other groups, it is *fady* to work the land on Tuesdays; Thursday is also a *fady* day for some people, both for funerals and for farming.

A *fady* is not intended to restrict the freedom of the Malagasy but to ensure happiness and an improved quality of life. That said, however, there are some cruel *fady* which Christian missionaries have been trying, over the centuries, to eliminate. One is the taboo against twins among the Antaisaka people of Mananjary. Historically twins were killed or abandoned in the forest after birth. Today this is against the law but still persists and twins may not be buried in a tomb. Catholic missionaries have established an orphanage in the area for the twins born to mothers torn between social tradition and maternal love. Many mothers who would otherwise have to suffer the murder or abandonment of their babies can give them to the care of the Church.

Many *fady* benefit conservation. For instance the killing of certain animals is often prohibited, and the area around a tomb must be left undisturbed. Within

THE INTRUDERS AND THE GEESE During the rule of King Andrianampoinimerina, thieves once attempted a raid on the village of Ambohimanga. The residents, however, kept geese which caused a commotion when the intruders entered the compound, thus alerting the people who could take action. Geese are therefore not eaten in this part of Madagascar.

THE BABY AND THE DRONGO Centuries ago the communities of the east coast were persecuted by pirates who made incursions to the hills to pillage and take captives. At the warning that a pirate band was on its way the villagers would flee into the jungle. When pirates approached the village of Ambinanetelo the women with young children could not keep up with the others so hid in a thicket. Just as the pirates were passing them a baby wailed. The men turned to seek the source of the cry. It came again, but this time from the top of a tree: it was a drongo. Believing themselves duped by a bird the pirates gave up and returned to their boats. Ever since then it has been *fady* to kill a drongo in Ambinanetelo.

THE TORTOISE AND THE POT A Tandroy man put a tortoise in a clay pot of boiling water to cook it, but the tortoise kicked so hard that the pot shattered to smithereens. The man declared that his descendants would never again eat tortoise because it broke his pot.

these pockets of sacred forest, *ala masina*, it is strictly forbidden to cut trees or even to burn deadwood or leaf litter. In southeast Madagascar there are *alam-bevehivavy* (sacred women's forests) along a stretch of river where only women may bathe. Again, no vegetation may be cleared or damaged in such localities.

For an in-depth study of the subject try to get hold of a copy of *Taboo* (see page 460).

Vintana Along with *fady* goes a complex sense of destiny called *vintana*. Broadly speaking, *vintana* is to do with time – hours of the day, days of the week, etc – and *fady* usually involves actions or behaviour. Each day has its own *vintana* which tends to make it good or bad for certain festivals or activities. Sunday is God's day; work undertaken will succeed. Monday is a hard day, not a good day for work although projects undertaken (such as building a house) will last; Tuesday is an easy day – too easy for death so no burials take place – but all right for *famadihana* (exhumation) and light work; Wednesday is usually the day for funerals or *famadihana*; Thursday is suitable for weddings and is generally a 'good' day; Friday, *Zoma*, is a 'fat' day, set aside for enjoyment, but is also the best day for funerals; Saturday, a 'noble' day, is suitable for weddings but also for purification.

As an added complication, each day has its own colour. For example Monday is a black day. A black chicken may have to be sacrificed to avoid calamity, dark-coloured food should not be eaten and people may avoid black objects. Other day-colours are: Tuesday multicoloured, Wednesday brown, Thursday black, Friday red, Saturday blue.

Tody and Tsiny A third force shapes Malagasy morality. In addition to *fady* and *vintana*, there is *tody* and its partner *tsiny*. *Tody* is somewhat similar to the Hindu/Buddhist kharma. The word means 'return' or 'retribution' and indicates that for any action there is a reaction. *Tsiny* means 'fault', usually a breach of the rules laid down by the ancestors.

After death Burial, exhumation and second burial are the focus of Malagasy beliefs and culture. To the Malagasy, death is the most important part of life, when a person abandons his mortal form to become a much more powerful and significant ancestor. Since a tomb is for ever whilst a house is only a temporary dwelling, it follows that tombs should be more solidly constructed than houses.

Burial practices differ among the various tribes but all over Madagascar a ritual known as *sasa* is practised immediately after a death. The family of the deceased go to a fast-flowing river and wash all their clothes to remove the contamination of death.

Funeral practices vary from clan to clan. The Antankarana (in the north) and Antandroy (south) have 'happy' funerals during which they may run, with the

TOMB ARCHITECTURE AND FUNERARY ART

In Madagascar the style and structure of tombs define the different clans or tribes better than any other visible feature, and also indicate the wealth and status of the family concerned. Below is a description of the tombs.

MERINA In early times burial sites were near valleys or in marshes. The body would be placed in a hollowed-out tree trunk and sunk into the mud at the bottom of a marsh. These *fasam-bazimba* marshes were sacred. Later the Merina began constructing rectangular wooden tombs, mostly under the ground but with a visible structure above. In the 19th century the arrival of the Frenchman Jean Laborde had a profound effect on tomb architecture. Tombs were built with bricks and stone, no longer just from wood. It was Laborde's influence which led to the elaborate structure of modern tombs, which are often painted with geometric designs. Sometimes the interior is lavishly decorated.

SAKALAVA During the *Vazimba* period, the Sakalava tombs were simple piles of stones. As with the Merina the change occurred with the introduction of cement and a step design was added. At a later stage, wooden stelae, *aloalo*, were placed on the tombs, positioned to face east. These were topped with carvings of a most erotic nature. Since Sakalava tombs are for individuals and not families, there is no attempt at maintaining the stelae as it is believed that only when the wood decays will the soul of the buried person be released. Not all the carvings, however, are erotic – they may just depict scenes from everyday life or geometric paintings.

Tomb construction commences only after the person's death and can take up to six weeks, the body meanwhile being kept in a house. While a tomb is under construction, many zebu are sacrificed to the ancestors. The Sakalava call their tombs *izarana*, 'the place where we are separated'.

ANTANDROY AND MAHAFALY The local name of these tombs is *fanesy* which means 'your eternal place'. Zebu horns are scattered on the tomb as a symbol of wealth (on Sakalava tombs, zebu horns are only a decoration, not an indication of status). The Antandroy and Mahafaly tombs have much the same architecture as those of the Sakalava, but are more artistically decorated. The Mahafaly *aloalo* bear figures depicting scenes from the person's life, and the entire length is often carved with intricate designs. These tombs are carefully maintained, and it is probably the Mahafaly tombs in the southern interior which are the most colourful and striking symbols of Malagasy culture. Antandroy tomb paintings tend to be merely decorative and do not represent scenes from the deceased person's life.

coffin, into the sea. An unusual ritual, *tranondonaky*, is practised by the Antaisaka of the southeast. Here the corpse is first taken to a special house where, after a signal, the women all start crying. Abruptly, after a second signal, they dance. While this is happening the men are gathered in the hut of the local chief from where, one by one, they go to the house where the corpse is lying and attach money to it with a special oil. The children dance through the night, to the beat of drums, and in the morning the adults wrap the corpse in a shroud and take it to the *kibory*. These tombs are concealed in a patch of forest known as *ala fady* which only men may enter, and where they deliver their last messages to the deceased. These messages can be surprisingly fierce: 'You are now at your place so don't disturb us any more' or 'You are now with the children of the dead, but we are the children of the living.'

More disturbing, however, is the procedure following the death of a noble of the Menabe Sakalava people. The body may be placed on a wooden bench in the hot sun until it begins to decompose. The bodily fluids which drip out are collected in receptacles and drunk by the relatives in the belief that they will then take on the qualities of the deceased.

It is after the first burial, however, that the Malagasy generally honour and communicate with their dead, not only to show respect but to avoid the anger of the *razana* who dwell in the tombs. The best-known ceremony in Madagascar is the 'turning of the bones' by the Merina and Betsileo people: *famadihana* (pronounced 'famadeean'). This is a joyful occasion which occurs from four to seven years after the first burial, and provides the opportunity to communicate with and remember a loved one. The remains of the selected relative are taken from the tomb, rewrapped in a new burial shroud (*lambamena*) and carried around the tomb a few times before being replaced. Meanwhile the corpse is spoken to and informed of all the latest events in the family and village. The celebrants are not supposed to show any grief. Generous quantities of alcohol are consumed amid a festive atmosphere with much dancing and music. Women who are trying to conceive take small pieces of the old burial shroud and keep these under their mattresses to induce fertility.

By law a *famadihana* may take place only in the dry season, between June and September. It can last up to a week and involves the family in considerable expense, as befits the most important celebration for any family. In the Hauts Plateaux the practice of *famadihana* is embraced by rich and poor, urban and rural, and visitors fortunate enough to be invited to one will find it a strange but very moving occasion; it's an opportunity to examine our own beliefs and rituals associated with death. For an account of what *famadihana* means to a sophisticated London-based Merina woman, see box on pages 18–19.

Variations of *famadihana* are practised by other tribes. The Menabe Sakalava, for example, hold a *fitampoha* every ten years. This is a royal *famadihana* in which the remains of deceased monarchs are taken from their tomb and washed in a river. A similar ritual, the *fanampoambe*, is performed by the Boina Sakalava further north.

HEALERS, SORCERERS AND SOOTHSAYERS The 'Wise Men' in Malagasy society are the *ombiasy*; the name derives from *olona-be-hasina* meaning 'person of much virtue'. Traditionally they were from the Antaimoro clan and were the advisors of royalty: Antaimoro *ombiasy* came to Antananarivo to advise King Andrianampoinimerina and to teach him Arabic writing.

The astrologers, *mpanandro* ('those who make the day'), work on predictions of *vintana*. There is a Malagasy proverb, 'Man can do nothing to alter his destiny'; but the *mpanandro* will advise on the best day to build a house, or hold a wedding or *famadihana*. Though nowadays *mpanandro* do not have official recognition, they are present in all levels of society. A man (or woman) is considered to have the powers

Seraphine Tierney Ramanantsoa

I travelled across the seas to be here today. This day was long awaited, I would soon be in contact with my mother again. She had died seven years previously and I had not been able to be at her funeral. Tradition had always been so important to her so I knew she would be happy that I have come for her *famadihana*.

The meeting point is at 6am outside Cinema Soa in Antananarivo. My household woke up at about 4am to pack the food that had been prepared during the previous week. Drinks and cutlery are all piled into the car. A great number of people are expected as it is also the *famadihana* of the other members of my mother's family.

Fourteen cars and a big *taxi-brousse* carrying in all about 50 people, squashed one on top of the other, turn up. Everybody is excited. It is really great to see faces I haven't seen since my childhood. Everybody greets each other and exchanges news.

At 8am we all set off. We are heading towards Ifalimanjaka (meaning 'Joy Reigns Here'), in the *fivondronana* of Manjakandriana. Driving through villages with funny names like Ambohitrabiby (the 'Town of Animals') brings me back to the time when such names were familiar. We make one stop at Talatan'ny volon'ondry for a breakfast of rice cakes and sausages: another opportunity to re-acquaint myself with long lost cousins with whom I spent the long summer holidays as a child. We used to run around together playing games like catching grasshoppers and then finding carnivorous plants and dropping the insect in to see how long it took the plant to close its top to eat its prey.

10am. We arrive at the tombs. Faces are bright, full of expectancy. I ask what the day means to them. They all agree that it's a day for family togetherness, a day for joy, for remembrance.

We are in front of my mother's tomb. It is made out of stone and marble, very elegant. The family will have spent more money on keeping that tomb nice and well maintained than on their own house.

Everybody stands around in front of the tomb waiting for the main event to start: the opening of the tomb door. We have to wait for the president of the *fokon'tany* ('local authority') to give permission to open the tomb. Although it had been arranged beforehand he cannot be found anywhere. This wait, after such anticipation, is taken patiently by all – just one of those things.

Mats are laid on the ground on one side of the tomb. The atmosphere of joy is so tangible! Music is blaring out. Permission is finally granted to enter the tomb. The *ray aman-dreny* ('the elders') are the first to enter.

The inside of my mother's tomb looks very comfortable with bunk beds made out of stone. It is very clean. There are names on the side of the beds. The national flag is hoisted on top of the tomb as a sign of respect. The conversation goes on happily on the little veranda outside the tomb's door, people chatting about the event and what they have been doing in the last few days.

They start to take the bodies out. Voices could be heard above the happy murmur: 'Who is this one? This is your ma! This one your aunt! Here is your uncle! Just carry them

of a mpanandro when he has some grey hair – a sign that he is wise enough to interpret *vintana*. Antandroy soothsayers are known as *mpisoro*.

The Malagasy have a deep knowledge of herbal medicine and all markets display a variety of medicinal plants, amulets and talismans. The Malagasy names associated with these are *ody* and *fanafody*. Broadly speaking, *ody* refers to fetishes such as sacred objects in nature, and *fanafody* to herbal remedies – around 60% of the plants so far catalogued in Madagascar have healing

around!' The closest relations carry the body but others could touch and say hello. When carrying them, they make sure that the feet go first and the head behind. Everybody carries their loved ones out of the tomb in a line, crying but happy.

When all the bodies are out, they are put on the ground on the front side of the tomb, the head facing east, with their immediate family seated around their loved one. This is a very important moment of the *famadihana*: the beginning of the wrapping of the body. The old shroud in which the body was buried is left on and the new silk shroud put on top of it, following the mummified shape and using baby safety pins to keep it in place. There are three new silk shrouds for my mother which have been donated in remembrance and gratitude. The belief is that she won't be cold and the top shroud befits her, being of top quality silk with beautiful, delicate embroidery. This is the time to touch her, give her something, talk to her. Her best friend is there, making sure that my mother is properly wrapped, as the ritual has to follow certain rules. Lots of touching as silent conversation goes on, giving her the latest news or family gossip, and asking for her blessing. Perfume is sprinkled on her and wishes made at the same time.

The music plays on, everyone happily sitting around the mummified bodies. Flowers are placed on the bodies. The feeling of togetherness and love is so strong. This occasion is not just for the immediate family, but for cousins, and cousins of cousins, uncles and aunts and everybody meeting, bonded by the same ties, belonging to one unique extended family.

Photographs of the dead person are now put on top of each body. There is a photograph of a couple on top of one body: they were husband and wife and are now together for ever in the same silk shroud.

Food is served in the forest area just next to the tombs. The huge feast and celebration begins.

Back to the bodies. We lift them, carrying them on our shoulders. We sing old rhymes and songs and dance in a line, circling the tomb seven times, moving the body on our shoulder and making it dance with us.

The last dance ends. The bodies have to be back inside the tombs by a precise time and the tomb is immediately closed after a last ritual cleaning. This moment of goodbye is very emotional. The next time the tomb will be opened will not be for happiness but grief because it will be for a burial. *Famadihana* happens only once every seven or ten years.

Everybody returns to the cars and drives to the next meeting place – my uncle's, where a huge party finishes the day. Everyone is happy at having done their duty, *Vita ny adidy*!

It has been a very special day for me. My mother was extremely traditional, spending endless energy and money during her lifetime to keep the traditions. It all makes sense now because this *famadihana* brought so much joy, a strong sense of belonging and identity, and give a spiritual feeling that death is not an end but an extension into another life, linked somehow with this one.

Misaotra ry neny ('Thank you Mum').

properties. Travellers will sometimes come across conspicuous *ody* in the form of stones or trees which are sacred for a whole village, not just for an individual. Such trees are called *hazo manga*, 'good tree', and are presided over by the *mpisoro*, the senior man of the oldest family in the village. Another type of *ody* is the talisman, *aoly*, worn for protection if someone has transgressed a *fady* or broken a promise. *Aoly* are sometimes kept in the house or buried. *Ody fiti* are used to gain love (white magic) but sorcerers also sell other forms of *ody* for black magic and are paid by clients with either money, zebu or poultry (a red rooster being preferred).

Mpamonka are witch doctors with an intimate knowledge of poison and *mpisikidy* are sorcerers who use amulets, stones, and beads (known as *hasina*) for their cures. Sorcerers who use these in a destructive way are called *mpamosavy*.

On their death, sorcerers are not buried in tombs but are dumped to the west of their villages, barely covered with soil so that feral dogs and other creatures can eat their bodies. Their necks are twisted to face south.

Thanks to Nivo Ravelojaona, of Za Tours, who provided much of the above information.

THE WAY IT IS... Visitors from the West often find the beliefs and customs of the Malagasy merely bizarre. It takes time and effort to understand and respect the richness of tradition that underpins Malagasy society, but it is an effort well worth making.

Leonard Fox, author of *Hainteny*, sums it up perfectly:

> Whoever has witnessed the silent radiance of those who come to pray… at the house of Andrianampoinimerina in Ambohimanga and has experienced the nobility, modesty, unobsequious courtesy, and balanced wholeness of the poorest Merina who has remained faithful to his heritage can have no doubt as to the deep integrative value of the Malagasy spiritual tradition.

MALAGASY SOCIETY

MARRIAGE AND CHILDREN The Malagasy have a strong sense of community which influences their way of life. Just as the ancestors are laid in a communal tomb, so

MALAGASY HATS

Camilla Backhouse

During my year working in Madagascar I was particularly struck by the wonderful array of different hats that were worn there. Market stalls were piled high with hats of all shapes, colours and sizes. I had done some millinery before and was extremely interested in all the different weaves and so spent time learning about them.

Little had been noted about Malagasy headwear until the missionaries came in the early 19th century. At that time, apparently, few hats were worn as a person's hairstyle was regarded as more important and a sign of beauty. People from each region of Madagascar had different ways of plaiting their hair and they would often incorporate shells, coins or jewels. Oils and perfumes were massaged into the hair – the richer people used *Tseroka*, a type of castor oil mixed with the powdered leaf of *Ravintsara*, which produced a nutmeg scent, while the poorest population were satisfied with the fat of an ox or cow.

The chiefs wore simple headdresses but it was not until the Europeans came that hats became more popular. Although plaiting and the art of weaving were already very well established, there was little or no evidence of woven hats. The cutting of hair was introduced in 1822 which may have changed the Malagasy attitudes to wearing hats – to cover an unplaited head certainly would not be any detriment to their beauty. Initially hats were worn by the more wealthy people. Chiefs could be seen wearing caps made of neatly woven rushes or coarse grass and the people of Tana began to wear hats of more costly and durable material (often imported from overseas). It was Jean Laborde in the 1850s who started the industry of hat-making and helped to increase the production of them.

In each region the hats vary – they use different plant fibres (depending on what

their descendants share a communal way of life, and even children are almost considered common property within their extended family. Children are seldom disciplined but learn by example.

Marriage is a fairly relaxed union and divorce is common. There is no formal dowry arrangement or bride price, but a present of zebu cattle will often be made. In rural communities the man should bring his new wife home to his village (not vice versa) or he will lose face. You often see young men walking to market wearing a comb in their hair. They are advertising their quest for a wife.

Most Malagasy (and all Christians) have only one wife, but there are exceptions. There is, for example, a well-known man living in Antalaha, in the northeast, who has 11 wives and 120 children. This arrangement seems to work surprisingly well, with each wife working to support her own children, and a head wife to whom the others defer. The man is wealthy enough to provide housing for all his family.

THE VILLAGE COMMUNITY Malagasy society is a structured hierarchy with two fundamental rules: respect for the other person and knowing one's place. Within a village, the community is based on the traditional *fokonolona*. This concept was introduced by King Andrianampoinimerina when these councils of village elders were given responsibility for, among other things, law and order and the collection of taxes. Day-to-day decisions are still made by the *fokonolona*.

Rural Malagasy houses are always aligned north/south and generally have only one room. Furniture is composed of mats, *tsihy*, often beautifully woven. These are used for sitting and sleeping, and sometimes food is served on them. There are often *fady* attached to *tsihy*. For example you should not step over a mat, particularly one on which meals are eaten.

grows well near them), different weaves and occasionally dyes. The colours used are not the vegetable or plant dyes I had imagined but imported from China. The fibres are usually from palms (raffia, *badika*, *manarana*, *dara*), reeds (*penjy*, *harefo*) or straw. Some of the best regions that I came across for seeing weaving were near Lac Tritriva (straw), Maroantsetra (raffia), Mananjary (*penjy*, *dara*), Mahsoabe near Fianarantsoa (*badika*) and Vohipeno (*harefo*).

The ways of preparing the fibres differ, but in general they are dried, flattened and then, if necessary, using a sharp knife, are stripped into thin fibres. They are then ready for weaving. Some are woven into strips which are eventually machined together, while other regions use a continuous weave method to make the entire hat. The latter method can be extremely complicated and is an amazing art to watch. The weaver will place their foot on the central part of the woven circle and gradually intertwine hundreds of different fibres into position. One of my lasting memories was spending time in Maroantsetra where they make the most beautiful crochet-style raffia hat. Women sit on palm mats outside their houses weaving, while children play, plait hair or busily prepare food for the next meal. Occasionally the hats are blocked (a method of shaping a crown or brim over a wooden block). There are places in Tana where they heat steel blocks on a fire and then press the woven hat into a trilby style for example. This was a fascinating sight to see as normally these blocks are electrically heated.

The variety of hats is astounding. It can take a day for a woman to weave a hat, and this can be a main source of family income. If you are interested in getting a Malagasy hat, it is worthwhile getting to know a weaver so they may be able to make one large enough for the *vahaza* head!

Part of the Malagasy culture is the art of oratory, *kabary*. Originally *kabary* were the huge meetings where King Andrianampoinimerina proclaimed his plans, but the word has now evolved to mean the elaborate form of speech used to inspire and control the crowds at such gatherings. Even rural leaders can speak for hours, using highly ornate language and many proverbs; a necessary skill in a society that reached a high degree of sophistication without a written language.

The market plays a central role in the life of rural people, who will often walk 15–20km to market with no intention of selling or buying, but simply to catch up on the gossip or continue the conversation broken off the previous week. You will see well-dressed groups of young people happily making their way to this social centre. Often there is a homemade tombola, and other outlets for gambling.

FESTIVALS AND CEREMONIES Malagasy Christians celebrate the usual holy days, but most tribes or clans have their special festivals.

Ala volon-jaza This is the occasion when a baby's hair is cut for the first time. With the Antambahoka people in the south the haircut is performed by the grandparents. The child is placed in a basin filled with water, and afterwards bathed. Among the Merina the ceremony is similar but only a man whose parents are still alive may cut a baby's hair. The family then have a meal of rice, zebu, milk and honey. Coins are placed in the bowl of rice and the older children compete to get as many as possible.

Circumcision Boys are usually circumcised at the age of about two; a baby who dies before this operation has been performed may not be buried in the family tomb.

The operation itself is often done surgically, but in some rural areas it may still be performed with a sharpened piece of bamboo. The foreskin is not always simply discarded. In the region of the Antambahoka it may be eaten by the grandparents, and in Antandroy country it could be shot from the barrel of a gun!

Different clans have their own circumcision ceremonies. Among the Antandroy, uncles dance with their nephews on their shoulders. But the most famous ceremony is *Sambatra*, which takes place every seven years in Mananjary.

Tsangatsaine This is a ceremony performed by the Antankarana. Two tall trees growing side by side near the house of a noble family are tied together to symbolise the unification of the tribe, as well as the tying together of the past and present, the living and the dead.

Fandroana This was the royal bath ceremony which marked the Malagasy New Year. These celebrations used to take place in March, with much feasting. While the monarch was ritually bathed, the best zebu was slaughtered and the choicest rump steak presented to the village nobles. The day was the equivalent of the Malagasy National Day, but the French moved this to 14 July, the date of the establishment of the French Protectorate. This caused major resentment among the Malagasy as effectively their traditional New Year was taken from them. After independence the date was changed to 26 June to coincide with Independence Day. These days, because of the cost of zebu meat and the value attached to the animals, the traditional meat has been replaced by chicken, choice portions again being given to the respected members of the community. In the absence of royalty there is, of course, no royal bath ceremony.

This section was originally taken from A Glance at Madagascar *by Ken Paginton in 1973 (and at that time the only authoritative source on Madagascar) and has subsequently been added to from a variety of sources.*

The different clans of Madagascar are based more upon old kingdoms than upon ethnic grouping. Traditions are changing: the descriptions below reflect the tribes at the time of independence, rather than in the more fluid society of today.

ANTAIFASY (PEOPLE-OF-THE-SANDS) Living in the southeast around Farafangana, they cultivate rice, and fish in the lakes and rivers. Divided into three clans, each with its own 'king', they generally have stricter moral codes than other tribes. They have large collective burial houses known as *kibory*, built of wood or stone and generally hidden in the forest.

ANTAIMORO (PEOPLE-OF-THE-COAST) These are among the most recent arrivals and live in the southeast around Vohipeno and Manakara. They guard Islamic tradition and Arab influence and still use a form of Arab writing known as *sorabe*. They use verses of the Koran as amulets.

ANTAISAKA Centred south of Farafangana on the southeast coast but now fairly widely spread throughout the island, they are an off-shoot of the Sakalava tribe. They cultivate coffee, bananas and rice – but only the women harvest the rice. There are strong marriage taboos amongst them. Often the houses may have a second door on the east side which is used only for taking out a corpse. They use the *kibory*, communal burial house, the corpse usually being dried out for two or three years before finally being put there.

ANTANKARANA (THOSE-OF-THE-ROCKS) Living in the north around Antsiranana (Diego Suarez) they are fishermen or cattle raisers whose rulers came from the Sakalava dynasty. Their houses are usually raised on stilts. Numerous *fady* exist amongst them governing relations between the sexes in the family; for example a girl may not wash her brother's clothes. The legs of a fowl are the father's portion, whereas amongst the Merina, for instance, they are given to the children.

ANTAMBAHOAKA (THOSE-OF-THE-PEOPLE) The smallest tribe, of the same origin as the Antaimoro and living around Mananjary on the southeast coast. They have some Arab traits and amulets are used. They bury in a *kibory*. Group circumcision ceremonies are carried out every seven years.

THE *VAZIMBA*

Vazimba is the name given to the earliest inhabitants of Madagascar, pastoralists of the central plateaux who were displaced or absorbed by later immigrants. Once thought to be pre-Indonesian aboriginals from Africa, it is now generally accepted that they were survivors of the earliest Austronesian immigrants who were pushed to the west by later arrivals.

Vazimba come into both the legends and history of the Malagasy. *Vazimba* tombs are now places of pilgrimage where sacrifices are made for favours and cures. It is *fady* to step over such a tomb. *Vazimba* are also thought to haunt certain springs and rocks, and offerings may be made here. They are the ancestral guardians of the soil.

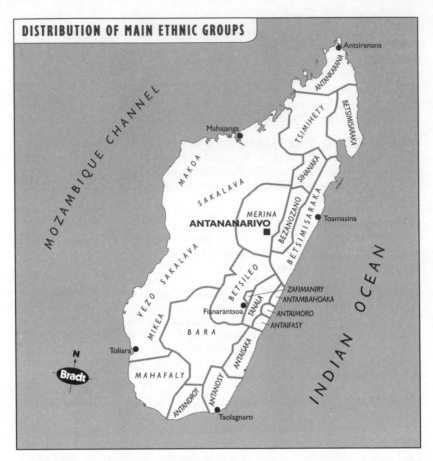

DISTRIBUTION OF MAIN ETHNIC GROUPS

(Map of Madagascar showing: Antsiranana, ANTANKARANA, BETSIMISARAKA, TSIMIHETY, Mahajanga, MAKOA, SIHANAKA, SAKALAVA, BEZANOZANO, MERINA, ANTANANARIVO, BETSIMISARAKA, Toamasina, SAKALAVA, VEZO, BETSILEO, ZAFIMANIRY, ANTAMBAHOAKA, Fianarantsoa, TANALA, ANTAIMORO, MIKEA, BARA, ANTAIFASY, Toliara, ANTAISAKA, MAHAFALY, ANTANOSY, ANTANDROY, Taolagnaro, MOZAMBIQUE CHANNEL, INDIAN OCEAN, Bradt)

ANTANDROY (PEOPLE-OF-THE-THORNS) Traditionally nomadic, they live in the arid south around Ambovombe. A dark-skinned people, they wear little clothing and are said to be frank and open, easily roused to either joy or anger. Their women occupy an inferior position, and it is *fady* for a woman to milk a cow. The villages are often surrounded by a hedge of cactus plants. Until recently they ate little rice, their staples being maize, cassava and sweet potatoes. They believe in the *kokolampo*, a spirit of either good or bad influence. Their tombs are similar to those of the Mahafaly tribe. Sometimes it is *fady* among them for a child to say his father's name, or to refer by name to parts of his father's body. Thus he may say *ny fandiany* (the-what-he-moves-with) for his feet, and *ny amboniny* (the-top-of-him) for his head.

ANTANOSY (PEOPLE-OF-THE-ISLAND) The island is a small one in the Fanjahira River. They live in the southeast, principally around Taolagnaro (Fort Dauphin). Their social structure is based on clans with a 'king' holding great authority over each one. There are strict *fady* governing relationships in the family. For example, a brother may not sit on or step over his sister's mat. As with many other tribes there are numerous *fady* regarding pregnancy: a pregnant woman should not sit in the doorway of the house; she should not eat brains; she should not converse with men; people who have no children should not stay in her house overnight. Other *fady* are that relatives should not eat meat at a funeral and the diggers opening a tomb should not wear clothes. When digging holes for the corner posts of a new house it may be *fady* to stand up so the job must be performed sitting down.

BARA Originally in the southwest near Toliara, these nomadic cattle raisers now live in the south-central area around Ihosy and Betroka. Their name has no special meaning but it is reputed to derive from an African (Bantu) word. They

THE MALAGASY *LAMBA*

Joseph Radoccia

Lambas are the most distinctive item of traditional Malagasy clothing, and among one of the island's most vibrant forms of artistic expression. There are many types of *lamba*, each with its own role in Malagasy culture. The Merina highlanders have a long tradition of handweaving; the *lamba* is the fruit of this tradition. However, the variety most often encountered is not handwoven, but rather the machine-manufactured *lamba* hoany.

This, the category designated for everyday use, is a large decoratively printed rectangular cotton cloth. Some feature brilliantly hued repetitive patterns surrounding a central medallion, while others, printed in two or three colours, depict a rural or coastal scene within an ornate border. You may also find some with images of Malagasy landmarks, the annual calendar, or historic events such as the election of President Ravalomanana. A consistent feature of the various styles of *lamba hoany* is one essential recurring element that makes each unique: in a narrow box along the bottom you will find a Malagasy proverb or words of wisdom. For this reason the *lamba hoany* are often referred to as 'proverb cloths'.

As you travel the island you will discover that this seemingly simple wraparound cloth is adapted for many purposes. It is an invaluable essential for almost every citizen of rural Madagascar. As clothing, it is worn in coastal regions as a sarong, while in the highlands *lambas* are draped around shoulders as shawls for added warmth in the evening chill. Everywhere on the island the *lamba hoany* is employed as a sling to carry a child on a mother's back or rolled up to cushion the weight when carrying a large basket on one's head. You may also encounter a *lamba* used as a light blanket, curtains in a window or door, and on occasion as a wall-hanging or tablecloth.

You can purchase a *lamba* at almost any market. The souvenir vendors usually carry a few, but you will find a much wider selection – at better prices – with the textile merchants. By far the widest choice is to be found at the fabric stores just north of the Analakely market pavilions in Antananarivo. Here hanging from the ceiling in each shop is row after row of gorgeously coloured *lambas*. Point one out and the merchant will spread it out for your perusal. Be sure to look at a few, because each one is a unique piece of art. Take your new purchase to one of the tailors in the market to have the edges hemmed for a small fee.

Another significant type is the *lumbamena* (literally 'red cloth,' although not necessarily red in colour). These are handwoven from the silk of an indigenous Malagasy silkworm and used primarily as burial shrouds in funerary ceremonies. If you prefer a traditional handwoven *lamba*, a nice colourful selection can be found at the Anosy flower market in Tana.

Joseph Radoccia is an artist and Malagasy art enthusiast who visits Madagascar frequently to paint. His paintings inspired by his lamba collection can be viewed at www.radoccia.com.

may be polygamous and women occupy an inferior position in their society. They attach importance to the *fatidra* or 'blood pact'. Cattle stealing is regarded as proof of manhood and courage, without which a man cannot expect to get a wife. They are dancers and sculptors, a unique feature of their carved wooden figures being eyelashes of real hair set into the wood. They believe in the *helo*, a spirit that manifests itself at the foot of trees. In the past a whole village would move after somebody died owing to the fear of ghosts. They use caves in the mountains for burial. It is the custom to shave the head on the death of a near relative.

BETSILEO (THE-MANY-INVINCIBLES) They are centred in the south of the Hauts Plateaux around Fianarantsoa but about 150,000 of them also live in the Betsiboka region. They are energetic and expert rice-producers, their irrigated, terraced rice-fields being a feature of the landscape. *Famadihana* was introduced to their culture by the Merina at the time of Queen Ranavalona I. It is *fady* for the husband of a pregnant woman to wear a *lamba* thrown over his shoulder. It may be *fady* for the family to eat until the father is present or for anyone to pick up his fork until the most honourable person present has started to eat.

BETSIMISARAKA (THE-MANY-INSEPARABLES) They are the second largest tribe and live on the east coast in the region between Nosy Varika and Antalaha. Their culture has been influenced by Europeans, particularly pirates. They cultivate rice and work on vanilla plantations. Their clothes are sometimes made from locally woven raffia. Originally their society included numerous local chiefs. The *tangalamena* is the local official for religious rites and customs. The Betsimisaraka have many superstitious beliefs: *angatra* (ghosts), *zazavavy an-drano* (mermaids), and *kalamoro*, little wild men of the woods, about 25 inches high with long flowing hair, who like to slip into houses and steal rice from the cooking pot. In the north coffins are generally placed under a shelter, in the south in tombs. It may be *fady* for a brother to shake hands with his sister, or for a young man to wear shoes while his father is still living.

BEZANOZANO (MANY-SMALL-PLAITS) The name refers to the way in which they do their hair. They were probably one of the first tribes to become established in Madagascar and now live in an area between the Betsimisaraka lowlands and the Merina highlands. Like the Merina, they practise *famadihana*. As with most of the coastal tribes their funeral celebrations involve the consumption of considerable quantities of *toaka* (rum).

MAHAFALY (THOSE-WHO-MAKE-TABOOS OR THOSE-WHO-MAKE-HAPPY) The etymology of the word is sometimes disputed but the former meaning is generally regarded as being correct. They probably arrived around the 12th century and live in the southwest desert area around Ampanihy and Ejeda. They are farmers, with maize, sorgho and sweet potatoes as their chief crops; cattle rearing occupies a secondary place. They kept their independence under their own local chiefs until the French occupation and still keep the bones of some of their old chiefs – this is the *jiny* cult. Their villages usually have a sacrificial post, the *hazo manga*, on the east side where sacrifices are made. Some of the blood is generally put on the foreheads of the people attending.

The tombs of the Mahafaly attract a great deal of interest. They are big rectangular constructions of uncut stone rising some three feet above the ground and decorated with *aloalo* and the horns of the cattle slain at the funeral feast. The tomb of the Mahafaly king Tsiampody has the horns of 700 zebu on it. The *aloalo* are sculpted wooden posts set upright on the tomb, often depicting scenes from the person's life. The burial customs include waiting for the decomposition of the body before it is placed in the tomb. It is the practice for a person to be given a new name after death – generally beginning with 'Andria'.

The divorce rate is very high and it is not at all uncommon for a man to divorce and remarry six or seven times. It is very often *fady* for children to sleep in the same house as their parents. Their *rombo* (very similar to the *tromba* of the Sakalava) is the practice of contacting various spirits for healing purposes. Amongst the spirits believed in are the *raza* who are not real ancestors and in some cases are even supposed to include *vazaha* (white foreigners), and the *vorom-be* which is the spirit of a big bird.

MAKOA The Makoa are descended from slaves taken from the Makua people of Mozambique, and although sometimes classified as Vezo, they maintain a separate identity. Typically of larger stature than most Malagasy, Makoa men were often employed by the French as policemen and soldiers, thus reinforcing their distinction from other Malagasy.

MERINA (PEOPLE-OF-THE-HIGHLANDS) They live on the Hauts Plateaux, the most developed area of the country, the capital being 95% Merina. They are of Malayo-Polynesian origin and vary in colour from ivory to very dark, with straight hair. They used to be divided into three castes: the Andriana (nobles), the Hova (freemen) and the Andevo (serfs); but legally these divisions no longer exist. Most Merina houses are built of brick or mud; some are two-storey buildings with slender pillars, where the people live mainly upstairs. Most villages of any size have a church – probably two, Catholic and Protestant. There is much irrigated rice cultivation, and the Merina were the first tribe to have any skill in architecture and metallurgy. *Famadihana* is essentially a Merina custom.

MIKEA The term 'Mikea' refers not so much to a tribe as to a lifestyle. They subsist by foraging in the dry forests of the west and southwest. Various groups of people along the west coast are called Mikea, although their main area is the Forêt des Mikea between Morombe and Toliara. The Mikea are Malagasy of various origins, having adopted their particular lifestyle (almost unique in Madagascar) for several reasons, including fleeing from oppression and taxation etc exerted on them by various powers: Sakalava, French, and the Government of the 2nd Republic. (Information from Dr J Bond.)

SAKALAVA (PEOPLE-OF-THE-LONG-VALLEYS) They live in the west between Toliara and Mahajanga and are dark skinned with Polynesian features and short curly hair. They were at one time the largest and most powerful tribe, though disunited, and were ruled by their own kings and queens. Certain royal relics remain – sometimes being kept in the northeast corner of a house. The Sakalava are cattle raisers, and riches are reckoned by the number of cattle owned. There is a record of human sacrifice amongst them up to the year 1850 at special occasions such as the death of a king. The *tromba* (trance state) is quite common. It is *fady* for pregnant women to eat fish or to sit in a doorway. Women hold a more important place amongst them than in most other tribes.

SIHANAKA (PEOPLE-OF-THE-SWAMPS) Their home is the northeast of the old kingdom of Imerina around Lake Alaotra and they have much in common with the Merina. They are fishermen, rice growers and poultry raisers. Swamps have been drained to make vast rice-fields cultivated with modern machinery and methods. They have a special rotation of *fady* days.

References in this book to the Merina have hitherto been focused on their military abilities, but this tribe has a rich and complex spiritual life. Perhaps the shortest route to the soul of any society is through its poetry, and we are fortunate that there is a book of the traditional Malagasy poetry, *Hainteny*. Broadly speaking, *hainteny* are poems about love: love between parent and child, between man and woman, the love of nature, the appreciation of good versus evil, the acceptance of death. Through the sensitive translations of Leonard Fox, the spiritual and emotional life of the Merina is made available to the reader who cannot fail to be impressed by these remarkable people. As Leonard Fox says: 'On the most basic level, *hainteny* give us an incomparable insight into a society characterised by exceptional refinement and subtlety, deep appreciation of beauty, delight in sensual enjoyment, and profound respect for the spiritual realities of life.'

Here are two examples of *hainteny*. There are others on pages 176, 357 and 363.

What is the matter, Raivonjaza,
That you remain silent?
Have you been paid or hired and your mouth tied,
That you do not speak with us, who are your parents?
– I have not been paid or hired
and my mouth has not been tied,
but I am going home to my husband
and am leaving my parents,
my child, and my friends,
so I am distressed,
speaking little.
Here is my child, dear Mother and Father.
If he is stubborn, be strict, but do not beat him;
and if you hit him, do not use a stick.
And do not act as though you do not see him
when he is under your eyes, saying:
'Has this child eaten?'
Do not give him too much,
Do not give him the remains of a meal,
and do not give him what is half-cooked,
for I will be far and will long for him.

———

Do not love me, Andriamatoa, as one loves
the banana tree exposed to the wind,
overcome and in danger from cold.
Do not love me as one loves a door:
It is loved, but constantly pushed.
Love me as one loves a little crab:
even its claws are eaten.

ST MARIANS The population of Ile Sainte Marie (Nosy Boraha) is mixed. Although Indonesian in origin there has been influence from both Arabs and European pirates.

TANALA (PEOPLE-OF-THE-FOREST) These are traditionally forest-dwellers, living inland from Manakara, and are rice and coffee growers. Their houses are usually built on stilts. The Tanala are divided into two groups: the Ikongo in the south and the Menabe in the north. The Ikongo are an independent people who never submitted to Merina domination, in contrast to the Menabe. Burial customs include keeping the corpse for up to a month. Coffins are made from large trees to which sacrifices are sometimes made when they are cut down. The Ikongo usually bury their dead in the forest and may mark a tree to show the spot.

Some recent authorities dispute that the Tanala exist as a separate ethnic group.

TSIMIHETY (THOSE-WHO-DO-NOT-CUT-THEIR-HAIR) The refusal to cut their hair (to show mourning on the death of a Sakalava king) was to demonstrate their independence. They are an energetic and vigorous people in the north-central area and are spreading west. The oldest maternal uncle occupies an important position.

VEZO (FISHING PEOPLE) More usually referred to as Vezo–Sakalava, they are not generally recognised as a separate tribe but as a clan of the Sakalava. They live on the coast in the region of Morondava in the west to Faux Cap in the south. They use little canoes hollowed out from tree trunks and fitted with one outrigger pole and a small rectangular sail. In these frail but stable craft they go far out to sea. The Vezo are also noted for their tombs, which are graves dug into the ground surrounded by wooden palisades, the main posts of which are crowned by erotic wooden carved figures.

ZAFIMANIRY A clan of some 15,000 people distributed in about 100 villages in the forests between the Betsileo and Tanala areas southeast of Ambositra. They are known for their woodcarvings and sculpture, and are descended from people from the Hauts Plateaux who established themselves there early in the 19th century. The Zafimaniry are thus interesting to historians as they continue the forms of housing

SOME MALAGASY PROVERBS

Tantely tapa-bata ka ny foko no entiko mameno azy.
This is only half a pot of honey but my heart fills it up.

Mahavoa roa toy ny dakam-boriky.
Hit two things at once like the kick of a donkey.

Tsy midera vady tsy herintaona.
Don't praise your wife before a year.

Ny omby singorana amin' ny tandrony, ary ny olona kosa amin' ny vavany.
Oxen are trapped by their horns and men by their words.

Tondro tokana tsy mahazo hao.
You can't catch a louse with one finger.

Ny alina mitondra fisainana.
The night brings wisdom.

*Aza manonofy harena aombin. *
If you are just a dung beetle don't try to move mountains.

Aza midera harena, fa niter-day.
Do not boast about your wealth if you are a father.

Ny teny toy ny fonosana, ka izay mamono no mamaha.
Words are like a parcel: if you tie lots of knots you will have to undo them.

and decoration of past centuries. Their houses, which are made from vegetable fibres and wood with bamboo walls and roofs, have no nails and can be taken down and moved from one village to another.

In the last few years there have been several anthropological books published in English about the people of Madagascar. See *Books* on page 59.

The tribes may differ but a Malagasy proverb shows their feeling of unity: *Ny olombelona toy ny molo-bilany, ka iray mihodidina ihany*; 'Men are like the lip of the cooking pot which forms just one circle'.

MALAGASY WITHOUT (TOO MANY) TEARS

Janice Booth

Once you've thrown out the idea that you must speak a foreign language correctly or not at all, and that you must use complete sentences, you can have fun with only a few words of Malagasy. Basic French is understood almost everywhere, but the people – particularly in villages – warm instantly to any attempts to speak 'their own' language.

If you learn only three words, choose *misaotra* (thank you), pronounced 'misowtr'; *veloma* (goodbye), pronounced 'veloom'; and *manao ahoana* (pronounced roughly 'manna owner'), which is an all-purpose word meaning 'hello', 'good morning' or 'good day'. If you can squeeze in another three, go for *tsara* (good); *aza fady* (please), pronounced 'azafad'; and *be* (pronounced 'beh'), which can be used – sometimes ungrammatically, but who cares! – to mean 'big', 'very' or 'much'. Thus *tsara be* means very good; and *misaotra be* means a big thank you. Finally, when talking to an older person, it's polite to add *tompoko* (pronounced 'toompk') after 'thank you' or 'goodbye'. This is equivalent to Madame or Monsieur in French. If your memory's poor, write the vocabulary on a postcard and carry it round with you.

In a forest one evening, at dusk, I was standing inside the trunk and intertwining roots of a huge banyan tree, looking up through the branches at the fading sky and a few early stars. It was very peaceful, very silent. Suddenly a small man appeared from the shadows, holding a rough wooden dish. Old and poorly dressed, probably a cattle herder, he stood uncertainly, not wanting to disturb me. I said '*Manao ahoana*,' and he replied. I touched the bark of the tree gently and said '*tsara*'. '*Tsara*,' he agreed, smiling. Then he said a sentence in which I recognised *tantely* (honey). I pointed questioningly to a wild bees' nest high in the tree. '*Tantely*,' he repeated quietly, pleased. I pointed to his dish – '*Tantely sakafo?*' Yes, he was collecting wild honey for food. '*Tsara. Veloma, tompoko.*' I moved off into the twilight. '*Veloma*,' he called softly after me. So few words, so much said.

Another day, in Tana, a teenaged girl was pestering me for money. She didn't seem very deserving but wouldn't give up. Then I asked her in Malagasy, 'What's your name?' She looked astonished, eyes suddenly meeting mine instead of sliding furtively. 'Noro.' So I asked, very politely, 'Please, Noro, go away. Goodbye.' Nonplussed, she stared at me briefly before moving off, the cringing attitude quite gone. By using her name, I'd given her dignity. You can find that vocabulary in the language appendix on page 452.

'What's your name?' is probably the phrase I most enjoy using. Say it to a child and its eyes grow wider, as a timid little voice answers you. Then you can say '*Manao ahoana*', using the name, and you've forged a link. Now learn how to say 'My name is…' – and you're into real conversation!

When I'm in Madagascar I still carry a copy of the language appendix in my bag. It's dog-eared now, and scribbled on. But it's my passport to a special kind of contact with friendly, gentle and fascinating people.

LANGUAGE

The Indonesian origin of the Malagasy people shows strongly in their language which is spoken, with regional variations of dialect, throughout the island. (Words for domestic animals, however, are derived from Kiswahili, indicating that the early settlers, sensibly enough, did not bring animals with them in their outrigger canoes.) Malagasy is a remarkably rich language, full of images, metaphors and proverbs. Literal translations of Malagasy words and phrases are often very poetic. 'Dusk' is *Maizim-bava vilany*, 'Darken the mouth of the cooking pot'; 'two or three in the morning' is *Misafo helika ny kary*, 'When the wild cat washes itself'. The richness of the language means that there are few English words that can be translated into a single word in Malagasy, and vice versa. An example given by Leonard Fox in his book on the poetry of Madagascar, *Hainteny*, is *miala mandry*. *Miala* means 'go out/go away' and *mandry* means 'lie down/go to sleep'. Together, however, they mean 'to spend the night away from home, and yet be back in the early morning as if never having been away'!

Learning, or even using, the Malagasy language may seem a challenging prospect to the first-time visitor. Place names may be 15 characters long (because they usually have a literal meaning, such as Ranomafana: hot water), with seemingly erratic syllable stress. However, as a courtesy to the Malagasy people you should learn a few Malagasy words. There is a Malagasy vocabulary on page 452 and a recommended phrase book in *Appendix 4*.

3

Natural History

Daniel Austin & Kelly Green

INTRODUCTION

Isolated for 65 million years, Madagascar is the oldest island on earth. As a result its natural history is unique. There are over 200,000 species on the island, living in habitats ranging from rainforests to deserts and from mountain tops to mangrove swamps. The residents are as unique as they are diverse – a list of Malagasy species reads like a hurried appendix tagged on to the end of a catalogue of the world's wildlife. Eight whole plant families exist only on Madagascar, as do close to 1,000 orchid species, many thousands of succulents, countless insects, at least 350 species of frog, around 370 kinds of reptile, five families of birds and approaching 200 different mammals, including an entire branch of the primate family tree, the order to which we ourselves belong.

This magnificent menagerie is the product of a spectacular geological past. About 167 million years ago Madagascar was a land-locked plateau at the centre of the largest continent the Earth has ever seen: Gondwana. This was during the age of the reptiles at about the time when flowering plants were beginning to blossom and primitive mammals and birds were finding a niche among their giant dinosaur cohabitants. With a combination of sea-level rises and plate movements Gondwana subsequently broke apart. Madagascar, still attached to present-day India, drifted away from Africa. Then, around the time of the mass dinosaur extinction, Madagascar broke completely free, setting itself adrift as one of the earth's great experiments in evolution.

Some of the plants and animals present on the island today are the results of adaptation from the original, marooned Gondwana stock. Ancient groups such as the ferns, cycads, palms and screw pines, and primitive reptiles such as the boas and iguanids, are descendants of this relic community. Yet the magic of Madagascar is that a select band of species has enriched the community by arriving *since* the break-up. Flying, swimming, journeying as seeds or riding the floodwaters of the east African rivers in hollow trunks, wave after wave of more recent plants and animals came from over the horizon during a period of 100 million years, bringing with them the latest adaptations from the big world beyond. Colonisers, such as the lemurs and carnivores, may have had a helping hand from a partial land-bridge which is thought to have appeared from beneath the waves of the Mozambique Channel about 40 million years ago.

Yet, whatever their mode of transport, upon landfall each species spread outwards in every direction, through the tremendous range of habitats, changing subtly as they encountered new environments, frequently to the extent that new species were formed. This evolutionary process is termed 'adaptive radiation' and it results in the creation of an array of new species found nowhere else.

The patterns in the island's diversity tell us something of the timing of these colonisations. A large number of unique succulent plants indicates an early arrival from Africa in the dry west, followed by a radiation eastwards ending in the rainforests. On the other hand, the two Malagasy pitcher plants found on the east coast probably arrived at about the same time as the people, and from the same direction.

From this great evolutionary melting pot has emerged the bewildering array of animals and plants that bless Madagascar today; most are unique to the island and countless still await discovery.

MADAGASCAR'S EXTINCT MEGAFAUNA

Madagascar is famed for its bizarre and unique wildlife today, but many of the island's most fascinating animal inhabitants have long since disappeared.

Recently a truly remarkable discovery was made in southern Madagascar. Scientists unearthed two prosauropods (herbivorous dinosaurs) that dated back 230 million years, making them not only the earliest fossils ever to be found in Madagascar, but also probably the oldest in the world.

Another unusual find was of a very strange blunt-snouted, herbivorous crocodile in northwest Madagascar, dating from the late Cretaceous (97–65 million years ago). Prior to the discovery of this beast (*Simosuchus clarki*) experts had believed ancient crocodiles to resemble more closely those alive today.

In 2001 a new species of dinosaur was found and is thought to be the first animal to take its name from a pop star. Palaeontologists named *Masiakasaurus knopfleri* after the lead guitarist of Dire Straits because whenever they played his music they struck lucky finding fossils! *M. knopfleri* was a ferocious little bipedal carnivore (the genus name *Masiakasaurus* comes from *masiaka*, Malagasy for 'violent') whose larger cousin *Majungatholus atopus* was discovered by the same team from the State University of New York, Stony Brook. This lived around 70–65 million years ago and is believed to have been cannibalistic. An examination of distinctive marks on the fossilised bones suggests that they could only have been caused by the teeth of the same species, though it is still a matter of debate whether the victim was alive at the time. (Cannibalism has been documented in only one other species of dinosaur: *Coelophysis bauri*. A specimen was found with the remains of juvenile individuals preserved in its stomach.)

Until very recently, Madagascar had a flourishing megafauna (a word used to refer to all large animals). When humans first settled on the island less than 2,000 years ago, they would have been greeted with great forests populated by huge tortoises, dwarf hippos and lemurs the size of gorillas. Around 16 species of lemur are known to have been bigger than the indri, the largest alive today, but all are now extinct as a result of the arrival of man.

Perhaps the most amazing of Madagascar's extinct animals is still fresh in Malagasy folklore. Tales of this creature were passed along to Marco Polo who wrote extravagantly of an awesome bird, the giant roc, capable of carrying off an elephant. This majestic animal was, in fact, the flightless elephant bird or *Aepyornis*. Standing over 3m tall, it would have made an ostrich seem like a goose. The largest, *Aepyornis maximus*, weighed in at more than 500kg and is thought to have been the largest bird ever to have lived. Sadly, like the famous dodo of neighbouring Mauritius, it was driven to extinction by humans in the last few centuries.

The roc as visualised by an artist in 1598

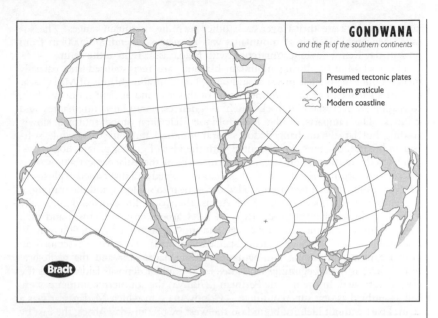

GONDWANA
and the fit of the southern continents

- ▨ Presumed tectonic plates
- ✕ Modern graticule
- ▨ Modern coastline

Bradt

BIODIVERSITY In recognition of its massive wealth of endemic flora and fauna, Madagascar has been designated a Biodiversity Hotspot by Conservation International – and as hotspots go, Madagascar is considered one of the hottest.

Biodiversity Hotspots cover less than 1% of the earth's surface, yet are home to well over half of its plant and animal species. Although it is not entirely understood why Madagascar has so many species, two factors have helped: it is near to the Equator and it contains an astonishing array of habitats. The tropical climate is a perfect host to the processes of life – far more living things survive within the tropics than in cooler regions – and the habitat variety provides greater opportunity for animal and plant variation.

GEOLOGY *With information from Tim Ireland*

Note: mya = million years ago

The story of Madagascar's astonishing natural history begins millions of years ago. The island's geology raises plenty of interesting questions – many still unanswered – and attracts geologists and mining companies from around the world. Madagascar comprises three main geological terranes: a **crystalline core** comprising the central highlands, a **sedimentary shelf** that flanks this core on the west, and dispersed **volcanic edifices**.

The **crystalline core** dates to the Late Proterozoic (900–550mya), a period long before the evolution of complex life, and before the assembly of the continents as we know them. Yet these rocks contain tiny crystals of zircon which testify to a far greater antiquity (2,600mya). It is thought that this zircon records the formation of a continent that would later become part of Gondwana. Other continental masses also existed, several that would later become the northern continents, and one that would split and become South America and Africa.

Two of these (South America-Africa and Australia-Antarctica-India-Madagascar) had been drifting slowly closer together until they collided 690mya, just as the first large multicellular marine creatures were beginning to evolve. During such collisions the edges of the continents crumple and sheets several kilometres thick are thrust over each other forming mountain ranges. The so-called Mozambique Belt of mountains was immense, extending 7,000km from present-day Kenya down to Antarctica, with Madagascar right at the centre.

The rocks buried during mountain-building are recrystallised and partially melted under the intense pressure and heat. The central highlands of Madagascar are just a small part of the exhumed roots of this vast and ancient mountain belt, consisting of recrystallised rocks such as gneisses, granulites, migmatites and granites. The ramparts of the Mozambique Belt then stood sentinel, slowly eroding but largely unchanged, for several hundred million years, while soft-bodied life in the oceans experimented with the idea of greater progression.

The **sedimentary shelf** began to form early in the Palaeozoic (500mya), as macroscopic organisms with external skeletons evolved and diversified explosively. The old mountain belt had been eroded down near to sea level, and the waning of an ice age caused flooding of the land. Across the world, life evolved dramatically towards a climax of plant productivity in the Carboniferous (320mya) and then shivered through its most severe ice age and most catastrophic extinction only 30 million years later (96% of marine species vanished). That ice age scraped all evidence of the preceding sedimentation from Madagascar and the geological record there is reset, beginning with gravel and boulder deposits laid down as the glaciers retreated. In the middle Permian (270mya) the southern continents were still assembled as one supercontinent – Gondwana – in which Madagascar was a central part without identity, bound on the west by present-day Africa, the east by India and the south by Antarctica.

Gondwana began to split apart soon after, towards the modern continental distribution. As a continent divides, rifts form, gradually becoming seas, then oceans. The rocks of the sedimentary shelf record 100 million years of deposition spanning that cycle for the rift separating Madagascar from Africa. The earliest sediments are mixed glacial, river and lake deposits that contain a fossil flora common to all the modern southern continents. Later, the land was inundated and marine carbonates were deposited in this new shallow sea preserving the remains of some primitive fish. During the Triassic (240–210mya) the landscape was uplifted and terrestrial gravels and sands were deposited, including those exposed in Isalo National Park. A major rise in sea level followed, and from this time until after the demise of the dinosaurs (63mya) fossil-bearing limestone sedimentation dominated in the growing Mozambique Channel. These sediments today make up the Bemahara Plateau and the *tsingy* landscapes of western Madagascar. The shallow marine ecosystems were characterised by a great abundance of ammonites, and today the sedimentary carbonates of west Madagascar are an incredible repository of these fossils. Uplifting occurred again 50–30mya as a major eastern rift developed between India and Madagascar, ending sedimentation on the shelf.

The **volcanic edifices** of Madagascar are less obvious than the volcanoes responsible for the islands of the Comoros, Réunion and Mauritius. They are widespread in the north and along the east coast, and inland they make up the Ankaratra Massif, Itasy highlands and Montagne d'Ambre. Underwater volcanic activity began during the Cretaceous (120mya) and has persisted off the north coast up to the present day. The lavas and intrusive rocks produced have a bizarre and unique chemistry. The most recent major volcanic activity occurred less than 2mya, giving rise to Nosy Be, where modern hot springs testify to the island's relative youth. There are suggestions that the volcanic focus is moving southeast towards Madagascar; the volcanic record in the island is potentially far from over.

Significant **landscape evolution** has occurred over the last 40 million years. Since India began to head northeast, the rift between Africa and Madagascar stabilised and mountains were regenerated by activity on major NNE- and NNW-

Hundreds of thousands of animals and plants are known to science but most do not have common names. Those that do may have many common names, or the same name could be used for multiple plants or animals. To avoid confusion, scientists use scientific names (sometimes called 'Latin names'). These are unambiguous and universal across languages, which is why we have often used them in this book. For those who are not familiar with the system, here is a brief explanation.

All life is divided into *kingdoms* including Plantae (plants) and Animalia (animals). Each of these groups is divided, then further subdivided, through several levels of classification, right down to individual species. The bottom two levels (*genus* and *species*) together form the scientific name. For example, mankind belongs to the genus *Homo* and the species *sapiens*. Our species can be written as *Homo sapiens* (often abbreviated to *H. sapiens*). Sometimes species are further divided into *subspecies*. Humans belong to a subspecies (also called *sapiens*) so if we want to be really specific, we refer to ourselves as *Homo sapiens sapiens*.

You will encounter scientific names for plants and animals throughout this book, especially where there is no universally accepted common name.

oriented faults. These orientations can be recognised across the country bounding smaller sedimentary basins and mountain ranges, and most noticeably control the strikingly linear geometry of the east coast. The centre and east were uplifted more than the west, providing the basis for the modern shape of the island. Completely emergent for the first time for several hundred million years, land plants and animals proliferated and evolved towards the island's present flora and fauna. Local lake and river deposits developed in the lowlands and erosion cut back the highlands. In the centre and east, the entire marine record was stripped away, revealing the crystalline core and resulting in undulating dome-like mountains, such as Pic d'Imarivolanitra (formerly Pic Boby). In the west the sedimentary rock was eroded flat to near sea level. Tectonic activity in the last million years has again uplifted the Malagasy terrain, and this ancient erosional surface now defines the plateaux of the west, including Bemaraha.

HUMAN COLONISATION The final chapter starts just 2,000 years ago, when skilled Malay boatmen found their way to then-uninhabited Madagascar and began a dramatic demonstration of how humans can affect geological processes. Reduction in primary forest since the colonisation of Madagascar has indisputably influenced the shape of the land. Soils once stabilised by deep root systems became susceptible to erosion, and the sediment load in the rivers increased. In the 50 years to 1945, 40m of clay was deposited in the delta of the Betsiboka River at Mahajanga, immensely more than the underlying sedimentary record suggests was usual prior to deforestation. Ubiquitous hillside scars (called *lavaka*) are the inland testimony to this accelerated redistribution of material from highlands to coast, an inexorable environmental response to deforestation that is sending the Malagasy highlands towards eventual peneplanation (flattening) at an incredible rate. Even with an average annual erosion of 1mm taking place continuously, Madagascar will be reduced to near sea level in a geologically short three million years.

FLORA

Madagascar and its adjacent islands harbour some 13,000 species of flowering plants of which a staggering 89% are endemic. Although some other regions of the

Clare & Johan Hermans

Like so many other living things on the island, the orchids of Madagascar are extremely varied; and well over three-quarters are endemic. More than 950 different species have been recorded so far and new ones are still being discovered. The orchids have adapted to every possible habitat, including the spiny forest and the cool highland mountain ranges, but their highest density is in the wet forests of the east. Whilst orchid habitats are becoming scarcer, one or other of them can be seen in flower at most times of the year; the best season for flowers is the rainy season from January to March.

Some of the most memorable orchids are to be found in the eastern coastal area, which is the habitat of large *Angraecums*, *Eulophiellas* and *Cymbidiellas*. Many orchids here are epiphytes – they live on tree branches or trunks, anchored by their roots (but, although they scramble over their host collecting moisture and nutrients, they are not parasites).

Angraecum eburneum can be seen in flower from September to May, its thick leathery leaves forming a half-metre-wide fan shape; the flower stems reach above the leaves carrying a number of large greenish-white fragrant flowers. Like many Malagasy orchids the blooms are strongly scented and white in colour to attract pollinating moths at night.

The comet orchid, *A. sesquipedale*, is one of the most striking. It flowers from June to November and the plants are similar to *A. eburneum* but are slightly more compact. Individual flowers can be 26cm across and over 30cm long including the lengthy nectary spur, characteristic for the angraecoid orchids, at the back of the flower. The flower was described by Charles Darwin at the end of the 19th century when he predicted that there would be a moth with a very long tongue that could reach down to the nectar at the bottom of the spur. This idea was ridiculed by his contemporaries, but in 1903 – more than two decades after his death – he was proved right: a hawk moth with a proboscis of over 30cm (*Xanthopan morganii praedicta*) was discovered, and it has recently been caught on film pollinating this orchid.

Aeranthes plants look similar to *Angraecums*. Their spider-like greenish flowers are suspended from long thin stems, gently nodding in the breeze.

Eulophiella roempleriana, which can reach almost 2m tall, is now very rare. One of the few remaining plants can be seen on Ile aux Nattes, off Ile Sainte Marie. The large, deep pink flowers are well worth the pirogue trip to the island. A few more of these plants survive in the reserves around Andasibe. They normally flower from October onwards.

Cymbidiella orchids are also very striking; they generally flower from October to

world (such as the Tropical Andes, Indonesia and Brazil) have more plant species, they have substantially lower rates of endemism, typically below 50%. Madagascar is the world's number one floral hotspot for an area its size. The fortuitous break from Africa and Asia at a time when the flowering plants were just beginning to diversify allowed many groups to develop their own lineage, supplemented occasionally by the later colonisations of more advanced forms.

FERNS AND CYCADS Ferns were in their heyday before Gondwana was even formed. Their best efforts were the impressive **tree ferns**, which had large spreading fronds sprouting from a tall, scaly stem. These structures created vast forests in all warm, humid areas during the Carboniferous, 350 million years ago. Although they eventually lost ground to seed-bearing plants during the age of the dinosaurs, it is a credit to their design that they are still abundant and successful. Indeed the soft, symmetrical foliage of ferns very much epitomises the lushness of hot, wet places. It's true that they have been relegated to a life in

January. *C. pardalina*, with its huge crimson lip, cohabits with a staghorn fern, while *C. falcigera*, with large black-spotted yellow flowers, prefers the exclusive company of the raffia palm.

The highlands of Madagascar with their cooler and more seasonal climate are inhabited by numerous terrestrial orchids, growing in soil or leaf litter; underground tubers produce deciduous leaves and flower stems – not dissimilar to orchids seen in temperate regions.

Eulophia plantaginea is a relatively common roadside plant; large colonies can sometimes be found, especially in boggy areas.

Cynorkis can also be seen along the roads. Many are terrestrials, others grow on wet rock or in swamps. Epiphytes like *Angraecum* and *Aeranthes* can still be found in the few remaining pockets of forest in the highlands.

Aerangis plants are instantly recognisable by their shiny, dark green foliage. The flowers superficially resemble those of *Angraecum* but they are often much smaller, carried on elegant racemes, and their scent is exquisite. The plants are commonly seen in the wet shade of the rainforest reserves of Andasibe and Ranomafana.

Jumellea are again similar but have a more narrow, folded-back single flower on a thin stem.

Bulbophyllum orchids are easily missed by the untrained eye; their rounded, plump pseudo-bulbs are often seen on moss-covered trees. They are always worthwhile to investigate: small gem-like blooms may be nestled amongst the foliage.

Oeonia with its huge white lip and two red dots on its throat can be found rambling amongst the undergrowth.

The apparently bare higher peaks of the *hauts plateaux*, like Ibity near Antsirabe, also contain a very specialised community of orchids. The thick-leaved, sun-loving angraecoids and *Bulbophyllums* share the rock faces with succulents; these rock-dwellers are known as lithophytes.

One of the best and easiest places to see orchids – including *Angraecum*, *Cymbidiella* and *Gastrorchis* – is in the grounds of hotels and private gardens, but one must be aware that these domestic collections may contain the odd foreign interloper. Orchids from the Orient and South America are brought in as pot plants, the flowers often being bigger and brighter than the natives'.

Note that import and export permits are required when transporting orchids out of Madagascar.

the shade of more recently evolved plants, but here they excel, out-competing all others.

Although some species are present in dry habitats, the vast majority of Madagascar's ferns decorate the branches and trunks of the eastern rainforests. One eye-catching species is the huge **bird's nest fern** (*Asplenium nidus*) which adorns many large trunks with luxuriant balconies of leaves. The ancient tree ferns (*Cyathea* spp) that once supplied the forest canopy are still present on its floor, contributing to the prehistoric atmosphere of the forest.

Often mistaken for a tree fern, the **cycad** (*Cycas* spp) is in fact one of the original seed-bearing plants. The evolution of seed propagation eventually led to the flowering plants that currently dominate all of the world's habitats, marking the end of the ferns' reign on earth. Resembling a tree fern with palm-like leaves, the single Malagasy representative of the genus, *Cycas thouarsii*, is found only in the eastern rainforests. Look closely at its cone: it holds seeds which, 30 million years ago, became the most significant single plant adaptation in the history of life.

PITCHER PLANTS There are only two species of insect-eating pitcher plant (*Nepenthes* spp) in Madagascar, but they are spectacular enough to deserve a mention. In wetlands in the south they poke out of the marsh beds like triffids planning an ambush. One of their leaves wraps upon itself to create a fly trap, which then serves up trace elements, from the flies' remains, unobtainable from the mud below. The rest of the family live thousands of miles away in southeast Asia, and it is thought that the arrival of Madagascar's two species stemmed from a fortuitous migration along the same path that originally brought the first people – perhaps they inadvertently shared the boats.

SUCCULENTS *With information from Gavin Hart*
In Madagascar, wherever rainfall is below about 400mm a year, succulents reign. The entire southwest of the island is dominated by their swollen forms. Further north they decorate the natural rock gardens of Isalo, Itremo and the countless outcrops on the central plateau. They also appear within the sparse dry forests of the west, among the stony chaos of the *tsingy* (see box opposite), and even venture onto the grasslands and into the rainforests. About 150 succulent species occur in Madagascar, distributed widely across the island.

Euphorbia is one of the largest genera of flowering plants with over 2,000 species worldwide. Almost 500 are succulent species occurring predominantly in Africa and Madagascar. They have diversified into countless different forms, from bushes resembling strings of sausages, and trees sprouting smooth leafless green branches, to spiny stalks emerging from swollen underground tubers. Many species shed their leaves at the start of the dry season, but when present they are swollen with water and shining with wax. To replace the leaves they often yield wonderful flowers and in so doing brighten up the landscape.

E. *oncoclada* is sometimes called the sausage bush because of the regular constrictions along its cylindrical green stems, giving a string-of-sausages appearance. E. *stenoclada* is a large shrub with flattened spiny branches. By contrast there are dwarf prostrate species, such as E. *decaryi* and E. *ambovombensis*, often with swollen underground roots

The E. *milii* complex (a group of closely related forms) is undoubtedly the most prominent euphorbia in Madagascar, lining the streets of many cities and towns. These are small shrubby plants with spiny stems (hence the common name: crown of thorns) and a few terminal leaves. The most dominant feature, however, is the bright red bracts surrounding the flowers which produce a blaze of colour from the mass plantings. All euphorbias have white milky sap which is toxic on skin contact, and can cause temporary blindness, so caution is urged in handling these plants.

Pachypodium is a genus of five species from southern Africa and about 20 from Madagascar. The Malagasy pachypodiums have an unusual flower structure in that the stamens are covered by a segmented cone which must be penetrated to achieve pollination. They vary from tree-like species to caudiciforms (stem succulents) with white, red or yellow flowers. They are mostly quite spiny when young but tend to lose their spines as they mature.

The bizarrely compressed P. *brevicaule*, which has been likened to a sack of potatoes, has most of its large mass beneath the ground. P. *lamerei* – widespread in the southwest – is the most common species in cultivation, often sold under the name Madagascar palm. P. *rutenbergianum* is widely distributed from the mid-west coast to the north and is the largest of the pachypodiums, reaching up to 15m tall with a heavily branched crown.

Unlike animals, plants cannot escape harsh environments. The plants of Madagascar's dry southwest have therefore had to adapt to tolerate strong sunlight, high temperatures and – most restrictive of all – desiccation. These high demands have produced unusual-looking and fascinating plant species called **xerophytes**.

All xerophytes have deep root systems to acquire what little water there is available. Their leaves are usually small and covered in hairs, and much of their photosynthesis is done by the green stems. This design lowers the surface area of the plant and traps still air adjacent to the leaf, reducing water loss – the key aim. In addition to desiccation, overheating is as much a problem for plants as it is for animals. Xerophytes have therefore evolved various techniques to minimise heating: usually they have their narrowest edge facing the sun and they often add grey pigments to their leaves to deflect the harsh rays of midday.

The most extreme adaptations for a dry life are to be seen in the **succulents**. This general term describes all xerophytes which store water in their waxy leaves, roots or stems. Water is a valuable commodity in a dry habitat, and one that must be protected from thirsty grazers, so succulents usually employ toxins or spines as a defence. This is evident in many of the island's spectacular plants, not least the octopus trees (*Didierea*) of the spiny forest.

Didiereaceae of the arid southwest are the most intriguing plants in Madagascar, for they are an entire family of bizarre plants found nowhere else on earth. They look similar to cacti, but their tiny deciduous leaves – and the immense thorns that protect them – indicate that they are not (cacti don't have thorns; their spines are modified leaves). Of this family's four genera, **Alluaudia** contains six species, **Alluaudiopsis** and **Didierea** each contain two species and **Decaryia** is monotypic.

The octopus trees (*Didierea* spp) are the most famous members of this group. Species vary greatly in form and flower colouration within the family. *Alluaudia ascendens* is the largest, growing initially as a single stem, but then branching from the base forming massive V-shaped plants 10–15m tall with white to reddish flowers. *Alluaudia comosa* also branches from the base, but forms a wide, flat-topped shrub 2–6m tall. The single spines are up to 2cm long and white flowers cover the ends of its shoots. The beautiful *Alluaudiopsis marnieriana* grows to 4m and has the most colourful flowers of the whole family. They are up to 3cm across with bright crimson petals.

Aloe is a genus containing about 450 species occurring in southern and eastern Africa and Madagascar. Over a hundred are recognised in Madagascar but there are distinct differences between African and Malagasy species. Madagascar does not have any grass aloes or spotted aloes, but has numerous species which differ markedly from those growing elsewhere. Even though aloes are known as low-growing plants, some species have stems to raise their broad foliage above the ground. The largest aloes have stocky 3m stems covered in untidy dead scales which sport huge succulent leaves and, in June and July, a large red inflorescence. *A. divaricata* is a fast-growing species common in the southwest. Its single or branched stems are 2–6m long with narrow blue-grey leaves and red-brown marginal teeth, scattered along the whole length. Highly branched inflorescences of up to 1m bear coral-red flowers. *A. suzannae* is unique among aloes in being a night-bloomer; flowers open before midnight and close the following morning. Flowers (which only appear on plants at least ten years old) are pollinated by the souimanga sunbird and Madagascar white-eye as well as by bats and mouse lemurs.

Kalanchoe contains 143 species of succulent perennials distributed through Africa, Madagascar, Arabia and Asia – with 63 occurring in Madagascar. The most well known is the panda plant (*Kalanchoe tomentosa*) a shrub with dense rosettes. The species are highly variable in form (from low leafy succulents to tall tree-like plants), leaf shape, size and colour. *Kalanchoe* flowers have parts in multiples of four – four connected petals forming a tube, four sepals, four carpals and eight stamens – whereas most other genera in the Crassulaceae family have floral parts in multiples of five. In Madagascar the largest species (eg: *K. arborescens, K. beharensis, K. grandidieri*) tend to be restricted to the semi-arid regions of the south and southwest, while the smaller species occur mostly in the more humid areas up to 2,000m.

Adenia is a genus of about 150 species in the passionflower family. Most are deciduous vines, climbing with the aid of tendrils, extending from a swollen stem base. They are usually dioecious – that's to say individual plants are either male or female – with inconspicuous creamy greenish flowers and fruit that's often vividly coloured when ripe.

Uncarina is an endemic genus of 13 species in the Pedialaceae family. The plants are deciduous shrubs or small trees up to 8m tall with a substantial underground tuber. Flowers may be yellow, white, pink or violet, and the fruits are large capsules covered with numerous, ferociously hooked thorns, which aid dissemination by attaching to the hairy coats of animals.

Cyphostemma (family Vitaceae) is a genus with over 300 species (a minority of which are succulent). Twenty-four occur in Madagascar. *Cyphostemma sakalavense* is bottle-shaped with a stem up to 3m tall. It can be found on the limestone rocks of the *tsingy* in northwest Madagascar.

Senecio is a genus of leaf succulents, existing essentially as a collection of swollen leaves sprouting from the earth. The leaves are often ornamental, tinged with terracotta and bearing harsh spines, but also display showy red flowers during times of drought.

PALMS Madagascar is home to one of the world's richest palm floras. There are around 170 species – three times more than in the rest of Africa put together – and 165 of these are found nowhere else.

A lack of large herbivores in Madagascar has left its palms – with no need for defences – spineless and without poisons. Pollination is mostly by bees and flies, but some have tiny flowers to entice unknown insect guests. For seed dispersal lemurs are often employed. Ring-tailed, black, red-ruffed and brown lemurs all assist in scattering the seeds. The bright colours of some fruits serve to attract birds and forest pigs, while the handful of African palms, which normally use elephants as dispersers, presumably make do with zebu.

The dominance of species with Asian relatives betrays the fact that Madagascar severed with India millions of years *after* it broke away from African shores.

The species present range from the famous to the recently discovered, from dwarf to giant, and almost all have intriguing characteristics. One palm has led to a Malagasy word entering the English language – the **raffia palm** (*Raphia ruffia*). The fibres from its leaves are woven into the hats, baskets and mats. Of the 50 new palm species discovered in the last decade, one is worth particular attention: *Ravenea musicalis*, the world's only water palm. It starts life underwater in only one of Madagascar's southeastern rivers. As it grows, it surfaces, eventually bears fruit, and then seeds. Its discoverer named it *R. musicalis* after being charmed by the

Jamie Spencer

Slash-and-burn farming, *tavy* in Malagasy, is blamed for the permanent destruction of the rainforest. Even those practising *tavy* agree with this. They also respect the forest and they can see that *tavy* greatly jeopardises the future for the next generations. So why destroy what you love and need?

One answer to a very complex question is the practical need. In Madagascar poverty is extreme and there are few options. Life's priority is to feed your family and children. Rice, the food staple, is grown both on the flat ground in sustainable paddy fields, and on the steep slopes of slashed and burned forest. Cyclones often wash away much of the paddy rice crop and wipe out the earth dams and irrigation waterways built at great cost and effort. Some farmers have invested a lifetime's savings employing labour for their construction. So if floods strike, people rely on the hill rice. Fertility in these fields is not replenished as in paddies where nutrients are carried in the water. The soil quickly becomes unproductive so new slopes must be cut after a few years.

The cultural explanation for *tavy* is less obvious. The people of 'my' village, Sandrakely, are Tanala (meaning 'people of the forest'). The forest is their world and to survive in this surprisingly harsh environment they clear the land with fire – the ancient agricultural technique brought by the original immigrants from Indonesia perhaps 2,000 years ago. In more recent history the Tanala were forced into the forest by warring neighbours and colonial occupants of more fertile areas.

As the traditional means of survival and provision, *tavy* can be seen as central to society's make-up and culture. The calendar revolves around it, land ownership and hierarchies are determined by its practice, and politics are centred on it. It is the pivot and subject of rituals and ceremonies. The forest is the domain of the ancestors and site of tombs and religious standing stones. *Tavy* is an activity carried out between the living and the dead: the ancestors are consulted and permit its execution to provide for the living. The word *tavy* also means 'fatness', with all the associations of health, wealth and beauty.

If they have the choice, many people are happy to pursue the sustainable agricultural alternatives, so Feedback Madagascar is ready to help them. But the practical and cultural context must always be respected. The new alternatives must be rock solid when people's lives are at stake and to be truly enduring they must be accommodated within the culture by the people themselves. It is they who understand the problems and know the solutions that are acceptable. They must not be forced.

Jamie Spencer is the founder of the charity Feedback Madagascar; see page 146.

chimes of its seedpods as they hit the water below. There are other riverside palms in Madagascar adapted to tolerate the recurrent floods of the island's lowland rainforest, but none as perfectly as the musical water palm.

Another unusual group is the **litter-trapping palms**. The crown of their leaves is arranged like an upturned shuttlecock, sprouting at first from the forest floor, and then gaining height as the stem grows from below. Its watertight crown catches leaves falling from the canopy, perhaps to obtain trace minerals, but no one knows for sure. A strange consequence of this growth is that the roots of other plants, which originally grew through the soil into the crown by mistake, later dangle down from its heights as alabaster-white zigzags.

Although the vast majority of palms live among the hardwoods of the lowland rainforests, there are species which brave the more arid environments, notably the feather palms (*Chrysalidocarpus* spp) which nestle in the canyons of Isalo National Park and stand alone amongst the secondary grasslands of the west.

Looking like a messy cross between a palm and a pine tree, **pandan palms** or screw pines (*Pandanus* spp) are different from those above, but equally fond of Madagascar. Their foliage consists of untidy grass-like mops which awkwardly adorn rough branches periodically emerging from their straight trunks. Common in both rainforests and dry forests there are 75 species, only one of which is found elsewhere, placing the country alongside Borneo in the pandan diversity stakes.

Note: The word palm is often used rather liberally. The **traveller's palm** (*Ravenala madagascariensis*), symbolic of Madagascar, is not a palm at all (see *Trees* below). In fact it is in the same family as the bird of paradise flower (Strelitziaceae). A second 'false palm' is the **Madagascar palm**, which is actually a spiny succulent *Pachypodium lamerei* (page 40).

TREES Until the arrival of humans, Madagascar is thought to have been largely cloaked in forest. There remain examples of each of the original forests, but vast areas have become treeless as a result of *tavy* (slash-and-burn agriculture; see box on page 43) and soil erosion.

Most of the remaining **evergreen trees** form the superstructure of the rainforest. They are typically 30m high, with buttressed roots, solid hardwood trunks and vast canopies. There can be up to 250 species of tree in a single hectare of lowland rainforest, but from the ground they all look very similar. To identify a species, botanists must often wait for flowering, an event that is not only extremely difficult to predict, but also one that takes place 30m high, out of sight.

One notable and obvious tree is the **strangler fig** (*Ficus* spp), which germinates up in the canopy on a branch of its victim, grows down to the floor to root, and then encircles and constricts its host leaving a hollow knotted trunk. The Malagasy prize the forest hardwoods; one canopy tree is called the 'kingswood' because its wood is so hard that, at one time, any specimens found were automatically the property of the local king.

The only evergreen species to be found outside the rainforest are the **tapia tree** (*Uapaca bojei*), the nine species of **mangrove tree** and some of the **succulent trees** in the extreme southwest where sea mists provide water year-round. In tolerating the conditions of west Madagascar, these evergreens have borne their own unusual communities.

The rest of Madagascar's trees are **deciduous**, ie: they lose their leaves during the dry season. The taller dry forests of the west are dappled with the shadows of **leguminous trees** such as *Dalbergia* and *Cassia*, characterised by their long seedpods and symbiotic relationships with bacteria which provide fertilisers within their roots. Sprawling **banyan figs** (*Ficus* spp) and huge **tamarind trees** (*Tamarindus indica*) create gallery forest along the rivers of the west and south, yielding pungent fruit popular with lemurs. In drier woodland areas Madagascar's most celebrated trees, the **baobabs** (*Adansonia* spp), dominate. See the next section for a rundown of the baobabs.

One last species deserves a mention. The **traveller's palm** (*Ravenala madagascariensis*) is one of Madagascar's most spectacular plants. It is thought to have earned its name from the relief it affords thirsty travellers: water is stored in the base of its leaves and can be released with a swift blow from a machete. Its elegant fronds are arranged in a dramatic vertical fan, which is decorative enough to have earned it a role as Air Madagascar's logo. Its large, bulbous flowers sprout from the leaf axils and, during the 24 hours that they are receptive, are visited by unusual pollinators – ruffed lemurs. The lemurs locate flowers which have just opened, and literally pull them apart to get at the large nectary inside. Keeping a lemur fed puts quite a demand on the tree, but it produces flowers day after day for several months, and during this time the lemurs eat little else. The traveller's palm is perhaps the only native species to have benefited from *tavy* agriculture – it dominates areas of secondary vegetation on the central plateau and east coast.

This secondary rainforest that grows back after *tavy* is called *savoka*. Aside from the traveller's palm, these areas of *savoka* are sadly dominated by foreign tree species which will eventually infest all returning forest, changing Madagascar's rainforest communities forever. A handful of native plants have managed to compete with these exotics but relatively few animals live in this vegetation.

BAOBABS *With information from Jim Bond*

The baobab – a freak among trees with its massively swollen trunk and sparse stubby branches – is emblematic of Madagascar. This is the motherland of baobabs. Of the eight species found worldwide, six grow exclusively in Madagascar. The others (one in Australia and one across Africa) are believed to have originated from seedpods that were swept away from Malagasy shores around 10mya and survived the ocean crossings. Even the African species can be seen in Madagascar today, for it was introduced by Arab traders as street planting in towns including Mahajanga and Antsiranana.

The reason for the baobab's extraordinary girth – sometimes exceeding 30m – is that it is well adapted to inhospitably dry conditions. It is capable of taking up and storing water from sporadic downpours very efficiently, its porous wood acting like a huge sponge. No doubt inspired by the great size of some specimens, claims have been made that these giants can live for many thousands of years. In fact, recent studies suggest that few are older than 500, but it is difficult to be certain because unlike other trees baobabs do not produce growth rings.

Floral groups The six Malagasy species can be divided into two groups based on floral characteristics: the Brevitubae (short-tubed) and Longitubae (long-tubed). Baobabs have large, showy flowers – up to 30cm long – that open at dusk and are receptive for one night only.

Brevitubae This group comprises *Adansonia grandidieri* in the south and *A. suarezensis* in the north. They typically have flat-topped crowns of predominantly horizontal branches, emerging just above the canopy of the surrounding forest. This arrangement is thought to assist their favoured pollinator, a fruit bat, in hopping between flowers. The cream-coloured flowers, which are held erect rather like a cup and saucer, and have a foul carrion-like smell, are also visited by fork-marked lemurs, giant mouse lemurs, sunbirds and bees.

Longitubae The remaining Malagasy species, *A. za* and *A. rubrostipa* in the south, and *A. perrieri* and *A. madagascariensis* in the north, have long floral parts, which in contrast to the Brevitubae are red and yellow and have a sweetly fragrant scent. They dangle downwards concealing the nectar at the end of an elongated tube. Only the long tongues of certain hawk moths – commonly reaching 25cm unfurled – can reach it. These trees tend to be smaller than the Brevitubae because, being pollinated by hawk moths, they have less need to emerge above the canopy.

Species of baobab Even to the expert eye, individual species can be tough to identify. Their form is highly dependent on environmental factors meaning there can be massive variation within one species. Grandidier's baobabs near Morondava, for example, are smooth, columnar giants up to 30m tall. But in the spiny scrub at Andavadoaka, mature trees of the same species are quite knobbly and almost spherical, often reaching no more than 3m in height. Nevertheless, the following descriptions should help you to determine which are which.

Adansonia grandidieri These, the most majestic and famous of the Malagasy baobabs, were named in honour of French naturalist Alfred Grandidier. They may reach 30m in height and 7.5m in diameter, with some large hollow ones reportedly having been used as houses. The best-known specimens form the Avenue des Baobabs near Morondava (one of the most photographed sights in Madagascar). The isolated trees in this area would once have been surrounded by dense forest; but today their silhouettes can be seen for miles across the flat, featureless rice fields. Better examples (being in relatively intact forest) can be seen in the Mangoky Valley. Grandidier's baobabs tend to be found on flood plains or near rivers. Malagasy names: *renala*, *reniala* (literally 'mother of the forest'); flowers: May–Aug; distribution: Manambolo lakes system down to Mikea Forest.

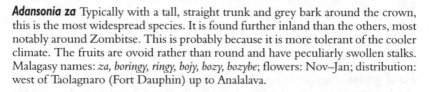
A. grandidieri
Andavadoaka

A. grandidieri
Morondava

Adansonia za Typically with a tall, straight trunk and grey bark around the crown, this is the most widespread species. It is found further inland than the others, most notably around Zombitse. This is probably because it is more tolerant of the cooler climate. The fruits are ovoid rather than round and have peculiarly swollen stalks. Malagasy names: *za, boringy, ringy, bojy, bozy, bozybe*; flowers: Nov–Jan; distribution: west of Taolagnaro (Fort Dauphin) up to Analalava.

Adansonia rubrostipa (formerly A. fony) Preferring sandy soil, this is the smallest of the baobabs. In the spiny forest they assume a bottle shape, but at Kirindy they are taller and more slender. The fruits are rather thin-walled and do not carry far without breaking open. This may explain why clusters of *A. rubrostipa* are often found growing in relatively high concentrations. Identifying features include serrated leaf edges and bark that tends to have a reddish tinge. Malagasy names: *fony, zamena, boringy, ringy*; flowers: Feb–Mar; distribution: along the west coast from Itampolo to Soalala.

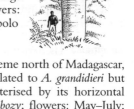

Adansonia suarezensis Restricted to a few sites in the extreme north of Madagascar, this is the world's second rarest baobab. It is closely related to *A. grandidieri* but specimens tend to be somewhat smaller. It is characterised by its horizontal branches and smooth red bark. Malagasy names: *bojy, bozy*; flowers: May–July; distribution: areas near Antsiranana and the forests of Mahory and Analamera.

Adansonia perrieri Some people call this the 'rainforest species' for it shuns the drier habitats where its siblings thrive. It occupies a specialised niche on the sheltered banks of small streams running down from Montagne d'Ambre. It is the largest of the three northern baobabs, and with just a few dozen specimens remaining it is also one of the rarest trees in the world. One of the best sites to see it in its full glory is by the stream that runs down from the Grande Cascade in the

National Park. You will need to set aside a half-day, but the sight of these tall trees rising majestically from the steep valley floor is well worth the walk. Malagasy names: *bojy, bozy*; flowers: Nov–Dec; distribution: a few very small populations near Montagne d'Ambre.

Adansonia madagascariensis This is the most variable and consequently the most difficult to identify of the baobabs. Given favourable soil and water conditions, such as at the east entrance to Ankarana, it may reach an imposing 20m in height, while on the nearby karst the same species is squat and pear-shaped. The bark is pale grey and the flowers are dark red. The fruits are smaller, rounder, less furry, and narrower-stalked than in most species. Malagasy names: *zabe, renida, bojy, bozy*; flowers: Mar–Apr; distribution: Ankara plateau northwards.

Adansonia digitata Although an introduced species, the African baobab has become naturalised in several parts of Madagascar. The best known specimen grows in the middle of a road at the western side of Mahajanga, where it has a role as a traffic island! This is the fattest tree in Madagascar with a circumference of 22m. In Africa it grows in 31 countries. Malagasy names: *sefo, bontona, vontona*; flowers: Nov–Dec.

Uses and conservation Baobabs provide a number of resources for humans. The seeds are eaten and used for cooking oil; the bark is used to make rope and roofing materials; and the leaves are fed to cattle, as is the wood in times of drought. Baobab wood is neither strong enough for building nor particularly good for burning, so the trees tend to be left standing when the surrounding forest is cleared. Removal of the bark does little damage since baobabs possess the rare ability to regenerate it. Mature trees are even quite resistant to fire and so rarely succumb to the regular burning of undergrowth carried out to stimulate new grazing.

Nevertheless, the outlook for the Malagasy baobabs is bleak. Half of the species are listed as endangered and all are recognised as threatened by habitat loss. The main problem is that there is virtually no new growth. Deprived of the protection afforded by the surrounding forest, those seedlings that escape burning are promptly devoured by zebu. Furthermore, two species (*A. grandidieri* and *A. suarezensis*) are thought to depend on animals to disperse their seeds. But since no living Malagasy creature is known to eat the fruit of the baobab, it can only be assumed that these seed dispersers are now extinct – very bad news indeed for the future of these species.

If these trees were allowed to die out it would be a terribly sad loss. But the impact penetrates much deeper than that. Baobabs provide food, support and homes for a plethora of creatures, both directly and indirectly, including: lemurs, bats, birds, insects, geckos, humans and even other plants and fungi. Treat these majestic giants with respect and remember that many are honoured as *faly* (sacred) – so try to ask permission before you take photos.

FOREIGN INVADERS In common with many islands around the globe, Madagascar has suffered from accidental and intended introductions of alien species. Sometimes referred to as weeds, because they do not really belong there, they can cause havoc when they arrive.

Out-competing native species, sharp tropical grasses from South America permanently deface the burnt woodlands of the west. And their populations explode because zebu do not find these exotic species appetising. Where thick forest is cleared, fast-growing *Eucalyptus* and *Psidium* trees step in. The trumpet lily (*Datura* spp) is now rampant in localised areas. Another growing problem is the

3

Many Malagasy plants crop up in garden centres throughout Europe. Familiar to horticulturalists are the dragon tree (*Dracaena marginata*), the crown of thorns (*Euphorbia millii*), the Areca palm, the flamboyant tree (*Delonix regia*) and the Madagascar jasmine (*Stephanotis floribunda*) of bridal bouquet fame. Other natives are valued for their uses rather than their aesthetic qualities. Recent interest has grown in Madagascar's various wild coffees (Rubiaceae family). Many are naturally caffeine-free and hybrids with tastier coffees are currently being produced to exploit this trait. (Naturally caffeine-free coffees are highly desirable because artificial decaffeination processes tend to leave toxic residues in the finished product.)

The Madagascar rosy periwinkle (*Catharanthus roseus*) is a champion of those who campaign to conserve natural habitats. The plant has a long history of medicinal use the world over. In India, wasp stings were treated with juice from the leaves; in Europe, it was long used as a folk remedy for diabetes; in Hawaii, the plant was boiled to make a poultice to stop bleeding; in China, it was considered a cough remedy; in Central and South America, it has also been used in homemade cold remedies to ease lung congestion, inflammation and sore throats; and in the Caribbean, an extract of the flower was used to treat eye infections. Most importantly, however, it is now used in chemotherapy. Substances called vinblastine and vincristine extracted from the rosy periwinkle have proved effective in the treatment of leukaemia and Hodgkin's disease.

There are certainly many other plants with equally life-saving chemical properties yet to be found, but the rate of forest destruction may be driving these to extinction before we have a chance to appreciate them or even discover the species at all.

rubber bush *(Calotropis procera)*, which is native to tropical Africa and Asia; this has become the dominant plant in some areas around Antsiranana. They either suffocate competitors with their dense growth or poison the soil with their toxins. In drier areas, superbly adapted and profoundly damaging *Opuntia* cacti spread from the nearby sisal plantations and flourish where there was once spiny forest.

Needless to say, the native animal populations, unable to adapt to these invaders, also suffer – and this, perhaps even more than the endangerment of plant species, has prompted action from conservation bodies.

FAUNA

Compared with the breathtaking ecosystems of mainland Africa, Madagascar's fauna has far more subtle qualities. A combination of ancient Gondwana stock and 165 million years of isolated evolution has created a haven for a plethora of strange and unusual creatures. Here are a seemingly random collection of animal groups that had the opportunity to prove themselves in the absence of large predators and herbivores. The resulting 180,000 species, existing in habitats from rainforests to coral reefs, bring human opportunity too: for numerous truly unique wildlife encounters.

INVERTEBRATES There are well over 150,000 species of invertebrate in Madagascar, the majority in the eastern rainforests. To spot them turn over leaves and logs on the forest floor, peer very closely at the foliage or switch on a bright light after dark. Although perhaps creepy, and undeniably crawly, they do contribute substantially to the experience of wild areas on the island and – provided you can suppress the spine shivers – your mini-safaris will be hugely rewarding.

It is a difficult task to pick out the most impressive invertebrates, but notable are the hugely oversized **pill millipedes** (*Sphaerotherium* spp) which roll up when threatened to resemble a stripy brown or green golf ball. Among the forest foliage are superbly camouflaged **praying mantises**, **net-throwing spiders** that cast their silk nets at fliers-by, and **nymphs** and bugs of all shapes, colours and adornments. Among the leaf litter there are spectacular striped and horned

CURIOUS ARACHNIDS

Len de Beer & John Roff

LOOKING LIKE ... You're walking through a patch of forest and stop to photograph an unusual flower, when you notice some thoughtless bird has relieved itself on a leaf you were about to lean on. You're about to wipe it off when you have a hunch that you should look closer. What looked like a bird dropping turns out to be a fine specimen of *Phrynarachne* – a specialised crab spider that spends its time sitting on top of a leaf looking like poo. Some even emulate the scent of urine and faeces.

Why? Flies delight in landing on faeces and other choice decomposing substances; bird droppings are a fine source of nutrition for forest flies. Bird-dung crab spiders like *Phrynarachne* take full advantage of this, waiting on leaves or other prominent surfaces for hungry flies to come and investigate the latest tempting blob of excrement. Once the fly is within reach, the spider seizes it with lightning speed and administers a deadly bite.

A FREAK BACK FROM THE DEAD In 1881 a spider hunter with the charming moniker of Octavius Pickard-Cambridge was staring at a 'fossil' that had come crawling out of the substrate as if to proclaim: 'Hah! You thought I had gone!' in much the same way that Prof J L B Smith would later stare at the resurrected coelacanth as it received instant worldwide recognition as a living fossil.

The archaea – or pelican spider – has languished in obscurity, a victim of its small size, northern hemisphere bias and irrational arachnophobia. The archaeid spiders with their giraffe necks and cannibalistic natures were first described from Baltic amber in 1854. Imagine Octavius's rapture when 27 years later, on an expedition to the dripping escarpments of the red isle, archaea tiptoed back into the list of species with which humans are privileged to share the earth.

'Bizarre' seems too mild an adjective for an arachnid that does not build a web, has massively elongated, spiked jaws that can extend outward at right angles, and stilt-like legs that enable it to hover over its prey. The fact that the victims are exclusively other spiders just adds to the archaea's mystique. Living archaeids have only been found on the southern landmasses of Madagascar, Africa and Australia, yet more evidence that these places were once a continuous continent. Is it a coincidence that both archaea and the coelacanth are associated with an island renowned for the freakier designer labels of creation that so fascinate us?

SPIDER-WATCHING Madagascar's spiders are well worth a closer look. You never know what you may find. They show an incredible range of design and diversity. Keep an eye out for the iridescent jumping spiders, the giant orb-web weavers and the multi-coloured lynx spiders. Who knows – you could even find a new species.

Spider-watching in Madagascar is particularly enjoyable because you can do it anywhere. Even most hotels have at least one tree or bush in the garden where you can find extraordinary spiders easily before you even get to the national parks.

flatworms, the otherworldly **ant lions** (see boxes on pages 51 and 434) and vast numbers of wonderful **weevils**, the most spectacular being the bright red giraffe-necked weevil (most easily seen at Ranomafana National Park). The species gets its name from the male whose tremendously long neck is almost three times the length of his body!

One invertebrate whose presence will not be welcomed by most visitors is the **leech**, but it is a more fascinating creature than you might at first imagine; turn to the box on page 346 to discover why.

There are around 300 species of **butterfly** in Madagascar, 211 of which are endemic to the island. The most eye-catching are the heavily-patterned swallowtails, and the nymphalids with their dominant blue and orange liveries. Madagascar's **moths** are significantly older in origin and are probably descendants of the Gondwana insects marooned on the island. This explains the diversity – 4,000 species – including many groups active during the day, filling niches that elsewhere are the realm of butterflies. Most dramatic is the huge yellow comet moth (*Argema mittrei*) with a wingspan of up to 25cm, and the elaborate urania moths (*Chrysiridia* spp), which look just like swallowtails decorated with emeralds. A very close relative is found in the Amazon rainforest.

There's one impressive invertebrate which you will encounter almost everywhere you go; all you need do is look up. The huge **golden orb-web spiders** (*Nephila madagascariensis*) string together massive webs often extending between trees and telephone wires. Along Fianar's telegraph cables hundreds of *Nephilas* string their webs together forming an impressively huge net several hundred metres long! Their silk is so strong that it was once woven into a fabric; Queen Victoria even had a pair of *Nephila* silk stockings. For more spider oddities see the box on page 49.

BUGS, DRUGS AND LEMURS

John Roff & Len de Beer

A couple of fascinating stories have recently emerged from Madagascar concerning the relationship between bugs and drugs – and both involve lemurs too.

The first relates to lemur hygiene. In 1996 black lemurs (*Eulemur macaco*) were being studied at Lokobe on Nosy Be as part of research into seed dispersal. A mature female was observed to grab a millipede (*Charactopygus* sp), bite it and rub the juices of its wounded body vigorously over her underside and tail. While enacting this strange ritual she half closed her eyes and salivated profusely with a silly grimace on her primate face. She was seen to do this a second time and it is speculated that the toxins in the millipede serve to protect her against parasites such as mosquitoes. Or maybe she just needed a fix?

In a relationship that goes the other way, the golden bamboo lemur – a species unknown to science until 1984 – has developed a startling specialism. These furry honey-coloured characters avoid competition with other resident species of lemur at Ranomafana by feeding exclusively on the shoots of *Cephalostachyum viguieri* – a giant bamboo that contains about 150mg of cyanide per kilogramme of fresh shoots. In so doing each individual consumes 12 times the theoretical lethal dose for a primate of it's size per day – that's enough cyanide to kill three grown men. High concentrations of this deadly chemical are found in its dung and it turns out that this is the exclusive food source of a very specialised rainforest dung beetle. It is currently not known how either creature manages to survive this poisonous diet, but one thing is fairly certain: were the golden bamboo lemur to become extinct, the fascinating beetle that relies on its toxic excrement would follow suit.

Angus McCrae

Should you come across perfectly conical little craters up to 5cm across in dry, sandy places, you are looking at traps built by ant lions. Out of sight at the bottom of each pit lurks the strange and ravenous ant lion larva, buried but for the tips of its needle-sharp mandibles. Should an unwary ant or other small prey stray over the brink, a blur of action may suddenly erupt: showers of sand are hurled back by the ant lion's jerking head and the resultant landslide carries the intruder helplessly down into the waiting jaws.

Seen close up, the larval ant lion is a termite-like alien with a flattened head attached, apparently upside down, to its hunched body. It has eyes arranged in groups either side of the head, and thin whiskers sprout from around its sickle-like jaws. Its mouth is permanently sealed, so it feeds through a narrow groove along each mandible. It is thus incapable of chewing or taking in anything but liquid. (With no solids to be excreted the stomach ends blindly, disconnected from the hind-gut.)

The adults, which superficially resemble clumsy dragonflies, are seldom noticed by non-specialists as most are dull in colour and usually fly only at night. About 20 ant lion species are known from Madagascar, but probably many more remain undescribed.

Other arachnids in Madagascar include **scorpions** and **tarantulas**, though neither is frequently encountered.

FISH *With information from Derek Schuurman*

Freshwater species The inhabitants of Madagascar's abundant lakes, marshes, estuaries, rivers and mountain brooks have been as much isolated by history as those of the land. The most interesting species are the **cichlids** (known locally as *damba*) with their huge variety, colourful coats and endearing habits of childcare – they protect their young by offering their mouths as a retreat in times of danger. Other Malagasy species demonstrate the parental instinct, a feature rare in fish. Some of the island's **catfish** are also mouth-brooders, and male **mudskippers** in the mangroves defend their nest burrows with the vigour of a proud father.

Another major group is the **killifish**, which resemble the gouramis found in pet shops. Specialised **eels** live high up in mountain brooks, and blind **cave fish** are to be found in the underground rivers of western Madagascar, in some cases surviving entirely on the rich pickings of bat guano. The one problem with the island's fish is that they are not big and tasty. Consequently many exotic species have been introduced into the rivers and are regularly on display in the nation's markets. These new species naturally put pressure on the native stock and, as is so often the story, the less-vigorous Malagasy species have been all but wiped out. The main culprit seems to be the Asian snakehead (*Channa* spp). North Koreans farmed them in Madagascar in the 1980s, but following the first floods they spread and are now present in all the major lakes of Madagascar. The snakehead is a voracious predator and has severely reduced populations of endemic fish wherever it occurs. The other predatory fish which has decimated indigenous species is the largemouth bass, *Micropterus salmoides*.

Marine species More robust are the marine species to be found swimming off the island's 4,000km of coastline. Madagascar is legendary for its **shark** populations and a quick dip off the east coast should be considered carefully. On the opposite side, the Mozambique channel is the most shark-infested stretch of water in the world, both in terms of number of species and number of individuals. However, swimming on this west coast is generally safe because the inshore waters are mostly shallow and protected by fringing **coral reefs**. Much of this reef is in good condition and bursting with life, outdoing even the Red Sea for fish diversity. The reefs are host to a typical Indo-Pacific community of clownfish, angelfish, butterflyfish, damselfish, tangs, surgeonfish, triggerfish, wrasse, groupers, batfish, blennies, gobies, boxfish, lionfish, moray eels, flutefish, porcupinefish, pufferfish, squirrelfish, sweetlips and the Moorish idol.

Scuba-diving in Madagascar can therefore be very rewarding; see page 88 for practical information.

FROGS Madagascar is home to a staggering 230 recorded frog species, but it seems that is just the tip of the iceberg. The island's amphibian population has never been thoroughly investigated. However, in recent years herpetologists Miguel Vences and Frank Glaw have been carrying out intensive research and at the time of writing are beginning the unenviable and gargantuan process of describing more than 120 new species that they have identified!

The box opposite describes a selection of Madagascar's most interesting ranine inhabitants.

REPTILES The unique evolutionary history of Madagascar is typified by its reptiles. There are around 365 endemic species, representing 96% of the island's reptilian population. Some are derived from ancient Gondwana stock, many of which are more closely related to South American or Asian reptiles than to African ones. There are also large groups of closely related species marking the radiations that stemmed from African immigrations in more recent times. This is illustrated most dramatically by the **chameleons**. Madagascar is home to about half the world's chameleon species including the smallest and the largest. With impressive adaptive dexterity, they have dispersed throughout the habitats of the island to occupy every conceivable niche.

Similar in their success have been the **geckoes**. The hundred or so gecko species in Madagascar seem to be split between those that make every effort imaginable to camouflage themselves and those that go out of their way to stick out like a sore thumb. The spectacular **day gecko** (*Phelsuma madagascariensis*) and its relatives can be seen by passing motorists from some distance. Their dazzling emerald coats emblazoned with Day-Glo orange blotches are intended for the attentions of the opposite sex and competitors. Once in their sights they bob their heads and wave their tails as if an extra guarantee of visibility is needed. In contrast a magnificently camouflaged **leaf-tailed gecko** (*Uroplatus* spp) could easily be resting on a tree trunk right under your nose without being noticed. With its flattened body, splayed tail, speckled eyes, colour-change tactics and complete lack of shadow, you may remain ignorant of its presence unless it gets nervous and gapes its large, red tongue in your direction.

A quiet scuttle on the floor of a western forest may well be a **skink**, while louder rustlings are likely to be one of the handsome **plated lizards**. However, the most significant disturbances, both in the forest and the academic world, are made by the **iguanids**. This group of mostly large lizards is primarily found in the Americas but no evidence of their presence has ever been discovered in Africa. The question of how some came to be in Madagascar has not yet been answered convincingly.

Madagascar's three **boas** are in the same boat. They exist only as fossils in Africa, supplanted by the more stealthy pythons, but they do have distant relatives in South America. Most often seen is the Madagascar tree boa (*Sanzinia madagascariensis*), which although decorated in the same marbled glaze, varies in

THE FROG CHORUS

Kelly Green & Daniel Austin

Stop and listen to the sounds of the rainforest. You may think those mysterious chirps, squeaks and clicks are birds and insects, but in most cases you would be wrong. Unlike the stereotypical Amazon jungle, where birdcalls permeate the air, the dominant sound in the Malagasy rainforest is the frog chorus. Yet these remarkable creatures are largely overlooked by tourists.

Frogs are the only amphibians in Madagascar – no toads, newts, or salamanders here – but with over 230 described species, and countless more in the pipeline, they outnumber Madagascar's lemurs, chameleons and snakes combined. Compare this to Britain with just one native frog (plus three introduced by man).

All but two of Madagascar's frogs (99%) are endemic. These frogs come in all colours and sizes: from tiny *Stumpffia pygmaea* measuring just 1cm fully grown to the giant *Hoplobatrachus tigerinus* reportedly reaching 17cm in length. In their struggle for survival Malagasy frogs have evolved numerous ingenious forms of protection. In Masoala we stumbled across *Mantidactylus webbi*, looking for all the world like a tuft of moss – the perfect camouflage amongst the damp green rocks of its habitat. In contrast, the eye-catching mantellas are anything but camouflaged. Their dramatic colours warn predators that they contain alkaloid toxins, making them a rather unpleasant snack. Another frog it would be wise to avoid eating is the aptly named tomato frog. When attacked these obese, bright red frogs gum up the predator's mouth with a thick gluey substance secreted from their skin. The unfortunate attacker is forced to release its prey and cannot eat for some days after.

Each December, for just three or four days, *Aglyptodactylus madagascariensis* frogs gather in huge numbers to mate. Males and females alike turn a bright canary yellow for the occasion. With hundreds of thousands of individuals gathered in a single marshy pool the noise of their croaking is deafening. This bizarre sound, coupled with the carpet of garishly coloured pairs of mating frogs stretching off into the distance in every direction, makes for a truly bewildering spectacle. After this colourful orgy each female will produce a clutch of up to 4,130 eggs. At the other end of the spectrum, green climbing mantellas lay just one egg at a time. A male will defend his waterlogged bamboo stump which he hopes will attract a female. If successful the female will lay her egg and leave it in his care. This can be risky as the egg may not be alone – on Nosy Mangabe we saw many males defending their wells, only to discover that the egg had been eaten by another tadpole (probably from the same male) or by other predators.

Frogs here also have a widely varied diet. They are well-known to eat flies, ants, slugs and other small invertebrates, but scientists have discovered that some Malagasy frogs will even eat scorpions, young chameleons, tadpoles and occasionally other frogs. Most surprising, however, are the reports from Malagasy farmers that *Hoplobatrachus tigerinus* – apparently introduced to control the rat population around Mahajanga – can even eat snakes and birds!

New frog species are constantly being discovered in Madagascar, with at least 40 described so far this decade. But for many it is a race against extinction. More than 50 of Madagascar's frog species are considered vulnerable or endangered (nine critically so) and over a quarter have yet to be assessed. Despite this, until recently only three species were protected by international law. However, in 2000, restrictions on the trade of mantellas were imposed, bringing the total number of protected Malagasy frogs to 19.

Daniel Austin and Kelly Green have spent many months in Madagascar researching wildlife. They have a particular interest in Malagasy frogs and have photographed more than 60 species in the wild.

Hilary Bradt

Everybody thinks they know one thing about chameleons: that they change colour to match their background. Wrong! You have only to observe the striking Parson's chameleon (*Calumma parsonii*), commonly seen at Andasibe, staying stubbornly green while transferred from boy's hand to tree trunk to leafy branch, to see that in some species at least this is a myth. Most chameleons are cryptically coloured to match their preferred resting place (there are branch-coloured chameleons, for instance, and leaf-coloured ones) and some do respond to a change of background, but their abilities are mainly reserved for expressing emotion. An anxious chameleon will darken and grow stripes and an angry chameleon, faced with a territorial intruder, will change his colours dramatically. The most impressive displays, however, are reserved for sexual encounters. Chameleons say it with colours. Enthusiastic males explode into a riot of spots, stripes and contrasting colours, whilst the female usually responds by donning a black cloak of disapproval. Only on the rare occasions that she is feeling receptive will she present a brighter appearance.

Chameleons use body language more than colour to deter enemies. If you spot a chameleon on a branch you will note that his first reaction to being seen is to put the branch between you and him and flatten his body laterally so that he is barely visible. If you try to catch him, he will blow himself up, expand his throat, raise his helmet (if he has one) and hiss. His next action will be to bite, jump, or try to run away. Fortunately they must be the slowest of all lizards, are easily caught, and pose for the camera with gloomy resignation (who can resist an animal that has a constantly down-turned mouth like a Victorian headmistress?). This slowness is another aspect of the chameleon's defence: when he walks, he moves like a leaf in the wind. This is fine when the danger is an animal predator, but less effective when it is a car. In a tree, his best protection is to keep completely still. He can do this by having feet shaped like pliers and a prehensile tail so he can effortlessly grasp a branch, and eyes shaped like gun-turrets which can swivel 180 degrees independently of each other, enabling him to view the world from front and back without moving his head. This is the chameleon's true camouflage.

The family Chamaeleonidae is represented by three genera, the true chameleons – *Calumma* and *Furcifer* – and the little stump-tailed chameleons, *Brookesia*. Unlike the true

colour from orange or green (when juvenile) to grey and black, brilliant green or brown and blue, depending on the location. Its larger relative the ground boa (*Acrantophis madagascariensis*) is also often spied at the edge of waterways in the humid east and north. Of the remaining species of snake, the metre-long **hog-nosed snake** (*Leioheterodon madagascariensis*), in its dazzling checkerboard of black and yellow, is one of the most frequently encountered, usually gliding across a carpet of leaves on the lookout for frogs.

Despite the fact that none of the island's snakes poses a danger to humans, the Malagasy are particularly wary of some species. The blood-red tail of one harmless tree snake (*Ithycyphus perineti*), known to the Malagasy as *fandrefiala*, is believed to have powers of possession. It is said to hypnotise cattle from up high, then drop down tail-first to impale its victim. Similar paranormal attributes are bestowed on other Malagasy reptiles. The chameleons, for example, are generally feared by the Malagasy, and when fascinated *vazaha* go to pick one up, this is often met with surprised gasps from the locals. Another reptile deeply embedded in the folklore is the **Nile crocodile** (*Crocodilus niloticus*) which, although threatened throughout the island, takes on spiritual roles in some areas (see *Lake Antanavo*, page 368).

A number of Madagascar's **tortoises** are severely threatened with extinction.

chameleons, the *Brookesia's* short tail is not prehensile.

In chameleons there is often a striking colour difference between males and females. Many males have horns (occasionally used for fighting) or other nasal protuberances. Where the two sexes look the same you can recognise the male by the bulge of the scrotal sac beneath the tail, and a spur on the hind feet.

It is interesting to know how the chameleon achieves its colour change. It has a transparent epidermis, then three layers of cells – the top ones are yellow and red, the middle layer reflects blue light and white light, and the bottom layer consists of black pigment cells with tentacles or fingers that can protrude up through the other layers. The cells are under control of the autonomic nervous system, expanding and contracting according to a range of stimuli. Change of colour occurs when one layer is more stimulated than others, and patterning when one group of cells receives maximum stimulation.

In the early 17th century there was the firm conviction that chameleons subsisted without food. A German author, describing Madagascar in 1609, mentions the chameleon living 'entirely on air and dew' and Shakespeare refers several times to the chameleon's supposed diet: 'The chameleon ... can feed on air' (*Two Gentlemen of Verona*) and 'of the chameleon's dish: I eat the air promise-crammed' (*Hamlet*). Possibly at that time no-one had witnessed the tongue flash out through the bars of its cage to trap a passing insect. This tongue is as remarkable as any other feature of this extraordinary reptile. It was formerly thought that the club-shaped tip was sticky, allowing the chameleon to catch flies, but researchers discovered that captive chameleons had been catching much larger prey – lizards, intended to coexist as cage-mates. These animals were far too heavy to be captured simply with a sticky tongue, so a high-speed video camera was brought into use. This showed that a chameleon is able to use a pair of muscles at the tip of its tongue to form a suction cup milliseconds before it hits its prey. The whole manoeuvre, from aim to mouthful, takes about half a second.

The name apparently comes from Greek: *chamai leon* – 'dwarf lion'. I suppose a hissing, open-mouthed reptile could remind one of a lion, but to most visitors to Madagascar they are one of the most appealing and bizarre of the 'strange and marvellous forms' on show.

Captive breeding programmes at Ampijoroa are currently successfully rearing the ploughshare (*Geochelone yniphora*) and flat-tailed tortoises (*Pyxis planicauda*) and further south, the Beza-Mahafaly reserve is protecting the handsome radiated tortoise (*Geochelone radiata*). Four species of freshwater **turtle** inhabit the western waterways, the only endemic species being the big-headed or side-necked turtle (*Erymnochelys madagascariensis*), now also being bred at Ampijoroa. Beyond, in the Mozambique Channel, there are **sea turtles** (hawksbill, loggerhead, olive ridley, leatherback and green turtles) which periodically risk the pot as they visit their nesting beaches.

BIRDS *With information from Derek Schuurman*

Madagascar's score sheet of birds is surprisingly short: of 283 species recorded there, only 209 regularly breed on the island. However 51% of these are endemic, including five endemic families and 37 endemic genera – rendering Madagascar one of Africa's top birding hotspots.

Key endemics include the three rail-like **mesites** – the brown mesite (*Mesitornis unicolor*) in the rainforests, the white-breasted mesite (*M. variegata*) in the western dry woods and the subdesert mesite (*Monias benschi*) in the southwestern spiny

Derek Schuurman

To see a fair spectrum of Madagascar's endemic birds, visit at least one site in each in the island's three chief climatic/floristic zones: eastern rainforest, southern spiny forest and western dry deciduous forests. Each holds its own complement of regional endemics. In addition, a select band of birds is dependent on the dwindling wetlands, so include these in your itinerary. The transition forest of Zombitse should be visited. During a stay of two or three weeks and armed with two helpful field guides (see page 461) you should be able to tick off most of the island's sought-after 'lifers'.

The standard birding route is as follows:

EASTERN RAINFOREST Rainforest birding is best in spring and early summer (mid September to January).

Andasibe-Mantadia National Park (Périnet) and surrounds (Mitsinjo and Maromizaha) At Andasibe you can see most of the broadly distributed rainforest endemics. Specials include collared nightjar, red-fronted coua, Rand's warbler, coral-billed nuthatch vanga and Tylas vanga. In rank herbaceous growth, look for Madagascar wood-rail, white-throated rail and Madagascar flufftail.

In Mantadia, the pitta-like, scaly (rare) and short-legged ground-rollers occur, as do velvet asity, common sunbird asity and brown emutail. Two wetlands nearby, the Torotorofotsy Marsh (a four-hour walk) and the more accessible Ampasipotsy Marsh, hold Madagascar rail, Madagascar snipe, grey emutail and Madagascar swamp warbler.

Ranomafana National Park Above all, Ranomafana is known for its ground-rollers (pitta-like and rufous-headed especially). Other 'megaticks' include brown mesite, yellow-browed oxylabes, Crossley's babbler, grey-crowned tetraka (greenbul), forest rock-thrush and Pollen's vanga. Velvet and common sunbird asities are plentiful. On high ridges, look for yellow-bellied sunbird asity, brown emutail and cryptic warbler.

Masoala National Park Birding in this lowland rainforest is exceptional. Aside from nearly all the broadly distributed rainforest endemics, specials include brown mesite, red-breasted coua, scaly ground-roller and the helmet and Bernier's vangas. The extremely rare Madagascar serpent eagle and Madagascar red owl have a stronghold here but seeing them is extremely difficult: both are highly elusive.

bush. A similar allocation of habitats is more generously employed by the ten species of **coua**, which brighten forests with their blue-masked faces. Six species are ground-dwellers, occupying roles filled elsewhere by pheasants and roadrunners. Difficult to see are the **ground-rollers**, which quietly patrol the rainforest floor in their pretty uniforms. One member of the family, the long-tailed ground-roller (*Uratelornis chimaera*), inhabits the south-western spiny bush. The two **asities** (*Philepitta* spp) resemble squat broadbills, to which they are related. In the eastern rainforests, the **sunbird-asities** (*Neodrepanis* spp) appear as flashes of blue and green in the canopy, their down-turned beaks designed for the nectaries of canopy flowers.

Beak variation is remarkable among Madagascar's most celebrated endemic family, the **vangas**. All species have perfected their own craft of insect capture, filling the niches of various absent African bird groups, which they may resemble superficially. Vangas often flock together or with other forest birds, presenting a formidable offensive for local invertebrates. Most prominent is the sickle-billed

TROPICAL DRY DECIDUOUS FORESTS (WESTERN REGION)

Ankarafantsika National Park (Ampijoroa) An outstanding birding locality year-round, this forest holds most of the specials of western Madagascar. They include white-breasted mesite, Coquerel's coua, Schlegel's asity and Van Dam's vanga. Several other vangas (sickle-billed, rufous, Chabert's, white-headed, blue and rufous) abound. Raptors include the critically endangered Madagascar fish eagle, Madagascar harrier-hawk and Madagascar sparrow-hawk. Other sought-after species often seen include Madagascar crested ibis and Madagascar pygmy kingfisher. In the Betsiboka Delta (Mahajanga) look for Humblot's heron, Madagascar teal, Madagascar white ibis and Madagascar jacana.

TRANSITION FOREST

Zombitse-Vohibasia National Park A serious 'OOE' (Orgasmic Ornithological Experience) year-round and included in all birding itineraries for its 'megatick': the Appert's tetraka. Zombitse also holds an impressive variety of other endemics, like giant and crested couas. Look out for Madagascar partridge, Madagascar buttonquail, Madagascar sandgrouse, greater and lesser vasa parrots, grey-headed lovebird, Madagascar green pigeon, Madagascar hoopoe, Thamnornis warbler, common newtonia, common jery, long-billed green sunbird, white-headed and blue vangas, and Sakalava weaver.

Southern sub-arid thorn thicket (spiny bush/spiny forest) Excellent birding year-round; start just before daybreak.

Ifaty/Mangily (The protected portion of the PK 32 spiny bush parcel). Ifaty's bizarre *Euphorbia-Didiereaceae* bush holds some extremely localised birds, notably sub-desert mesite, long-tailed ground-roller, Lafresnaye's vanga and Archbold's newtonia. Look for running coua and subdesert brush-warbler. Excellent for banded kestrel and Madagascar nightjar too.

St Augustine's Bay and Anakao The coral ragg scrub here is lower than Ifaty's spiny bush and holds Verreaux's coua, littoral rock thrush and the recently described red-shouldered vanga (La Table is a good site for these birds). At puddles along the road look for Madagascar plover.

vanga (*Falculea palliata*) which parallels the tree-probing habits of Africa's wood hoopoes. The heavily carnivorous diet of shrikes is adopted by – among others – the hook-billed vanga (*Vanga curvirostris*) and the dramatic, blue-billed helmet vanga (*Euryceros prevostii*) which resembles a small hornbill. Other vangas mimic nuthatches, flycatchers and tits. In short, if *The Beagle* had been caught by the West Wind Drift and Darwin had arrived in Madagascar instead of the Galapagos, the vangas would certainly have ensured that his train of thought went uninterrupted.

Malagasy representatives of families found elsewhere make up the bulk of the remaining birdlife. Herons, ibises, grebes, ducks and rails take up their usual positions in wetlands, including endemics such as the endangered Madagascar teal (*Anas bernieri*) of some western mangroves, and the colourful Madagascar malachite kingfisher (*Alcedo vintsioides*). Game birds include the attractive Madagascar partridge and Madagascar sandgrouse. The impressive Madagascar crested ibis (*Lophotibis cristata*), Madagascar blue and green pigeons and tuneful vasa parrots (*Coracopsis* spp) occupy the various strata of vegetation. More colourful birds include the grey-headed lovebird (*Agapornis cana*); the Madagascar bee-eater (*Merops superciliosus*); the Madagascar paradise flycatcher (*Terpsiphone mutata*); the Madagascar hoopoe (*Upupa marginata*); the Madagascar red fody (*Foudia madagascariensis*) dressed in scarlet during the breeding season (October to March); souimanga and long-billed green sunbirds; and the crested drongo (*Dicrurus forficatus*), with its black plumage, forked tail and silly crest. The four **rock thrushes** (*Monticola* spp) look like European robins in morning suits. The confiding endemic Madagascar magpie robin (*Copsychus albospecularis*) sports black-and-white attire and flirts fearlessly with humans.

The Madagascar kestrel (*Falco newtoni*) is joined by other **raptors** such as the banded kestrel (*Falco zoniventris*), the exceptionally handsome Madagascar harrier-hawk (*Polyboroides radiatus*), Frances's sparrow-hawk (*Accipiter francesii*), Madagascar buzzard (*Buteo brachypterus*), Madagascar cuckoo-hawk (*Aviceda madagascariensis*) and seven species of owl. The two endemic eagles – the critically endangered Madagascar fish eagle (*Haliaeetus vociferoides*) of the west coast and the Madagascar serpent eagle (*Eutriorchis astur*) of the northeastern rainforests – are among the world's rarest raptors. Like the Madagascar red owl (*Tyto soumagnei*), the serpent eagle had managed to escape detection for several decades and was feared extinct, until both species were found thriving discretely in various rainforest sites. The ultra-rare Sakalava rail (*Amaurornis olivieri*) was also recently rediscovered in the Mahavavy Delta, which holds a small breeding population. But the most sensational avian news to emerge from Madagascar in recent years was the discovery, in November 2006, of 13 **Madagascar pochards** (*Aythya innotata*) living on a remote northern lake. This diving duck, previously thought to have been confined to Lake Alaotra, had not been seen alive since 1992 and was thought likely to be extinct.

MAMMALS Madagascar's mammals are the prize exhibit in the island's incredible menagerie. They exist as an obscure assortment of primates, insectivores, carnivores, bats and rodents, representing the descendants of parties of individuals who, curled up in hollow trunks or skipping across temporary islands, accidentally completed the perilous journey from eastern Africa to the island beyond the horizon at different times over the last 100 million years. Once established, they gradually spread through the diverse habitats of their paradise island, all the time evolving and creating new species.

Biologists often refer to Madagascar as a museum housing living fossils. This is because almost all the mammals on the island today closely resemble groups that once shone elsewhere but have since been replaced by more advanced species. Although evolution has certainly occurred on the island, it seems to have plodded on with less momentum than back in Africa. Hence, while their cousins on the mainland were subjected to extreme competition with the species that were to develop subsequently, the Malagasy mammals were able to stick more rigidly to their original physiques and behaviours.

The word 'cousins' is especially poignant when applied to the lemurs, for across in Africa primate evolution was eventually to lead to the ascent of humankind. How opportune then for an understanding of our own natural history that one of our direct ancestors managed to end up on this island sanctuary and remain, sheltered from the pressures of life elsewhere, relatively true to its original form for us to appreciate 35 million years later.

Lemurs Lemurs are to a biologist what the old masters are to an art critic: they may not be contemporary, but historically they are very important and they are beautiful to look at. Lemurs belong to a group of primates called the prosimians, a word which means 'before monkeys'. Their basic body design evolved about 40 to 50 million years ago. With stereoscopic colour vision, hands that could grasp branches, a brain capable of processing complex, learned information, extended parental care and an integrated social system incorporating a wide range of sound and scent signals, the lemurs were the latest model in evolution's comprehensive range of arboreal (tree-living) mammals. Their reign lasted until about 35 million years ago, when a new model – the monkey – evolved. Monkeys were superior in a number of ways: they were faster, could think more quickly, used their vision more effectively and were highly dextrous. Their success rapidly drove the less adaptable prosimians to extinction across most of the world. A few stowaways managed to take refuge in Madagascar, a corner of the world never reached by more advanced primates (until the recent arrival of humans). Today we see the results of 35 million years of leisurely evolution. The single ancestral species has adapted into more than 80 recognised varieties and instead of gazing at inanimate rocks we have the luxury of being able to watch, hear and smell the genuine article.

Smell is an extremely important aspect of lemur lives. Through scents, lemurs communicate a wide range of information, such as who's in charge, who is fertile, who is related to whom and who lives where. They supplement this language with a vocal one. Chirps, barks and cries reinforce hierarchies in lemur societies, help to defend territories against other groups and warn of danger. Socially the lemurs show a great variety of organisational skills and the strategy used by each species is largely dependent on the nature of their diet. The small, quick-moving, insectivorous lemurs such as the mouse lemurs and dwarf lemurs are nocturnal and largely solitary except during the mating season when they pair up with a member of the opposite sex. Literally surrounded by their insect food, they require only small territories, hence they never cover large distances and spend their entire lives in the trees. A different way of life is led by the larger leaf-eating species such as the indri. In a rainforest there is no shortage of leaves; however, as a food source leaves are poor in nutrients, so each lemur needs to consume a large amount. Leaf-eaters therefore tend to collect in small groups, together defending their territory of foliage with scents and often loud calls which in the dense forests are the best forms of communication.

Their sex lives vary, but most of these species have family groups in which a single male dominates. The most social lemurs on the island are those with a more varied diet concentrating on fruit, but also including seeds, buds and leaves. These include

Nick Garbutt

Diurnal (day-active) lemurs are the largest and easiest to identify. They are usually found in groups of between three and 12 individuals. In many of the island's renowned wildlife locations two or more species can been seen relatively easily.

RING-TAILED LEMUR (*Lemur catta*). Instantly recognisable by its banded tail. More terrestrial than other lemurs and lives in troops of up to 20 animals in the south and southwest, notably in Isalo, Andohahela and Andringitra National Parks, and Berenty Reserve.

RUFFED LEMURS (genus *Varecia*) are large lemurs commonly found in zoos but difficult to see in the wild. There are two species and both live in eastern rainforests: black-and-white ruffed lemur is found sporadically in pristine areas and can sometimes be seen in Mantadia and Ranomafana National Parks, and on Nosy Mangabe, while the red ruffed lemur is restricted to Masoala.

Ring-tailed lemur

Black-and-white ruffed lemur

TRUE LEMURS (genus *Eulemur*) are all roughly cat-sized, have long noses, and live in trees. A confusing characteristic is that males and females of most species have somewhat different markings and coat colours. The well-known black lemur (*E. macaco*; called *maki* by the Malagasy), from northwest Madagascar, notably Nosy Komba and Lokobe, is perhaps the best example. Only males are black; females are chestnut brown. Visitors to Ranomafana and Mantadia often see red-bellied lemurs; males have white tear-drop face-markings, while females have creamy-white bellies. In far northern reserves crowned lemurs (*E. coronatus*) are common: males are sandy-brown, females are grey.

The six species of brown lemur present the ultimate challenge, but fortunately their ranges do not overlap, so locality helps identification. In most cases males are more distinctively marked and look quite different from females which tend to be uniformly brown. Two neighbouring male brown lemurs have beautiful cream or white ear-tufts and side whiskers: Sanford's brown lemur (*E. sanfordi*) is found in far northern reserves, while the white-fronted brown lemur (*E. albifrons*) occurs in the northeast and males

Collared brown lemur

have bushy white heads and Santa-Claus-like side whiskers. Further south you will find common brown lemur (*E. fulvus*) in both the east (eg: Andasibe-Mantadia National Park) and also the northwest (eg: Ankarafantsika). Red-fronted brown lemurs (*E. rufus*) live in the southeast and southwest. The males of the two variations of collared brown lemur (*E. collaris* and *E. albocollaris*) unsurprisingly have distinctive tufty fur collars and both occur in far southeastern areas, but the white-collared brown lemur (*E. albocollaris*) has an extremely restricted range and is very rare.

BAMBOO LEMURS (genera *Hapalemur* and *Prolemur*) are smaller than the true lemurs, with short muzzles and round faces. They occur in smaller groups (one to four animals), cling to vertical branches, and feed mainly on bamboo. You may see the commonest species, grey bamboo lemur (*Hapalemur griseus*), in several eastern parks including Marojejy, Andasibe-Mantadia and Ranomafana. The very much rarer golden bamboo lemur (*H. aureus*) and greater bamboo lemur (*Prolemur simus*) are, realistically, only seen at Ranomafana.

Bamboo lemur

Indri

INDRI (*Indri indri*). The largest lemur and the only one with virtually no tail. This black-and-white teddy-bear lemur is unmistakable, having a characteristic eerie wailing song. It is seen in Andasibe-Mantadia National Park.

SIFAKAS (genus *Propithecus*) belong to the same family as the indri, and have characteristic long back legs. Some sifakas (pronounced *sheefahk*) are the famous dancing lemurs that bound upright over the ground and leap spectacularly from tree to tree. The commonest sifakas are white or mainly white and are quite unmistakable. Verreaux's sifaka (*P. verreauxi*) shares its southern habitat with the ring-tailed lemur, while its cousin the Coquerel's sifaka (*P. coquereli*), which has chestnut-maroon arms and legs, is seen at Ankarafantsika in the northwest. You may also see the stunningly beautiful diademed sifaka (*P. diadema*) in Mantadia and the rich chocolate-coloured Milne-Edwards' sifaka (*P. edwardsi*) at Ranomafana.

Verreaux's sifaka

Nick Garbutt

Because they are generally smaller than the diurnal lemurs (sometimes *very* tiny) and active primarily after dark, the various types of nocturnal lemur are often more challenging to identify. However, night walks in Madagascar's forests are safe and very exciting as you can never really be sure what you might discover. Two types of nocturnal lemur – sportive lemurs and woolly lemurs – often helpfully sleep or doze in the open during the day so are regularly seen by tourists.

Brown mouse lemur

MOUSE LEMURS (genus *Microcebus*) are the smallest of all primates: the most minuscule is Madame Berthe's mouse lemur (*M. berthae*) which could sit in an egg cup and weighs 30g. As a group these are the most abundant type of lemur and are generally common in virtually all native forests types, they even survive in some forest fragments where other lemurs have disappeared. There are now a number of species (16 at the last count), which makes accurate identification confusing and difficult. The easiest places to see them are Andasibe-Mantadia and Ranomafana National Parks in the east and Ankarafantsika, Ankarana and Berenty Reserves in drier areas.

DWARF LEMURS (genera *Cheirogaleus, Mirza* and *Allocebus*) are mostly squirrel-sized and run along branches in a similar fashion. Some, like the fat-tailed dwarf lemur (*Cheirogaleus medius*), become dormant during the winter, sleeping in tree holes and surviving on reserves of fat stored in their tails.

Greater dwarf lemur

Dwarf lemurs from the genus *Cheirogaleus* have distinctive dark spectacle-like rings around their eyes which helps identification. Giant dwarf lemurs (genus *Mirza*) are unusual as they are sometimes predatory and eat baby birds, frogs, lizards and even small snakes. For a long time it was through the hairy-eared dwarf lemur (*Allocebus trichotis*) was exceedingly rare, it now turns out to have been overlooked and is actually quite widespread; it can even be seen in Andasibe-Mantadia National Park. It is about the size of a large mouse lemur, but look out for its distinctive ear-tufts.

Eastern fork-marked dwarf lemur

FORK-MARKED LEMURS (genus *Phaner*) prefer to live high in the canopy so are often rather difficult to see and identify. Their distribution is also somewhat sporadic. Perhaps the best places to look are the dry western forests like Kirindy and Zombitse. The dark fork markings on the face are highly distinctive.

SPORTIVE LEMURS (genus *Lepilemur*) mostly spend the day in tree-holes from which they peer drowsily. Their name is something of a misnomer as they are rarely particularly energetic, even at night. They cling vertically to tree trunks and, after dark, their high pitched calls are often a feature of the forests they inhabit. Recently scientists have described many new species (the genus now contains 23 species) and in appearance they are often very similar. The best guide for identification is locality.

WOOLLY LEMURS (genus *Avahi*) also adopt a vertical posture and are similar in size to sportive lemurs, but have round, owl-like faces and conspicuous white thighs. They often sleep in the tangled branches of trees. Many park guides use 'woolly lemur' and 'avahi' interchangeably as the common name.

Western woolly lemur

Small-toothed sportive lemur

One recently described species is named after British comic actor John Cleese: Cleese's woolly lemur (*Avahi cleesei*) is currently known only from Tsingy de Bemaraha National Park.

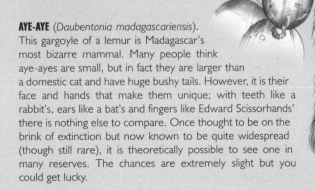

AYE-AYE (*Daubentonia madagascariensis*). This gargoyle of a lemur is Madagascar's most bizarre mammal. Many people think aye-ayes are small, but in fact they are larger than a domestic cat and have huge bushy tails. However, it is their face and hands that make them unique; with teeth like a rabbit's, ears like a bat's and fingers like Edward Scissorhands' there is nothing else to compare. Once thought to be on the brink of extinction but now known to be quite widespread (though still rare), it is theoretically possible to see one in many reserves. The chances are extremely slight but you could get lucky.

Aye-aye

THE AYE-AYE

Hilary Bradt

The strangest lemur is the aye-aye, *Daubentonia madagascariensis*. It took a while for scientists to decide that it was a lemur at all: for years it was thought to be a peculiar type of squirrel. Now it is classified in a family of its own, Daubentoniidae. The aye-aye seems to have been assembled from the leftover parts of a variety of animals. It has the teeth of a rodent (they never stop growing), the ears of a bat, the tail of a fox and the hands of no living creature, since the middle finger is like that of a skeleton. It's this finger which so intrigues scientists, as it shows the aye-aye's adaptation to its way of life. In Madagascar it fills the ecological niche left empty by the absence of woodpeckers. The aye-aye evolved to use its skeletal finger to winkle grubs from under the bark of trees. The aye-aye's fingers are unique among lemurs in another way – it has claws not fingernails (except on the big toe). When searching for grubs the aye-aye taps on the wood with its finger, its enormous ears pointing like radar dishes to detect a cavity. It can even tell whether this is occupied by a nice fat grub. Another anatomical feature of the aye-aye that sets it apart from other primates is that it has inguinal mammary glands. In other words, its teats are between its back legs.

This fascinating animal was long considered to be on the verge of extinction, but recently there have been encouraging signs that it is more widespread than previously supposed. Although destruction of habitat is the chief threat to its survival, it is also at risk because of its supposedly evil powers. Rural people believe the aye-aye to be the herald of death. If one is seen near a settlement it must be killed, and even then the only salvation may be to burn down the village.

'I WANT TO SEE AN AYE-AYE' A glimpse of Madagascar's weirdest lemur is a goal for many visitors. And many go away disappointed. When weighing up whether to try to see one in the wild or to settle for a captive animal, you should bear in mind that the aye-aye is a rare, nocturnal and largely solitary animal. Most of its waking hours are spent foraging for food in the upper canopy; only occasionally does it descend to the ground. So even in the reserve of Nosy Mangabe, which was created for aye-ayes, your chance of seeing more than two distant shining eyes in the beam of your torch is very small. I know of more than one visitor who spent a week on Nosy Mangabe and never saw this animal.

That leaves the choice between the semi-wild aye-aye on the eponymous island at Mananara or those caged in the two Malagasy zoos: Tsimbazaza in Tana and Ivoloina near Toamasina. Mananara seems to satisfy most people, providing they know what to expect. The animals are 'wild' in that they live free and find some of their food in their environment, but they are thoroughly accustomed to people so are easy to approach and photograph. Don't assume, however, that aye-aye sightings are guaranteed here. Some visitors are unlucky and see nothing.

Of the two zoos, Ivoloina is my choice because there are fewer visitors, which means the animals are less stressed. At the time of writing they have just one female. You can usually arrange to see the aye-aye at dusk as it starts to become active. Tsimbazaza now has a day-to-night aye-aye house, allowing you to see the creatures awake.

Outside Madagascar, an increasing number of zoos have night-reversed aye-aye cages. The best are London, Bristol and Jersey (the late Gerald Durrell's zoo) in the UK and Duke University Primate Center in the USA.

the ring-tailed lemur, ruffed lemur and true lemurs *(Eulemur* spp). The diet of these species requires active foraging over large areas during the day, so in order to defend their expansive territory, and to protect themselves in daylight, these lemurs form distinctive troops. The societies are run by matriarchs, who organise the troop's movement, courtship and defence. But there are also whole groups of males, which often separate for week-long excursions away from the home base. Usually operating in more open country, these lemurs use a wide range of visual signals to accompany their scents and sounds, making them particularly entertaining to watch.

Perhaps the most entertaining of all is the ring-tailed lemur (*Lemur catta*). Among lemurs it forms the largest and liveliest troops. Each troop typically stirs at dawn, warms up with a period of sunbathing and then, guided by the matriarchs, heads off to forage, breaking at noon for a siesta. The troop moves along the ground, each individual using its distinctive tail to maintain visual contact with the others. If out of eyesight, the troop members use the cat-like mews that prompted their scientific name. By dusk they return to the sleeping trees which they use for three or four days before the females move the group off to another part of the territory to harvest the food there. During the April breeding season the males become less tolerant of each other and engage in stink fights where, after charging their tails with scent from glands on their wrists, they waft them antagonistically at opponents. Similar aggressive interactions occur when two troops of ring-tails meet, sometimes leading to serious injury or death, but usually one side backs down before it reaches this stage.

Identifying species Even for a keen naturalist, sorting out Madagascar's 86 varieties (species and subspecies) of lemur can be challenging. The two illustrated layman's guides on pages 60–3 should help you put names to faces. The first box covers diurnal (day-active) species; the second describes the nocturnal ones more likely encountered on a night walk. For an explanation of scientific classification turn to the box on page 37.

See also *Appendix 3* for details of where to see the main lemur species. Serious naturalists should consider purchasing a field guide (see page 461).

Tenrecs Employing one of the most primitive mammalian body plans, the tenrecs have been able to fill the vacancies created by an absence of shrews, moles and hedgehogs, and in doing so have diversified into about 27 different species. Five of these are called the spiny tenrecs, most looking just like hedgehogs, some with yellow and black stripes. However, the largest, the tailless common tenrec (*Tenrec ecaudatus*), has lost the majority of its spines. Not only is this species the largest insectivore in the world at 1.5kg, but it can also give birth to enormous litters which the mother feeds with up to 24 nipples. The 19 species of furred tenrecs are mostly shrew-like in stature, although three species look and act more like moles, and one has become aquatic, capturing small fish and freshwater shrimps in the fast-flowing streams of the *hauts plateaux*.

Rodents Highly successful elsewhere, rodents have made little impression on Madagascar. There are 20 species, most of which are nocturnal. The easiest to see is the red forest rat (*Nesomys rufus*) which is active during the day. The most unusual are the rabbit-like giant jumping rat (*Hypogeomys antimena*) from the western forests and the two tree-dwelling *Brachytarsomys* species which have prehensile tails.

Civets and mongooses The island's eight carnivores belong to the civets and mongooses, Viverridae, which evolved 40 million years ago at about the same time as the cats. The largest, the fossa (*Cryptoprocta ferox*), is very cat-like with an extremely long tail which assists balance during canopy-based lemur hunts. This

Richard Jenkins, Madagasikara Voakajy

DIVERSITY Bats make a significant contribution to tropical diversity but in Madagascar they have only recently received the concerted attention of biologists. New species of Malagasy bat continue to be discovered. Five new endemic bats have been described since 2004, bringing the total to at least 37 species (24 of which are thought to be endemic). The megachiropterans (fruit bats) are represented by three endemic species (*Pteropus rufus, Eidolon dupreanum* and *Rousettus madagascariensis*); they feed on flowers, fruits and leaves. Six families of insectivorous microchiropterans (*ramanavy, kinakina* or *kananavy* in Malagasy) are also found in Madagascar, including the endemic family of sucker-footed bats (genus *Myzopoda*).

CONSERVATION Bats are threatened in Madagascar from habitat loss, persecution (as fruit crop pests and unwanted house guests), hunting (bushmeat) and roost site disturbance. Bats are not protected under Malagasy law and only populations inside reserves or at sacred sites receive any protection. Many species are gregarious and roost in cavities (eg: caves, tree-holes, roofs) or on vegetation.

BAT-WATCHING The Madagascar flying fox *P. rufus* (*fanihy* in Malagasy) is large (wingspan 1.2m) and forms colonies of up to 5,000 individuals. It makes short flights during the day and excellent viewing rewards patient observers. Good tourist sites to see them include Berenty Reserve, Nosy Tanikely, Nosy Mangabe, the mangroves near Anjajavy and independent travellers can visit other sites, such as near Moramanga. The Madagascar straw-coloured bat *E. dupreanum* (*angavo* in Malagasy) is best seen in the Grotte des Chauve-souris at Ankarana or flying around rock overhangs at Cap Sainte Marie.

The smallest Malagasy fruit bat *Rousettus madagascariensis* (*matavikely* in Malagasy) lives in caves and a large colony is resident at the aforementioned Ankarana cave. These bats betray their presence by noisy chattering and reflective orange eye-shine. The best time to view fruit bats is during June and July when the kapok trees are flowering in western Madagascar. All three species flock to these trees at night to feed on nectar and can be observed in torchlight at close quarters.

The circuits at Tsingy de Bemaraha offer the chance of seeing some roosting microchiropterans. Other reserves with bat caves include Ankarana, Tsingy de Namoroka and Tsimanampetsotsa. House-roosting bats can be seen at dusk as they emerge to feed; a good site to watch this is at the post office in Andasibe. There are three new colour

extremely shy creature is quite widespread but rarely seen – except in November, see page 431. The size of a chubby cat, the striped civet (*Fossa fossana*) hunts in the eastern rainforests for rodents, and a third, very secretive animal, the *falanouc* (*Eupleres goudotii*) inhabits the northeastern rainforests where it lives almost entirely on earthworms. Each of Madagascar's forest types plays host to mongooses. There are five species in all, the most commonly seen being the ring-tailed mongoose (*Galidia elegans*) which varies in colour but is typically a handsome, rusty red.

Bats Possessing, among mammals, the unique gift of flight, it is not surprising that most of Madagascar's bats are also found on mainland Africa or Asia. There are three species of fruit bat which are active during the day, very noisy, large and unfortunately often on the Malagasy menu. If the fruit bats look like flying foxes (their alternative name), then the remaining 30 or so species are not unlike flying mice. These are nocturnal, prefer moths to figs and find them by echolocation. They tend to have shell-like ears and distorted noses. It is known that some moths

interpretation boards located around the post office to raise the awareness of tourists and local people to bats. Mauritian tomb bats can be seen in a rock crevice on the Manambolo circuit at Tsingy de Bemaraha and also roosting on tree trunks in the camp site at Ankarafantsika.

Bats are sensitive to disturbance whilst roosting. Always ask advice from your guide and use common sense: avoid handling bats, avoid shining bright lights at roosting bats, keep quiet at roosts and don't try to provoke resting bats into flight.

Bats are key species in Madagascar's fragile environment; they disperse seeds over vast distances and pollinate trees such as baobabs. They don't have it easy. They tend to be vilified by most people, eaten by some and ignored by the rest. By showing a genuine interest in bats when you visits protected areas you can help Madagasikara Voakajy and its partners to raise bats onto the conservation agenda.

MADAGASIKARA VOAKAJY This Malagasy conservation organisation is dedicated to conserving the island's bats and their habitats. Our Malagasy bat experts study all aspects of bat ecology and operate a conservation awareness campaign. There are many bat roosts in Madagascar that remain unknown to conservationists and we would very much like to hear from anyone who finds a bat cave or tree roost that is not mentioned in this article (e *voakajy@wanadoo.mg*).

SPECIFIC SITES
Cap Sainte Marie There is a roost site of the Madagascar straw-coloured fruit bat *E. dupreanum* that can be seen from one of the tourist trails as it passes a deep valley. The bats are sometimes active in the day and can be seen flying between different rock overhangs.

Mananara-Nord There is a *Pteropus rufus* roost reported from Nosy Antafana, an offshore island in the marine reserve.

Moramanga A Malagasy NGO called ACCE, based in Moramanga, is conserving a number of Madagascar flying fox roosts in the Mangoro Valley. Visits to their sites often allow excellent views of roosting bats (4x4 or motorcycle required). Arrangements can be made through Ndriana at their office (m *033 05 017 89*; e *ACCE@isuisse.com. No English spoken*).

outwit these bats by chirping back at them in mid-flight, scrambling the echo and sending the aggressor off into the night.

Marine mammals Antongil Bay marks the northern extent of **humpback whale** migrations. The whales calve just beyond the coral reefs in July and August, and after this period migrate south as far as the Antarctic coast to feed. **Dugongs** (sea cows) are extremely rare. The Vezo of the west coast share their fishing grounds with an abundance of **dolphins**, and regard them as kin. If a dolphin is discovered dead they wrap it in shrouds and bury it with their ancestors.

MADAGASCAR'S ECOSYSTEMS
Madagascar's amazing array of habitats is the result of the effects of ocean currents, prevailing winds and geological forces. Rain is heaviest in the north and east, and lightest in the south and west. Rainfall is the single most significant

factor in creating habitat characteristics, so a complex spectrum of habitat types has resulted within Madagascar's relatively small area. Madagascar's geology brings further variety by creating undulating coastlines, broad riverbeds and estuaries, shallow ocean shelves for coral reefs, high mountainous slopes and plateaux, a wealth of soil types and even bizarre limestone 'forests' riddled with caves. These various habitats house a wealth of ecosystems, the most important of which are described below.

RAINFORESTS The spine of mountains which border the central plateau forces the saturated air arriving from over the Indian Ocean to drop its moisture onto the east coast of the island. Madagascar's rainforests therefore form in a distinct band adjacent to the east coast where the continuous rainfall is high enough to sustain the evergreen canopy trees. Known as the Madagascar Sylva, this band of forest – now seriously fragmented by deforestation – extends inland only as far as the mountain range, so it is broadest in the northeast. The southern end of the range near Taolagnaro forms a unique but fragile divide between the evergreen rainforest to the east and the arid spiny forest beyond.

Littoral rainforest (sea level) Very little of Madagascar's unique coastal, or littoral, rainforest remains. Rooted in sand, washed with salty air, battered by cyclones and bordering lagoons and marshes, coastal forests harbour a very unusual community. The architecture of the forest is similar to the more widespread lowland forest, but the plants are different: they are salt-tolerant and highly efficient at extracting water and nutrients from the shallow, porous sand beneath. *Good example: Tampolo Forestry Station.*

Lowland rainforest (0–800m) Most of the rainforest in Madagascar is lowland, that is, below around 800m. This type of forest is hot and sticky, with humidity at 100% and annual rainfall of up to 5,000mm. The forest canopy is 30m above the ground, with few trees emerging beyond this level. Butterflies flutter as monstrous beetles and myriad ants and termites patrol the forest floor.

Lemurs skip among the branches and lianas which serve as highways between the forest floor and the world above. Preying on the lemurs, the fossa is at home among the canopy branches, while above the leaves birds of prey and fruit bats patrol. Tenrecs and forest birds rummage through the leaf litter, and the Madagascar striped civet and mongooses wait to pick off any unsuspecting prey. *Good examples: Masoala, Nosy Mangabe and the lower parts of Marojejy.*

Montane rainforest (800–1,300m) As altitude increases and air temperature drops, the tree species of the lowland rainforests give way to those more able to tolerate the cooler conditions. These species have lower canopies and are the foundation of the montane rainforest. The change from lowland to montane forest is a gradual one influenced by a number of factors. In southern Madagascar, montane forest occurs lower down; in the warmer north lowland forest may continue up to around 900m.

Once in true montane forest the landscape is very different. Not only is the canopy lower and the temperature much cooler, the understorey is far more dense. Tree ferns and bamboos litter the forest floor and there is a tight tangle of trunks, roots and woody lianas, all sporting furry lichens and lines of bright fungi.

Montane reserves are excellent places to spot mammals and birds including many lemur species. *Good examples: Ranomafana, Andasibe-Mantadia, Montagne d'Ambre and parts of Marojejy.*

Cloudforest (above 1,300m) The forest beyond 1,300m has an even lower canopy and is characteristically thick with ferns and mosses. It is properly called high-altitude montane rainforest, but because it is often cloaked in mists it is also known as cloudforest. The low temperatures slow down decomposition, creating waterlogged peaty soils in valleys. Termites cannot live at these altitudes, so large earthworms and beetles take their place as detritivores. The canopy can be as low as 10m, and in places the understorey gives way to a thicket of shrubs. Mosses, lichens and ferns inhabit every branch and stone, and cover the floor along with forest succulents and *Bulbophyllum* orchids. *Good examples: Marojejy and Andringitra.*

DRY DECIDUOUS FOREST The magnificent dry forests of the west once covered the vast lowland plain west of the *hauts plateaux*. Now only a few patches remain, sharing the coast with the mangroves, bordering the largest rivers of the south and dotted about the plains near Isalo and inland from Mahajanga. The forest supports far fewer species than the eastern rainforests but has higher levels of endemism. The trees are less densely arranged and the canopy is typically 12–20m high.

The canopy leaves are shed during the seven or eight months of the dry season and a carpet of leaves begins to accumulate on the forest floor shortly after the rains stop in May. These decompose creating a thick humus layer in the soil. During this dry period much of the wildlife goes to ground, quite literally: amphibians and insects bury themselves in the soil to await the return of the rains.

Sifakas, sportive lemurs, brown lemurs and the ubiquitous mouse lemurs are particularly in evidence. Vangas live in the canopy and tuneful vasa parrots make territories in the understorey. The deep litter layer is home to tenrecs, tortoises, boas and hog-nosed snakes. Fossas and mongooses regularly run along their patrol trails, sometimes pursuing their prey up into the canopy. *Good examples: Kirindy, Ankarafantsika and Berenty.*

INSELBERG AND *TSINGY* COMMUNITIES In the west, where the underlying rocks are exposed, localised communities of specialised plants and animals develop. Since rain simply drains off, or through, the rocks, all the residents must be tolerant of desiccation. Magnificent *Euphorbias*, *Aloes*, *Kalanchoes* and *Pachypodiums* grip on to tiny crevices, bringing foliage and flowers to the rock face. The insects, birds and lemurs rely on these for sustenance, only retreating in the heat of the day to rest beneath the trees in nearby canyons.

Plants and animals are also to be found among the knife-edge pinnacles of the spectacular limestone karst massifs known as *tsingy* (see *Plants of the tsingy*, page 430). These bizarre eroded landscapes enable a complex mosaic of communities to live side-by-side. The towering pinnacles which sport the succulents are in fact the ornate roofs of extensive cave systems below. These caves are inhabited by bats and rodents, with millions of insects and arachnids feeding on the bat guano and each other. Blind cave fish share these dark subterranean rivers with lurking cave crocodiles.

This diverse habitat supports numerous birds and mammals. It has even been claimed that Ankarana has the highest density of primates on earth. *Good examples: Isalo, Ankarana, Bemaraha and Namoroka.*

SPINY FOREST Whenever photographers wish to startle people with the uniqueness of Madagascar they head for the spiny forest. Its mass of tangled, prickly branches and swollen succulent trunks creates a habitat variously described by naturalists as 'a nightmare' and 'the eighth wonder of the world'. Stretching in a band around the southwest coast from Morombe to Taolagnaro, the spiny forest is the only primary community able to resist the extremely arid environment. All the plants here are beautifully adapted to survive on the sporadic rainfall, sometimes going without water for more than a year. The unworldly landscape of this community is a result of the dramatic and striking forms of tall *Aloes*, broad-leaved *Kalanchoe* 'trees', octopus trees, *Pachypodiums*, *Euphorbias*, endemic orchids and palms – all extremely specialised to withstand the harsh dry conditions.

The most evident animal life, aside from reptiles and desert arthropods, are the groups of sifakas which somehow avoid the vicious spines of the *Didierea* as they leap from one trunk to another. *Good examples: Berenty, Ifaty, Beza-Mahafaly and along the road from Taolagnaro to Ambovombe.*

WETLANDS Wetlands everywhere are regarded as important habitats. The plants here are terrestrial species adapted to tolerate waterlogging. Lakes, swamps and marshes all over the island are popular with birds, attracted by the shelter and materials of the reeds and rushes, and the sustenance to be gained from the insect life. On open water and lagoons near the coast, large flocks of flamingoes gather, accompanied in their feeding by various waders.

But in Madagascar it is not only birds that make their homes among the reeds. In the reed beds of Lake Alaotra, a rare species of bamboo lemur, *Hapalemur alaotrensis*, has given up bamboo for papyrus to become the world's only reed-dwelling primate. Lakes and waterways also play host to sometimes-sacred populations of crocodiles. *Good examples: Tsimanampetsotsa, Lake Alaotra, Lake Ravelobe, Lake Ampitabe and Ankarafantsika.*

MANGROVES Where trees dominate the wetlands instead of grasses, there are swamps. The most important of these are the mangrove swamps. Madagascar possesses the largest area of mangroves in the western Indian Ocean – about 330,000ha. The aerial roots of their characteristic salt-tolerant trees are alternately submerged and exposed twice daily with the tide. Some of the trees get a head start in life by germinating their seeds whilst still on the parent tree.

Mangroves are important and rich ecosystems. They support a wealth of bird species, which feast on the swarms of insects above the water and shoals of fish below. Many marine fish and crustaceans use mangroves as a nursery, coming in from the open sea to mate, breed and rear their young in relative safety. However, mangroves are now under threat in Madagascar. *Good examples: Anakao, Katsepy, Marovoay and Morombe.*

CORAL REEFS Madagascar has about 1,000km of coral reefs. Most of the species they support come from a community of globetrotting fish, corals and invertebrates, which crop up wherever the environment is just right.

The 1,600km difference in latitude between north and south Madagascar results in a subtle temperature gradient. The slightly cooler waters of the south are dominated by different corals and other species from those found in the north.

The continental shelf surrounding Madagascar also contributes to diversity. A sharp drop-off on the east coast limits fringing reef growth, while the west coast's vast and shallow shelf – spreading out under the Mozambique Channel and warmed by the Agulhas Current – is much better suited to coral reef development. Along this coast there are fringing and barrier reefs sporting remote cays and a wealth of fish and invertebrates. Loggerhead, green and hawksbill turtles cruise the underwater meadows between reefs and nesting beaches, and from July to September migrating humpback whales use the warm waters of eastern Madagascar for breeding. *Good examples: Ile Sainte Marie, islands off Nosy Be, Ifaty, Anakao and Lokaro.*

AN AGE-OLD PROBLEM When people first settled in Madagascar, the culture they brought with them depended on rice and zebu cattle. Rice was the staple diet and zebu the spiritual staple, the link with the ancestors. Rice and zebu cannot be raised in dense forest, so the trees were felled and the undergrowth burned.

Two hundred or so years ago King Andrianampoinimerina punished those of his subjects who wilfully deforested areas. The practice continued, however. In 1883, a century later, the missionary James Sibree commented: 'Again we noticed the destruction of the forest and the wanton waste of trees.' The first efforts at legal protection came as long ago as 1927 when ten reserves were set aside by the French colonial government, which also tried to put a stop to the burning. Successive governments have tried – and failed – to halt this devastation.

Since independence in 1960, Madagascar's population has more than doubled (to nearly 17 million) and the remaining forest has been reduced by half. Only about 10% of the original cover remains and an estimated 2,000km² is destroyed annually – not by timber companies (although there have been some culprits) but by impoverished peasants clearing the land by the traditional method of *tavy*, slash-and-burn (see box on page 43), and cutting trees for fuel or to make charcoal. However, Madagascar is not overpopulated; the population density averages only 21 people per square kilometre (compared to 228 in the UK). The pressure on the forests is because so much of the country is sterile grassland. Unlike in neighbouring Africa, this savanna is lifeless because Malagasy animals evolved to live in forests; they are not adapted to this new environment.

Change in Madagascar's vegetation is by no means recent. Scientists have identified that the climate became much drier about 5,000 years ago. Humans have just catalysed the process.

THE RACE AGAINST TIME Madagascar has more endangered species of mammal than any other country in the world. The authorities are well aware of this environmental crisis: as long ago as 1970 the Director of Scientific Research made this comment in a speech during an international symposium on conservation: 'The people in this room know that Malagasy nature is a world heritage. We are not sure that others realise that it is *our* heritage.' Resentment at having outsiders make decisions on the future of their heritage without proper consultation with the Malagasy was one of the reasons there was little effective conservation in the 1970s and early 1980s. This was a time when Madagascar was demonstrating its independence from Western influences. Things changed in 1985, when Madagascar hosted a major international conference on conservation for development. The Ministry of Animal Production, Waters and Forests, which administered the protected areas, went into partnership with the World Wide Fund for Nature (WWF). Their plan was to evaluate all protected areas in the country, then numbering 37 (2% of the island), and in their strategy for the future to provide people living near the reserves with economically viable alternatives. They have largely achieved their aims. All the protected areas have been evaluated and recommendations for their management are being implemented. These original protected areas are now the responsibility of the National Association for Management of Protected Areas (ANGAP) which was established under the auspices of the Environmental Action Plan (EAP) sponsored by the World Bank working together with many other donors. Among their successes has been the establishment of a number of new national parks and several Debt for Nature swaps, in which international debts are cancelled in return for some of Madagascar's repayments going into conservation projects.

Joanna Durbin, Madagascar Programme Director

Durrell Wildlife Conservation Trust is an international conservation organisation with its headquarters in Jersey, Channel Islands. It was established by the visionary conservationist and renowned author Gerald Durrell in 1963. The organisation, with the mission 'to save species from extinction', has pre-eminent expertise in hands-on management of endangered species and a global reputation for its work through its field conservation projects, captive breeding, re-introduction and research (in the wild and under conservation care). Durrell currently has 40 conservation projects in 18 countries, as well as an extensive programme of research, training, conservation and breeding of endangered species. Our largest programme is in Madagascar, where we have been working for over 20 years in a range of different locations and habitats. Our current efforts are concentrated on eight sites in western dry forests, wetlands and fragmented lowland rainforest – fragile and poorly studied ecosystems with their own complement of Madagascar's endemic species, which have often been neglected by other conservation programmes.

The Menabe forests near Morondava on the west coast contain a remarkable cluster of locally endemic, endangered species including the giant jumping rat, the flat-tailed tortoise and the narrow-striped mongoose. They are threatened by slash-and-burn maize cultivation, which has created vast holes in the forest, and by unsustainable logging operations that damage the forest's structure and open up trails that lead to increased hunting and other extractive uses. Our work has been focused on raising awareness of the locally endemic species by defining their conservation status and threats; on working with local communities using traditional laws called *dina* to agree on limits to cultivated areas in exchange for rights to cultivate on illegally deforested land; and working with government and NGO partners to create a new protected area to ensure the survival of Menabe's forests and species. Durrell's partnership approach is starting to show success

Numerous projects in Madagascar are funded by many conservation NGOs and other agencies including WWF, Durrell Wildlife Conservation Trust (UK), German Primate Centre – DPZ, Conservation International, Missouri Botanical Garden, Duke University Primate Center, Wildlife Conservation Society, Madagascar Fauna Group and The Peregrine Fund; also USAID (US Agency for International Development), Cooperation Francaise, GTZ and KfW (German government), UNDP (United Nations Development Programme) and UNESCO. One of the most active Malagasy NGOs is FANAMBY.

TRIPLING MADAGASCAR'S PROTECTED AREAS – THE DURBAN VISION In a dramatic announcement at the 5th World Parks Congress in Durban, South Africa, in September 2003, President Marc Ravalomanana promised to more than triple the area of Madagascar's protected reserves from 1.7 million to six million hectares over the next five years. That's an increase from 3% to 10% of the country's total area.

Under the plan, the government will expand its terrestrial coverage from 1.5 million to five million hectares and its coastal and marine-area coverage from 200,000 to one million hectares. Deforestation, the president said, has taken its toll on the island, reducing the country's forest by nearly half over the last 20 years. 'We can no longer afford to sit back and watch our forests go up in flames,' he said. 'This is not just Madagascar's biodiversity; it is the world's biodiversity. We have the firm political will to stop this degradation.'

The government with all their conservation partners launched a science-based process to choose the best sites for protection, including the identification of 'gaps'

with a halt to deforestation in this area since 2003. The Malagasy government decided to legally protect the Menabe forests in March 2006.

The Durrell Madagascar programme has been working to conserve endemic wetland species through two projects. The Western Wetland Project concentrates on species such as Madagascar teal, side-necked turtle and sacred ibis, while the Eastern Wetland Project includes action for the Lac Alaotra gentle lemur (bamboo lemur), Meller's duck and nineteen endemic species of fish found in the Nosivolo river near Marolambo. In addition to their biodiversity importance, wetlands are highly productive and sustain large human populations through fisheries and agriculture. Our wetland conservation campaign at Lac Alaotra has also been a success (see page 280).

The ploughshare tortoise is a prime example of an extremely rare species – occurring only at a single site – that is vulnerable to a variety of pressures such as uncontrolled bush fires and collection for international trade. Our conservation action for this species, in Baie de Baly National Park, which includes all remaining tortoise habitat, demonstrates how concentrating on a single species can provide multiple benefits for the conservation of a range of endangered species typical of the highly threatened western dry forest and coastal habitats. In particular, we have helped to revive a traditional fire management technique based on burning firebreaks at the start of the dry season. We also run a captive breeding centre for the ploughshare tortoise, the flat-tailed tortoise and the side-necked turtle at Ampijoroa forestry station in Ankarafantsika National Park. Captive-bred juveniles are being returned to the wild to reinforce the depleted populations.

We recently extended our conservation actions to Manombo forest in southeastern Madagascar, a lowland rainforest patch which is home to the southernmost population of black-and-white ruffed lemurs and is the only protected site for the critically endangered white-collared brown lemur.

where threatened species are currently outside the protected area network. The government will also create wildlife corridors that connect existing parks, preserve rare habitats and protect watersheds. The new protected areas and the existing ANGAP-managed ones are all grouped into the new System of Protected Areas of Madagascar (SAPM) which has three major objectives: to conserve Madagascar's unique biodiversity; to conserve Madagascar's cultural heritage; and to enable sustainable use and maintain ecosystem services to contribute to poverty alleviation. The government aims to turn the country into a regional leader in ecotourism through sustainable conservation, helping to achieve its goal of reducing poverty by 50% over the next ten years. The new protected areas are in the process of negotiation and at the time of writing around 2 million hectares in 19 sites are already under temporary protection as a step towards their official creation.

FANAMBY

This Malagasy NGO is at the forefront of conservation, being particularly involved in establishing protected areas in the new category Paysages Harmonieux Protégés (protected landscapes). The development of sustainable tourism falls into their remit, and you will often see their name associated with the exciting new reserves that are being created as part of the Système d'Aires Protégées de Madagascar (SAPM).

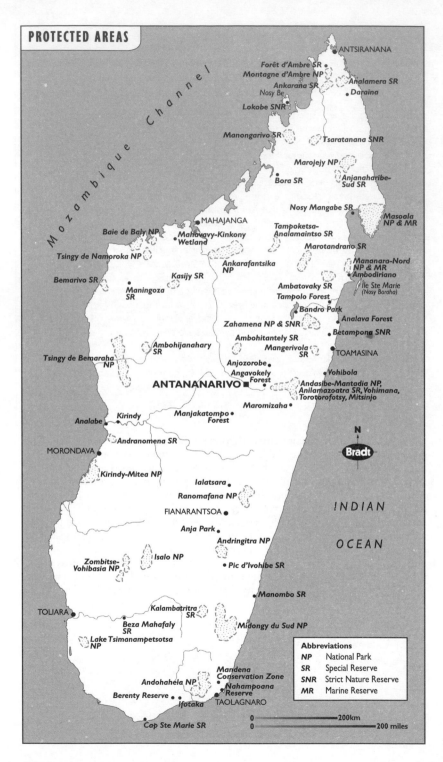

PROTECTED AREAS

ANTSIRANANA

Forêt d'Ambre SR
Montagne d'Ambre NP
Ankarana SR
Nosy Be
Lokobe SNR

Analamera SR
Daraina

Manongarivo SR

Tsaratanana SNR

Marojejy NP

Bora SR

Anjanaharibe-Sud SR

Nosy Mangabe SR

Masoala NP & MR

Tampoketsa-Analamaintso SR

MAHAJANGA
Mahavavy-Kinkony Wetland
Baie de Baly NP

Marotandrano SR

Tsingy de Namoroka NP

Ankarafantsika NP

Mananara-Nord NP & MR
Ambodiriano
Île Ste Marie (Nosy Boraha)

Bemarivo SR

Kasijy SR

Maningoza SR

Ambatovaky SR
Tampolo Forest
Bandro Park

Analava Forest

Zahamena NP & SNR

Betampona SNR

Tsingy de Bemaraha NP

Ambohijanahary SR

Ambohitantely SR

Mangerivola SR

TOAMASINA

Anjozorobe

Angavokely Forest

ANTANANARIVO

Vohibola

Andasibe-Mantadia NP,
Anilamazoatra SR, Vohimana,
Torotorofotsy, Mitsinjo

Maromizaha

Analabe
Kirindy
Manjakatompo Forest

Andranomena SR

MORONDAVA

Kirindy-Mitea NP

Ialatsara
Ranomafana NP

FIANARANTSOA

Anja Park

Andringitra NP

Isalo NP
Zombitse-Vohibasia NP

Pic d'Ivohibe SR

Manombo SR

TOLIARA

Kalambatritra SR

Beza Mahafaly SR

Midongy du Sud NP

Lake Tsimanampetsotsa NP

Mandena Conservation Zone
Nahampoana Reserve

Andohahela NP

Berenty Reserve

Ifotaka

TAOLAGNARO

Cap Ste Marie SR

Mozambique Channel

INDIAN OCEAN

N

Bradt

Abbreviations
NP	National Park
SR	Special Reserve
SNR	Strict Nature Reserve
MR	Marine Reserve

0 — 200km
0 — 200 miles

PROTECTED AREAS

CATEGORIES Four new categories of protected area have been added to the original three to encompass the new range of objectives. More and more of the original reserves – and many of the new areas – are being opened up to tourism.

1 Réserves Naturelles Intégrales (strict nature reserves)
2 Parcs Nationaux (national parks)
3 Réserves Spéciales (special reserves)
4 Parcs Naturels (natural parks)
5 Monuments Naturels (natural monuments)
6 Paysages Harmonieux Protégés (protected landscapes)
7 Réserves de Ressources Naturelles (natural resource reserves)

The first three categories are those managed by ANGAP which were established by French colonial governments, and subsequent Malagasy ones, to protect natural ecosystems or threatened species. The new categories protect natural sites of cultural importance and enable greater levels of sustainable use while still maintaining biodiversity. They will mostly be managed collaboratively with local people, local authorities and NGOs. Several of the former strict nature reserves that denied access to tourists have now been gazetted as national parks. These protect ecosystems and areas of natural beauty, and are open to the public (with permits and accompanied by guides). At the time of writing there are 18 national parks: Montagne d'Ambre, Marojejy, Masoala, Mananara-Nord, Zahamena, Andasibe-Mantadia, Andringitra, Ranomafana, Midongy du Sud, Andohahela, Lake Tsimanampetsotsa, Zombitse-Vohibasia, Isalo, Kirindy-Mitea, Tsingy de Bemaraha, Tsingy de Namoroka, Ankarafantsika and Baie de Baly.

A letter from an American adventurer prompts me to point out that national parks in Madagascar are very different to those in North America or even Europe. They are not huge areas of wilderness with a network of hiking trails where you can wander at will, but carefully controlled places which you may visit only with a guide who will require you to stick to prescribed circuits. If you want to get off the beaten track, don't try to do it within a national park.

There are 20 or so special reserves, of which Ankarana, Cap Sainte Marie, Beza-Mahafaly, Analamerana, Andranomena, Anjanaharibe-Sud and Nosy Mangabe are described in this book. These reserves are for the protection of specific habitats or threatened species. Not all are supervised. Access may be limited to authorised scientific research.

The new areas coming under protection include some vast corridors along the eastern rainforest belt such as Makira, Ankeniheny-Zahamena, Fandriana-Vondrozo, as well as important wetlands at Lake Alaotra, Mahavavy-Kinkony and a plethora of other sites conserving important species and habitats. Most are not yet able to accept visiting tourists.

There are also an increasing number of private reserves, the most famous of which are Berenty and Anjajavy, and the NGO-run protected areas which welcome tourists. These include Ambodiriano Reserve, Analabe, Analalava Forest, Angavokely Forest Reserve, Anja Park, Anjozorobe, Ankafobe, Association Mitsinjo, Bandro Park, Daraina, Ialatsara Lemur Forest Camp, Ifotaka Community Forest, Kirindy, Mahavavy-Kinkony Wetland Complex, Mandena Conservation Zone, Manjakatompo Forestry Station, Maromizaha, Nahampoana Reserve, Tampolo Forestry Station, Torotorofotsy, Vohibola and Vohimana.

PERMITS The cost of permits to visit the reserves and national parks varies, according to which one you are visiting and the number of days spent there.

Current permit prices for adult foreign tourists are shown below. (There are concessions for children, residents, nationals and researchers.)

For these popular parks – Isalo, Andasibe-Mantadia, Ranomafana, Montagne d'Ambre, Ankarana and Tsingy de Bemaraha – the rates are (with approximate euro equivalents):

1 day	25,000Ar (€10)	3 days	40,000Ar (€17)
2 days	37,000Ar (€15)	4 days or more	50,000Ar (€21)

For all other parks and reserves these cheaper rates apply:

1 day	10,000Ar (€4)	3 days	20,000Ar (€8)
2 days	15,000Ar (€6)	4 days or more	25,000Ar (€10)

Half of this entrance fee goes to ANGAP and half to local communities, so each visitor is playing his or her part. Permits are always available at the park/reserve entrance (be sure to get a receipt) but you may wish to visit the ANGAP office in Antananarivo or www.parcs-madagascar.com.

GUIDES It is obligatory to be accompanied by a guide in all parks and reserves. Note that the permit price does not include their fee. Guide prices vary from park to park but a list of agreed rates is normally on display at each ANGAP office. Additionally it is usual to tip your guide if you are satisfied with his or her service.

HAINTENY

Consider, children, the conditions here on earth:
The trees grow, but not unceasingly,
For if they grew unceasingly, they would reach the sky.
Not only this,
but there is a time for their growing,
a time for their becoming old,
and a time for their breaking.
So it is, too, for man: there is a time for youth,
a time for old age,
a time for good,
a time for evil,
and a time for death.

4

Practical Information

WHEN TO VISIT

Read the section on climate (page 3) before deciding when to travel. Broadly speaking, the dry months are in the winter between April and September, but rainfall varies enormously in different areas. The months you may want to avoid are August and during the Christmas holidays, when popular places are crowded, and February and March (the cyclone season) when it will probably rain – and worse. However, the off-peak season can be rewarding, with cheaper international airfares and accommodation and fewer other tourists. September is nice, but often windy in the south. April and May often have lovely weather, and the countryside is green after the rainy season.

Keen naturalists have their own requirements: botanists will want to go in February when many of the orchids are in flower, and herpetologists will also prefer the spring/summer because reptiles are more active – and brightly coloured – during those months. Bear in mind that giant jumping rats, dwarf lemurs, tenrecs and some reptiles are less active and so harder to see during the cool dry months of June to September. Alasdair Harris reported, after a January visit: 'I just returned from a research trip in the southwest where there has been some very heavy rain recently. It was quite extraordinary to see the spiny forest looking so lush and wet. The scenery changed completely, and within hours of the first rains arriving took on a deep leafy green, resonating at night time to the deafening chorus of relieved amphibians.'

My favourite months to visit Madagascar are October and November, when the weather is usually fine but not too hot, the jacarandas are in flower, the lemurs have babies, and lychees are sold from roadside stalls in the east. However, word has got out that this is the best time, and so popular places and flights tend to be booked up.

WAYS AND MEANS

Over the years I've come to believe that everyone *can* enjoy Madagascar but not everyone does because they do not take sufficient care in matching the trip to their personality. When planning a holiday most people consider only their interests and how much they are prepared to spend. I feel that a vital component has been missed out.

WHAT SORT OF PERSON ARE YOU? The Catch 22 of tourism in Madagascar is that the type of person who can afford the trip is often the type least suited to cope with the Malagasy way of life. In our culture assertiveness, a strong sense of right and wrong, and organisational skills are the personality traits which lead to success in business, and thus the income to finance exotic travel. But these 'A' type personalities often find Madagascar unbearably 'inefficient' and frustrating. By having control over their itinerary through a tailor-made tour, or by renting a vehicle and driver, such people are more likely to get the most out of their trip. A group tour, where they must 'go with the flow', may be the least successful option.

Conversely, the happiest travellers are often either those who choose to travel on a low budget (providing they're not obsessed with being ripped off) or those who can adopt the attitude of one elderly woman on a group tour who said 'I'm going to give up thinking; it doesn't work in Madagascar.' It doesn't, and she had a great time!

These days there is a trip to suit everyone in this extraordinary country. It won't be a cheap holiday, but it will be one you never forget, so choose wisely.

Below are the main options, in descending order of price and comfort.

The luxury package Four-star hotels are no longer unusual in Madagascar, and luxury seekers will have no problem planning their tour around the new upmarket 'boutique' hotels. These include Nosy Iranja and Tsarabanjina (Nosy Be), Anjajavy (north of Mahajanga), Jardin du Roy (Isalo) and Domaine de Fontenay (Joffreville, near Antsiranana), but this is by no means the complete list. The fly-in hotels even shield you from the realities of Madagascar by whisking you off to their resort by private plane.

Expedition cruising On a ship you know that you will sleep in a comfortable bed each night and eat familiar food. It is thus ideal for the adventurous at heart who are no longer able to take the rigours of land travel. It is also sometimes the only way of getting to remote offshore islands. In the UK try Noble Caledonia (↘ 020 7752 0000; www.noble-caledonia.co.uk). And in the US, Zegrahm Expeditions (↘ 1 800 628 8747 or 206 285 4000; www.zeco.com) are recommended.

Tailor-made tours This is the ideal option for a couple or small group who are not restricted financially. It is also the best choice for people with special interests or who like things to run as smoothly as possible. You will be the decision-maker and will choose where you want to go and your preferred level of comfort, but the logistics will be taken care of.

You can organise your tailor-made trip through a tour operator in your home country, in which case you will have the benefit of legal protection if things go wrong, or use email to contact some Malagasy tour operators. Let the tour operator know your interests, the level of comfort you expect, and whether you want to cram in as much as possible or concentrate on just a few centres.

Tour operators which specialise in tailor-made tours in Madagascar are listed later in this chapter.

Group travel Group travel is usually a lot of fun, ideal for single people who do not wish to travel alone, and if you choose the tour company and itinerary carefully you will see a great deal of the country, gain an understanding of its complicated culture and unique wildlife, and generally have a great time without the need to make decisions (but you need to be able to relinquish the decision-making; not everyone can do this).

A Madagascar specialist which does a variety of set-departure trips is Unusual Destinations in South Africa.

Semi-independent travel If you have email, and are willing to persevere with Madagascar's erratic telecommunications (which are rapidly improving), you can save money by dealing directly with a tour operator in Madagascar. The ones that I know or that have been recommended are listed later in this chapter, but there are many more. Now tourism is established in Madagascar, local operators have a clear understanding of tourists' needs and are impressively efficient. The downside to using a local operator is that they won't be bonded. If things go wrong there is no redress: you will not get a refund nor be able to sue the company.

Perhaps the ideal do-it-yourself trip is to hire a local driver/guide and vehicle when you arrive in Tana. This way you are wonderfully free to stop when you please and stay where you wish. There are some drivers listed in the Antananarivo chapter but some people have written to me happily about their experiences after being approached by a man with a car at Ivato Airport.

Independent travel Truly independent travellers usually have a rough idea of where they want to go and how they will travel but are open to changes of plan dictated by local conditions, whim and serendipity. Independent travellers are not necessarily budget travellers: those who can afford to fly to major towns, then rent a vehicle and driver, can eliminate a large amount of hassle and see everything they set out to see – providing they set a realistic programme for themselves. What they may miss out on is contact with the local people, and some of the smells, sounds and otherness of Madagascar.

The majority of independent travellers use public transport and stay in middle-range or budget hotels. They are exposed to all Madagascar's joys and frustrations and most seem to love it. The key here is not to try to do too much, and to speak at least some French. Chapter 4 tells you about the trials and tribulations of travelling by *taxi-brousse*: no problem providing you allow time for delays.

Independent travellers can save money and help Madagascar by avoiding the more expensive 'big six' national parks and visiting the less-known but equally rewarding ones, often run by NGOs, listed in Chapter 3.

The seriously adventurous Madagascar must be one of the very few countries left in the world where large areas are not yet detailed in a guidebook. A study of the standard 1:2,000,000 map of Madagascar reveals some mouth-watering possibilities, and a look at the more detailed 1:500,000 maps confirms the opportunities for people who are willing to walk or cycle. Or drive. Two of my most adventurous correspondents, Valerie and John Middleton, have travelled all over Madagascar by 4x4 vehicle and their trusted Madagascar Airtours guide and driver. I asked them why they keep coming back. 'Why do we go where we do? Well, I have had a passion for worldwide cave and karst exploration for well over 40 years and in plants, and in particular their adaptation to extreme conditions.' As John says, having a focus helps, especially when explaining your presence to bemused locals.

Serious adventurers will need to plan their trip beforehand with the FTM regional maps. The Middletons tell me: 'It is possible to obtain photocopies of the 1:100,000 maps that cover Madagascar plus a few of the 1:25,000 that cover only a small area. These can be obtained in person only from The Institute Geographique National, 2–4 Av Pasteur, 94165 Saint-Mande, Paris. This also applies to maps for other French ex-protectorates. ID is needed before entry is permitted. It may seem a long way to go but it does make an excellent excuse for a trip to Paris!' If you don't live within reach of Paris you will have to purchase the maps in Tana. See page 172.

Valerie and John also support my theory that the seriously adventurous are often 'pensioners'. Not that the youngsters don't do their bit for exploring Madagascar's uncharted areas. Throughout this book there are quotes from people who did just that, sometimes after a lot of preparation and sometimes on a whim.

Not everyone is courageous enough to step or pedal into the unknown like this, but in fact it's one of the safest ways to travel: the Malagasy that you meet will, once they have got over the shock of seeing you, invariably be welcoming and hospitable. The risk of crime is very low.

It's how I first saw Madagascar and why I fell in love with the place.

Travelling alone To travel alone may be a matter of choice or necessity. The trick is to make the necessity into choice by revelling in the opportunity to get close to the local people and to immerse yourself in their culture.

Lone travellers need to be prepared for the long evenings. Robert Bowker found nights at national parks particularly lonely: 'Dinner is early, and after that nothing to do but go to your bungalow. Take a powerful torch and lots to read. I got through a fair number of crossword puzzles. Also take music...' For budding writers evenings alone are the perfect time to develop your diary skills.

Another problem which needs to be borne in mind when planning a solo trip is that national parks and reserves will be expensive unless you team up with other travellers, because guides charge for a group of three. Trips like the Masoala Peninsula, where boat hire is involved, will be prohibitive. Conversely, one person can squeeze into any *taxi-brousse*.

Solo travellers should consider avoiding the usual tourist routes where the local people will be less friendly and the prices higher. The real rewards come when you travel off the beaten track; here you'll meet genuinely hospitable locals still leading traditional lives.

Safety aspects of travelling alone are covered on page 136.

Disabled travel With careful planning and help from a local tour operator, even wheelchair users can see something of the landscape and wildlife. See box on page 134.

Working holidays and volunteering There is a growing interest in paying to be a volunteer in a scientific or community project in Madagascar. This is an excellent way of 'giving something back' while enjoying a learning experience which will stay with you much longer than the normal holiday memories. There are also some opportunities of working as a volunteer for local charities or NGOs. These volunteers still need to pay for their air fare and basic living costs, and are sometimes only accepted if they have a skill that is needed by that particular organisation.

A volunteer with an NGO in Madagascar advises: 'You don't get much training. This can be daunting, but to be honest I preferred the challenge of having to figure things out for myself. Sometimes it can be a little boring and frustrating, so you definitely need to be able to motivate yourself. But if you do, you will find lots of unexpected rewards. There is also a nice pioneering feeling, though also a feeling of disorganisation. Overall, I suppose it depends on the attitude of the individual whether or not they will enjoy it.'

Earthwatch 267 Banbury Rd, Oxford OX2 6HU, England; ℡ 01865 318838; www.earthwatch.org/europe/ & 3 Clock Tower Pl, Suite 100, Box 75, Maynard, MA 01754, USA; ℡ 1 800 776 0188 or 978 461 0081; e info@ earthwatch.org. Pioneers in upmarket scientific research trips. In Madagascar you can work with Dr Alison Jolly on lemur research in Berenty.
World Challenge Expeditions, Black Arrow Hse, 2 Chandos Rd, London NW10 6NF; ℡ 020 8728 7200;

e welcome@world-challenge.co.uk. While Earthwatch tends to attract mature travellers, this organisation is aimed at students.
Blue Ventures ℡ 0208 341 9819; madagascar@blueventures.org; www.blueventures.org. This responsible & highly effective organisation is based in Andavadoaka. It coordinates teams of volunteers, working with local biologists, NGOs & communities whose livelihoods depend on marine ecosystems. See boxes on pages 440 & 444.

Peter Jourdier

Akany Avoko, where I worked as a volunteer, was originally set up as a refuge for young girls 'who would otherwise be in prison, awaiting trial to prove their innocence against allegations of petty crime'. That was 40 years ago. Now most of the children either have no family or are separated from what family they have by poverty or domestic problems. Despite this, it is an amazingly happy place. At the moment the centre is near full capacity with about 140 children up to 18 years old.

The thought of bio-gas loos and outdoor showers did not excite me too much, but when I arrived I was pleasantly surprised. The place was clean, bright and everyone was incredibly friendly.

It took a while for me to get used to the life. They get up extremely early and go to bed at around 6pm when the sun goes down, but I soon found my feet and saw that there were plenty of things I could do to help. Before going out to Madagascar I had been sent rather a worrying e-mail saying 'we are thrilled to read you have carpentry skills, there is much to do in the way of fixing and making items around Akany Avoko' … and there was. Many of the windows had warped so much that they couldn't shut, furniture needed to be made, doors repaired, leaking pipes fixed. I had done some woodwork at school, but was certainly not a plumber, carpenter, electrician or cabinet maker when I arrived, and I'm still not now. However, this was a large part of what I did during my stay there. The windows now close, some furniture is made, most of the doors now lock and the pipe still leaks (I did try!)

I also gave some computer lessons to some of the children in the evenings, when the electricity was strong enough to keep the computer going. Here there was a great difference in the levels of the children, depending on their background. To make matters a little more interesting, it was generally the ones with less education who couldn't use a computer, meaning they also spoke little or no French, and I didn't speak Malagasy.

Overall I had a fantastic three months there, as well as (I hope) being useful to them. I would strongly recommend Akany Avoko or simply Madagascar to anyone. The country is incredibly beautiful (as are the beaches), the people are so friendly and they need, and are very grateful for, all the help we can offer. The orphanage has a website with lots of information. www.akanyavoko.com.

Practical Information **WAYS AND MEANS**

4

Frontier 50–52 Rivington St, London EC2A 3QP; 020 7613 2422; www.frontierprojects.ac.uk. Also works in marine conservation, taking paying volunteers for their marine research programmes.

Azafady Studio 7, 1a Beethoven St, London W10 4LG; 020 8960 6629; f 020 8962 0126; e info@ azafady.org; www.madagascar.co.uk. This registered UK charity & Malagasy NGO works in southeast Madagascar to tackle human poverty & suffering, & protect unique environments. It runs 2 volunteer schemes, Pioneer Madagascar which offers the opportunity to work alongside village communities, & Lemur Venture which is a volunteering initiative set up in collaboration with Tsimbazaza (see above and page 144), Madagascar's national botanical & zoological gardens. Azafady also takes on independent volunteers on a short- or long-term basis.

People and Places 01795 535 718; e madagascar@travel-peopleandplaces.co.uk; www.travel-peopleandplaces.co.uk. With their team of local people, this company offers community-led placements to volunteers with a few years under their belt.

Akany Avoko (00216 20) 22 441 58; e akany.avoko@wanadoo.mg; www.akanyavoko.com. This wonderful children's organisation welcomes volunteers with suitable skills. See boxes on pages 83 & 144.

The Dodwell Trust www.dodwell-trust.org. Volunteers spend 1–6 months living in a village or small town, taking part in community life & working to assist English teachers. They can also work at the Zoo looking after lemurs, or in the Botanical Gardens, hold a Sports Day, plant tree nurseries, make radio shows in English, hold English Club meetings in villages, & set up & decorate new local cultural centres. No skills are required, & weekends are free. Conservation & biology research work is available to graduates. In addition, the Dodwell Trust has cheap clean accommodation in Tana & Ampefy with part-time volunteer activities,

£6 per night with minimum 3 nights stay. Reservations in advance to dodwell@madagascar.freeserve.co.uk **Arboretum d'Antsokay** ꝳ 032 02 600 15; e andry.petignat@caramail.com. This splendid arboretum, near Toliara (see page 234) welcomes botanist volunteers.

SPECIAL INTERESTS: HIKING, TREKKING AND ROCK-CLIMBING Madagascar now has several wonderful options for enthusiastic hikers: organised trekking in the national parks or hiking in remote areas.

Trekking It's a misnomer to call it trekking because Madagascar is not like the Himalayas or Andes where your gear is carried by porters or pack animals to a different campsite each night. There are two national parks that are specifically set up for hiking, Andringitra and Isalo, but you usually do a circular hike and return to the same campsite at night. This does not diminish the experience, however. I count Andringitra as one of my best hiking trips anywhere (see page 215) and Marojejy (page 343) is one of the most exciting mountains I have (nearly) climbed. There are a growing number of national parks and reserves that offer good hiking – but remember, you must always be accompanied by a guide (see page 76).

Hiking My advice to people wanting to strike out on their own is to bear in mind that many of Madagascar's 'roads' are overgrown tracks, and ideal for hiking. There are a couple of well-known routes, the Smugglers' Path and the Trans-Masoala Trail, but these do not appeal to me nearly as much as the huge regions that have seen few, if any, foreigners. The country is well mapped and the local people are accustomed to travelling on foot. I find the FTM 1:500,000 maps mouth-watering in their possibilities – talking of which, be sensible about water supplies. Hiking in the south is fascinating from a cultural perspective but you will need to carry a lot of water. Conversely, if hiking in the east you will get very wet but never be short of a drink! Read the advice on page 143 on the cultural aspects of travelling off the beaten path safely and enjoyably.

Rock-climbing The centre for rock-climbing is Andringitra and Camp Catta. See page 214.

Mountain biking Madagascar is becoming increasingly popular for travelling using your own muscle-power. The advantages are obvious: bad roads and broken-down vehicles do not delay you, con-men will not overcharge you and – most important – by passing slowly through Madagascar's small villages and communities you will experience the Malagasy culture in an unforced way. These advantages far outweigh the inevitable security risks of being totally at the mercy of local people. You are far more likely to be overwhelmed by hospitality than robbed.

Several readers have written to me about their experiences of cycling in Madagascar. Some of these are incorporated into the text and the box on page 322. Bill and Nina French, who have made two trips in Madagascar by bicycle, recommend the following routes:

Manompana to Mananara Especially Antanambe–Mananara (approx. 52km). Some very difficult stretches, particularly north of Ivontaka, with big boulders. We did this route in autumn 2005; building of a proper road was going on, with concrete bridges over small creeks.

Masoala Peninsula Particularly good from Ratsianara, where the dirt track for vehicles stops, and all the way south to Cap Masoala and Masoala village. There is access only for bicycles, motorbikes and walkers. (Cap Est–Ratsiananara 30km; Ratsiananara–Ampanavoana 64km; Ampanavoana–Masoala village 24km; Masoala village–Cap Masoala–Ampanavoana 35km).

Other recommended routes Ambalavao–Fianarantsoa; Manakara–Sahasinaka; Ranomafana–Fianarantsoa; Fianarantsoa–Soatanana–Route National 42 (northbound); Lac Tritriva–Marinanpona (to the main road leading to Betafo); Ambatolampy–Antananarivo.

See box overleaf for some practical hints on cycling in Madagascar.

Caving Madagascar has some fabulous caves, and several expeditions have been mounted to explore them. Caving is not a popular Malagasy pursuit, however, so cavers should take particular care to explain what they are doing and get the necessary permits for exploring protected areas. An experienced local tour operator will help with the red tape.
   The best karst areas are in the north and west, as follows.

Ankarana Known for its *tsingy*, this is the best explored and mapped of all karst areas. More than 100km of subterranean caves have been explored here, and it is thought that the total may be 200–300km.

Narinda The longest cave, Anjohibe, is 5,330m.

Bemaraha Another potentially good area now tourism is well established.

Toliara region Mickoboka Plateau to the north has pits to a depth of 165m, and the Mahafaly Plateau to the south contains numerous small caves.

Diving Liz Bomford, an experienced diver who has been visiting Madagascar for 25 years, provided the following information.
   'By far the best and most exciting diving is around Nosy Be and its galaxy of islands and reefs. The biodiversity in this area is outstanding. Coral bleaching caused by global warming has not affected the reefs to any great degree and you can find almost every hard coral species known in the western Indian Ocean. You may see humpback whales as well as dolphins from the

DIVE SITES

ANTSIRANANA

Nosy Be   Iharana (Vohemar)

Antalaha

MAHAJANGA

Ile Ste Marie

TOAMASINA

ANTANANARIVO

MORONDAVA

FIANARANTSOA
MOROMBE
Ampasilava

Ifaty
TOLIARA
Anakao

Lokaro
TAOLAGNARO

Practical Information   WAYS AND MEANS

4

Lex Cumber with additional recommendations from Bill French & Julian Cook

If you are thinking of taking a bike to Madagascar, do it, you'll love it. On most of the roads you will be more comfortable than anyone in motorised transport. The simplicity and strength of the humble bike will get you virtually anywhere, bring you closer to the wonderful people of the island and allow you to see things that you would miss if you travelled any other way.

If you intend to cycle between the major centres and in the more developed parts of the island, then you can plan as for touring but in tough conditions. You will need a mountain bike as the tarred roads can be broken, especially after rains, and there are many unmade roads. You should carry a good supply of spares and tools, some food and plenty of container capacity for water, though you probably will find enough to eat and drink in most areas, as well as places to stay. If you plan to go into more remote areas and to tackle the smaller roads, then here are some tips.

THE BIKE What you need to think is simplicity, strength and self sufficiency. Don't take it if it can't be fixed with the tools you carry yourself, or with a hammer by a Malagasy mechanic. Fit a new chain and block, carry spare spokes, brake blocks, cables, inner-tubes and take plenty of oil (the dust is unbelievable). Go with the strongest wheels you can afford, and the fattest tyres you can fit (1.95 minimum). You can pick up cheap bike parts in the larger towns. Bill adds: 'Take at least two dozen patches for punctures, a chain riveter, a few dozen plastic cableties plus ten jubilee clips.'

ON THE BIKE Lex: 'Forget panniers unless you are staying on good roads. A 20–35 litre backpack held away from your back with mesh for ventilation is ideal: it's more flexible, stays with you at all times, and you do get used to it. A rear rack with a rack bag is a good addition, and allows you to carry heavy tools/food/water away from your back.' Bill: 'Only front panniers break off, they tend not to survive Malagasy roads. Sturdy back panniers are necessary – tie them together so you don't lose them on bumpy roads; a backpack makes you more tired.'

CLOTHING You need two sets, one for cycling and one for socialising/resting. If you are going to explore the deserts, I advise the 'Beau Geste' style of hat with peak on front, and flap on back. General purpose shorts, with cycling short inners underneath (two pairs minimum) are ideal. Also take leather cycling gloves (artificial materials disintegrate with the sweat and the heat); footwear of the trainer/walking boot variety is ideal, again go for natural materials; lightweight socks, with a clean set of underwear spare at all times. I find an Arabic scarf a fantastic all-purpose bit of kit: sleep under it, dry yourself with it, use it as a picnic blanket or head covering for dust-storms etc. Bandannas are a useful addition and keep the sweat out of your eyes. Just think tough kit for your contact points on the bike, and breathable kit everywhere else. The rule to apply for your clothing is 'one set wet, one set dry'. At night consider a clean T-shirt/vest with a cotton or similar shirt, and lightweight trousers. Your appearance is always worth considering, as you never know who you are going to meet! Finally, take a lightweight fleece as it can get cold at night, and some sort of wind breaker/waterproof shell.

PERSONAL HYGIENE Take a good first-aid kit, and Savlon for your backside. My colleague on our 3,000km Madagascar adventure had golf-ball sized boils on his behind for 3–4 weeks as a result of a) lots of saddle time b) sweat c) lack of 'arse discipline' (as we called it). Apply Savlon liberally, and if you get the chance to wash, take your time and be particular down below. Anti-fungal creams are a good idea as well. Take dehydration salts, Imodium type pills and laxatives. Your body will not know what's hit it, and you never know how it will react. Salt pills are useful as well. Remember to drink as much as you can at night. Take water purifiers.

REMOTE TOWNS When pulling into a town/village, think of riding right the way through it first, to select your likely bar/bunkhouse, and then cycle back to it. You don't want to miss the heavenly spot 500m up the road because you pulled over early. If in doubt look for a village elder. If you are really remote, the locals will often run away, but just wait and the relevant person will find you. You may not always be able to buy food. If you do buy food in remote villages make sure you give the women-folk the money, not the men. Bear in mind villagers will often offer you food, and as result go without themselves.

RIDE ROUTINE Be moving before sunrise if you're in the desert: 05.00 is about right. If you can finish your riding for the day by 11.00–12.00, that's perfect, but be realistic. Don't ride in the middle hours of the day unless you really have to. Just find or make some shade and rest. You'll probably be exhausted by then anyway, but after a short while you should be able to put in 6–8 hours' riding per day. Rest days are vital, and give you the benefit of time in great places..

FOOD Carry two days' rations if you can, because you just never know when you may have to spend a night out. Try peanuts, raisins, dates, processed cheese, salt, couscous, muesli with powdered milk and boiled sweets. Take some with you or pick it up in Tana or the larger towns. This food stash will supplement your basic rice diet, which soon becomes boring, and lacks the calories required for hard riding. Otherwise, watch where the locals eat and don't be afraid of the road-side stands, they are fantastic. Carry a lightweight stove that does not rely on gas.

CAMPING Strangely in Madagascar there is a totally different attitude to camping. It is viewed as suspicious behaviour by many rural communities. Where possible avoid it. However, you need to carry a sleeping bag and mat anyway, so a poncho or tent will allow you the flexibility to camp out should you need to, or just take a mossie net if in the dry season. Best advice: try not to be too obvious or you will attract a lot of unwanted attention.

SECURITY As a rule Madagascar is a very safe place, but on a bike you are exposed. Your best defence is learning some of the language, using humour and keeping some small denomination notes handy. Note that outside the four or five main towns you will not find banks that know what a credit card is, so you will have to carry cash – though your costs will be low. Spread it around, hide some in your bike, etc. Have photocopies of documentation on you, as well as originals. Leave details in Tana, and inform your national consulate or someone of an approximate return date. If in trouble, don't raise your voice, and negotiate calmly with the head man, be patient, and keep smiling.

NAVIGATION Even the best maps available in Madagascar are inaccurate. Rely on local knowledge when navigating the minor roads. If you are travelling cross country, good compass work and the ability to read the terrain is essential. Again local knowledge and the ability to stay calm when lost, are essential.

Biking in Madagascar is breathtaking in every sense of the word. It's not easy, but you don't go to Madagascar to be pampered! I can promise you will see the country at its best, and the desert sunrises are worth the journey alone. Go for it!

Tim Healy

The coast and islands of Madagascar can be divided into key regions based upon the principal marine ecosystems and the presence of important species of fish, birds, turtles and marine mammals.

NORTH COAST Composed principally of coral reefs, lagoons, mangroves and an abundance of small islands. One of the richest in marine life of all the regions in Madagascar. Important species seen in this area include the whale sharks, turtles and manta rays. Due to the variety of sites and beauty of this region, tourism is well established and is supported by several hotels and dive centres which offer diving and snorkelling excursions.

Sites Islands and coral reefs: Archipelago of Nosy Mitsio including Ilots des Quatres Frères, Nosy Hara, Nosy Be, Nosy Manitse and Nosimborona, Nosy Ratafanika, Nosy Iranja, Nosy Haramy & Nosy Milomboka, Nosy Faho, Nosy Mangabe, Nosy Tanikely (unofficially protected area), islands of the Baie d'Emeraude (Nosy Antaly-Be, Nosy Suarez, Nosy Lava), Nosy Lowry, and Nosy Ankao.

Continental shelf from Nosy Be to Antsiranana (sites with specific coral and topographic formations).

Mangroves and estuaries: Ambanja and Antsiranana.

WEST COAST Characterised by extensive beaches, several rocky rivers and large estuaries supporting extended mangroves. Most of this region's small islands and coral reefs are seldom visited. Its coast offers enormous potential for quality dive tourism. Hotels and dive centres are limited.

Sites Islands and coral reefs: Kirindy-Mitea coast and small islands, and Nosy Barren (several small islands).

Mangroves and estuaries: Tsiribihina, Betsiboka, Mahajamba, Manambolomaty, and Mahavavy estuary.

SOUTHWEST COAST Composed of a variety of habitats including large areas of mangroves and vast lagoons lined with endless beaches. Some of the most notable sites are located within one of the largest coral reef systems in the world stretching over 150km from the coastal town of Toliara northwards. Tourism is well developed in this region, where access to various marine sites is assured.

boat. Underwater you could get lucky and find whale shark. Nosy Be is extraordinarily good for nudibranchs so there's something for everyone. The diving operators in Nosy Be work with local fishermen to protect the environment with the aim of providing good diving conditions for tourists. You won't be disappointed.

'At Ile Sainte Marie, off the east coast, there are several good dive sites, and the dive operators are a responsible bunch. However, visibility is often limited due to heavy rainfall in this area.

'The west coast around Toliara used to offer very good diving (I first dived there in 1976) but these days over-fishing has taken its toll and the diving is a shadow of what it used to be.

'The water is colder in August and September (take a hood or a sweat) but the rest of the year a 3 or 5mm suit will do. Men will have no trouble hiring a suit but if you're a woman, consider taking your own wetsuit – otherwise you may have trouble finding one to fit.'

Sites Islands and coral reefs: Mikea coastal reef, islands and lagoons, Toliara's Grand Récif (frontal reef wall and pools), Nosy Ve and reefs, and Nosy Manitse.

Continental shelf from Toliara to Morombe (sites with specific coral and topographic formations).

SOUTHEAST COAST Composed of principally rocky shoreline with some isolated coral reefs supporting Madagascar's largest lobster fishery. There are a few dive good sites which benefit from both a diverse and picturesque coastline. Tourism is being developed, offering opportunities for diving.

Sites Coral and rocky reefs: Between Lokara and St Luce.

Offshore: migrating humpback whales.

EAST COAST Composed of long beaches divided by rivers running down from the rainforest. There are some patches of coastal forest and a natural river network known as the Pangalanes. Diving opportunities are limited along this coast, which is well known for its spices and rainforest.

Sites Islands: Nosy Fonga and Dombola, and Nosy Faho.

Wetland: Pangalanes Canal and coastal forest.

NORTHEAST COAST Composed of a diverse range of habitats from rocky shores to long sandy beaches and impressive coral reefs circling several small islands. This is an important area for the breeding of humpback whales during Madagascar's winter months. Equally, this area's coastline is located near some of Madagascar's most impressive rainforests.

Sites Islands, wrecks and reef: Ile Ste Marie (coastal wrecks and reef), Nosy Atafana (attached to Mananara–Nord National Park), Masoala Marine Reserve (three small islands) and Cap Est reef.

Offshore: breeding humpback whales (Ile Ste Marie and Antongil Bay).

Tim Healy is an environmental consultant, regular radio broadcaster for the BBC and a keen diver based in Madagascar for over 10 years. He is compiling information for a dive and snorkelling guide with WWF. This is his overview of places where you can definitely snorkel, whilst at other sites you have to either organise trips with the nearest dive centre or take along your own kit. For more information e aquater@wanadoo.mg.

If you are considering diving in Madagascar, read the box on *Diving Safety* on page 128.

River trips Madagascar has some splendid rivers, particularly in the west. Some offer the perfect means to pass through otherwise inaccessible areas of the country. The range includes extended calm water floats to exciting white-water sections. See *River trips* on page 446 for a description of the western rivers. Close to Tana there are some great white-water trips on the highland rivers coming off the plateau. Many of these offer medium and extreme white-water runs to challenge rafters and kayakers of all skill levels. Gondwana Explorer is one tour operator that offers white-water excursions.

Birdwatching There are several tour operators that specialise in birding trips. 'Twitchers' travel with such a different focus to other wildlife viewers that it's well worth going with a like-minded group and an expert tour-leader.

See pages 56–7 for full details on the best birding places.

Having sorted out the 'whats' and 'hows' of travelling in Madagascar you must turn your attention to the all-important subject of 'where'. One of the hardest decisions facing the first-time visitor to a country as large and diverse as Madagascar is where to go. Even a month is not long enough to see everything, so itineraries must be planned according to interests and the level of comfort wanted.

HIGHLIGHTS

Wildlife The following well-established reserves and national parks have comfortable accommodation nearby, easy access and experienced guides (starting from the north and going clockwise): Montagne d'Ambre, Nosy Mangabe, Andasibe-Mantadia (Périnet), Ranomafana, Berenty and Ankarafantsika (Ampijoroa). Isalo, which used to be noted more for hiking than wildlife, now has habituated lemurs.

Others, with more difficult access and simple accommodation or camping, include (again, starting from the north and going clockwise): Daraina, Marojejy, Masoala, Andohahela, Beza-Mahafaly, Kirindy and Ankarana.

Scenery The central highlands between Fianarantsoa and Ambalavao, Andringitra, Isalo and Andohahela National Parks, Avenue of the Baobabs (Morondava), Tsingy de Bemaraha, Ankarana, Montagne d'Ambre and the Andapa region.

Beaches and watersports Madagascar's best beaches are on the west coast, but many people are disappointed because of the shallow water (it is often impossible to swim at low tide). The beautiful beaches of the east coast offer better swimming but the weather is uncertain and strong currents and sharks are occasionally a danger. The very best beaches are in remote areas such as Anjajavy, islands around Nosy Be, Ile Sainte Marie and south of Toliara.

Diving is covered under *Special Interests*. Surfing is a growing sport in the southwest and sport fishing can be organised from Nosy Be.

Nightlife The people of southern Madagascar are the most outgoing on the island, with good discos in Taolagnaro and Toliara, but Nosy Be (and specifically Ambataloaka) is undoubtedly where the action is for tourists.

Museums Madagascar has only a few good museums so it is worth listing them here. The best by far – really excellent! – is the Museum of the Antandroy in Berenty Reserve. Toliara has a good ethnological museum, as has the Museum Akiba in Mahajanga. Moramanga has a unique and fascinating police museum. The only natural history museum that I am aware of is in Tsimbazaza in Tana.

People and tombs Your tour operator may be able to organise a visit to a *famadihana* (only in the highlands and only between June and September). An unforgettable experience. Merina tombs can be seen easily between Antananarivo and Antsirabe, but the most intriguing and interesting tombs are those of the Mahafaly in the Toliara region. Many are well off the beaten track and make this a particularly interesting area to explore by mountain bike.

Finally... Remember that you are in Madagascar to enjoy yourself. Here's a comment from a traveller who spent eight days in Ranomafana: 'Now I will make my confession: I never actually went into the park itself! ... I'm not that keen on

Frances Kerridge worked for several years in the southeast of Madagascar, studying carnivores with the organisation MICET. Her letters from the field were a regular source of entertainment. Here are some extracts:

[After setting my tent on fire] I stayed in the guide's tent overnight. This was indeed an experience and not one I wish to repeat ever. Iato lit the candle every 15 minutes to see what time it was (as he has to get up first to start cooking breakfast) but as he can't tell the time he had to wake Baby to read the watch. Zaman'dory got up every 15 minutes to go for a pee and Baby alternatively ground his teeth and talked in his sleep. I was very relieved when the night was over …

The next drama involved Baby, who was complaining of toothache. I got a shock when I looked inside his mouth – one tooth had a massive hole in it, another was just a splintered fragment and there were quite a few missing (remember he is only 22). I walked down to Vondrozo with him (25km) to see if the hospital would pull his tooth out, there being no dentist there. However, they were not very helpful so I arranged for him to go to Farafangana with me. This was to be his first trip beyond Vondrozo and his first sight of the sea, which he found suitably impressive; in fact he lost the power of speech for quite a while.

Zely's wife gave birth to their sixth offspring – a messenger arrived to say she was in labour and I sent down a knitted baby jacket and some sardines and chocolate to sustain her through the ordeal. When Zely returned from paternity leave he said we should choose his new son's name. I tried to make something suitable from our initials but the best I could manage was Frisbe, so we all chose a name and put them in a hat. Zely chose mine which was 'Faly' which means happy in Malagasy. It could have been much worse – we had run out of glue and a guide was going to Vondrozo to do some shopping. I had written down 'Araldite' on a piece of paper and somehow that got into the hat!

lemurs anyway – they look like half monkeys and half cat and I don't much like either animal. I absolutely love the thermal baths, though!'

Good for Sarah for knowing what she wants and doesn't want to do!

ITINERARIES The information above should enable you to plan your itinerary with a degree of confidence. Beware of trying to cram too much into your visit – this is a huge island and even though the roads are improving, it still take a while to get from place to place. Bear in mind also that tour operators usually divide the country into north and south (with Tana as the centre) because there are no connecting domestic flights linking the two halves. You often have to spend a night in Tana. If your time is limited you should choose either the north or the south.

TOUR OPERATORS

UK The internet is the ideal way of finding out the best tour operator for your purposes. ATTA (African Travel and Tourism Association) has a comprehensive listing for Madagascar, separated into different interests: www.atta.co. Safaribookers (www.safaribookers.com) has a listing of Madagascar specialists; check out their 'Last Minute' area for good deals at short notice. The organisation Responsibletravel.com promotes ethical tour operators.

The listings below are the specialists.

Aardvark Safaris ✎ 01980 849160; **f** 01980 849161; **e** mail@aardvarksafaris.com; www.aardvarksafaris.com. Exclusive tailor-made holidays.
Africa Travel Centre ✎ 0845 450 1520; **f** 0207 383 7512; **e** info@africatravel.co.uk; www.africatravel.co.uk. Flights & tailor-made holidays.
Audley Travel ✎ 01993 838044; **e** africa@audleytravel.com; www.audleytravel.com
Discovery Initiatives ✎ 01285 643333; www.discoveryinitiatives.co.uk. Wildlife specialists. Group & tailor-made holidays.
Explore Worldwide Ltd ✎ 0870 333 4001; **f** 01252 391110; **e** res@explore.com; www.exploreworldwide.com. Regular Madagascar trips; no special focus.
Gane and Marshall ✎ 020 8445 600; **e** holidays@ganeandmarshall.co.uk
Naturetrek ✎ 01962 733051; **f** 01962 736426; **e** info@naturetrek.co.uk; www.naturetrek.co.uk. Special focus: birds & mammals.
Okavango Tours & Safaris Ltd; ✎ 020 8343 3283; **f** 020 8343 3287; **e** info@okavango.com; www.okavango.com
Papyrus Tours ✎ 01405 785 211; **f** 01405 785 232; **e** info@papyrustours.co.uk, www.papyrustours.co.uk. Wildlife tours led by Nick Garbutt.
Pulse Africa ✎ 0208 995 5909; **e** pulseafricauk@easynet.co.uk; www.africansafari.org.uk. Beaches & lemurs galore!
Rainbow Tours ✎ 020 7226 1004; **f** 020 7226 2621; **e** info@rainbowtours.co.uk; www.rainbowtours.co.uk. Tailor-made trips for individuals & for small groups, with an emphasis on wildlife, birding, culture & community tourism. They

also offer small group departures including wildlife & birding tours led by experts such as Nick Garbutt, Lyn Mair & Roger Garina.
Reef & Rainforest Tours ✎ 01803 866965; **f** 01803 865916; **e** mail@reefandrainforest.co.uk, www.reefandrainforest.co.uk. Specialists in Madagascar with a wide variety of tours, including Family Adventures itineraries for children under 12 yrs old.
Safari Consultants ✎ 01787 888590; **f** 01787 228096; **e** bill@safariconsultantuk.com; www.safari-consultants.co.uk. Private holidays through southern Madagascar.
Steppes Africa ✎ 01285 650011; **e** africa@steppestravel.co.uk; www.steppestravel.co.uk. Tailor-made holidays to Madagascar.
Sunbird ✎ 01767 262522; **f** 01767 262916; **e** sunbird@sunbirdtours.co.uk; www.sunbirdtours.co.uk
The Ultimate Travel Company ✎ 020 7386 4646; **e** enquiry@theultimatetravelcompany.co.uk; www.theultimatetravelcompany.co.uk. Upmarket, tailor-made tours; leader Nick Garbutt.
Wildlife Worldwide ✎ 0845 130 6982; **f** 0845 130 6984; **e** sales@wildlifeworldwide.com Tailor-made wildlife tours with expert naturalists.
World Odyssey ✎ 01905 731373; **f** 01905 726872; **e** info@world-odyssey.com; www.world-odyssey.com. Private, tailor-made, guided tours.
World Primate Safaris ✎ 0870 850 9092 or 01273 691 941; **e** sales@worldprimatesafaris.com; www.worldprimatesafaris.com. Contact Will Bolsover. A specialist operating tailor-made trips to see the world's primates, including lemurs. A percentage of profits goes towards primate conservation.

USA The website for the Madagascar embassy has a selection of US tour operators: www.embassy.org/Madagascar/tours.html. Below are the specialists I know and trust.

Blue Chameleon Ventures PO Box 516, Alva, FL 33920, USA; ✎ +239 697 4414; **e** bill@bluechameleon.org; www.bluechameleon.org. 'Herp' trips with an expert.
Cortez Travel, Inc PO Box 1699, Solano Beach, CA 92075; ✎ 619 755 5136 or 1 800 854 1029; **f** 1 858 481 7474; **e** info@cortez.usa.com. Cortez is the specialist Madagascar operator in the US; Monique Rodriguez has been running trips there for over 2 decades & probably knows the

practicalities better than anyone else in the travel business.
Field Guides, Inc 9433 Bee Cave Rd, Austin, Texas 78733; ✎ 512 327 4953 or 800 728 4953; **e** fieldguides@fieldguides.com; www.fieldguides.com. Birding tours.
Remote River Expeditions PO Box 544, Boulder, CO 80306; **e** gary@remoterivers.com; www.remoterivers.com. Specialising in river journeys, birding & wildlife tours.

AUSTRALIA

Adventure Associates Pty Ltd Level 7, 12–14 O'Connell St, Sydney, NSW 2000 (PO Box 4414, Bondi Junction, NSW 2001); ✆ 02 8916 3000; f 02 8916 3090; e mail@adventureassociates.com; www.adventureassociates.com
Heritage Destinations Suite 102, 379 Pitt St, Sydney NSW 2000 ✆ 61 2 9267 0129; f 61 2 9267 2899; e heritagedest@bigpond.com. Contact: Ray Boniface.
Wildlife Safari 213 Railway Rd; Subiaco WA 6008; ✆ 61 08 9388 9900; f 61 08 9388 9232; e info@wildlife-safari.com.au; www.wildlife-safari.com.au

SOUTH AFRICA

Birding Africa 21 Newlands Rd, Claremont 7708; ✆ 021 531 9148; e info@birdingafrica.com; www.birdingafrica.com. Specialist for birding trips.
Falcon Safaris (Pty) Ltd Shop 8C, Landela Complex, Livingstone Way, Victoria Falls, Zimbabwe; ✆ +263 13 42695; f +263 13 42695; e info@falconsafaris.com; www.falcon-safaris.co.za. 10 yrs experience of running trips into Madagascar.
Jenman African Safaris Tel: 021 683 7826; email: enquries@jenmanafricansafaris.com; www.jenmansafaris.com. Island-hopping trips by dhow in the Nosy Be region. Tailor-made & scheduled travel.
Pulse Africa ✆ 011 325 2290; e info@pulseafrica.com; www.pulseafrica.com. Beaches & lemurs.
Unusual Destinations PO Box 97508, Petervale 2151, Johannesburg; ✆ 011 706 1991; f 011 463 1469; e info@unusualdestinations.com; www.unusualdestinations.com. The SA experts in Madagascar. Very helpful & knowledgeable. Regular group departures & specialist natural history trips.

MADAGASCAR There are many tour operators in Madagascar. This is by no means a complete list, just a selection of those that I can recommend. The telephone code for Madagascar is (+261 20) followed by the number.

Boogie Pilgrim BP 12149, Galerie Zoom, Antananarivo 101; ✆ 22 530 70; f 22 530 69; e boogie@simicro.mg. One of the leading tour operators in Madagascar, organising tours of every sort including by light aircraft. Own lodges & some private reserves. Recommended.
Cortez Expeditions 25 Rue Ny' Zafindraindiky, Antanimena, Antananarivo; ✆ 22 219 74; f 22 247 87; e cortezexpeditions@simicro.mg. One of the most experienced tour operators in Madagascar & owner of the Relais du Masoala in Maroantsetra.
Destination Mada 32 Rue Andrianary Ratianarivo, Antananarivo; ✆ 22 310 72; f 22 310 67; e destmada@malagasy.com; www.madanet.com.
Gondwana Explorer (formerly Voyages Bourdon) ✆ 22 296 96; www.gondwanaexplorer.com. One of Madagascar's oldest tour operators. Highly praised by more than one reader.
Mad Caméléon Lot II K6, Ankadivato, Antananarivo; ✆ 22 630 86; f 22 344 20; e madcam@dts.mg. Specialise in river trips.
Madagascar Airtours 33 Av de l'Indépendance, Antananarivo; ✆ 22 241 92/22 627 99; f 22 641 90; e office@airtours.mg or airtours@wanadoo.mg; http://takelaka.dts.mg/airtours. Also at the Hilton Hotel. The most experienced agency, with offices in most major towns, they can organise a wide variety of specialist tours including natural history, ornithology, speleology, trekking, mineralogy, river trips, sailing, etc. Michel Rakotonirina is the very experienced guide used by contributors John & Valerie Middleton for all their serious adventures. 'His knowledge of all things Malagasy is exceptional & we found him invaluable.'
Madagascar Discovery ✆ 22 351 65; f 22 351 67; e mda@mda.mg; www.madagascar-discovery.com. Booking agent for Terres Blanches & other lodges.
Madagascar Expedition Agency ✆ 22 261 14; e mea@wanadoo.mg. Agents for Masoala Forest Lodge.
Madamax Tours ✆ 22 351 01; www.madamax.com. Specialise in 'high-adrenaline adventures' including white-water rafting.
Magical Madagascar ✆/f 22 545 42; e magical.madagascar@netclub.mg; www.magical-madagascar-travel.com. A new company run by one of the most popular & experienced guides in Madagascar, Hery Andrianiantefana (see advert on page 218).
Malagasy Tours Lot VX29, Avaradrova, Antananarivo; ✆ 22 627 24/22 356 07; f 22 622 13; www.malagasy-tours.com. The owner, Olivier Toboul, runs specialised itineraries for ethnobotany (amongst other things) using local people who can explain the complexities of the Malagasy culture. Good for off-the-beaten-track exploration, too.

PRIORI ↘ 22 625 27; e priori@wanadoo.mg; www.priori.ch. Located in the centre of Antananarivo (opposite the White Palace Hotel), this Swiss-owned, Malagasy-run agency is recommended by a reader for their knowledge & efficiency.
Remote River Expeditions ↘ 95 543 27; e gary@remoterivers.com; www.remoterivers.com
Roadhouse Voyages ↘/f 44 492 26; e roadhouse@simicro.mg; http://www.simicro.mg/roadhouse. Located in Antsirabe (see page 190).
SETAM Madagascar 56 Av du 26 Juin, Antananarivo 101; ↘ 22 324 31/33; e setam@wanadoo.mg; www.setam-madagascar.com. Very helpful & efficient.

Transcontinents 10 Av de l'Indépendance, Antananarivo; ↘ 22 223 98; f 22 283 65; e transco@dts.mg. Efficiently run. Recommended.
Visit Mada Tours 071 KI, Ivato Airport; m 033 11 319 24; e visitmadatours@yahoo.com; www.madagascar-tour.com. English-speaking tour operator offering various tours: car rental, canoeing, trekking. Contact Mr Benjamin.
Za Tour II J 178 AB Bis Ambodivoanjo Ambohijatovo Farango, 101 Antananarivo; ↘ 24 253 08/22 424 22/24 253 07; m 032 40 376 44; f 22 422 86; e zatour@iris.mg; www.zatours-madagascar.com. One of the most experienced & conscientious operators in Madagascar. Highly recommended.

RED TAPE

VISAS A visa is required by everyone and is normally issued for a stay of 30 days. However, visas for 90 days are also issued, exceptionally, by the London embassy and at the airport on arrival in Madagascar. A tourist visa costs about €12 or the equivalent in US dollars. If buying it on arrival note that the exact amount fluctuates so bring some additional low-denomination bills. Although long-term visas are usually available for stays of more than 90 days, most travellers prefer to take a trip to Mauritius or Réunion and ask for another 90 days on arrival back in Madagascar.

If you find yourself unexpectedly needing a visa extension, go to the Ministry of the Interior, five minutes from the Hilton Hotel in Antananarivo. For your *prolongation* you will need three photos, a photocopy of your currency declaration, a typewritten declaration (best done at home) of why you want to stay longer, a *Certificat d'Hébergement* from your hotel, your passport, your return ticket and the fee. Every provincial town has an immigration office, or at least a Commissariat de Police, so in theory you can extend your visa anywhere.

ⓔ EMBASSY AND CONSULATE ADDRESSES

Australia Consulate: 3rd level, 100 Clarence St, Sydney, NSW 2000; ↘ 02 9299 2290; f 02 9299 2242; e tonyknox@ozemail.com.au. Hours 09.00–13.00. The Consul-General, Anthony Knox, is very enthusiastic & helpful. He is also the agent for Air Madagascar.
Austria Consulate: Pötzleindorferstr 94, A-1184 Wien; ↘ 47 91 273; f 47 91 2734
Belgium Embassy; 276 Av de Tervueren, 1150 Bruxelles; ↘ 770 1726 & 770 1774; f 722 3731; e ambassade.madagascar@skynet.be
Canada Embassy: 649 Blair Rd, Gloucester, Ontario KIJ 7M4; ↘ 613 744 7995; f 613 744 2530; e ambmgnet@inexpres.net. Honorary Consulate: 8530 Rue Saguenay, Brossard, Québec, J4X IM6; ↘/f 450 672 0353. Honorary Consulate: 8944 Bayridge Drive SW, Calgary, Alberta T2V 3M8; ↘ 403 262 5576; f 403 262 3556
France Embassy: 4 Av Raphael, 75016 Paris; ↘ I 45 04 62 11; f I 45 03 31 75 Consulate: 234 Bd Perrier, 13008 Marseille; ↘ 4 91 15 16 91; f 4 91 53 79 58
Germany Consulate: Seepromenade 92, D-14612 Falkensee; ↘ 03322 23 140; f 03322 23 14 29
Italy Embassy: Via Riccardo Zandonai 84/A, Roma 400194; ↘ 36 30 77 97; f 396 329 43 06
Kenya Honorary Consulate: First floor, Hilton Hotel (PO Box 41723), Nairobi; ↘ 225 286; f 252 347
Mauritius Embassy: Av Queen Mary, Port Louis; ↘ 686 3956; f 686 7040
Réunion Consulate: 73 Rue Juliette Dodu, 97461 Saint-Denis; ↘ 21 05 21/21 65 58
South Africa Consulate: No 13 6th St, Houghton Estate, Johannesburg; ↘ 442 3322; f 442 6660; e consul@infodoor.co.za; www.madagascarconsulate.org.za. Consulate; Hon Consul: David Fox; 201 Percy Osborne Rd, Morningside, Durban; ↘/f 31 312 9704; e mdconsul@icon.co.za

Spain Honorary Consulate: Lluria 85 pal 2a, 08009, Barcelona; ☎ 93 272 2125
Switzerland Honorary Consulate: 2 Theaterplatz, 3011 Bern; ☎ 311 3111; f 311 0871; e Hocomad@Datacomm.ch
United Kingdom Embassy: 8-10 Hallam St, London W1W 6JE; ☎ 020 3008 4551; f 020 3008 4551; e embamadlon@yahoo.co.uk; www.embassy-madagascar-uk.com
United States Embassy: 2374 Massachusetts Av NW, Washington DC 20008; ☎ 202 265 5525;

e malagasy@embassy.org. Permanent Representative of Madagascar at the UN: 820 Second Ave, Suite 800, New York, NY 10017; ☎ 212 986 9491; www.embassy.org/madagascar. Honorary Consulate: The Hon Consul in California is Monique Rodrigues, who runs the specialist tour operator, Cortez Travel, 124 Lomas Santa Fe Dr, No 208, Solana Beach, CA 92075; ☎ 619 792 6999; e info@madagascar-consulate.org. Also 123 South Broad Street, Philadelphia, PA 19109; ☎ 215 893 3067.

GETTING THERE

✈ **BY AIR** If you are planning to take several domestic flights during your stay, Air Madagascar should be the international carrier since they offer a 'Visit Madagascar Pass' giving a 50% discount on domestic flights, providing visitors also book their international flight (at the same time) on Air Madagascar. The rules governing this discount – and the percentage itself – are liable to change so it's best to check the latest information on the Air Madagascar website or through one of their agents. Those on an extended visit pay the full rate. Also South Africa and Kenya count as 'regional' not international (so no discount).

Note that flights towards the end of the year are heavily booked (it's the most popular season and also the start of the off-peak cheaper tickets). Book as far in advance as possible.

From Europe As with any longhaul flight it is often cheaper to book through an agency such as Trailfinders (☎ 020 7938 3366), WEXAS (☎ 020 7581 8768), STA (☎ 020 7361 6262), or the Flight Centre (☎ 01892 530030) rather than phoning the airline direct. At the time of writing only Air France flies to Madagascar from the UK (via Paris). Air Madagascar is the preferred alternative (from Paris) in order to take advantage of the discount on domestic fares. Both airlines charge roughly the same price: between £800 and £1,000 depending on the season and the agency issuing the ticket. However, promotional fares are sometimes available for as little as £500.

Air Madagascar (*Headquarters: 31 Av de l'Indépendance, Antananarivo;* ☎ *+261 20 22 222 22;* f *+261 20 22 337 60;* e *airmad@wanadoo.mg; www.airmadagascar.mg*) The country's national airline is now owned by Lufthansa. Their UK contact details remain the same, however (*Air Madagascar, Oak House, County Oak Way, Crawley, West Sussex RH11 7ST;* ☎ *01293 596 665;* e *info@aviareps-group.com*). Schedules are updated regularly but the website does not give prices. New routes are frequently introduced, often at a promotional price, so keep an eye on their website.

There are no Air Madagascar flights from London – it is necessary to fly (or take the train) to Paris and connect with the Air Madagascar flight from CDG Airport (section 2a). Currently there are daily flights from Paris except for Tuesdays and Saturdays. They leave CDG at 16.55, arriving too early to check into most hotels in the capital. From Paris to Antananarivo is 10½ hours. Paris – Antananarivo is not the only route: there are now direct flights from Milan to the islands of Nosy Be or Ile Sante Marie, as well as Rome or Munich to Antananarivo.

For information on domestic flights see page 107.

Air France (*www.airfrance.com*) Flights depart from Heathrow via Paris on Tuesday, Wednesday, Friday and Sunday (low season – there are more flights in July and

August). These are day flights (leaving CDG at 10.15), in contrast to Air Madagascar which flies overnight. The suffering comes on the return home: flights leave Antananarivo at 01.30 on Monday, Wednesday, Thursday and Saturday. The advantage of Air France is that you book your luggage straight through from London. The disadvantage, apart from the inferior service, is that you must pay in full within a week of booking the ticket.

Corsair This is the cheapest option but tickets can be purchased only through Nouvelles Frontières (*3 Bd Saint-Martin, 75003 Paris;* ✎ *01 4027 0208;* f *01 4027 0019; www.nouvelles-frontieres.fr*). A word of warning from a recent user: 'We were 15 hours delayed going out and 30 hours delayed returning. Apparently this is not uncommon…'

On most airlines serving Madagascar there are different rates according to the season (based on popularity). High season is usually July and August, and the Christmas holiday, and low season from January to the end of June.

From other Indian Ocean islands
Réunion The following airlines fly from Paris to Réunion: Air France, AOM French Airlines, Air Liberté, and British Airways. From Réunion there are almost daily Air Madagascar flights to Antananarivo, and also to Toamasina, Mahajanga and Taolagnaro (Fort Dauphin). Air Austral flies three times a week to Nosy Be.

Mauritius Air Mauritius and Air Madagascar fly between Mauritius and Antananarivo.

Comoro Islands Air Madagascar flies from Mayotte and Air Mauritius from Moroni.

Seychelles There is one flight a week (Tuesday) from the Seychelles.

From Africa
Ethiopia Ethiopian Airlines are due to start flights from Addis Ababa in 2007.

Kenya There are several flights per week (Air Madagascar, Air Mauritius and Air France) from Nairobi. With so many cheap flights from London to Nairobi, this may be a good option. Try to book a seat on the right-hand side of the plane for the wonderful view of Kilimanjaro shortly after take off.

South Africa For travellers coming from the UK, flights from Johannesburg offer a good alternative to the London-Paris-Antananarivo option. There are five flights a week from Jo'burg, two with **Air Madagascar** (✎ *011 289 8222*) and three with their partner **InterAir** (✎ *011 616 0636; www.interair.co.za*). All flights leave Jo'burg at 08.30, getting you to Tana in the early afternoon – a much more civilised time than the pre-dawn arrivals from Europe. Airlink also now flies to Nosy Be. The flight takes four hours and, at a discounted rate through a tour operator, costs about R5,000 (about £380) high season. In 2007 Air Madagascar instituted a new flight between Jo'burg and Taolagnaro (Fort Dauphin) in the south.

InterAir can be contacted in London (✎ *0208 283 9742;* f *0208 562 3600;* e *gsa.1.gsa@britishairways.com*).

From the USA Madagascar is about as far from California as it is possible to be. Indeed, San Francisco and the southern Malagasy town of Toliara *are* as far apart as it is possible to be. Understandably, therefore, fares from the USA are expensive.

Air France is probably the best carrier, or via United or Delta to Paris to connect with the Air Madagascar flight. From California you can travel west via Hong Kong or Bangkok (from where there are Air Madagascar flights). Check the excellent website of Air Madagascar agent Cortez Travel: www.air-mad.com.

From Australia Air Madagascar has an office in the same building as the Sydney consulate. Flights are usually routed via Hong Kong or Bangkok, from where there is an Air Madagascar flight to Antananarivo. Alternatively you can go from Melbourne or Perth to Mauritius (Air Mauritius) connecting with an Air Madagascar flight to Antananarivo, or fly from Perth via Johannesburg.

BY SEA

From South Africa There are no passenger-carrying boats running from Durban, but many people sail their own yachts to Madagascar.

Yacht clubs

Royal Natal Yacht Club PO Box 2946, Durban 4000;
☏ 031 301 5425; f 031 307 2590
Point Yacht Club PO Box 2224, Durban 4000; ☏ 031 301 4787; f 031 305 1234

Zululand Yacht Club PO Box 10387, Meer'en'see 3901;
☏ 035 788 0256; f 035 788 0254
Royal Cape Yacht Club PO Box 777, Cape Town 8000;
☏ 021 4211 354; f 021 4216 028

Many yachts sail from Natal to Madagascar and the Durban consulate was set up to cope with their visas. It takes six or seven days to sail to Anakao, the most popular port (south of Toliara). Most stop en route at Europa Island, where a French garrison will advise on the next stage. Experienced sailors and divers will want to reach the atoll of Bassas da India which offers superb diving but has been responsible for the shipwreck of numerous vessels.

Because of the increasing number of yachts visiting the northwest of Madagascar, I give information for 'yachties' in the *Nosy Be* chapter.

WHAT TO TAKE

LUGGAGE A soft bag or backpack is more practical than a hard suitcase (and you may not be allowed to take a suitcase on a Twin Otter plane). Backpackers should consider buying a rucksack with a zipped compartment to enclose the straps when using them on airlines. Or – a cheaper option – roll up the straps and bind them out of the way with insulating tape. Bring a light folding nylon bag for taking purchases home, and the largest permissible bag to take as hand baggage on the plane. Pack this with everything you need for the first four days or so (security restrictions permitting). Lost or delayed luggage is then less of a catastrophe.

CLOTHES Before deciding what clothes to pack, take a look at the *Climate* section on page 3. There is quite a difference between summer and winter temperatures, particularly in the highlands and the south where it is distinctly cold at night between May and September. A fibre-pile jacket or a body-warmer (down vest) is useful in addition to a light sweater. In June and July a scarf (muffler) can give much-needed extra warmth. At any time of the year it will be hot during the day in low-lying areas, and very hot between October and March. Layers of clothing – T-shirt, sweatshirt, light sweater – are warm and versatile, and take less room than a heavy sweater. Don't bring jeans, they are too heavy and too hot. Lightweight cotton or cotton mix trousers such as Rohan Bags are much more suitable. The Bags have a useful inside zipped pocket for security. At any time of year you will need a light shower-proof jacket, and during the wet season, or if spending time in the rainforest, appropriate raingear and perhaps a small umbrella. A light cotton jacket is always useful for breezy evenings by the coast. Don't forget a sunhat.

For footwear, trainers (running shoes) and sandals are usually all you need. 'Sports sandals' which strap securely to the feet are better than flip-flops. Hiking boots are necessary for Marojejy and may be required in places like Ankarana, Andringitra and Isalo but are not necessary for the main tourist circuits.

Give some thought to beachwear if you enjoy snorkelling. You may need an old pair of sneakers (or similar) to protect your feet from coral and sea urchins, and a T-shirt and shorts to wear while in the water to prevent sunburn.

TOILETRIES Although you can buy just about everything in Madagascar, it's still best to bring all you need. My indulgence is bringing a roll of my favourite brand of soft toilet paper; the local stuff is adequate, but that's all, and you can't rely on the local WCs having any sort of paper. A correspondent notes with satisfaction that condoms are very cheap and reliable. Certainly Madagascar is addressing the problem of AIDS with enthusiasm: in the drawer of my posh hotel in Antananarivo was a Gideon's Bible and a condom!

Bring baby-wipes or – better – moist toilet tissues for freshening up during a long trip, and hand-gel which cleans and disinfects your hands. When used regularly, especially after shaking hands or handling money, I have found this a real help in preventing traveller's diarrhoea.

Some toilet articles have several uses: dental floss is excellent for repairs as well as for teeth, and a nail brush gets clothes clean too.

Don't take up valuable space with a bath towel – a hand towel or even face-flannel (washcloth) is perfectly adequate. Or take Daniel's advice: 'I never travel with a towel. A sarong (or *lamba*) is more absorbent than you'd think, very lightweight, incredibly fast-drying (which can be really useful), and more multi-purpose than a hand towel: you can lie on it on the beach, sleep under it, use it for shade, hang it up for a bit of privacy to change behind, wear it, and probably even use it as a parachute if you fall out of a plane. Maybe.'

ELECTRICAL EQUIPMENT The voltage in Madagascar is 220v. Outlets (where they exist) take 2-pin round plugs. If you use a 3-pin fused plug plus adapter, bring a spare fuse for the plug.

PROTECTION AGAINST MOSQUITOES

Repellents With malaria on the increase, it is vital to be properly protected (see page 121). Buzz-Bands (made by Traveller International Products) which slip over the wrists and ankles are recommended as easy to use and effective. For hotel rooms, pyrethrum coils which burn slowly through the night and repel insects with their smoke are available all over Madagascar. They really do work. Plug-in repellents which work in a similar way are also effective.

Mosquito nets Most upper- and mid-range hotels either have effective screening or provide mosquito nets, but if you are staying in budget hotels or travelling by overnight *taxi-brousses* (which may stop or break down) you should consider bringing a mosquito net. Because most hotels do not have anything to hang a net from, a free-standing net is more practical (though a lot more expensive). They generally have a built-in groundsheet giving protection from bed bugs and fleas as well as mosquitoes. This means, however, that you must use your own sleeping bag inside it. You should also treat these nets with Permethrin, which kills bugs on contact.

A range of mosquito nets and other anti-bug devices, plus advice, can be had from Nomad Travel Store in London (✆ 020 8889 7014; e orders@nomadtravel.co.uk; www.nomadtravel.co.uk).

BACKPACKING EQUIPMENT Basic camping gear gives you the freedom to travel adventurously and can add a considerable degree of comfort to overland journeys.

The most important item is your backpack: this should have an internal frame and plenty of pockets. Protect it from oil, dirt and the effluent of young or furry/feathered passengers with a cover. You can buy a commercially-made one or make your own: the plastic woven rice sacks sold in Madagascar markets are ideal for this purpose (bring a large needle and dental floss to do the final custom-fitting in Antananarivo). For security consider bringing a lockable mesh backpack cover.

In winter (June to August) a lightweight sleeping bag will keep you warm in cheap hotels with inadequate bedding, and on night stops on – or off – 'buses'. A sheet sleeping bag plus a light blanket (buy it in Tana) or space blanket are ideal for the summer months (October to May) and when the hotel linen may be missing or dirty.

An air-mattress or pillow pads your bum on hard seats as well as your hips when sleeping out. One of those horseshoe-shaped travel pillows lets you sleep sitting up (which you'll need to do on *taxi-brousses*).

A lightweight tent allows you to strike out on your own and stay in national parks, on deserted beaches and so forth. It will need to have a separate rain-fly and be well-ventilated.

Most people forgo a stove in order to cut down on weight, but if you will be camping extensively bring a stove that burns petrol (gasoline) or paraffin (kerosene). Meths (*alcohol à bruler*) is usually available as well. Fuel quality in Madagascar is poor so make sure your stove will burn local fuel while you are still in Tana.

Daniel Austin and Kelly Green, who used Camping Gaz stoves, give this information: 'Gas canisters can be very difficult to find in Madagascar. You will only find one type of canister there: the Camping Gaz C206 (and compatible models of other brands). Do not bother to bring a camp stove that requires any other sort of canister. Note that it is illegal to send gas canisters by mail or to take them on an aircraft, so the only option would be to buy them in Madagascar if you plan on using a camp stove. We found canisters in the following towns: Toliara in the large hardware store Quincaillerie du Centre; Fianarantsoa at Supermarché 2000; Antsiranana (Diego Suarez) at Brico-Nord, the big hardware store opposite the new Grand Hotel on Rue Colbert. Oddly we never did succeed in locating any in Tana, despite extensive efforts.'

There are always fresh vegetables for sale in the smallest village so bring some stock cubes to make vegetable stew.

Take your own mug and spoon (and carry them with you always). That way you can enjoy roadside coffee without the risk of a cup rinsed in filthy water, and market yoghurt without someone else's germs on the spoon. Milk powder tastes (to most people) better in tea or coffee than condensed milk. You can buy it locally, or bring it from home. Don't forget a water-bottle and water-purifiers.

Give some thought to ways of interacting with the locals. A Malagasy phrase-book (see page 459) provides lots of amusement as you practise your skills on fellow-passengers, and playing-cards are universally understood.

A good book allows you to retreat from interaction for a while (but you won't be able to read on a *taxi-brousse*). Bring enough reading matter with you – English-language books are not easy to find in Madagascar. If you want to read at night, buy a 100-watt bulb (bayonet type) to substitute for the 40-watt one supplied by the cheaper hotels.

MISCELLANEOUS ITEMS FOR BUDGET TRAVELLERS Bring a roll of insulating tape or gaffer tape which can be used for all manner of things. Blu-Tack is equally versatile; bring enough to make a plug for your sink, to stop doors banging or to hold them open. A Swiss Army knife (or similar) is essential (but remember not to pack it in your hand luggage). A rubber wedge will secure your hotel door at night, and a combination lock is useful in a variety of ways (see the section on safety, page 132). Other useful items are a light tarpaulin (multiple uses) and a length of strong, nylon cord (ditto). It's worth bringing two torches (flashlights) in case one breaks or is lost.

Earplugs are just about essential, to block out not only the sounds of the towns but those of enthusiastic nocturnal animals when camping in reserves! (Personally I think it's worth being kept awake by these, but it can pall after several nights.) A large handkerchief or bandanna has many uses, from mopping your streaming face to protecting your neck from the sun or your hair and lungs from dust.

If you are travelling independently or want to keep in touch with family and friends at home, bring your mobile phone (see page 118).

PHOTOGRAPHIC EQUIPMENT These days most people use digital cameras. Apart from the obvious advantages it is great to be able to show local people their photo. Most travellers just show the image on their cameras, but Derek Antonio Serra writes: 'I bought the portable Canon Selphy photo printer that prints colour postcards directly from your digital camera in 90 seconds. On arriving in a village, I'd take a stroll with my camera, and ask one or two people if I could photograph them. I then rushed back to my hotel and printed their photographs. Imagine their amazement when I returned minutes later and presented them with these valued gifts. From then on I had no problems finding subjects to photograph.'

Don't overburden yourself with camera equipment – there's no substitute for the eye/brain combination!

Batteries Battery sizes other than AA can be hard to find in Madagascar. AA batteries, although sold everywhere, are almost universally of poor quality, which will not be a problem for low-drain applications like alarm clocks or small torches, but will work for barely five minutes in a digital camera. So it is best to bring good-quality spare batteries from home. That said, there is a serious environmental consideration to chucking away disposable batteries, so rechargeable ones should be used if possible.

CHECKLIST Small torch (flashlight) with spare batteries and bulb, or headlamp (for nocturnal animal hunts), travel alarm clock (or alarm wristwatch), penknife, sewing kit, scissors, tweezers, safety pins, insulating tape or Sellotape (Scotchtape), string, felt-tipped pen (the permanent type so you can write on Zip-loc bags, CDs, etc), ballpoint pens, a small notebook, a large notebook for diary and letters home, envelopes, plastic bags (all sizes, sturdy; Zip-loc are particularly useful), universal plug for baths and sinks (though Blu-Tack does the job just as well), elastic clothes line or cord and pegs, concentrated detergent, ear plugs, insect repellent, sunscreen, lipsalve, spare glasses or contact lenses, sunglasses, medical and dental kit (see *Chapter 5*), dental floss, a water bottle, water purifying tablets or other sterilising agent, compact binoculars, camera and film, books, miniature playing cards, Scrabble/pocket chess set, French dictionary, Malagasy phrasebook and a star chart for the southern hemisphere.

GOODS FOR PRESENTS, SALE OR TRADE This is a difficult area. In the past tourists have handed out presents to children and created the tiresome little beggars you will encounter in the popular areas (if you don't now know the French for pen or sweets, you soon will). They have also handed T-shirts to adults with similar consequences. For more on this subject see *Chapter 6*. There are, however, plenty of occasions when a gift is appropriate, although as Will Pepper points out, 'On a number of occasions people said this souvenir of Ireland is all well and good but I would prefer cash.' Giving money in return for services is entirely acceptable so in rural areas it's best to pay cash and refrain from introducing a new consumer awareness.

In urban areas or with the more sophisticated Malagasy people, presents are a very good way of showing your appreciation for kindness or extra good service. Music cassettes often go down well with *taxi-brousse* drivers, but only pop music.

If you want to contribute something a little more intellectually satisfying, here is a suggestion from Dr Philip Jones, who travels in Madagascar on behalf of the charity Money for Madagascar. 'I was asked several times for an English Grammar, so any such books would be valued gifts. If visitors take a French–English dictionary, why not leave it in Madagascar?'

The most deserving of your gifts are the hard-pressed charities who work with the very poor. So why not contact Money for Madagascar (see page 146) and see if there are any urgently-needed goods you can take to the organisations they support.

$ MONEY

TRAVELLERS' CHEQUES In the old days everyone brought travellers' cheques, but now these are rarely seen and consequently are difficult to cash. If you do opt for travellers' cheques (and it is the safest option) they should be in euros or US dollars. Sterling travellers' cheques are almost impossible to change.

CASH It is far easier to change cash (euros or US dollars) so this is the best option if you are on a prepaid group tour. Be wary of bringing US$100 bills – these are not always accepted because of the large number of counterfeit ones doing the rounds. Bring $50 and $20 bills (or the equivalent in euros), and about 10 single dollar bills which are ideal for tips or handicrafts if you don't have local currency handy.

CREDIT CARDS Most of the large hotels now accept credit cards, **but Visa only**. There are some notable exceptions (these are detailed under hotel listings) and the rate of exchange/charges can be exorbitant. Credit and debit cards may be used to draw cash at many banks and *Bureaux de Change* (remember your PIN code).

☞ *WARNING!* Very few businesses or ATMs accept MasterCard. However, in Maroantsetra it is currently the *only* credit card accepted. American Express is rarely accepted but, when it is, the rate of exchange for dollars is better.

CASH MACHINES (ATM) These not only exist but often work! But they are not found in every town so don't rely on them.

In summary, when I travel in Madagascar I bring my money in cash and credit cards (in a money belt). For independent travel (no pre-booked hotels) I would add some euro travellers' cheques.

TRANSFERRING FUNDS Now that you can draw cash from many banks using your credit card you are less likely to need money transferred from home. If you are staying a long time in Madagascar, however, it's advisable to make the transfer arrangement beforehand. The best bank for this is Banque Malgache de l'Océan

4

Indien, Place de l'Indépendance, Antananarivo. Its corresponding bank in the UK is Banque Nationale de Paris (*8–13 King William St, London EC4P 4HS;* ↘ *020 7895 7070*).

If you need cash in a hurry there are Western Union offices in Madagascar to which money can be transferred from home in a few hours, or in minutes if your nearest and dearest are willing to go to a Western Union office with cash. The fee (in the UK) is £32 if done with a credit card but, for the obliging mum, partner or whoever in your home country, it is a simple procedure which can be done over the phone, saving the journey to a Western Union office. They need to phone Western Union on↘ 0800 833 833 (in the USA: ↘ 800 325 6000) and know the town from where you wish to pick up the money. There are Western Union offices in Antananarivo, Mahajanga, Toamasina, Fianarantsoa and Nosy Be. Phone ↘ +261 20 22 313 07 for addresses or further information or check their website: www.westernunion.com.

THE CURRENCY Madagascar's currency has always been difficult to cope with. Here is an extract from an account written over a hundred years ago:

> The French five-franc piece is now the standard of coinage in Madagascar; for small change it is cut up into bits of all sizes. The traveller has to carry a pair of scales about with him, and whenever he makes a purchase the specified quantity of this most inconvenient money is weighed out with the greatest exactness, first on his own scales, and then on those of the suspicious native of whom he is buying.

So it is perhaps not surprising that the present government has kept up the tradition of confusing foreigners, and its own people, by changing the currency. The *franc malgache* (Fmg) has been replaced by the traditional Malagasy currency of *Ariary* (which was still in use in Madagascar when I first went there). This move was initiated in 2003 and, predictably, only the larger towns and tourist centres have adapted to the new currency. Although the Franc is no longer legal tender, in rural areas the locals still give prices in the old currency. One Ariary is 5Fmg, so if the price you are quoted seems unreasonably high you can assume it is Francs not Ariary. Note that the Fmg amount is still printed (in small type) on the Ariary bank notes.

EXCHANGE RATE AND HARD CURRENCIES The Ariary floats against hard currencies and the exchange rate changes frequently. For this reason most upper-range hotels quote their prices in euros, the most commonly-used hard currency.

Exchange rates in June 2007:

£1 = 4,087 Ariary
€1 = 2,771 Ariary
US$1 = 2,064 Ariary

HOW MUCH WILL IT COST? The airfare is the most expensive part of your trip. Once there, you will find Madagascar a relatively cheap country. Travel by *taxi-brousse*, and eat and sleep like the locals, and you can keep your costs down to about £15/€23/US$30 per day for a couple. Note that couples can travel almost as cheaply as singles, since most budget and mid-range hotels charge by the room (with double bed). Sleep cheap and eat well is a good recipe for happy travels.

However, fuel is expensive in Madagascar, with petrol prices equivalent to those in Europe, roughly one euro per litre, so car hire is expensive, especially since you normally have to hire a driver as part of the deal. Costs also mount up if you are visiting many national parks or reserves, where you have the park fee plus the cost of a guide. The 'big six' most popular parks cost £6/€9/US$12 per day, but the less popular parks and reserves are considerably cheaper. See page 75 for further details.

The easiest way to save money on a day-to-day basis is to cut down on bottled water: a bottle of *Eau Vive* costs over £1/€1.50/US$1.90 in smart hotels (but half the price in a shop). Bring a water container and sterilising agent (and some herbal tea bags to make it taste nicer). If you are a beer drinker, be careful where you buy it: from a supermarket it costs one third of the price you'd pay in a fancy hotel.

TIPPING I (and even *vazaha* residents) find this an impossible subject on which to give coherent advice. Yet it is the one that consistently causes anxiety in travellers. The problem is you have to balance up the expectation of the tip recipient – who is probably used to generous tippers – and the knowledge of local wages. Ponder the following. A policeman, school teacher or junior doctor will earn around US$100 a month, while an experienced doctor or a university professor might get US$200. At the other end of the scale, although the minimum wage is 49,000Ar (US$125) per month, many manual workers are paid far less in the private sector; a waiter or labourer would be lucky to be paid US$15 and some girls working as maids receive no payment at all, just board and lodging. Near Toamasina is a small community where every member of the family breaks rocks for road-building. They are paid $1 for 10 buckets of broken rocks. No wonder everyone in Madagascar dreams of finding a job in tourism.

Some tipping is relatively simple: a service charge is added to most restaurant meals so tipping is not strictly necessary though waiters in tourist hotels now expect it. About 10% is ample; Malagasy would tip far less. Taxi drivers should not expect a tip, though you may want to add something for exceptional service.

The most manipulative people are baggage handlers, because they usually catch you before you are wised up to Madagascar, and are masters at the disappointment act. That said, a dollar is easily found (by you) and easily spent (by them) so in a stressful situation you might as well take the easy way out.

The hardest tipping question is how much to pay guides, drivers … people who have spent several days with you and given excellent service. Here I err on the generous side, because I am coming back, because the tour operator I work for needs to maintain good relations, and because these people are accustomed to generous tips. However, I do try to ensure that the people who work behind the scenes, such as cooks and cleaners, get tipped and not just the guides and drivers. Guides know, and accept, that independent travellers often cannot afford to tip with the same generosity as those on an organised tour. Generally speaking, 10,000Ar (roughly £3/€4/US$5) per person per day is a starting point. You can tip more or less than that according to your means and inclination. Bear in mind that the work is seasonal, and that their high-season earnings must support them during the three or four months when there are few tourists and little work.

It's always useful to get the Malagasy perspective of such things. 'I recommend that tourists should always err on the generous side regardless of the danger of setting unrealistic expectations. These are the rare opportunities where the income generated by tourism actually reaches the intended beneficiaries. Malagasy people have had their expectations raised and crushed several times over the centuries through various economic and social reforms; your generous tip will not phase them. The chances are they will hardly believe their luck, and will never dare to expect the same again with the next tourist.

'To put figures into perspective, anyone who pays the 10% tip is correct and ethical. There is nothing ethical about calculating a pro-rata of a global tip rate when Madagascar is not paying a pro-rata rate of its oil and food imports. You should aim to help feed a family of five each time you tip, which is around £1 or US$2 in a restaurant.

'Tourism is one of the main pillars for growth in Madagascar. The other is mining. Tipping is your chance to promote the tourism industry and to improve the service and competition in that sector. So if you liked what you experienced and would like to keep it that way, tip as if you were in your own country.'

Where it is essential not to over-tip is when travelling off the beaten track, where you could be setting a very dangerous precedent. It can cause problems for *vazaha* that follow who are perhaps doing research or conservation work and who cannot afford to live up to these new expectations.

Finally, when tipping guides working in national parks away from the main cities, do pay in Ariary. There are no banks in, say, Andasibe where they can change the euros or dollars into local currency.

GETTING AROUND

PUBLIC TRANSPORT You can get around Madagascar by road, air and water. And by rail. Whatever your transport, you'd better learn the meaning of *en panne*; it is engine trouble/breakdown. During these *en panne* sessions one can't help feeling a certain nostalgia for the pre-mechanised days when Europeans travelled by *filanzana* or palanquin. These litters were carried by four cheerful porters who, by all accounts, were so busy swapping gossip and telling stories that they sometimes dropped their unfortunate *vazaha* in a river. The average distance travelled per day was 45km – not much slower than a *taxi-brousse* today! The *filanzana* was used for high officials as recently as the 1940s. To get around town the locals depended on an earlier version of the current rickshaw, or *pousse-pousse*. The *mono-pousse* was a chair slung over a bicycle wheel. One man pulled and another pushed. The more affluent Malagasy possessed a *boeuf-cheval*: a zebu trained to be ridden. (I've seen a photo; the animal looks rather smug in its saddle and bridle.)

🚗 BY ROAD

'If I make roads, the white man will only come and take my country. I have two allies – hazo [forest] and tazo [fever]…'

King Radama I

Coping with the 'roads' used to be one of the great travel challenges in Madagascar. It's not that the royal decree has lasted 200 years but there's a third ally that the king didn't mention – the weather: torrential rain and cyclones destroy roads as fast as they are constructed. However, under President Ravalomanana road building has been given priority, and it will soon be quite difficult to find the truly awful roads that used to typify Madagascar.

Taxi-brousse is the generic name for public transport in Madagascar. *Car-brousse*, *camion-brousse*, *taxi-be* and *kat-kat* are also used, but they all refer to the 'bush-taxis' which run along every road in the country. These have improved a lot in recent years, especially along tourist routes. A comfortable alternative is MadaBus (www.madabus.com) which runs a fleet of buses along the popular tourist routes. Their office is in Antananarivo and more details are given in the *Getting there* sections in this book.

TAXI-BROUSSE
Vehicles *Taxi-brousses* are generally minibuses or sometimes Renault vans with seats facing each other (sometimes known as *kat-kat*). A *baché* is a small van with a

canvas top. More comfortable are the Peugeot 404s or 504s designed to take nine people, but often packed with 14 or more. A *car-brousse* is usually a Tata sturdy enough to cope with bad roads. *Kat-kat* is also used in the northeast for the 4x4 vehicles which are needed to cope with the atrocious roads. The back is covered with a tarpaulin and there are no seats: you sit on your luggage. For even worse conditions, you may find a *tracteur-brousse*!

Practicalities Vehicles leave from a *gare routière* (bus station) on the side of town closest to their destination. You should try to go there a day or two ahead of your planned departure to check times and prices, and for long journeys you should buy a ticket in advance (from the kiosk – don't give your money to a ticket tout). Daniel and Kelly, who made 'several dozen' *taxi-brousse* journeys in 2006 comment: 'Arriving at a *taxi-brousse* station can be a scary experience. You are likely to get mobbed by people demanding to know where you are going and insisting they know the best service for you. Some of the mob will even jump into a moving taxi with you! I generally tell them I already have a ticket, then walk determinedly to one of the offices before starting discussions with someone I know is official. Most offices display a board showing the official prices to different towns. It is often a lottery when choosing which company to use. MAMI seems to be a particularly reliable choice. On one occasion when they were forced to cancel a departure on which we had reserved seats, the MAMI official immediately organised a *taxi-brousse* with a different company, and we left almost on our original schedule.

'I would advise paying a deposit in advance – to secure the seat – but it's safest not to pay in full till the actual day, once you're sitting in the actual seats you booked. *Taxi-brousse* staff are generally honest and won't try to run off with your money or overcharge you, but you will sometimes find that your booking gets moved to a different seat or even onto a different *taxi-brousse* service.'

Frances Kerridge adds: 'Never be late for a *taxi-brousse*. Some of them do leave on time, especially on popular journeys or if the departure time is horrendous, eg: 2am. Get there early to claim your seat, then read your book, write your diary or whatever. Be ready with soap and towel for a bath stop. Follow the women and children to get some degree of privacy.'

Stuart Riddle adds this advice on how to survive a long-distance *taxi-brousse* journey. 'The priority is to choose your seat carefully. The best seats are on the row behind the driver because there is more leg room. The worst seats for leg room are the back row of Toyotas. This is also the noisiest area and you will be fighting for space with children and chickens.

'On overnight journeys prepare for the cold nights even though the sun may be beating down when you leave. Try to get a window seat so you can control the temperature. The warmest seat is next to the driver, because of the heat of the engine, but this can be uncomfortably hot and the driver will wake you each time he changes gear. The dazzle of oncoming headlights is also a problem.

'Your driver will play loud music throughout the night. The speakers are usually at the back so sitting near the front brings some relief. [Some travellers

DISTANCES FROM TANA IN KILOMETRES

Antananarivo–Ambositra	259km	Antananarivo–Morondava	701km
Antananarivo–Antsirabe	169km	Antananarivo–Andasibe	142km
Antananarivo–Fianarantsoa	412km	Antananarivo–Toamasina	360km
Antananarivo–Mahajanga	561km	Antananarivo–Toliara	952km

Taxi-brousses are improving, especially on the main tourist routes, but I couldn't resist repeating these entertaining stories!

At about 10 o'clock we (two people) went to the *taxi-brousse* station. "Yes, yes, there is a car. It is here, ready to go." We paid our money. "When will it go?" "When it has nine passengers." "How many has it got now?" "Wait a minute." A long look at notebooks, then a detailed calculation. "Two." "As well as us?" "No, no, including you." It finally left at about 7 o'clock.'

Chris Ballance

After several hours we picked up four more people. We couldn't believe it – the driver had to sit on someone's lap!

Stephen Cartledge

At last we were under way. I had my knees jammed up against the iron bar at the back of the row in front where sat a very sick soldier, who spent most of the journey with his head out of the window spewing lurid green bile at passers-by like something from a horror-movie… After about 20 minutes we had to stop at a roadside stall to buy mangoes. Since I was now on the sunny side of the vehicle the temperature of my shirt rose to what, had it been made of polyester, would have been melting point. Our next stop was Antsirabe where we were surrounded by about 50 apple vendors and all and sundry went absolutely berserk. I hadn't seen so many apples since…since we left Ambositra. At about 5pm the radio was turned on so we could listen to two men shouting at each other at a volume which would have caused bleeding of the eardrums in Wembley Stadium. When one passenger complained, our driver managed to find a few extra decibels. At about 6pm it started to get decidedly brisk, and since the ailing squaddie in front of me showed no sign of having rid himself of toxic enzymes I now had to endure an icy blast in my face. Our next stop was for grapes. We now had enough fruit on board to start a wholesale business in Covent Garden, and I was a bit tetchy.

Robert Stewart

We eventually made it after an eventful four-hour *taxi-brousse* journey which entailed the obligatory trawl around town for more passengers, selling the spare tyre shortly after setting off, a 30-minute wait outside the doctor's as the driver wasn't feeling very well, and all of us having to bump-start the vehicle every time we stopped to pick anyone up.

H & M Kendrick

I woke up nice and early to get my *taxi-brousse* to Mahamasina from Diego. I clambered on to a nice new minibus, eager to hit the open road. There was one other passenger. We cruised around for three hours, frequently changing drivers, trying to get more customers. In this time our driver got into three fights, one lasting half an hour. There was even a tug-of-war with passengers, which looked quite painful, to persuade them to use their *taxi-brousse*.

Ben Tapley

On one memorable trip from Fianar to Tana the back three seats were stacked high with crates of chicks which chirped noisily for the full ten hours. In addition to the breakdowns we've come to expect, we drove through a fire, came close to colliding with at least one oncoming vehicle, dodged an exploding tyre from the truck in front, and a chicken lost its life under our wheels!

Kelly Green

recommend bringing your own favourite cassettes and hoping to persuade the driver to play them.]

'Motion sickness is often a problem even if you've never experienced it before. Be prepared with pills as well as waterproof plastic bags and tissues.' The front window seat is probably the best for people prone to motion sickness.

On short journeys and in remote areas, vehicles simply leave as soon as they fill up. Or if they have a schedule expect them to leave hours late, and always be prepared (with warm clothing, fruit, water etc) for a night trip, even if you thought it was leaving in the morning.

There is no set rate per kilometre; fares are calculated on the quality of the vehicle, the roughness of the road and the time the journey takes. They are set by the government and *vazaha* are only occasionally overcharged. Ask other passengers what they are paying, or trust the driver. *Taxi-brousses* are very cheap. It should not cost you more than US$10 for an all-day journey. Faster routes (tarred roads) may be a bit more expensive. Passengers are occasionally charged for luggage that is strapped on to the roof, but this is not how the system works so refuse politely.

Drivers stop to eat, but usually drive all night. If they do stop during the night most passengers stay in the vehicle or sleep on the road outside.

There is much that a committed overland traveller can do to soften his/her experiences on *taxi-brousses* – see page 99. If you're prepared for the realities, an overland journey can be very enjoyable and gives you a chance to get to know the Malagasy. And before you get too depressed and cancel your trip, remember that on the popular routes there are normal buses with one seat per passenger. The above (and the box) mainly pertains to adventurous journeys away from the *Routes Nationales*.

✈ **BY AIR** Air Madagascar started its life in 1962 as Madair but understandably changed its name after a few years of jokes. Most people now call it Air Mad. Since coming under the control of Lufthansa the unprofitable domestic routes have been reduced or cancelled. See map on page 108 for their current destinations. At the time of writing the cost of flying from Tana to Toliara, Taolagnaro or Nosy Be (one way) was US$130 low season or US$150 high season. Remember that you can get a 50% discount on domestic flights providing you chose Air Mad as your international carrier.

Air Madagascar has the following planes: Boeing 767 for international routes, two Boeing 737s, with 130 seats, to the larger cities and Nosy Be, the smaller ATR 49-seater turbo props, and the little 19-seater Twin Otters to the smaller towns. The recent rise in tourism in Madagascar has brought more passengers than Air Mad can cope with, particularly at peak holiday times. Try to book in advance through a tour operator. If you are doing your bookings once you arrive, avoid the crush by getting to the Air Mad office when it opens in the morning, or use one of the many very competent travel agents in the capital.

Often flights which are said to be fully booked in Antananarivo are found to have seats when you reapply at the town of departure. Rupert Parker, a frequent traveller to Madagascar, reveals his secret: 'Because you are still allowed to make a reservation without payment, flights always appear full, but the trick is to go to the airport two hours in advance and put your ticket on the counter. The *liste d'attente* works on a first-come-first-served basis and half an hour before the flight is due to leave they start filling the empty seats, taking the tickets in order of arrival. We have never, in ten years, been disappointed.' Conversely, passengers with booked seats who check in late will find their seats sold to waiting-list passengers. Always arrive at least an hour before the scheduled departure, and add your ticket to the 'queue' of tickets on the counter.

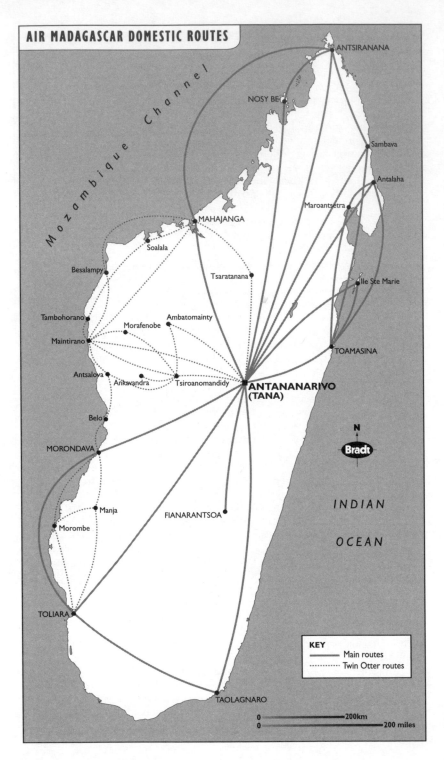

AIR MADAGASCAR DOMESTIC ROUTES

ANTSIRANANA

NOSY BE

Sambava

Antalaha

Maroantsetra

MAHAJANGA

Soalala

Besalampy

Tsaratanana

Ile Ste Marie

Tambohorano

Morafenobe

Ambatomainty

Maintirano

TOAMASINA

Antsalova

Ankavandra

Tsiroanomandidy

ANTANANARIVO
(TANA)

Belo

MORONDAVA

N

Bradt

Manja

FIANARANTSOA

INDIAN

Morombe

OCEAN

Mozambique Channel

TOLIARA

KEY
—— Main routes
.... Twin Otter routes

0 ——————— 200km
0 ——————— 200 miles

TAOLAGNARO

Hand luggage should weigh no more than 5kg. Passengers should not be surprised if they are weighed *themselves* before a Twin Otter flight. It's not that there's a tax on fat people; they're just gathering the info for some take-off weight calculations. It is useful to know that *Enregistrement Bagages* is the check-in counter and *Livraison Bagages* is luggage arrival.

There are no numbered seats on internal flights, which are non-smoking. And a warning: there are no toilets in a Twin Otter!

Although no longer a requirement, you are recommended to reconfirm your seat a day before departure.

Air Madagascar schedules are reviewed twice-yearly, at the end of March and the end of October, but are subject to change at any time and without notice. Their website is regularly updated (www.airmadagascar.mg). The phone number in Antananarivo is ✆ +261 20 22 22 222.

With a shortage of aircraft and pilots, planes are sometimes delayed or cancelled. Almost always there is a perfectly good reason: mechanical problems, bad weather. Air Mad is improving and on the whole they provide as reliable a service as one can expect in a poor country.

A new private company, ATTR (Air Transport et Transit Régional) is launching flights between 11 airports: Antananarivo, Antalaha, Antsiranana, Mahajanga, Maroantsetra, Nosy Be, Sainte-Marie, Sambava, Taolagnaro, Toamasina and Toliara. They are using SAAB aircraft and a mixture of Malagasy and South African pilots.

BY BOAT The Malagasy are traditionally a seafaring people (remember that 6,000km journey from Indonesia) and in the absence of roads, their stable outrigger canoes are used to cover quite long sea distances. Pirogues without outriggers are used extensively on the rivers and canals of the watery east. Quite a few adventurous travellers use pirogues for sections of their journeys. Romantic though it may be to sail in an outrigger canoe, it can be both uncomfortable and, at times, dangerous.

Ferries and cargo boats travel to the larger islands and down the west coast (see box on page 423).

River journeys are becoming increasingly popular as a different way of seeing the country.

BY RAIL After years of deterioration, Madagascar's railways have been privatised. The line between Fianarantsoa and Manakara on the east coast is giving a reliable, enjoyable service, and there is talk about the line from Antananarivo to Toamasina being restored.

TRANSPORT WITHIN CITIES

Buses Most cities have cheap buses but few travellers use them because of the difficulty in understanding the route system. No reason not to give it a try, however. Andrew Shimmin says: 'I would strongly recommend travelling around Tana and Antsirabe by bus – an absolute bargain, people smiley, and really seeing the real city.'

Taxis Taxi rates have gone up in recent years because of a sharp rise in fuel prices, but they are still reasonable. Taxis have no meters, so you must agree on the price before you get in. However, within most cities taxis operate at a set rate.

Rickshaws (Pousse-pousses) *Pousse-pousses* were introduced into Madagascar by British missionaries who wanted to replace the traditional palanquin with its association with slavery. The name is said to originate from the time they operated in the capital and needed an additional man behind to push up the steep hills. They are now a Madagascar speciality and are mostly pulled by a running man, although pedal rickshaws have been introduced to Toamasina. Most towns have *pousse-pousses* – the exceptions are the hilly towns of the highlands.

Many Western visitors are reluctant to sit in comfort behind a running, ragged, sweating man and no-one with a heart can fail to feel compassion for the *pousse-pousse* pullers. However, this is a case of needing to abandon our own cultural hang-ups. These men want work. Bargain hard (before you get in) and make sure you have the exact money. It would be optimistic to expect change. A medium-length journey will generally cost around 4,000Ar. If you don't feel like bargaining, two dollars will do nicely. *Pousse-pousse* pullers love carrying soft-hearted tourists and have become quite cunning – and tiresome – in their dealings with *vazaha*. However, remember how desperately these men need a little luck – and an innocent tourist could make their day!

HIRING (OR BRINGING) YOUR OWN TRANSPORT Tim Ireland puts it succinctly: 'The great pity is watching so many magnificent landscapes tear past your eyes as you strain your neck trying to get a better view past 15 other occupants of a *taxi-brousse*.' He goes on to recommend a mountain bike as the perfect means of transport, but a hired vehicle will achieve the same flexibility.

Car hire You would need to be a competent mechanic to hire a self-drive car in Madagascar, and generally cars come with chauffeurs (providing a local person with a job and you with a guide/interpreter). A few days on Madagascar's roads will cure you of any regret that you are not driving yourself. Night-time driving is particularly challenging: headlights often don't work or are not switched on. Your driver will know that the single light bearing down on you is more likely to be a wide truck than a narrow motorbike and react accordingly. The Merina Highway Code (informal version) decrees that drivers must honk their horns after crossing a bridge to ensure that the spirits are out of the way.

There are car-hire firms in most large towns. The regional tourist offices have information on these, or a local tour operator can organise it.

Peter Jourdier reports on his experiences of hiring a car plus driver. 'We hired a Nissan Patrol jeep from Budget Cars at a cost of 160,000Ar per day (€60); with tax at 18% the price was 188,000Ar per day. This included the driver plus his accommodation and food, but not fuel. We discovered on the first night that the driver was however not given enough money by Budget for both food and accommodation (he was going to sleep in the car), so we put him up, and he paid his food. (May have been a ploy to get more money, but we didn't think so). The fuel cost us about 300,000Ar each way (at 2,130Ar per litre). This was high as it was a huge and very thirsty 4x4.

'We only wanted to take the vehicle down to Tulear as we were flying back, but (as with all the rental companies I looked at) we had to pay an extra two days' rental after we left the jeep so that the driver could get it back to Tana. We also had to pay for the fuel both ways. Budget also put an extra charge of about 3% on if you pay by card.

'I did find other companies/individuals that were cheaper, but I when I asked, I found out the car would be about 10 years old, having spent its whole life on dodgy roads I was also slightly wary of insurance and the legality if we were stopped by police, so decided not to take the chance. Budget was then the cheapest of the more expensive group – Hertz was considerably more expensive, Dodo Travel had one for €70 a day (smaller car but same conditions as Budget).'

Peter goes on to praise his driver for his helpfulness and resourcefulness. The whole experience was very positive. I have had equally positive reports from readers who took the chance and hired a driver who approached them at the airport on arrival, or who arranged car hire through their hotel or B&B. For a saloon car, €60 per day including fuel and driver seems about average. See *Chapter 7* for more information.

Driving licence Here's some advice from Daniel Austin: 'Whilst hiring self-drive cars in Madagascar is unusual (and perhaps unwise), smaller vehicles like quads and buggies are hired a lot by visitors, and of course a driving licence will be required to take these on the roads. Apparently a British driving licence alone is acceptable in Madagascar, but we would recommend taking an International driving licence. They are more likely to be recognised by the police and so reduce possible complications. (The Malagasy love their bureaucracy – forms, signatures, stamps – so if you are stopped by police while driving, the more official-looking documents you can show them, the more impressed they will be, and the sooner you'll be on your way.) IDLs are available for about £5 from the AA, RAC, and a few post offices.'

Bicycle The French for mountain bike is VTT. Bikes can usually be hired in Antananarivo, Antsirabe, Taolagnaro (Fort Dauphin), Antsiranana (Diego Suarez) and Nosy Be. Or you can bring your own bike (see page 86) or buy one in Antananarivo.

ACCOMMODATION

Hotels in Madagascar are classified by a national star system – five star being the highest. There is, at present, no five-star hotel in Madagascar, although the soon-to-be-opened lodge in Nosy Iranja aims to be the first.

In recent years upper- and mid-range hotels have been brought up to international standard, and visitors looking for comfort should not be disappointed.

There is a tourist tax, *vignette touristique*, of between 3,000Ar and 600Ar per person per night. This is sometimes absorbed into the price, but is often added separately.

Outside the towns, hotels in the form of a single building are something of a rarity. Accommodation is usually in bungalows which are often constructed of local materials and are quiet, atmospheric and comfortable.

A word about bolsters. Visitors using mid-range hotels, who are not accustomed to the ways of France, may be disconcerted to find a firm, sheet-covered sausage anchored to the top of the bed. In the better hotels you can usually find a pillow hidden away in a cupboard. Failing that, I make my own pillow with a sweater stuffed into a T-shirt.

Breakfast is rarely included in the room price, and if it is it'll be continental breakfast or Malagasy breakfast (just dry bread and black coffee). Exceptions to this general rule are always mentioned in the hotel listings.

PRICING IN THIS BOOK Lists of accommodation rank hotels in strict decreasing order of price (based on a typical double room). Larger hotel lists are subdivided by price-category headings: Luxury, Top end, Upper range, Mid range, Budget and Penny-pincher.

Luxury 👑	250,000Ar (€95/£65/US$127 & up)
Top end €€€€€	150,000–250,000Ar (€57/£40/US$77 & up)
Upper range €€€€	65,000–250,000Ar (€25/£17/US$33 & up)
Mid range €€€	25,000–65,000Ar (€10/£6.50/US$13 & up)
Budget €€	10,000–25,000Ar (€3.80/£2.61/US$5.00 & up)
Penny-pincher €	Below 10,000Ar

This key is repeated inside the front cover.

HOTEL CATEGORIES: WHAT YOU GET FOR YOUR MONEY

Luxury The top hotels and lodges are truly luxurious, and will cost around € 150. They are, without exception, foreign-owned, but most show a good sensitivity to the needs of the local people. One such French owner explained that as foreigners their conscience dictates that they do not appear as neo-colonials so go out of their way to contribute to community-based projects.

Top end These are either a cut above the average upper-range hotel or are in an expensive part of Madagascar, such as Nosy Be, where all prices are higher than average.

Upper range These are very comfortable hotels which can be found in all major towns and tourist centres. They have all the trappings that upmarket tourists expect: TV, mini-bar, and perhaps a business centre with internet connections. All have en-suite bathrooms and spacious restaurants with good food. The larger ones are popular with groups, so check the number of rooms if you're looking for a more intimate atmosphere.

Mid range These are often just as clean and comfortable, and most have en-suite bathrooms. There will be no TV beaming CNN into your bedroom, but you should have comfortable beds though bolsters are the norm. The hotels are often family-run and very friendly. The average price is about £15/€21/US$28.

Budget and penny-pincher In early editions I described these as 'exhilaratingly dreadful at times' until a reader wrote: 'We were rather disappointed by the quality of these hotels … We found almost all the beds comfortable, generally acceptably clean, and not one rat. We felt luxuriously cheated!' However, the following description from Rupert Parker of a hotel in Brickaville should gladden the masochistic heart, '… a conglomeration of shacks directly beneath the road bridge. The rooms are partitioned-off spaces, just large enough to hold a bed, in a larger wooden building – the partitions don't reach to the ceiling and there is only one light bulb for all the rooms – the hotel manageress controls the switch. Not only can you hear everyone's conversation and what they're up to, but when there is a new arrival, at whatever time of the night, the light comes on and wakes everyone up – that is if you've managed to ignore the rumbling and revving of trucks as they cross the bridge above you, or the banging on the gate which announces a new arrival. Suffice to say the toilet and washing facilities are non-existent.' It would be rather a shame if they've improved it in the intervening years!

Such hotels certainly give the flavour of how Madagascar used to be, and in remote areas you will still find the occasional sagging double bed and stinking hole toilet. Usually you can find the toilet by the smell, but ask for the WC ('dooble vay say'), not *toilette* which usually means shower or bathroom. In these hotels used toilet paper should not be thrown into the pan but into the box provided for it. Not very nice, but preferable to a clogged loo.

Most of the Budget hotels in this book are clean, friendly and excellent value. In an out-of-the-way place you will pay as little as £1/€1.50/US$2 for the most basic room. For this you get a bed, candle, mozzie coil, and ripped mozzie net. In small towns about £2.50/€3.75/US$5 would be average. For this price you will get a shared toilet – of sorts.

Hotely usually means a restaurant/snack bar rather than accommodation, but it's always worth asking if they have rooms.

Most *Mid-range* and *Budget* hotels will do your washing for you at a very reasonable price. This gives employment to local people and is an important element of responsible travel. In *Upper-range* and *Top-end* hotels laundry can be disproportionately expensive!

WEBSITES If you want to check hotel listings the following are good general websites:

www.madagascar-guide.com
www.tourisme.gov.mg
www.vanilland.com/hotelcentremada.html

⚠ CAMPING Until very recently Madagascar had no official campsites, although backpackers with their own tent were often allowed to camp in hotel gardens. National parks-style camping is usually on a wooden platform with a thatched roof above. Very comfortable, but if you have your own tent make sure it is self-standing since there is nowhere to drive in the tent pegs..

Self-contained backpackers will know the wonderful sense of freedom that comes with carrying their own tent – there is all of Madagascar to explore!

African-style mobile safari camping has recently been introduced to Madagascar. See www.madaclassic.com.

✗ EATING AND DRINKING

FOOD Eating well is one of the delights of Madagascar, and even the fussiest tourists are usually happy with the food. International hotels serve international food, usually with a French bias, and often do special Malagasy dishes. Lodges and smaller hotels serve local food which is almost always excellent, particularly on the coast where lobster (crayfish), shellfish and other seafood predominates. Meat lovers will enjoy the zebu steaks, although they are often tougher than we are used to (free-range meat usually is). Outside the capital, most hotels offer a set menu (*table d'hôte* or *menu*) to their guests. This can cost as little as 5,000Ar/€2.00/£1.35/US$2.50. At the upper end you can expect to pay around 30,000Ar/€11.50/£7.80/US$15.30 for that special treat.

Where the menu is *à la carte* it is a help to have a French dictionary or phrasebook.

The national dish in Madagascar is *romazava* (pronounced 'roomazahv'), a meat and vegetable stew, spiced with ginger and containing *brèdes* (pronounced 'bread'), tasty, tongue-tingling greens. Another good local dish is *ravitoto*, shredded manioc leaves with fried beef and coconut. Volker Dorheim adds: 'If you like your food really spicy ask for *pimente verde*. If this isn't hot enough ask for *pimente malgache*.' And Sebastian Bulmer tells me that all Malagasy restaurants grind to a halt when the nation's favourite soap, *Terra Nostra*, comes on!

Independent travellers on a tight budget will find Chinese restaurants in every town; these are almost always good and reasonably priced. *Soupe Chinoise* is available nearly everywhere, and is filling and tasty. The Malagasy eat a lot of rice, but most restaurants cater to foreign tastes by providing chips (French fries). Away from the tourist routes, however, most dishes are accompanied by a sticky mound of rice, sometimes embellished with small stones, so chew with caution!

For a real Malagasy meal, eat at a *hotely*. These are often open-sided shacks where the menu is chalked up on a blackboard: *henan-omby* (or *hen'omby*) – beef, *henan-borona* (or *hen'akoho*) – chicken, *henan-kisoa* – pork, *henan-drano* (or *hazan-drano*) – fish. Other dishes include: *tsaramasy* (rice with beans and pork), *vary sosoa* (rice pudding), *mofo boule* or *mofogasy* (slightly sweet bread rolls), and *koba* (rice and banana, wrapped in a leaf and served in slices). The menu may end with *Mazotoa homana*. This is not a dish, it means *Bon appétit*!

Along with the meat or fish and inevitable mound of rice (*vary*) comes a bowl of stock. This is spooned over the rice, or drunk as a soup.

Thirst is quenched with *ranovola* (pronounced 'ranoovool') obtained by boiling water in the pan in which the rice was cooked. It has a slight flavour of burnt rice, and since it has been boiled for several minutes it is safe to drink.

For do-it-yourself meals there is a great variety of fruit and vegetables, even in the smallest market. A selection of fruit is served in most restaurants, along with raw vegetables or *crudités*. From June to August the fruit is mostly limited to citrus and bananas, but from September there are also strawberries, mangoes, lychees, pineapples and loquats. As an extra special treat you may come across mangosteen (see box on page 291). Slices of coconut are sold everywhere, but especially on the coast where coconut milk is a popular and safe drink, and toffee-coconut nibbles are sold on the street, often wrapped in paper from school exercise books.

Madagascar's dairy industry is growing (not surprising – it was the former occupation of President Ravalomanana). There are some good, locally produced cheeses and Malagasy yoghurt is excellent and available in even the smallest shops. Try the drinking yoghurt, *yaourt à boire*.

Finally, if you're a chocoholic, you'll be happy to learn about Madagascar's award-winning chocolate. The very best chocolate is for export only, so if you've bought this book in the fond hope that one day you'll get to Madagascar you can get a taste of the country by buying the Mora Mora or Sambirano chocolate bars in Waitrose or on-line from www.malagasy.co.uk. When in the country look out for Chocolat Robert. It's excellent!

Vegetarian food Madagascar is becoming more accustomed to *vazaha* vegetarians and with patience you can usually order meatless dishes even at small *hotelys*. *Tsy misy hena* means 'without meat'. Stuart Riddle, a vegetarian, 'had all sorts of problems, but also found some gems'.

DRINK The most popular drink, Three Horses Beer (THB), is wonderful on a hot day. I think it's wonderful on a cold day, too. The price goes up according to the surroundings: twice as much in the Hilton as in a *hotely* and there is always a hefty deposit payable on the bottle. A newish beer is Queens, which is slightly weaker, and there is also Gold. Why does the Star brewery give its beer English names that the Malagasy can't pronounce? And why horses and queens when the country has few of either (and not much gold)? I don't know. Actually I do – it was a marketing ploy.

Madagascar produces its own wine in the Fianarantsoa region, and some is very good. L'azani Betsileo (*blanc* or *gris*, *reservé*) is recommended.

A pleasant aperitif is Maromby (the name means 'many zebu') and I have been told that Litchel, made from lychees, is good. Rum, *toaka gasy*, is very cheap and plentiful, especially in sugar-growing areas such as Nosy Be; and fermented sugar cane juice, *betsabetsa* (east coast), or fermented coconut milk, *trembo* (north), make a change. *Rhum arrangé* is found in most locally-run hotels: fruit slices soaked in rum. The best cocktail is *punch coco*, with a coconut-milk base, which is a speciality of the coastal areas. Yummy!

The most popular mineral water is called Eau Vive, but other brands are now available: Olympiko and La Source. Tiko, which produces Olympiko and cartons of very good fresh juice, also make their own Cola and some nice Classico soft drinks (their lemon-lime is recommended by a reader). It's nice to be able to support a local company rather than the internationals, although Coca-Cola and other popular soft drinks such as Sprite and Fanta are available. Fresh is an agreeable shandy, and Tonic is – you guessed it – tonic water. The locally produced *limonady* sadly bears no resemblance to lemons, and Bon Bon Anglais is revolting (although I do know one *anglaise* who rather likes it!). Caffeine-addicts have a problem. The coffee is OK – just – if taken black, but often only condensed milk is available. I find that one quickly regresses to childhood and surreptitiously spoons the condensed milk not into the coffee but into the mouth. If you prefer unsweetened white coffee it might be better to bring your own powdered milk.

The locally grown tea is very weak, the best quality being reserved for export. A nice alternative is *citronelle*, lemon-grass tea, which is widely available.

☞ *WARNINGS!* If you are travelling on a prepaid packaged tour, you may be disconcerted to find that you are charged for coffee and tea along with drinks. These beverages count as 'extras' in Madagascar.

The Malagasy are enthusiastic smokers and non-smoking restaurants, or sections in restaurants, are a rarity.

PUBLIC HOLIDAYS

The Malagasy take their holidays seriously. In every town and village there will be a parade with speeches and an air of festivity. 'New Year was celebrated throughout the night, and on New Year's Day everyone paraded their new clothes through the streets in a Malagasy version of an Easter Parade. New Year parties were held by every conceivable organisation during the next two months.' (Bryan and Eve Pinches)

OFFICIAL HOLIDAYS

1 January	New Year's Day
29 March	Commemoration of 1947 rebellion
Easter Monday (movable)	
1 May	Labour Day
Ascension Day (movable)	
Whit Monday (movable)	
26 June	Independence Day
15 August	Feast of the Assumption
1 November	All Saints' Day
25 December	Christmas Day
30 December	Republic Day

When these holidays fall on a Thursday, Friday will be tacked on to the weekend. Banks and other businesses often take a half-day holiday before the official holiday.

SHOPPING

You can buy just about everything in the handicrafts line in Madagascar. Most typical of the country are woodcarvings, raffia work (in amazing variety), crocheted and embroidered table-cloths and clothes, leather goods, carved zebu horn, *Antaimoro* paper (with embedded dried flowers) marquetry and so on. The choice is almost limitless, and it can all be seen in the handicrafts markets and shops in Antananarivo and throughout the country.

In the south you can buy attractive heavy silver bracelets that are traditionally worn by men. In Tana, and the east and north (Nosy Be), you will be offered vanilla pods, peppercorns, cloves and other spices, and honey.

Almost anywhere you will find shops selling *lambas*.

Do not buy products from endangered species. That includes tortoiseshell (turtle shell), snake skins (now crocodiles are farmed commercially, their skins may be sold legally), shells and coral and, of course, live animals. Butterflies are farmed commercially so buying mounted specimens is permitted. Also prohibited are endemic plants, fossils and any genuine article of funerary art. To tell turtle shell from zebu horn, hold it up to the light: turtle shell is semi-transparent.

To help stamp out the sale of endangered animal products, tourists should make their feelings – and the law – known. If, for instance, you are offered tortoise or turtle shell, tell the vendor it is *interdit*; and to push the point home you could say it is *fady* for you to buy such a thing.

The luggage weight-limit when leaving Madagascar is normally 20kg – bear this in mind when doing your shopping.

BARGAINING It always seems strange to me that people who think nothing of slipping a dollar to the doorman who heaves their bags from the pavement to the hotel lobby will spend five minutes trying to cut the same amount off a beautifully crafted woodcarving that may have taken its maker weeks to complete. Yes, in my early days of travelling on a tight budget I too bargained hard. I had no option. Now, if I think the price is fair, I'm quite happy to pay it. If it's really true that you lose the respect of the vendor if you don't bargain – well, I can cope with that. There'll be plenty of Real Travellers boasting about how they beat him down to less than half to balance my foolishness. And after all, no-one really minds getting more money than they expected.

SEMI-PRECIOUS STONES Madagascar is a rewarding place for gem hunters, with citrin, tourmaline and beryl inexpensive and easy to find. The solitaire sets using these stones

THE MUSIC OF MADAGASCAR

Derek Schuurman & Paddy Bush

Like everything else in Madagascar, the island's music portrays characteristics from other parts of the world but the end result is uniquely Malagasy.

Justin Vali (Justin Rakotondrasoa) – a Merina from the *hauts plateaux* – is today the country's best-known Malagasy musician outside of his country. Apart from Vali, other Malagasy musicians who have enjoyed success abroad include D'Gary, who has a huge following in Canada and USA; Regis Gizavo; Jojoby, the King of *Salegy*, who is once again performing after a near-fatal car accident; the band Tarika, which was highly rated in an international *Time Magazine* poll a few years ago; and Mahaleo, the Malagasy version of the Beatles, who have been going strong since the 1970s and whose songs contain profound lyrical content.

Many western instruments have found their way into Malagasy music. It is not uncommon to see accordions in particular, but also clarinets and certain brass instruments, being played at the colourful *hira gasy* events. On the other hand, visit a vibrant nightclub and you'll very likely see contemporary musicians belting out thumping dance tracks using modern electric and bass guitars and synthesisers.

The national instrument is the *valiha*, which belongs to the family of tube and box zithers. This fascinating instrument goes back generations in Justin Vali's family, who both make and play it. The original or 'ancestral' form of valiha is constructed from certain rare species of bamboo, known as volo ('hair from the ground' – a wonderful way to describe bamboo!). *Valiha* are of great spiritual significance and have been played for centuries in ceremonies sacred to the razana (ancestors).

The *valiha* is thought to have arrived some 2,000 years ago from southeast Asia, where various forms of the instrument are still to be found in the Borneo and Philippines region. In these areas it is also an instrument of the spiritual world, being used in ceremonies to appease animistic forest spirits.

are typical and most attractive. The centre for gems is traditionally Antsirabe but they are for sale in many highland towns, and now Ilakaka, the town that has sprung up at the centre of the sapphire rush, is the main hub. If you buy uncut stones bear in mind the cost of having them cut at home. Better to have it done in Tana, if you have time.

🎭 ARTS AND ENTERTAINMENT

MUSIC Malagasy music is distinctive and justly famous. See box opposite.

Finding good local music is a hit and miss affair when travelling. Often your best bet is to look out for posters advertising concerts. These are often put up near the *gare routière*.

CINEMA Films are dubbed into French; Bruce Lee is one of the most popular stars.

TELEVISION Posh hotels have CNN but the local station shows BBC World Service news at 09.00.

MEDIA AND COMMUNICATION

NEWSPAPERS AND MAGAZINES The main daily newspapers are the *Madagascar Tribune* (in French; www.madagascar-tribune.com) which tends to follow the government line and is relatively upmarket, and *Midi Madagasikara* the paper with the highest circulation but little international news. *L'Express* (in French and

The bamboo from which *valiha* is made must be cut during the three-day period during a full moon, which is when the plants are apparently free of certain insects – otherwise months later they will emerge from eggs laid inside and destroy the instrument. (I have seen this happen when a friend tried to import a huge consignment of *valiha*, only to have them ruined by the insects; we were forced to make an enormous bonfire consisting of hundreds of contaminated *valiha*!)

The *valiha* has a royal heritage: according to Justin Vali, King Radama II was a superb composer. During his reign Queen Victoria gave him a piano, which resulted in the standardising of *valiha*-tuning into diatonic form – called *lalandava* ('straight road') – corresponding to the white notes on a keyboard. One of the most legendary players of the instrument, the late Rakotozafy, built himself a *marovany*-like *valiha* out of sheet iron, and today his music is still widely played on the island's radio stations.

The *marovany*, unlike the tube *valiha*, appears to have African origins. It is tuned in a very different way and is played in the coastal regions where the African influence is more apparent than in the highlands. If you happen to be in the right places in Madagascar, searching for recordings of Malagasy music, and you want to hear phenomenal *marovany* players, ask for Madame Masy, Bekamby, Daniel Tomo or Albi, to name a few of the best.

In recent years, there has been an explosion of CDs of Malagasy music; good websites on which to find these include:

www.discovermadagascar.co.uk – from which you can order, among others, The Sunshine Within, a beautiful album by Justin Vali.

www.madagate.com
www.frootsmag.com/content/madagascar/cdography

Paddy Bush is a musicologist. He is one of very few westerners to have mastered playing the marovany and valiha, and has performed in the UK with Justin Vali.

Malagasy; www.midi-madagasikara.mg) is a daily newspaper read mainly by intellectuals (in French and Malagasy; www.lexpressmada.com). A similarly intelligent paper is *La Gazette de la Grande Ile* (www.lagazette-dgi.com) which often has articles on local culture.

Dans les Média Demain is an independent weekly magazine, and *Revue de l'Océan Indien – Madagascar* appears monthly. For wildlife enthusiasts and conservationists, the WWF publishes *Vintsy* (see *Further Information*, page 462).

✆ **TELEPHONE** You can buy phone cards for 25, 50, 100 and 150 units and use them for overseas calls from most public phone boxes (Publiphone). Only cream-coloured phones do international calls. Rates are much cheaper in the evenings after 22.00 and on Sundays.

The telephone code for landlines in Madagascar is 261 20 (+ town code + the number). If calling from a cellphone, replace the 20 with 30, 32, 33 or 34.

Below are the phone codes for all of Madagascar (this information is repeated under the relevant town information).

Antananarivo (Tana)	➘ 22 or 24	Manakara	➘ 72
Antsirabe	➘ 44	Moramanga	➘ 56
Antsiranana (Diego Suarez)	➘ 82	Morondava	➘ 95
Farafangana	➘ 72	Nosy Be	➘ 86
Fianarantsoa (Fianar)	➘ 75	Sambava	➘ 88
Ile Sainte Marie	➘ 57	Taolagnaro (Fort Dauphin)	➘ 92
Mahajanga (Majunga)	➘ 62	Toamasina (Tamatave)	➘ 53
Maintirano	➘ 69	Toliara (Tulear)	➘ 94

Cellphones Cellphones (mobile phones) are very popular in Madagascar, leading to the incongruous scene of a *pousse-pousse* passenger deep in phone-conversation. Kim Loohuis reports: 'I took my mobile phone to Madagascar and bought a new prepaid SIM-card (Orange or Madacom). Everywhere in the country you will find recharges for your phone. The network is more or less the same for Orange or Madacom and works only in the bigger towns. It is much cheaper to call or text with a Malagasy SIM that with your own.'

 MAIL The mail service is reasonably efficient; letters take about two weeks to reach Europe and a little longer to North America. Stamps are quite expensive and postcards do not always arrive (some postal workers prefer to steam off the stamps and chuck the cards). The smaller post offices often run out of stamps, but some hotels sell them.

COURIER SERVICE Colis Express hooks up with DHL. There is an office in Tana (see page 173) and in all the large towns.

e **INTERNET** Cybercafés or internet offices are established in all major towns and tourist centres, with Broadband increasingly available. The prices vary a lot, depending on the competition. Be warned that the keyboards are usually French, not English-Qwerty, which is intensely frustrating if you are normally a fast typist. Also the offices in coastal towns are always stiflingly hot; I drip steadily over the keyboard while searching for the elusive y that forms part of my name.

BUSINESS HOURS

Most businesses open 08.00–12.00 and 14.00–18.00. Banks are open 08.00–16.00, and are closed at weekends and the afternoon before a holiday.

5

Health and Safety

Dr Jane Wilson-Howarth

BEFORE YOU GO

MALARIA PREVENTION Take advice from a travel clinic, your GP or the website www.fitfortravel.scot.nhs.uk. Malaria (including cerebral malaria) is a risk in Madagascar including in the High Plateau and it is crucial to protect yourself by avoiding bites especially between dusk and dawn and also by taking tablets. There is chloroquine resistance so it is important to take one of the kinds of prescribed antimalarial tablets. The choice is between weekly mefloquine (Lariam) or daily Malarone or daily doxycycline. Lariam and doxycycline cost about £25 for a two-week trip. Perhaps around one quarter of people who try Lariam will experience unacceptable side effects, so take it for two and a half weeks (three doses) before departure and if it makes you feel weird or gives you nightmares stop it and take another regime. A good alternative, although unsuitable in pregnancy, while breast-feeding or in children under 12, is doxycycline capsules daily. There is a possibility of photosensitivity (in up to 5% of users) and so this may not be the best prophylactic if you plan to do a lot of sunbathing. Ensure that you use factor 15+ SPF suncream and long clothes to protect you. Malarone, a once a day preparation, is another good alternative although few doctors will prescribe it for more than three months because of current licensing restrictions. It is by far the most expensive prophylactic: it will cost you about £90 for a two-week trip.

All prophylactics have the potential to cause side effects and are best taken after food (or milk or biscuits); nausea is more likely if they are taken on an empty stomach. If pregnant or planning a pregnancy take medical advice before travelling. Some travellers like to carry tablets for the emergency treatment of malaria; if you choose to do this make sure you understand when and how to take them, and carry a digital thermometer.

Take plenty of insect repellent; DEET-based is best; try some before you go and if it irritates your skin look for a product based on Merck 3535. Loose-fitting outfits with long-sleeved shirts and long trousers will allow you to cover up at dusk; for additional protection you can spray your evening clothes with permethrin (eg: Bug Proof from Nomad). Consider carrying a mosquito net (see page 98). Bed-nets are most effective if treated with permethrin or a similar contact insecticide. Such treatment remains effective for six months; kits are sold at many travel clinics.

IMMUNISATIONS Seek advice about immunisations at least a couple of months before travel; in the UK you can see your GP or visit a travel clinic which offer frequently updated health briefs as well as immunisations. There is a list of vaccination centres at the end of this section. It is important that your immunisations for tetanus, polio and typhoid are up to date. The hepatitis A jab is recommended and two shots provide protection for at least ten years.

If you are flying to Tana from Nairobi you will need a certificate of immunisation against yellow fever. Consider shots against rabies if you are

Dr Jane Wilson-Howarth

Long-haul air travel increases the risk of deep vein thrombosis. This has been understood since 1946 when a doctor reported his own thrombosis after a 14-hour non-stop flight. Fortunately he survived, as do the vast majority of people who develop clots in their leg veins. Indeed recent research has suggested that most of us develop clots when immobilised but nearly all of them resolve without us ever having been aware of them. In certain susceptible individuals, though, large clots form and these can break away and lodge in the lungs. This is dangerous but happens in a tiny minority of passengers. Several conditions make the problem more likely. Immobility is the key and factors like reduced oxygen in cabin air and dehydration may also contribute. Moving about the cabin hourly should help avoid the problem and abstaining from excessive alcohol will prevent sedation and also dehydration which both exacerbate the situation. Taking sleeping pills on long flights is also unwise.

Studies have shown that flights of over five-and-a-half-hours are significant; also people who take lots of shorter flights over a short space of time form clots. People at highest risk are:

- Those who have had a clot before – unless they are now taking warfarin
- People over 80 years of age
- Anyone who has recently undergone a major operation or surgery for varicose veins
- Someone who has had a hip or knee replacement in the last three months
- Cancer sufferers
- Those who have ever had a stroke
- People with heart disease
- Those with a close blood relative who has had a clot – they may have an inherited tendency to clot because of LeidenV factor.

Those with a slightly increased risk:

travelling in remote areas. The disease is a problem in Madagascar because of the half-wild dogs found in many parts of the island; there is also a theoretical risk of rabies after lemur bites (see box on page 124).

TEETH If travelling off the beaten track, have a dental check-up before you go and if you have a lot of fillings and crowns carry a Dental Emergency Kit (from some pharmacies or ask your dentist).

INSURANCE Make sure you have insurance covering the cost of an air ambulance and treatment in Réunion or Nairobi, which offer more sophisticated medical facilities than are available in Madagascar. Europ Assistance International, which has an office in Antananarivo, gives cover for scuba-diving. Divers Aware Network (DAN) is the best insurance available for scuba-diving. With all insurance make sure that you tell them about any pre-existing problems when applying.

WATER STERILISATION Most traveller's diarrhoea comes from inadequately cooked, or reheated, contaminated food – salads, ice, ice cream etc – rather than from disobeying the 'don't drink the water' rule. Even so it is best to take care with what you drink. Bringing water to the boil kills all the microbes that are likely to make you ill so tea, coffee or *ranovola* (the water rice is boiled in) bought in *hotelys*

- People over 40
- Women who are pregnant or have had a baby in the last couple of weeks
- Women taking the combined oral contraceptive pill or HRT
- Heavy smokers
- Those who have very severe varicose veins
- The very obese
- People who are very tall (over 6ft/1.8m) or short (under 5ft/1.5m)

A deep vein thrombosis (DVT) is a clot of blood that forms in the deep leg veins. This is very different from irritating but harmless superficial phlebitis. DVT causes swelling and redness of one leg and there is usually heat and pain in one calf and sometimes the thigh. A DVT is only dangerous if a clot breaks away and travels to the lungs (pulmonary embolus). Symptoms of a pulmonary embolus (PE) include chest pain which is worse on breathing in deeply, shortness of breath and sometimes coughing up small amounts of blood. The symptoms commonly start three to ten days after a long flight. Anyone who thinks that they might have a DVT needs to see a doctor who will arrange a scan.

Treatment is usually to take warfarin tablets for six months or more.

PREVENTION OF DVT To reduce the risk of thrombosis on a long journey:
- Take a meal of oily fish in the 24 hours before departure
- Exercise before and after the flight
- Keep mobile during the flight; move around every 1-2 hours
- During the flight drink plenty of water or juices
- Avoid taking sleeping pills and excessive tea, coffee and alcohol
- Perform exercises that mimic walking and tense the calf muscles
- Consider wearing flight socks or support stockings (see www.legshealth.com)

The jury is still out on whether it is wise to take aspirin. If you think you are at increased risk of a clot ask your doctor if it is safe to travel.

are safe and convenient drinks. Mineral water is not always available, causes a litter problem and can be quite expensive, and studies in other countries suggest it may be contaminated. Chemical sterilisation methods do not render water as safe as by boiling, but it is good enough for most purposes. The cheapest and most effective sterilising agent is iodine (preferable to chlorine and silver because it kills amoebic cysts). Iodine comes in liquid or tablet or crystal form. To make treated water more palatable, add vitamin C after the sterilisation time is complete or bring packets of powdered drink. Silver-based sterilising tablets (sold in Britain under the trade name Micropur) are tasteless and have a long shelf life but are less effective than both iodine and chlorine products. An alternative is a water filter such as the Pur system or Aqua-pure Traveller, which provide safe water with no unpleasant flavour; they are expensive, however, and – like any filter – are prone to blockage, or to being lost! Cheaper and more versatile is a plug-in immersion heater, so that you can have a nice hot cuppa (bring teabags).

SOME TRAVELLERS' DISEASES

MALARIA AND INSECT-BORNE DISEASES Tablets do not give complete protection from malaria (though it will give you time to get treatment if it does break through) and there are other insect-borne diseases in Madagascar so it is important to protect yourself from being bitten. The *Anopheles* mosquitoes that spread malaria usually bite in the evening (from about 17.30) and throughout the night, so it is wise to dress in long trousers and long-sleeved shirts, and to cover exposed skin with insect repellent. These mosquitoes generally hunt at ankle level, and tend to bite the first piece of exposed flesh they encounter, so applying an effective repellent (DEET is best) to feet and ankles is important in reducing bites. In most countries, malaria transmission is rare in urban environments, but it does occur around Antananarivo because rice fields are so close to the city. Most hotels have screened windows or provide mosquito nets. Bring your own net if staying in cheap hotels. Burning mosquito coils reduces but does not eliminate the risk of bites.

Be sure to take your malaria tablets meticulously for the requisite time after you get home. Even if you have been taking your malaria prophylaxis carefully, there is still a slight chance of contracting malaria. The symptoms are fevers, chills, joint pain, headache and sometimes diarrhoea – in other words the symptoms of many illnesses including flu. Malaria can take as little as seven days to develop. Consult a doctor (mentioning that you have been abroad) if you develop a flu-like illness within a year of leaving a malarious region. The life-threatening cerebral malaria will become apparent within three months and can kill within 24 hours of the first symptoms.

Mosquitoes pass on not only malaria but also Rift Valley fever, elephantiasis, dengue and other serious viral fevers. By avoiding mosquito bites you also avoid illness, as well as those itching lumps which so easily become infected. Once you've been bitten, tiger balm or calamine lotion help stop the itching.

TRAVELLER'S DIARRHOEA Diarrhoea is very common in visitors to Madagascar, and you are more likely to suffer from this if you are new to tropical travel. The new oral Dukoral cholera vaccine gives partial protection (see www.medsafe.govt.nz/Consumers/cmi/d/dukoral.htm) against traveller's diarrhoea. Tourists tend to be obsessed with water sterilisation but, contrary to popular belief, traveller's diarrhoea usually comes from contaminated food not contaminated water. ice cream, sadly, is risky, especially if it is homemade and even factory-made ice creams can be bad news if they are stored badly. So, especially if you have a sensitive stomach and/or haven't travelled much before, you should avoid ice cream, and also ice, salads, fruit with lots of crevices such as strawberries, uncooked foods and cooked food that has been hanging around or has been inadequately reheated. Sizzling hot street food is likely to be far safer than the food offered in buffets in expensive hotels, however gourmet the latter may look. Yoghurt is usually safe, as are sorbets. Remember: peel it, boil it, cook it or forget it!

The way to the quickest recovery from traveller's diarrhoea is to reduce your normal meals to a few light or high carbohydrate items, avoid milk and alcohol and drink lots of clear fluids. You need to replace the fluids lost down the toilet, and drinks containing sugar and/or salt are most easily absorbed. Add a little sugar to a salty drink, such as Marmite (available in Tana!) or Oxo, or salt to a sugary drink like non-diet Coca-Cola. Sachets of rehydration mixtures are available commercially but you can make your own by mixing a rounded dessertspoon (or four teaspoons) of sugar with a quarter-teaspoon of salt and adding it to a glass of boiled and cooled water. Drink two glasses of this every time you open your bowels – more often if you are thirsty. Substituting glucose for sugar will make you feel even better. If you are in a rural area drink young coconut water or *ranovola* (water boiled in the pot that rice is cooked in).

Hot drinks and iced drinks cause a reflex emptying of the bowel and cause belly-ache, so take drinks tepid or at room-temperature while the diarrhoea is at its worst. Once the bowel has ejected the toxic material causing the diarrhoea, the symptoms will settle quite quickly and you should begin to feel better again after 24–36 hours. Should the diarrhoea be associated with passing blood or slime, it would be sensible to have a stool check at some stage, but provided you continue to drink clear fluids, no harm will come from waiting for a few days.

Holiday schedules often make it impossible to follow the 'sit it out' advice. When a long bus journey or flight is anticipated you may wish to take a blocker such as Imodium, but if you are tempted to do that it is better to take an antibiotic with it. 'Blockers' are dangerous if you have dysentery and work best if combined with an antibiotic such as Ciprofloxacin (500mg twice daily for at least three days). The three-day course used to be highly effective but resistance is developing. It is probably best, therefore, to take local advice and try to find a clinic rather than treating yourself. Drink lots whatever treatment you are taking and if you are worried or feel very ill, find a local medic. As long as you keep well hydrated the symptoms will usually settle by themselves. Even bacillary dysentery and cholera will usually resolve within a week without treatment, as long as you drink plenty of clear fluids.

CHOLERA In the last few years cholera has been a problem in Madagascar. By the end of 2000, 39,400 cases had been reported and 2,245 Malagasy had died. Although it has a fearsome reputation, cholera doesn't usually make healthy people ill. It takes the debilitated, poor and half-starved of famine or conflict zones, or it is present along with other gastro-intestinal infections. Cholera is avoided in the same way as other 'filth-to-mouth' diseases and – if there are symptoms – it can be treated with the usual oral rehydration fluids that all wise travellers know about (see above).

OTHER HITCHHIKERS There is a high prevalence of tapeworm in Malagasy cattle, so eat your steaks well done. If you do pass a worm, this is alarming but treatment can wait.

BILHARZIA (SCHISTOSOMIASIS) This is a nasty, debilitating disease which is a problem in much of lowland Madagascar. The parasite is also carried by pond snails and is caught by people who swim or paddle in clean, still or slow-moving water (not fast-flowing rivers) where an infected person has defecated or urinated. The parasite causes 'swimmer's itch' when it penetrates the skin. Since it takes at least ten minutes for the tiny worm to work its way through your skin, a quick wade across a river, preferably followed by vigorous towelling off, should not put you at risk. Bilharzia is cured with a single dose of Praziquantel. If you think you may have been exposed to the disease, ask your doctor to arrange a blood test when you get home. This should be done more than six weeks after the last exposure.

SEXUALLY TRANSMITTED INFECTIONS These are common in Madagascar and AIDS is on the increase. If you enjoy nightlife, male or female condoms will make encounters less risky. The femidom doesn't rustle as much as it used to.

RABIES (LA RAGE) Rabies is a disease that is feared wherever it occurs – and it occurs on Madagascar. However there are highly effective vaccines that give absolute protection.

The rabies virus can be carried by any mammal, and the commonest route of infection is from a dog bite. It is likely that lemurs could pass on rabies, and bats can certainly carry the disease. Unfortunately, most rabid animals do not look mad or froth at the mouth so it is important to assume that any mammal bite sustained

Hilary Bradt

When I was leading a trip in Madagascar a few years ago one of my group was bitten on the forearm by a female ring-tailed lemur. The animal was carrying a baby and was startled. It bit in self-defence. The skin was broken and there was a small amount of bleeding. In the days and weeks that followed, Susanne and I agonised about the possibility of rabies and what to do about it.

We asked advice from a local hotel manager (French) who reassured her that there was almost no possibility of the lemur being rabid. I felt the same way so Susanne decided to wait until she returned to Germany, but the uncertainty spoiled the rest of her trip. Even the tiniest chance of catching rabies is too terrible to contemplate – and she couldn't stop contemplating it.

She saw her doctor 18 days after the bite and was started on a course of anti-rabies injections. Rather than being reassuring, her doctors told her that she'd left it much too late, and that she would not know for three months whether or not she would get rabies – and die from it. Of course she is fine now, but what should we have done?

I've talked to several people about this dilemma including Madagascar residents. They all know that lemurs could carry rabies but what interests me is the likelihood of the animal becoming infected and then surviving long enough to bite a human. Lemurs tame enough to bite a tourist are found only in private reserves where dogs are excluded. Even if a rabid dog did get into the reserve would it be able to catch a lemur? And if it did catch one, would it inflict a bite which infected the animal but didn't kill it? The likelihood seems very small.

Alison Jolly, who has been studying lemurs for 40 years, says: 'I have never heard of anyone catching rabies from a lemur. I think that the chances are so small that I wouldn't dream of getting rabies shots after a lemur bite – as you say, the chance of a rabid dog catching a lemur which then got away seem not worth worrying about – except in one circumstance. If the lemur was hand-raised, either a current pet or a pet released into the wild, it may attack a human without provocation. In that case you get a deep bite with no warning. It probably is just misguided "normal" behaviour, treating you as one of its own species, but you can't be sure, so I would go and get shots. A bite in self-defence, though, isn't worth bothering about.'

Dr Jane comments: 'I have now been involved in quite a number of cases of tourists who have been bitten overseas and then are badly scared by the prospect of the disease and/or seeking/finding clinical services abroad. Increasingly I encourage travellers to pay out for the jabs before they travel.'

anywhere in Africa could potentially be dangerous. It is not safe to wait and see because once the symptoms of hydrophobia become apparent, the victim is doomed and the mode of death is terrible.

After any animal bite it is wise to administer good first aid because infection is likely. Vigorously clean the wound with plenty of soap under running water (from a tap or poured from a water bottle) for five minutes – timed with a watch. Scrubbing under running water – if a brush can be found – will clean out even more virus. After the cleaning process, the wound should be flooded with rum, whisky, vodka or any strong antiseptic solution. Next the victim should get the wound dressed – but not stitched – and post-bite jabs need to be arranged. Tetanus jabs, and sometimes antibiotics, may be needed to treat wound infection.

If rabies virus enters the body, it slowly progresses along the nerves until it gets to the brain at which point it causes encephalitis and hydrophobia – fear of water including one's own saliva. The incubation period for rabies depends upon the severity of the bite and also the distance from the brain. If a toddler gets savaged on the face the child will become ill in as little as four days.

The dilemma is what to do if you have a small skin-break on a limb. Treatment clearly needs to be given, and as promptly as possible, but the options available in remote parts of Madagascar are less than ideal. Malagasy health assistants will still administer the less-than-safe and out-dated Semple vaccine but for those with the money and resources to get something better it is not a wise option. Semple vaccine is a 5% suspension of sheep or goat brain given – painfully – into the abdomen on 21 consecutive days followed by booster doses. Semple isn't used in many hospitals in Tana but it is outside the capital, eg: in Toliara. Serious reactions to it happen as frequently as 1 in 76 courses (with 41% of those affected dying), and its efficacy is poor. I have heard of people receiving Semple vaccine after a dog bite and dying of rabies anyway. There is also HIV/AIDS in Madagascar and so any treatment involving injections could give you HIV, as well as hepatitis B.

Because of the anxiety a rabies-prone bite causes and because of the risks of accessing treatment locally, being immunised before travel is wise. If you are unimmunised you have less time to get to somewhere with rabies vaccine and you'll also have the complication of needing rabies immune globulin, and there is a world shortage: there have been difficulties obtaining this lately, even in Europe. Reputable travel health insurers should be able to advise where the nearest source of safe vaccine and immune globulin might be. Sometimes embassies can help with such information.

INFECTION AND TRIVIAL BREAKS IN THE SKIN The skin is very prone to infection in hot, moist climates: even the smallest nick or graze allows bacteria to enter and cause problems. Mosquito bites – especially if you scratch them – are a common route of infection, so apply a cream to reduce the itching. White toothpaste helps if you are stuck for anything better. Cover any wounds, especially oozing ones, so that flies don't snack on them. Antiseptic creams are not advised, since they keep the wounds moist and this encourages further infection. A powerful antiseptic, which also dries out moist wounds, is potassium permanganate crystals dissolved in water. Another alternative is diluted tincture of iodine (which you may be carrying anyway as a water steriliser) or povidone-iodine. Large bottles of the latter are available at a reasonable price in the many pharmacies in Madagascar or can be bought in spray form as Betadine or Savlon Dry before arrival. Bathe the wound twice a day, more often if you can, by dabbing with cotton wool dipped in dilute potassium permanganate, or iodine solution. Bathing in sulphur springs cures too.

SUNBURN Light-skinned people, particularly those with freckles, burn remarkably quickly near the Equator, especially when snorkelling. Wearing a shirt, preferably one with a collar, protects the neck and back, and long shorts can also be worn. Use a sunscreen with a high protection factor (up to 25) on the back of the neck, calves and other exposed parts.

PRICKLY HEAT A fine pimply rash on the trunk is likely to be heat rash; cool showers, dabbing (not rubbing) dry and talc will help relieve it. Treat the problem by slowing down to a relaxed schedule, wearing only loose, baggy 100% cotton clothes and sleeping naked under a fan; if it is bad, check into an air-conditioned hotel room for a while.

FOOT PROTECTION Wearing shoes or sandals even on the beach will protect the feet from injury and from parasites. Old trainers (running shoes) worn when you are

Marko Petrovic

With less than a week left until the end of my seven months in Madagascar I fell ill with a serious infection. About a fortnight earlier, during an evening spent in the company of particularly aggressive mosquitoes, I had scratched a bite on my ankle just a bit too vigorously and it had turned septic. I treated it with antiseptic powder and covered it with plasters and it almost healed. All that was left was a small spot which in Europe I would have simply left to dry out. So I went out with no plaster and while engaged in conversation the infernal flies found the minute spot and had a feast ...

The next day I found I could hardly walk because the infection had spread to the muscle. I obtained some antibiotics and had a good dressing put on it and continued my beloved work as a truck driver despite the discomfort. By evening the whole foot had ballooned and looked quite frightening. The next two days I spent mainly in bed because even sitting put me in great discomfort as the blood rushed down into the foot. I had high fever and couldn't eat. But with my visa running out and my flight back booked I had to get to Tana. The two day car or *taxi-brousse* journey from Vangaindrano was out of the question so I flew from Farafangana via Taolagnaro to Tana. The steward in the Air Mad Twin Otter was very friendly and helpfully folded down the seat in front of me so I could keep my leg up. I was very impressed with how quickly I was provided with a wheelchair at both Taolagnaro and Ivato without even having asked for one.

My flight back to Paris was on the following evening but an 11-hour flight in a sitting position was completely out of the question and, having no insurance, I didn't want to pay for extra seats. So I decided to stay in Madagascar and have treatment there. By this time the infection was already creeping up the leg and on the foot an enormous sausage-like blood blister spanning the whole length of the foot had formed. The first doctor that saw me at the Clinique St Francois d'Assise Ankadifotsy in Tana (a private clinic) where I was taken was so fascinated by the sight that the first thing he did was to take out his mobile phone, and take pictures of it! I was given a bed in a room on my own. Everything was wonderfully clean and new. The following day an old, greying doctor performed an operation under local anaesthetic to remove the worst infected tissue. He told me that he'd studied neo-natal surgery at Great Ormond Street Hospital and therefore spoke English well.

in the sea will help you avoid getting coral or urchin spines in the soles of your feet and give some protection against venomous fish spines. Booties, which can be bought for about £25, will protect from coral but not venomous fish. If you tread on a venomous fish or stingray, or are charged by a lionfish, soak the foot (or affected part) in hot (up to 45°C) water until some time after the pain subsides; this may mean 20–30 minutes' immersion in all. If the pain returns re-immerse. Once the venom has been heat-inactivated, get a doctor or paramedic to check and remove any bits of fish spines in the wound.

THE NASTY SIDE OF NATURE

Animals Malagasy land-snakes are back-fanged, and so are effectively non-venomous. Sea-snakes, although venomous, are easy to see and are rarely aggressive. However, if you are bitten then seek immediate medical treatment; try to keep the bitten part as still and as low as possible to slow the spread of venom. Large spiders can be dangerous – the black widow is found in Madagascar, as well as an aggressive hairy spider with a nasty bite. Navy digger wasps have an unpleasant sting, but it is only scorpions that commonly cause problems because they favour hiding places where one might plunge a hand without looking. If you

Despite having large doses of intravenous antibiotics the infection spread up as far as my knee and it was four or five days before it showed signs of receding. Meanwhile the big blood blister had burst, dried and formed a large scab which the doctor now wanted to remove (under general anaesthetic) because it was sealing in the infected tissue underneath. I became scared, both about having an open wound covering half my foot, as well as the expense of the operation, and decided to risk the flight back to Paris. I had spent exactly a week in hospital, at the end of which the infection had been successfully driven down and confined to the foot and my body temperature was brought down to normal. I paid only about £200.

The people looking after me all this time were a Slovenian missionary priest who works in the capital, a French nun who has good government contacts and made sure I didn't get into trouble about the out-of-date visa and I'm especially grateful to the parishioners of another Slovenian missionary (Père Pedro) who took me to this hospital and provided me with a 'guarde' (a lad who was with me all the time and helped me in my bed-ridden state – this appears to be normal practice in Malagasy hospitals). The parishioners visited me every day and brought me things to eat and drink. Unfortunately I couldn't eat anything, not even the hospital dinners which looked wonderful. The nurses, in an effort to get me to eat, were even so kind as to ask me what I liked and, being fed up with rice, I said mashed potatoes. I felt ashamed when I couldn't eat them. I think the doctors and nurses were rather disappointed that I decided to go and I almost felt sorry for them – it would have been a nice victory for them to have successfully got a *vazaha* back on his feet! Before I was discharged the nurses took pains over my dressing saying: 'We don't want people to think we're under-developed'! The awful treatment I later got from the *vazahas* at Charles de Gaulle airport where I waited three hours for a wheelchair made me wonder who was the more developed.

At the end the parishioners took me to the airport in their Land Rover Ambulance. I lay on the stretcher in the back and there were children on both sides singing all the way to the airport. It had been worth staying in Madagascar just for that experience!

Marko is back in Madagascar working in the southeast for his missionary uncle. He agrees that he was lucky with his contacts in Tana and that medical insurance really is a good thing!

sleep on the ground, isolate yourself from these creatures with a mat, a hammock or a tent with a sewn-in ground sheet.

Scorpion and centipede stings are very unpleasant and worth avoiding. Scorpions often come out after rain. They are nocturnal but they like hiding in small crevices during the day. People camping in the desert or the dry forest often find that a scorpion has crept into the pocket of a rucksack – despite taking the sensible precaution of suspending their luggage from a tree. Scorpion stings are very painful for about 24 hours. After a sting on the finger, I had an excruciatingly painful hand and arm for several days. The pain was only eased with morphine. My finger had no feeling for a month, and over 20 years later it still has a slightly abnormal sensation.

Leeches can be a nuisance in the rainforest, but are only revolting, not dangerous (AIDS is not spread via leeches). They are best avoided by covering up, tucking trousers into socks and applying insect repellent (even on shoes – but beware, DEET dissolves plastics). Once leeches have become attached they should not be forcibly removed or their mouthparts may remain causing the bite to itch for a long time. Either wait until they have finished feeding (when they will fall off) or encourage them to let go by applying a lit cigarette, a bit of tobacco, chilli, salt

Liz Bomford with additional information by Rob Conway

Madagascar has some truly wonderful underwater opportunities but divers need to be cautious. There is no hyperbaric chamber in the country; diving casualties must be evacuated overseas by air. The nearest recompression facilities are in Kenya, South Africa, Réunion and Mauritius. As flying exacerbates decompression sickness, this is not an ideal situation so you need to keep risks to the minimum. Divers Aware Network (DAN) offers comprehensive diving insurance for evacuation from Madagascar and has experience in doing this.

If you are going to dive Madagascar you should be an experienced diver, taking responsibility for your own dives. Madagascar is not suitable for newly qualified PADI open-water divers. It is essential to dive within guidelines and take your own computer so you do not depend blindly on the local dive leaders. Do not dive with any outfit that does not carry oxygen on the boat. Make sure you ask about this; your life may depend on it.

There are no regulations in Madagascar and dive operators are not obliged to provide good quality octopus rigs, or to service equipment regularly, or indeed to carry out any of the 'housekeeping' that is required to provide safe diving. If you can manage it, bring your own equipment. Also make sure that you are conservative with your dive profiles and take an extra long safety stop on ascending.

Don't be afraid to ask about safety issues. You are not being a wimp. I had a 'bend' in Madagascar in 2003. If my instructor had not been equipped with oxygen, I would be dead. As it was, he didn't have enough and I now have mild but permanent neurological injuries. Don't let them tell you 'there are no accidents in Madagascar'. I was that statistic and I feel sure I'm not the only one.

or insect repellent. A film canister is a convenient salt container. The wound left by a leech bleeds a great deal and easily becomes infected if not kept clean. For more on leeches see box on page 346.

Beware of strolling barefoot on damp, sandy riverbeds and areas of beach where locals defecate. This is the way to pick up jiggers (and geography worms). Jiggers are female sand fleas, which resemble maggots and burrow into your toes to incubate their eggs. Remove them, using a sterilised needle, by picking the top off the boil they make and teasing them out (this requires some skill, so it is best to ask a local person to help). Disinfect the wound thoroughly to avoid infection.

Plants Madagascar has quite a few plants which cause skin irritation. The worst one I have encountered is a climbing legume with pea-pod-like fruits that look furry. This 'fur' penetrates the skin as thousands of tiny needles, which must be painstakingly extracted with tweezers. Prickly pear fruits have the same defence. Relief from the secretions of other irritating plants is obtained by bathing. Sometimes it is best to wash your clothes as well, and immersion fully clothed may be the last resort!

MEDICAL KIT

Apart from personal medication taken on a regular basis, it is unnecessary to weigh yourself down with a comprehensive medical kit, as many of your requirements will be met by the Malagasy pharmacies.

Expeditions or very adventurous travellers should contact a travel clinic (see *Travel clinics and health information*, opposite). The absolute maximum an ordinary traveller needs to carry (I always carry less) is: malaria tablets; insect repellent; condoms (useful emergency water carriers), lots of plasters (Band-Aid/Elastoplast) to cover broken skin, infected insect bites etc; antiseptic (potassium permanganate crystals to dissolve in water are best, or povidine-iodine); sterile dressings (eg: Melolin) and adhesive plaster; soluble aspirin or paracetamol (Tylenol) – good for fevers, aches and for gargling when you have a sore throat; Anusol or Sudocrem or some kind of soothing cream for a sore anus (after diarrhoea); also useful in cases of severe diarrhoea where a cough or sneeze can be disastrous are panti-liners or sanitary pads (these are also excellent for covering wounds); Canesten for thrush and athlete's foot; foot powder; Vaseline or Heel Balm for cracked heels; a course of Amoxicillin (or Erythromycin if you're penicillin-allergic) which is good for chest infections, skin infections and cystitis; Cicatrin (neomycin) antibiotic powder for infected bites etc; antibiotic eye drops; antihistamine tablets; travel sickness pills (for those winding roads); tiger balm or calamine lotion for itchy bites; pointed tweezers for extracting splinters, sea urchin spines, small thorns and coral.

✚ TRAVEL CLINICS AND HEALTH INFORMATION

A full list of current travel clinic websites worldwide is available on www.istm.org/. For other journey preparation information, consult ftp://ftp.shoreland.com/pub/shorecg.rtf or www.tripprep.com. Information about various medications may be found on www.emedicine.com/wild/topiclist.htm.

Your Child Abroad: a travel health guide is a useful resource for those travelling with children or Bugs Bites & Bowels: the Cadogan guide to travel health contains information and treatment guidelines for adults.

UK

Berkeley Travel Clinic 32 Berkeley St, London W1J 8EL (near Green Park tube station); ☏ 020 7629 6233

Cambridge Travel Clinic 48a Mill Rd, Cambridge CB1 2AS; ☏ 01223 367362; e enquiries@travelcliniccambridge.co.uk; www.travelcliniccambridge.co.uk. ⊕ Tue–Fri 12.00–19.00, Sat 10.00–16.00.

Edinburgh Travel Clinic Regional Infectious Diseases Unit, Ward 41 OPD, Western General Hospital, Crewe Rd South, Edinburgh EH4 2UX; ☏ 0131 537 2822; www.link.med.ed.ac.uk/ridu. Travel helpline (☏ 0906 589 0380) open weekdays 09.00–12.00. Provides inoculations & antimalarial prophylaxis, & advises on travel-related health risks.

Fleet Street Travel Clinic 29 Fleet St, London EC4Y 1AA; ☏ 020 7353 5678; www.fleetstreetclinic.com. Vaccinations, travel products & latest advice.

Hospital for Tropical Diseases Travel Clinic Mortimer Market Bldg, Capper St (off Tottenham Ct Rd), London WC1E 6AU; ☏ 020 7388 9600; www.thehtd.org. Offers consultations & advice, & is able to provide all necessary drugs & vaccines for travellers. Runs a healthline (☏ 0906 133 7733) for country-specific information & health hazards. Also stocks nets, water purification equipment & personal protection measures.

Interhealth Worldwide Partnership Hse, 157 Waterloo Rd, London SE1 8US; ☏ 020 7902 9000; www.interhealth.org.uk. Competitively priced, one-stop travel health service. All profits go to their affiliated company, InterHealth, which provides health care for overseas workers on Christian projects.

Liverpool School of Medicine Pembroke Pl, Liverpool L3 5QA; ☏ 051 708 9393; f 0151 705 3370; www.liv.ac.uk/lstm

MASTA (Medical Advisory Service for Travellers Abroad) Moorfield Rd, Yeadon LS19 7BN; ☏ 0870 606 2782; www.masta-travel-health.com. Provides travel health advice, anti-malarials & vaccinations. There are over 25 MASTA pre-travel clinics in Britain; call or check online for the nearest. Clinics also sell mosquito nets, medical kits, insect protection & travel hygiene products.

NHS travel website www.fitfortravel.scot.nhs.uk. Provides country-by-country advice on immunisation & malaria, plus details of recent developments, & a list of relevant health organisations.

Nomad Travel Store/Clinic 3–4 Wellington Terrace, Turnpike Lane, London N8 0PX; ☏ 020 8889 7014; travel-health line (office hrs only) ☏ 0906 863 3414; e sales@nomadtravel.co.uk;

Samantha Cameron

Faced with environmental degradation and increasing exposure to Western medicine, there are many people who fear for the future of ethnobotanical knowledge. However, recent research in rural southeast Madagascar found that traditional healing practices continue to be widespread and that, although older people generally have more faith in them, the younger generation are also very knowledgeable about traditional remedies.

Many people consult both healers and the hospital, the decision depending on the type of illness they are suffering from and, to a lesser extent, the cost of treatment. Often healers are seen when people have an illness that they believe Western medicine cannot cure. The two are also used in combination, or people resort to one having found the other ineffective. If symptoms of a disease are recognised, treatment is often self-administered. Some health problems of a sensitive nature, such as gynaecological problems and sexually transmitted diseases, are commonly treated by healers; women being afraid or too embarrassed to go to the hospital. Other conditions are often of a more psychological or supernatural nature, such as phobias and spirit possessions.

Healers commonly first receive their powers on the death of another healer, usually their parent or grandparent, and often through a dream. Many practise clairvoyance, using cards or mirrors in order to communicate with their ancestors so as to diagnose illness and treatment. Sometimes, even if the disease is known, there is no fixed recipe but treatment varies according to what is identified as the cause of that disease. So two people with the same illness would not necessarily be administered the same treatment. These diagnostic powers of healers are all-important, and are the reason why they could never be replaced. Some healers update treatments annually, on the advice of their ancestors, and many are blessed with healing hands; so the medicinal plants they use would not be as effective if self-administered. It is therefore difficult to know to what extent people are successfully cured by a plant's medicinal properties and how much is due to the healer's power or is just psychological.

Despite evident deforestation in the area, people living close to the forest do not suggest any consequent dramatic change in the abundance of medicinal plants, only stating that they have to go slightly further afield to find them. In fact, users of medicinal plants originating from secondary vegetation note that their abundance has actually

---

www.nomadtravel.co.uk. Also at 40 Bernard St, London WC1N 1LJ; ☎ 020 7833 4114; 52 Grosvenor Gdns, London SW1W 0AG; ☎ 020 7823 5823; & 43 Queens Rd, Bristol BS8 1QH; ☎ 0117 922 6567. For health advice, equipment such as mosquito nets & other anti-bug devices, & an excellent range of adventure travel gear.

Trailfinders Travel Clinic 194 Kensington High St, London W8 7RG; ☎ 020 7938 3999; www.trailfinders.com/clinic.htm

Travelpharm The travelpharm website, www.travelpharm.com, offers up-to-date guidance on travel-related health & has a range of medications available through their online mini-pharmacy.

IRISH REPUBLIC
Tropical Medical Bureau Grafton Street Medical Centre, Grafton Bldgs, 34 Grafton St, Dublin 2;

☎ 1 671 9200; www.tmb.ie. A useful website specific to tropical destinations. Also check website for other bureaux locations throughout Ireland.

USA
Centers for Disease Control 1600 Clifton Rd, Atlanta, GA 30333; ☎ 800 311 3435; travellers' health hotline ☎ 888 232 3299; www.cdc.gov/travel. The central source of travel information in the USA. The invaluable *Health Information for International Travel*, published annually, is available from the Division of Quarantine at this address.

Connaught Laboratories PO Box 187, Swiftwater, PA 18370; ☎ 800 822 2463. They will send a free list of specialist tropical-medicine physicians in your state.

IAMAT (International Association for Medical Assistance to Travelers) 1623 Military Rd, 279,

increased as a direct result of environmental degradation. Other healers are unaware of availability since they are not responsible for plant collection. Some even claim to know nothing about medicinal plants or where they are found, being led to them whilst in a trance, their body possessed by ancestral spirits.

Although use of forest plants is generally higher in villages near the forest, some healers living near the forest use exclusively savannah-originating medicinal plants, and some living far from the forest use forest plants. Such patterns of medicinal-plant use can result from the method of plant collection; some healers have plants come to them overnight by a supernatural force, some send people to harvest them, and some buy in the market or elsewhere. Many healers also conserve plants by drying them, thus making frequent collection unnecessary. Migration is another cause, some healers originating from forested areas and later moving away but continuing to use the forest plants that tradition has passed on to them. Medicinal plant knowledge therefore changes more according to the speciality of the healer, and the healer's origin, as opposed to their proximity to the forest.

Although traditional healing does not appear to be dying out and Western medicine does not seem to pose a real threat, perhaps its greatest threat is from religion. Common belief has it that traditional healing is the devil's work as it comes from the power of the ancestors rather than the power of God. The risk is that young people may resist the healing power they inherit. Recording traditional medicine practices enhances understanding of the context in which it is used in Madagascar, by distributing the results to local communities, authorities and scientists. It is also necessary to increase appreciation and valuation of these secondary forest products, with the aim of conservation and sustainable natural resource management.

The author is a volunteer for the NGO Feedback Madagascar, and is co-ordinator of their health programme in the Fianarantsoa region. She led an RGS-supported expedition researching ethnobotanical knowledge in an area bordering the rainforest, and hopes that findings can be used to ease collaboration and understanding between traditional healers and the medical establishment, in the same way as is being done with traditional birth attendants. Anyone interested in borrowing an extensive photo exhibition, complete with captions, about village life in Madagascar, should write to: samcam77@hotmail.com.

Niagara Falls, NY14304-1745; ✆ 716 754 4883; e info@iamat.org; www.iamat.org. A non-profit organisation that provides lists of English-speaking doctors abroad.
International Medicine Center 920 Frostwood Drive, Suite 670, Houston, TX 77024; ✆ 713 550 2000; www.traveldoc.com

CANADA
IAMAT Suite 1, 1287 St Clair Av W, Toronto, Ontario M6E 1B8; ✆ 416 652 0137; www.iamat.org
TMVC Suite 314, 1030 W Georgia St, Vancouver BC V6E 2Y3; ✆ 1 888 288 8682; www.tmvc.com. Private clinic with several outlets in Canada.

AUSTRALIA, NEW ZEALAND, THAILAND
IAMAT PO Box 5049, Christchurch 5, New Zealand; www.iamat.org

TMVC ✆ 1300 65 88 44; www.tmvc.com.au. Clinics in Australia, New Zealand & Singapore, including:
Auckland Canterbury Arcade, 170 Queen St, Auckland; ✆ 9 373 3531
Brisbane 6th floor, 247 Adelaide St, Brisbane, QLD 4000; ✆ 7 3221 9066
Melbourne 393 Little Bourke St, 2nd floor, Melbourne, VIC 3000; ✆ 3 9602 5788
Sydney Dymocks Bldg, 7th floor, 428 George St, Sydney, NSW 2000; ✆ 2 9221 7133

SOUTH AFRICA
SAA-Netcare Travel Clinics P Bag X34, Benmore 2010; www.travelclinic.co.za. Clinics throughout South Africa.

SWITZERLAND
IAMAT 57 Chemin des Voirets, 1212 Grand Lancy, Geneva; www.iamat.org

5

Before launching into a discussion on crime, it's worth reminding readers that by far the most common cause of death or injury while on holiday is the same as at home: road accidents. No-one seems to worry about this, however, preferring to focus their anxieties on crime. I have been taken to task by some readers for over-emphasising the danger of robbery, and certainly it is true that most visitors to Madagascar return home after a crime-free trip. However, this is one area where being forewarned is forearmed: there are positive steps that you can take to keep yourself and your possessions safe, so you might as well know about them, while knowing also that the vast majority of Malagasy are touchingly honest. Often you will have people call you back because you have overpaid them (while still unfamiliar with the money) and every traveller can think of a time when his innocence could have been exploited – and wasn't. In my experience, too, hotel employees are, by and large, trustworthy. So try to keep a sense of proportion. Like health, safety is often a question of common sense. Keep your valuables hidden, keep alert in potentially dangerous situations, and you will be OK.

Bear in mind that thieves have to learn their profession so theft is common only where there are plenty of tourists to prey on. In little-visited areas you can relax and enjoy the genuine friendliness of the people.

BEFORE YOU GO You can enjoy peace of mind by giving some time to making your luggage and person as hard to rob as possible before you leave home. Also make three photocopies of all your important documents: passport (information page and visa), airline ticket (including proof of purchase), travellers' cheques (sales advice slip), credit cards, emergency phone number for stolen credit cards, emergency phone number of travel insurance company and insurance documents. Leave one copy with a friend or relative at home, one in your main luggage and one in your handbag or hand luggage. A simpler alternative is to have a hotmail or yahoo account and email yourself scans of all these documents to access if necessary.

- Leave your valuable-looking jewellery at home. You do not need it in Madagascar. Likewise your fancy watch; buy a cheap one.
- Lock your bag when travelling by plane or *taxi-brousse*; combination locks are more secure than small padlocks. Make or buy a lockable cover for your backpack.
- Make extra deep pockets in your travel trousers by cutting the bottom off existing pockets and adding an extra bit. Fasten the 'secret' pocket with velcro.

CRIME PREVENTION Violent crime is still relatively rare in Madagascar, and even in Antananarivo you are probably safer than in a large American city. The response to a potentially violent attack is the same in Madagascar as anywhere: if you are outnumbered or the thief is armed, it is sensible to hand over what they want.

You are far more likely to be robbed by subterfuge. Razor-slashing is very popular (with the thieves) and is particularly irritating since your clothes or bag are ruined, maybe just for the sake of the used tissue that caused the tempting-looking bulge in your pocket. When visiting crowded places avoid bringing a bag (even a daypack carried in front of your body is vulnerable, as is a bum-bag); bring your money and passport or ID in a moneybelt under your clothes, or in a neck pouch. Women have advantages here: the neck pouch can be hooked over their bra so no cord shows at the neck and a moneybelt beneath a skirt is safe since it needs an unusually brazen thief to reach for it! If you must have a bag, make sure it is difficult to cut, and that it can be carried across your body so it cannot be snatched.

Passengers in taxis may be the victims of robbery: the thief reaches through the open window and grabs your bag. Keep it on the floor by your feet.

Having escorted scores of first-timers through Madagascar, I've learned the mistakes the unprepared can make. The most common is wearing jewellery ('But I always wear this gold chain'), carelessness with money etc ('I just put my bag down while I tried on that blouse'), and expecting thieves to look shabby ('But he was such a well-dressed young man').

PASSPORTS AND IDS If you prefer to leave your passport in a safe place in your hotel room when you go out, carrying a photocopy of your passport is no longer sufficient for ID purposes, unless it is an authorised copy, with red stamps all over it, available either from the police (supposedly free) or from the office of the mayor for a small payment. You must provide your passport (photo page and visa page) and as many photocopies of it as you think you might need. This authorised copy is then valid for the police, for banks, for Western Union, or anyone else who might demand your ID. This is all quite a hassle, but losing your passport is worse. I've never been stopped in all my trips to Madagascar, but have had plenty of reports of people (mostly young) who have.

TIPS FOR AVOIDING ROBBERY

- Remember that most theft occurs in the street not in hotels; leave your valuables hidden in a locked bag in your room or in the hotel safe.
- If you use a hotel safe at Reception, make sure your money is in a sealed envelope that cannot be opened without detection. There have been cases of the key being accessible to all hotel employees, with predictable results.
- If staying in budget hotels bring a rubber wedge to keep your door closed at night. If you can't secure the window put something on the sill which will fall with a clatter if someone tries to enter.
- Pay particular attention to the security of your passport.
- Carry your cash in a moneybelt, neck pouch or deep pocket. Wear loose trousers that have zipped pockets. Keep emergency cash (eg: a US$100 bill) in a Very Safe Place. Keep a small but reasonable amount of cash in a wallet that you can give away if threatened.
- Divide up travellers' cheques so they are not all in one place. Keep photocopies of important documents in your luggage.
- Remember, what the thief would most like to get hold of is money. Do not leave it around (in coat pockets hanging in your room, in your hand while you concentrate on something else, in an accessible pocket while strolling in the street). If travelling as a couple or small group have one person stand aside to keep watch while the other makes a purchase in the street.
- In a restaurant never hang your bag on the back of a chair or lay it by your feet (unless you put your chair leg over the strap). When travelling in a taxi, put your bag on the floor by your feet.
- For thieves, the next best thing after money is clothes. Avoid leaving them on the beach while you go swimming (in tourist areas) and never leave swimsuits or washing to dry outside your room near a public area.
- Bear in mind that it's impossible to run carrying a large piece of luggage. Items hidden at the bottom of your heaviest bag will be safe from a grab-and-run thief. Couples or small groups can pass a piece of cord through the handles of all their bags to make them one unstealable unit when waiting at an airport or *taxi-brousse* station.
- Avoid misunderstandings – genuine or contrived – by agreeing on the price of a service before you set out.

Gordon Rattray www.able-travel.com

Discovering the flora and fauna of Madagascar's rainforests can be a physical challenge for any travellers, but don't let this put you off. With some effort, those less fleet of foot can also appreciate much of what this unique country has to offer, and there are at least two reserves with features favouring people with limited mobility.

PLANNING AND BOOKING There are, as yet, no UK operators running specialised trips to Madagascar for disabled people, and although many travel companies will listen to your needs and try to create a suitable itinerary, independent travellers can just as easily plan their trip by contacting local operators and establishments directly, in advance by email.

ACCOMMODATION In general, it is not easy to find disabled-friendly accommodation; only top of the range lodges and hotels have 'accessible' rooms, and even here, I've yet to hear of anywhere with grab-handles, roll-under sinks and a roll-in shower. Occasionally (more by accident than through design), bathrooms are wheelchair accessible, but where this is not the case, you should be prepared to be lifted, or do your ablutions in the bedroom. It is worth mentioning that many toilets in out of the way places are of the squat variety, so if this is a problem for you it may be worth asking your tour organiser to have an easily transportable commode frame made, or do this yourself if travelling independently.

TRANSPORT

Air travel Irrelevant of how much help you need, there will always be assistance at airports, although it is not guaranteed to be as slick or efficient as you may be used to. This is especially true of smaller provincial terminals where, if you cannot walk at all, you may need to be manhandled (without an aisle chair) to and from the aircraft.

One contributor reports that because he had a serious leg infection, he needed a wheelchair to get him on a domestic flight and then the international one. He has nothing but praise for Air Madagascar but only condemnation for Air France, who made him wait three hours in Paris for a wheelchair, thus missing his flight to the UK.

Buses and trains There is no effective legislation in Madagascar to facilitate disabled travellers' journeys by public transport, so if you cannot walk at all, then both of these options are going to be difficult. You will need to ask for help from fellow passengers to lift you to your seat, it will often be crowded and there will be no accessible toilet.

- Enjoy yourself. It's preferable to lose a few unimportant things and see the best of Madagascar than to mistrust everyone and ruin your trip!

... AND WHAT TO DO IF YOU ARE ROBBED Have a little cry and then go to the police. They will write down all the details then send you to the chief of police for a signature. It takes the best part of a day, and will remind you what a manual typewriter looks like, but you will need the certificate for your insurance. If you are in a rural area, the local authorities will do a declaration of loss.

WOMEN TRAVELLERS Things have changed a lot in Madagascar. During my travels in the 1980s my only experience of sexual harassment (if it could be called that) was when a small man sidled up to me in Nosy Be and asked: 'Have you ever tasted Malagasy man?'

Sadly, with the increase of tourism comes the increase of men who think they may be on to a good thing. A firm 'no' is usually sufficient; try not to be too

MadaBus (see page 104) on the other hand, is an efficient, comfortable means of road travel which, although it does not have vehicles fitted with lifts and ramps, should be able to accommodate most mobility problems.

By car It is possible to hire a car, with driver, through reliable tour operators. 4x4 vehicles are often higher than normal cars making transfers more difficult and although drivers and guides are always willing to help, they are not trained in this skill. You must therefore explain your needs thoroughly and always stay in control of the situation. Distances are great and roads are often bumpy, so if you are prone to skin damage you need to take extra care. Place your own pressure-relieving cushion on top of (or instead of) the original car seat and, if necessary, pad around knees and elbows.

ACTIVITIES Although the majority of Madagascar's wildlife highlights are not disabled-friendly, there are two outstanding exceptions. The luxurious Anjajavy resort has villas, of which the nearest to the dining area is officially accessible (see page 416), and for the more budget conscious, Berenty (page 262) has broad, smooth, well-maintained forest paths (even possible for wheelchairs). Although the latter has no designated disability rooms, there will always be plenty of willing hands to help lift you over obstacles.

The ideal route for a disabled traveller would be Route National 7 (RN7) from Antananarivo to Toliara, either by MadaBus or, preferably, by hired car and driver. See *Chapters 8, 9* and *10*. The trip would be worth it for scenery alone. For lemurs try Lemurs Park (see page 177).

HEALTH AND INSURANCE Doctors will know about 'everyday' illnesses, but you must understand and be able to explain your own particular medical requirements. Rural hospitals and pharmacies are often basic, so it is wise to take as much essential medication and equipment as possible with you, and it is advisable to pack this in your hand luggage during flights in case your main luggage gets lost. If heat is a problem for you then try to book accommodation with fans or air-conditioning, and a useful cooling aid is a plant-spray bottle.

Travel insurance can be purchased from Age Concern (\ *0845 601 2234; web: www.ageconcern.org.uk*), who have no upper age limit, and Free Spirit (\ *0845 230 5000; www.free-spirit.com*), who cater for people with pre-existing medical conditions. Most insurance companies will insure disabled travellers, but it is essential that they are made aware of your disability.

offended: think of the image of Western women that the average Malagasy male is shown via the cinema or TV. A woman Peace Corps volunteer gave me the following advice for women travelling alone on *taxi-brousses*: 'Try to sit in the cab, but not next to the driver; if possible sit with another woman; if in the main body of the vehicle, establish contact with an older person, man or woman, who will then tend to look after you.' All women readers agree that you should say you are married, whether or not you wear a ring to back it up.

Lone travellers, both male and female, seem to have a better time well off the beaten track. My correspondent 'FRB' (see box overleaf) is not alone in saying that the true warmth of ordinary Malagasy is more likely to be found away from tourist areas. But here's a recent comment from a woman who travelled down RN7 last year: 'I can tell you, from my experience … travelling in Rwanda, Tanzania, Malawai, Uganda and Zambia, that the people I encountered in Madagascar three weeks ago – travelling as a lone woman the entire time – were wonderful. I always felt comfortable and respected.'

FRB

I had a fantastic time travelling alone for a few weeks in rural Madagascar! Making a journey between S-Ivongo and Maroantsetra I'd expected to be left with overwhelming impressions of beautiful coastlines, an extraordinary ecosystem, improbable fauna and near-impossible transport conditions. I wasn't disappointed! Just as special though were the warmth and hospitality of the Malagasy people.

I'd landed in Tana with the doubtful benefit of four months' (poorly) self-taught French and only the vaguest idea of an itinerary, having booked the flight on a whim to satisfy a long-standing but uninformed curiosity about the island. In an almost *vazaha*-free area I must have been quite a novelty but I learnt a few words of Malagasy and tried to take an interest in everything – although after attempting to de-husk rice grains with a giant (6ft) pestle and mortar, I decided that this was best left to the experts!

Travelling alone is perhaps nobody's ideal but I really wouldn't have missed the experience for the world, at least in this part of the world; I was constantly touched by the friendship and companionship extended by local people. My limited linguistic skills were no bar to laughter and camaraderie in the back of a *camion*, as our lurching vehicle threw us among the sacks of rice, flour and sugar, the cooking pots and tomatoes, whilst the beer crates crashed alarmingly on shelves just above our heads … although it was sometimes difficult to see each other through the diesel fumes! My (all male) companions on this journey were unfailingly charming, lowering a plank which I used to enter and exit more easily as we made the numerous stops required to rebuild bridges and take on/offload people, poultry and produce … and I found this pattern of courtesy and kindness repeated again and again in so many situations as I progressed via *kat-kats* and ferries, pirogues, on foot, by boat and even, briefly, on the back of a motorbike.

I should have at least one cautionary tale to tell of an intimidating experience – but I haven't! I enjoyed myself far more than I'd anticipated and am left humbled by the simple humanity of the people who made this possible. I never felt unsafe and while eating in *hotelys* or having bread and coffee from a roadside stall would generally find people willing to chat.

Having said that, it was a relief to speak English when happy chance found me a travelling companion! I think the solo experience might have been more uncomfortable among the groups of *vazaha* present in the more tourist-orientated areas. But if you're thinking of seeing Madagascar alone – do it! I found that the rural Malagasy respond with relief to someone who trusts them and will make you welcome. If you're in a touristy area, try to find a like-minded *vazaha* to enjoy it with – and don't forget to exchange email addresses, sharing the memories afterwards is as important as living them!

MEN TRAVELLERS To the Malagasy, a man travelling alone is in need of one thing: a woman. Lone male travellers will be pursued relentlessly, particularly in beach resorts. Prostitutes are ubiquitous and very beautiful. Venereal disease is common. A recent added danger from prostitutes is lacing a tourist's drink with the 'date-rape' drug Rohypnol to render their victim unconscious in his room, then rob him of all his possessions.

The government is clamping down hard on sex tourism. Considering the risks you would be foolish to succumb to temptation.

6

Madagascar and You

YOUR CARBON FOOTPRINT

When I published the last edition of this guide in 2005 this heading would have mystified my readers. Now, in 2007, it's the question I'm most often asked by journalists: how do I deal with the dilemma of encouraging people to fly halfway across the world while knowing that this contributes to carbon emissions and global warming? I reply that to me it's no dilemma. The following stories explain why.

Earlier this year I was the lecturer on board an expedition cruise ship, *The Island Sky*. Yes, a long flight then a ship which also contributed its share of CO_2 to the atmosphere, so thumbs down. But one of my lectures was on *Giving Something Back* where I described the work done by the Ivoloina Zoo and the charity HELP in Toamasina, and invited passengers to see the work for themselves and perhaps to make a donation. About one third of the passengers signed up for the visit to the charity; afterwards some told me it was one of the highlights of the trip, and the outcome was a combined on-the-spot donation to the Zoo's educational programme and to HELP of about $1,500. In my experience this sort of generosity is not unusual once people can see for themselves the work done in Madagascar in conservation and educating the next generation. There's a huge reservoir of goodwill among visitors and, yes, even among the 'tourists' so despised by 'travellers'.

The budget travellers' contribution is equally valuable because they bring goodwill and an enthusiasm for breaking down cultural barriers. The backpackers who contribute their stories and philosophies to this book may be the politicians or businessmen and women of the future. Their experiences in Madagascar will help inform the decisions they make as leaders.

And even those visitors who simply enjoy Madagascar, relaxing on the beaches, visiting the national parks, buying handicrafts and gaining a little understanding of what makes the average Malagasy tick, have made a contribution to the economy of the country. The term 'Giving something back' is perhaps misleading: it suggests that we visitors have taken something from the country in the first place. I don't believe this, so 'Getting involved' is a better heading.

So my position is clear. Although I admire those conscientious people who are prepared to make the sacrifice of not flying, I think they're wrong. The best way to save Madagascar is to go there – and that means taking a plane. If you want to offset your carbon emissions do it by contributing to one of the reforestation programmes in Madagascar. See pages 287, 296, and 417 for just some of the NGOs and businesses in the country which are actively involved in planting trees.

Alasdair Harris – Blue Ventures

Madagascar's coastal environments comprise some of the most ecologically sensitive areas of the country. Throughout their trip visitors should be aware of the intrinsic effect that their presence and activities will have on local habitats. We encourage you to plan your holiday in a way that minimises your impact on the environment.

When trekking, try to avoid sensitive habitats and vegetation types, reducing the impact of your movement and access to and from campsites. All waste should be sorted and disposed of sensibly. In arid environments such as the southwest, freshwater use should be kept to a minimum.

In the water, swimmers, snorkellers and divers should avoid all physical contact with corals and other marine life. Divers should take care to avoid any damage to reefs, maintaining good buoyancy control at all times in order to avoid accidental contact with the reef, or stirring up bottom sediment.

In coastal hotels and restaurants, seafood is commonly caught to order, regardless of the sustainability of the catch. In some tourist areas it is not uncommon to see critically endangered species such as the humphead or Napolean wrasse served up in a restaurant kitchen. Shellfish should not be bought out of season, since this can have devastating consequences on the reproductive success of species.

The marine curios trade is equally driven by tourism, and hard as it may seem, visitors should refrain from purchasing all forms of shells that have been gleaned from reefs. In Toliara alone, almost 150 species of gastropods are exploited for the ornamental shell trade. Several of these species – notably the magnificent helmet shell and the cowries – are now threatened with extinction. Similarly, the exploitation of sea turtles is increasingly focused at the tourist market, turtle shells now fetching staggering prices in markets and bijouteries. After the day's catch has been brought in, it's an all-too-common sight to see the lines of gasping turtles baking slowly in the sun in fishing villages adjacent to tourist areas.

RESPONSIBLE TOURISM

In recent years there has been a welcome shift of attitude among visitors to developing countries from 'What can I get out of this trip?' to 'How can I give something back?' This chapter addresses those issues, and suggests ways in which you can help this marvellous, but sometimes tragic, country.

THEY DO THINGS DIFFERENTLY THERE I once caught our Malagasy guide scowling at himself in the mirror. When I teased him he said: 'As a Malagasy man I smile a lot. I can see that if I want to work with tourists I must learn to frown.' He knew that the group considered him insufficiently assertive. Tolerance and the fear of causing offence is an integral part of Malagasy social relationships. So if a tourist expresses anger in a way that is entirely appropriate in his or her own culture, it may be counterproductive in Madagascar. It is deeply unsettling to the person at the receiving end who often giggles in response, thus exacerbating the situation. If you are patient, pleasant and keep your temper, your problem will be solved more quickly.

Avoid being too dogmatic in conversation (you do not have exclusivity of the truth). Make use of 'perhaps' and 'maybe'. Be excessive in your thanks. The Malagasy are very polite; we miss the nuances by not understanding the language. Body language, however, is easier to learn. For instance, 'Excuse me, may I come through?' is indicated by a stooping posture and an arm extended forward. Note how often it is used.

Part of responsible tourism is relinquishing some of our normal comforts. Consider this statistic: fuelwood demand in Madagascar has far outstripped supply. Wood and charcoal are the main sources of energy, and the chief users are city dwellers. In rural areas, tourist establishments may be the main consumers. Do you still feel that hot water is essential in your hotel? Another source of energy is hydroelectric power, so drought – as is common in these times of climate change – causes electricity cuts. So think again before leaving the air-conditioning and lights on when absent from your hotel room.

One of the keys to responsible tourism is ensuring that as much as possible of the money you spend on your holiday remains in Madagascar. Independent travellers should try, whenever possible, to stay at small hotels run by Malagasy. Madagascar now has a home-stay programme – see page 213. Tourists on an organised tour will probably find themselves in a foreign-owned hotel, but can do their bit by buying handicrafts and perhaps donating to local charities.

Madagascar's shortcomings can be infuriating. Sometimes a little reflection reveals the reasons behind the failure to produce the expected service, but sometimes you just have to tell yourself 'Well, that's the way it is'. After all, you are not going to be able to change Madagascar, but Madagascar may change you.

TOURIST POWER I recently learned that a hotel which used to keep caged lemurs as an attraction has now released them after some customers complained (although release is not that straightforward; see page 233). We can sometimes be too cautious about making our feelings felt because so often the hotel management is only trying to please us. So, if your chambermaid leaves the lights or air-conditioning on in your room, it's worth explaining to the manager that you would rather save Madagascar's precious resources. If a smart new hotel has proudly stated that they use the valuable – and highly endangered – hardwoods such as rosewood or *pallisandre* for their furniture or – worse – their floors, you could get into a conversation about sustainability.

There is, of course, a big difference between complaining about bad service and informing the management about a shift in tourist values. Even your disapproval of caged lemurs should be expressed tactfully, and your views about sustainable tourism needs even more care. Your green views won't be shared by all tourists and it's not a conversation you can have in a hurry when paying your bill. Take some time to discuss it over a drink.

PHOTOGRAPHY Lack of consideration when taking photos is perhaps the most common example of irresponsible tourist behaviour – one that each of us has probably been guilty of at some time. It is so easy to take a sneak photo without first establishing contact with the person, so easy to say we'll send a print of the picture and then not get round to it, so easy to stroll into a market or village thinking what a wonderful photo it will make and forgetting that you are there to experience it.

The rules are not to take people's photos without permission, and to respect an answer of 'no'. Give consideration to the offence caused by photographing the destitute. Be cautious about paying your way to a good photo; often a smile or a joke will work as well, and sets no precedent. People love to see pictures of themselves, and in these days of digital photography you can show them the photo immediately. Or you can go further, as one reader did (see page 100) and bring a small photo printer so you can hand out prints the same day that you took the photos. Otherwise be sure to write down the addresses of the people in your photos and honour your promise to send them prints.

Philip Thomas writes: 'A Malagasy, for whom a photograph will be a highly treasured souvenir, will remember the taking of the photograph and your promise to send them a copy, a lot longer than you might. Their disappointment in those

6

Bill Love

My last trip was unforgettable! I once again contacted 'my' little school in Ankify, c/o of Le Baobab Hotel nearby, to arrange a cultural visit for my group during our stay. We visited the two-room school on the morning of 4 November. Monsieur Farajao, a teacher, helped us exchange questions and answers about life in the USA and Madagascar. Everyone with me packed half their suitcase with school supplies, sports gear, and toys and games to donate. These went a long way, even among the 160+ school kids ranging from six to 15 years old.

As a special treat this year I also brought in a six-foot long ground boa, the largest kind of snake found in Madagascar. Our guide, Angelin Razafimanantsoa, found it the previous evening and knew I'd want to show the kids. I kept it hidden for most of the hour, saving it for the grand finale of a live Show & Tell style 'biology lesson'. That turned out to be the most memorable part of all!

The kids went wild when I suddenly lifted the four-inch thick snake out of an Eau Vive box on the floor. Some ran for the door while others leaped out of open windows. But soon the whole class was back crowding around to touch the tail end of the huge boa. Malagasy boas are usually very mellow, but just to be safe, I held its head up and out of reach just in case the commotion upset it. That proved to be wise because the snake quickly tired of the handling, sunk its teeth into my armpit, and held on. I shielded the bite from view and tried not to wince as I continued to smile and allow everyone to quench their curiosity. I don't think anyone realised what was actually happening, which is good because I certainly didn't want to give anyone a bad impression of this beautiful and essentially harmless local snake that was only reacting to the hundreds of hands touching it.

I've made visiting L'Ecole Primaire Publique d'Ankify an annual event since I always return to this magical area with my tours. Besides Madagascar's unique animals, the people are a true treasure that I proudly include in interactions as often as possible as we rove the countryside seeing and photographing nature.

Bill Love is a photographer, writer, and tour operator (www.bluechameleon.org) who regularly runs eco-tours to Madagascar. The northwest of Madagascar, including Ambanja, is his favourite stopover area. This is how he is 'giving something back' to the region.

who say one thing and do another is great, so if you think you might not get it together to send the photograph then do not say that you will.'

A responsible attitude to photography is so much more fun! And it results in better pictures. It involves taking some time getting to know the subject of your proposed photo: making a purchase, perhaps, or practising your Malagasy greetings.

BEGGARS Whether or not to give to professional beggars (but not children) is up to you. My policy is to give to the elderly and, on an extended trip, I also single out 'beggar days' when I fill my pockets with small change and give to every beggar who looks needy and over school age. And if I make some trickster's day, so be it.

It is important to make up your mind about beggars before you hit the streets so you can avoid standing there riffling through a conspicuously fat wallet for a low-denomination bill.

THE EFFECTS OF TOURISM ON LOCAL PEOPLE The impact of foreigners on the Malagasy was noted as long ago as 1669 when a visitor commented that formerly the natives were deeply respectful of white men but were changed 'by the bad examples which the Europeans have had, who glory in the sin of luxury in this country …'.

In developing countries tourism has had profound effects on the inhabitants, some good, some bad. Madagascar seems to me to be a special case – more than any other country I've visited it inspires a particular devotion and an awareness of its fragility, both environmental and cultural. Wildlife is definitely profiting from the attention given it and from the emphasis on ecotourism. For the people, however, the blessings may be very mixed: some able Malagasy have found jobs in the tourist industry, but for others the impact of tourism has meant that their cultural identity has been eroded, along with some of their dignity and integrity. Village antagonisms are heightened when one or two people gain the lion's share of tourist revenue and gifts, leading in one case to murder, and hitherto honest folk have lapsed into corruption, alcoholism or thievery.

DEALING WITH CHILD BEGGARS The unintentional effect of giving sweets, pens, money or whatever to children can be seen in any popular resort. Kids trail after you,

'PLEASE SEND ME A PHOTO'

It is not always easy to keep a promise. Of course we intend to send a print after someone posed cheerfully for the photo, but after we get home there are so many other things to do, so many addresses on torn-out pages of exercise books. I now honour my promises. Here's why.

I was checking my group in to a Nosy Be hotel when the bellboy asked if he could speak to me. He looked nervous, so suspecting a problem with the bookings I asked him to wait until everyone was in their rooms.

When we were alone he cleared his throat and recited what was obviously a carefully prepared speech: 'You are Mrs Hilary Bradt. Ten years ago you gave your business card to the lady at Sambava Voyages and she gave it to a schoolboy who wrote to you. But you were away so your mother answered the letter. She wrote many letters. My name is Murille and I am that boy. And now I want to talk to you about Janet Cross and Brian Cross and Andrew and...' There followed a list of every member of my family. As I listened, incredulous, I remembered the original letter. 'We love England strongly,' he wrote, 'especially London, Buckingham, Grantham, Dover...' I remembered passing it to my mother saying I was too busy for such a correspondence but maybe she'd like to write. She kept it up for several years, answering questions such as 'How often does Mrs Hilary go to Grantham and Dover?' and she sent a photo of the family gathering at Christmas, naming every member on the back of the photo.

This brought an indignant letter from a cousin. 'I have seen your photo. It is a very nice one. I asked Murille if he would lend it for one day only because we all study English so we must have photo of English people more to improve this language, but he refused me strongly because they are only his friends not mine...'

Murille brought out the treasured photo. It had suffered from the constant handling and tropical heat and was peeling at the edges. He wanted to trim it, he explained, 'but if I do I will have to cut off a bit of your mother's beautiful chair and I can't do that.'

Later that year I sent Murille a photo album filled with family photos. I never heard from him again – that's the way it is in Madagascar – but the story has a twist to its tail. I returned to Sambava 12 years after the original visit, and found myself addressing a classroom of eager adult students of English and their local teacher. Searching for something interesting to say, I told them about the time I was last in their town and the series of letters between Murille and my mother. And I told them about the cousin who also wrote to her. 'I think his name was Patrice,' I said. The teacher looked up. 'I'm Patrice. Yes, I remember writing to Janet Cross ...'

grabbing your hands and beseeching you for gifts. Many tourists are simply worn down by their persistence and give in, thus perpetuating the problem. Bill French who, with his wife Nina has made two long trips by bicycle to Madagascar, offers the following advice: 'Just don't give anything. Ignore their begging and change the subject, eg: do *cinque, cinque* (fist to fist), amuse them – sing, play, do tricks or just chatter away. These are skills you have to work on. Just don't give to anybody. Salve your conscience by giving a larger lump of money to an organised charity that will distribute more fairly and where needed. (We donated to the orphanage of Frères Missionnaires de la Charité (Charity of Mother Theresa).' (See page 158.)

GIVING PRESENTS This is a subject often discussed among experienced travellers who cannot agree on when, if ever, a present is appropriate. Most feel that giving presents is appropriate only when it is in exchange for a service.

My repeat visits to Madagascar over the course of 31 years have shaped my own view: that giving is usually done for self-gratification rather than generosity, and that one thoughtless act can change a village irreparably. I have seen the shyly inquisitive children of small communities turn into tiresome beggars; I have seen the warm interaction between visitor and local turn into mutual hostility; I have seen intelligent, ambitious young men turn into scoundrels. What I haven't sorted out in my mind is how much this matters. Thieves and scoundrels make a good living and are probably happier than they were in their earlier state of dire poverty. Should we be imposing our cultural views on the Malagasy? I don't know.

But giving does not have to be in the form of material gifts. 'Giving something back' has a far broader meaning. We should never underestimate our value as sheer entertainment in an otherwise routine life. We can give a smile, or a greeting in Malagasy. And we can learn from people who in so many ways are richer than us. Paul Atkinson, a much loved and respected former Peace Corps volunteer in the Andapa region, supports this view: 'Tourists don't realise that the best present they can give the villagers (and the *only* present they need give!) is a warm and friendly smile. Material presents are almost always destructive.'

MORE AND MORE ... Visitors who have spent some time in Madagascar and have befriended a particular family often find themselves in the 'more and more and more' trap. The foreigner begins by expressing appreciation of the friendship and hospitality he or she received by sending a gift to the family. A request for a more expensive gift follows. And another one, until the luckless *vazaha* feels that she is seen as a bottomless cornucopia of goodies. The reaction is a mixture of guilt and resentment.

Understanding the Malagasy viewpoint may help you to come to terms with these requests. You may be considered as part of the extended family, and family members often help support those who are less well-off. You will almost certainly be thought of as fabulously wealthy, so it is worth dispelling this myth by giving some prices for familiar foodstuffs at home – a kilo of rice, for instance, or a mango. Explain that you don't have servants, that you pay so much for rent, and that you have a family of your own that needs your help. Don't be afraid to say 'no' firmly.

It is sensible to be cautious about giving your name and address to local people with whom you have only a passing acquaintance. Women may be surprised – and possibly delighted – to receive a letter declaring undying love, but it's just possible that this comes with a few strings attached.

... AND THE MOST I know two couples, one in America and the other in Australia, who have translated their wish to help the Malagasy into airfares to their home country. This is not to be undertaken lightly – the red tape from both governments is horrendous – but is hugely rewarding for all concerned.

OFF THE BEATEN PATH Travellers venturing well off the beaten path will want to do their utmost to avoid offending the local people, who are usually extremely warm and hospitable.

Unfortunately, with the many *fady* prohibitions and beliefs varying from area to area and village to village, it is impossible to know exactly how to behave, although *vazaha* and other outsiders are exempt from the consequences of infringing a local *fady*.

Sometimes, in very remote areas, Malagasy will react in sheer terror at the sight of a white person. This probably stems from their belief in *mpakafo* (pronounced 'mpakafoo'), the 'stealer of hearts'. These pale-faced beings are said to wander around at night ripping out people's hearts. So it is not surprising that rural Malagasy often do not like going out after dark – and it's a problem if you are looking for a guide. In the southeast it is the *mpangalak'aty*, the 'taker of the liver', who is feared. The adventurous *vazaha* is not helped by the fact that mothers still threaten that 'If you don't go to bed now (fetch the water, or whatever) the *vazaha* will get you' to gain the obedience of their children. No wonder the poor things burst into tears at the sight of a white stranger.

Villages are governed by the Fokonolona, or People's Assembly. On arrival at a village you should ask for the Président du Fokontany. Although traditionally this was the village elder, these days it is more likely to be someone who speaks French – perhaps the schoolteacher. He will show you where you can sleep (sometimes a hut is kept free for guests, sometimes someone will be moved out for you). You will usually be provided with a meal. Now travellers have penetrated most rural areas, you may be expected to pay. Certainly you should offer, and if the answer is vague, make a donation of an appropriate amount. Philip Thomas, a social anthropologist who has conducted research in the rural southeast, points out several ways that tourists may unwittingly cause offence. 'People should adopt the common courtesy of greeting the Malagasy in their own language. 'Salama', 'manahoana' and 'veloma' are no more difficult to say than their French equivalents.

'*Vazaha* sometimes refuse food and hospitality, putting up tents and cooking their own food. But in offering you a place to sleep and food to eat the Malagasy are showing you the kindness they extend to any visitor or stranger, and to refuse is a rejection of their hospitality and sense of humanity. You may think you are inconveniencing them, and this is true, but they would prefer that than if you keep to yourselves as though you were not people (in the widest sense) like them. It may annoy you that it is virtually impossible to get a moment away from the gaze of the Malagasy, but you are there to look at them and their activities anyway, so why should there not be a mutual exchange? Besides, you are far more fascinating to them than they are to you, for their view of the world is not one shaped by mass education and access to international images supplied by television.

'It is perfectly acceptable to give a gift of money in return for help. Gifts of cash are not seen by the Malagasy as purchases and they themselves frequently give them. Rather, you give as a sign of your appreciation and respect. But beware of those who may try to take advantage of your position as a foreigner (and you may find these in even the remotest spot), those who play on your lack of knowledge of language and custom, and their perception of you as extremely wealthy (as of course you are by their standards).'

Valerie and John Middleton, who have travelled more adventurously and successfully in Madagascar than anyone else I know, add this advice: 'In three long visits to Madagascar we have never had a bad experience anywhere. We have, however, noted several people who have not fared so well and feel that we could possibly pass on some advice for anyone wanting to go off the beaten path.

1 To prevent misunderstanding always take a guide with you at least for communication as many isolated peoples speak only Malagasy.
2 Always introduce yourself to the local 'Président' and explain why you are in his village or even just passing through – you will never cease to be amazed at how helpful they wish to be once your purpose is fully understood and perhaps even more importantly the authority of his backing confers a considerable degree of protection in that area (it does always help to have a purpose).
3 Always defer to his advice.
4 Find out about local *fady* before doing anything.'

Waste disposal Madagascar has no mechanised recycling plants. Instead, the poorest of the poor scavenge the rubbish dumps in the larger towns. Clothes, containers and suchlike will be found and reused. In rural areas rubbish is simply dumped on the beach or on wasteland. Therefore whenever possible take your rubbish home with you, or at least back to the city. The exception is plastic bottles. Rural people in Madagascar need all the containers they can get for carrying or storing water or other liquids. So whenever possible, give your empty water bottles to villagers.

HOW YOU CAN HELP

There are several ways in which you can make a positive contribution. By making a donation to a local project you can help the people – and the wildlife – without creating new problems.

AKANY AVOKO

Akany Avoko is a Children's Home caring for around 150 abandoned and impoverished children. For over 40 years Akany Avoko has fed, clothed, educated and given a secure home to orphans, street kids, children from broken families, young people with disabilities, teenage girls on remand and teenage mums with their babies. It is run by the Malagasy Church in co-operation with the Malagasy Government and is sustained solely by charitable donations and income-generating projects within the centre itself.

As well as providing food, shelter, schooling and primary healthcare to the children who live there, Akany Avoko works to ensure that the children are capable of supporting themselves in the future and also to provide environmental education, enabling future generations of Malagasy people to help both themselves and Madagascar's precious environment.

Akany Avoko's 'green' projects are an inspiration: they use solar cooking, organic food production, and sustainable waste and water management. The compost toilet provides methane gas for cooking as well as fertiliser, carbonised pine-needles are mixed with clay for fuel.

Vocational training includes cookery, dressmaking, metal and wood workshops, and traditional dance, sports, games, and fun are also very much part of the centre's weekly routine.

The cost of caring for the orphans and abandoned children who end up at Akany Avoko is very high and the centre is always short of money. Do try to pay a visit when you are in Tana – you won't regret it.

Contact details: Akany Avoko, BP29 Ambohidratrimo 105, Madagascar; ✆ +216 20 22 441 58. Steve and Hardy Wilkinson: e akany.avoko@wanadoo.mg; Irenee Rajaona Horne: e horne@wanadoo.mg.

My initiation to the concept of 'giving something back' was over a dozen years ago when I met a couple of English teachers, Jill and Charlie Hadfield, who told me how they has started The Streetkids Project. Visiting a charity run by the Sisters of the Good Shepherd in Tana, they could see where a little money could go a long way and they started raising money for the Centre Fihavanana (see page 146). The nuns run – amongst other things – a preparatory school for the very poor. When the children are ready to go on to state school, however, the parents can't afford the £15 a year they must pay for registration, uniform and books, so the children are condemned to return to the streets as beggars. The Streetkids Project raises money to continue their education. Tourists have sometimes been so affected by what they experience in Madagascar that they team up with local people to found a charity. One example is the Dutch organisation Fazasoma in Ambositra (see page 194). Anything is possible if you care enough.

Here's a contribution to the subject by Nina French: 'There are lots of charities all over Madagascar. If you really want to make a little difference in lives of ordinary people you should do a bit of research. Look for help organisations, pop in local schools, find out what is being done for feral kids and old people, especially in big towns. Try to find the less-visible charities. Or just buy a proper meal for a child on the street – it is still better than giving them something.'

The organisations and charities listed below are all working with the people of Madagascar, and, by extension, habitat conservation. Most of them are very small, run by dedicated volunteers who would welcome even modest donations. Other charities work specifically for wildlife. What better way to channel your empathy for Madagascar and its problems?

UK AND US CHARITIES ASSISTING MADAGASCAR
People

Andrew Lees Trust 0207 4249256; www.andrewleestrust.org.uk. Set up in 1995, this charity helped to launch & support training at the Libanona Ecology Centre. Named after the international environmental campaigner Andrew Lees, the Trust develops social & environmental education projects in the south, specifically to increase access to information & education that empowers local populations to improve food security, reduce poverty & manage natural resources more sustainably. Project Radio, recently shortlisted for the UNESCO international prize for rural development communications, works with a network of 16 local partners & 14 radio stations across the south to produce & broadcast vital information & educational radio programmes to isolated rural communities. A sister programme, Project Energy, has trained women in the south to build over 32,000 wood-efficient stoves that reduce domestic fuel consumption by over 50% & help reduce pressure on forest resources. Tree planting follows the stove trainings & over 1,800 trees are already growing in a drought area.

Azafady Studio 7, 1a Beethoven St, London, W10 4LG; 020 8960 6629; f 020 8962 0126; e mark@azafady.org, or azafady@easynet.co.uk;

www.madagascar.co.uk. Works mainly in the southeast of Madagascar, aiming to break the cycle of poverty & environmental degradation so apparent in that area. Projects include tree planting & facilitation of small enterprises such as village market gardens, bee farming, basket making, & fruit drying. They fund a Health & Sanitation Programme to improve access to clean drinking water & basic healthcare. Conservation Projects include studies of the remaining littoral forest in southeast Madagascar & of endangered loggerhead turtle populations. The also run the Pioneer scheme for volunteers (see page 83).

The Dodwell Trust 16 Lanark Mansions, Pennard Rd, London W12 8DT; e dodwell@ madagascar.freeserve.co.uk; www.dodwell-trust.org. A British-registered charity founded by Christina Dodwell, running a radio project designed to help rural villagers, through the production & broadcast of a drama & magazine radio series for family health, AIDS prevention, poverty issues, & environment (similar to *The Archers* on BBC Radio). The Trust has set up 1,000 listener-groups with donated wind-up/solar radios, to send back useful information & take part in programmes. In collaboration with the Ministry of Education, the Trust also sends any donated computers from the UK to Madagascar &

assists with the twinning of schools in the UK. There is also a volunteer programme (see page 83). The Trust is currently building a new learning centre near Tana. Donations can be made through The Dodwell Trust (who charge no fee). Just mark your envelope 'to help the learning centre'.

Feedback Madagascar 5 Lyndale Av, London NW2 2QD; \f 020 741 7853; e info@ feedbackmadagascar.org; www.feedbackmadagascar.org. Head office in Madagascar: 1er étage, Lot IB 65 Bis Isoraka, 6 rue Raveloary, Antananarivo 101; \f 261 20 22 638 11; e feedback@simicro.mg. Other regional offices are in Fianarantsoa & Ambositra. A small, but highly effective Scottish charity that has worked to alleviate poverty & environmental degradation in Madagascar for over 10 yrs. Projects focus on improving primary healthcare & education, & promoting natural resource management & income-generating schemes. They are currently working with the Malagasy organisation Ny Tanintsika on revitalizing the silk industry & other traditional crafts, community forest management & beekeeping,

social action & awareness campaigns through adult literacy programmes, & capacity-building of communities on health, agriculture, environment & good governance.

Money for Madagascar LLwyncelyn Isaf, Carregsawdde, Llangadog SA19 9BY; e theresa@mfmcar.fsnet.co.uk; www.moneyformadagascar.org. This long-established & well-run Welsh charity funds rural health & agricultural projects & supports deprived groups in urban areas. It also provides funds for cyclone relief & other natural disasters. MfM sends funds on a regular basis to The Streetkids Project described below & to Akany Avoko (page 144) both of which run child sponsorship schemes. As with MOSS (see below), the staff are all volunteers & they don't even have an office, so the overheads are very low. Thus you can be confident that almost all the money you give will go direct to the project you want to support. If you are singling out the Streetkids Project or Akany Avoko, write the cheque to Money for Madagascar but enclose a note saying where you want it to be sent.

CENTRE FIHAVANANA (THE STREETKIDS CENTRE)

Run by the Sisters of the Good Shepherd (*Centre Fihavanana (Soeurs du Bon Pasteur), 58 Lalana Stephani, Amparibe, 101 Antananarivo;* \ *22 299 81;* e *bpfihavanana@netclub.mg*) their activities are aimed mainly at women and children. About 300 children aged 3–12 are taught in four classes and many do well enough to get into state primary school. Undernourished babies are fed and their destitute mothers given training in childcare. Teenagers come to the centre to learn basic skills and handicrafts. Elderly people come twice a month for a little food, company and care. Food is taken weekly to over 300 women, teenagers and children in prison. 82 children at the centre are being helped by the Child Sponsor Programme, but there is a growing number still needing sponsors. The Centre also has a scheme called Wheels4Life which provides bicycles for young men who need them to earn a living. There are photos of these boys beaming from ear to ear on their shiny new bikes. Finally, a group of 86 women do beautiful embroidery at home while caring for their families, which provides an income both for them and for the centre.

A recent project is housing for needy women and their children; 27 simple houses have been built on donated land on the outskirts of Tana and this is now a thriving community with its own livestock and kitchen gardens. Added to this is the new Fanilo Crisis Home for girls and women who have been battered, abandoned or sexually abused.

The challenges of working with the destitute was brought home to me on a recent visit, when Sister Jeanette (who speaks English) told that women enrolling in the embroidery programme have first to be shown how to hold a pen, and then how to take measurements, before they can even begin to be taught how to sew. They also need to be 'paid' in food during their training to compensate for loss of earnings as beggars. Hard to believe when you see the exquisite work done by these former street-women.

If you live in the UK and have fallen in love with Madagascar, why not join the Anglo-Malagasy Society? Regular meetings with speakers are held in London, along with a delicious Malagasy buffet. A quarterly newsletter keeps members informed of events on the island. For more information see www.anglo-malagasysociety.co.uk.

MOSS c/o Oliver Backhouse, Denby Hse, Minskip, York, North Yorkshire YO51 9JF; e obackhouse@doctors.org.uk; www.mossuk.net. MOSS (Madagascan Organisation for Saving Sight) was set up in 1993, following a year's work by ophthalmologist Oliver Backhouse & his wife. Approximately 250,000 people in Madagascar are blind. Research undertaken by MOSS has shown that 70% of adult blindness is treatable & 90% of childhood blindness is preventable. MOSS is currently involved in a Childhood Refraction project in Fianarantsoa & an Outreach Cataract programme to run for 3yrs, delivering ophthalmic services in remoter areas. A recent similar project in Antsirabe was very successful: of the 65,000 children & teachers screened, 3,000 required spectacle correction.

Population Concern Studio 325, Highgate Studios, 53–79 Highgate Rd, London NW5 ITL; ☎ 020 7241 8500; f 0207267 6788; e info@populationconcern.org.uk; www.populationconcern.org.uk. 'Working for the right to reproductive healthcare worldwide.' At present this organisation, relatively new to Madagascar, is working in Toliara & Antsiranana on a variety of initiatives to improve the sexual health of young people. They also aim to reduce the incidence of teenage pregnancies. Doing similar work is **Population Services International** (www.psi.org). See page 172.

Water Aid A UK-based NGO, which works to help poor communities gain access to drinking water, safe sanitation & good hygiene. In Madagascar, where the majority of the population has none of these vital services, they have been working since 1999 with local partner organisations & the national government. In the highlands they support programmes in rural parts of Antananarivo & Fianarantsoa provinces, as well as parts of Toliara & the city of Toamasina. If you would like to know more, please contact wateraidmg@dts.mg or visit www.wateraid.org.

Mad Imports 262 Court St, Suite 3, Brooklyn, NY 11231; ☎ 718 802 9757; e laurel@madimports.org; www.madimports.org. A socially responsible company that imports & sells handmade art & accessories from Madagascar. The sale of these products supports community & economic development in Malagasy communities including Akany Avoko. They work with individual & collective groups of artists to import fine quality handmade art & accessories for sale in the US. This enables families to gain economic independence.

Wildlife

Conservation International (USA) 1015 18th St NW, Washington DC, 20003, USA; www.conservation.org. One of the most active conservation organisations in Madagascar.

Durrell Wildlife Conservation Trust Les Augres Manor, Trinity, Jersey JE3 5BP, Channel Islands, British Isles; ☎ 01534 860000; f 01534 860001; www.durrell.org.

Wildlife Conservation Society www.wcs.org. A US-based organisation at the Bronx Zoo in New York City which supports a wide range of conservation projects in Madagascar.

WWF Av du Mont-blanc, 1196 Gland, Switzerland (International Office); Panda Hse, Weyside Park, Godalming, Surrey GU7 IXR, UK; 1250 24th St NW, Washington DC 20037-1175, USA; Aires Protégées, BP738, Antananarivo 101, Madagascar. www.wwf.org

Part Two

THE GUIDE

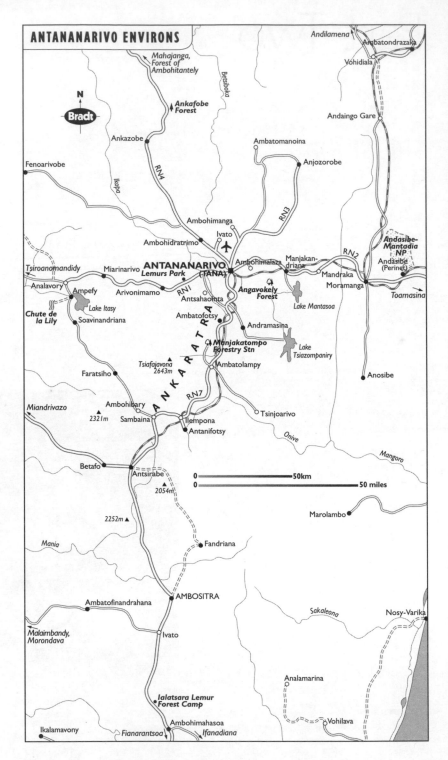

ANTANANARIVO ENVIRONS

N

Bradt

*Mahajanga,
Forest of
Ambohitantely*

Betsiboka

Andilamena

Ambatondrazaka

Vohidiala

*Ankafobe
Forest*

Andaingo Gare

Ankazobe

Ambatomanoina

Anjozorobe

Fenoarivobe

Ikopa

RN4

RN3

Ambohimanga

Ivato

Andasibe-
Mantadia
NP

RN2

Ambohidratrimo

Andasibe
(Perinet)

**ANTANANARIVO
(TANA)**

Ambohimalaza

Manjakan-
driana

Mandraka

Tsiroanomandidy

Lemurs Park

Miarinarivo

Moramanga

Analavory

Ampefy

Arivonimamo

RN1

Antsahaointa

*Angavokely
Forest*

Lake Mantasoa

Toamasina

*Chute de
la Lily*

Lake Itasy

Soavinandriana

Ambatofotsy

Andramasina

A
N
K
A
R
A
T
R
A

Faratsiho

*Tsiafajavona
2643m*

*Manjakatompo
Forestry Stn*

Lake
Tsiazompaniry

Ambatolampy

Miandrivazo

Ambohibary

2321m

Sambaina

RN7

Tsinjoarivo

Anosibe

Ilempona

Antanifotsy

Onive

Mangoro

Betafo

Antsirabe

0 ————— **50km**

0 ————————— 50 miles

2054m

Marolambo

2252m

Mania

Fandriana

*Malaimbandy,
Morondava*

Ambatofinandrahana

AMBOSITRA

Sakaleana

Nosy-Varika

Ivato

Analamarina

**Ialatsara Lemur
Forest Camp**

Ambohimahasoa

Ikalamavony

Fianarantsoa

Ifanadiana

Vohilava

7

Antananarivo and Area

Looking down from the plane window as you approach Antananarivo you can see how excitingly different this country is from any of its near neighbours. Clusters of red clay houses and steepled churches stand isolated on the hilltops overlooking a mosaic of green and brown paddy fields. Old defence ditches, *tamboho*, form circles around villages or estates, and dotted in the empty countryside are the white concrete Merina tombs from where the dead will be exhumed in *famadihana* ceremonies.

Most people stay only a day or so in Tana (as Antananarivo is often called), but there is plenty to see in the city and the surrounding *hauts plateaux*. A week would not be too long to experience the cultural, historical and natural sites which lie within a day's excursion from the capital. The kingdom of Imerina thrived for over a century before French colonisation, so it is here that the rich and fascinating history and culture of the Merina people are best appreciated.

HISTORY

At the end of the 16th century the Merina king Andrianjaka conquered a Vazimba town called Analamanga, built on a great rock thrusting above the surrounding plains. He renamed it Antananarivo and ordered his palace to be built on its highest point. With its surrounding marshland, ideal for rice production, and the security afforded by its position, this was the perfect site for a Merina capital city.

In the 18th century there were two centres for the Merina kingdom: Antananarivo and Ambohimanga. The latter became the more important and around 1787 Ramboasalama was proclaimed king of Ambohimanga and took the name of Andrianampoinimerina. The name means 'the prince in the heart of Imerina' which was more than an idle boast: this king was the Malagasy counterpart of the great Peruvian Inca Tupac Yupanqui, expanding his empire as much by skilful organisation as by force, and doing it without the benefit of a written language. (History seems to demonstrate that orders in triplicate are not essential to efficiency.) By his death in 1810 the central plateau was firmly in control of the Merina and ably administered through a mixture of old customs and new. Each conquered territory was governed by local princes, answerable to the king, and the system of *fokonolona* (village communities) was established. From this firm foundation the new king, Radama I, was able to conquer most of the rest of the island.

Antananarivo means 'city of the thousand', supposedly because a thousand warriors protected it. By the end of the 18th century Andrianampoinimerina had taken Antananarivo from his rebellious kinsman and moved his base there from Ambohimanga. From that time until the French conquest in 1895 Madagascar's history centred around the royal palace or *rova*, the modest houses built for Andrianjaka and Andrianampoinimerina giving way to a splendid palace designed for Queen Ranavalona I by Jean Laborde and later clad in stone by James Cameron. The rock cliffs near the palace became known as Ampamarinana (the place of hurling) as Christian martyrs met their fate at the command of the queen.

There was no reason for the French to move the capital elsewhere: its pleasant climate made it an agreeable place to live, and plenty of French money and planning went into the city we see today.

IVATO AIRPORT

The airport has been extensively modernised, with the international and domestic sections separated by a long corridor. Each has its own restaurant. The main one is upstairs in the international section. It's quite smart with waiter service and a self-service buffet for 15,000Ar. Nearby is a snack bar. In the domestic arrivals/departure area there is a café which serves tasty food from 06.00. As in all airports there are plenty of (expensive) souvenir shops and money-changing facilities. SOCIMAD in International Departures gives a better rate of exchange than the Bank of Africa in Arrivals.

ARRIVING In the good old days Ivato was like the cottage of a wicked witch, seducing innocent visitors through its beguiling doors. Once inside, only the good and the brave emerged unscathed. Now (sigh) it is much the same as other international airports in the developing world. On arrival the procedure is as follows:

1 Join the correct queue: with visa/no visa.
2 Fill in the Disembarkation/Embarkation Card. This should be handed to you on the plane (usually as part of a handy little booklet about Madagascar) but you may need to obtain one from an official by the immigration desk. The questions are straightforward, but be prepared to say where you'll be staying in Tana.
3 If you do not have a visa, fill in the appropriate form and have the required amount (currently €12) ready. This payment is made at a separate desk where the official will stick stamps inside your passport as proof of payment. The police official at the visa desk will also want to see your return flight tickets. Note that visas of up to 90 days can now be issued in the airport.
4 Shuffle forward in your queue to be processed. When you hand in your passport watch its progress to the next official and move to the appropriate window.
5 Pick up luggage. There are trolleys to take your bags through customs. If you are carrying a video camera or something of value such as jewellery or a laptop computer you should pass through the red channel and declare it. Failure to do this may cause problems on departure. Otherwise try to get behind other tourists who are usually waved through the green 'Nothing to Declare' channel without having to open their bags.

Be warned that the porters at Ivato are quite aggressive. Be on your guard and, unless you need help, insist on carrying your own stuff. Daniel Morgan warns: 'They jump on you like leeches. Mine kept saying "give me euro". Having just come from exchanging money, the smallest notes we had were 5,000Ar (about €2); you give one and later realise the phenomenal disparity of what should have been given and how this can only lead to the continued harassment of the embarrassed and bewildered newly-arrived traveller. If you are being met by a tour operator you won't need a porter, so be firm. If you do need one, have ready some single dollar bills – one per porter.

CHANGING MONEY On arrival most people will need to change money at the airport to pay for a taxi into the city. The banks are always open for international flight arrivals. There are two banks, and it's as well to compare exchange rates. At the time of writing BNI-Crédit Lyonnaise gave better rates than SOCIMAD. Daniel offers this warning: 'Falling off an aeroplane after an 11hr flight, you must guess how much local money you might need. Not easy in Madagascar. We handed over €350, then watched, stunned, as the cashier gave us huge handfuls of ariary. In that little booth, with a queue behind you, is your one chance to check the amount. The size of the bundles of notes evokes immediate insecurity. My partner sat with the luggage while I counted out (thankfully as an ex-bank-clerk) three quarters of a million ariary. I feel that people should be forewarned.'

I know of only one incidence of a traveller being short-changed, but it's as well to be on your guard. My own ploy is to change a small amount at the airport and the rest of my needs at the hotel or SOCIMAD (see page 174). Note that the airport banks are reluctant to change travellers' cheques.

LEAVING This has been streamlined and is now a normal procedure. You no longer need to reconfirm your flight, although you may wish to be on the safe side and also ask for a seat allocation. You can also change your ariary back into hard currency (minimum €40–50).

The Departure Lounge has some souvenir shops (hard currency only), a bar and an internet café. The women minding the toilets can often change a small amount of ariary into hard currency.

LOST LUGGAGE Sometimes your luggage doesn't arrive. These days there is a relatively efficient procedure: find the lost-luggage kiosk, fill in a form and they'll phone your hotel when the bag arrives. To be on the safe side ask for the phone number at the kiosk so you can find out if your luggage has been traced yet. If you have moved on they will usually send your bag to the nearest airport.

TRANSPORT TO THE CITY CENTRE (12KM) There is no airport bus service. Most mid- and upper-range hotels offer an airport transfer service. Otherwise official taxis will cost you 20,000–30,000Ar (€7–11). If you walk purposefully across the car park you will find some lurking unofficial taxis which are cheaper. Experienced travellers can go for the local bus which stops at the road junction about 100m from the airport. It costs only 400Ar and you can pay for an extra seat for your luggage. This bus takes you to the Vasakosy area behind the train station.

ANTANANARIVO (TANA) TODAY

From the right place, in the right light, Antananarivo is one of the most attractive capitals in the developing world. In the evening sunshine it has the quality of a child's picture book: brightly coloured houses stacked up the hillsides with mauve jacarandas and purple bougainvillea against the dark blue of the winter sky. Red crown-of-thorns euphorbias stand in rows against red clay walls, rice paddies are tended right up to the edge of the city, clothes are laid out on canal banks to dry, and zebu carts rumble along the roads on the outskirts of town. It's all deliciously foreign and can hardly fail to impress the first-time visitor as he or she drives in from the airport. Indeed, this drive is one of the most varied and interesting in the highlands. The good impression is helped by the climate: during the dry season the sun is hot but the air pleasantly cool (the altitude is between 1,245m and 1,469m).

Sadly, for many people this wonderful first impression does not survive a closer acquaintance. Tana can seem squalid and dangerous, with conspicuous poverty,

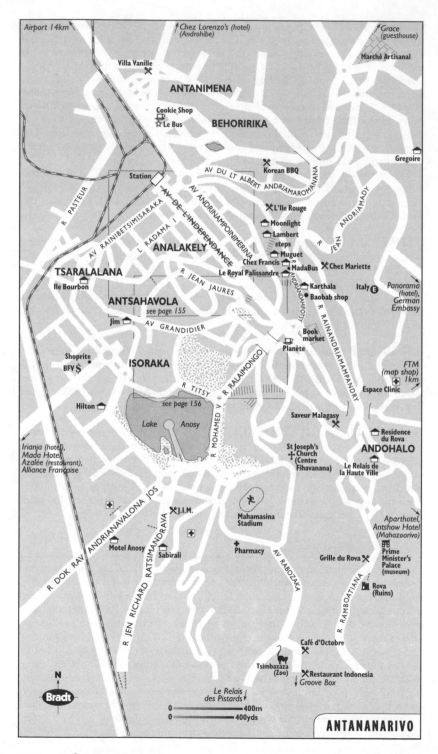

Airport 14km

Chez Lorenzo's (hotel)
(Androhibe)

Grace
(guesthouse)

Marché Artisanal

Villa Vanille ✗

ANTANIMENA

Cookie Shop
☆ ✕ Le Bus

BEHORIRIKA

Gregoire

Station

AV DU LT ALBERT ANDRIAMAROMANANA

Korean BBQ ✗

R PASTEUR

AV ANDRINAMPOINIMERINA

AV DE L'INDEPENDANCE

AV RAINIBETSIMISARAKA

L RADAMA I

✗ L'Ile Rouge

Moonlight
Lambert
steps
Muguet

ANALAKELY

Chez Francis
Le Royal Palissandre

MadaBus
✗ Chez Mariette

R JEN ANDRIAMADY

R ANDRIANDAHIFOTSY

TSARALALANA

Ile Bourbon

R JEAN JAURES

Karthala
Baobab shop

Italy Ⓔ

Panorama
(hotel),
German
Embassy

ANTSAHAVOLA
see page 155

AV GRANDIDIER

Jim

R RAINANDRIAMAMPANDRY

Book
market

Shoprite

BFV $

ISORAKA

R TITSY

R RALAIMONGO

Planète

FTM
(map shop)
1km

Espace Clinic

Hilton

see page 156

Lake
Anosy

R MOHAMED V

Saveur Malagasy
✗

Residence
du Rova

Irianja (hotel),
Mada Hotel,
Azalée (restaurant),
Alliance Française

ANDOHALO

St Joseph's
✝ Church
(Centre
Fihavanana)

Le Relais de
la Haute Ville

R DOK RAV ANDRIANAVALONA JOS

✗ J.I.M.

Mahamasina
Stadium

Aparthotel,
Antshow Hotel
(Mahazoarivo)

Prime
Minister's
Palace
(museum)

Motel Anosy

Sabirali

Pharmacy

AV RABOZAKA

Grille du Rova ✗

R JEN RICHARD RATSIMANDRAVA

Rova
(Ruins)

R RAMBOATIANA

Café d'Octobre
✗

Tsimbazaza
(Zoo)

✗ Restaurant Indonesia
↓ Groove Box

N

Bradt

Le Relais
des Pistards ↓

0 ——————— 400m
0 ——————— 400yds

ANTANANARIVO

154

persistent beggars and a worrying crime rate. However, in the late 1990s the then mayor of Tana, Marc Ravalomanana (now president), launched a clean-up campaign which has had a noticeable effect. Many foreigners mourn the passing of the *zoma* (street market) but the central areas of the city are undoubtedly cleaner and safer.

The geography of the city is both simple and confusing. It is built on two ridges which meet in a 'V'. On the highest hill, dominating all the viewpoints, is the ruined queen's palace or *rova*. Down the central valley runs a broad boulevard, Avenue de l'Indépendance (sometimes called by its Malagasy name Fahaleovantena), which terminates at the railway station. It narrows at the other end to become Rue du 26 Juin. To escape from this valley means climbing steps if you are on foot, or driving through a tunnel if you are in a vehicle.

It is convenient to divide Tana into the two main areas most often wandered by visitors: Avenue de l'Indépendance and the side streets to its southwest (districts Analakely and Tsaralalana, or the lower town) and the smarter area at the top of the steps leading up from Rue du 26 Juin (districts Antaninarenina and Isoraka, or the upper town). Of course there are lots of other districts but most tourists will take taxis to these rather than going on foot. This can be a challenging city to explore; streets are often unnamed, or change name several times within a few hundred metres, or go by two different names. When reading street names it's worth knowing that *Lalana* means street, *Arabe* is avenue and *Kianja* is square.

TELEPHONE CODE The area codes for Tana are 22 and 24.

ANALAKELY AND TSARALALANA (LOWER TOWN) Analakely (which means 'little forest') used to be famous for its large forest of white umbrellas, under which every product imaginable (and many unimaginable) used to be sold. Tana's *zoma* market

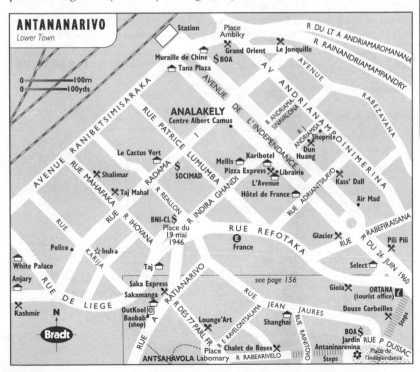

was famous worldwide. Now it has all gone (though illicit, dawn markets are still held in the side streets) and traffic and pedestrians can move more freely.

Avenue de l'Indépendance is a broad boulevard (grassed in the centre) with shops, snack bars, restaurants and hotels along each side. If you start at the station and walk up the right-hand side you will pass the Tana Plaza hotel, Librairie de Madagascar (a good bookshop) and Hôtel de France. Continuing south you reach one of Tana's liveliest bars (Le Glacier) and then you're at the steps up to Antaninarenina.

This is not a street for strolling – there are too many persistent beggars and souvenir vendors. And thieves, so walk briskly. Shopwise, the north side of the avenue is less interesting, but it does have several excellent snack bars, and the Air Madagascar office is here.

Tsaralalana is a more relaxing area of side streets to the south of Avenue de l'Indépendance (although maps do not indicate the steep climbs involved if you go too far). Walk down Rue Indira Gandhi (Rue Nice), past the shoe shop Aigle d'Or and Hôtel Mellis, to the cumbersomely named Place du 19 Mai 1946. Beyond it is Hôtel Taj and the very popular Sakamanga hotel/restaurant. The excellent Baobab souvenir shop is here and, at the top of the road, is BioAroma, which sells beauty products and herbal remedies. But to avoid this steep (rather dull) climb to Isoraka you could double back on one of the parallel streets to Avenue de l'Indépendance.

ANTANINARENINA AND ISORAKA (UPPER TOWN) This is the Islington of Tana; or the Greenwich Village. Here are the jewellers, the art shops and craft boutiques, the atmospheric hotels, the inexpensive guesthouses and a little-known museum. There is also a rose garden where, in October, the jacaranda trees drip their nectar onto the heads below. The beggars are persistent here too, but once you leave the hotel/post office area you can relax.

Start at the bottom of the steps by Select Hotel on Avenue de l'Indépendance and, as you climb up, marvel that so many men can make a living selling rubber

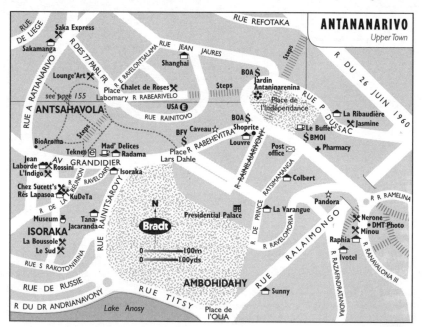

Stroll around Tana – or anywhere in Madagascar – and you'll come across groups of men and boys clustered round a board marked with squares and criss-crosses. Sometimes the 'board' is scratched in the earth. They are playing a game unique to Madagascar: *fanorona*. It is a game of strategy; in its simplest version it has some similarities to draughts/chequers but for advanced players it is more like chess. In Tana the best place to watch a game in progress is the Esplanade de la Pergola. Carved *fanorona* boards can be purchased (with instructions) at the Andravoahangy craft market.

stamps. Visit the Tana tourist office (ORTANA) on the right near the bottom of the steps, and check out their leaflets and tourist information. At the top of the steps is Place de l'Indépendance, and Jardin Antaninarenina with its jacarandas and rose bushes. And benches. Nearby is Le Buffet du Jardin where you can sip a fruit juice in the sun. Other landmarks are Hôtel du Louvre and Shoprite supermarket. Turn left and you'll come to the post office where, if you go through a side door to the philatelic counter, you can buy special-issue Malagasy stamps. If you feel like a coffee, yummy cake or ice cream, cross the road to Hôtel Colbert. The street-side bar/café is where conservationists and other expats meet to discuss their latest challenges, and the patisserie is where tourists come to indulge their cravings.

Now it's time to explore Isoraka. A 30-minute walk is enough to take in the main sights. Start up Rue Rabehevitra, past Radama Hotel, Hôtel Isoraka and Arts Malagasy which has a good selection of crafts. Turn left onto Rue Raveloary, continue over the next intersection and you'll pass a very nice little restaurant: Chez Sucett's. Before that there's a cobbler's shop with a group of men sitting outside chatting and stitching. If you have anything that needs repairing, this is the place. On a corner is Résidence Lapasoa. At this point (opposite) look out for a bronze 'tree' hung with clay pots which marks the Musée d'Art et Archéologie. On the way back, drop in at Galerie Yerden, one of Tana's best craft shops, on Rue Dr Villette, then pick whatever street you fancy to get you back to Place de l'Indépendance.

GETTING AROUND

Traffic jams and pollution are major problems in Tana. Traffic is often gridlocked on the narrow, hilly streets so it makes sense to avoid vehicular transport when possible. Get to know the city on foot during the day (but carry nothing of value); use taxis for long distances, unknown destinations and always at night.

Taxis are easily recognised by their cream colour. Tough bargainers will pay no more than 4,000Ar for a short trip but most *vazaha* end up paying around 5,000Ar. Prices are much higher after dark. Taxis do not have meters so agree the price before you get in. The taxis that wait outside posh hotels like the Colbert are more expensive but also more reliable than those cruising the streets. (Check the fare with the hotel receptionist if you think you are being ripped off.) The cheaper option is to take one of the battered, old vehicles which wouldn't dare go near a hotel and you have the extra bonus of watching the street go by through the hole in the floor, or being pushed by helpful locals when the vehicle breaks down or runs out of fuel.

The advantage of having no meters is that if the driver gets lost (not unusual) you won't pay any more for the extra journey. In my experience Tana's taxi drivers are honest and helpful, and can be trusted to get you to your destination – eventually. They will also pick you up at an agreed time.

Buses are much cheaper, but sorting out the destinations and districts can be difficult. A good map of Tana is helpful here.

☞ **WARNING!** Sadly robbery has become quite common in Tana. Leave your valuables in the hotel (preferably in a safe or locked in your bag) and carry as little as possible. Avenue de l'Indépendance seems particularly risky. One scam is the 'ballet of the hats': kids in wide-brimmed straw hats encircle you and, using the hats to obscure your view, work through your pockets, money belt, neck pouch or whatever. If you can manage to carry nothing at all – no watch, no camera, no money ... not even a paper tissue in your pocket – you will bring back the best souvenirs: memories. But few people (myself included) heed this advice, so just be on your guard and never wander around with passports or flight tickets unless they are safe in a money belt.

WHERE TO STAY

New hotels and restaurants are opening all the time in Tana. This selection is by no means complete – be adventurous and find your own!

Note that the better hotels charge a tourist tax of around 2,000Ar.

LUXURY ♔

⌂ **The Caravon Annex** At Hôtel Colbert (see below). The only truly luxury accommodation in Tana. Beautiful views & separate, comfy sitting-rooms (Senior Suite only). The marble-dressed bathrooms are almost embarrassingly opulent, with his-&-hers washbasins, deep bathtubs & separate showers.

⌂ **Hilton Hotel** (171 rooms) Rue Pierre Stibbe, Anosy; ☎ 22 260 60; f 22 260 51; e sales_madagascar@hilton.com. On west side of Lake Anosy. Skyscraper with lovely views. Its advantages are the offices & shops in the building, 4 restaurants, cybercafé, ATM & swimming pool (a real

bonus in the dry season). Some way from town centre but the walk in is enjoyable. Most credit cards accepted. Airport transfers inc.

⌂ **Hôtel Colbert** (140 rooms) Rue Printsy Ratsimamanga, Antaninarenina; ☎ 22 202 02; f 22 340 12/254 97; e colbert@wanadoo.mg; www.colbert-hotel.com. In a prime location in the upper town, the main hotel has standard, comfortable accommodation (inc suites with separate sitting-room), plus indoor pool, sauna, fitness centre, cybercafé, business centre & casino. Very French. Recommended for its central location, nice atmosphere, excellent food & decadent patisserie. Most credit cards accepted.

⌂ **Hôtel Le Royal Palissandre** (36 rooms) 13 Rue Andriandahifotsy (Rue Romain Desfossés), Faravohitra; ↘ 22 605 60; f 22 326 24; e hotelpalissandre@simicro.mg; www.hotel-palissandre.com. Recommended;

TOP END €€€€€

⌂ **Hôtel du Louvre** (60 rooms) 4 Pl Philibert Tsiranana; ↘ 22 390 00; f 22 640 40; e hoteldulouvre@simicro.mg; www.hotel-du-louvre.com. Convenient, safe upper-town location. Comfortable & well-run, with very pleasant rooftop bar, good restaurant, free internet facilities & massage room. Expanding into current Shoprite premises in 2007. Airport transfers.

⌂ **Hôtel de France** (30 rooms) 34 Av de l'Indépendance; ↘ 22 213 04; f 22 201 18; e hdf_tana@wanadoo.mg. Very pleasant with large rooms (some with terrace), convenient central location

UPPER RANGE €€€€
Town centre

⌂ **La Varangue** (7 rooms) 17 Rue Printsy Ratsimamanga, Antaninarenina; ↘ 22 273 97; f 22 552 30; e varangue@simicro.mg. Charming, traditional, Creole-style home; interesting décor. Comfortable rooms with fan, heating, safe, satellite TV & minibar. Secure parking. Excellent restaurant. 'Amazing food & generally a lovely, very friendly place' (PJ). Visa accepted.

⌂ **Hôtel de l'Avenue** (7 apartments & 8 studios) Av de l'Indépendance (near Hôtel de France); ↘ 22 228 18; f 22 356 24; e bj-karim@malagasy.com or kamoula@blueline.mg. Self-catering apartments with satellite TV. Clean with English-speaking staff. Long-stay discounts. Bar/restaurant & popular internet café on 1st floor. B/fast inc. Airport transfer.

⌂ **Résidence Lapasoa** (10 rooms) 15 Rue de la Réunion, Isoraka; ↘ 22 611 40; e corossol@malagasy.com. Friendly guesthouse in a pleasant part of town, ideal for lone travellers. Sgl, dbl, twin, tpl & family en-suite rooms with TV, phone & safe. 'I had a most comfortable stay here. It is tastefully decorated & furnished, immaculately clean, with overall simple elegance. A common room with free internet connection encourages interaction with other guests. Breakfast is in the equally pleasing downstairs restaurant KuDeTa' (Lee Miller).

⌂ **Sakamanga** (32 rooms) Rue Andrianary Ratianarivo; ↘ 22 358 09; m 032 02 668 34/033 11 769 27; f 22 245 87; e saka@malagasy.com; www.sakamanga.com. Lovely French-run hotel

popular with tourists & businesspeople. All comforts, good food, lovely views & pleasant location within walking distance of town centre. Bar, meeting room, swimming pool & fitness centre. Massage available. B/fast inc.

& very good food. Internet facilities. B/fast inc.

⌂ **Tana Plaza** (75 rooms) 2 Av de l'Indépendance (near the station); ↘ 22 218 65; f 22 642 19; e hdf_tana@wanadoo.mg. Upmarket but rooms facing street can be noisy. Conference room & private internet room. Good restaurant. B/fast inc. Airport transfer.

⌂ **Sunny Hotel** (16 rooms) Rue Ralaimongo (northeast of Lake Anosy); ↘ 22 263 04; f 22 290 78; e sunny@wanadoo.mg. A good location (though not sunny!), handy for both lower & upper town; friendly staff; good food.

decorated throughout with interesting historic photos & artefacts. Rooms en suite with fan, phone, safe & satellite TV. Also suite with AC, balcony & minibar. Usually full so booking is essential. The excellent, lively restaurant/bar is popular & also heavily booked. Movies shown (in French) at 17.00 every Sun (for programme see website). *Cheapest rooms from 34,000Ar (€12).*

⌂ **Radama Hotel** (16 rooms) 22 Av Ramanantsoa, Isoraka; ↘ 22 319 27; f 22 353 23; e radama@simicro.mg; www.radama-hotel.com. A small hotel in a great location down from the Colbert. Sgl, twin & dbl rooms with hot water, satellite TV, phone & minibar; some with AC, balcony & view. Ideal for businesspeople (conference room) or independent travellers. No elevator. **Tatao** restaurant features rather indifferent Malagasy & international cuisine with live music in the evenings. Airport transfer. Most credit cards accepted.

⌂ **Hôtel Raphia** (11 rooms & 1 bungalow) Rue Ranavalona III, Ambatonakanga; ↘ 22 253 13; e hotelraphia@wanadoo.mg; www.hotels-raphia.com. Nice hotel with lovely views over Lake Anosy from 3rd & 4th floors; bungalow in garden. Sgl, dbl & tpl rooms at various prices. B/fast inc. Airport transfer. Tours organised in the south from Tana to Ifaty for groups of 10–15: €99 pp for 10 days.

⌂ **Karibotel** (25 rooms) Av de l'Indépendance; ↘ 22 665 54/629 31; m 033 11 665 54; f 22 629 32; e karibotel@wanadoo.mg;

7

http://takelaka.dts.mg/karibotel/. Clean, comfortable rooms with bath/shower; some with balcony. Lively folk music every Fri night. Airport transfer. Visa accepted.

🏠 **Le Cactus Vert (Indri Hotel)** (15 rooms) 15 Rue Radama I, Tsaralalana; ☎ 22 209 22/624 41; f 22

Outskirts

🏠 **Résidence du Rova** Pl Ratsimandrava, Ambohijatovo (near the Queen's Palace); ☎ 22 341 46; f 22 239 12; e residence.rova@wanadoo.mg; www.residence-antananarivo.com. Self-catering apartments with fully equipped kitchen, TV, phone & small sitting-room. Secure parking.

🏠 **Hôtel Panorama** (55 rooms) Rte d'Andrainarivo; ☎ 22 412 44/412 45/409 65; m 033 11 054 35/033 07 054 35; f 22 412 47; e panorama@wanadoo.mg; www.panoramatana.com. Spacious, comfortable rooms with AC. Swimming pool & conference room. Good quality but not conveniently located.

🏠 **Chez Lorenzo's** (5 rooms) Lot II M 35 N, Androhibe (Rue des Hydrocarbures); ☎ 22 427 76; f 22 421 71; e lorenzo@wanadoo.mg. A peaceful place away from city bustle, 8km from town centre on road to Ivandry. Satellite TV. Good restaurant & pizzeria with international & Malagasy food. B/fast inc.

🏠 **Aparthotel (Radama House)** (14 rooms/apartments) Rte d'Ambohipo, Ambatoroka; ☎ 22 334 71/249 84; f 22 334 94; e radama.house@wanadoo.mg; Caters mainly for business travellers with apartments that can be

624 40; e lecactusvert@wanadoo.mg. Comfortable, friendly, medium-sized hotel in a convenient location. Rooms have TV, phone & safe. Small craft shop & lively cocktail bar. Restaurant serves Malagasy & international cuisine. Airport transfers.

taken by the week as well as hotel rooms. Secure parking. Conference facilities. Excellent **Tranovola** restaurant.

🏠 **Antshow Madagascar** (5 rooms) Lot VK67 Ter AC, Ambatolava, Morarano; ☎ 22 565 47; e info@antshow.nu; www.antshow.nu. Not just a hotel but a complete Malagasy experience. Tpl rooms. Malagasy meals served with 24hrs notice. If your visit coincides with one of the twice-monthly musical events you're in for a treat! Artists from all over the world perform here from time to time. 'A really superb place to stay' (K Harvey).

🏠 **La Ribaudière** (11 rooms) Rue Paul Dussac, Analakely Sud (behind BNI bank); ☎ 24 215 25; e laribaudiere@wanadoo.mg. New centrally located hotel; very comfortable with TV & impeccable bathrooms. Pleasant, inexpensive restaurant; booking essential.

🏠 **Hôtel Gregoire** (30 rooms) Lot II M 53, Ter Mahavoky, Besarety; ☎ 22 222 66; f 22 292 71; e gregoir@bow.dts.mg; www.madagascar-contacts.com/gregoire/. Near Andravoahangy craft market. Comfy rooms with AC, minibar, satellite TV & safe.

MID RANGE €€€
Town centre

🏠 **Ivotel** (20 rooms) Rue Razafindratandra, Ambohidahy; ☎ 22 227 16; e sitivoltel@wanadoo.mg. Sgl, dbl & twin rooms & suites.

🏠 **La Muraille de Chine** (20 rooms) 1 Av de l'Indépendance; ☎ 22 230 13; f 22 628 82; e murchine@wanadoo.mg. One of Tana's longest-established hotels. Clean, bright rooms with TV, hot water & toilet. Friendly staff. Chinese restaurant (☎ 22 281 41) & **Montana Voyage** travel agency on premises. A small free book of useful Malagasy words is available at reception.

🏠 **White Palace Hotel** (75 rooms) 101 Rue de Liège, Tsaralalana; ☎ 22 664 59/669 98; f 22 602 98; e white-palace@malagasy.com. Conveniently located in lower town. Sgl, dbl & tpl rooms in 3 categories: gold, silver (with bath) & bronze. B/fast inc. Airport transfers.

🏠 **Hôtel Mellis** (50 rooms) 3 Rue Indira Gandhi; ☎ 22 234 35/660 70/625 35; e resa@

madagascar-hotel-mellis.com; www.madagascar-hotel-mellis.com. A perennial favourite in a good location with rooms ranging from dbl to suite. Some with AC & balcony.

🏠 **Tana-Jacaranda** (7 Rooms) 24 Rue Rainitsarovy, Antsahamanitra; ☎ 24 235 77; m 032 07 056 51; f 22 562 40; e tana-jacaranda@tana-jacaranda.com; www.tana-jacaranda.com. Modern, clean sgl, dbl & twin rooms with shared bathroom. Very friendly owner & staff. Use of kitchen & dining room with wonderful views from balcony. Free Wi-Fi internet access. Airport transfer. Visa accepted.

🏠 **Hôtel Shalimar** (25 rooms) 5 Rue Mahafaka, Tsaralalana; ☎ 22 640 03; f 22 689 93. Dbl, twin & tpl rooms with AC, satellite TV & hot water. Some with shower/bath. Its restaurant next door offers Indian & mixed cuisine.

🏠 **Hôtel Sabirali** (18 rooms) Soanierana; ☎ 22 621 52; e hotelsabirali@yahoo.fr. Handily situated near the south *taxi-brousse* station. Dbl rooms, some en suite.

🏠 **Hôtel Restaurant Chez Francis** (16 rooms) Rue Andriandahifotsy; ✆ 22 613 65; f 22 613 65; e hotelchezfrancis@mel.wanadoo.mg or francisvacheresse@yahoo.fr. Super little place in a good location; lovely views over Tana from back rooms (could be noisy at front). Rooms have bathroom with hot water. Some with shared toilet, others en suite with TV. There is also an annexe with spacious rooms.

🏠 **Hôtel Taj** (23 rooms) 69 Rue de Liège, Tsaralalana (near Pl du 19 Mai 1946); ✆ 22 624 09/10; f 22 331 34; e taj@wanadoo.mg. Comfortable sgl & dbl rooms with hot water. Good restaurant. But 2 readers warn: '6 floors & no lift, so choose your room wisely!' & 'The red light district seems to be right across the street. If sex tourism isn't your bag, you might want to stay somewhere else.'

🏠 **Ile Bourbon** (9 rooms) 12 Rue Benyowski, Tsaralalana; ✆ 22 279 42; f 22 624 96; e hotelbourbon@freenet.mg. The owner is from Réunion. This Creole-style house has dbl & tpl rooms with hot water & TV.

Outskirts

🏠 **Le Relais de la Haute Ville** (9 rooms) Rue Pierre Rapiera, Ambohijatovo; ✆ 22 604 58; m 033 11 755 42/033 11 776 20; e rhvl@mel.wanadoo.mg. An old colonial house on the way to the Queen's Palace. Comfortable rooms with TV, internet access & minibar. Restaurant with Malagasy & European food.

🏠 **Le Relais des Pistards** (8 rooms) BP 3550, Rue Fernand Kasanga (1km past Tsimbazaza zoo); ✆ 22 291 34; f 22 629 56; e pistards@simicro.mg. A friendly, family-style hotel run by Florent & Jocelyn Colney. Sgl & dbl rooms, some en suite. Pleasant dining room & excellent cooking. Florent is an avid mountain biker, so a stay here is a must for those cycling in Madagascar. Car, minibus & 4x4 rental.

🏠 **La Karthala** (8 rooms) 48 Rue Andriandahifotsy; ✆ 22 248 95; f 22 272 67; e le_karthala@yahoo.fr. A short walk from Av de l'Indépendance. A secluded enclave in central Tana, the traditional Malagasy home of Mme Rafalimanana. English spoken. B/fast inc.

BUDGET €€

🏠 **Hôtel Isoraka** (7 rooms) 11 Av Gal Ramanantsoa; ✆ 22 355 81; f 22 355 81. Recently refurbished. Basic but bright rooms with safe & fan; some en suite with hot water. Reasonable sgl rooms; better rooms up to 56,000Ar. Staff friendly & helpful but little English spoken. Can be noisy.

🏠 **Hôtel Jean Laborde** (13 rooms) 3 Rue de Russie, Isoraka; ✆ 22 330 45; f 22 327 94. Very conveniently located with rooms ranging from en-suite ones with phone, table & balcony to basic ones with hot shower & basin but shared toilets (accessible only through restaurant!). Rooms fronting the street can be noisy. No credit cards.

🏠 **Hôtel Anjary** (133 rooms) 89 Rue de Liège, Tsaralalana; ✆ 22 244 09/279 58; f 22 234 18; e anjary-hotel@wanadoo.mg; www.anjary-hotel.com. Clean, large, secure & friendly. Rooms with fan, AC, fridge, safe & reliable hot water. Room service & elevator. Rooms on 4th floor are best but avoid those facing the (noisy) street. Massage available. Their 7th-floor **Terrasse Exotique** restaurant (m 033 11 358 29) offers Indian & Malagasy cuisine. *Restaurant open daily, evening only on Sun.*

🏠 **Select Hotel** (20 rooms) 54 Av de l'Indépendance; ✆ 22 629 16; m 032 07 965 18. En-suite rooms with TV. An ugly tower block with little to commend it but its prime location. 'Very run down with visibly sagging beds.'

🏠 **Grace Guest House Ankanin'ny Soa** (8 rooms) Ambatobe (near Lycée Français); ✆ 24 326 80; m 033 12 010 52/033 11 658 85; e akany_soa@yahoo.fr. Comfortable & peaceful in a quiet residential area 10mins from town centre & 25mins from airport. Sgl, twin & family rooms, en suite with hot water, lounge with minibar & satellite TV. Malagasy décor, beautiful garden & views from terrace. Car rental. Airport transfer.

🏠 **Motel Anosy (Solimotel)** (32 rooms) Route d'Arivonimamo, RN1, Anosy (opposite flower market & hospital); ✆ 22 670 83/89/96; e motelanosy@wanadoo.mg. Rooms have phone & satellite TV. Swimming pool & tennis court at extra cost. Good restaurant serving European & Malagasy cuisine; good pizzas.

🏠 **Hôtel Shanghai** (19 rooms) 4 Rue Rainitovo, Antsahavola (near US Embassy); ✆ 22 314 72/675 13; f 22 315 61; e shanghai@malagasy.com. Very competitive rates.

🏠 **Mada Hotel** (18 rooms) Rue Agosthino Neto Andavamamba (opposite Alliance Française); ✆ 22 636 90. Sgl, dbl, twin & tpl rooms with TV, fan/AC, hot shower/bath & phone. Also family suites (up to 6 people) for 42,000Ar.

🏠 **Hôtel Lambert** (24 rooms) Lot SIAC 3, Ambondrona; ☎ 22 229 92; m 032 40 904 95; e hotellambert@yahoo.fr; www.hotellambert.tk. Basic, clean, convenient, good value & popular, but be prepared to climb a lot of stairs! Free aperitifs on Sun for guests.

🏠 **Moonlight Hotel** (10 rooms) SIAB 10, Rue Rainandriamampandry, Ambondrona; ☎ 22 268 70; e hasinaherizo@yahoo.fr. This old refurbished Malagasy house retains much of its former charm; recommended by several readers. Good for lone travellers (cheap sgl rooms & dorm beds) from 8,000Ar. Airport transfer.

🏠 **Chambres d'Hôte 'Jim'** (4 rooms) Rue Grandidier (at intersection with Rue Andrianary); ☎ 22 374 37. Clean balconies with sunset views. En-suite showers; shared toilet.

BED AND BREAKFAST Staying with a family, bed-and-breakfast style, is an excellent introduction to Madagascar.

🏠 **Country View B&B** (7 rooms) Off road to Mahajanga, 5mins beyond Ambohidratrimo; ☎ 22 582 78; m 033 12 591 00; f 22 582 78; e cview@netclub.mg. A spacious, comfortable South-African-owned house, but quite far from Tana centre. Some rooms en suite. Airport transfer. €€€€

🏠 **Irianja Guest House** (5 rooms) Lot AVB 100, Avarabohitra, Itaosy; m 033 11 546 56; e info@irianja.com; www.irianja.com. En-suite dbl & twin rooms in a large, comfortable home set in a splendid tranquil garden; warm hospitality. Traditional Malagasy cuisine. Massage & botanical garden tours for guests. A day's notice required for meals & airport transfer (25mins by car). B/fast inc. €€€€

🏠 **Villa Soamahatony** (5 rooms) BP 11044, Rte Digue, Ankadivory; ☎ 24 900 60/22 585 18; m 033 11 033 37; e soamahatony@wanadoo.mg; http://takelaka.dts.mg/soamahatony/. A delightful villa set in 2ha of grounds with fantastic views over the rice paddies. Owned by a French-Malagasy couple who can arrange car rental for short excursions. Sgl & dbl rooms with shared facilities; 2 en-suite rooms under construction. Airport transfers (10mins by car). €€€

🏠 **Soamiandry Sarl** (7 rooms) Ankadivory, Talatamaty; m 033 14 882 28; e soamiandry@yahoo.fr. Family-run (so book ahead). 'Joshua & Fara try to do everything for you; it's one of those places you remember.' Garden with swimming pool. €€€

ACCOMMODATION NEAR THE AIRPORT It can take 45 minutes to get to the airport from the centre of town, so staying nearby is a sensible option, especially when you have an early-morning flight.

🏠 **Relais des Plateaux** (19 rooms) Lot 66 B, Antanetibe, Ivato; ☎ 22 441 18/22; f 22 444 76; e relaisdesplateaux@wanadoo.mg; www.relais-des-plateaux.com. Just 5mins from airport in a rural setting. Sgl & dbl rooms with AC, minibar, safe, direct international calls & satellite TV. Children's playground; heated pool. Large restaurant (fast service). Malagasy craft boutique. Minibus rental. Airport transfers inc. €€€€€

🏠 **Mahavelo** (18 rooms) Off Rte de l'Aeroport (near Club du Car), Ivato; ☎ 22 004 64; m 032 07 720 68; e hotelmahavelo@netclub.mg or hotelmahavelo@yahoo.fr. Quiet, comfortable, en-suite sgl, dbl & twin rooms with garden view. Restaurant **Alamanda** offers tropical & French dishes. Airport transfer. €€€

🏠 **Sifaka Auberge** (8 rooms) Lot 152 A, Antanetibe, Antehiroka, Ivato; ☎ 22 481 32; f 22 441 74; m 032 07 174 67; e sifaka.auberge@wanadoo.mg. Peaceful, pleasant surroundings. Dbl & twin rooms, some en suite. Good restaurant **Clos Semillon** with English menu. Airport transfer. €€€

🏠 **Tonga Soa** (4 rooms & 1 bungalow) Mandrosoa; ☎ 22 442 88; m 032 02 181 11; f 24 254 50; e tongasoahotel@mel.wanadoo.mg. This pleasant place is only 5mins from the airport. 'Managed by Ninah, a warm & very active person. Clean, very nice accommodation with the best breakfast we had in Madagascar & very good Malagasy food' (Silke Rother). The Tonga Soa is also well-known for its garden full of endemic plants, birds & jewel chameleons. Advance booking essential. Euro accepted. €€€

🏠 **Hôtel Ivato** (26 rooms) Lot K6 28, Imotro, Ivato; ☎ 22 445 10; f 22 586 93; e ivatotel@wanadoo.mg. Only 900m from airport. Friendly, clean & comfortable. Dbl, twin & family rooms with hot showers. Secure parking. Restaurant specialises in Malagasy & Chinese food. Airport transfer inc (arrival only; additional charge for departure transfer).

Restaurant open daily 06.30–10.00, 11.30–14.30 & 18.00–23.00. €€€

🏠 **Hôtel Restaurant Farihy** (15 rooms & 5 bungalows) ME 475, Mandrosoa, Ivato; ✆ 22 580 76; m 032 40 263 31/032 04 586 73/033 12 727 31. Dbl & twin rooms & bungalows. Meals available. €€€

🏠 **Auberge du Cheval Blanc** (33 rooms) BP 23, Ivato; ✆ 22 446 46; e chevalblanc@wanadoo.mg; www.cheval-blanc-madagascar.com. This is one of Madagascar's longest-established hotels, just 1km from the airport. Sgl & dbl rooms set in a pleasant garden. TV lounge. Recently renovated restaurant with live music nightly & a buffet Sun eve. Airport transfers inc. €€€

🏠 **Le Manoir Rouge** (35 rooms) Lot K IV 023, Ivato; ✆ 24 576 96/22 441 04; f 22 482 44; m 032 40 260 97; e madatana@wanadoo.mg; www.manoirrouge.com. A mere 600m from airport. Fairly basic rooms for 1–6 people, some en suite. Snack bar & take-away food. Cybercafé & satellite TV. Camping permitted. Airport transfers inc. €€–€€€€

🏠 **Residence Hôtelière Raphia** (6 rooms) Mandrosoa, Ivato; ✆ 22 452 97; m 033 12 191 73; e hotelraphia@wanadoo.mg; www.hotels-raphia.com. Same ownership as Hôtel Raphia in Isoraka. En-suite dbl, twin & tpl rooms with hot water. TV for extra fee. Restaurant serves Indian & French food. Airport transfer (5mins by car). €€–€€€

🏠 **Motel au Transit** (16 bungalows & 6 rooms) Antanetibe, Ivato; m 033 11 338 31. Near airport. Basic but good value. Meals available. €–€€€

✕ WHERE TO EAT

HOTEL RESTAURANTS Most of the better hotels serve good food. Expats and Malagasy professionals favour the **Colbert**. The all-you-can-eat Sunday buffet is good value (but beware of the health risks of eating cold buffets). There are two restaurants at the Colbert; the **Taverne** (✆ *22 202 02*) is the smartest and imposes a dress code on its diners. The food and service are excellent – this is the place to go for that special treat. Bring your French dictionary – menus are not translated.

The **Hilton** does a whole series of buffets which in the past were very good; standards seem to have declined recently, however. A better bet is **Tana Plaza** which has an excellent restaurant with live music (traditional) in the bar. On Av de l'Indépendance there is the popular **O! Poivre Vert** (✆ *22 213 04*), next to Hôtel de France, and a short walk away is the **Sakamanga** restaurant: crowded and lively, with excellent food, though almost exclusively European clientele. Book ahead (✆ *22 358 09*). Finally **La Varangue** (*Rue P Ratsimamanga, Antaninarenina;* ✆ *22 273 97/251 74;* e *varangue@moov.mg*) is rated by Lorna Gillespie as the best of all Tana's restaurants: 'sophisticated surrounds, exceptionally well-presented food, well-trained and professional staff.'

SPECIAL TREAT

✕ **Villa Vanille** Pl Antanimena; ✆ 22 205 15. A fine old Tana house, about 100yrs old, specialising in Creole food. Music (traditional Malagasy & jazz) every evening. 'Exceptionally good: wonderful food, wine, service & local music. The lady owner very much in evidence, talking to every guest & making sure that everything was A1' (Daniel Morgan). 🕐 11.30–23.00.

✕ **La Table d'Hôte de Mariette (Chez Mariette)** 11 Rue George V, Faravohitra; ✆ 22 216 02; f 22 277 19; www.sinergic.mg. Beautifully prepared Malagasy food, traditionally served. Described by one visitor as 'caught in a time warp' but I loved this elegant stylisation when I last ate there. Advance booking essential.

✕ **Restaurant Tranovola** Rte d'Ambohipo, Ambatoroka; ✆ 22 334 71/249 84; f 22 334 94. Opened in 2003, this is the place to go for an end-of-the-trip treat. Superb & unusual Malagasy cooking & music. The manager, Elyane Rahonintsoa, ensures that this is an evening to remember. Malagasy buffet Thu eve with traditional *valiha* musicians; piano bar with happy hour Fri eve.

✕ **Le Grill du Rova** About 100m down from the queen's palace; ✆ 22 627 24; f 22 622 13. Excellent food, eaten indoors or outside, with a view over the city. Traditional Malagasy music every Sun noon–sunset; piano bar Wed eve. Good English spoken. Recommended. 🕐 Mon–Sat 10.00–22.00; Sun 10.00–18.00.

SERIOUS EATING AND MID RANGE
Upper town

✗ **Le Rossini** Rue Général Ramanantsoa, Isoraka (opposite Espace Mada); ☎ 22 342 44. Upmarket French restaurant in a good location. Meat dishes particularly recommended.

✗ **La Boussole** 21 Rue de Dr Villette, Isoraka; ☎ 22 358 10. Stylish French restaurant with excellent food, cosy bar & charming patio for outdoor dining. The best restaurant in Isoraka. Especially lively Fri eve. ⊕ daily.

✗ **KuDeTa** 15 Rue de la Réunion, Isoraka; ☎ 22 281 54. 'Food is upmarket, stylish & the waiters fun if you speak French' says one reader; 'dire' says another. You decide.

✗ **L'Indigo** 5 Rue Raveloary, Isoraka; ☎ 24 220 52; e fhorm@simicro.mg. Tex-Mex speciality restaurant with Algerian owner/chef. Fantastic food; vibrant & colourful décor; excellent service.

✗ **Nerone** 28 Rue Ratsimilaho, Ambatonakanga; ☎ 22 231 18; e smietana@wanadoo.mg. Small, upmarket Italian restaurant offering a variety of à la carte dishes & Italian wines. Sometimes live music. ⊕ 10.00–14.00 & 18.00–23.00.

✗ **Le Sud** 23 Rue Dr Villete, Isoraka; ☎ 22 310 22. Specialises in grills but also serves European food. W/end cabaret & concerts. ⊕ 12.00–14.30 & 18.00–23.00.

✗ **Restaurant Chez Sucett's** 23 Rue Raveloary, Isoraka; ☎ 22 261 00; Pleasant, small restaurant specialising in Creole food. Universally praised; excellent service.

✗ **Restaurant Jasmin** 8 Rue Razanatseheno; ☎ 22 342 96. Good Chinese food. ⊕ 12.00–14.00 & 19.00–22.00.

Lower town

✗ **Le Grand Orient** Place Ambiky (near the station); ☎ 22 202 88. One of Tana's long-established restaurants. Chinese, fairly expensive, but extensive menu, nice atmosphere & piano music at w/end.

✗ **Le Kashmir** 5/7 Rue Dr Ranaivo; ☎ 22 328 42; m 032 04 009 19. Muslim-run, very good & reasonably priced food. Malagasy, French & Indian cuisine. ⊕ 07.30–21.00.

✗ **La Jonquille** 7 Rue Rabezavana, Soarano; ☎ 22 206 37. A small restaurant with imaginative menu, mainly Chinese; especially good seafood. Reasonable prices. Booking recommended, particularly w/end.

✗ **El Pili Pili** 39 Av de l'Indépendance, Analakely; ☎ 22 556 14. Popular with locals. Low prices & good pizzas. ⊕ daily 09.00–24.00.

Outskirts

✗ **Restaurant J.I.M** III N 77 Bis Bd Ratsimandrava, Soanierana; ☎ 22 655 15; m 033 02 788 88. Serves good, though rather overpriced Chinese food. Plush décor with casino.

✗ **La Saveur Malagasy** 56 Rue Tsiombikibo, Ambatovinaky; ☎ 22 613 91. About 10mins walk from upper town post office towards the rova. European & Malagasy food in a romantic setting. ⊕ Mon–Sat 10.00–22.30; closed Sun.

BUDGET
Upper town

✗ **Chalet des Roses** 13 Rue Rabary, Antsahavola (opposite US Embassy); ☎ 22 642 33. 'Delicious & affordable pizzas.' Other dishes served too.

✗ **Minou** Rue Ratsimilaho, Ambatonakanga; ☎ 22 288 62. Very good budget restaurant with inexpensive, tasty food. A range of dishes: Malagasy,

Chinese & European. ⊕ from 08.00.

✗ **Restaurant aux Douze Corbeilles** On the steps up to Antaninarenina. A Malagasy-run, non-smoking restaurant (quite a rarity!); excellent food at very reasonable prices.

Lower town

✗ **Lounge'Art** Rue des 77 Parlementaires Français, Antsahavola (near Air Mauritius); ☎ 22 612 42. Pub & Restaurant. European food served in a nice open area.

✗ **Murraille de Chine** Av de l'Indépendance (near station); ☎ 22 281 41. Good, reasonably priced

Chinese food.

✗ **Dun Huang** 1 Rue J Andriamisa, Analakely (near Shoprite); ☎ 22 669 65; f 22 669 67; m 033 11 188 42. Good Chinese food, large portions. A new annexe of Dun Huang is opening at the Centre Commercial CAP 3000, Rue Dr Raseta, Andraharo.

✘ **Restaurant Taj Mahal** 15 Rue Mahafaka, Tsaralalana; ✆ 22 309 02. Specialises in Indian but Malagasy & European dishes also served, inc vegetarian. ⏲ 08.00–22.00.

✘ **Pizza Express** Galerie Kamoula, 26 Av de l'Indépendance, Analakely; ✆ 22 228 18/310 30; f 22 356 24. Good pizzas! ⏲ very late (usually until 02.00 at w/end)

✘ **Le Saka Express** (near Sakamanga); ✆ 24 334 39. Small but good. Pizzas, sandwiches & salads.

✘ **Shalimar** 5 Rue Mahafaka, Tsaralalana; ✆ 22 260 70. Good curries & a selection of vegetarian dishes. Popular place for b/fast. Good family restaurant; often busy.

Outskirts

✘ **Restaurant Café d'Octobre** Tsimbazaza (opposite the zoo); ✆ 24 200 27; m 032 40 009 63/032 02 400 32. European & Malagasy cuisine. ⏲ 11.30–22.00 or later.

✘ **Restaurant Indonesia** 35 Rue Kasanga, Tsimbazaza (near zoo entrance); m 032 40 066 42/032 04 807 27. Surprisingly, given Madagascar's history, this is the country's only Indonesian restaurant. Recommended. Serves seafood if pre-ordered. Evening karaoke. ⏲ 09.00–24.00.

✘ **Chez Arnaud** 21 Rue Rabozaka (the road to the zoo); ✆ 22 226 49. 'Without doubt the best pizza in town!' Also a good French menu & pasta dishes, but quite pricey. ⏲ Tue–Sun 11.30–14.30 & 18.00–22.00; closed Mon.

✘ **La Chaumière** Rte d'Ivato (towards Club du Car); ✆ 22 442 30; f 22 489 64. Well signposted on the left as you drive to the airport. Specialises in Réunionese cuisine. Delightful surroundings, good value meals. Very popular with locals & expats from Réunion.

Snack bars

🍴 **Le Buffet du Jardin** Pl de l'Indépendance. This fast-food restaurant is a convenient place for lunch, beer or coffee. Pleasant outdoor tables ideal for people-watching & meeting other vazaha. The food is mediocre.

🍴 **Le Planète** Pl MDRM (near secondhand book market). Good value fast food. Filling burgers, fries & sandwiches for hungry tourists.

🍴 **Pandora** 1 Rue Rabobalahy, Antaninarenina; ✆ 22 377 48. This nightclub serves pizzas, hamburgers & other fast food. ⏲ 18.30–dawn.

✘ **Hôtel Glacier** Av de l'Indépendance. This old hotel has been a prostitutes' hang-out for years but is lively & fun. Rupert Parker reports: 'Music every night, well organised. The cheaper of the 2 restaurants (on the left) is good value & does great Malagasy food.'

✘ **Kass' Dall** 4 Rue Andriantsilavo, Analakely (opposite Hôtel de France); ✆ 22 308 13; m 032 41 471 13. Specialises in French salads & sandwiches.

✘ **Gioia Restaurant** 15 Rue de Liège, Ambatomena (behind Select Hotel); m 033 11 943 24. On 1st floor; serves great cheap food to locals & vazaha. Good pasta. The owner, Marie-Ange, speaks some English & is very friendly. Closed Sun.

✘ **Korean BBQ** Lot IVD 48 F Ter Behoririka (Lalana Ranarivelo, near Lake Behoririka); ✆ 22 681 88; m 033 07 033 07/033 12 666 88. A traditional Korean restaurant recommended by Sil Westra as 'the best in Tana'. Customers choose & grill their own food. This is the place for sushi. & for something different: 'there is sake with snakes & zebu dicks inside ... yummy!' ⏲ 10.00–14.00 & 17.00–20.00.

✘ **Bar Restaurant l'Ile Rouge** Lot II D 29, Ambondrona (opposite Moonlight Hotel); m 032 04 059 86/032 04 685 96. Small French-Malagasy restaurant with a good food at low prices.

✘ **Azalée** Lot 192 Cité 67ha Sud (near CENAM crafts market); m 033 12 167 10. A small budget restaurant with good food & fast service. All cuisines but Chinese a speciality.

✘ **Le Muguet** Rue Razafindriantsoa. A cheap & cheerful Chinese restaurant at the bottom of the steps up to Hôtel Lambert.

🍴 **Mad' Delices** 29 Av Général Ramanantsoa, Isoraka (opposite Hôtel Isoraka); ✆ 22 266 41; m 032 02 546 73. 'Very good pizzas, a selection of Malagasy food, luscious pastries & ice cream. Friendly service; spotless restaurant! Really good b/fast. We liked it so much we ate almost every meal there.' Branches in Ampefiloha & Ankadifotsy. ⏲ daily; no pastries on Sun.

🍴 **The Cookie Shop** 14 Rue Rainizanabololona, Antanimena. American-style coffee, muffins, cookies & bagels for homesick vazaha. English spoken. ⏲ daily 08.00–19.00.

Avenue de l'Indépendance has a number of eateries: **Tropique** (good pastries and ice cream; also Chinese food), **Honey** (very good for breakfast and ice cream; closed Tue), and **Blanche Neige** (for ice cream and pastries; closed Mon). Try

Shalimar for tamarind juice, **Le Croissanterie** for fresh fruit juice, and **La Potinerie** (near Air Mad). In the upper town both the **Patisserie Suisse** (Rue Rabehevitra) and the **Patisserie Colbert** do excellent pastries and teas. **Patisserie Suisse** serves a delicious range of cakes and tarts, but closes at midday for up to three hours.

And for something a little different ...

📺 **Akany Avoko Café** ☎ 22 441 58. A meal at the café is a natural extension of a visit to this inspiring place (see page 144). The café showcases Malagasy cooking by the domestic science girls. Vegetarians are especially catered for. The café manager, Nirina, speaks English as do many of the young girls. It is essential to pre-book your visit by phone at least a day in advance.

NIGHTLIFE

Cohiba at the Hilton is a popular nightclub. Also **Le Caveau** (*4 Rue Jeneraly Rabehevitra, Antaninarenina;* ☎ *22 343 93*) and the **Indra** nightclub in Tsaralalana are recommended. In Antaninarenina, near the Colbert, is the nightclub 'a'.

Bars and discos include **Le Bus** in Antanimena (☎ *22 691 00*) and **Pandora** (*1 Rue Rabobalahy, Antaninarenina;* ☎ *22 377 48*).

Another option is **Groove Box**, near Tsimbazaza, which draws the crowds (live band: Thu jazz, Fri international music, Sat dance music).

Finally, it's worth having a drink at **Hôtel Glacier**, on Avenue de l'Indépendance, to admire the wonderful 1930s décor and to observe the more disreputable side of Tana's nightlife!

☞ *WARNING!* Some male travellers have spent the night with prostitutes, only to wake up with a headache and minus their wallets and other possessions. Be cautious about accepting a drink: it may be drugged.

ENTERTAINMENT If you are in Tana for a while, buy a local newspaper to see what's on or keep an eye out for posters advertising special shows or events. Or drop into the Centre Albert Camus on Avenue de l'Indépendance to pick up a programme of concerts and films.

For a truly Malagasy experience go to a performance of *hira gasy* (pronounced heera gash) – see box on page 168. There are regular Sunday performances at Andavamamba, in the front yard of a three-storey grey concrete house set back from the street that goes past Alliance Français. A few Malagasy flags fly above the high, red brick wall and the entrance is via an unsignposted footpath. It starts at 10.00 and finishes around 16.00. Tickets cost 800Ar. Part of the seating is under a tarpaulin canopy and the rest is in the open. It's an exciting and amusing day out. Have plenty of small-denomination notes ready to support the best performers. There are food stalls with drinks.

Any entertainment that allows you to join a Malagasy audience will be worth the entrance fee.

Films are dubbed into French.

WHAT TO SEE AND DO

As if to emphasise how different it is to other capitals, Tana has relatively little in the way of conventional sightseeing. However, there's quite enough to keep you occupied for a couple days. Your first stop should be to the regional tourist office, ORTANA.

ROVA (*Closed for restoration at the time of writing; check at the tourist office (ORTANA) for current status*) The queen's palace, or *rova*, the spiritual centre of the Merina people, dominates the skyline of Tana – even though it was destroyed by fire in 1995, leaving only the stone shell – an act of arson unprecedented in Madagascar's history.

The palace is being painstakingly reconstructed and should soon reopen to visitors. It is anyway worth the walk up to the palace for the view and to imagine its former grandeur.

PRIME MINISTER'S PALACE (PALAIS D'ANDAFIAVARATRA) (⊕ *Sat–Thu 10.00–17.00; closed Fri pm. Entry 3,000Ar.*) This former residence of Rainilaiarivony (he who married three queens) has been restored and now houses the few precious items that were saved from the *rova* fire, mostly gifts from foreign prime ministers and monarchs (including Queen Victoria). It was built in 1872 by the British architect William Pool. After independence it became in turn an army barracks, law courts, school of fine arts, the presidential palace and (again) the prime minister's palace. It was burned in 1975.

TSIMBAZAZA (✆ 24 517 78/510 74. ⊕ *daily 09.00–17.00. Entry for tourists 10,000Ar*) This comprises a museum, botanical garden and zoo exhibiting – with a few exceptions – only Malagasy species.

The zoo and botanical garden The **zoo** at Tsimbazaza (pronounced tsimba*zaz*, and meaning 'where children are forbidden', dating from when it was a sacred site) has an extensive collection of animals so is worth a visit providing you don't expect it to measure up to Western standards. We need to consider the importance of Tsimbazaza to the local people. They love coming here, and put on their best clothes for the occasion. The chief attraction is the ostriches! And why not? An ostrich is a far more extraordinary animal to a Malagasy child than a lemur. An example of the difference between the Western and Malagasy views of animal management, and life in general, was the argument some years ago over a project to have a free-ranging group of lemurs in the park. There was no problem agreeing on the desirability and visitor appeal of this, the conflict was about the components of the group. The American co-ordinator insisted on single-sex lemurs ('One thing we do not want are babies when we have a surplus of lemurs') whilst the Malagasy were holding out for a proper family unit: mother, father and children, because that's what happiness is all about.

Among the animals on display in the zoo are four aye-ayes, now displayed in a new day-to-night house which also has some mouse lemurs and other nocturnal animals.

You can take a guided tour of the zoo (be sure to agree the fee first). This may discourage the sort of 'help' offered to a recent visitor: 'A shabbily dressed man approached us shortly after we arrived and surreptitiously produced a colourful chameleon from under his coat. Apparently it was for sale! Rather more disturbing though was the zoo employee who spotted us watching the sleeping fossa. He came over and began throwing stones at the animal to wake it up so that we could get a better photograph. We were even more shocked when he insisted we pay him for this service! (We didn't.)'

A visit to a session of *hira gasy* provides a taste of genuine Malagasy folklore – performed for the locals, not for tourists.

In the British magazine *Folk Roots*, Jo Shinner describes a *hira gasy*: 'It is a very strange, very exciting affair: a mixture of opera, dance and Speaker's Corner bound together with a sense of competition.

'The performance takes place between two competing troupes of singers and musicians on a central square stage. It's an all-day event so the audience packs in early, tea and peanut vendors picking their way through the throng. Audience participation is an integral part – the best troupe is gauged by the crowd's response. Throughout the day performers come into the crowd to receive small coins offered in appreciation.

'The most immediate surprise is the costumes. The men enter wearing 19th-century French, red, military frock-coats and the women are clad in evening dress from the same period. Traditional *lamba* are carefully arranged around their shoulders, and the men wear straw Malagasy hats. The musicians play French military drums, fanfare trumpets, flutes, violins and clarinets. The effect is bizarre rather than beautiful.

'The *hira gasy* is in four parts. First there are the introductory speeches or *kabary*. Each troupe elects a speaker who is usually a respected elder. His skill is paramount to a troupe. He begins with a long, ferociously fast, convoluted speech excusing himself and his inadequacy before the audience, ancestors, his troupe, his mother, God, his oxen, his rice fields and so on – and on! Then follows another speech glorifying God, and then a greeting largely made up of proverbs.

'The *hira gasy* pivots around a tale of everyday life, such as the dire consequences of laziness or excessive drinking, is packed with wit, morals and proverbs and offers advice, criticism and possible solutions. The performers align themselves along two sides of the square at a time to address different parts of the audience. They sing in harsh harmony, illustrating their words with fluttering hand movements and expressive gestures, egged on by the uproarious crowd's appreciation. Then it is the dancers' turn. The tempo increases and becomes more rhythmic as two young boys take to the floor with a synchronised display of acrobatic dancing that nowadays often takes its influence from karate.'

The botanical garden is spacious and well laid out, and its selection of Malagasy endemics is being improved with the help of advisers from Kew (UK) and the Missouri Botanical Garden (USA). There's a new and interesting palm garden. The botanical area provides a sanctuary for numerous birds – indeed, this is an excellent place for birders – including a huge colony of egrets. There are also some reproduction Sakalava graves.

The Museum of Ethnology and Paleantology This is an excellent museum for gaining an understanding of Madagascar's prehistoric natural history as well as the traditions and way of life of its inhabitants. Skeletons of now-extinct animals, including several species of giant lemur and the famous elephant bird, provide a fascinating glimpse of the Malagasy fauna that the first humans helped to extinction (explanations in French only). There are also displays of stuffed animals, but the efforts of the taxidermist have left little to likeness and a lot to the imagination. It's worth taking a close look at the aye-aye, however, to study its remarkable hands.

The room housing the ethnological exhibits has been modernised, with clear explanations of the customs and handicrafts of the different ethnic groups.

Practicalities Tsimbazaza is about 4km from the city centre. There are buses from Avenue de l'Indépendance (number 15), but it is easier to take a taxi there and bus back. Keep your ticket stub which you may need to show when entering the nocturnal house.

There is a souvenir shop with a good selection of high-quality T-shirts and postcards, and a couple of snack bars. It's also a fine place for a picnic or you can ask to have your ticket clipped so you can pop across the road to a restaurant. The toilets are behind the café at the entrance.

CROC FARM (↘ 22 030 71/007 15; f 22 070 49; e reptel@wanadoo.mg; www.reptel.mg. ⊕ daily 09.00–17.00 inc gift shop & restaurant-bar. Entry 6,000Ar) I have been convinced by zoo expert Catherine Brinkley, as well as other readers, that this place near the airport is worth a visit. 'Croc Farm is a French-owned zoo. In addition to a variety of reptiles, fossas and free-range lemurs, the zoo hosts an impressive number of crocodiles, which are raised for meat, leather and other products. Visitors can try grilled crocodile in vanilla sauce at the zoo's restaurant while looking over the main lake. Unlike crocodile exhibits in zoos, the hundreds of crocodiles in the lake ensure that visitors are likely to see movement and interaction – especially during feeding time (midday). In addition, standing so close to Madagascar's only human predator is quite a thrill. The farm warns that the 30,000 crocodiles left in Madagascar are continually under threat from habitat destruction and illegal hunting. The zoo informs visitors of superstitions surrounding crocodiles while at the same time searching for a balance between wild crocodile populations and villages' (CB).

There is also a terrarium which contains smaller reptiles and mouse lemurs.

Croc Farm is at the end of a very poor road; it takes about 20 minutes to reach from the main airport road.

MUSEUM OF ART AND ARCHAEOLOGY (17 Rue Dr Villette, Isoraka; e icmaa@dts.mg or musedar@syfed.refer.mg. ⊕ Tue–Fri 12.00–17.00; closed Mon & w/ends) This lovely little museum in Isoraka is supported by the University of Antananarivo and has changing exhibitions of archaeology and ethnology, as well as art. Well worth checking at ORTANA what, if anything, is on.

ANTSHOW (Androndra, about 20mins southeast of city centre; ↘ 22 565 47; m 033 11 258 68; e hmblanche@simicro.mg; www.antshow.nu) This Malagasy Arts and Cultural Centre is the brainchild of Hanitrarivo Rasoanaivo, the lead singer of Tarika, who also founded the charity Valiha High to promote the teaching of the valiha (see page 116). It comprises a large exhibition space, a performance area, the first professional music studio in Madagascar, and a restaurant serving Malagasy food. Five rooms provide luxury accommodation (see hotel listings). 'Great home-cooked food and all the local music you could wish for, playing live downstairs' (K Harvey).

MAHAMASINA MARKET (⊕ daily, but best on Fri) Now that the zoma is closed, this street market on the western side of the stadium is the place to come for the familiar variety and bustle of a typical Malagasy market. You can buy anything here – except for souvenirs.

FLOWER MARKET A colourful flower market is held at the northwestern edge of Lake Anosy. There's something happening here every day but on Sundays it's buzzing.

SHOPPING

Note that bargaining is expected only in the handicrafts markets. It is neither customary nor appropriate to bargain in shops.

THE HANDICRAFTS MARKETS (⊕ *Mon–Sat 09.00–17.00*) The **Marché Artisanal** on Rte Digue in District 67 (a major bus stop when approaching the city from the airport) showcases the enormous range and quality of Malagasy handicrafts. Most noteworthy is the embroidery and basketry, woodcarving, minerals, leatherwork (stiff cowhide, not soft leather) and the unique *Antaimoro* paper embedded with pressed flowers. Bargain hard and beware of pickpockets.

A second **Marché Artisanal**, accessible from Rue Ramananarivo in Andravoahangy, offers similar wares. There is a particularly good selection of carved games here, including solitaire, chess and the traditional Malagasy *fanorona* (sellers can provide a sheet explaining the rules). It is about 30 minutes' walk northeast of the centre.

There's also a **bamboo market** near the Hilton hotel.

SERIOUS SHOPPING The best-quality goods are sold in specialist shops. In the centre of town, within walking distance of most hotels, is the excellent **Baobab Company**. Their two shops, one near Hôtel Palissandre and the other (better, I think) near the Sakamanga, sell a wonderful variety of high-quality goods and T-shirts. Other good craft outlets, especially for T-shirts, are **Maki** and **Kameleon** on the road up to Ambatonakanga near Hôtel Raphia. **Just' Original** is in the same area, as is **Sandra Boutique**.

Town centre

Galerie d'Art Malgache Yerden 9 Rue Dr Villete, Isoraka (opposite Japanese Embassy); ☎ 22 244 62; f 22 240 86. Sells a huge variety of quality products. ⊕ *Mon–Sat.*

Viva Home 23 Rue Ramelina, Antaninarenina (near the Colbert); ☎ 22 692 71. An excellent place for wood crafts.

Malagasy Arts 26 Av Gal Ramanantsoa Isoraka (next to Radama Hotel); ☎ 22 295 13; m 033 05 041 74; e artetjardinmalagasy@yahoo.fr. Sells a good range of crafts. ⊕ *Mon–Sat from 08.30.*

La Flamant Rose 45–47 Av de l'Indépendance, Analakely; ☎ 22 557 76/24 268 04; m 032 02 354 19; e flamant.rose@simicro.mg. A good art gallery. ⊕ *daily 09.00–18.00.*

BioAroma 54 Av Gen Ramanantsoa; ☎ 22 545 57/326 30; m 032 02 575 23/033 14 383 74; e bioaroma@simicro.mg. Up the hill from the Sakamanga, this shop has a huge selection of their own brand of natural remedies, essential oils, cosmetics & other beauty products. You can also have aromatherapy, a manicure or a massage here. It's all quite clinical with assistants dressed in white coats. ⊕ *Mon–Fri 08.00–18.00, Sat 09.00–17.00, Sun 09.00–12.00.*

Outskirts

Lisy Art Gallery Rte de Mausolée (opposite Cercle Mess de la Police, near Hôtel Panorama); ☎ 22 277 33; m 032 02 444 16/033 14 085 00; e lisy@wanadoo.mg. 'A delightful shop, very large, with non-aggressive but helpful staff & an excellent range of Malagasy products. If you only have time for one shopping stop, this should be the one' (Anne Gray). ⊕ *Mon–Fri 08.30–18.30, Sat 08.30–12.30 & 14.00–18.30.*

Vatosoa Boutique Lot IV2 3A Ilanivato; ☎ 22 320 01. Bus no 138, terminus Tsaralalana, goes there.

This is the place for exquisite *lamba*. English spoken. In the same block is **Lambamena** Boutique.

Galerie Le Bivouac Antsofinondry (on the road to Ambohimanga); ☎ 22 429 50; e bivouac@dts.mg. Beautiful painted silk items, woodcarvings & other handicrafts of a high quality. Restaurant le Bivouac is also here.

Atelier Jacaranda Near Le Bivouac. This place specialises in batik. The quality here is excellent & the prices low. The Jacaranda workshop is next to Le Bivouac (worth visiting if you have time), but

John Grehan

During the early years of World War II, the Royal Navy placed Madagascar under a strict maritime blockade. This resulted in many imported goods becoming very scarce, especially gasoline. The inventive Malagasy, however, found a solution to the shortage of fuel by mixing 10% petrol with 90% sugar-alcohol.

Soon Tana's bustling streets were enveloped in a dense rum-laden cloud. Visitors to the capital reported seeing pedestrians staggering around stupefied by the misfiring vehicles belching their explosive mixtures into the air.

sales are made from the gallery 1km down the road, on the other side of the canal.

Gasyk' Art 62B Talatamaty; ℡ 22 447 53; ℮ gasykart@simicro.mg. It has a nice variety of crafts in its shop on the way to Ivato, as well as an outlet at the airport.

Sataria 2 families from Ambalavao make *Antaimoro* paper. Look for a small green building on the right on the way to the airport. Ask for Tsaramila or Rasoa. The other business is run by Mr Iarivo (m 033 11 386 58).

Le Village Lot 36F, Ambohibao (on the left as you go to the airport); m 032 07 129 50; ℮ village@wanadoo.mg; web: www.maquettesdebateaux.com. This unusual place makes & sells scale models of famous ships such as *The Mayflower, The Bounty & The Victory*, as well as more modest designs. Prices range from €115 to €1,507. They can be shipped home by DHL or carefully packaged to be carried as hand luggage. 'We bought a sailed lobster boat & their packaging protected it perfectly as checked baggage ...' Get a duplicate receipt from Le Village in case you need to show it at the airport on departure. There is also a showroom at the Hilton (m 032 07 775 73). ⊕ *Mon–Sat 07.30–17.00, Sun by appointment only.*

Artisanat Aina Opposite Le Village; m 033 11 076 16; ℮ aina.sarl@dts.mg; www.ainamadagascar.com. They make raffia work & other crafts.

SUPERMARKETS Instead of buying the usual T-shirts and carvings, how about taking back some of the local consumables? If you have a sweet tooth, Robert chocolate is recommended. On my last visit I bought some very good tea (Sahambavy) which is also produced flavoured delicately with vanilla. Similarly flavoured coffee is also available. I always buy wine as well. OK, it's not the most superior wine in the world, but it'll impress your guests. The most convenient supermarket is **Shoprite**, adjacent to Hôtel du Louvre in the Upper Town. There is another branch half way along Avenue de l'Indépendance (but avoid this area after dark). Other stores are at Talatamaty on the way to Ivato, near the Hilton in a big glass building called Fiaro, and at Ambodivona on the way to the *gare routière* serving the east, north and northwest of the country. The latter has a nice T-shirt shop and a restaurant.

Leader Price supermarkets in Tanjombato, on the way to Antsirabe, and Ankorondrano, *en route* to Ivato, have a good range of food if you are stocking up for an excursion. **Jumbo Score** has the biggest selection of goods at the lowest prices.

YOUR LAST DAY IN TANA? There are two places which sell high-quality handicrafts as well as welcoming donations of your leftover ariary, clothes or medical supplies, plus an interesting NGO working with reproductive health which also welcomes visitors.

If you visit one of the centres that provide work and hope for the disadvantaged girls and women of Tana, make sure you allow time for a tour as well as for shopping; this visit could be one of the highlights of your trip to Madagascar. Seriously.

Akany Avoko (see page 144) sells a range of handicrafts produced at its heart-warming halfway house. Phone to book a visit (℡ 22 441 58). It's located in Ambohidratimo, the last suburb on RN4 towards Mahajanga, about 15km from Tana centre. A taxi there from central Tana costs 15,000–20,000Ar. AA is on the

Antananarivo and Area **SHOPPING**

7

left, 1km past Ambohidratrimo on a corner (look for the sign with the small waving hands logo). Make sure you explain your visit as there is a guardhouse. If you are brave and want to take a *taxi-be*, get on the Mahitsy or Alakamisy (next towns after Ambohidratrimo) service and ask for the bus stop 'l'école Ambohidratrimo' (fare 400Ar); walk ahead 10m and AA is on your left. The handicrafts are varied and very well made. And you can also give something back by having a meal at the café.

Easier to get to is the **Centre Fihavanana** (see page 146) in Mahamasina, near the stadium, which is run by the Sisters of the Good Shepherd. The centre is in a building set back from the road, just to the right of an orange-painted church. Ask the taxi driver to take you to the Eglise St Joseph. The women here work to a very high standard, producing beautiful embroidery and greetings cards. Judith Cadigan writes: 'We are so glad you suggested visiting the Sœurs du Bon Pasteur in Tana. We bought lots of embroidered linens and were shown around the school, shook hands with what felt like most of the 200 children there, were serenaded by one of the classes, and were altogether greatly impressed by what the nuns are doing. We waited to go there until almost our last day, so that we could take along unused antibiotics, and they were indeed glad to have them.' Most of the sisters speak some English. To make an appointment phone Sister Jeanette (22 299 81) or simply turn up.

Population Services International If you are interested in the work done by this internationally active NGO in Madagascar, visit their office near the Hilton. Catherine Brinkley reports: 'On my last day I made a trip to the PSI office at Immeuble-Fiaro, Rue Jules Ranaivo (stairway D, 2nd floor). I was their first walk-in donation ever in Madagascar. They graciously explained their programmes and gave me a receipt for my donation to family planning (a donation motivated towards alleviating the problem of starving or unwanted children, and giving Malagasy women some control over their lives). They encouraged me to spread the word that tourists are welcome to visit their office to learn more about the problems and solutions in Madagascar and to make on-the-spot donations.' For more information see their website: www.psi.org.

MAPS A large selection of maps (and also old photo prints) can be bought at the **Institut Géographique et Hydrographique National** (its long Malagasy name is shortened to FTM) (*Rte Circulaire, Ambanidia;* *22 229 35;* e *ftm@wanadoo.mg; www.ftm.mg.* ⊕ *Mon–Fri 07.30–16.00*) They produce a series of 12 folded 1:500,000 maps, together covering Madagascar and the Comoro Islands, mostly costing 10,000Ar each. Also, for 10,000Ar each is a set of four rolled maps which cover the whole island at 1:1,000,000 scale. The staff are pleasant and helpful. FTM maps of the more popular tourist areas can usually be bought in bookshops in the town centre, where you can also buy good maps of Tana.

BOOKSHOPS The best bookshop is probably **Librairie de Madagascar** on Avenue de l'Indépendance, although the shelves were surprisingly bare when I visited late 2006. There is another large bookshop opposite. Also recommended is **Librairie Md Paoly** opposite Hôtel Mellis, a well-stocked Catholic bookshop with a section of books and maps for tourists. **BiblioMad**, also near Hôtel Mellis, is smaller but worth a visit. In Isoraka, near the Résidence Lapasoa, there's a good bookshop that specialises in academic books but also has many books about Madagascar. Two more are located near Hôtel Isoraka on opposite sides of Rue Ramanantsoa.

Lovers of used books should visit the secondhand book market by the monument at the opposite end of Avenue de l'Indépendance from the station. 'A great experience, though be sure to go with your haggling hat on because these bookstall-holders can smell a *vazaha* wallet a mile off. On one occasion, I went there seeking back issues of *Vintsy* and discovered a few scattered around. I was soon mobbed by stallholders and middlemen demanding 5,000Ar or more a piece – too much. Later, when I made to leave, I was mobbed once again, the prices having miraculously fallen to less than 500Ar each!' (DA).

PHOTOGRAPHY Several **Fuji** shops in Tana cater for digital camera users. Among other services they can transfer your photos to a CD. There is a convenient one just past Hôtel Mellis on Rue Indira Gandhi. Also recommended is **DMT Photo** opposite Restaurant Nerone on Rue Ratsimilaho in the upper town. The **Photorama** shops also cater efficiently for digital camera users. There are branches throughout the city including one near the Ataninarenina steps.

MEDIA AND COMMUNICATION

COURIERS

Colis Express 11 Rue Randrianary Ratianarivo, Ampasamadinika; ☎ 22 272 42. The main office is at Lot II W 27 D, Ankorahotra; ☎ 24 521 94. There's a branch in Andrefan' Ambohijanahary at Lot 3 E 54 Bis; ☎ 22 623 05/557 42.

Midex Madagascar Located in the building of Orange Mobile at Galaxy Andraharo Bâtiment 48 AB; ☎ 23 649 77/301 66; e rakotoarivony.sandrine@midextnr.com.

INTERNET If cost is your main concern, the cheapest internet access is at the main **post office** in the upper town, but there is often a queue. For efficiency the best option is **Teknet** (*32 Av du Gal Ramanantsoa, Isoraka (opposite Hôtel Isoraka);* ☎ *22 313 59;* f *22 642 95; www.teknetgroup.com*). Internet access costs 9–30Ar/min (depending on how many hours you prepay). They have many more computers than most cybercafés (18 plus an overspill backroom with a further ten) including four with QWERTY keyboards, a godsend for Brits and Americans! They are even open Sunday (afternoon only) and the computers are new and fast. Teknet also has a small cybercafé in the departure lounge at Ivato airport.

There are good computers with smart flat screens in the cybercafé upstairs at **Hôtel Colbert**, but connection costs 100Ar/min here (minimum charge 1,500Ar). The **Outcool Web Bar** (*a few doors up from the Sakamanga.* ⊕ *Mon–Sat till 23.00 and Sun 15.30–21.00*) has seven computers (30Ar/min; cheaper if you prepay) plus additional sockets for laptops.

HT Technology on Avenue de l'Indépendance (on the right as you walk towards the station) is also highly rated.

If your first introduction to the Malagasy internet, and therefore French keyboards, is in Tana, prepare yourself by reading page 118.

POST OFFICE (⊕ *Mon–Sat 07.00–15.00*) The main post office is opposite Hôtel Colbert. There is a separate philately section where you can buy attractive stamps. The post office is open non stop for outgoing phone calls – useful in an emergency and much cheaper than phoning from a hotel. You can send faxes from here and it has the cheapest internet facilities in Tana. Post offices in Analakely, Ambatomena and District 67 also have inexpensive internet facilities (called *cyberpaositra*).

MEDICAL

CLINICS (PRIVATE)

✚ **Mpitsabo Mikambana** Rte de l'Université; ☎ 22 235 55; e mm24@wanadoo.mg. Inexpensive & very good.

✚ **Espace Medical** Lot IVO 110 GA, Ambodivona; ☎ 22 625 66; m 032 02 088 16;

e esmed@wanadoo.mg. Run by Dr Arilaza Razafimahaleo. Provides a complete medical service inc ambulance, helicopter evacuation & a clinical laboratory.

PRIVATE HOSPITALS

✚ **Clinique des Sœurs Franciscains** Ankadifotsy; ☎ 22 235 54/695 20; f 22 230 95. Its main English-speaking doctor is Dr Louis Razafinarivo.

MILITARY HOSPITAL

✚ **Le Centre Hospitalier de Soavinandriana** ☎ 22 397 53. All facilities such as medical consultation, dentistry, X-ray, surgery, clinical laboratory etc. The cost of hospitalisation is very low, but most *vazaha* would prefer to return home or at least seek treatment in

DENTIST

✚ **Dr Mariane Ottoni** ☎ 22 529 70.

PHARMACIES

✚ **Pharmacie Principale** Rte des Hydrocarbures, Ankorondrano (opposite big Digital building); ☎ 22

✚ **Medical Plus** 1118 Ankaditoho, Rte Circulaire; ☎ 22 567 58; f 22 629 71. Highly recommended by Stuart Cassie: 'They do 24hr home/hotel visits & ambulance service. A doctor arrived within 30mins. She charged 60,000Ar for a 45min visit & thorough examination.'

✚ **Polyclinique d'Ilafy** ☎ 22 425 66/69. Modern facilities and equipment, helpful staff. Recommended.

Réunion. 'This hospital is the most set up for emergencies & accidents. As with most hospitals in Madagascar you will need someone to stay with the patient all the time & act as nurse & assistant' (R Conway). See page 126 for a hospital story.

533 93/439 15; e pharm.s@dts.mg. The largest pharmacy in the city.

For normal requirements the pharmacy opposite the post office in the upper town and the chemists in the Jumbo Score supermarkets have most things.

MISCELLANEOUS

AIRLINE OFFICES

✈ **Air Madagascar** 31 Av de l'Indépendance; ☎ 22 222 22. ⊕ Mon–Fri 07.30–17.00, Sat 08.30–12.00.
✈ **Air France** Tour Zital (2nd floor), Rte des Hydrocarbures, Ankorondrano; ☎ 23 230 01/41 (bookings: ☎ 23 230 23); f 23 230 41. ⊕ Mon–Fri 08.30–17.00, Sat 08.30–12.30.
✈ **Interair** Hilton Hotel; ☎ 22 224 06/52; f 22 624 21; e interair@mel.wanadoo.mg. ⊕ Mon–Fri 08.00–17.00, Sat 08.30–12.30.

✈ **Corsair** 1 Rue Rainitovo, Antsahavola; ☎ 22 633 36; f 22 626 76; e corsair@wanadoo.mg. ⊕ Mon–Fri 08.30–16.30, Sat 08.30–12.00.
✈ **Air Mauritius** & **Air Austral** Immeuble Marbour, 77 Rue Solombavambahoaka (Allée des Palmiers), Antsahavola; ☎ 22 359 90/604 46/634 26; www.ario-madagascar.com. ⊕ Mon–Fri 08.30–12.30 & 13.30–17.30, Sat 08.30–12.00.

LAND TRANSPORT OFFICES

MadaBus ☎ 24 222 72. The office is in Ambondrona, opposite the hotel Chez Francis. For details of *taxi-brousse* stations see page 176.
Madarail Rumour has it that passenger trains may

run again from Tana so it's worth checking the situation at the rail company which has offices behind the station – the unmissable landmark at the end of Av de l'Indépendance.

MONEY Banking hours are usually 08.00–15.00. The best place to change money, both for exchange rate and service, is SOCIMAD on Rue Radama I. They will change travellers' cheques as well as hard currencies. The UCB bank in Antashavola, near Air Mauritius, will also change travellers' cheques, as well as accepting MasterCard. The BOA bank in Antaninarenina next to the Shoprite supermarket will let you draw up to US$200 a day on MasterCard. Go there in the morning as you need to wait three hours before you can pick up your money. Closed on Saturdays.

There's a **Western Union** office on Lalana Generaly Rabehevitra in Antaninarenina and also near the Hilton, at the BFV bank.

Cash machines You can use your credit or debit card to get cash at the following banks.

UCB Antsahavola, near the American Embassy. Accepts MasterCard.

BFV-SG 14 Rue General Rabehevitra, Antaninarenina. **Hilton Hotel**

EMBASSIES

🇪 **UK** Honorary Consul (the embassy is closed) Richard W Hyde MBE, BP 12193 Zoom, Villa Ricana, Lot 187A, Manjaka-Ilafy; ☎ 22 014 85.

🇪 **USA** BP 620, Antsahavola; ☎ 22 200 89/212 57. For visa/passport business it is open Mon/Wed/Fri.

🇪 **France** 3 Rue Andriantsilavo, Ambatomena; ☎ 22 000 08.

🇪 **Germany** Rue Pasteur Rabeony, Ambodiroatra; ☎ 22 216 91.

🇪 **Italy** BP 16, Rue Pasteur Rabary, Ankadivato; ☎ 22 665 80.

ENGLISH-SPEAKING UNION The chairman is Mrs Anna Hyde (*BP 12193, Zoom, Ankorondrono;* ☎ *24 521 80*).

FIXERS A local guide/fixer can take a lot of hassle out of planning an independent trip, but bear in mind that anyone recommended here will charge more than newcomers whom you have found yourself!

Pierrot (Solofonirina Pierrot Patrick) Lot près VE 38, Ambohijatovo; ☎ 22 697 27 (office); m 032 40 699 66. Pierrot often meets international flights & will identify himself.

Henri Serge Razafison Lot 1384 Cité 67ha; ☎ 22 341 90.

Christophe Andriamampionona ☎ 22 445 08. 'Very knowledgeable.'

Serge Razafison ☎ 22 341 90; m 032 02 811 80; e razafisonserge@yahoo.fr

VEHICLE HIRE Full details on hiring a car or motorbike are given in *Chapter 4*. Details of car hire companies in Tana are available from ORTANA (see page 167). Large hotels will also have car-hire agencies, as does Grace Guest House.

Quite a few visitors find their own driver, rather than hiring a car and driver through an agency. Marja and Wim, from the Netherlands, have used the same driver for both their trips to Madagascar: **Justin Randrianarison** (☎ 22 472 46; m 032 07 532 19). 'He owns a 1989 (but looks brand new) Peugeot 505 and works independently. He lives 10km outside Tana on the way to Antsirabe and is a very pleasant and reliable person, a good driver and speaks some English.'

Another reader highly recommends the company **Tanalahorizon** and their driver Michael Rakotomavo. The tour co-ordinator was Patrick Andriamihaja (m *032 07 545 29;* e *madhorizon@yahoo.com*). 'Michael was the perfect companion for me on this car trip: he readily offered commentary on what I was seeing and answered my questions thoughtfully; played a variety of Malagasy music (and later helped me choose some to bring home); listened to my ideas about hotels and offered his advice when solicited; and showed me shops and roadside stands, but never pushed them on me. Equally important to me, given that we spent 3–4 hours together in the car every day, he was also very comfortable being silent.' This reader paid € 60 per day including fuel, which is a pretty good rate.

INFORMATION AND PERMITS FOR NATURE RESERVES

ANGAP Main office: BP 1424, Ambatobe (near Lycée Français & SNGF: Silo National des Graines Forestières); ✆ 22 415 54. There's a more conveniently located branch office in the tour operator Océane Aventures, 22 Rue Andrianary Ratianarivo, Ampasamadinika; ✆ 22 312 10; f 22 312 22. ⏱ Mon–Fri, 08.00–12.00 & 14.00–18.00. ANGAP is the organisation responsible for the administration of almost all the protected areas of Madagascar. Permits for the national parks &

reserves may be purchased here (see page 76 for prices), although they are also available at the town serving each reserve. It is worth visiting the Tana office, however, for the latest information on the reserves. There is also an excellent reference library adjacent to the main office. ANGAP website: www.parcs-madagascar.com.
WWF Lot près II M 85 Ter, Rue Hugues Rabesahala, Antsakaviro; ✆ 22 255 41.

VISA EXTENSION A visa extension can be obtained overnight from the Ministry of the Interior near the Hilton Hotel (see page 94).

CHURCH SERVICES

Anglican Cathedral St Laurent, Ambohimanoro; ✆ 22 262 68. *Service Sun 09.00.*
Roman Catholic ✆ 22 278 30. 3 churches have

services in Malagasy & 3 in French. Phone for details.
Scriptures Union Antaninarenina. *English service Sun 09.30.*

GOLF COURSE There is a good golf course, the **Club de Golf de Rova** at Ambohidratrimo, 20km out of town on the road to Mahajanga. It is open to visitors except at the weekend. Good meals are served at the club house and the Wednesday buffet is particularly recommended.

EXCURSIONS FROM ANTANANARIVO

BUS STATIONS (*GARES ROUTIERES*) The *gares routières* for *taxi-brousses* are on the outskirts of the city at the appropriate road junctions. Fasan'ny Karana, on the road to the airport, is the *gare routière* serving the south, southeast and southwest of the country. Gare de l'Ouest, Anosibe (Lalana Pastora Rahajason on the far side of Lake Anosy) serves the west and Gare du Nord (at Andravoahangy behind the craft market) takes care of the north.

DAY EXCURSIONS

Ambohimanga (⏱ *Tue–Sun 09.00–11.00 & 14.00–17.00, closed Mon. Entry 7,000Ar*) Lying 21km northeast of Antananarivo, accessed by RN3 – Madagascar's first dual-carriageway! – Ambohimanga (pronounced am*boo*imanga), meaning 'blue hill', was for a long time forbidden to Europeans. From here began the line of kings and queens who were to unite Madagascar into one country, and it was here that they returned for rest and relaxation among the forested slopes of this hill-top village. These days tourists find the same tranquillity and spirit of reverence and this recently named World Heritage Site is highly recommended as an easy day trip. It is accessible on a good road by private taxi or *taxi-brousse*. The journey takes about 30 minutes.

Ambohimanga has seven gates, though some are all but lost among the thick vegetation. By the main entrance gate is an enormous stone disc which was formerly rolled in front of the gateway each night. Just inside are some useful small shops selling drinks and snacks. Climb up the stairs to the ceremonial courtyard shaded by two giant fig trees. Ambohimanga still retains its spiritual significance for the Malagasy people. On the slope to the left of the entrance to the compound is a sacrificial stone. Melted candle wax and traces of blood show that it is still used for offerings, particularly in cases of infertility. Rituals involving the placing of seven small stones in the 'male' or 'female' hole will ensure the birth of a baby boy or girl.

Inside the compound The centrepiece here is the wooden house of the great king Andrianampoinimerina, who reigned from 1787 to 1810. This simple one-room building is interesting for the insight it gives into daily (royal) life of that era. There is a display of cooking utensils (and the stones that surrounded the cooking fire), weapons, and the two beds – the upper one for the king and the lower for one of his 12 wives. The roof is supported by a 10m rosewood pole. A visit here can be full of surprises: 'Remember this is not a museum, it is the king's palace: he is there. On all my visits there were always several people asking the king for favours. On one memorable occasion I entered his hut to find what seemed like a party in full flow. A man had been possessed by the spirit of a king from the south and he had come to the palace to greet, and be greeted by, King Andrianampoinimerina. The man had gone into a trance and a group of mediums were assisting him. They had found an accordion player and the man was dancing to get the king's attention. We were spellbound by all this, but the Malagasy visitors totally ignored what was going on and continued to look round the hut as though nothing was happening!' (Alistair Marshall)

With British help Andrianampoinimerina's son, Radama, went a long way to achieving his father's ambition to expand his kingdom to the sea. His wife succeeded him as Queen Ranavalona. Three more queens followed and, although the capital had by that time been moved to Antananarivo, they built themselves elegant summerhouses next to Andrianampoinimerina's simple royal home. These have been renovated and provide a fascinating glimpse of the strong British influence during those times, with very European décor and several gifts sent to the monarchs by Queen Victoria. French influence is evident too: there are two cannons forged in Jean Laborde's Mantasoa iron foundry. Here also is the small summerhouse belonging to Prime Minister Rainilaiarivony. Understandably cautious about being overheard (he wielded more power than the queens he married) he chose an open design with glazed windows so that spies could be spied first.

Also within the compound is a mundane-looking concrete pool (the concrete is a recent addition) which was used by the queens for ritual bathing and had to be filled, so they say, by 70 virgins, and a corral where zebu were sacrificed. An enclosing wall built in 1787, and faced with a rock-hard mixture of sand and egg, completes the tour.

From a high point above the bath you can get a superb view of the *hauts plateaux* and Tana in the distance, and on an adjacent hill the white mausoleum of the king's *ombiasy*.

✖ **Where to eat** Ambohimanga is an ideal place for a picnic. There is no longer a restaurant here, although a *hotely* by the car park serves Malagasy food. Visitors with their own transport could try **Relais du Rova**, situated about 5km away at the main turn-off to Ambohimanga.

Lake Alarobia/Tsaraotra (www.boogie-pilgrim.net. Entry 12,000Ar w/days, 14,000Ar w/ends) This private wildfowl reserve, owned by the Ranarivelo family, is only 8km from the centre of Tana and is well worth a visit for any birders with a few hours to spare in the capital. White-faced ducks and red-billed teal are very common, and hottentot teal, comb duck and fulvous ducks should be seen too. The heronry includes the sought-after Madagascar pond heron and dimorphic egret. There is an information centre at the site.

Lemurs Park (✆ 22 234 36; m 033 11 728 90; e info-lemurs@lemurspark.com; www.lemurspark.com. ⊕ Tue–Sun 10.00–16.00, closed Mon; restaurant open Tue–Sat 12.00–16.00, closed Sun/Mon. Entry 10,000Ar inc guide) This 'zoo' (but no cages),

22km west of Tana, makes a good day trip for those on a quick visit who are not able to see lemurs in their natural habitat. 'After some disappointments in the national reserves it was really great to see so many lemurs so close. Especially the jumping sifakas were really great.' Ten species of lemur live free in the 4ha park; many of them are confiscated pets, and this is the first step towards rehabilitation. Feeding times are 09.00, 12.00, 14.00 and 16.00; if you can visit just before these times the lemurs will be more active.

The park is on RN1 (the road to Arivonimamo). The entrance is on the right and clearly signposted.

Ambohimalaza (La Nécropole Royale) Situated 17km east of Tana, off RN2 to Toamasina, is a remarkable cemetery. Ambohimalaza ('notorious hill') was one of the 12 sacred hills of King Andrianampoinimerina, and only the Merina aristocracy are buried here. Their tombs are topped by a *tranomanara* or 'cold house' resembling a little chalet, which indicates that the deceased was of royal blood, as does the red colour of some of the tombs. Nearby are the tiny graves of uncircumcised children who are not allowed to be buried in the family tombs. Around the perimeter you can see the remains of the deep moat and traces of a retaining wall. There is even one of those huge circular stones for closing off the entrance.

The whole area is resonant with atmosphere. Rupert Parker writes: 'It's difficult not to feel the presence of the ancestors of the royal family. My camera certainly felt them and gave up the ghost in the middle of the film – back in the UK they said it couldn't be fixed and my Malagasy friends gleefully pointed out that the ancestors had had their revenge.'

Taxi-brousses run every day except Sunday from Ampasampito, on the east of Tana, to the village of Ambohimalaza; from here it's a 2km walk to the site.

Angavokely Forestry Station Clare and Johann Herman recommend this day trip from Tana. 'At Carion, 30km from Tana on RN2, you follow the track to Angavokely which takes about 30 minutes down a rutted track which had once been cobbled. It ends at an extraordinary turreted barrier which will be opened after you have applied at the office (a ten-minute walk away located in a large set of buildings amongst a defunct sawmill). Faded direction signs and a map indicate the way to the arboretum with picnic tables and parasols, and you can camp. Mt Angavokely is a fair climb up past the eucalyptus plantation and takes about 30 minutes. Thoughtfully, steps with railings are built into the rock face so that you can enjoy the splendid views from the top of the Ankaratra mountains and Lake Mantasoa. A wide track leads back down through the arboretum to the offices.'

TWO- TO THREE-DAY EXCURSIONS In recent years the region around Tana has been developed for tourism. Travel-worn visitors with some time to spare at the end of their trip should consider spending a few days winding down in one of the resort-style lake hotels at Itasy or Mantasoa.

Lake Mantasoa Some 70km east of Antananarivo is Mantasoa (pronounced manta*soo*) where in the 19th century Madagascar had its first taste of industrialisation. Indeed, historians claim that industrial output was greater then than at any time during the colonial period. It was thanks to Jean Laborde that a whole range of industries were started, including an iron foundry which enabled Madagascar to become more or less self-sufficient in swords, guns and gunpowder, thereby increasing the power of the central government. Jean Laborde was soon highly influential at court and he built a country residence for the queen at Mantasoa.

Many of the buildings remain, and although a one-day visit to Mantasoa is rewarding, a stay of a few days would be even better.

Getting there Mantasoa can be reached by *taxi-brousse* from Tana in about four hours. The village and its attractions are quite spread out, but it is a very pleasant area for walking.

Where to stay/eat

🏠 **Domaine de l'Ermitage** (31 rooms) ↘ 42 660 54. The rooms are so-so but the meals & old-fashioned atmosphere make it well worth a stay. The Sunday buffet is excellent value with a small band playing 1950s songs. It is set up as a country club & offers recreational activities inc riding, tennis, boating, country walks etc. €€€–€€€€

🏠 **Le Riverside** (12 bungalows) ↘ 42 660 85; m 033 12 640 21; e riversidehotel@wanadoo.mg; www.mantasoa.com. A resort-style hotel with an outdoor eating area overlooking the lake; the hotel of choice in Mantasoa. 'Great food & nice bungalows close to the lake. If you have some time left & don't want to stay in Tana you can get here in about 3hrs for a relaxing end to your holiday' (P van der Bij). Billiards, ping-pong, bowling, jet ski, canoeing & bike hire available. €€€–€€€€

🏠 **Motel le Chalet/Le Chalet Suisse** (8 bungalows) ↘ 42 660 95. Still Swiss-owned but now managed by Mme Lala Razanadraibe. 'There's a lovely Swiss restaurant serving cheese fondue & raclette – funny place to find it, but delicious.' Meals must be eaten there. The walk here from the *taxi-brousse* drop-off point is a pleasant 1½hrs. €€–€€€

What to see Beside the school playing field is a chimney, once part of the china factory. The cannon factory still stands (part of it is lived in) and the large furnace of the foundry remains. All are signposted and fascinating to see; you can just imagine the effort that was required to build them.

Jean Laborde is buried in the cemetery outside the village, along with 12 French soldiers; there is an imposing mausoleum with a strikingly phallic monument.

The very active *Les Amis de Jean Laborde* are developing the area for tourism. If you have a special interest in this fascinating man, do contact them (↘ 42 402 97; e topoi@dts.mg).

The first project was to restore Laborde's house. It is now a very interesting museum set in a lovely garden. All the labels are in French but a guide may be available to translate. It is worth making the effort to follow Laborde's remarkable story and achievements (see box on page 181).

Anjozorobe This FANAMBY-run reserve on the northeast of Tana is reached via RN3. Formerly owned by the tour operator Boogie Pilgrim, who run the nearby Mananara Camp, it comprises 2,500ha of the Anjozorobe–Angavo Forest Corridor, one of the last vestiges of dense forest in the central plateau of Madagascar. Established as a protected area in 2005, the Corridor covers an area of 52,200ha, and stretches for over 80km. Nine species of lemur are found here including indri and diademed sifaka. It is also rich in birdlife (82 recorded species) and has 550 species of plant. The reserve itself has a variety of hiking trails and a mountain-bike track.

Mananara Camp is 10km from RN3, a beautiful drive through typical highland villages. 'The camp is terrific: six igloo tents with beds, mounted on a wooden platform and standing under a thatched roof. Well-maintained, clean and attractive. The food is good – served in a tented dining room with "lounge area". There is also a small library and bar. Roland, the camp manager, does a great job.'

Boogie Pilgrim is currently refurbishing the camp so contact them for further details (↘ 22 530 70; e contact@boogie-pilgrim.net; www.boogie-pilgrim.net).

Ampefy and the Lake Itasy area Approximately 2½–3 hours' drive west of the capital, this region offers much of interest as well as a chance to relax in one of the comfortable hotel complexes. Great strides have been made in the last couple of years to make Lake Itasy tourist-friendly. There are now comfortable resort-style hotels and the roads have been improved. The drive there along RN1 is interesting: 'One of the first things I noticed, on the western outskirts of Antananarivo, are some marvellous examples of Merina tombs. About 40km further along RN1, we stopped by at the farmers' market at **Mangatary**, which takes place on Thursdays. The local farmers sell produce from their colourful zebu-drawn wagons. Another noticeable feature of this part of the highlands is the groves of tapia trees, much like around Isalo but seemingly even more extensive' (Derek Schuurman).

In addition to the hotels listed below, the Dodwell Trust (e *dodwell@madagascar.freeserve.co.uk*) has clean, budget-priced accommodation with part-time volunteer activities. Advance booking essential.

⌂ Where to stay/eat

⌂ **Hôtel Kavitaha** (21 rooms) ☎ 48 840 04; e bicrakotomavo@wanadoo.mg. The hotel offers a range of activities: pedalos, kayaks, pirogues, table tennis, fishing etc. Ideal for families. Coming from Tana turn left off RN1 at Analavory to Ampefy. €€€

⌂ **La Terrasse** (10 bungalows) Ampefy; ☎ 48 840 28; m 032 07 167 80; e laterrasse.ampefy@wanadoo.mg; http://laterrasse.ampefy.com. This resort-style hotel is on the right as you drive through Ampefy. Run by Mash (from Tana) & Claude (from France), it has simple en-suite bungalows set in a garden; more are being built on the lake shore. Activities range from hiking to river-rafting. Highly praised by all: 'The food is really great & the owners are very kind. The specialty of the restaurant is the *rhum arrangé*' (Roelf Mulder & Paul Janssen). €€€

⌂ **Relais de la Vierge** (6 rooms & 7 bungalows) Ilot Boisé Antanimarina, Ampefy (on the way to Soavinandriana); m 032 02 796 20/032 41 085 29; www.relaisdelavierge.com. Ping-pong, tennis, billiards etc; also children's activities. A relaxing & enjoyable place. €€€

Lake Itasy Once you've had your fill of watersports you can do some walking: 'From Ampefy continue south and 1km from the hotel is a turn-off (to the left) to a peninsula. A 5km-long route takes you along the edge of the lake with beautiful views. But the best view is on top of the hill of the peninsula, where a shrine of the Virgin Mary overlooks the lake' (R Mulder & P Janssen).

Chute de la Lily This large waterfall is 7km from Ampefy. It can be reached by *taxi-brousse* if you don't have your own vehicle. Guides are available but not really necessary. Going towards Tana turn left along the river before crossing it. Keep going till you reach the falls. There is a second large and lovely waterfall about 20 minutes downstream. 'The surrounding rock faces are composed of (typically) hexagonal basalt columns, which makes the scene, especially for a geologist, even more interesting' (R Mulder & P Janssen).

The Geysers of Andranomandraotra Getting here is no longer a challenge. 'You can take a *taxi-brousse* from Analavory and get off at a junction from where the geysers are a mere 1.3km walk. Not only have the roads been improved, but there is now a bridge over the river to the geysers. They are really spectacular, especially if you have never seen a geyser before. The site was improved even more by some facilities: toilets and a picnic table. You can give a donation to sponsor the maintenance of the bridge and the other facilities' (R Mulder & P Janssen).

Tsiroanomandidy Lying about 200km to the west of Tana, on a surfaced road (four hours), this town is a pleasant and attractive place to spend a day or two. Its main

Technology was largely introduced to Madagascar by two remarkable Europeans: James Cameron, a Scot, and Jean Laborde, a Frenchman.

JAMES CAMERON arrived in Madagascar in 1826 during the country's 'British phase' when the London Missionary Society (LMS) had attempted to set up local craftsmen to produce goods in wood, metal, leather and cotton. Cameron was only 26 when he came to Madagascar but was already skilled as a carpenter and weaver, with a broad knowledge of other subjects which he was later to put to use in his adopted land: physics, chemistry, mathematics, architecture and astronomy. Cameron seemed able to turn his hand to almost anything mechanical. Among his achievements were the successful installation and running of Madagascar's first printing press (by studying the manual – the printer sent out with the press had died with unseemly haste), a reservoir (now Lake Anosy), an aqueduct, and the production of bricks.

Cameron's success in making soap from local materials ensured his royal favour after King Radama died and the xenophobic Queen Ranavalona came to power. But when Christian practice and teaching were forbidden in 1835, Cameron left with the other missionaries and went to work in South Africa.

He returned in 1863 when the missionaries were once more welcome in Madagascar, to oversee the building of stone churches, a hospital, and the stone exterior to the *rova* or queen's palace in Antananarivo.

JEAN LABORDE was even more of a renaissance man. The son of a blacksmith, Laborde was shipwrecked off the east coast of Madagascar in 1831. Queen Ranavalona, no doubt pleased to find a less godly European, asked him to manufacture muskets and gunpowder, and he soon filled the gap left by the departure of Cameron and the other artisan-missionaries. Laborde's initiative and inventiveness were amazing: in a huge industrial complex built by forced labour, he produced munitions and arms, bricks and tiles, pottery, glass and porcelain, silk, soap, candles, cement, dyes, sugar, rum … in fact just about everything a thriving country in the 19th century needed. He ran a farm which experimented with suitable crops and animals, and a country estate for the Merina royalty and aristocracy to enjoy such novelties as firework displays. And he built the original queen's palace in wood (in 1839), which was later enclosed in stone by Cameron.

So successful was Laborde in making Madagascar self-sufficient, that foreign trade was discontinued and foreigners – with the exception of Laborde – expelled. He remained in the queen's favour until 1857 when he was expelled because of involvement in a plot to replace the queen by her son. The 1,200 workmen who had laboured without pay in the foundries of Mantasoa rose up and destroyed everything – tools, machinery and buildings. The factories were never rebuilt, and Madagascar's Industrial Revolution came to an abrupt end.

He returned in 1861 and became French consul, dying in 1878. A dispute over his inheritance was one of the pretexts used by the French to justify the 1883–85 war.

attraction is the large cattle market, held on Wednesdays and Thursdays. The Bara people of the south drive huge herds of cattle through the Bongolava plateau to sell at the market.

There are two hotels. **Chez Marcelline**, north of the market and near the airport, seems to be the better.

Jolijn Geels

From Tsiroanomandidy we went to Belobaka by *taxi-brousse*, and that is where the road ends – in a small town with no electricity, no toilets and no hotels. After presenting ourselves to the *maire* and the *gendarmerie*, we were offered a room in the newly built 'city hall' which was not yet in use. The room was on the first floor and it was completely empty. Water was provided in a bucket, and the 'toilet' was 'past the *gendarmerie* to the left behind the bushes'. From Belobaka we would have to walk to Ankavandra, the starting point of our Manambolo River trip.

Most of the time Belobaka is very dark at night, with only candles and oil lamps to provide a little light. However, on a clear night when the moon is full, a bluish light casting sharp shadows shines over Belobaka and the streets that are otherwise so quiet come alive. In this remote town the children sing and dance to a full moon!

It was our first night in Belobaka. After our evening meal and a bucket shower in a hidden corner, we retreated to the balcony on the first floor where we sat and talked for a while. Then we heard singing, clapping, drumming and a lot of laughter! On the square just next to our 'hotel' many children of all ages and some adults were dancing, clearly visible in the light of the full moon. Running up and down the street, challenging a second group of kids to improve on their performance, they seemed to make up their game as they went along. All of a sudden they were chanting '*vazaha! vazaha!*' and the whole spectacle moved towards our balcony where they put on a real show for us. Of course we sang along as best as we could when they started singing some well-known French songs. Did we understand Malagasy, they asked. Well, not really, but we told them what words we knew, and every attempt we made to say something in their language triggered outbursts of laughter. It was just wonderful! At times we felt a bit silly, like a king and queen being cheered by a crowd, but what a happy crowd it was!

Then, without warning, the party was over and the children dispersed. Within minutes the streets of Belobaka were completely empty and silent.

8

The Highlands South of Tana

Many visitors drive the full length of Route Nationale 7 (RN7) to Toliara, either by hired car or by public transport. It is a delightful journey, providing an excellent overview of the *hauts plateaux* and Merina and Betsileo culture, as well as spectacular scenery, especially around Fianarantsoa. More and more excursions off this main route are opening up, ideal for cyclists or backpackers.

FROM TANA TO ANTSIRABE

It takes about three hours to drive to Antsirabe non stop, but there are numerous suggested pauses and diversions so most people take the best part of a day to do the 169km. The photo opportunities are terrific: all along this stretch of road you will see Merina tombs, and can watch the labour-intensive cultivation of rice paddies.

About 15km from Tana look for the huge, white replica of the *rova* (as it was before it burned) across the paddy fields on the right. This was ex-president Didier Ratsiraka's palace, funded by North Korea.

AMBATOFOTSY An interesting diversion for those with their own vehicle is this lakeside resort some 20km south of Tana. There's a small nature park here with around 160 plant species, a few lemurs and one or two snakes and other reptiles. There is also a museum. The entrance fee is 5,000Ar.

Where to stay
🏠 **Resto les Mitas & Chalet Bonne Place** (4 bungalows) Lot XV 100 Anosibe, Ambatofotsy (opposite entrance to 'Eaux et Fôrets', PK 22); m 032 07 792 30/033 11 788 65/033 12 863 88; e restomitas@yahoo.fr. Panoramic views.

Bungalows with bathroom & toilet. €€€
🏠 **Hôtel Restaurant Le Carat** (19 bungalows) ➘ 22 297 80; m 030 23 812 22. Meals served. €€–€€€

AMBATOLAMPY AND REGION Ambatolampy lies some two hours (68km) from Tana and has a colourful market as well as several hotels. It is also the starting point for

DISTANCES IN KILOMETRES			
Antananarivo–Ambatolampy	68km	Antsirabe–Miandrivazo	246km
Antananarivo–Antsirabe	169km	Antsirabe–Ihosy	449km
Antananarivo–Ambositra	259km	Ambositra–Ranomafana	138km
Antananarivo–Fianarantsoa	412km	Fianarantsoa–Mananjary	197km
Antsirabe–Ambositra	90km	Fianarantsoa–Manakara	254km
Antsirabe–Fianarantsoa	243km	Fianarantsoa–Ihosy	206km

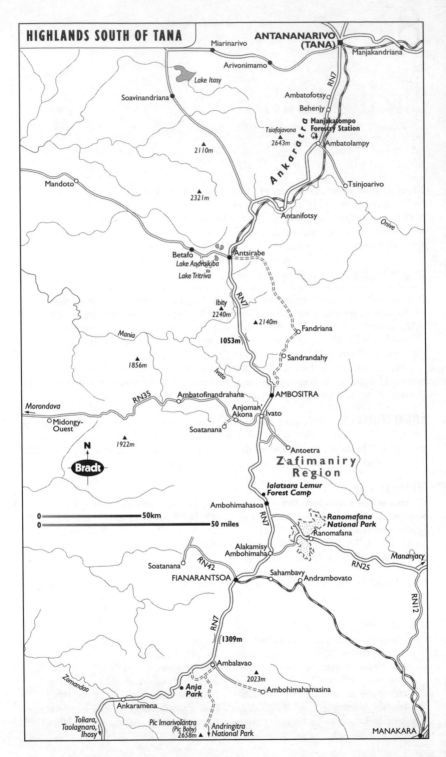

HIGHLANDS SOUTH OF TANA

ANTANANARIVO (TANA)

Miarinarivo
Manjakandriana
Arivonimamo
Soavinandriana
Lake Itasy
Ambatofotsy
Behenjy
Manjakatompo Forestry Station
Tsiafajavona 2643m
Ambatolampy
2110m
Mandoto
Tsinjoarivo
2321m
Onive
Antanifotsy
Betafo
Antsirabe
Lake Andraikiba
Lake Tritriva
RN7
Ibity 2240m
2140m
1053m
Fandriana
Mania
Sandrandahy
1856m
Ivato
RN35
Ambatofinandrahana
AMBOSITRA
Morondava
Anjoman' Akona
Ivato
Midongy-Ouest
Soatanana
N
1922m
Antoetra
Bradt
Zafimaniry Region
Ialatsara Lemur Forest Camp
0   50km
Ambohimahasoa
RN7
Ranomafana National Park
0   50 miles
Alakamisy Ambohimaha
Ranomafana
Soatanana
RN42
Sahambavy
Andrambovato
RN25
Mananjary
FIANARANTSOA
RN7
RN12
1309m
Ambalavao
2023m
Ambohimahamasina
Zomandao
Anja Park
Ankaramena
Toliara, Taolagnaro, Ihosy
Pic Imarivolantra (Pic Boby) 2658m
Andringitra National Park
MANAKARA

two interesting excursions to Tsinjoarivo, with its summer *rova*, and the forestry station of Manjakatompo.

Telephone code The area code for Ambatolampy is 42.

 **Where to stay/eat**

Hôtel Antsaha (27 bungalows) ☎ 44 050 02; m 032 40 564 69/033 12 220 46; e antsaha@freenet.mg. Off RN7 near **Tombotsoa**, this is a relaxing place to get away from the city. Numerous activities: tennis, ping-pong, badminton, bowling, bikes, swimming pool etc. Restaurant with Malagasy, European & Chinese food. €€€–€€€€

Hôtel au Rendez-vous des Pecheurs (7 rooms) ☎ 42 492 04. Albanian-owned; renowned for its large restaurant which caters to tour buses, so very crowded at lunchtime. Rooms are simple but comfortable, mostly with shared bathrooms (with a

big bathtub) & hot water, but there are a few en-suite rooms. €€

Manja Ranch Lot B 153, Mandrevondry; m 033 11 993 70/032 04 648 57; e bijouxline@yahoo.fr. About 2km south of town. Owned by American Doug Cook & his Malagasy wife Bijou. Rooms (shared bathrooms, unreliable water) & bungalows. Camping permitted. Bike hire. Set menu. B/fast inc. €€

Hôtel Njara The cheapest place in Ambatolampy, close to the market. Recommended by Nina French: 'the best room with a balcony is upstairs'. €

TSINJOARIVO From Ambatolampy a road leads southeast to Tsinjoarivo. Johan and Clare Hermans write: 'Check conditions before setting out; although only about 50km it takes a good three to four hours by car and is not an all-weather road (an alternative road on higher ground bypasses some of the boggiest stretches). The journey is worthwhile for the series of waterfalls and the *rova* of Queen Rasoherina; in her time it took three days from Tana by palanquin. There is a guardian who will show you round the buildings: one for the queen with the remains of some fine wooden carving from her bed, and others for the prime minister, chancellor and guard. Situated on a promontory overlooking the falls, the site has spectacular views and an incredible atmosphere. There are stone steps down from the *rova* to the viewpoint at the falls, complete with spray.'

MANJAKATOMPO FORESTRY STATION A road leads west and then north from Ambatolampy to Manjakatompo, an hour's drive (17km). 'The road passes through aluminium smelting villages – worth a stop to watch them making cutlery and cooking pots. Permits for the Manjakatompo Forest are obtainable at the gate: about 5,000Ar. Guides not obligatory (ours was not worth the money). Well-signposted walks; sights include a small waterfall and an interesting lichen forest with two royal tombs, circa 1810, near the encampment. It is a four-hour hike to Tsiafajavona, the tallest peak of the Andringitra range.' (Johan and Clare Hermans)

Taxi-brousses go here Monday, Wednesday and Thursday only. The reception at Rendez-vous des Pêcheurs can contact a local driver who will take you here for 15,000Ar. It is best to give them a day's notice to track him down.

MERINA TOMBS About 15 minutes beyond Ambatolampy are some fine painted Merina tombs. These are on both sides of the road, but the most accessible are on the right.

ANTSIRABE

Antsirabe lies 169km south of Antananarivo at 1,500m. It was founded in 1872 by Norwegian missionaries attracted by the cool climate and the healing properties of the thermal springs. The name means 'place of much salt'.

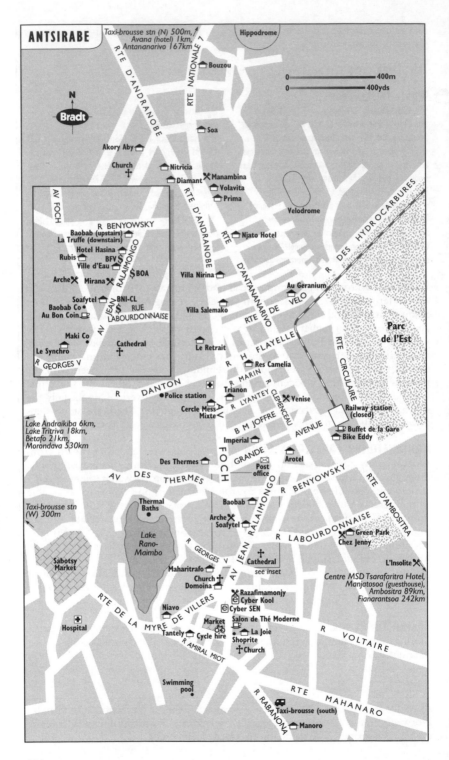

ANTSIRABE

Taxi-brousse stn (N) 500m,
Avana (hotel) 1km,
Antananarivo 167km

Hippodrome

Bouzou

Soa

Akory Aby

Church

Nitricia

Diamant   Manambina
           Volavita
           Prima

Velodrome

RTE D'ANDRANOBE

RTE NATIONALE 7

RTE D'ANDRANOBE

RTE

Njato Hotel

0 ——————— 400m
0 ——————— 400yds

R BENYOWSKY
Baobab (upstairs)
La Truffe (downstairs)
    Hotel Hasina
Rubis   BFV
    Ville d'Eau
              BOA
Arche   Mirana

    Soafytel   BNI-CL
Baobab Co   RUE
Au Bon Coin   LABOURDONNAISE

    Maki Co
Le Synchro   Cathedral
R GEORGES V

AV FOCH

AV JEAN RALAIMONGO

Villa Nirina

Villa Salemako

Le Retrait

RTE D'ANTANANARIVO

Au Geranium

RTE DE VELO

Parc
de l'Est

R DES HYDROCARBURES

R H FLAYELLE

Res Camelia

R MARIN

R DANTON

Police station
Cercle Mess
Mixte

Trianon

R LYANTEY

B M JOFFRE

Venise

AV FOCH

R CLEMENCEAU

AVENUE

GRANDE

RTE CIRCULAIRE

Railway station
(closed)

Buffet de la Gare
Bike Eddy

Lake Andraikiba 6km,
Lake Tritriva 18km,
Betafo 21km,
Morondava 530km

Des Thermes

Imperial

Arotel

Post
office

AV DES THERMES

Taxi-brousse stn
(W) 300m

Thermal
Baths

Lake
Rano-
Maimbo

Sabotsy
Market

Baobab

Arche
Soafytel

R GEORGES V

Maharitrafo
Church
Domoina

Niavo

RTE DE LA MYRE DE VILLERS

Hospital

R RALAIMONGO

R BENYOWSKY

R LABOURDONNAISE

Green Park
Chez Jenny

L'Insolite

RTE D'AMBOSITRA

Centre MSD Tsarafaritra Hotel,
Manjatosoa (guesthouse),
Ambositra 89km,
Fianarantsoa 242km

AV JEAN

Cathedral
see inset

Razafimamonjy
Cyber Kool
Cyber SEN

Salon de Thé Moderne

Market

Tantely   Cycle hire
           Shoprite
           Church

La Joie

R AMIRAL MIOT

R VOLTAIRE

Swimming
pool

R RABANONA

RTE MAHANARO

Taxi-brousse (south)

Manoro

Bradt

N

For Madagascar, this is an elegant city. A broad avenue links the handsome (though now unused) railway station with Hôtel des Thermes, an amazing building in both size and architectural style. There is nothing else like it in Madagascar; it would not be out of place along the French Riviera and is set in equally elegant gardens (see *Where to stay*). At the station end is a monolith depicting Madagascar's 18 main ethnic groups. Antsirabe is the agricultural and industrial centre of Madagascar. It is also the centre for beer: you can smell the Star Brewery as you enter the town. These days the town is equally celebrated for its connection with Tiko dairy products, and thus the President. He owns several factories in Antsirabe. The cool climate also allows it to produce apples, pears, plums and other temperate fruit.

If you are travelling between May and September you will need a sweater in the evening. It gets quite cold.

TELEPHONE CODE The area code for Antsirabe is 44.

GETTING THERE AND AWAY Antsirabe is three hours by road from Tana, and there's a good choice of public transport. Madabus leaves at 06.00 and costs € 9. Buses and *taxi-brousses* leave from Fasan'ny Karana in Tana. Continuing south to Ambositra takes two hours, while travelling from Antsirabe to Fianarantsoa (non stop) by private car takes five hours.

Note that there are three *taxi-brousse* stations in Antsirabe: north, south and west.

GETTING AROUND This is the *pousse-pousse* capital of Madagascar. There are hundreds, perhaps thousands of them. The drivers are insistent that you avail yourself of a ride, and why not? But be very firm about the price. Now that lots of tourists come to Antsirabe, the drivers have found they can make a dollar just by posing for pictures. To actually have to run somewhere towing a large *vazaha* for the same price must seem very unfair.

Daniel and Kelly add this warning: 'On all three occasions that we arrived in Antsirabe and took a *pousse-pousse* to a hotel from the *taxi-brousse* station, the *pousse-pousse* drivers stopped halfway saying "I know a much better hotel: Hôtel Video. It is much cheaper and better. I will take you there." Each time they were very persistent and we had to lie that we had already reserved a room at our chosen hotel to get them to take us there. Evidently Hôtel Video must pay *pousse-pousse* drivers a commission for bringing new customers in.'

Andrew Shimmin points out that 'not only are none of the streets labelled with their "names", but no-one knows them anyway!'

WHERE TO STAY A special feature of Antsirabe is the private guesthouses. These offer a friendly and economical alternative to hotels.

Upper range €€€€

⌂ **Arotel** (45 rooms & 2 apartments) Rue Ralaimongo; ☎ 44 481 20/485 73/485 74; f 44 491 49; e arotel.inn@wanadoo.mg. Well-situated & comfortable with luxurious bathtubs, though has reportedly gone downhill a little in recent years. A secluded garden at the back has a swimming pool open to non-residents for 2,000Ar.
⌂ **Hôtel des Thermes** (32 rooms) ☎ 44 487 61/62; f 44 497 64; e sht@wanadoo.mg. Amazing from the outside; pleasant en-suite rooms with

balconies. Cosy bar & restaurant (though overpriced). Silke Rother stayed here when ill: 'It is really perfect if you need a little bit of European comfort. You get a nice view & it is really quiet in the garden.' Swimming pool (6,000Ar for non-residents), tennis, mini-golf, billiards, volleyball & meeting room. Visa & MasterCard accepted.
⌂ **Le Trianon** (6 rooms) ☎ 44 051 40; e letrianon@wanadoo.mg. Comfortable rooms with facilities. TV & safe. Excellent restaurant.

Mid range €€€

⌂ **Résidence Camélia** (10 rooms) North of Grande Av; ☎ 44 488 44; e camelia@simicro.mg. A converted villa set in lovely gardens in the French part of town. Rooms in the main house are small, with shared bathrooms; there's an annexe with 2 spacious en-suite rooms with verandas. Some sgl rooms.

⌂ **Manjatosoa Guest House** (5 rooms) Rte d'Ambositra, Ambalavato; m 032 04 165 35; e zo_soa@yahoo.fr. Rooms with facilities; good view from terrace. Can organise Antsirabe tours.

⌂ **Soa Guest House** (5 rooms) Lot 0910 E 101, Vatofotsy, Mahafaly; m 032 02 279 90/033 15 279 90; e soa_guesthouse@hotmail.com. Restful, quiet house decorated with Malagasy crafts.

⌂ **Avana Hotel** (27 rooms) Lot 540 A 290 B, Mahafaly; ☎ 44 492 99; e avana_hotel2000@mel.wanadoo.mg. A large hotel near the north *taxi-brousse* station. Comfortable & competitively priced.

⌂ **Imperial Hotel** (24 rooms) Grande Av; ☎ 44 483 33. 'Soulless oriental with Eastern Bloc influence. The "casino" is a few slot machines' (S Bulmer). But rooms are comfortable with en-suite bathrooms, some with TV & balcony. Good food.

⌂ **Hôtel Le Retrait** (13 rooms) Rte d' Andranomadio; ☎ 44 050 29. Down a small path opposite the Total filling station. Comfortable, nice rooms with TV & en-suite bathrooms. Extensions underway. Studio for 178,500Ar.

⌂ **Villa Nirina** (5 rooms) Rte d'Andranobe; ☎ 44 485 97/486 69; e zanoa@blueline.mg. Run by Mrs Zanoa Rasanjison, who speaks fluent English, French & survival German. Sgl rooms available.

⌂ **Hôtel Hasina** (31 rooms) Rue Jean Ralaimongo (same building as Courts); ☎ 44 485 56; f 44 483 55; e hotelhasina@yahoo.fr. Same owner as Razafimamonjy restaurant. Some rooms en suite.

⌂ **Prima Guest House** (4 rooms) Lot 0906 B 270, Rte d'Antananarivo; ☎ 44 493 02; e rest.manambina@yahoo.fr. Safe parking; 2 en-suite sgl rooms. Incorporates **Restaurant Manambina**.

⌂ **Villa Salemako** (5 rooms) RN7; ☎ 44 495 88. Recognisable by the Malagasy motif on the chimney. A good-value private home run by Julia-Brigitte Rakotonarivo. Spacious lounge; comfortable rooms; beautiful garden.

⌂ **Hôtel Diamant** (65 rooms) 110 Rte d'Andranobe; ☎ 44 488 40/493 72; e diamant@madawel.com. Good selection of rooms inc spacious suite. Internet available, 20Ar/min.

⌂ **Le Bouzou (Shanti)** (10 rooms) Lot 0910 A 85, Mahafaly, Vatofotsy; ☎ 44 932 44; m 032 0230 552. Indian hotel about 450m from north *taxi-brousse* station. Restaurant serves European, Chinese & Malagasy food inc pizzas! Warm & welcoming. Sgl rooms available.

⌂ **Green Park** (8 rooms) Tsarasaotra; ☎ 44 051 90. Restaurants L'Auberge & Chez Jenny are next door. Order b/fast in advance.

Budget €€

⌂ **Hôtel Soafytel** (15 rooms) Lot 22 J 60, Av Ralaimongo (opposite BNI bank); ☎ 44 480 55. Cheap but reportedly run-down. Rooms with hot shower; most have en-suite toilet. Malagasy craft boutique.

⌂ **Hôtel Niavo** (10 rooms) Rue Rakotondrainibe Daniel; ☎ 44 484 67. The full name is Hôtel/Restaurant Fitsangatsanganana Niavo! Convenient location close to market & south *taxi-brousse* station. Some rooms en suite with hot water & TV.

⌂ **La Joie** (6 rooms) Antsenankely, Rue Duplex; ☎ 44 962 47. TV use extra. Some cheap rooms from 7,000Ar.

⌂ **Akory Aby** (5 rooms) Lot 1120 A 403, Miaramasoandro; m 033 12 845 10/032 40 878 73; e akory_aby@yahoo.fr; near north *taxi-brousse* station. Sgl & dbl rooms. Order b/fast in advance. Internet access for 20Ar/min. Car hire available.

⌂ **Ville d'Eau** (10 rooms) Lot 22 J 80, Rue Ralaimongo; ☎ 44 499 70; e villedeau@simicro.mg. Dbl & twin rooms, some en suite.

⌂ **Au Geranium** (8 rooms) Rte du Vélodrome; ☎ 44 497 31; m 032 07 045 44. A pleasant guesthouse. Dbl rooms, some en suite.

⌂ **Hôtel Volavita** (20 rooms) Rte d'Antananarivo; ☎ 44 488 64; f 44 489 60; e volavita@blueline.mg. A good variety of rooms at different prices. Sgl room available. TV use extra.

⌂ **Centre MSD Tsarafaritra** Mandanitresaka, off the road to Ambohimena; ☎ 44 481 62; m 033 14 120 27; e bettylauber@wanadoo.mg. A Christian retreat centre, about 40mins from the town centre, highly recommended by Andrew & Catherine Shimmin. 'It is an absolute haven. Comfortable rooms in the main house, with shared bathrooms. Lovely gardens, home-grown food. The centre is run by Betty Lauber, an incredible Swiss lady, who speaks about a million languages, & is an absolute star!'

Dbl rooms & self-catering apt.

🏠 **Maharitrafo** (5 rooms) Lot 01 C 30, Antsenakely, Rue Rakotondraibe Daniel; ✆ 44 052 15; m 033 12 039 47/032 43 306 10. Dbl rooms at various prices.

🏠 **Pension de Famille Nitricia** (8 rooms) Lot 1118 P 261, Miaramasoandro; ✆ 44 493 02/963 80; m 033 14 349 20. Friendly, relaxing atmosphere in a family home with terrace near north *taxi-brousse* station. Safe parking. Cooking facilities; b/fast to order. Larger rooms for up to 4 people. Shared facilities.

🏠 **Nouveau Synchro Pub** (6 rooms) Rue Pastuer Antsenakely, Voasaribe; ✆ 44 962 24; m 033 02 266 36/033 14 212 09. Down a path near the

Cathedral. Extensions underway, inc a craft outlet. Dbl rooms; also studios for 30,000–40,000Ar.

🏠 **Nouveau Baobab** (8 rooms) Rue Jean Ralaimongo; ✆ 44 483 93. Sgl & dbl rooms, some en suite.

🏠 **Manoro Hotel** (10 rooms) Ambavahadimangatsiaka; ✆ 44 944 15; m 032 207 624 44; /033 14 905 69; e edm@wanadoo.mg. En-suite dbl & family rooms with TV.

🏠 **Cercle Mess Mixte** (29 rooms) Av Maréchal Foch; ✆ 44 483 66. One of Antsirabe's longest-established hotels — it appeared in the 1st ed of this guide! Good value sgl & dbl rooms. Cyber Snack Club internet & Malagasy craft boutique with precious stones.

Penny-pincher €

🏠 **Hôtel Restaurant Tantely** (6 rooms) Rue Ernest Renan; ✆ 44 491 37. One of the oldest houses in Antsirabe (1920); retains its Malagasy features. Comfortable sgl, dbl & family rooms.

🏠 **Hôtel Restaurant Domoina** (4 rooms) Rue Kleber Antsenakely; m 032 07 961 39/032 02 129 80. A simple hotel. Rooms with shared facilities.

🏠 **Hôtel Restaurant Domoina Annexe** (7 rooms) Lot 24 B 21, Mahazoarivo; m 032 07 961 39/032 02

129 80. Rooms with shared facilities.

🏠 **Njato Hotel** (10 rooms) Located near Hôtel Diamant on the left of the filling station as you come from the north. A very simple hotel.

🏠 **Hôtel Rubis** (4 rooms) Rue Stavanger. A very simple hotel behind Soafytel. Dbl rooms, some with facilities.

🏠 **Hôtel Bike Eddy** ✆ 44 495 91. Near the railway station; central & very cheap. Restaurant.

✗ **WHERE TO EAT** Some of the hotel restaurants serve very good food. Particularly recommended is the **Trianon,** which specialises in French food but also serves Malagasy and Italian. The **Nouveau Synchro Pub** serves good European, Malagasy and Chinese food.

✗ **Arche** Rue Stavanger; m 032 02 479 25. 'On a little street leading from Av M Foch to Av J Ralaimongo. Small, French-owned, good food, live music in the evenings, good atmosphere' (S Bulmer). 'The speciality is chicken with lemon, also famous for its fresh fillet, the best Malagasy food in Antsirabe' (LG). Exhibition of paintings for sale in the restaurant.

✗ **Bar-Restaurant Razafimamonjy** Antsenankely; ✆ 44 483 53. Opposite the market on Av Jean Ralaimongo. Good value excellent food & sometimes live music.

✗ **Restaurant Manambina** Rte d'Antananarivo. Lot 0906 B 270; ✆ 44 493 02. Malagasy, French, Chinese & vegetarian dishes. German spoken. ⊕ *11.00–14.30 & 19.30–21.00.*

✗ **Mirana** Av Jean Ralaimongo; ✆ 44 491 81; m 033 11 199 87. Good for b/fast & take-away meals.

✗ **La Truffe** Lot 22 J 14, Rue Jean Ralaimongo; ✆ 44 978 95; m 033 11 335 55;

e bakoliarisoaemily@yahoo.fr. Downstairs from the Nouveau Baobab hotel.

✗ **Chez Jenny** A highly recommended restaurant & bar. 'The speciality is pizzas cooked in sight of the diners. A cosy place with friendly staff. Their 2 adorable dogs are often to be seen chasing one another beneath the tables!' (D&K).

✗ **L'Insolite** Rte d'Ambositra, Village Artisanal; m 032 02 158 14. Bar & restaurant with recreation park (mini-golf, bowling, badminton etc). It serves Malagasy & European food; draught THB. ⊕ *11am–late.*

✗ **Le Venise** Lot 0912 C 021 (near railway station); m 033 11 411 61. New bar & restaurant; good service & pleasant venue. Excellent European & Malagasy food at reasonable prices. ⊕ *daily 08.00–24.00.*

🍽 **Au Bon Coin** Lot 01E 20, Rue Stavanger; ✆ 44 492 48. Same ownership as the Nouveau Baobab hotel. Simple but tasty Malagasy & Chinese food. Inexpensive.

🍽 **Buffet de la Gare** This café is part of the railway station. Drinks & snacks.

🍽 **Salon de Thé Moderne** A pleasant snack bar opposite the Pharmacie Mahasoa.

NIGHTLIFE

☆ **Tahiti nightclub** At Hôtel Diamant. 'Worth a visit' (SB).

INTERNET

🌐 **Cyber Kool** (next to Bar-Restaurant Razafimamonjy) Has 11 computers & costs 30Ar/min. The connections are quite fast & if you stay long enough (3hrs) they'll give you a free drink. ⏲ *daily 08.00–24.00.*

🌐 **Cyber SEN** Antsenankely (opposite Razafimamonjy Restaurant) 30Ar/min.

BICYCLE HIRE Rabemananjara Mamisoa is your man. Find him at the hotel Green Park (*or* m *032 02 176 05;* e *rabemananjaram@yahoo.fr*). 'He has a stack of good bikes which he hires out for a reasonable price. He provided a good map and even gave me a puncture repair kit and tools for no extra cost. A lovely bloke!' (Stuart Riddle). Mamisoa can also organise excursions on foot, by bike or by car, or even trekking trips further afield.

WHAT TO SEE AND DO Saturday is market day in Antsirabe, an echo of Tana before they abolished the *zoma* but with an even greater cross section of activities. It's enclosed in a walled area of the city on the hill before the road to Lake Tritriva. 'The entire back wall of the market is a row of open barber stalls. Each has a small mirror, a chair and a little peg for one's hat. There are a few local gambling places nearby, too. They're hard to find and the stakes can get pretty high' (Maggie Rush).

I used to recommend a visit to the thermal baths (*thermes*) but recent reports are that these are now quite grubby (⏲ *07.00–21.00. Price 1,300Ar*).

Artisan workshops Antsirabe has a thriving handicrafts sector and it's well worth visiting the workshops to see the skill and ingenuity of the craftsmen. Silke Rother recommends a *pousse-pousse* tour: 'We made a very nice trip to some places where local art is made. We saw carved zebu horn, jewellery, things made out of old tin cans, and a lot of embroidered tablecloths and clothing. It was fascinating to see how these arts were done. After the (free) demonstrations you can (and should) buy some souvenirs, but be advised that they can be much more expensive than in Tana. You can bargain [but bear in mind that the makers may need the money more than you do – HB]. Make sure that you set a price for the *pousse-pousse* tour, otherwise there will be arguments for a higher price at the end. We paid 16,000Ar for two *pousse-pousses* to take us on a two-hour tour.'

TOURIST OFFICE AND TOUR OPERATOR

🛈 **ORTVA** (regional tourist office) m 032 07 186 42; e etravel@wanadoo.mg.
Roadhouse Voyages ✆/f 44 492 26; e roadhouse@simicro.mg; www.simicro.mg/roadhouse. Bill Love, an experienced American tour operator, writes: 'The manager, Klaus Sperling, is German & is the most organised person I've ever met for getting things accomplished, especially in remote places. Klaus's English is excellent, & his team of mostly Malagasy guides & drivers are very good. I'd highly recommend them to anyone planning an adventure trip, especially if they wish to explore not-so-popular areas.'

EXCURSIONS FROM ANTSIRABE

Lakes Andraikiba and Tritriva Andraikiba is a large lake 7km west of Antsirabe, often overlooked in favour of the more spectacular Lake Tritriva. 'One of the few moments when you stepped back into another world. Very laid back, very few people. Tranquil and picturesque' (Volker Dornheim).

Taxi-brousses heading for Betafo pass close to the lake, or you can go by hired bicycle – worth considering. Cyclist Nina French reports: 'From Antsirabe we did a day trip to the volcanic lakes and to Betafo. We enjoyed the views from the crater of Lac Tritriva and the downhill dirt road continuing northwest and to Betafo. Fantastic scenery!'

Where to stay

Hôtel Dera (6 bungalows & 6 rooms)
44 052 42/938 01. Tpl bungalows have en-suite

bathrooms & lake views; dbl & tpl rooms have shared bathrooms. €€–€€€

Lake Tritriva's name comes from *tritry* – the Malagasy word for the ridge on the back of a chameleon (!) – and *iva*, deep. And this emerald-green crater lake is indeed deep – 80m, some say. It is reached by continuing past Lake Andraikiba for 12km on a rough, steep road (4x4 only) past small villages of waving kids. You will notice that these villages are relatively prosperous-looking for Madagascar; they grow the barley for the Star Brewery.

Apart from the sheer beauty of Lake Tritriva (the best light for photography is in the morning), there are all sorts of interesting features. The water level rises in the dry season and debris thrown into the lake has reappeared down in the valley, supporting the theory of underground water channels.

Look across the lake and you'll see two thorn trees with intertwined branches growing on a ledge above the water. Legend has it that these are two lovers, forbidden to marry by their parents, who drowned themselves in Lake Tritriva. When the branches are cut, so they say, blood oozes out, not sap. You can walk right round the lake for impressive views of both the lake and the surrounding countryside.

The local people have not been slow to realise the financial potential of groups of *vazaha* corralled at the top of a hill. There is an 'entrance charge' and once through the gate don't think you will be alone at the lake.

Getting to Tritriva without a vehicle is difficult. The best way is to take a bus to Lake Andraikiba and then walk. Or rent a bike and make it a day trip.

Betafo About 22km west of Antsirabe, off the tarred road that goes as far as Morondava, lies Betafo, a town with typical highlands red-brick churches and houses. Dotted among the houses are *vatolahy*, standing stones erected to commemorate warrior chieftains. A visit here is recommended. It is off the normal tourist circuit, and gives you an excellent insight into Merina small-town activities. Monday is market day. There is no hotel in Betafo but you should be able to find a room by asking around.

At one end of the town is the crater lake **Tatamarina**. From there it is a walk of about 3km to the **Antafofo** waterfalls among beautiful views of rice fields and volcanic hills. You will need to find someone to show you the way. 'It's very inviting for a swim but they told me there are ghosts in the pool under the falls. If you go swimming they will grab your legs and pull you to the bottom' (Luc Selleslagh).

On the outskirts of Betafo there are hot springs, where for a few ariary you can have a hot bath with no time limit.

CONTINUING SOUTH ON RN7

Leaving Antsirabe you continue to pass through typical highland scenery of rice paddies and low hills.

An interesting side trip from this stretch is to **Mount Ibity**. Valerie Middleton writes: 'About 15km south of Antsirabe on RN7 a large white sign points westwards to the "Holcim Cement Works". This good dirt road can be followed to the village of Ibity opposite the works, above which rears Mt Ibity. This mainly quartzite massif provides excellent walking opportunities as it naturally has few trees, thus allowing panoramic views from almost any point. Many small footpaths cross and circumnavigate the hills (about ten hours, all between 1,600m and 1,900m). Unusual caves formed in quartzite can also be visited (a six-hour round-trip to 2,000m). Large, rounded boulders dominate the lower slopes whilst highly eroded blocks create a wilderness higher up. The flora is particularly fascinating and includes many endemics only to be found on the quartzite of Mt Ibity. Small quarries for semi-precious stones scar the mountain and the surrounding hills; we visited several including tourmaline, rose quartz and talc. The best access is to turn left immediately before the village, go past a new church, and then fork right on a rough track up to the house of the man in charge of the communications dish and antennae. His son is a good guide.'

Some 20km south of Antsirabe you enter the Amoron'ny Mania region, Betsileo country, and the province of Fianarantsoa. It's another 76km to Ambositra.

AMBOSITRA

Ambositra (pronounced am*boo*str) is a friendly little Betsileo town. Many of the 30,000 inhabitants are students so in July and August the population is much reduced. Most visitors stop only briefly, but the countryside around the town is very scenic and the local people are renowned for being talkative, so it merits a few days' stay if you have time.

Ambositra is the centre of Madagascar's woodcarving industry. Even the houses have ornately carved wooden balconies and shutters. There is an abundant choice of carved figures and marquetry, and the quality is improving although there are occasional lapses into pseudo-Africana (see *Shopping*).

Ambositra produces more than woodcarvings: 'Some of the best cheese in Madagascar is made by the cloistered nuns at the Benedictine convent. The chapel and convent are architecturally stunning. Stepping into the courtyard feels like you've wandered into 17th-century France.' (Mark Shehinian)

Several readers have complained that this town has more persistent beggars than anywhere else in Madagascar. The problem area is in front of the Grand Hotel with its profusion of tour buses. You are unlikely to be bothered in other parts of the town, which is notably safe and friendly.

TELEPHONE CODE The area code for Ambositra is 47.

WHERE TO STAY

🏠 **Angelino Tsaralaza** (8 rooms) 🕿 47 711 92; m 032 07 868 81; e angelino-hotel@ wanadoo.mg; www.angelino-hotel.com. The best guesthouse in town, in a traditional Malagasy house. Mountain bikes for rent. The shop in the same building sells excellent silk goods. €€–€€€€

🏠 **Hôtel Violette** (6 rooms & 6 bungalows) Madiolahatra; 🕿 47 710 84. North of the town. Elegantly furnished bungalows with TV. Great views from 2nd-floor balcony, but cheaper rooms face the road. Popular with tour groups. Being extended at time of writing. €€–€€€

🏠 **Residence Mahatsinjo** 🕿 47 710 36; jeannoeltours@yahoo.fr. A short walk up the hill, 1st left after Hotel Violette. 'Easily the most attractive place to stay in town. Very quiet & rural while only a short walk from town. Wonderful service from the charming family who run it. Chantal will cook a delicious meal to order & her father, Jean-Noel, organises trips locally or further afield. A real find' (HD). €€

🏠 **Hôtel Restaurant Jonathan** (8 rooms) A new hotel; rooms are en suite. €€

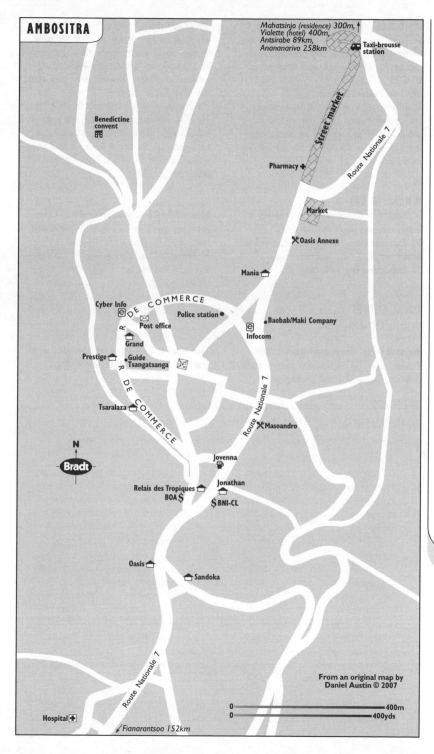

AMBOSITRA

Mahatsinjo (residence) 300m,
Violette (hotel) 400m,
Antsirabe 89km,
Anananarivo 258km

Taxi-brousse
station

Benedictine
convent

Street market

Route Nationale 7

Pharmacy ✚

Market

✕ Oasis Annexe

Mania 🏠

Cyber Info
🄴 R DE COMMERCE

Police station ●

Baobab/Maki Company ●

Post office ✉

🄴 Infocom

Grand 🏠

Prestige 🏠

Guide
Tsangatsanga

R DE COMMERCE

Tsaralaza 🏠

Route Nationale 7

N

Bradt

✕ Masoandro

Jovenna ⛽

Relais des Tropiques 🏠

Jonathan 🏠

BOA $

$ BNI-CL

Oasis 🏠

🏠 Sandoka

From an original map by
Daniel Austin © 2007

0 ──────── 400m
0 ──────── 400yds

Hospital ✚

Route Nationale 7

Fianarantsoa 152km

The Highlands South of Tana AMBOSITRA 8

193

🏠 **Le Relais des Tropiques** (12 rooms) ⚲ 47 711 26. Simple rooms, some with shared facilities. 'Ask for the cool, artsy, sky-lit room outside the main building' (MS). Indian-owned. Good restaurant. €–€€

🏠 **Hôtel Mania** (11 rooms) ⚲ 47 711 21; e toursmania@wanadoo.mg. Malagasy-owned, central; clean, en-suite rooms. 'The entrance is pedestrian only via a gate off the main street, locked at night so you have to ring the bell.' Tours organised; bikes & cars for rent. €€

🏠 **Grand Hotel** (13 rooms). ⚲ 47 712 62. The only Ambositra hotel in the 1st ed of this guide – it's been around a long time & has a loyal clientele. It's a beautiful old building: 'very woody' as one enthusiast described it. Some rooms en suite, others with bidet & basin. €–€€

🏠 **Prestige** (7 rooms) Andrefan' i Vinani; ⚲ 47 711 35. A charming, small *auberge* with a garden & beautiful views. The owner, Francis Rakotonisa, is very helpful. Sgl, dbl, twin & family rooms. Booking advised, especially for w/ends. Restaurant open high season only. €–€€

✗ WHERE TO EAT

✗ **Hotely Gasy Masoandro** Rue de Commerce. A budget restaurant which also has rooms.
✗ **Restaurant Oasis** Mid-range restaurant with nice seating upstairs & tasty food.
✗ **Oasis Annexe** Very good, cheap food.

✗ **Grand Hotel** A hangout for travellers, so even if you're not staying here it's useful to have a drink & swap stories. The food is (usually) good.
✗ **Restaurant Voajanahary** At Angelino Tsaralaza. Very basic food, but with a lovely view.
🕓 08.00–22.00.

LOCAL GUIDES There are a few guide services in Ambositra that take tourists out to nearby Betsileo villages.

Maison de Guide 'Tsangatsanga' Opposite Hôtel Prestige; ⚲ 47 714 48. Organises tours in & around Ambositra; English- & French-speaking guides.

Tours Mania At Hôtel Mania. Organises tours in & around Ambositra; also to Zafimaniry villages.

INTERNET Two cybercafés, **Infocom** and **Cyber Info** are located on the Rue de Commerce. 150Ar/min if you can get a connection.

FAZASOMA

This inspiring organisation demonstrates how visitors can work with local people to make a real difference in Madagascar. Fazasoma was founded in 2000 by three Malagasy women in Ambositra who used their own money to help needy children in their town. They were joined by three Dutch women who, after their visits to Madagascar, wanted to do something for the Malagasy children. They founded their organisation (with the same name) in the Netherlands to raise funds for the projects in Ambositra.

In 2003 they had raised enough funds to build an orphanage for 17 children (not all of these children are strictly orphans; some have mothers who are unable to care for them properly). By 2006 the group had built another three houses for homeless women, which include a crèche and a sewing room. Gradually these women are rebuilding their lives, and their children (now more than 40) are provided with clothes, schooling and medical care. Fazasoma has also helped families repair their houses and built two new classrooms for the local school.

The organisation provides microcredit finance to many women, so that they can start small businesses.

For further information or to arrange a visit contact Eva Hassambay (the owner of Hôtel Mania and President of the Malagasy branch of Fazasoma) or Remi Doomernik at e remi.madagaskar@gmail.com.

SHOPPING Most of the stores selling woodcarving and other handicrafts – nearly 30 in total – are on the 'ring road' running round Ambositra's central hill (this circuit is an easy 1.4km walk). There are ethical problems when buying palisander and rosewood carvings – these endemic trees are becoming very rare. That said, wood carving is the main source of income for the town, so it's a typically Malagasy dilemma. Also avoid buying all your souvenirs at Chez Victor's, opposite the Grand Hotel. He has a commercial arrangement with drivers who dump tour groups at the shop, depriving the other shopkeepers of their custom. Try to spread your custom around as many shops as possible.

Clare Hermans recommends 'Mr Randrianasolo's workshop at **Ilaka Centre**, just north of Ambositra. He has 25 apprentices working for him and has some artefacts that are different from the usual run-of-the-mill stuff.'

There's a workshop below the boutique and restaurant Voajanahary/Angelino Tsaralaza (✆ *47 711 92*) where you can see demonstrations of the different silk production techniques. This initiative is supported by Ny Tanintsika (e *nytk@simicro.mg*) and Mondo Giusto (e *fabio@simicro.mg*), providing an outlet for some of the wild silk and domestic silk products produced by women's associations. If you want to shop ethically, this is the place to do it.

PLACES OF INTEREST NEAR AMBOSITRA

ROYAL PALACE On a hill east of the town is a renovated royal palace. It is a beautiful 1½ hours' walk up (there's no shortage of guides to show you the way) through rice fields with superb views across the valley. The 'palace' used to consist of two houses, but one burned down a few years ago. Two flagpoles remain, two tombs and a rock on which the king stood to make his speeches. There is a small museum which contains the story of the place in some detail. Remi Doomernik, who knows the area well, suggests descending on the other side of the hill, where the road down is even more beautiful. 'A very nice way to get to know Ambositra and its environment.'

SANDRANDAHY AND FANDRIANA A tarmac road northeast of Ambositra leads to Fandriana, well known for its raffia work. It takes about 1½ hours to cover the 45km from Ambositra. Roughly halfway is Sandrandahy which holds a huge Wednesday market.

In Fandriana, cyclist Nina French recommends **Hôtel Sariaka** near the market: 8,000Ar for a small room, 10,000Ar for the big room with the balcony. 'Good security. Peace Corps leave their bikes there when they travel by *taxi-brousse* to Ambositra. Take a walk around the town and admire weekend houses of members of the government.'

If you are in a private vehicle or on a bicycle, the dirt road from Fandriana to Antsirabe is said to be very beautiful.

SOATANANA In the last edition two Peace Corps volunteers wrote about their work with the silk-weavers of Soatanana, 38km west of Ambositra (not to be confused with another Soatanana a little further south – see page 203): 'The village is nestled in picturesque rice paddies surrounded by granite peaks. The scenery alone is worth the trip. Soatanana is a traditional highlands village with rice farming and oxcart building, but what makes it outstanding is its silk cloth production. We are working to help these women develop a sustainable business based on their weaving. The Soatanana weavers make the finest cloth we've seen in Madagascar.'

The region has the largest remaining area of *tapia* forest in Madagascar – *tapia* is the staple diet of the endemic silkworm (*Borocera madagascariensis*). Feedback

Madagascar, Ny Tanintsika, oversees a project in this area to reintroduce the wild silkworm to the *tapia* forest and supports a weavers' union, Tambatra. A tour of this area provides the opportunity to see all the stages in silk production, from the cocoon to weaving, including dyeing of the threads using natural dyes.

The trip to Soatanana can be made in an hour in private transport (the road is tarred for the first 30km). You can organise a tour from Ambositra or hire a taxi. Or cycle. To get there, first go 12km south from Ambositra on RN7 and take the paved RN35 15km west to Anjoman' Akona. Then ask for directions to Soatanana – you will need to take the dirt road that goes to Ambohimahazo. Alternatively you can get as far as Anjoman' Akona or Ambohimahazo by *taxi-brousse* from Ambositra. Another reader 'took the northbound RN42 that after a while changed to a rough track. Quite remote and very pretty scenery. We returned by the southbound road (much flatter than the northbound road but not as pretty). This road joined the main road at Soendranana, 11.5km south of Fianar.'

For more information contact Feedback Madagascar in Tana (✆ 22 638 11; e *nytk@simicro.mg*).

AMBATOFINANDRAHANA If you want to explore more of the area, Mark and Kyley provide the following information: 'If you continue on RN35 west past Anjoman' Akona, 50km down the paved road is Ambatofinandrahana (place where stone is cut). Much of Madagascar's marble and granite is cut and processed here in a factory 3km south of town. Some of the stone is quarried 5km from the factory, but most comes on flatbed trucks from the hinterlands west of 'Ambato' (as the locals call it). MAGRAMA is the name of the factory and they are happy to give free tours. The finished stone is sold to wealthy Tana residents and some is exported to Europe.

'Just north of Ambato (5km on a dirt road) are some wonderful hot springs. Buildings put up by the French have fallen into disrepair and now look like Roman ruins, lending the place a charming sense of disorientation. Go in the early morning, when the air is cool and the water is clean. Ask anybody in town how to get to the *ranomafana*.'

There is one tourist hotel in Ambato – **Hôtel du Marbre**. The rooms are nice and the hotel has a garden full of native plants. Doubles with shower and toilet down the hall cost about 15,000Ar.

ANTOETRA AND THE ZAFIMANIRY VILLAGES For the past few editions I have downplayed the attractions of the Zafimaniry region following reports in the 1990s of severe deforestation. This woodcarving region is now benefiting from controlled ecotourism and I am grateful to Peace Corps volunteer Tony Quintero for this update.

One of the reasons I stopped recommending visits here was because readers complained that the constant begging was spoiling their visit. Tony requests: 'Please mention to your readers *not* to distribute money or candy to the people or children in Antoetra and other villages because it makes them very greedy and dependent, and you will get hassled by "*Vazaha, omeo vola*" (*vazaha* give me money)!' The community charge, payable to each village, is a much fairer way of giving to the villagers.

Getting there There is only one official *taxi-brousse* which runs regularly from Ambositra to Antoetra. 'It's a white pick-up truck with a blue strip on its side, owned by a man named Doda (Dudà). Doda works from his home in Ambositra and travels to Antoetra every day except Monday, leaving around 07.30. The journey takes about two hours. On Wednesday, market day, he leaves at 06.30, returning at about 15.00. Other days he waits 2–5 hours in Antoetra before heading back to Ambositra.' The journey costs 5,000Ar each way. Doda can be contacted by phone (m *032 41 789 16*) between 05.00 and 19.30 to arrange to be picked up the next day from your hotel. 'His French is limited, so if you cannot understand each other, ask a Malagasy person to assist you.'

Where to stay

🏠 **Sous le Soleil de Mada** (8 bungalows) m 032 40 735 62; e souslesoleildemada@voila.fr. A new hotel situated between Ivato & Antoetra, the first Zafimaniry village. Built in the traditional Zafimaniry style, with its own restaurant; organises tours of the region. €€€

🏠 **Gîte Papavelo** (5 dorm beds) In Antoetra, this new hotel has 1 dormitory room but plans to expand. The owner, Mme Fleur, speaks French & some English. The hotel has running water, flush toilets & generator-powered electricity at night. Treks through the Zafimaniry villages can be organised from here. Camping permitted (2,000Ar); tents for hire. €

Antoetra village This is no longer a typical Zafimaniry village, but nevertheless is worth a visit for the chance to see woodcarvers at work and to buy their crafts. All the villages require visitors to pay a community charge of 3,000Ar and this is no exception. French is spoken, but not English.

Trekking circuits Guides can be hired at the two hotels, or in Antoetra; the cost is 15,000Ar per day for up to five people. Apart from their craft, the Zafimaniry are known for their unique houses, making this region a UNESCO World Heritage Site.

Here are Tony's recommendations: 'My favourite village is **Sakaivo Nord**, approximately two hours from Antoetra. It's a small village at the foot of a mountain, next to a small river. Near the village is a waterfall and a mountain that is said to look like a gorilla. Be careful, the track is somewhat difficult, so bring good walking shoes and plenty of water.

'The nearest village to Antoetra is **Ifasina** (place of dirt), a 1½ hour walk. It receives lots of visitors, but is a small quaint village where you can observe the original way of life and see people at work with their woodcarvings. Other villages that are cool to visit are **Faliarivo**, **Fempina** and **Tetazandrotra**.'

James Brehaut, who did a three-day trek in 2005, reports: 'We thought the trek was the perfect length. Be warned the hygiene in the villages is very minimal and fresh water only available from outlets nearby the villages. We did not find any of these villages ruined by tourism; in fact the locals were some of the most curious but shy that I've ever come across.'

SOUTH FROM AMBOSITRA ON RN7

From Ambositra, the scenery becomes increasingly spectacular. You now pass remnants of the western limit of the rainforest (being systematically destroyed). The road runs up and down steep hills, past neat Betsileo rice paddies interspersed with eucalyptus and pine groves. The steepest climb comes about two hours after Ambositra, when the vehicle labours up an endlessly curving road, through thick forests of introduced pine, and reaches the top where stalls selling oranges, honey or baskets provide an excuse for a break. Then it's down to Ambohimahasoa. **Hôtel Nirina** serves good snacks. Leaving Ambohimahasoa you pass more remnants of forests, then open country, rice paddies and houses as you begin the approach to Fianarantsoa.

IALATSARA LEMUR FOREST CAMP (e *kimbaforest@mel.wanadoo.mg; www.madagascar-guide.com/lemurcamp/. Entry: 8,000Ar pp; guided walks 15,000Ar per group (up to 4).*

The Malagasy have an almost mystical attachment to rice. King Andrianampoinimerina declared: 'Rice and I are one,' and loyalty to the Merina king was symbolised by industry in the rice paddies.

Today the Betsileo are masters of rice cultivation (they manage three harvests a year, not the normal two) and their neat terraces are a distinctive part of the scenery of the central highlands. However, rice is grown throughout the island, either in irrigated paddies or as 'hill rice' watered by the rain. Rice production is labour-intensive. First the ground must be prepared for the seeds. Often this is done by chasing zebu cattle round and round to break and soften the clods – a muddy, sticky job, but evidently great fun for the boys who do it. Seeds are germinated in a small plot and replanted in the irrigated paddies when half grown. In October and November you will see groups of women bent over in knee-deep water, performing this back-breaking work.

The Malagasy eat rice three times a day, the average annual consumption being 135kg per head (about a pound of rice per day!) although this is declining because of the availability of other foods and reduced productivity. Rice marketing was nationalised in 1976, but this resulted in such a dramatic drop in the amount of rice reaching the open market that restrictions were lifted in 1984. By that time it was too late to reverse the decline in productivity, which was mainly due to the decay of irrigation works. Despite a steady increase in acreage at the expense of the precious forest, production is continuing to fall.

Small farmers grow rice only for their own consumption but are forced to sell part of their crop for instant cash. Richer families in the community store this grain and sell it back at a profit later. To solve this small-scale exploitation, village co-operatives have been set up to buy rice and sell it back to the farmer at an agreed price, or at a profit to outsiders if any is left over.

Sgl/dbl chalets 17,000/30,000Ar. B/fast 6,000Ar; meals 14,000Ar) This private reserve is on RN7, 65km north of Fianar and 84km south of Ambositra (just north of Ambohimahasoa). It has 2,500ha of forest to the south of the road, comprising 1,000ha natural forest and 1,500ha of managed pine and eucalyptus, and a separate 600ha on the north side. Several species of lemur can be seen here, including Milne-Edwards' sifaka.

Daniel and Kelly report: 'We saw plenty of lemurs, chameleons, snakes, tenrecs, frogs, geckos and birds. Seven wood-frame canvas chalets have been built on stilts in the forest. Although these are very basic, we found the bed here to be without doubt the softest and most comfortable we slept on in all of Madagascar! It was a very successful visit in terms of number of species seen.'

The walk from the road to the bungalows is just 200m. Toilets and showers are communal; hot water can be provided on request.

FIANARANTSOA

The name means 'place of good learning'. Fianarantsoa (Fianar for short) was founded in 1830 as the administrative capital of Betsileo. It is built on a hill, like a small-scale Antananarivo. The attractive upper town (old town), reachable only on foot, is small; and the lower town, with most of the hotels and restaurants, is quite dreary, although there have been recent efforts to improve it. Fianar is an ideal base from which to do a variety of excursions: Andringitra, Ranomafana and Andrambovato are within easy(ish) reach.

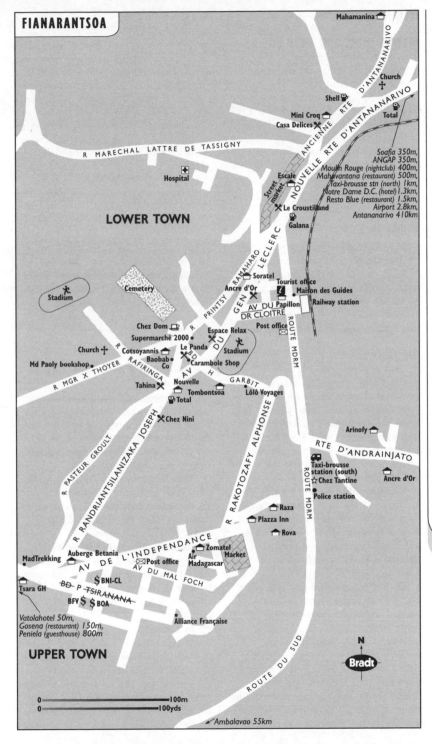

FIANARANTSOA

Mahamanina

Church

Shell

D'ANTANANARIVO

Mini Croq
Casa Delices

RTE ANCIENNE

NOUVELLE RTE D'ANTANANARIVO

Total

R MARECHAL LATTRE DE TASSIGNY

Hospital

Soafia 350m,
ANGAP 350m,
Moulin Rouge (nightclub) 400m,
Mahavantana (restaurant) 500m,
Taxi-brousse stn (north) 1km,
Notre Dame D.C. (hotel) 1.3km,
Resto Blue (restaurant) 1.5km,
Airport 2.8km,
Antananarivo 410km

LOWER TOWN

Escale

Street market

Le Croustilland

Galana

Cemetery

Stadium

RAMAHARO

GEN LECLERC

PRINTSY

Soratel

Ancre d'Or

Tourist office

Maison des Guides

Railway station

AV DU Papillon
DR CLOITRE

Chez Dom

Supermarché 2000

Church

Cotsoyannis

Md Paoly bookshop

R MGR X THOYER

RAFIRINGA

Baobab
Co

Le Panda

Carambole Shop

Espace Relax

Stadium

Post office

ROUTE MDRM

Tahina

Nouvelle

Tombontsoa

Total

AV H

GARBIT

Lôlô Voyages

Chez Nini

Arinofy

RTE D'ANDRAINJATO

R PASTEUR GROULT

R RANDRIANTSILANIZAKA JOSEPH

R RAKOTOZAFY ALPHONSE

AV DE L'INDEPENDANCE

ROUTE MDRM

Taxi-brousse
station (south)

Chez Tantine

Police station

Ancre d'Or

Raza

Plazza Inn

Rova

MadTrekking

Auberge Betania

Post office

Air
Madagascar

Zomatel

Market

AV DU MAL FOCH

Tsara GH

BD P TSIRANANA

BNI-CL

BFV

BOA

Vatolahotel 50m,
Gosena (restaurant) 150m,
Peniela (guesthouse) 800m

Alliance Française

N

UPPER TOWN

Bradt

0 — 100m
0 — 100yds

Ambalavao 55km

TELEPHONE CODE The area code for Fianar is 75.

GETTING THERE AND AWAY The easiest way to reach Fianar is by MadaBus, leaving Tana at 06.00 and arriving at 14.30; price €23. You can pick up the bus at Antsirabe or Ambositra. There are also minibuses running between Fianar and Tana with a lunch stop in Ambositra. The journey by *taxi-brousse* takes between six and ten hours from Tana, arriving at the north *taxi-brousse* depot, 20 minutes' walk north from the train station. The current cost is about 13,000Ar.

For the onward journey to Toliara, MadaBus leaves at 14.30 arriving at 23.45. A *taxi-brousse* takes from nine to 14 hours. 'MadTrekking (see *Tour operators*) will make the arrangements for you for a slightly higher price which includes free pick up at your hotel and drop off at the TB station.' (HD)

GETTING AROUND The average taxi fare was 2,500Ar in early 2007 but this varies according to the price of fuel.

WHERE TO STAY
Upper range €€€€
🏠 **Tsara Guest House** (16 rooms) Ambatolahikosoa; 📞 75 502 06; f 75 512 09; e tsaraguest@ wanadoo.mg; www.tsaraguest.com. For over a decade this has been the most popular *vazaha* place in Madagascar, universally praised by readers. The old house & garden began life as a church; its terrace has a wonderful view of the town. Owner Jim Heritsialonina works unstintingly to provide all the comforts & atmosphere that travellers desire. Good restaurant. Many tours offered. Some profits go to support good causes. Visa & MasterCard accepted.

Mid range €€€
🏠 **Zomatel** (34 rooms) Place du Zoma; 📞 75 507 97; f 75 513 76; e zomatel@altern.org; www.zomatel-madagascar.com. Comfortable but rather characterless. Sgl, dbl, tpl & family rooms with TV, en-suite bathroom, minibar & AC. Good restaurant. Secure parking. Internet café. 'The only problem is that most rooms have windows that open directly onto the corridor. Some face the road, with excellent views over town, so ask for those' (SC).

🏠 **Hôtel Cotsoyannis** (21 rooms) 4 Rue de Prince Ramaharo; 📞 75 514 72; e cotso@malagasy.com. A long-established hotel; recently extended. Pleasant sgl, dbl & twin rooms with en-suite bathrooms & good views. Restaurant with good pizzas.

🏠 **Hôtel Soafia** (83 rooms) Zorozoroana Ambalakisoa; 📞 75 503 53/513 13; e soafia.hot@wanadoo.mg. A large hotel with all sorts of unusual features. 'Looks like a cross between Disney World, a Chinese temple & a gigantic doll's house' (J Hadfield). 'A veritable rabbit warren. Walking around the spartan corridors made me feel I was going to round a corner & meet Jack Nicholson wielding an axe! A bizarre place' (Jerry Vive). 'Faded grandeur. Definitely one for those who fancy something a bit different' (S Bulmer). It has its fans but few people really like this hotel. However, everyone loves its wonderful patisserie & there's all sorts of useful goodies in the shop.

🏠 **Hôtel Tombontsoa** (8 rooms) Bd Hubert Garbit; 📞 75 514 05; www.hotel-tombontsoa.com. A newish hotel & restaurant with swimming pool, sauna, tennis court & conference centre. All rooms are en suite with TV. Some with kitchenette & fridge. Beautiful views. Sgl rooms available for 21,000Ar.

🏠 **Plazza Inn** (38 rooms) 📞 75 515 72. Sgl, dbl, twin & family rooms, some en suite with TV.

🏠 **Peniela Guest House** Rue du Rova (opposite the church); m 032 40 486 56/032 02 739 63; e tsaraguest@wanadoo.com or heritsialonina@yahoo.com. A lovely, brand new renovation of a traditional house in the (pedestrians only) old town; same ownership as the Tsara. On the left before the viewpoint; great position: quiet, environmentally & aesthetically sensitive. Dbl & family rooms.

🏠 **Hôtel Soratel (Sorako)** (26 rooms) Immeuble SORAKA, Ampazambazaha; 📞 75 516 66; f 75 516 78; e info@soratel.com; www.soratel.com. Near the train station, this hotel delights some: 'Double rooms with wonderful huge bath, hot water, minibar, fridge stocked with cold drinks; extremely helpful, friendly staff' (DF) but others are more cautious: 'Rooms are nice but overlook a busy road & can be overlooked

The children of Fianar have learned (from whom?) an irresistible method of getting money – and more – from tourists. When my group met for dinner, each had a similar story and each (including myself) was charmed by it. A little boy came up to me in the street and said, in impeccable English: 'Excuse me, I wonder if you would be willing to buy these cards I have made. I shall use the money to buy a copybook for school. I also collect foreign coins. Perhaps you have one for me?' I asked his age (12) and a few questions about his family. Each question was answered courteously and in the same fluent English. I gladly bought some of his nicely drawn cards and found a shiny English penny for him. Every town in Madagascar has its child beggars, but only Fianar seems to have these courteous, well-educated ones. I would love to know who taught them that courtesy succeeds better than aggression. A recent visitor to Fianar reports being followed by one such child for some distance: 'This cute kid was just staring at my feet, then eventually – in timid but flawless English – said, "Excuse me, can I have your shoes?" What do you say to that?'

when the curtains are open! It has an indoor car park but no restaurant (only a coffee shop)' (SC).

🏠 **Hôtel Mahamanina** (23 rooms) Rte d'Andriamboasary; ✆ 75 521 11/502 50; e hotel-mahamanina@wanadoo.mg. Very pleasant sgl, dbl & family rooms; good views from the balcony. Excellent restaurant. B/fast inc.

Budget €€

🏠 **Arinofy Hotel** Ivory Sud; ✆ 75 506 38; e arinofy@vitelcom.mg. Perennially popular with (most) travellers. Communal dining room. Hot water. Sgl, dbl & twin rooms; some en-suite dbls. Camping permitted in the garden when hotel is full (2- & 3-man tents can be hired).

🏠 **Raza Hotel** (3 rooms) Quartier Anjoma; ✆ 75 519 15. Large, quiet, well-furnished & spacious dbl & tpl rooms with shared bathroom. Garden. Recommended, but book ahead.

Penny-pincher €

🏠 **Auberge Betania** (5 rooms) Ambatolahikisoa (near Cinema Rex); ✆ 75 520 79. Entry via a stairway to the right of a bookshop (no sign). Mostly sgl rooms; 1 dbl. A Norwegian reader raves about this private home & the couple who own it, Mamy & Hasina Randriamahazo, who will double as guide & driver to take you anywhere in the country. Ideal for solo travellers. 'Hasina is the always-helping (with a smile) lady that solves the problems before we know they are happening.' There are plans to extend in 2007.

🏠 **Vatolahotel** ✆ 75 515 98. 'The most marvellous hotel in all of Madagascar. The Malagasy owner, Fidy, has lived there for 3 generations. His shy mother is the chef. Fidy speaks a little English & we spent an evening talking about his family history & about our

🏠 **Mini Croq Hôtel-Restaurant** (17 rooms) Ancienne Rte d'Antananarivo; ✆ 75 505 87; f 75 501 72; e minicroqhotel@dts.mg. Near the large pharmacy on the top of the hill. Off-street, secure parking. Clean, bright & cheerful. Excellent value rooms, some en suite. Popular with tour groups so can get booked up even in the low season.

🏠 **Hôtel Chez Papillon** (12 rooms) ✆ 75 508 15; f 75 518 76. Near the station – handy for the early train. Sgl, dbl & family rooms, inc a reasonably priced suite of 2 dbl bedrooms, bathroom, hallway & balcony.

countries, Sweden & America. Each day he would ask what we wanted for dinner which, with all the works, was never more than 3,000Ar. He made our departure from Fianarantsoa tearful' (Catherine Brinkley).

🏠 **Ancre d'Or** (see Where to eat) has some rooms in Ivory, up from the Arinofy hotel, behind the taxi-brousse station. Enquire at the restaurant.

🏠 **Hôtel Escale** Simple but cheap & adequate accommodation between Ampazambazaha & Antarandolo.

🏠 **Notre Dame de Cenacle** (6 rooms) Maison d'Accueil; ✆ 75 514 23. 'These nuns in Talatamaty have rooms for 7,000Ar & dormitories for 5,000Ar; clean, quite & pleasant, but there is a 22.00 curfew. They also serve meals' (SC).

✕ WHERE TO EAT

✕ **Chez Papillon** 🕾 75 500 03. Back in the 1980s & 1990s this restaurant basked in its reputation as the best in Madagascar. Now a reader complains: 'we found their restaurant to be poor with bad service, mediocre food & no English spoken.' So it goes.

✕ **Gosena** Up the hill from the Tsara Guest House on the old road to the old town. 'A charming, well-lit, family-owned place specialising in Vietnamese soups, sandwiches & pastries. Prices were very reasonable & it was filled with Malagasy families. Great food & as an added bonus, it's non-smoking!' (Tom Voth).

✕ **Le Panda** 🕾 75 505 69. Bd Hubert Garbit. Very good Chinese meals & a startling selection of game dishes: bat, frog, pigeon, crocodile & wild boar. 'The menu specifically points out that the bats served are not a protected species! Some visitors may be put off by the croc skin menu covers & the décor of crocodile skins & turtle shells. Note that most of the "adventurous" dishes seem generally unavailable, at least in the low season' (D&K).

✕ **Espace Relax** Av du General Leclerc. A restaurant-bar with a small but very smart interior. The 7 or 8 tables fill up quickly so book ahead or arrive early. Excellent pizzas (inc take-away).

✕ **Le Croustilland** An excellent Chinese/Cantonese restaurant with good prices. They also sell some cakes & pastries.

✕ **Mini Restau Tahina** 📱 032 04 421 24. A pleasant pizza & grill restaurant.

✕ **L'Ancre d'Or** Ampazambazaha (opposite the Soratel). Spacious bar. Sometimes live music at w/ends. Silke Rother reports: 'This is a very nice place to sit & eat in the evenings. The staff are very friendly & the meals are fantastic.'

✕ **Resto Blue** Very good, inexpensive food. Friendly.

✕ **Chez Nini** Good, cheap Malagasy food in pleasant surroundings.

✕ **Zomatel** Excellent pizzas & ice cream.

✕ **Casa Delices** Antarandolo (on the corner near Mini Croc). Good value food.

✕ **Mahavantana** Antsororokavo. Malagasy, Chinese & European dishes.

🖳 **Chez Dom** A fast-food café & bar; popular *vazaha*. Internet access (1 computer). Some local guides base themselves here. Browse their itinerary list during lunch then discuss your requirements over a drink afterwards.

NIGHTLIFE The area of Tambohobe (up the hill behind Antarandolo, on the road to the hospital) is good for late night bars and kebabs.

☆ **Moulin Rouge** 'A fantastic nightclub on the outskirts of town. The place to be at the weekend. Varied music: Malagasy, African, Reggae, funny Euro-pop disco.' That comment was from a few years ago; since then it has declined in popularity & is only busy on Sun.

☆ **Soafia Dance** For a hot sweaty experience, slightly more upmarket than the Moulin Rouge.

☆ **Chez Tantine** By the *taxi-brousse* station. Very Malagasy & fun.

INTERNET

📧 **Post Office** There's 11 computers for 30Ar/min. They also have printing & scanning services.

📧 **Fianar Online** Inside the **Carambole** boutique.

Connection 40Ar/min. Facilities for burning digital photos onto a CD-ROM. ⊕ *daily* 08.00–22.00.

SHOPPING

Md Paoly Bookshop Sells beautiful handmade greeting cards, wooden carvings, a massive range of postcards, books, maps, religious items & other handicrafts. Well worth a visit.

Labo Men This photo shop at Hôtel Soafia is home to internationally renowned photographer Labo Men, creator of the majority of Madagascar's postcards. There is a huge selection of postcards & a nice variety of posters for sale.

WHAT TO SEE AND DO Take time to explore the old town and then visit the market. This is best on Tuesday and Friday. When walking, check out the telegraph wires – they are festooned with the webs of *Nephila* spiders!

A couple of readers have recommended an *Antaimoro* paper-making business run by Maurice Razafimahaleo. 'This is a family concern and they are most happy to show you the process. The prices are very reasonable and the product more interesting than most.' From the old *taxi-brousse* station follow the signs to Arinofy Hotel, go over the bridge and take the road to your right following the power lines. It's a bit of a climb; don't give up! Go past the *gendarmerie*, turn right at the top of the hill and the house is on the left, just past the communal water tap. You will see the paper drying on frames.'

LOCAL GUIDES/TOUR OPERATORS

ORTF (regional tourist office) m 032 04 630 26; e tsaraguest@wanadoo.mg.

La Maison des Guides ↘ 75 517 30. This is a new initiative of the Association 'Cœur Malgache' for professionally trained guides specialising in mountain treks & community tourism. It's situated in front of the train station.

Marao de Fianar m 032 04 064 95; e aurelienmada@yahoo.fr. Highly praised by a reader as being extremely reliable & professional.

Lôlô Voyages ↘ 75 520 80; e lolovoyages@wandadoo.mg. Lôlô has been organising excursions in

Fianar for many years, & can arrange car hire. Popular & reliable.

MadTrekking. ↘ 75 503 73; m 032 02 221 73; e mad.trekking@wanadoo.mg. Opposite Tsara Guest House & the Fianar stop for MadaBus. Universally recommended by readers for its helpful & knowledgeable staff. Organises trips in the local area & further afield. Can also help with the intricacies of ongoing transport.

ANGAP ↘ 75 512 74. The office is 200m up the dirt track opposite the Jovenna fuel station on the road near the Soafia.

EXCURSIONS FROM FIANARANTSOA

Sahambavy This pretty valley with its lake and tea estate, some 25km east of Fianar, now has its own resort-style hotel, making it well worth a stay of a day or two if you want to relax.

Getting there If you don't have your own transport, the easiest way to get here is by train to the Sahambavy station on the way to Manakara (see page 205 for times). The hotel is directly opposite the train station. There is also a regular *taxi-brousse* service from the *taxi-brousse* station near the post office.

Where to stay

Lac Hotel (31 bungalows) ↘ 75 518 73; f 75 519 06; e lachotel@wanadoo.mg; www.lachotel.com. A lakeside resort with 2 sets of bungalows in a

peaceful location. All with en-suite facilities. Very friendly. No English spoken. 'Lovely, romantic, efficient – but wine surprisingly expensive' (DM). €€€

Sahambavy Tea Estate (↘ 75 521 91/511 56. ⊕ 07.30–15.30. *Guided tours 7,000Ar pp inc tasting*) Around 75% of the tea is exported to Kenya and the rest is for local consumption in Madagascar. The plantation is under Greek/Mauritian management (all the packaging comes from Mauritius). Tours demonstrate the process from picking to packing.

SOATANANA Not to be confused with the silk-weaving village of the same name near Ambositra, this little town was sought out by Bill and Nina French for its unique religious group (see box on page 204). Bill and Nina cycled there on RN42, which runs northwest of Fianar. The scenery *en route* is beautiful and the village itself remarkable.

ANDRAMBOVATO Peace Corps volunteers Ben and Kendall Badgett sent me this information about a new ecotourism project 45km from Fianar and accessible by rail.

'Andrambovato is a small village in the rainforest. Currently there is a Malagasy NGO working with the locals in the village to establish ecotourism at this site. The villagers are very excited about the project and welcoming to all visitors. The emphasis is on hiking, with short and long walks to suit all levels of fitness and ability.

'The easiest hike, which can be done as a day trip from Fianar, is an hour's walk to a gorgeous waterfall. Bring a picnic lunch and soak your feet in the cool streams.

'Much more strenuous is the hike to the top of the granite rock face. You'll get to see wildlife as well as a breathtaking view of the valley below – with binoculars you can see all the way to the ocean on a clear day. On a historical note the current trail is the same as that used in colonial times by the villagers to extract timber from the forest for the construction and use of the FCE railway company.

'Another hike takes you down into the valley to visit the Tanala village of Ambalavero. Here you can see traditional village life and meet the local *mpanjaka* (king).

'Finally there's a two- to three-day trek through the forest corridor from Andrambovato to **Ranomafana**. Along this trek you will see typical Tanala villages, wonderful flora and fauna, and traditional agriculture.'

Practicalities You must employ a local guide for the required time – from a half day to three days or more. There is an entrance fee which is under the control of the local COBA (community based management association) of Andrambovato and Ambalavero.

Be flexible with time; access is dependent on the FCE train, which does not always run on time. For most of the treks you'll need hiking boots. As in all rainforest hikes you can expect leeches.

The local guides are learning English as well as basic guiding skills, so don't be afraid to help them with their English or let them know if there is a specific interest you have, eg: birdwatching.

THE FANDRAHARANA SECT OF SOATANANA

Nina & Bill French

We cycled onto a dirt road and entered a different world! People were extremely friendly, asking us where we were going; kids were jumping up and down with excitement at the rare sight of a *vazaha* on the road. The reason we cycled to Soatanana was not only remoteness and stunning scenery but the existence of a small religious Lutheran sect, Fandraharana, purely Malagasy. About a fifth of all people here wear white clothing and pray by singing beautiful songs. When we were sitting by the side of the road eating baguettes for breakfast, a minibus full of white-clad singing people passed by – wonderful! We stayed with the mayor's family. They put us up in their daughter's house; she was confined for a month, having given birth to a little girl. She was staying in a dark room and her mum was doing everything for her. She cooked special food for her and washed nappies ... until the baby was vaccinated a month later and would then be allowed to see the outside world. This is an old Malagasy custom, done because of high infant mortality.

We arrived on Monday which, like Wednesday, is a day of prayer when groups of people walk around the town and sing. We missed the huge Sunday mass, but at least we experienced this. Then we passed a private *lycée* run by the sect, and were invited in by a bunch of young boys. The most fluent in English, and the least shy, was 18-year-old Dominique who became our guide. The following morning we sat in the class for morning prayer – a class full of teenagers singing beautifully. In the evening we were invited for dinner; it is their custom to welcome strangers not only with prayers but by washing their feet and hands (taken from the Bible). And all of this by candlelight, because there's no electricity here.

There are limited local provisions available in Andrambovato at the Sunday market, but you would be safer to bring your food with you. There are no restaurants or *hotely* here, but one *epicerie* sells dried goods, biscuits, drinks, etc.

🏠 **Where to stay** If you have your own tent there are plenty of places to camp or find lodging with a local family.

🏠 **Gîte Lac Hotel.** This is a bungalow-style extension of the Lac Hotel in Sahambavy (see page 203). The rooms are very nice with solid walls, flush toilets & hot showers. Book through the hotel in Sahambavy. The Gîte Lac also has tents for budget travellers or backpackers with no reservations. The guardian of the Gîte Lac Hotel also serves as your cook (you supply the food).

🏠 **Tsara Guest House Cabin** Book in advance at the Tsara in Fianar. This wooden cabin nestles close to the forest & away from the village. Basic amenities. You must prepare your own meals.

Getting there and away The FCE railway from Fianarantsoa to Manakara is the only mode of transport that gets you to Andrambovato (unless you hike in from Ranomafana or Sahambavy), as there are no roads. The village is the fifth stop from Fianar, and the 07.00 departure arrives at about 09.00. The train from Manakara usually arrives in Andrambovato between 12.30 and 14.00, but sometimes runs late.

If you want to come to Andrambovato as a day trip, the trains run in both directions on Wednesday, Thursday and Sunday, crossing in Manampatrana (east of Andrambovato).

TRAIN TO MANAKARA This line was privatised in 2000, ending decades of deterioration. The 163km trip is currently the only rail journey in Madagascar now open to passengers and is justifiably popular. The train leaves for Manakara on Sunday, Tuesday, Wednesday and Saturday at 07.00 and the journey takes ten hours. Tickets can be bought in advance: 24,000Ar for first class (including seat reservation); 16,000Ar for second class.

If travelling second class, Stuart Riddle recommends boarding the train just before departure and standing by the open doors for the whole journey (you can sit on the step if you get tired): 'That way you will not only get the best views but will avoid the smell from the toilet which pervades the carriages.' Stuart also points out that the windows are tinted, making it impossible to see the spectacular view from your seat.

You can buy a nice little booklet, produced by the ADI-FCE (railway users' association), which describes the history of this railway, the villages on the way, and various statistics about the line (it was constructed between 1926 and 1936, there are 67 bridges and 48 tunnels, the longest of which is 1,072m long). The train stops frequently, allowing time for photography and for buying fruit, snacks and drinks from vendors. 'Most of all it is the people on the railway stations and in the villages that make this trip unforgettable, and as a bonus the landscape is beautiful. And as you near Manakara the railway crosses the airport runway!' reports Marja van Ipenburg, who adds this warning: 'On arriving at Manakara, one should be prepared to deal with at least a hundred *pousse-pousse* men waiting for you at the railway station.'

RANOMAFANA

The name Ranomafana means 'hot water' and it was the waters, not the lemurs, that drew visitors in the colonial days and financed the building of the once-elegant Hôtel Station Thermale de Ranomafana.

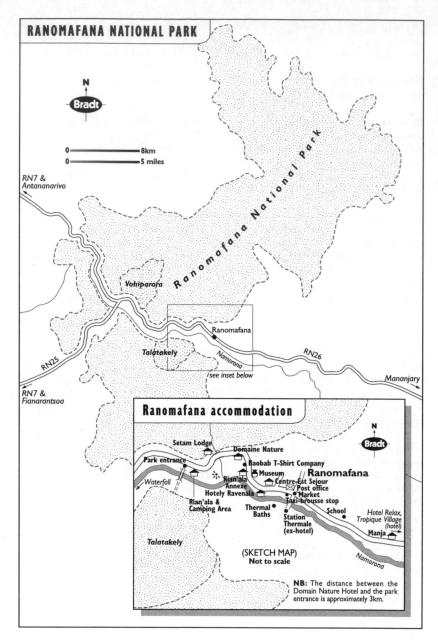

RANOMAFANA NATIONAL PARK

N

8km
5 miles

RN7 &
Antananarivo

Ranomafana National Park

Vohiparara

Ranomafana

Talatakely

Namorona

RN26

see inset below

Mananjary

RN25

RN7 &
Fianarantsoa

Ranomafana accommodation

N

Setam Lodge

Domaine Nature

Park entrance

Baobab T-Shirt Company

Museum

Ranomafana

Centre-Est Sejour

Waterfall

Rian'ala
Annexe

Post office

Market

Hotely Ravenala

Taxi-brousse stop

Rian'ala &
Camping Area

Thermal
Baths

School

Hotel Relax,
Tropique Village
(hotel)

Station
Thermale
(ex-hotel)

Manja

Talatakely

(SKETCH MAP)
Not to scale

Namorona

NB: The distance between the
Domain Nature Hotel and the park
entrance is approximately 3km.

These days the baths are often ignored by visitors anxious to visit Ranomafana
National Park, which was created in 1991. This hitherto unprotected fragment of
mid-altitude rainforest first came to the world's attention with the discovery of the
golden bamboo lemur in 1986 and is particularly rich in wildlife.

Ranomafana has experienced a welcome explosion of accommodation in recent
years (for nearly a decade after it opened there was just one, dire hotel) so now
pleases almost everyone. I have always loved it! First you have the marvellously

scenic drive down, with the dry highland vegetation giving way to greenery and flowers. Then there are the views of the tumbling waters of the Namorona River, and the relief when the hillsides turn to that lovely unbroken, knobbly green of virgin forest that indicates you are nearing the park. Hidden in these trees are 12 species of lemur: Milne-Edwards' sifaka, red-fronted brown lemur, red-bellied lemur, black-and-white ruffed lemur and three species of bamboo lemur. At night you can add mouse lemur, woolly lemur (avahi), sportive lemur (*Lepilemur*), greater dwarf lemur and even aye-aye. Then there are the birds: more than 100 species with 36 endemic. And the reptiles. And the butterflies and other insects. Even if you saw no wildlife, there is enough variety in the vegetation and scenery, and enough pleasure in walking the well-constructed trails, to make a visit worthwhile. And – I nearly forgot – in the warm summer months you can swim in the cold, clear water of the Namorona while a malachite kingfisher darts overhead. Some negative things: the trails are steep and arduous, it often rains and there are leeches.

GETTING THERE AND AWAY Good news! For 20 years the road to this, one of Madagascar's most popular national parks, was so pot-holed and furrowed that passengers in tour buses often chose to walk the worst stretches. Now the road from Alakamisy Ambohimaha, about 26km north of Fianar, is in the process of being surfaced and, by the time you read this, may be glorious smooth macadam. Furthermore, the northern access road from Ambohimasoa has been improved, shortening the journey for those travelling south. The journey time should now be cut to about 1½–2 hours from Fianar and 3½ hours from Ambositra.

Public transport can be a problem since vehicles are so often full. The trick is to leave Fianar early in the morning: be at the *gare routière* at 06.00 to ensure a good seat. At least two *taxi-brousses* leave between 07.00 and 09.00. There are also *taxi-brousses* in the afternoon. If you are coming from Antsirabe, James Brehaut recommends looking for a *taxi-brousse* to Mananjary and ask to be dropped off at Ranomafana. An alternative is to take a *taxi-brousse* to Fianar and ask to be dropped off at Alakamisy Ambohimaha. 'With a bit of luck, a *taxi-brousse* with free seats will come by; if not it's a lovely walk!' (But note: at least 25km!)

For the seriously fit and adventurous, you can walk (with a guide) from Andrambovato (see page 203). If time is short, consider taking a package tour with one of the tour operators in Fianar, such as MadTrekking.

WHERE TO STAY
Upper range €€€€
Setam Lodge (14 bungalows) ☎ 24 310 71/22 324 31; f 22 324 31; e setamlodge@wanadoo.mg; http://lodge.setam-madagascar.com. The best hotel in Ranomafana, about 1km from the park entrance. Spacious semi-detached bungalows built on 3 levels, plus a restaurant & bar, with stunning views of the forest & Namorona valley. Good food, though limited choice.

Hôtel Domaine Nature (20 bungalows) Book through Destinations Mada in Tana; ☎ 22 310 72; f 22 310 67. Well-managed, friendly & popular. Halfway between the village & park. Recently renovated bungalows provide very pleasant accommodation with gorgeous views over the river. Good food served in a spacious restaurant. Set on a steep hillside so not a good choice for people with difficulty climbing steps – there are a lot!

Mid range €€€
Ihary (14 bungalows) Located just beyond the village of Ranomafana; ☎ 75 523 02. Bungalows in a nice riverside setting; en-suite facilities. Some visitors have complained that the rooms are noisy

(from the restaurant & adjacent rooms) & service is slow.

Centrest Hotel (8 bungalows & 13 rooms) ☎ 75 523 02 (ex 13)/513 47 (ex 13). Beyond the museum, on the left as you enter Ranomafana. Sgl, dbl, twin & tpl en-suite rooms; very pleasant & reasonably priced thatched bungalows with shared bathrooms. Well-run with a good restaurant.

Budget €€
🏠 **Palmerie Hotel** (6 rooms) A good budget option with hot water & shared toilets. Restaurant on opposite side of road.
🏠 **Hôtel Manja** (10 bungalows & some rooms). On the road to Mananjary (RN26), 5min walk east along

Penny-pincher €
🏠 **Rian'ala** (24 dorm beds) Dormitory accommodation (8 beds/room) near park entrance. If required, I room can be converted to a dbl or twin. The food is excellent & moths 'the size of frisbees' are attracted to the lamps! Staying here is

🏠 **Chez Gaspard** (5 bungalows but more being built) A variety of rooms at different prices; all but one have shared bathrooms.

the river. Food here is excellent: a good range of Malagasy & Western dishes to suit any budget.
🏠 **Hotely Ravenala** (9 rooms) Located opposite the museum. Basic, funky, very friendly, beautiful views & good food.

convenient for the park but quite isolated. Without your own transport this is by far the most convenient option, particularly if you want to do a night walk. Ask the *taxi-brousse* driver to stop at the park entrance.

Out of town For those with their own transport there are a couple of quiet hotels on the way to Mananjary which are recommended.

🏠 **Tropique Village** (14 rooms) ☎ 22 695 76; f 22 695 76; e tropic.r@wanadoo.mg. An upmarket hotel in Mahatsinjorano, about 9km from Ranomafana. Spacious rooms with nice view from the

veranda. Good restaurant. €€–€€€
🏠 **Hôtel Relax** Situated 5km from Ranomafana. Recommended with its restaurant **Le Terrace**. 'Lovely setting, away from the bustle of Ranomafana.' €€

⛺ Camping There is a very good campsite at the park entrance. There are six covered tent sites, with open-sided A-frame thatched shelters giving shade as well as protection from the rain, and one centrally located covered picnic table. There are basic toilets and showers, a tap for drinking water and a bungalow with kitchen facilities. There is no food available here, but the Varibolo restaurant is nearby.

This campsite was built by the villagers and is run by ANGAP; the money goes directly to the community.

✖ WHERE TO EAT
✖ **Restaurant Varibolo** Located just above the campsite near the park entrance, with nice views overlooking the park. An ideal place to have lunch

after hiking in the forest. B/fast available.
✖ **Chez Tantely & Claire** A nice little restaurant in the village of Ranomafana.

RANOMAFANA AND CONSERVATION The Ranomafana National Park Project, set up by Dr Patricia Wright, established a large range of activities, from education and health care for the villagers on the periphery of the park to an ecological monitoring team that works at several sites within the park. ANGAP and NGOs have continued this good work. The national park is one of the country's flagship conservation projects, with the involvement of local communities playing an important role.

Much scientific research takes place in the park and there have been some clashes between researchers and tourists. Tourists have been known to push researchers aside in order to get a better photo, and to encourage guides to shake or bang on trees to persuade a lemur to move. It goes without saying that this is irresponsible behaviour and is counter-productive since some researchers withhold information on the whereabouts of the rarer lemurs for fear of being disturbed in their work.

A world-class research station near the park entrance (the Centre Valbio) was completed in 2003 under the initiative of an international consortium from countries including Finland and Italy, along with UNESCO and Stony Brook University, New York. This new facility brings great possibilities for research and development in the area.

VISITING THE NATIONAL PARK

Getting there from your hotel The entrance to the park is over 6km west of the village of Ranomafana, on the main road. A *navette* (minibus) run by ANGAP leaves the village at 07.00 to take visitors and guides up to the park entrance. It returns at 16.00. If there is no bus, don't despair. 'I think the views *of* the park are far more spectacular than *in* the park,' says Stuart Riddle, who loved the 80 minutes it took him to walk up the hill to the park entrance.

Permits and guides Permits (see page 75 for prices) are obtainable from the park office. You are not allowed into the park without a guide. There is an official four-person limit per group but guides usually let you add a fifth. For larger numbers you need an additional guide. The quality of the guides at Ranomafana is now every bit as good as those from Andasibe. Guides will expect a tip in addition to the set fee which is fixed by the ANGAP office (and posted in the office at the park entrance). In theory the ANGAP office is there to help visitors but in practice they seem to have become a bit relaxed. 'We were disappointed with the lack of information available at the office. No maps of the different routes and staff did not speak English. The office was closed well before the advertised time of 17.00 and did not open until well after the official opening time of 07.30. The routes and prices listed in the office are not actually strictly what the guides can offer. They can do any length of day route you choose and their prices do not necessarily correspond with those on the office list' (J Brehaut). Perhaps this will have changed by the time you read this.

In the forest The paths in the forest have been improved in recent years, and the standard circuits supplemented by additional routes. Most of the standard routes take a few hours, but if you are fit you should opt for the longer tours taking 6–8 hours. You will see primary forest, where the vines are thicker, the trees bigger and it will be quieter. Even for the shorter walks you need to be reasonably fit – the paths are moderate to steep, and sometimes slippery. Your guide will assume that it is lemurs you have come to see; so, unless you stress that you are interested in other aspects such as botany or insects, he will tend to concentrate on mammals and birds. If you are keen on chameleons, arrange a night walk. You are most likely to see red-fronted brown lemurs, grey bamboo lemurs and the rarer red-bellied lemur. Star attractions such as greater bamboo lemur and golden bamboo lemur are now fairly frequently seen. There is also the spectacular Milne-Edwards' sifaka. Unlike the more familiar Verreaux's sifaka of the southern dry forests – which is largely white – this is dark brown with cream-coloured sides.

A delightful walk is to the Cascade of the River Namorona. If the circular route is taken it is quite strenuous, with a long steep descent to the waterfall. This is a dramatic and beautiful place and it's worth lingering to watch for kingfishers. A hydroelectric scheme diverts some of the water plunging over the cliffs, but this is not intrusive. The walk back, along the river, is outside the park boundary so gives you a chance to see small farming communities. Another waterfall, Le Petite Cascade, is hidden in the forest. A long ribbon of water falls into a deep pool which provides a chilly but invigorating swim (so bring your swimsuit). Allow three hours for this round-trip excursion.

Another trail system has been established on flatter ground at Vohiparara, near the boundary of the park, 12km west of Ranomafana on the main road. It only takes about three hours to do all the trails here with a guide. 'Vohiparara is good for birders. Among many others you may see the brown emutail, Madagascar snipe, Meller's duck and the extremely rare slender-billed flufftail. The song of the cryptic warbler was first recorded here in 1987' (Derek Schuurman). According to Nick Garbutt this is also the best place for the rufous-headed ground-roller, Pollen's vanga and yellow-bellied sunbird-asity.

A nocturnal visit to Belle Vue, a popular viewpoint, is now an established part of all tours. A viewing platform and shelter have been built here and the steep paths have been made as safe as possible, but even so negotiating them by torchlight can be tricky. Try to arrive early. By dusk there may be as many as 50 people with cameras at the ready waiting for the mouse lemurs, red-bellied lemurs and striped civet (*fanaloka*) to arrive for their supper. Which they do, with clockwork regularity. The animals seem oblivious to the flashes of cameras, outstretched hands and squeals of delight, and are certainly appreciative of this effortless meal. Everyone leaves happy, including the 'wild' life, so it seems snooty to be disapproving. And you won't get a better chance of getting a close-up view of mouse lemurs and *fanaloka* in Madagascar. That said, it is rumoured that there will soon be restrictions on the Belle Vue spectacle.

The Global Canopy Programme (*www.globalcanopy.org*) is assessing Ranomafana as a possible site for Madagascar's first canopy walkway. That would be quite something!

Museum and gift shop This is part of the Ranomafana National Park Project to improve visitor understanding of the area. It is an interesting museum and the handicrafts for sale are of a high standard including beautifully embroidered T-shirts.

THERMAL BATHS (⊕ *08.00–16.30; closed Tue*) These are close to the former Station Thermale hotel. For a minimal payment you can have a wonderful warm swim in the pool. I love it, but be warned: the pool water is not chlorinated so there's algae on the bottom and sides.

CONTINUING SOUTH ON RN7

The next leg of the journey, to Ihosy, is 206km. Coming from Fianar the landscape is a fine blend of vineyards and terraced rice paddies (the Betsileo are acknowledged masters of rice cultivation), then after 20km a giant rock formation seems almost to hold the road in its grasp. Its name is, appropriately, Tanan' Andriamanitra, or 'hand of God'. From here to Ihosy is arguably the finest mountain scenery in Madagascar.

AMBALAVAO

Some 56km southwest of Fianarantsoa is my favourite highlands town, Ambalavao. The road drops steeply down to the town providing excellent views across the landscape. RN7 does not pass through the attractive part of Ambalavao, and I strongly urge people to stop here for a few hours or at least to amble through the car-free streets which are thronged with people, and take in the once-grand houses with their pillars, carved balconies, and steep, red-tiled roofs. If travelling south, this is the last time you'll see typical highland architecture. The town is famous as the centre for *Antaimoro* paper-making, so a lot of tour buses stop here.

Market day is Wednesday; the famous cattle market is Wednesday and Thursday.

GETTING THERE AND AWAY Although Ambalavao is on RN7, southbound travellers may prefer to make it an excursion from Fianarantsoa, since vehicles heading to Ihosy and beyond will have filled up with passengers in Fianar. Or reserve a seat on the MadaBus, which stops at Hôtel Bougainvillées

🏠 WHERE TO STAY

🏠 **Hôtel Snackbar aux Bougainvillées** (16 bungalows & 7 rooms) 📞 75 340 01. Adjacent to the *Antaimoro* paper shop. Bungalows have en-suite bathrooms & solar-heated water. Rooms have cold water & shared facilities. Clean & comfortable but rather characterless. Pleasant restaurant serving huge portions of good, plain food. Guide Adrien is based here & can organise a range of excursions inc the cattle market & Anja Park. €€€

🏠 **Hôtel Tsienimparihy** (14 rooms) 📞 75 341 28; e tsienimpari@mel.wanadoo.mg. 'Easy to spot as several storeys high & painted bright orange, behind the market? Nice en-suite dbl, twin & tpl rooms (but no mozzie nets). A very good restaurant & patisserie. Car park. €€–€€€

🏠 **La Résidence du Betsileo** (11 rooms) m 033

02 863 89; e sorafahotel@wanadoo.mg. New in 2006. Centrally located & recommended by Sam Cameron of Feedback Madagascar as her favourite hotel in Ambalavao. 'Tastefully decorated rooms with en-suite bathrooms (hot water), mosquito nets & choice of downstairs or upstairs rooms with street view or back view (but the water pump in these rooms can be noisy). Car park. Nice restaurant. €€–€€€

🏠 **Hôtel Samoina** (4 bungalows & 8 rooms) RN7; 📞 75 341 48. Northern edge of town. Bungalows have en-suite bathrooms; rooms share facilities. Good value. Restaurant recommended; also good value. €€

🏠 **Stop Hotel** (5 rooms) Town centre. Shared bathrooms. Basic but cheap & adequate. Camping permitted. €€

✖ WHERE TO EAT

✖ **Mano á Mano** A new snack bar next to Chez Notre. 'The owner is part of the Chan Foui family who have a vineyard near town. Their decent wine can be purchased at the snack bar from 3,200Ar. Snacks like samosas start from 150Ar; great pastries

700Ar; *soupe Chinoise* 1,500Ar & meals around 3,500Ar. This was one of the finds of our trip' (HD).
✖ **Mini-Restaurant Fraîche Heure** 'On right side of main street going south. Though grubby, it offers good food (inc pizza), value & service.'

WHAT TO SEE

Antaimoro paper Ambalavao is the original home of the famous Malagasy *Antaimoro* paper. This papyrus-type paper impregnated with dried flowers is sold throughout the island made into such items as wall-hangings and lampshades. The people in this area are Betsileo, but paper-making in the area copies the coastal Antaimoro tradition which goes back to the Muslim immigrants who wrote verses from the Koran on this paper. This Arabic script was the only form of writing known in Madagascar before the LMS developed a written Malagasy language nearly 500 years later using letters from the Roman alphabet.

Antaimoro paper is traditionally made from the bark of the *avoha* tree from the eastern forests, but sisal paste is now sometimes used. After the bark is pounded and softened in water it is smoothed onto linen trays to dry in the sun. While still tacky, dried flowers are pressed into it and brushed over with a thin solution of the liquid bark to hold them in place.

The open-air 'factory' (more flowerbeds than buildings) where all this happens is to the east of the town in the same compound as Hôtel Bougainvillées and is well worth a visit. It is fascinating to see the step-by-step process, and you get a good tour. A shop sells the finished product at reasonable prices.

EXCURSIONS FROM AMBALAVAO

Soavita winery (🕐 07.00–11.00, 13.00–17.00) This place offers free tours on weekdays where you will be shown the various stages of winemaking by one of the workers, followed by a tasting. They do expect you to buy some wine.

The humpbacked cattle, zebu, which nearly outnumber the country's human population, produce a relatively low yield in milk and meat. These animals are near-sacred and are generally not eaten by the Malagasy outside of important social or religious ceremonies. Zebu are said to have originated from northeast India, eventually spreading as far as Egypt and then down to Ethiopia and other parts of East Africa. It is not known how they were introduced to Madagascar but they are a symbol of wealth and status as well as being used for burden.

Zebu come in a variety of colours, the most sought-after being the *omby volavita*, which is chestnut with a white spot on the head. There are some 80 words in the Malagasy language to describe the physical attributes of zebu, in particular the colour, horns and hump.

In the south, zebu meat is always served at funerals, and among certain southern tribes the cattle are used as marriage settlements, as is done in Africa. Whenever there is a traditional ritual or ceremony, zebu are sacrificed, the heads being given to the highest-ranking members of the community. Blood is smeared on participants as it is believed to have purification properties, and the fat from the hump of the cattle is used as an ingredient for incense. I have seen a Vezo village elder wearing a domed hat apparently made from a zebu hump. Zebu milk is an important part of the diet among the Antandroy; it is *fady* for women to milk the cows but it is they who sell the curdled milk in the market.

Tourists in the south will see large herds of zebu being driven to market, a journey that may take several days. All cattle crossing regional borders must wear a 'zebu passport' in the form of yellow eartags. Cattle-rustling is now a major problem. Whereas before it was mainly confined to the Bara, as an initiation into manhood, it is now organised by large, Mafia-like gangs. In former times the punishment matched the crime: a fine of ten zebu would have to be paid by the thief, five for the family from whom the cattle were stolen and five for the king.

To the rural Malagasy a herd of zebu is as symbolic of prosperity as a new car or a large house in western culture. Government aid programmes must take this into account; for instance improved rice yields will indirectly lead to more environmental degradation by providing more money to buy more zebu. The French colonial government thought they had an answer: they introduced a tax on each animal. However, local politicians were quick to point out that since Malagasy women had always been exempt from taxation, the same rule should apply to cows!

Cattle market Held on Wednesday and Thursday on the outskirts of town. It gets going at about 03.00, so you need to be an early riser! To get there take RN7 south and after about 1km you'll see the zebu on a hill to the left.

After the market, the herdsmen take a month to walk the zebu to Tana, and you'll see these large herds on the road. Look out for the yellow eartags: these are 'zebu passports' giving the owner the right to take his cattle across regional boundaries.

Anja (Anjaha) Park About 13km south of Ambalavao is a community-run park which offers superb scenery, intriguing plants adapted to the dry southern climate, some interesting Betsileo history and several troops of cheeky ring-tailed lemurs.

The local people have long recognised the tourist potential here but it is only in the last few years that they have organised themselves into gaining some income from it. The region is sacred to the Betsileo; their ancestors are buried here and it has always been *fady* to hunt the lemurs. The caves have provided a useful sanctuary in times of trouble and were inhabited up to around 100 years ago.

The reserve covers 8ha and is home to about 300 ring-tails. Given the health problems affecting the lemurs of Berenty (see page 267) this park provides a worthwhile alternative for tourists wanting a lemur fix and to benefit the local people. It costs 7,000Ar to visit the park where you are provided with a guide (8,000Ar for two people). The well-maintained trail winds past some impressive rocks, topped by waiting lemurs, to a sacred cliff where there is an apparently inaccessible tomb high in the rock face. The tour takes one to two hours. 'The two-hour tour leads through bush to large rock formations, where you take one of two options depending on your fitness. We took the challenging route which involved scaling some impressive rock faces and a bit of climbing. Also had the chance to swing like Tarzan on vines and saw heaps of ring-tailed lemurs' (James Brehaut).

For more information contact the Association des Populations des Montagnes du Monde (APMM), Tambohivatro (✆ *75 514 68;* e *apmm-fia@wanadoo.mg*).

Adrien at Hôtel Bougainvillées (✆ *75 340 01*) organises visits from Ambalavao.

AMBOHIMAHAMASINA

Samantha Cameron provided the following information: 'A rural community 39km southeast of Ambalavao, Ambohimahamasina (literally 'at the sacred mountain') is home to Madagascar's most sacred mountain: Ambondrombe. It is believed that the spirits of all dead people reside here.

'Bordering the rainforest corridor that runs from Ranomafana to Andringitra, Ambohimahamasina is some spectacular scenery, with beautiful Betsileo villages, rice fields, and some interesting cultural sites. Weaving and basketry is traditional in the area.

'A community tourism committee has been running since 2003. Local guides have been trained and there are several guesthouses or 'homestays' giving travellers an opportunity to experience how rural Malagasy people really live. Various treks can be organised depending on interests, ability and time available. Views across the rainforest are breathtaking as you climb the mountain of Itaolana, and for the most adventurous there are various treks that can be organised which cut across to the eastern side of the rainforest. One takes you to **Ikongo** (from where you can get a *taxi-brousse* to the train station in **Manampatrana**) and another goes to **Ankarimbelo** (after which you can walk to **Ifanirea**, where there are *taxi-brousses* to **Vohipeno** and **Manakara**). Campsites are currently being established along these paths.

'There are fixed rates for guides as well as meals and accommodation at the homestays, and a tourist fee to pay at the commune office; these funds are managed by a local committee to improve amenities and benefit local communities.'

GETTING THERE There are daily *taxi-brousses* from Ambalavao to Ambohimahamasina, leaving very early in the morning on Monday and Thursday (market days). Make enquiries the day before to avoid long waits and disappointment. The road is semi-tarmacked and good year-round. It is best to arrive in Ambohimahamasina in the morning, in good time to contact guides and walk to your chosen homestay, but there are guides in Ambalavao and Fianarantsoa who can organise trips to Ambohimahamasina, including La Maison des Guides in Fianar. A website for Ambohimahamasina is currently under development. In the meantime, contact Ny Tanintsika (e *tany@netclub.mg*) or APMM (e *apmm-fia@wanadoo.mg*) for more information.

These spectacular granite peaks and domes have entranced me since I first travelled the length of RN7, so I am thrilled that they can now form the focus for a trekking holiday. The wonderful Andringitra National Park does not cover the entire area – there are other lodges and camps on the outskirts of the park which offer equally good scenery.

🏠 WHERE TO STAY/EAT

⋀ Tsara Camp (10 tents) e tsaracamp@simicro.mg; www.tsaracamp-madagascar.com. Owned by Boogie Pilgrim, this tented camp is located outside the park's northwest boundary. Access is by an unsignposted track off RN7 before Tanambao, 37km south of Ambalavao; in all it takes about 2hrs from the main road. The camp closes for 3 months in the rainy season. The large tents are pitched on wooden floors under thatched shelters, set in a spectacular plain bounded by the Andringitra Massif. Each tent has its own bathroom with basin & chemical toilet. The eating area is a bigger tent serving simple Malagasy food. Cold drinks are available. Although the main trekking routes of the national park are not easily accessible from here, trips can be arranged, eg: 5-day trek to Pic d'Imarivolanitra costs €288pp (in a group of 3). For the less energetic there is a half-day walk to the private reserve in the Tsaranoro valley to see ring-tailed lemurs. This walk can be extended to a tough all-day hike up the hill the locals call the Chameleon – 1,500m. €€€€

⋀ Camp Catta e campcatta@campcatta.com; www.campcatta.com. Up the road from Tsara Camp, this place has established itself as a centre for climbing & paragliding (note that technical climbing is not allowed in the national park). There are basic brick-built huts & a generator, & lots of ring-tailed lemurs, as the name implies. Arrangements to stay here can be made through Hôtel Cotsoyannis in Fianar. Those with their own tent may camp for 8,500Ar/night. €€€€

🏠 Tranogasy Ambalakajaha; m 033 11 264 27/033 14 306 78; e tranogasy@yahoo.fr. The ideal blend of comfort & scenery. A scatter of chalets overlooked by the Andringitra Massif; able to arrange a complete package for trekkers, inc transfer from Ambalavao (€50) plus guides & porters. There are 2 grades of chalet: more expensive ones have en-suite facilities. A restaurant provides good meals & caters for vegetarians. €–€€

🏠 Le Gîte If you want to sleep under a roof rather than in a tent, the gîte near Ambolamandary, 7km from the park entrance, is very comfortable. It costs 12,000Ar for a shared room & facilities (cold water). But it's a 1hr drive from the trail system so cuts into the day's hiking. You need to bring your own food, but there is a cook to prepare it for you. Book through the WWF in Ambalavao (📞 75 340 81). €

⋀ Camping There are four campsites within the national park, the most popular of which is Belambo (at 1,550m) in a wooded area close to the Zomandao River. There is a cooking hut with enough seats for a small group, level pitches for tents, and a long-drop toilet.

ANDRINGITRA NATIONAL PARK Created in 1999, this park protects the flora and fauna around Madagascar's second highest peak. The former Pic Boby (2,658m) has been renamed Pic d'Imarivolanitra, which means 'close to the sky': poetic but not half as easy for *vazaha* to remember. Andringitra (pronounced an*dring*tra) has some wildlife, but landscape, vegetation and trekking are the chief attractions. And what attractions! I would put Diavolana (see *Trekking* below) in the top ten of all mountain walks that I have ever done: the combination of granite peaks and gneiss formations, endemic succulent plants and ring-tailed lemurs (though at a distance) makes this an utterly different – and utterly marvellous – walking experience. Each circuit covers different terrain, from forest and waterfalls to the frosty peak of Imarivolanitra. In the warmer, wet season the meadows are carpeted with flowers, including 30 species of orchid.

The WWF and ANGAP must be commended for the care they have taken in creating the trails which are beautifully engineered through difficult terrain to make them as safe and easy as possible. Although the trail system covers a variety of ecosystems, the park also protects an area of montane rainforest in the east, which is closed to visitors. This provides a sanctuary for such rare species as golden and greater bamboo lemurs.

Local guides The guides are well-trained and knowledgeable, particularly on the medicinal use of plants, though few speak English. Fees vary from 7,000Ar for the longer circuits to 50,000Ar for a half day.

Getting there and away Travelling here by public transport is problematic, but for true backpackers, carrying a tent and food, it would be worth the effort. You may find a *taxi-brousse* to take you at least part of the way, but be prepared for a lot of walking. Alternatively hire a car and driver in Fianar.

The vast majority of visitors arrange an all-inclusive trip from Fianarantsoa (see page 203 for tour operators).

There are two entry points: east (Namoly) and west (Morarano). Access is usually via Namoly. All visitors need to go to the gîte where the ANGAP office is located to pick up their permit, a journey of around two hours. A map of the trail system and visitor guidelines are available here. It's another hour or more (depending on the condition of the road, and whether the four toll booths are manned) to the parking area and a further 20-minute walk to the campsite, so aim to leave Ambalavao by 14.00 at the latest to avoid setting up your tent in the dark.

Equipment There is no point in going to Andringitra unless you are equipped for walking. This means boots or tough trainers (running shoes), hiking poles, good raingear, and a water bottle. Plus a daysack. Remember also that at this altitude the nights can be very cold (close to freezing between June and September) so you need warm sleeping bags, thermal underwear, gloves and thick socks (to wear at night). Days are pleasantly warm, but it can rain – hard – at any time. It's worth bringing a swimsuit for the freezing (but refreshing) dip in the pool on the Diavolana circuit.

Trekking There are four main circuits: Asaramanitra, Imaitso, Diavolana and the route to the top of Pic d'Imarivolanitra. The times below are taken from the WWF map which errs on the cautious side. Fit people can cut an hour or so off.

Asaramanitra 6km/4hrs. This begins at the Belambo campsite and climbs up to two sacred waterfalls, Riambavy (the queen) and Riandahy (the king), which plunge 250m off the edge of the escarpment. These falls are said to be the embodiment of an ancient king and queen who could not conceive a child. They climbed up to the falls with an *ombiasy* (spiritual healer) and sacrificed a white-faced zebu to satisfy the gods. They were successful: now the waterfalls and streams that feed them are considered highly sacred. And if you want to get pregnant, this is the place to go.

Completing the circuit you pass through a large area of forest. This is where the guides show their knowledge of medicinal plants. Close to the campsite is the cave of Ijajofo, a former hiding place of cattle thieves.

Imaitso 9km/4hrs. In the extreme east of the park, this circuit takes you through a remnant of primary forest clinging to the side of a mountain and too steep for cultivation. Below are the rice fields of the local communities. There are some lovely views and the possibility of seeing five lemur species in the forest.

Diavolana 12km/10hrs. This is the real Andringitra – a close-up experience of the granite peaks and escarpments that have intrigued me for so many years. It's a

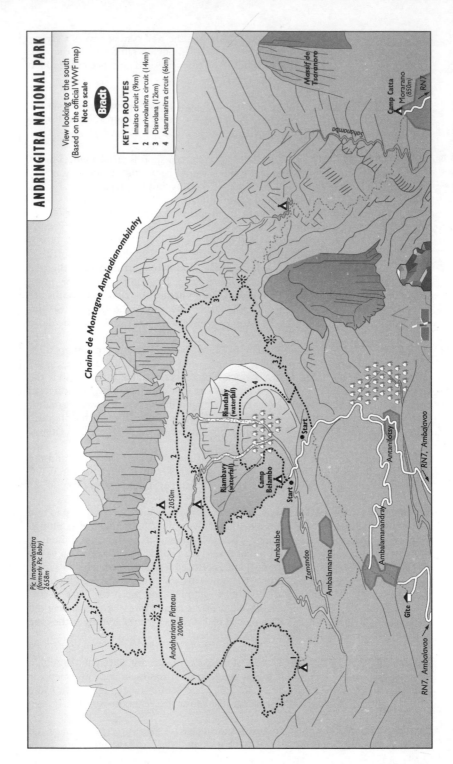

ANDRINGITRA NATIONAL PARK

View looking to the south
(Based on the official WWF map)
Not to scale

Bradt

KEY TO ROUTES

1 Imaitso circuit (9km)
2 Imarivolanitra circuit (14km)
3 Diavolana (12km)
4 Asaramanitra circuit (6km)

Pic Imarovolanitra
(formerly Pic Boby)
2658m

Chaine de Montagne Ampiadianombilahy

Andohariana Plateau
2000m

2050m

Riandahy (waterfall)

Riambavy (waterfall)

Camp Belambo

Start

Ambalabe

Zomandao

Ambalamarina

Antanifotsy

Ambalamanandray

Gite

Ambalamanandray

Sahorimba

Massif de Tsaranoro

Camp Catta
Morarano
(850m)

RN7

RN7, Ambalavao

RN7, Ambalavao

RN7, Ambalavao

When researchers first started investigating the fauna of Andringitra, in the early 1990s, they thought they'd found a subspecies of *Lemur catta*. The lemurs here look different from those in the southern spiny desert and gallery forest of Berenty. They appear slightly larger, their fur is thicker, and the colours seem more dramatic: a chestnut back, rather than grey-brown, with whiter whites and blacker blacks. And their behaviour is different. In the absence of trees these lemurs leap from rock to rock with great agility, often on their back legs like sifakas. It is now known that this variation is simply an adaptation to their cold, treeless environment, so the lemurs of Andringitra are an ecotype, not a subspecies.

tough walk, but our group of varying fitness did it in about seven hours including a lunch break. There's an altitude gain of 500m, but you hardly notice, so beautiful is the scenery. Leaving the campsite you walk up through forest to the junction of the trail to Pic d'Imarivolanitra. You soon cross the heads of the two sacred waterfalls and, if you're feeling courageous, you can swim in the icy pools. The trail then passes through tall, heather-like shrubs (*Phillipia* spp) and up towards the escarpment. The next stretch resembles a giant rock garden with colourful mosses and lichens decorating the boulders, succulents (Crassulaceae) nestling at their feet, and masses of daisy-like helichrysum flowers. Wonderful!

A viewpoint looks over the granite slabs near Camp Catta. Here you may see the characteristic Andringitra ring-tailed lemurs leaping around the rocks. A trail leads to the Mororano (western) park entrance (17km), but to complete the circuit you descend steeply – stopping at intervals to admire the view – to the forest and campsite. It was on this final stretch that our guide found a highland streaked tenrec – perhaps the most enchanting of all Madagascar's tenrecs.

Pic d'Imarivolanitra (Pic Boby) 14km (one way). This trek is usually done in two or three days so needs advance planning so porters are available to carry the tents and food. This is the ultimate Andringitra, with stunning views and all the high-altitude flora described above.

BEYOND AMBALAVAO ON RN7

The scenery beyond Ambalavao is marvellous. Huge domes of granite dominate the grassy plains. The most striking one, with twin rock towers, is called Varavarana Ny Atsimo (the door to the south) by the pass of the same name. Beyond is the Bonnet de l'Evêque (bishop's cap – but it looks more like a cottage loaf to me!) and a huge lump of granite shaped like an upturned boat, with its side gouged out into an amphitheatre; streams run into the lush vegetation at its base.

You will notice that not only the scenery but the villages are different. Bara houses are solidly constructed from red earth (no elegant Merina pillars here) with small windows. Bunches of maize are often suspended from the roof to dry in the sun.

Shortly after Ambalavao you start to see your first tombs – some painted with scenes from the life of the deceased.

Cyclists will find accommodation at **Zazafotsy** (the name means 'white child'!) at Hôtel Tongasoa. 'It was rather a private house as the owner's daughter moved out from her room. We learned later that most of cyclists stay in **Ankaramena** and it looked like a better option' (NF).

The next town of importance is Ihosy, described in *Chapter 9*.

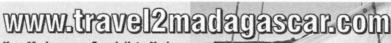

The South

This is the most exotic and the most famous part of Madagascar, the region of 'spiny desert' where weird cactus-like trees wave their thorny fingers in the sky, where fragments of 'elephant bird' eggshells may still be found, and where the Mahafaly tribe erect their intriguing and often entertaining *aloalo* stelae above the graves. Here also are some of the country's most popular national parks and reserves, as well as its best beaches and coral reefs. No wonder the south features on almost all tour itineraries.

BACKGROUND INFORMATION

HISTORY Europeans have been coming to this area for a long time. Perhaps the earliest were a group of 600 shipwrecked Portuguese sailors in 1527. Later, when sailors were deliberately landing in Madagascar during the days of the spice trade in the 16th and 17th centuries, St Augustine's Bay, south of the modern town of Toliara (Tulear), became a favoured destination. They came for reprovisioning – Dutch and British – trading silver and beads for meat and fruit. One Englishman, Walter Hamond, was so overcome with the delights of Madagascar and the Malagasy, 'the happiest people in the world', that fired by his enthusiasm the British attempted to establish a colony at St Augustine's Bay. It was not a success. The original 140 settlers were soon whittled down to 60 through disease and murder by the local tribesmen who became less happy when they found their favourite beads were not available for trade and that these *vazaha* showed no sign

DISTANCES IN KILOMETRES

Ihosy–Toliara	334km	Bezaha–Ampanihy	199km
Ihosy–Taolagnaro	506km	Bezaha–Ejeda	149km
Ihosy–Betroka	132km	Ampanihy–Berenty	273km
Ihosy–Ranohira	91km	Ampanihy–Taolagnaro	334km
Ranohira–Toliara	243km	Taolagnaro–Betroka	374km
Ranohira–Sakaraha	110km	Taolagnaro–Manantenina	110km
Sakaraha–Toliara	133km	Taolagnaro–Amboasary	75km
Toliara–Anakao	56km	Taolagnaro–Berenty	89km
Toliara–Ifaty	27km	Taolagnaro–Ambovombe	110km
Toliara–Andavadoaka	338km	Ambovombe–Tsiombe	67km
Toliara–Andranovory	70km	Tsiombe–Faux Cap	30km
Toliara–Ejeda	242km	Tsiombe–Lavanono	94km
Toliara–Bezaha	129km	Androka–Itampolo	56km
Toliara–Ampanihy	292km	Itampolo–Anakao	134km
Toliara–Morombe	290km		

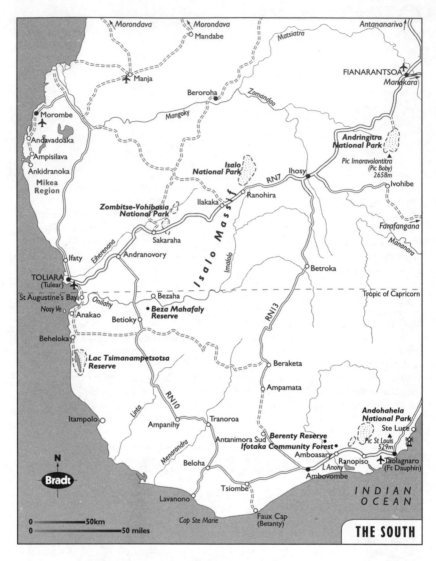

THE SOUTH

of going away. The colonists left in 1646. Fifty years later St Augustine was a haven for pirates.

THE PEOPLE TODAY Several ethnic groups live in the south: the Vezo (fishermen), Mikea and Masikoro (pastoralists) are subclans of the Sakalava. The Mahafaly, Antanosy, Antandroy and Bara all have their homes in the interior. These southern Malagasy are tough, dark-skinned people with African features, accustomed to the hardship of living in a region where rain seldom falls and finding water and grazing for their large herds of zebu is a constant challenge. The Bara are particularly known for their association with cattle – this warlike tribe resisted Merina rule and were never really subdued until French colonial times. Cattle rustling is a time-honoured custom – a Bara does not achieve manhood until he has stolen a few of his neighbour's cows.

In contrast to the highland people, who go in for second burial and whose tombs are the collective homes of ancestors, those in the south (with the exception of the Bara) commemorate the recently dead. There is more opportunity to be remembered as an individual here, and a Mahafaly or Masikoro man who has lived eventfully, and died rich, will have the highlights of his life perpetuated in the form of wooden carvings (*aloalo*) and colourful paintings adorning his tomb. Formerly the *aloalo* were of more spiritual significance; but just as we, in our culture, have tended to bring an element of humour and realism into religion, so have the Malagasy. As John Mack says (in *Island of the Ancestors*), '*Aloalo* have become obituary announcements when formerly they were notices of rebirth.'

Antandroy tombs may be equally colourful. They are large and rectangular (the more important the person the bigger his tomb) and, like those of the Mahafaly, topped with zebu skulls left over from the funeral feast. A very rich man may have over a hundred skulls on his grave. They usually have 'male and female' standing stones (or, in modern tombs, cement towers) at each side. Modern tombs may be brightly painted with geometric patterns or imaginative paintings (unlike those of the Mahafaly these do not necessarily represent scenes from the life of the deceased).

In Antandroy country, burial sometimes takes place several months after the day of death, which will be commemorated by the sacrifice of cattle and ritual mourning or wailing. A few days later the body is placed in the coffin – and more zebu are sacrificed. Meanwhile finishing touches will be made to the tomb, before the internment ceremony, which takes place over two days or more. The tomb is finally filled in with stones and topped with the horns of the sacrificed zebu. Then the house of the deceased is burnt to the ground. The burial ceremonies over, the family will not go near the tomb again.

The Antanosy have upright stones, cement obelisks or beautifully carved wooden memorials. These, however, are not over the graves themselves but in a sacred and secret place elsewhere.

GETTING AROUND Road travel in the south can be a challenging affair, but the roads are being improved and all of RN7 to Toliara is now paved. Cyclists and motorists alike will find the deep sand a problem on many of the unmade roads. Most visitors prefer to fly.

IHOSY

Pronounced ee*oosh*, this small town is the capital of the Bara tribe. It is about five hours from Fianar by *taxi-brousse* and lies a few kilometres north of the junction for Toliara and Taolagnaro (Fort Dauphin). The road to the former is good; to the latter, bad. An almost impassable road also runs from Ihosy to Farafangana on the east coast.

Ihosy is a medium-sized town whose role is to feed and accommodate those travelling south on RN7. Those staying longer can ask for the services of Alexandre Ralainandrasana, who is a regional tour guide with an office at Lot IM14 Andrefantsena. This is on the right on the road towards Toliara.

TELEPHONE CODE The area code for Ihosy is 75.

 **WHERE TO STAY/EAT**

⌂ **Zaha Motel** ↘ 75 740 83. Pleasant, comfortable bungalows with en-suite bathrooms. €€€

⌂ **Relais Bara** (16 rooms) A pleasant hotel with rooms of varying prices & facilities including 5 with en-suite bathroom & hot water & 5 with shared facilities & cold water. The remaining 6 rooms have a shower but shared toilet. Mozzie net provided. €€€

🏠 **Hôtel Chez Evah** (5 rooms) A reasonable budget hotel. Shared bathrooms. Quite a walk from the centre of town, however — about 400m down the road to Toliara, on the right. The restaurant serves very good Chinese & Malagasy food. €

🏠 **Hôtel Nirina** In the centre of town. Typical local restaurant serving good Malagasy dishes. €

In town there is a nice little square of open-sided *hotelys* serving good Malagasy food.

FROM IHOSY TO FARAFANGANA

This road has been impassable by car for over 20 years, but I have heard of someone getting through in a 4x4 and another on a motorbike. From Ihosy it is possible to drive as far as Ivohibe, and from Farafangana you can get to Vondrozo. It's the stretch in between those two towns which is tricky. Bridges have collapsed, some parts are very marshy, and the road has become overgrown with trees.

FROM IHOSY TO TAOLAGNARO (FORT DAUPHIN)

RN13 is in very poor condition. Adventurous travellers with a strong pair of legs or – better – a mountain bike, will enjoy the complete lack of tourist development. Nowadays anyone driving to Taolagnaro takes the better road via Andranovory. I have had no information about the route for several years and would love to hear from anyone who's done it.

FROM IHOSY TO TOLIARA (TULEAR)

After leaving Ihosy, RN7 crosses the Horombe Plateau. Some find these monotonous grasslands dull, others love it. 'It's all red quartz sand and whistling winds, with wonderful plants and fungi that you will miss unless you get down on your knees to look' (WA).

As you approach Ranohira, *Medemia* palms enliven the scenery. Henk Beentje of Kew Gardens writes: 'The palms are properly called *Bismarckia*, but the French didn't like the most common palm in one of their colonies being called after a German so changed the name, quite illegally according to the Code of Botanical Nomenclature!'

RANOHIRA AND ISALO NATIONAL PARK

The small town of Ranohira lies 91km south of Ihosy and is the base for visiting the popular Isalo National Park. It is also the nearest established town to Ilakaka, the relatively new settlement that is the base for the sapphire trade, which has transformed it from a sleepy little town to a bustling commercial centre.

GETTING THERE AND AWAY Getting to Ranohira is no problem. If coming from Toliara note that the *taxi-brousses* and buses depart early in the morning, so it is best to book your seat the day before. Continuing south can be difficult since *taxi-brousses* are usually full by the time they arrive in Ranohira. Local people may offer to stop one for you but will demand a high tip for the service. MadaBus is probably the best option; it arrives in the evening at 19.00.

WHERE TO STAY
Top end €€€€€
🏠 **Jardin du Roy** (15 bungalows) www.hotels-isalo.com. Book through Madagascar Discovery Agency, Tana (📞 22 336 23/351 65; f 22 351 67; e mda@wanadoo.mg). Under the same ownership as Relais de la Reine & even more luxurious! 'This family-run concern is set in 3 blocks, the split-level

bungalows offer savannah chic in their design, surrounded by sandstone outcrops. More upscale than Relais, the interior's rosewood furnishings are designed by the Colombie family themselves. The rooms have AC, unlike Relais, broad verandas, & large spacious en-suite bathrooms. Fine-dining is on offer in the restaurant & local sapphire-traders add to a lively atmosphere in the bar which has a stunning fireplace. A large swimming pool is also available.' (Mark Stratton)

Upper range €€€€
🏠 **Isalo Ranch** (19 bungalows) ☎ (Tana): 24 319 02; e info@isalo-ranch.com; www.isalo-ranch.com. About 2km southwest of Ranohira. Comfortable bungalows with solar-heated water. Swimming pool. Recommended by several readers. Food also reportedly very good. Transport provided to/from the

Mid range €€€
🏠 **Hôtel Orchidée d'Isalo** (31 rooms) m 032 44 676 89. At the centre of the village. Some very nice new rooms & some cheaper old rooms, available with hot or cold water. New luxurious restaurant. €€€–€€
🏠 **Motel d'Isalo** (60 bungalows, but more being built) ☎ 22 330 82. The 1st hotel coming from the north. Nice bungalows with en-suite rooms, solar heating & swimming pool. Much-praised, but it's some way from the centre of town.
🏠 **Les Toiles de l'Isalo** ☎ 22 245 34. Sgl, dbl &

Budget €€
🏠 **Chez Alice** e mariealice@wanadoo.mg. Alice, the gregarious, chain-smoking proprietor, has built a set of bungalows & Bara-style huts (*paillettes*) on a meadow 500m from the town centre. The huts (shared facilities) & restaurant overlook the Isalo

✗ WHERE TO EAT
✗ **Pakato** A new restaurant in Ranohira run by the brother of Clarisse, the only female guide in Isalo.
✗ **Hotely Aina** Recommended by Nina French.

🏠 **Relais de la Reine** (37 rooms) Contact/booking details as above. A lovely French-run hotel 9km southwest of Ranohira at Soarano, on the edge of the park. Blocks of 6 rooms grouped around a courtyard blend into the 40ha gardens. Solar-heated water. The water is drawn from a stream & fans cool the rooms in the hot season. Swimming pool, tennis court. Good-quality horses can be hired for riding tours in Isalo. Car transfers can be arranged from Toliara & the hotel even has a landing strip if you decide to splash out on their private plane!

park. Free accommodation & food for drivers.
🏠 **Le Palme de l'Isalo** (12 rooms) South of Isalo on the way to Ilakaka (turn left opposite the Fenêtre turnoff). Beautifully located amid typical Isalo landscape. Dbl & tpl rooms, en-suite bathrooms. Electricity by generator evenings only.

tpl rooms.
🏠 **Hôtel Berny** ☎ 75 801 76; f 94 419 20. Near ANGAP office. 'A great hotel with a very friendly French *patron*. The best rooms in a small chateau in the garden are fantastic. Pet lemurs in the garden like to play with tourists' (SR). Also cheaper rooms, some with cold water, others with hot shower & toilet. Very good food. English spoken.
🏠 **Momo Trek** (19 bungalows) These Bara-style huts are next to the ANGAP office (& the power plant, so noisy). Simple but clean. Camping permitted.

range & its spectacular sunsets. Excellent food. Camping permitted.
🏠 **Maison Jumelle Chez Thomas** (20 rooms) m 032 43 708 69. Basic rooms at a variety of prices, all with shared facilities.

'Situated below the post office on the same side of the road. A small restaurant run by Isalo guides. Several languages spoken.'

ISALO NATIONAL PARK The combination of sandstone rocks (cut by deep canyons and eroded into weird shapes), rare endemic plants and dry weather (between June and August rain is almost unknown) makes this park particularly rewarding. For botanists there is *Pachypodium rosulatum* or elephant's foot – a bulbous rock-clinging plant – and a native species of aloe, *Aloe isaloensis*; and for lemur-lovers there are sifakas, brown lemurs and ring-tails. Isalo is also sacred to the Bara tribe. For hundreds of years the Bara have used caves in the canyon walls as burial sites. Tourists who do not wish to hike (and this should not be undertaken lightly – it

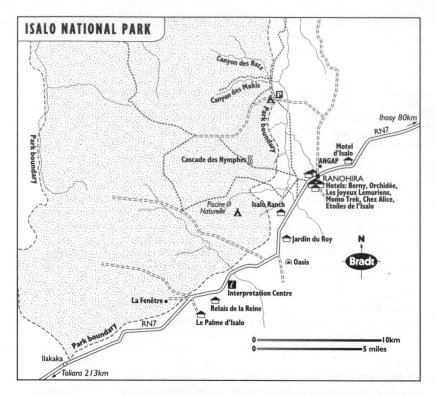

ISALO NATIONAL PARK

Canyon des Rats
Canyon des Makis
Park boundary
Ihosy 80km
RN7
Motel d'Isalo
ANGAP
Cascade des Nymphes
RANOHIRA
Hotels: Berny, Orchidée, Les Joyeux Lemuriens, Momo Trek, Chez Alice, Etoiles de l'Isalo
Piscine Naturelle
Isalo Ranch
Jardin du Roy
N
Oasis
Bradt
Park boundary
Interpretation Centre
La Fenêtre
Relais de la Reine
Park boundary
RN7
Le Palme d'Isalo
Ilakaka
Toliara 213km

0 ————— 10km
0 ————— 5 miles

can be very hot) or to pay the park fee have various options. Simply driving past the sandstone formations which can be seen from the road is exciting enough. Another popular visit – perhaps too popular at times – is to La Fenêtre, a natural rock formation providing a window to the setting sun. Walk behind the rocks for the proper Isalo feeling of space and tranquillity. Avoid bringing valuables; in 2007 there was a spate of muggings here.

Permits and guides For an excursion in the park you will need a permit (see page 75 for prices) which must be purchased at the ANGAP office in Ranohira, next to Hôtel Berny. Irritatingly, the office doesn't open until 07.00 so by the time you have organised the trip and set out, it's the hottest time of the day. If possible make your arrangements the day before. The park authorities have worked hard at rewarding the best guides by giving them a star rating which is posted outside the office. Charges are posted on the wall of the office. Prices depend on the length of tour. The price listings can be confusing, so it is important to clarify the total price for your circuit and guide before leaving the office. Schematic maps of the park are available from ANGAP.

Isalo Interpretation Centre (Maison de l'Isalo) Well worth a visit to learn more about the people who live around the park, as well as the wildlife in the national park itself. 'The most sophisticated I saw in Madagascar, with commentary in Malagasy, French and English throughout, modern interpretation boards and interactive displays.' The only negative is that it is poorly located some way south of the town.

Hiking in the park There are several established circuits, with campsites, and most guides are reluctant to deviate from these. No matter, they provide all the Isalo specials of lemurs, cool leafy canyons, and hot, dry plains with those extraordinary rock formations and accompanying succulent plants. If possible, arrange to camp overnight in the park. That way you can hike in the cooler parts of the day, avoiding the exhaustion of walking in the baking midday sun.

Circuit Namaza This has you following a stream (some scrambling) up a leafy canyon to the Cascade des Nymphes. The walk takes 30–45 minutes and you are rewarded at the end with a refreshing swim in surprisingly cold water. The pool is very deep, and you need to swim to see the waterfall and the imposing, fern-fringed black cliffs which almost hide the sky.

The campsite here is regularly visited by ring-tailed and brown lemurs. Hoopoes are also frequently seen in this lovely place.

Canyon des Makis (Canyon des Singes) This is 17km from Ranohira, accessible by a rough track (4x4 only, or on foot). At the canyon a path goes over rocks and along the edge of the tumbling river; there are pools into which you can fling yourself at intervals and, at the top, a small waterfall under which to have a shower. The sheer rocks hung with luxuriant ferns broaden out to provide views of the bare mountain behind, and trees and palms provide shade for a picnic. There is the added bonus of a troop of sifakas near the canyon entrance.

Piscine Naturelle This is justifiably the most popular destination for hikers in Isalo, so can be crowded. As the name implies, this is a natural swimming pool. Fringed with palm trees and constantly filled by a waterfall, it is both stunningly beautiful and wonderful for swimming, having been unobtrusively improved so that getting in and out of the water is easy. There is also an open-sided shelter where Benson's rock thrushes flirt with bathers. The nearby campsite has a flush (!) toilet and a shower.

Udi Columbus recommends: 'A one-day trip combining Canyon des Makis with the Namaza trail is very nice and diverse. After a two-hour visit to the magnificent canyon you start a somewhat strenuous climb up the hill, with a very rewarding viewpoint over the park. After that you go up and down for several hours, joining Namaza trail and have a nice (but cold) swim at the black cascade. Altogether it takes 5–6 hours to complete this 12km trail, including a lunch break and swimming/relaxing at the waterfall. You must have a driver drop you off next to the canyon and pick you up at the end (it's not a circular trail).'

Beyond the park Those with a 4x4 vehicle can explore some of the dirt roads bordering the national park. 'We got a guide from the park office in Ranohira and went up a dirt road west of the park towards the valley of the Malio River. In a small forest patch we rediscovered a liana previously known from only two 40- to 50-year-old collections. This is an interesting piece of forest. When you hit sand you have to park and walk through dense, liana-filled jungle with gigantic butterflies flitting through the gloom. Our guide told us that when he was a boy, they used to roast and eat the huge spiders that spin webs across the trail to catch *vazaha*. "But that was when I was a boy," he said while I was gagging. "I wouldn't do that now, of course … because they're endemic!" I thought this was a young man who had a real future in science.' (Wendy Applequist)

ILAKAKA

This extraordinary settlement has sprung up within the last few years as the centre of the sapphire trade. Tour buses now drive straight through with the windows closed for fear of bandits. However, providing you are sensible over security it is worth a visit for the Wild West atmosphere. There is, perhaps, nowhere else like it in the world: savour it while you can, in a couple of years it will probably be a ghost town. When I passed through in 2003 it was humming with life and full of swaggering men with guns on their hips. Every other shop has the word *Saphir* above its doorway, and the quantity of high-priced consumer goods for sale is remarkable. There are plenty of restaurants and hotels, if you decide to stay.

CONTINUING SOUTH

The drive from Isalo to Toliara (243km) takes a minimum of four hours. The sapphire rush is moving south and you will pass the temporary grass huts and piles of earth dug by fortune seekers for many kilometres. Other smaller versions of Ilakaka are springing up along this route.

Eventually the rugged mountains give way to grasslands, and following the rains there are many flowers – the large white *Crinum firmifolium* and the Madagascar periwinkle – but in the dry season it's quite monotonous. The next town of importance is Sakaraha, which has been transformed into another sapphire centre, and is convenient for Zombitse National Park.

SAKARAHA Daniel and Kelly, who supplied the hotel information, say: 'The post office is 120m from RN7 near the foot of a huge communications tower that can be seen from any point in town. (It can also usually be *heard*, for huge numbers of rowdy myna birds perch on its struts!)'

Where to stay/eat

⌂ **Le Relais de Sakaraha** (8 chalets) Hotel, bar, restaurant & disco. Each chalet has a dbl room upstairs, another downstairs & an en-suite squat toilet & bucket shower. The semicircular upper level with curved balcony is reminiscent of a lighthouse! It only comes alive in the evening, especially on disco nights. Very conveniently located for south *taxi-brousse* station. €

⌂ **Palace Club** (3 rooms) A French-run hotel on the southwest side of town with a bar & nightclub. They have 3 rooms with bucket showers. Shared toilets. They serve excellent food; staff are very helpful. €

⌂ **Hôtel Venus** (9 bungalows) A short walk out of town. Mostly en suite with shower, but 3 cheaper ones have shared facilities. Malagasy food served. €

ZOMBITSE-VOHIBASIA NATIONAL PARK
Zombitse is a stark example of the effects of deforestation. Years of continuous felling have turned the surrounding areas into an arid moonscape and what remains is an isolated pocket of forest, thankfully now protected. The park covers 21,500ha, straddling RN7 some 20km northeast of Sakaraha. It is an important example of a boundary zone

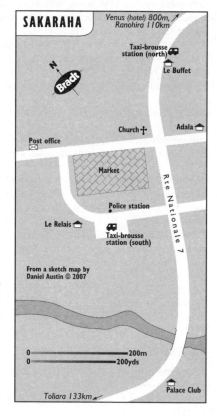

between the western and southern domains of vegetation and so has a high level of biodiversity.

Zombitse is of major significance to birdwatchers as it offers the chance to glimpse one of Madagascar's rarest endemics, Appert's greenbul, which is confined to this forest. In addition to birds you have a good chance of seeing sifaka, red-fronted brown lemurs, and the nocturnal sportive lemur peering out of its nest hole. 'Reptiles like the spectacular, locally endemic Standing's day gecko can be found resting on trunks. On one very lucky occasion, I even encountered a pair of mating fossas in a tree!' (Nick Garbutt).

The park office is on the southern side of RN7 and official guides will take you along the good paths and circuit trails. It takes just over an hour to reach the park from Isalo, or two to three hours from Toliara, so serious birdwatchers should leave as early as possible in the morning to avoid the heat. Better still, stay in Sakaraha.

Beyond Sakaraha you will start to see painted tombs, some with *aloalo*, near the road. Be wary of taking photographs, however. Some locals have become adept at materialising out of nowhere and demanding payment. As you get closer to Toliara you'll see your first baobabs and pass through a cotton-growing region. Look out for the enormous nests of hamerkop birds in roadside trees.

About two hours from Sakaraha is the small village of **Andranovory** which has a colourful Sunday market. Another hour and Toliara's table mountain, La Table, comes into view on the right; half an hour later you pass the airport and head for the town.

TOLIARA (TULEAR)

The pronunciation of the French, Tulear, and the Malagasy names is the same: tool*ear*. Toliara's history is centred on St Augustine's Bay, described at the beginning of this chapter, although the name of the town is thought to derive from an encounter with one of those early sailors who asked a local inhabitant where he might moor his boat. The Malagasy replied: *toly eroa*: 'mooring down there'. The town itself is relatively modern – 1895 – and was designed by an uninspired French architect. His tree planting was more successfully aesthetic, and the shady tamarind trees (*kily*) give welcome respite from the blazing sun.

There are three good reasons to visit Toliara: the rich marine life with good snorkelling and diving, the Mahafaly and Masikoro tombs with a museum that puts it all in context, and the remarkable spiny forest and its accompanying fauna. Don't miss a visit to the Arboretum d'Antsokay and/or the Reniala Nature Reserve. These two privately run places can give you an experience as good as many national parks, at a fraction of the cost.

The beaches south of the town have fine white sand, but those in the north are often rocky. Beyond the beaches is an extensive coral reef, sadly now suffering from coral bleaching so no longer particularly rewarding for snorkellers. Toliara itself, regrettably, has no beach, just mangroves and mud flats.

TELEPHONE CODE The area code for Toliara is 94.

☞ *WARNING!* In the cool season (June to September) the nights in Toliara are quite cold. The cheaper hotels rarely supply enough blankets. Businesses close between 12.00 and 15.00; banks are closed from 11.30–14.00.

GETTING THERE AND AWAY

By road Route Nationale 7 (RN7) is served by a variety of comfortable vehicles, including MadaBus which runs on Monday, Wednesday and Friday and costs €35 to Toliara from Tana.

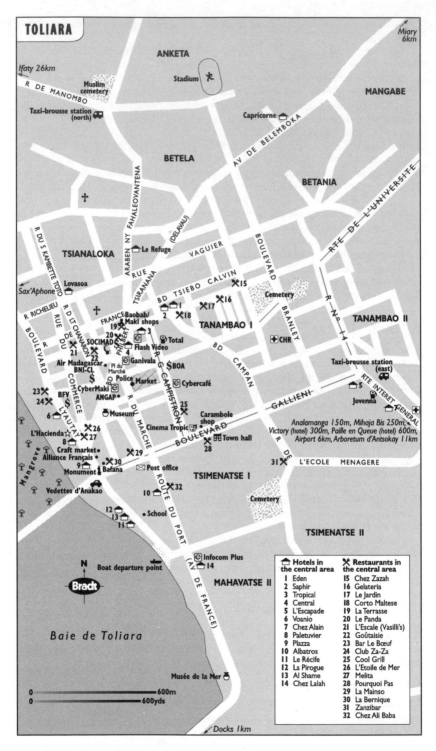

TOLIARA

Ifaty 26km

Miary 6km

ANKETA

Stadium

R DE MANOMBO

Muslim cemetery

Taxi-brousse station (north)

Capricorne

MANGABE

BETELA

AV DE BELEMBOKA

BETANIA

RTE DE L'UNIVERSITE

R DU S KAMBETTE TOTO

ARABEN NY FAHALEOVANTENA

Le Refuge

RUE TSIRANANA

(DELAVU)

VAGUIER

BOULEVARD

TSIANALOKA

R RICHELIEU

Sax'Aphone

Lovasoa

BD TSIEBO CALVIN

15

Cemetery

BRANLEY

R N° 4

TANAMBAO II

17 16

2 18 1

FRANCE Baobab/ Maki shops

RUE DE LT CHANARON

RUE DU

BOULEVARD

19

20

SOCIMAD

21

22

3

Total

Flash Video

4

TANAMBAO I

BD CAMPAN

CHR

Taxi-brousse station (east)

RTE INTERET GENERAL

Air Madagascar

BNI-CL

Ganivala

$BOA

Pl du Marché

RUE R GAMBETTA

Police Market

Cybercafé

GALLIENI

5

Jovenna

23

24

BFV

CyberMaki

ANGAP

Museum

25

Carambole shop

Analamanga 150m, Mihaja Bis 250m, Victory (hotel) 300m, Paille en Queue (hotel) 600m, Airport 6km, Arboretum d'Antsokay 11km

6

L'YAUTAU

RUE DU COMMERCE

RUE DU MARCHE

Cinema Tropic

BOULEVARD

26

27

8

Town hall

28

Craft market

Alliance Français

ROUTE DU PORT

29

L'Hacienda

9

30

31

L'ECOLE MENAGERE

Monument

Bafana

Post office

TSIMENATSE I

Vedettes d'Anakao

10

32

Mangrove

12

13

11

School

Cemetery

TSIMENATSE II

N

Bradt

Boat departure point

Infocom Plus

14

MAHAVATSE II

Baie de Toliara

AV DE FRANCE

Musée de la Mer

0 ——— 600m
0 ——— 600yds

Docks 1km

🏠 **Hotels in the central area**		✕ **Restaurants in the central area**	
1 Eden		15 Chez Zazah	
2 Saphir		16 Gelateria	
3 Tropical		17 Le Jardin	
4 Central		18 Corto Maltese	
5 L'Escapade		19 La Terrasse	
6 Voanio		20 Le Panda	
7 Chez Alain		21 L'Escale (Vasilli's)	
8 Paletuvier		22 Goûtaisie	
9 Plazza		23 Bar Le Bœuf	
10 Albatros		24 Club Za-Za	
11 Le Récife		25 Cool Grill	
12 La Pirogue		26 L'Etoile de Mer	
13 Al Shame		27 Melita	
14 Chez Lalah		28 Pourquoi Pas	
		29 La Mainso	
		30 La Bernique	
		31 Zanzibar	
		32 Chez Ali Baba	

Alternatively there are some reasonably comfortable buses which depart around 07.00 arriving in Toliara at 05.00 the following day (m *032 04 335 91/032 40 462 92*).

By air There are daily flights from Tana and Taolagnaro, but in the high season these tend to be fully booked. However, it's always worth going to the airport, whatever they say in the office. Depending on the season, it costs 200,000–220,000Ar.

GETTING AROUND Distances are quite large, but *pousse-pousses* are plentiful. They generally charge more at night or in the rain. A typical trip at the *vazaha*-price should cost around 1,500Ar. Make sure you have the right change. Don't grudge paying a bit more – a *pousse-pousse* driver's life is not easy and they are a friendly bunch. Taxis are plentiful. The going rate is 2,000Ar for any trip (except the airport where the starting price is 15,000Ar). If you stop anywhere – even briefly – *en route*, you will be charged for two trips.

Car hire
🚌 **Mihaja Bis Hotel** ☎ 94 445 43; e miharemana05@yahoo.fr. They can arrange car rentals.

🚌 **Les Vedettes d'Anakao** (formerly **Compagnie du Sud**) Mahavatse 2; ☎ 94 437 21; m 032 04 624 09; e vedettes@tulear-tourisme.com. 4x4 rentals.

WHERE TO STAY Most visitors spending any time in the Toliara area stay at the beach resorts (see pages 236–43) but there are some good-value hotels in or near the town.

Upper range €€€€
🏠 **Motel Le Capricorne** (10 rooms) ☎ 94 426 20; f 94 431 66; e capric@dts.mg. About 2km from the town centre on RN7. Lovely garden, well-run with a good restaurant.

🏠 **Le Paille en Queue** (18 bungalows) Andranomena; ☎ 94 446 99; f 94 447 00; e socoeto@ simicro.mg; www.pailleenqueue.com. Only 5mins from airport. Ideal if you need to make a quick getaway the following day. Owned by Bernard & Catherine Sanchis from Réunion. New, very pleasant, with rooms arranged round a central pool. All bungalows have TV & AC.

🏠 **Eden Hotel** (18 rooms) Tanambao; ☎ 94 415 66/442 59; f 94 442 60; e eden.hotel@yahoo.fr. Great central location opposite Corto Maltese restaurant. Very nice atmosphere; AC rooms. Bar & restaurant 'with real vanilla ice cream!'

🏠 **Hôtel Victory** (17 rooms) Rte de l'Aeroport; ☎ 94 440 64; m 032 02 068 19. 'A little haven away from the busy town. The owners are an Indian family; very friendly & welcoming. If you eat a meal there, you can use their pool & sit in the pleasant garden. The clean, airy rooms have AC, hot water, satellite TV, phone, fridge & safe. Nice family atmosphere' (Karen Paterson).

Mid range €€€
🏠 **Hôtel Plazza** (21 rooms) ☎ 94 903 06. One of Toliara's oldest & best-located hotels. Recently refurbished in spacious gardens facing the sea. Some rooms with AC. Visa & MasterCard accepted.

🏠 **Hôtel Palétuvier** (14 rooms) ☎ 94 440 35. A good hotel (the name means 'mangrove'). Sgl, dbl & tpl rooms.

🏠 **L'Escapade** (10 rooms) Bd Gallieni (eastern end). A newish hotel in a good location. Rooms arranged around a courtyard; plus bungalows with fans. Pool table.

🏠 **Hôtel Tropical** (20 rooms) Very clean; very good. Rooms have TV & AC. No restaurant but b/fast available.

🏠 **Le Recif Hotel** Bd Lyautey (southern end); ☎ 94 446 88; m 032 40 755 39. En-suite bathrooms, hot water, some with AC & ocean view. Nice swimming pool & restaurant.

🏠 **Hôtel Albatros** (12 rooms) Av de France (near post office); ☎ 94 432 10. A blue & white hotel with hot water & AC in some rooms.

Jilly Pollard

If you had walked into a jeweller's shop 30 years ago and shouted 'Madagascar!' the staff would probably have shuffled nervously waiting for your next trick. These days they would be more likely to approach you eagerly in the hope that you were a gem dealer with Malagasy stones to sell. Politically, much has changed. Madagascar's list of precious stones and mineral species is truly exciting and the quality of the specimens can be truly breathtaking. Nearly all the commercially famous stones are to be found on this large island, as are many rare stones and mineral species.

Tim Ireland appreciates the whole range of treasures, being both a geologist and gemmologist. On his recent visit to Madagascar he was able to explain the mineralogy of the area to his fellow travellers:

'The crystalline rocks and gravels available to today's miners, sifters and washers-of-gravel were once 10–30km deep within the earth – not necessarily underground but perhaps at the heart of ancient mountains now eroded away. Millions of years ago, too, the land flexed upwards so the rocks now on the surface were in fact formed under tens of kilometres of other rock in conditions of great pressure and great heat – ideal for the formation of crystalline gems. Gemstones are, by their nature, dense and durable, so they survive the ravages of time. Mountains and rocks were gradually ground down and washed away towards the sea and in some areas of the west coast gem-hunters have to trace and chase the old river channels in search of deposits of the hard, bright and valuable survivors of barely imaginable eruptions and upheavals.

'Elsewhere, traditional mining is necessary. To retrieve gemstones at Ilakaka, for example, an exploratory shaft is sunk until miners recognise a likely combination of

🏠 **Saphir Hotel** (16 rooms) Tanambao; 📞 94 436 79/446 31; e saphir.hotel@blueline.mg. Rooms with AC & hot water.

🏠 **Le Sax'Aphone** (4 bungalows & 3 rooms) Villa Soarimanga, Besakoa (western outskirts of Toliara, opposite a school); 📞 94 440 88; m 032 02 237 44; e sax.aphone@simicro.mg. A wonderful guesthouse run by the charismatic Alain & Michèle Bonard, who named it after a jazz club they used to run in Montpellier. They speak French, English &

German. More like a private home than a hotel; perfect for solo travellers. Lovely common room, bar & restaurant (excellent meals & great atmosphere).

🏠 **Chez Alain** (21 rooms) 📞 94 415 27; e c.alain@wanadoo.mg; www.chez-alain.net. Deservedly one of the most popular *vazaha* hotels in Madagascar, with rooms to suit almost every budget. Well-run & friendly. Excellent food (huge portions!). Mountain bikes for hire. Dive tourisme.gov.mg centre **L'Ancre Bleue** is based here.

Budget €€

🏠 **Le Refuge** (11 rooms) 📞 94 423 28; f 94 425 94. Very pleasant central hotel. Dbl & tpl rooms, some with AC. Small pool.

🏠 **Al Shame** (12 rooms) Bd Lyautey (southern end); 📞 94 447 28; m 032 05 267 24. A purple-painted hotel that, despite its name, isn't a bad

choice. Seafront location. Some rooms en suite.

🏠 **Arboretum d'Antsokay** (5 bungalows) The Arboretum (see page 234) has basic bungalows, some with en-suite bathrooms (cold water). Perfect for early-rising birdwatchers & other wildlife fans.

Penny-pincher €

🏠 **Hôtel Voanio** (4 bungalows) Bd Lyautey; m 033 14 088 73. Next to Club Za-Za (so likely to be noisy), these tin-roofed bungalows are surrounded by palm trees in a breezy setting. Cold showers & some with en-suite toilet.

🏠 **Hôtel Central** Aptly named, bang in the centre of town, so convenient for market & museum. Friendly owner, huge rooms with balconies, hot water & en-suite toilet. No restaurant. 'We would pop down to the market to buy fruit & eat it on our balcony

rock types. Then a few bags of local gravel are washed; if the results are good, a pit is sunk and more work begins. One miner said that half a dozen bags of gravel from an exploratory hole might yield four million ariary's worth of sapphires. The catch is that the payload layer is often around 15m deep in the earth, yet only about one metre thick – a big, deep hole for what might prove to be a small yield … or a fortune.

'When a find is made, the Malagasy miners will often arrive in great numbers from far away, willing to break their backs shifting dirt with shovels for the duration of the rush – two years? ten years? a hundred years? Curiously, the government has precluded the use of heavy machinery by the Malagasy people while outsiders are free to mine in whatever fashion they wish. Thai and Sri Lankan miners use earth-moving equipment to dig the efficient way. Strange enough; but add to this the shady nature of the gem industry: riches and smuggling. Instead of Madagascar getting rich now that its treasures are reaching the marketplace, money floods out of the country at a rate beyond anyone's wildest dreams. The richest Malagasies in the business seem not to be digging but instead are the ones providing security for the foreign buyers.

'The jewellery industry worldwide is trying to rebalance the distribution of money so that countries with a natural abundance of gemstones, and the indigenous miners of those riches, will get a better deal. The Kimberly Process is working well for the diamond industry and something might emerge from that for the coloured stone trade. In the mean time, if you are thinking of buying loose gemstones from Madagascar or anywhere else, remember that specialists and big business will have creamed the top off the supply. Buy something you fall in love with – there's plenty to choose from – but don't expect to get rich quick by selling it when you get home.'

while watching the life going on beneath' (Nina French).

🏠 **Chez Lalah** (15 rooms) Av de France. Probably the best bet in this category. Great location, quiet, inexpensive & comfortable. Some rooms en suite. 'Best espresso coffee in Madagascar!' Christophe, the manager, rents out quad bikes & is a mine of information.

🏠 **La Pirogue** (8 bungalows & 1 room) ☎ 94 415 37. Sgl & dbl bungalows & a twin room. Can be noisy. Restaurant serves Chinese, Malagasy & French cuisine.

🏠 **Hôtel Analamanga** (5 bungalows & 2 rooms)

RN7 ☎/f 94 415 47. On the outskirts of Toliara. Small, neat bungalows on stilts. Clean communal bathrooms. Nice quiet setting under shady trees; within walking distance of town.

🏠 **Hôtel Lovasoa** (9 rooms) ☎ 94 418 39. Basic rooms, some en suite, in a quiet street. Pleasant garden.

🏠 **Chez Micheline** (4 bungalows) Anketa; m 032 42 300 62. Within walking distance of the *taxi-brousse* station for Ifaty. Somewhat hidden away so ask locals for directions. 'Just about the cheapest place to stay in Toliara.' Outdoor toilet, bucket water, no electricity.

✕ WHERE TO EAT

✕ **L'Etoile de Mer** Bd Lyautey (opposite Hôtel Palétuvier). This place has maintained its high standards since I first visited Toliara in 1982 & deserves its success. They have some of the best pizza in Toliara, great seafood; also good Afghan & Indian dishes.

✕ **Le Jardin** An exceptional, Italian-run restaurant decorated in a pub style with a busy hodgepodge of artefacts adorning the walls & ceiling. Jovial owner; English & Italian spoken. The lasagne is especially

recommended. 'The giant seafood platter is awesome & they have big ice cream sundaes!'

✕ **Gelateria** Opposite the Memorial School. Nice outdoor seating area & fantastic ice creams; reported as 'The best ice cream & the best coffee in town.'

✕ **Club Za-Za** Serves particularly good fish & for chilli fans: excellent *sakay*.

✕ **Zanzibar** Rte de l'Ecole Ménagère. Huge pizzas, friendly atmosphere.

✕ **Corto Maltese** An upmarket restaurant serving really delicious Italian food.

✕ **La Bernique** Bd Gallieni. 'French-owned bar with snacks & the most comprehensive collection of malt whiskies I found in Madagascar. Well worth several visits!' (SB).

✕ **Le Panda** Excellent Chinese cuisine at good prices. Very similar to the restaurant of the same name in Fianar (presumably under the same ownership).

✕ **La Terrasse** Typical menu with some Malagasy dishes. They also serve English breakfast! The shady outdoor eating area is great for lunch.

✕ **Chez Zazah** Tanambao. Not to be confused with Club Za-Za on the other side of town. Specialises in Chinese food. 'Inexpensive & popular with locals. Wonderful gingery sweet-&-sour!'

✕ **The Cool Grille** Rue Campistron. A small restaurant close to Bd Gallieni. Similar to Chez Zazah, with tasty, inexpensive Malagasy & Chinese food.

✕ **Bar Le Boeuf** is a pleasant grill bar/restaurant. Great steak. Staff are enthusiastic & speak a little English.

✕ **Chez Ali Baba** Av de France. 'If you are tired of the tourist places, try this tiny restaurant. It's across the street from Hôtel Albatros & serves nice big salads, fish, meat & a lot of Malagasy dishes at very cheap prices' (Kim Loohuis).

✕ **Pâtisserie Le Goûtaisie** Just behind Le Panda. Canadian-owned. 'A wonderful place to have breakfast. Also good for lunch – & for chocolate & pastries. There is a little terrace outside' (Kim Loohuis). ⊕ 06.30–20.00.

✕ **L'Escale** Greek food (salads, pittas & other traditional dishes). The owner & chef is Greek & speaks English. A nice change from the usual Malagasy or Italian food.

✕ **La Maison** Bd Gallieni. Opposite post office. An open, airy wooden restaurant with a thatched roof & attractive dining area. Pizza, seafood, good steaks & bar.

✕ **Pourquoi Pas** Bd Gallieni. Why not (as the name says) try this pleasant little Malagasy restaurant? Good prices.

✕ **Melita American Bar and Grill** Bd Lyautey (opposite Hôtel Palétuvier). A very modern American restaurant. Food is reasonably priced.

NIGHTLIFE

☆ **Club Za-Za** This nightclub has been popular for years but has had poor reports recently. 'The music is a poor cross between Western & gasy. Most clientele are young local girls looking for *vazaha* men. However, it is possible to sit away from the loud music to have a conversation as there is loads of room' (TS). 'The "dancing competitions" are open to *vazaha* & you can put your name down on the night!' (SB).

☆ **L'Hacienda** A newer bar & disco on Bd Lyautey, next to Hôtel Palétuvier. 'It's supposed to be a more respectable place than Club Za-Za.'

INTERNET There are many internet places scattered round the town, but the following are favourites of the Peace Corps volunteers. And they should know.

🄴 **Cybersport** Ganivala Below Hôtel Central. Good internet with friendly staff; reasonably priced at 20Ar/min. *Closed 12.00–15.00 & all day Sun.*

🄴 **Infocom Plus** In front of Chez Lalah. Has 6 computers, facilities for printing; AC. Connection is slow when busy, but cheap at 20Ar/min. ⊕ *daily 08.00–18.00.*

🄴 **Cyber M@ki** Has 16 computers with broadband connection. 'Definitely the best internet café I saw in Madagascar! You buy your time online beforehand. 1hr costs 1,800Ar; 2hrs 3,400Ar. You can also burn CDs for 2,500Ar' (Kim Loohuis).

🄴 **Cyberpaositra** At the post office on Bd Gallieni. Usually has good connection; 30Ar/min. ⊕ *Mon–Fri 08.00–20.00; closed Sun.*

MONEY

$ **Tayyebi Change** Rue du Marché (near BFV bank); ☏ 94 442 51; ℻ 94 423 20. Recommended by the Tourist Office.

$ **BNI Crédit Lyonnaise** Pl du Marché.

$ **SOCIMAD** Corner of Rue Père Joseph Castan & Rue de l'Eglise; ☏ 94 216 91. Fast & efficient.

SHOPPING The main craft market in Toliara is towards the end of Bd Gallieni near the monument. There is also a shell market but buying these encourages the destruction of marine life.

Bafana This boutique near the craft market sells a range of good-quality local crafts; run on a co-operative basis.

Natur'ant Déco Essential oils & herbal remedies.

Craft Artisanat Carambole is part of the bright orange building ONG Bel Avenir on Bd Gallieni. They have a nice little boutique with a variety of Malagasy souvenirs. Normal *vazaha* prices.

MEDICAL

✚ **Clinique St Luc** Andabizy; ☎ 94 422 47; m 032 02 294 51; e cliniquesaint-luc@dts.mg. A private clinic that can handle most medical problems. Note, however, that it does not have oxygen for diving emergencies.

✚ **CHR** (Centre Hôpital Régional) Tsenengea; ☎ 94 418 55. Director: Dr Raymond Daniel. This is the main hospital for the southwest & can handle serious emergencies (including diving mishaps).

WATERSPORTS

Diving and snorkelling For many people the main reason to visit Toliara is for the coral reefs. The WWF recognises the importance of these in developing ecotourism in the area and a conservation programme is underway, centred at the University of Toliara. The goal of the project is 'to ensure that the coral reefs and coastal zone are effectively conserved through the establishment of a multiple-use marine park and sustainable economic development'. Certainly there is potential for marine ecotourism, although dead or dying coral is disturbingly evident and many areas which were impressive five years ago are unrecognisable now. See boxes on pages 440 and 444–5 for information on marine conservation.

Most diving centres are attached to beach hotels.

PET LEMURS

Several hotels in the Toliara region keep pet lemurs. The pathetic sight of these animals in cramped cages or tied by a cord around their loins upsets all visitors. Here's a report from a South African tour leader who decided that action speaks louder than words.

'The hotel has a cage with three ring-tails. I was shocked to see this and so were the clients so we designed this bold plan to liberate the lemurs. It was working like clockwork. Our transport was waiting and I had the clients in position. The manager, cooks, and receptionist all duly entertained by their barrage of questions as I slinked through the back and opened the cage door just enough to let the ringies out. Then we all casually made our way to the truck. I peeped over my shoulder and saw the lemurs come out, stand up and sniff the air – that sweet scent of freedom – and then the Helsinki Syndrome kicked in and they made a bee-line for the kitchen window. We drove off to screams and pots and pans clanging. I laughed but wanted to cry. Bloody idiots. Now I understand why they are "pre-simians".'

So what should we do in these circumstances? As this story demonstrates, you cannot 'liberate' an animal accustomed to captivity. It will literally not know what to do with itself and will return to its cage. The solution, as always in Madagascar, is more complicated than it seems. The reason these adorable animals are kept caged or tied is that as they grew from charming babies into assertive adults they started biting the hand that fed them.

'So what can we do?' a hotelier in Toliara asked me, her hands thrown wide in Gallic gesture. 'A kid brings us a little baby lemur and says that the mother is dead and do we want to buy it? I say yes because I think I will treat it more kindly than the kid. Maybe I shouldn't, because then he started biting my guests so now I have to keep him tied up.'

- **Atimoo Plongée** (Mangily) m 032 04 529 17; e info@atimoo.com; www.atimoo.com.
- **Club Nautique** (Dune Hotel); ☎ 94 428 85; e gino@wanadoo.mg.
- **Gipsy Club** (Hôtel Nautilus); ☎ 94 418 74; e nautilus@simicro.mg.
- **Centre de Plongée** €40–45/dive. €320 for a package deal of training, certification & 6 dives.
- **L'Ancre Bleue** (Hôtel Chez Alain); ☎ 94 415 27; e chez.alain@simicro.mg.
- **Le Grand Bleu** (Mangily); ☎ 032 07 822 12
- **Alizée Dive** (Safari Vezo, Anakao); hotel & diving.

- **L'Atlantide** (Trano Mena, Anakao); e lalbatross_8@yahoo.fr. Caters for most types of diving excursion; certified to do PADI training.
- **Centre Nautique et Touristique** (Ifaty); m 032 02 659 07; e fred.lucas1@caramail.com.
- **Ifaty Beach Club** m 032 02 600 47; e ifatybeachclub@wanadoo.mg.
- **Fifi Diving** (Bamboo Club) m 032 04 004 27; e bamboo.club@wanadoo.mg.
- **Lakana Vezo** ☎ 94 426 20; e lakanavezo@wanadoo.mg.

Sailing 'In places like Ifaty, Mangily and Anakao it is easy to arrange a one-day sailing trip once you arrive. There are plenty of fishermen with sailboats who are willing to take tourists out for sailing, snorkelling, and a lobster picnic on the beach. It usually costs around 15,000Ar per person. It's a very nice, relaxing experience' (CT).

▲ **Location Catamaran** ☎ 94 433 17. Organises catamaran trips to the Barren Islands, Belo-sur-Mer, Andavadoka, Ifaty, Anakao & Itampolo.

☞ **WARNING!** Sea urchins are a problem in the shallows off many of the beaches around Toliara. Be very careful not to touch them and wear some form of foot protection when swimming or snorkelling.

WHAT TO SEE AND DO

In town Toliara has more 'official' sightseeing than most Malagasy towns. Some places are worth the trip, others are not. In town the most interesting place to visit is the small **museum** on Bd Philbert Tsiranana, run by the University of Toliara, which is currently being renovated so should be better than ever. There are some remarkable exhibits, including a Mikea mask (genuine masks are rare in Madagascar) with real human teeth. These are well-displayed and labelled, and include some Sakalava erotic tomb sculptures. Marine enthusiasts should visit the **Musée de la Mer**, also run by the university, on Route de la Porte (☎ 94 41 612). The main attraction here is a preserved coelacanth – the only one now on view in Madagascar. 'Fascinating collection of crustacia and a couple of unexpected oddities. The coelacanth looks rather unwell' (S Bulmer). There is currently no entry fee.

The **market** is lively and interesting. This is one of the best places in all of Madagascar for *lambas* (see box on page 25). You can also find the mohair rugs that are made in Ampanihy, a terrific selection of herbal remedies (*fanafody*) and a wide range of fruit.

Day excursions from Toliara

Arboretum d'Antsokay (*12km from Toliara, just north of the turn to St Augustine on RN7*; m *032 02 600 15; www.antsokayarboretum.org. Entry inc tour 7,000Ar*) This botanical garden should not be missed by anyone with an interest in the flora – and its accompanying fauna – of the southwest. It was established in 1980 by the Swiss-born botanist Hermann Pétignat who died in 2000. His son, Andry, has carried on his work and is equally knowledgeable and helpful. There are nearly 900 species of plant here, 90% of which are endemic to the region. Around 80% have medicinal qualities.

A trained English-speaking guide takes you on a two-hour tour of the 'improved' area (7ha) of the 50ha arboretum where you will see around a hundred

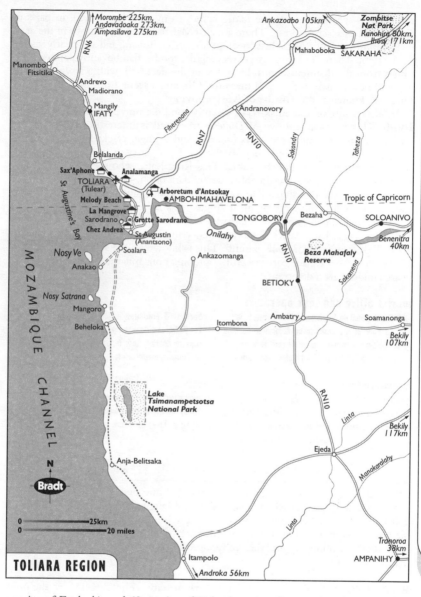

TOLIARA REGION

species of *Euphorbia* and 60 species of *Kalanchoe*, as well as an abundance of birds and reptiles. Indeed, with the spiny forest fast disappearing from the southwest, this is one of the best places in the region for birders. It's a really super place in every way!

Try to arrive as early as possible in the morning to miss the heat of the day. Better still, stay overnight in one of the bungalows. Excellent meals (10,000Ar) are served at the restaurant **Auberge de la Table**.

Tombs The most spectacular tombs within easy reach of the town are those of the Masikoro, a subgroup of the Sakalava. This small tribe is probably of African origin, and there is speculation that the name comes from *mashokora* which, in parts of Tanzania, means 'scrub forest'. There are also Mahafaly and Bara tombs in the area.

The tombs are off RN7, a little over an hour from Toliara, and are clearly visible on the right. There are several large, rectangular tombs, flamboyantly painted with scenes from the distinguished military life of the deceased, with a few mermaids and Rambos thrown in for good measure. Oh, and a scene from the film *Titanic*. These are known as the **Tombs of Andranovory**.

Another tomb, on the outskirts of town beyond the university, is **King Baba's Tomb**. This is set in a grove of *Didierea* trees and is interesting more for the somewhat bizarre funerary objects (an urn and a huge, cracked bell) displayed there and its spiritual significance to the local people (you may only approach barefoot) than for any aesthetic value. This King Baba, who seems to have died about a century ago, was presumably a descendant of one of the Masikoro kings of Baba mentioned in British naval accounts of the 18th century. These kings used to trade with English ships calling at St Augustine's Bay and gave their family and courtiers English names such as the Prince of Wales and the Duke of Cumberland.

On the way to King Baba's Tomb you may visit a little fenced-off park of banyan trees, all descending from one 'parent'. This is known as 'the sacred grove' and in theory would be a place for peaceful contemplation, but the hordes of tourist-aware children are a deterrent.

Tourist office and tour operators

⌨ Office Regional du Tourisme (ORTU) Located on the 2nd floor of the Chambre de Commerce building on Bd Gallieni; www.tulear-tourisme.com. Very helpful & sells an excellent map of RN7 plus many other booklets & brochures.

Les Vedettes d'Anakao See under *Car Hire*. Runs day trips to Anakao, Nosy Ve, Sarondrano & further afield to Tsimanampetsotsa etc.

Adventure tours

Trajectoire BP283, Toliara; ℣/f 94 433 00; e trajectoire@simicro.mg. Run by Bernard Forgeau, who owns a secluded hotel in Madiorano (see page 239). He runs small-group adventure tours throughout remote areas of the southwest, inc the Makay massif by motorbike & the descent of the Mangoky River by canoe.

RESORTS NORTH OF TOLIARA: IFATY AND MANGILY

Ifaty, and Mangily to its north, have now merged into one area offering sand, sea and snorkelling, plus beach bungalows. Ifaty/Mangily lies only 27km north of Toliara, but the road is in poor condition (though improved from the 'terrible' of the last few editions). This is the consequence of deforestation: with all the trees gone, there is nothing to hold the sandy topsoil, and no repair is going to last more than a few months.

☞ *WARNING!* Cell phones often don't work in Ifaty, so hotel radios are the only means of contacting the outside world. There are no money-changing facilities. When selecting a hotel, bear in mind that only those in the north of Ifaty/Mangily have sandy beaches. Mosquitoes are a problem in Ifaty, especially at dusk.

GETTING THERE AND AWAY It takes about two hours by *taxi-brousse*. *Vazaha* should only pay 2,000Ar, the same as the Malagasy in the same vehicle, but you need to be a persistent bargainer to achieve this. Private vehicles can be rented at a much higher cost, and hotels charge as much as 20,000Ar for the transfer.

Taxi-brousses from Ifaty to Toliara leave from opposite Chez Alex twice a day, in the early morning and around 13.00.

WHERE TO STAY/EAT Note that the hotels and beach bungalows are strung out over several kilometres of coastline. The cheaper ones are in the village itself, which has some food stalls selling grilled fish and some vegetables.

Top end €€€€€

⌂ **Dunes Hotel** Under new ownership at the time of writing. Was always good; now promises to be the best hotel in Ifaty.

⌂ **Hôtel Paradisier** (21 bungalows) ✆ 94 429 14; m 032 07 660 09; e paradisier@paradisier.com; www.paradisier.com. The most expensive hotel in Ifaty, with a luxury suite. Owned by Daniel Burkhalter. 'Staff friendly & obliging; bungalows very comfy with huge mozzie net & coil. Breezy veranda & an endless-horizon pool. Food good, too,' comments a reader.

Upper range €€€€

⌂ **Hôtel Lakana Vezo** (10 bungalows & 1 studio) Book through Motel Le Capricorne in Toliara (✆ 94 426 20; e capric@dts.mg). A 1hr's walk south of Dunes Hotel. The **Club Nautique** is probably the best in Ifaty. Powerboat excursions to Nosy Ve & Anakao.

⌂ **Hôtel de la Saline** (10 bungalows) ✆ 94 417 03; m 032 07 531 93; f 94 413 84; e issoufaly@simicro.mg. Facing the salt pans, rather than the beach, this French-managed hotel has a particularly good dining-room, with terrific views over the lagoon & superb food. Half the bungalows have AC.

⌂ **Club Bamboo** (23 bungalows) ✆ 94 427 17;

Mid range €€€

⌂ **Hôtel Vovo Telo** (16 bungalows) ✆ 94 439 69; m 032 02 621 48; e hotelvovotelo@simicro.mg; www.hotel-vovotelo.com. North of Dunes Hotel. Highly praised by all who stay there. Excellent (but fairly expensive) food & local dancing weekly. Also a noisy nightclub.

⌂ **Ifaty Beach Club;** m 032 02 600 47;

Budget €€

⌂ **Chez Alex** m 032 04 098 29. Beachfront bungalows with shared toilet/shower block. Reasonable restaurant. Dive centre. Can organise pirogue trips to the reef for snorkelling. 'Fri & Sat nights are party nights. Either join in or wear earplugs' (C Bulmer).

⌂ **Chez Freddy** ✆ 94 439 01. Bungalows & restaurant. Similar to Chez Alex.

Penny-pincher €

⌂ **Reniala Nature Reserve** (See below) Simple bungalows, with showers, in a prime spot for birders. Meals must be ordered in advance.

Fans, but no AC. B/fast inc. 'There is very nice littoral forest surrounding the hotel with good birdwatching (couas, vangas etc) & there is also good reptile-hunting, particularly after dark — I've found Dumeril's boa, *Paroedura* geckos & chameleons' (Nick Garbutt).

⌂ **Nautilus** (17 bungalows) ✆ 94 418 74; m 032 07 418 74; e nautilus@wanadoo.mg. An upmarket hotel on a nice beach. AC bungalows. Excellent restaurant, especially for seafood. **The Gipsy Club** dive centre is here.

m 032 04 004 27; e bamboo.club@wanadoo.mg; www.bamboo-club.com. Belgian-owned. Good value, though rather hot in summer. Book at the Bamboo shop (opposite Hôtel Central) in Toliara. Small pool; 14ha garden. Very good food, especially the fish. 'We thought the setting was much better than the other places.' **Fifi Diving**, next door, is a good diving club.

⌂ **Mangily Hotel** ✆ 94 421 97; m 032 02 197 65/032 02 554 28; f 94 414 19; e mangilyhotel@hotmail.com. French/Malagasy ownership. Next to Hôtel Vovo Telo. Bungalows right on the beach with shower, toilet & lovely views from the big terrace. Recommended dive centre.

e ifatybeachclub@wanadoo.mg. Restaurant with good but expensive meals. Dive centre. Also offers horseriding.

⌂ **Village Mora Mora** (10 rooms) The Mora Mora was just about the only hotel in Ifaty when I first visited in 1982, so I'm glad to hear that it's reopened.

⌂ **Chez Daniel** e bigorno@malagasy.com. Just north of Vovo Telo. '3 comfortable bungalows with electricity & occasional hot water. The patron is a friendly Frenchman whose Malagasy wife will provide breakfast on the terrace. Laid-back atmosphere. No English spoken' (S Bulmer).

⌂ **Chez Suzie** Family-run place. Squat toilets. Buckets are used for the shower. No electricity. Basic & cheap. Tpl bungalow.

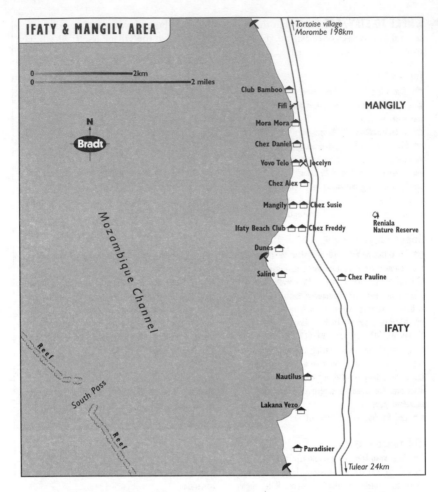

Tortoise village
Morombe 198km

IFATY & MANGILY AREA

0 ———————— 2km
0 ———————————— 2 miles

N

Bradt

Club Bamboo

Fifi

Mora Mora

Chez Daniel

Vovo Telo — Jocelyn

Chez Alex

Mangily — Chez Susie

Ifaty Beach Club — Chez Freddy

Dunes

Saline — Chez Pauline

MANGILY

Reniala
Nature Reserve

IFATY

Mozambique Channel

Reef

South Pass

Reef

Nautilus

Lakana Vezo

Paradisier

Tulear 24km

🏠 **Chez Pauline** On the main road to Toliara. Far from the beach, but cheap & clean.

🏠 **Chez Micheline** Mangily. Simple, thatched bungalows. Very cheap. No electricity (but candle & matches supplied); no running water (bucket showers); outdoor toilet. There's a small restaurant; the owner, Mme Micheline, is a good cook.

Restaurant

✗ **Jocelyn** Mangily (behind Vovo Telo). 'Small & relaxed with a seafood menu that changes daily according to the catch of the day' (SB).

WHAT TO SEE AND DO Diving is one of the main attractions of Ifaty-Mangily, but there are two super inland reserves that even non-naturalists will enjoy.

The Reniala Nature Reserve *(500m north of Mangily;* ☎ *94 417 56;* m *032 02 513 49;* e *reniala-mada@blueline.mg; www.reniala-madagascar.com.* ☺ *summer 08.00–18.00, winter 07.30–17.30. Entry 7,000Ar (inc tour)* This outstanding *Reserve Ornithologique et Botanique* is a small area (45ha) of protected spiny forest offering guided tours for birders, naturalists and interested tourists. An early-morning visit more or less guarantees long-tailed ground roller and subdesert mesite. Guides, who live at the reserve and can be arranged on arrival, are excellent at locating these two species and are also knowledgeable about the area's unique flora. In addition to birds there are many baobabs (including one 13 metres in circumference and said to be 1,000 years old), *Didierea* and *Euphorbia*. A visit here is highly recommended for anyone visiting Ifaty. Silke Rother adds her endorsement: 'A fantastic chance to see spiny forests and baobabs. Do not miss it. Even a day trip from Toliara is worth it, but you should start early in the morning. In the middle of the day and also in the afternoon the animals are hidden.'

There are bungalows and a campsite.

Le Village des Tortues (*94 425 67; www.villagetortues.com. Entry 4,000Ar*) 'Tortoise Village' was set up, with assistance from ANGAP and WWF, by SOPTOM, a French-based international organization for the protection of tortoises and turtles. They currently manage two such tortoise villages (the other is in Senegal).

The Madagascar project, within walking distance of Mangily, aims to protect the two southwestern species: spider tortoise and radiated tortoise. Both are seriously threatened by illegal trade (for pets abroad) and hunting (by locals for food).

Set in spiny forest with smaller baobabs, the guided tour will show you endemic Malagasy tortoises and explain the efforts to conserve them.

MADIORANO

This village a few kilometres north of Ifaty offers a more peaceful setting.

WHERE TO STAY

La Mira (9 rooms) m 032 02 621 44. Spacious & very comfortable. French/Malagasy ownership. 'Great food – always fresh because they do not have *à-la-carte* menus but only a daily one serving the catch of the day' (NR). €€€€

Chez Bernard (5 bungalows) 'Ideal for the discerning independent traveller – no tour groups. Comfortable bungalows near a quiet stretch of beach, but not far from the road. Excellent food; huge portions. Rustic douche facilities. Bernard Forgeau is a very pleasant & interesting Breton bush-hand & explorer. He can be contacted through Trajectoire (see page 236) in Toliara' (Jim Bond). €€€

NORTH TO MOROMBE AND MORONDAVA

A *camion-brousse* runs regularly along the coastal road to Manombo and then to Salary, which is about halfway between Ifaty and Andavadoaka. It's four hours to Manombo and another four to Salary with breathtaking views of the coastline and spiny forest. The onward journey to Andavadoaka and Morombe is possible by pirogue or speedboat.

An alternative is to contact Jean-Louis, a hotel owner, who frequently does the run between Salary and Andavadoaka by speedboat. His prices are high (25,000Ar pp) for the rather wet and crowded four-hour ride, but he has the monopoly. There are flights between Toliara and Morondava via Morombe.

Just south of Salary is **Tsiandamba**, where there's accommodation at **Chez Odilon** (12,000Ar).

SALARY A rather nondescript Vezo fishing town along a beautiful coastline with difficult access. It can be reached by boat or 4x4 from Ifaty. The town has no real centre, but is split up into Salary Avaratra (north) and Salary Atsimo (south). Information from Milo Mayr.

Where to stay/eat

🏠 **Salary Bay** (10 bungalows) Book at Hôtel Cotsoyannis, Fianar (✆ 75 514 86; f 75 505 68); e salarybay@malagasy.com; www.salarybay.com. An upmarket set of comfortable, thatched bungalows in a good beach location. Diving; snorkelling; pirogue & motorboat excursions; walks to Mikea forest. €€€€

🏠 **Chez Francesco** e salaryfrancesco@yahoo.it. Located in Salary Avaratra. Francesco is an ebullient Italian who has lived in the area for many years. Bungalows with bucket shower & squat toilets. The Italian-style food is reportedly very good. €€€

🏠 **Chez Jean-Louis** 2 sets of basic bungalows in Salary Atsimo. The first is grouped around the restaurant & is quite lively. Bucket showers & squat toilets. 'The bungalow we rented had a shared wall with Jean-Louis's pigsty, adding a rather delicate smell.' The second group of bungalows is more secluded & quieter. Food cheap, but poor quality; beer prices high. €

🏠 **Hôtel Takaliko** Reasonably priced bungalows. €

THE ONILAHY REGION

Two correspondents have raved about this unspoiled area northeast of Toliara. Valerie Middleton writes: 'By turning right some 17km from Toliara on RN7 it is possible to reach the Onilahy River at a point where virtually every salad and vegetable crop known is grown on the rich sediments. If the rough road is followed eastwards the attractively situated village of Tolikisy is reached (not 'Tokilisy' as shown on maps). A meeting with the village *président* may elicit an invitation to camp up the delightful Atsodroka Valley at the entrance to the village. Small cliffs and exotic trees like moringa and banyans dominate the hillsides. The many ring-tailed lemurs may also keep you awake at night with their continuous screaming! From the head of the valley a local guide, again with the good grace of the *président*, can take you on a 7km trip onto the plateau to visit the chasm of Ankikiky Velo. This is well worth the effort and measures around 80m diameter and 60m deep. A further 15 minutes away is the new village of Ankikymaty where another cave of impressive dimensions can be descended to nearly 90m in an enormous passage. This Ankikiky Plateau region was, until a couple of years ago, rich in forest cover and wildlife. There is now an exodus of people from Toliara wanting to cultivate this very poor and stony land. The forest now remains good only at the edge of the plateau and on the steep riverside slopes.

'Continuing upriver from Tolikisy the scenery becomes quite dramatic until, about 2km before Ifanato, a crystal-clear stream gushes beneath the road. There is a place to park here and by following the footpath on the left for 50m a superb flat campsite can be found above the first of the "Seven Lakes". These lakes are of a beautiful blue colour and are connected by yellow to orange tufa (a form of calcite) cascades and waterfalls extending for over 700m. This tufa is relatively soft and it is best to try to avoid walking on it where possible. Apart from the first lake upon which there is a *fady*, swimming can be done in most of them. The surrounding gallery forest is superb. There are more lakes further upstream but these are very difficult to get to and are not so beautiful. It is, however, possible to follow a zebu trail into the mountains where there is yet another vertical shaft known as Ankikiky lava. Ifanato, a couple of kilometres further on, has a couple of reasonable restaurants including one run by a Frenchman, but to follow the road further into Tongobory is extremely difficult, if not currently impassable. The "Sept Lacs" were apparently a very popular destination in the French colonial period.'

BEACH RESORTS SOUTH OF TOLIARA

The resorts south of Toliara now almost match Ifaty for comfort and some people prefer them because the beaches are better.

ST AUGUSTINE'S BAY (BAIE ST AUGUSTIN) This is an area of history and natural wonders, including dramatic sand dunes, and a cave swimming pool. It was the site of an ill-fated British colony, abandoned in 1646, and later frequented by pirates. St Augustine's Bay was mentioned by Daniel Defoe in *The King of Pirates*.

Getting there The hotels in the region will arrange transfers from Toliara, but there is a regular *taxi-brousse* to Sarodrano, leaving around midday from the main *taxi-brousse* station in Toliara. It costs 3,000Ar and returns early the following morning.

Where to stay

🏠 **Hôtel Melody Beach** (15 bungalows) m 032 02 167 57; e moukar@wanadoo.mg. Overlooking a sandy beach with good swimming, it is just 5km from the main road so is more easily accessible by public transport than St Augustine's Bay itself or Anakao. It is easy enough to walk in providing you have good footwear for the rough, rocky road. €€–€€€

🏠 **La Mangrove** (10 bungalows) ✆ 94 415 27; e c.alain@wanadoo.mg; www.chez-alain.net. Located 8km from RN7 (the turn-off is signposted). Under the same ownership as Chez Alain in Toliara. There's no beach, but a rocky access to the sea for swimming. This is a diving centre & boat excursions to Nosy Ve & Anakao can be arranged. Bookings & transfers (8,000Ar each way) through Chez Alain. €€€

🏠 **Chez Andrea** An Italian-owned hotel near Sarodrano. Thoughtfully designed, very friendly, excellent food & service. Book through Boogie Pilgrim in Tana. €€€

Excursions

Grotte Sarodrano Under a rocky overhang is a deep pool of clear blue water. Swimmers will find the top layer of water warm is only mildly salty, while the cooler lower layer is saline. Fresh water flows from the mountain into the pool, on top of the warmer, heavier layer of saltwater from the sea. Grotte Sarodrano is a 4km walk south from La Mangrove hotel (along an easy road). Kids with pirogues hang around there to take you back. Well worth it!

ANAKAO AND REGION

ANAKAO Anakao is a pretty little Vezo fishing village with colourful boats drawn up on the sands. Several new hotels, catering for all budgets, have opened in recent years so it now competes with Ifaty for tourists looking for a beach with snorkelling and some birdwatching within reach of Toliara. It has several advantages over its rival: isolation (Anakao is accessible only by boat or a very rough track), a much better beach, and the nearby island of Nosy Ve which has fine white sand and the world's southernmost breeding colony of red-tailed tropic birds (undiscovered until 1980).

Getting there Anakao is accessible from Toliara via a 56km dirt road, or by boat. All the hotels provide a transfer service, either by sea or a combination of road and sea.

For independent travellers, finding an affordable transfer is quite a challenge. Expect to pay about 40,000Ar, even for a pirogue. Because of the varying tides and wind, this journey usually involves a vehicle trip as well as the boat ride.

🏠 **Where to stay** Note that fresh water is a problem in Anakao – there is not enough of it, and only two hotels, the Prince Anakao and Club Resort Anakao have running water – but this doesn't always run.

🏠 **Club Resort Anakao** (6 bungalows) ✆ 22 336 28; e mda@wanadoo.mg; www.anakaoclubresort.com. Sophie & Peter Joudier warmly recommend this new 'boutique' hotel. 'It's run by a charming Italian called Valter who designed the hotel to perfection. It's expensive but well worth it;

one of the nicest places I've ever stayed in. Beautiful bungalows that would seem luxurious in any upmarket location, impeccable service, delicious food & a relaxed & peaceful atmosphere. Valter is a watersports enthusiast & will organise diving excursions & other activities.' Credit cards not accepted. *Kayaking 34,000Ar; sailing 84,000Ar; surfing 140,000Ar; fishing 140,000Ar; trips to Nosy Ve & Nosy Satrana 56,000Ar; trips to mangrove 84,000Ar.* €€€€€

⌂ **Prince Anakao** (27 bungalows) ✆ 94 439 57; e anakao@simicro.mg. One of only 2 hotels in Anakao able to take groups. Comfortable bungalows but no mosquito nets – mozzies are a problem here. No hot water. Good food. €€€€

⌂ **Bivouac Lalandaka/Chez Olivier** (6 bungalows) m 032 04 341 42 (Toliara)/032 02 275 20 (Anakao). A popular place, though recent reports are not so favourable, loud music being one problem. Bungalows have bucket showers (water can be heated on request) & shared toilets. €€€€

⌂ **Safari Vezo** (23 bungalows) ✆/f 94 413 81; m 032 02 638 87; e safarivezo@netclub.mg. For years this was the only hotel in Anakao & it has stood the test of time. Near the village so child beggars can be a problem. There is a good boutique & the Club Nautique is an excellent diving centre. *Whale-watching 84,000Ar; snorkelling at Nosy Ve 34,000Ar; trips to Nosy Ve, Nosy Satrana & mangrove 56,000Ar.* €€€

⌂ **Hôtel La Réserve** (6 bungalows) m 032 02 141 55; e quad@dts.mg. A few kilometres south of the village, so peaceful. Simple bungalows with en-suite shower (when there's water) & toilet, but not partitioned off from the room. French-run; excellent food, though very slow service. *Whale-watching 60,000Ar; fishing 60,000–100,000Ar.* €€€

⌂ **Longo Vezo** ✆/f 94 437 64; m 032 02 631 23; e longovezo@simicro.mg. A good dive centre & comfortable bungalows. *Whale-watching 50,000Ar; surfing 20,000Ar; trips to Nosy Ve 20,000Ar (2 people); trips to Nosy Satrana 40,000Ar (3 people).* €€€

⌂ **Chez Solange & Christophe** (3 rooms) ✆ 94 445 07; m 032 04 180 93; e lacombe-christian@voila.fr. A very small but cosy hotel recommended by Kim Loohuis. These bungalows are the closest to the beach in Anakao. No restaurant, but food can be delivered from Mme Coco or Chez Emile. Patron Fransisco is very nice & can arrange pirogue trips to Nosy Ve (16,000Ar inc lunch & snorkling gear). €€€

⌂ **Trano Mena/Chez Stoick** (6 bungalows) Run by Stoick, a mechanic from Taolagnaro. Each bungalow has a bucket shower. Communal squat toilet. Bar & terraced eating area. The beach is clean here. €–€€

⌂ **Chez Emile** (6 bungalows) Close to the village. Bucket showers & shared squat toilet. Very friendly. Bar popular with the locals. Shop sells snacks & a few postcards. €

✖ **Where to eat** James Brehaut reports: 'If you don't eat seafood, you're going to have a problem in Anakao. If you want to cut costs it is possible to buy fish and seafood from the local trading centre on the beach south of the market. We paid a small amount to our hotel to cook using their facilities. Langouste was out of season when we were in Anakao so most restaurants did not serve it. It was available though at some less reputable places and a fair number of tourists were eating it. This is obviously a very irresponsible attitude.'

Le Prince and **Safari Vezo** serve good food, but both have a fixed menu. **Chez Emile** is good and has a few non-seafood options, but service can be exceedingly slow. **Trano Mena** serves food if you book in advance. **Chez Mme Coco** (just north of Chez Emile) has good food and nice ambience. 'Her prawns with garlic and curry are recommended' (NF).

What to see and do

Tombs, wildlife and Aepyornis eggshells A day spent exploring on foot is rewarding. Take the track behind the village heading south. On the outskirts of Anakao you will find some interesting tombs – one has a satellite dish on the roof to provide eternal entertainment for the ancestors – and will then come to a small peninsula. This is being developed as an extension of Anakao, but it is still possible to find fragments of subfossil eggshell from the long-extinct *Aepyornis* (elephant bird). Please keep your collecting instincts under control so that others

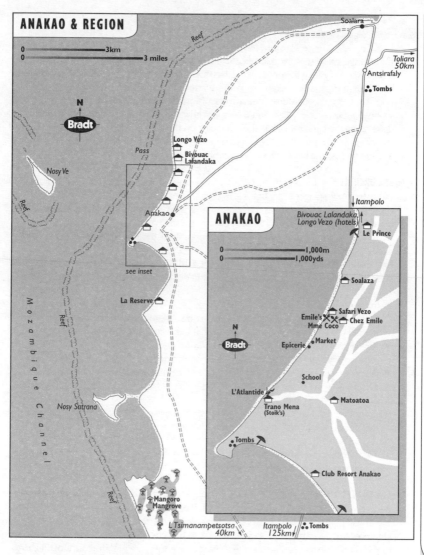

ANAKAO & REGION

0 ————— 3km
0 ————— 3 miles

N

Bradt

Soalara

Reef

Toliara
50km

Antsirafaly

Tombs

Longo Vezo

Pass

**Bivouac
Lalandaka**

Nosy Ve

↓ Itampolo

Anakao

see inset

La Reserve

M
o
z
a
m
b
i
q
u
e

C
h
a
n
n
e
l

Reef

Nosy Satrana

Reef

Mangoro
Mangrove

L Tsimanampetsotsa
40km

Itampolo
125km

Tombs

ANAKAO

Bivouac Lalandaka,
Longo Vezo (hotels)

0 ————— 1,000m
0 ————— 1,000yds

N

Bradt

Le Prince

Soalaza

Safari Vezo

Emile's
Mme Coco

Chez Emile

Epicerie **Market**

School

L'Atlantide

Matoatoa

Trano Mena
(Stoik's)

Tombs

Club Resort Anakao

can enjoy this extraordinary glimpse of the past. It is illegal to take these eggshells out of the country.

Diving With dead coral reducing the attraction of shallow reef for snorkellers, the emphasis has switched to diving. The best months for diving are between April and December when the water is clear of sediment from the Onilahy river. The highlight, for some, is diving with whales (between June and October).

NOSY VE AND NOSY SATRANA Nosy Ve (the name means 'is there an island?'!) lies 4km west of Anakao and is a sacred site for the Vezo people. It has a long history of European domination: the first landing was by a Dutchman in 1595, and Nosy Ve was officially taken over by the French in 1888 before their conquest of the mainland, although it is hard to see why: it is a flat, scrub-covered little island.

Rob Conway & Jane Wilson-Howarth

One of the main reasons that people enjoy snorkelling and diving is the contact with marine species within their natural habitats, and Madagascar has one of the most beautiful and diverse marine environments in the western Indian Ocean. But there is a negative side – not all these creatures are harmless. Most injuries from marine creatures are due to inexperienced snorkellers and divers, unfamiliarity with the local environment, or self defence on the part of the animal. Depending on the type of injury, the first aid treatment will differ. Below are some of the marine nasties that you may encounter in Madagascar and the first aid measures should you get hurt.

SEA URCHINS The most common injury to swimmers and snorkellers is from sea urchins, often from stepping on an urchin or part of one. Such injuries are painful but not dangerous. Treat by washing the wound and then remove as many of the spines as possible with tweezers or, if little bits remain in your sole and you have nothing else, use a toothpick or similar; the wound will not heal until all the bits are out.

RAY, SCORPIONFISH, LIONFISH AND STONEFISH STINGS Symptoms include immediate pain, laceration, nausea, vomiting, shock, swelling and occasionally collapse. First-aid treatment:

* Immerse wound in non-scalding hot water (43–45°C) for 30–90mins. The stung body part will be so painful that you won't be able to tell whether the water is too hot, so use a non-stung hand to check that the water isn't likely to scald.
* Repeat the immersion if pain recurs; it may be necessary to top up the water. But remove affected limb from the water before doing so.
* Remove any visible pieces of the stinger and irrigate vigorously with fresh water.
* Once the worst of the pain has subsided try to find someone to clean and dress the wound.
* Over the next several days look out for spreading redness, throbbing and/or fever; these symptoms imply infection which will need antibiotic treatment.

This situation is one where good first aid is probably going to be better for the patient than anything that will be offered by doctors.

SEA SNAKES The beautiful *Pelamis platurus* spends most of its life out at sea but they are occasionally encountered around the coasts of Madagascar. Sea snake venom is some of the most potent known to man. Fortunately for us they are usually timid, sluggish creatures that avoid humans. You are unlikely to be bitten unless you tease or handle one, or if you go close to a mating bundle of sea snakes – they resent disturbance of their orgy. If you are unfortunate enough to be bitten by a sea snake the following symptoms may occur: stiffness and aching, respiratory distress, difficulty swallowing or speaking, or weakness. First aid treatment:

What makes Nosy Ve special to modern-day invaders is the tranquillity of its white, shell-strewn beach, the snorkelling on its fringing reef, and the breeding colony of red-tailed tropic-birds. They breed year-round so you can be sure of seeing them at their nest sites under bushes at the southern end of the island, as well as flying overhead – a thrilling sight.

Camping is not allowed on the island, and visits are dependent for their success on wind and tide (strong wind makes snorkelling difficult; high tide is equally unrewarding for snorkellers and beachcombers). For this reason visits with Vezo

- Apply pressure bandage and immobilise limb.
- Seek medical attention.
- *Do not* use suction technique.

CONE SHELLS Cone shells are beautiful shells that contain a dart-like projection at the front. Do not touch as they can deliver a painful and potentially deadly sting. If stung:

- Apply pressure bandage and immobilise limb.
- Seek medical attention.

STINGS FROM FIRE CORAL, ANEMONE, HYDROID OR JELLYFISH Anemones are beautiful creatures that live amongst the coral and have stinging tentacles. Often small clown fish will live amongst these tentacles, protected by a mucous layer on their skin. Brushing against any coral will give a nasty abrasion which is inflamed and slow to heal. Fire coral looks like coral, but on closer examination there are fine stinging cells. Hydroids are small marine creatures, looking like plants, that again have stinging cells on their outer surface. Jellyfish are commonly encountered whilst diving or swimming in tropical waters and often do not sting; they may cause minor skin irritation.

If stung by any of these:

- Rinse with seawater. *Do not* use freshwater.
- If the stinger was a box jellyfish there will be characteristic cross-hatched tentacle-prints on the skin surface and irrigation with vinegar will inactivate the stingers. Vinegar actually makes things worse if the jellyfish is a Portuguese man-of-war but most stings are mild and the following treatments suffice.
- Shave off area with credit card to remove stinging cells, being very careful not to sting yourself.
- Apply hydrocortisone cream to reduce inflammation.
- If collapse occurs, offer cardio-pulmonary resuscitation since the severe effects of the venom fade quite quickly. Next get medical help as soon as you can.

BITES Most marine animals are not interested in human beings. The majority of bites are in self defence. The primary concern for the first-aider is to control bleeding and minimise the risk of infection. Sharks and moray eels are the two animals that could attack swimmers or divers on the reef, as well as titan triggerfish during the nesting season; the titan is up to 75cm long and will defend her nest ferociously.

- Control bleeding by applying firm bandages or strips of cloth.
- Clean wound and flood with lots of water to minimise infection.
- Seek medical advice.

fishermen using pirogues, which can land at low tide, are often more successful than those using large motorboats. With little natural shade on the island, make sure your boatman erects a sail on the beach to provide respite from the burning sun.

The island is illegally exploited by the local Vezo people but they do not harm the tropic-birds, the result of a fady originating in a great fire which destroyed much of the island's vegetation – except for the tropic-bird colony and the ancestors' tombs. Another (fortunate) fady is against defecating on the beach (unlike the main beach at Anakao where it is common practice). A boy angered an ancestor and went missing for doing just that. Tourists should also respect the ancestors and keep away from the tombs.

James Brehaut loved Nosy Ve: 'This island had one of the best beaches I've ever seen on the protected shore nearest to the mainland. A walk around the island takes about an hour and is beautiful. We paid 10,000Ar each for the return pirogue transfer from Anakao, including lunch which was caught in the sea just offshore from Nozy Ve whilst we snorkelled from the boat. You also have to pay 2,000Ar tax to visit the island. We used a pirogue 'office,' which doubles as a small restaurant, on the beach near the market. Other operators asked for 15,000Ar per person.' Note that there are plans to establish a much-needed marine protected area around Nosy Ve so fishing will be prohibited.

Nearby Nosy Satrana is a small peaceful island with some ancient tamarind trees. It offers excellent diving and good snorkelling, but no tropic-birds.

NAMAKIA

Mark Fenn writes: 'In 2005, a representative of WWF purchased a small parcel of coastal spiny forest and mangrove habitat 20km south of Toliara, adjacent to the hamlet of Namakia, and donated it to the Toliara Scout Association. Camp Namakia is also open to tourists. The campsite has water and simple toilet/shower facilities, and there are plans to build simple bungalows in 2008. It is a beautiful site that is easily accessible from Toliara by *taxi-brousse* and from the fishing village of Ankilibe, 2km to the north along the beach. This is a lovely natural area with a diversity of ecosystems and a beautiful beach. Aside from serving scouting groups across Madagascar, the camp uses proceeds to develop local community education programmes on natural resources conservation and adult literacy. Visitors to the camp can hike, swim, rent bicycles, or learn how to travel in a local dugout canoe. For more information see www.campnamakia.org.

'Adjacent to the camp is Resto Namakia, a small restaurant established by Simone Petignat (co-founder of the Arboretum d'Antsokay and Auberge de la Table). This provides simple yet great meals, snacks and cold drinks at a reasonable price, and is just a few steps off the beach. For those seeking a simple alternative to the tourist sites of Anakao and Ifaty, and with a wish to get to know the locals a little better, Camp Namakia is worth a visit.'

BEHELOKA

This small town currently acts as the dormitory for Tsimanampetsotsa National Park, and for rugged travellers making their way south along the almost impassable road to Itampolo.

The beaches are good, with clear water – although too shallow for proper swimming.

Note: There is no fresh water in Beheloka (other than the bottled water for sale), so coffee and tea have a salty flavour.

 WHERE TO STAY

🏠 **La Canne à Sucre/Chez Barnard** Beheloka; ✆ 94 437 21; m 032 04 624 09. Bookings can be made in Toliara through Chez Alain or Les Vedettes d'Anakao. Barnard is a friendly Frenchman whose little hotel sleeps 16. Clean & comfortable. Rooms considerably cheaper than the 4 bungalows. Good food. €€€

🏠 **Hôtel Finaritra** (6 rooms) Beheloka. Located on the beach. No electricity; outdoor latrine. Small restaurant with simple food. Very cheap. €

LAKE TSIMANAMPETSOTSA NATIONAL PARK

The large, shallow soda lake (pronounced tsimanampetsoots) is the focal point for this terrific national park of 45,604ha which was set up in 1999. The large calcareous (limestone) plateau here has some of the most striking spiny forest vegetation in Madagascar, much of it locally endemic. There are two quite extraordinary baobabs and also a magnificent banyan tree with its aerial roots hugging the side of a cliff face to find purchase in the soil some 20 metres below.

The park sits on a large underground aquifer that runs north, evidenced by the numerous sinkholes and caves. The lake is renowned for its waterfowl, notably flamingoes, and other rare endemic birds including the Madagascar plover (*Charadrius thoracicus*), but the emblem of the park is the very rare Grandidier's mongoose (*Galidictis grandidieri*).

The national park lies about 40km south of Anakao, down a very bad road, so is only just manageable as a day trip. To see the park properly you need to be pretty fit to cope with the heat, and carry enough water – at least two litres. Bring water-purifying tablets so you can top up from the well near the campsite. The lake, with its greater and lesser flamingoes, is starkly beautiful, but the dry forest is interesting at every step. You will be taken to Mitoho Cave (a sacred site) where a rare endemic species of blind fish, *Typhleotris madagascariensis*, is easily seen.

Under a generous grant from the German Development Bank (KfW), WWF and ANGAP have expanded the park south to the Linta River and subsequently created numerous community development programmes and are piloting a co-governance programme for the park.

The good news for visitors is that the grant has also provided for the development of several trail systems and camping areas, as well as providing finance for the construction of an interpretive centre and some tourist bungalows. These are scheduled for 2008.

The usual park fee must be paid at the ANGAP office a couple of kilometres from the park entrance. You pick up your guide here as well.

GETTING THERE AND AWAY Tsimanampetsotsa is not accessible by public transport. You need your own vehicle or to sign up for a tour from one of the hotels in Anakao, such as Trano Mena, (60,000Ar/day pp, min 2 people). Chez Alain also organises tours as does Les Vedettes d'Anakao in Toliara.

 WHERE TO STAY At present there are two camping areas in the reserve (water, but no other facilities) which are ideal for birders and other naturalists who want to see this extraordinary place when it's still cool enough to enjoy the flora and fauna at leisure. More are planned.

Meanwhile, if you don't want to camp, there's accommodation to be found in Beheloka (an hour's drive away), Ambola, or – at a stretch – Itampolo.

CONTINUING SOUTH

The far south is gradually being developed and you can drive on a barely motorable, sandy road until you join RN10, which links Toliara with Taolagnaro. The beaches is this region are littered with fragments of Aepyornis eggshell. Intrepid drivers with a 4x4 can continue to the very tip of Madagascar, Cap Sainte Marie (see page 252).

ITAMPOLO This small town, about 180km south of Toliara, is said by some to have the most beautiful beach in Madagascar, with pinkish-coloured sand. 'An interesting excursion can be made to a cenote (a vertical-sided collapsed doline – or sinkhole – floored by a lake whose surface is level with the local water table). This is situated barely 3km south of Itampalo and is just 50m east of the road. It is locally known as Vintana and measures around 35m in diameter and is 5m to the water surface at its lowest point. The water, of course, is bottomless!' (VM).

Where to stay

Gîte d'Etape 'Sud Sud' (4 bungalows & 3 rooms) Under same ownership as Chez Alain (✆ 94 415 27; e c.alain@wanadoo.mg; www.chez.com/photovoyage/itampolo.html). Simple, comfortable bungalows & rooms above restaurant (good food). Camping permitted. €€€

Chez Nany (1 bungalow & camping) Located 1–2km northwest of the village behind the dunes. 'There's a tiny, hard-to-see sign marking the opening in the dune vegetation, but don't count on it catching your eye.' Ask directions at the mayor's office or health clinic. 'They have 1 dbl bungalow & 4 little pop-up trailers. No electricity; outdoor latrine & bucket shower (a well provides fresh water). There is a small restaurant where you can order simple food in advance. The ocean is 75m away; the sand is soft, white & clean. Good swimming as the water isn't rough. It's a quiet place & I had the most enjoyable stay' (CT). Bill Love adds: 'It's a great place to see snail-shell spiders (Olios coenobita) in snail shells hanging in bushes around camp.' €

BEZA-MAHAFALY SPECIAL RESERVE

This reserve was the model for the WWF's integrated conservation and development efforts, and is now run by ANGAP and the University of Antananarivo. It was established at the request of local people who volunteered to give up using part of the forest, in return for help with a variety of social and agricultural projects such as schools and irrigation channels. It has recently been expanded from about 500ha to over 4,000ha as part of The Durban Vision.

The reserve protects two distinct types of forest: spiny forest and gallery (riverine) forest, with habituated ring-tailed lemurs and sifakas much in evidence. In this it mirrors Berenty, but there the comparison ends. In Beza-Mahafaly, researchers and the local Malagasy come first but visitors with a serious interest in natural history will find this a hugely rewarding place. In addition to lemurs, the forest has four species of tenrec including the rare large-eared one, Geogale aurita, three species of carnivores including the fossa, and lots of reptiles. About 90 species of birds have been recorded.

Dana Whitelaw, who spent a year there studying ring-tailed lemurs, can hardly contain her enthusiasm: 'Come here to enjoy the lemurs trooping into camp in the morning, and the well-cut trails in the reserve just across the road from your tent. Walk to the canyon, the sacred forest and visit a village. Hire the local cook and have someone (very inexpensively) clean your travel-worn clothes. Request a chicken, local tomatoes and some fruit to be brought from the local villages. These simple acts help ensure the economic viability of the reserve and keep money in the local people's pockets proving the value of this special reserve.

'Researchers, many from the University of Colorado at Boulder, come from about May till August, but at other times you will encounter the hapless, lonely graduate student who would love to share a meal, discuss their project and share their enthusiasm for the lemurs, birds, plants or insects they have chosen to study. Please say hi and make yourself at home on the cosy front porch of the research house/dining room.'

GETTING THERE Well, there had to be a downside! Beza-Mahafaly is 35km north of Betioky along a terrible – but very scenic – road. To get there you need a 4x4, motorbike, bicycle (maybe) or zebu cart. There are now signs directing you to the reserve so finding your way is no longer a challenge although Nina French, who tried to cycle there in 2006 says: 'There are lots of misleading side tracks at the beginning and stretches of killing sand.' She and Bill gave up and hitched a ride.

Dana reports that she met two groups of tourists who hired zebu carts from Betioky 'and absolutely loved their trip down. I used zebu carts to go back and forth to market day in Betioky and can honestly say it was one of my most memorable experiences in Madagascar. We were asked to leave in the middle of the night to make sure the zebu didn't overheat. A moonlit/starlit ride through the bush is enchanting! It takes about six hours. Take a cushion.

'Andry, the director of the reserve, lives in the house (white with red trim) across the street from the gas station and just past the main liquor store on the main drag in Betioky. He and his wife can help you get to Beza with a zebu cart or might know of a car coming through that you could squeeze into. Beza is worth the effort to get to!'

⛺ CAMPSITES The campsites are situated under groves of tamarinds which are the sleeping trees for the friendly groups of ring-tailed lemurs and Verreaux's sifakas. If you don't have your own tent, you can hire one or stay in a local house. There is water from a well for showers and to drink (but bring purifying tablets or a filter). Toilet facilities are simple but clean. Camping costs 10,000Ar per night.

WHAT TO SEE There are well-marked trails in the gallery forest directly across the road from the research camp, with habituated ring-tail and sifaka groups. The spiny forest is worth the hike and heat (but go early). You don't always need a guide as the trails are colour-coded and with the river and road bordering the reserve you can't get lost, but you'll see more if you hire a guide (5,000Ar a day). Elahavelo, Edabo and Enafa are local men (living in nearby villages) who are employed at the reserve to conduct censuses of the wildlife and phenology of all the plants – they have their finger on the pulse of this reserve and are very knowledgeable. Night hikes are not to be missed. Lepilemurs and mouse lemurs abound and their vocalizations are the last sound you'll hear as you drift to sleep under the tamarinds.

To fully appreciate Beza you need to stay a few days. Then there is time to visit Ehazoara Canyon, a 3km (1½hr) hike from the campsite which takes you through a local Mahafaly village. There is also a lovely sacred banyan forest 30 minutes' walk along the river to the northeast of the reserve, protected by a local fady. Several sifaka and ring-tailed lemur groups live here, although it is in the midst of agricultural fields.

THE ROAD TO TAOLAGNARO (FORT DAUPHIN)

A *taxi-brousse* from Toliara to Taolagnaro takes two to three days. It's a shame to pass straight through such an exciting area, however. Much more interesting is to rent a vehicle and driver, or to do the trip by *taxi-brousse* in stages, staying at Betioky, Ampanihy and Beloha or Ambovombe, or – most interesting of all – by a combination of walking and whatever transport comes along, taking pot luck on where you'll spend the night.

BEZAHA A side trip to this town, which lies east of the road to Betioky, is worth it if you have your own vehicle: 'A road full of botanical and scenic wonders' and there are some good Mahafaly tombs along the road.

BETIOKY Betioky is about four hours from Toliara by 4x4 (7–8hrs by *taxi-brousse*; 10,000Ar) on a very poor road. The market is on Tuesday.

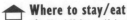

Where to stay/eat

🏠 **Hôtel Mahasoa** (4 bungalows & 4 rooms)
Thatched bungalows with outside toilet & shower.
Rooms are priced higher than bungalows because
the indoor toilets/showers are not as smelly! €
✗ **Mahafaly** A small *hotely* which sells low-priced
gasy food.

BETIOKY TO AMPANIHY Beyond Bekioky the bad road gets considerably worse. Some 20km south of Betioky is the small village of Ambatry. Next comes Ejeda, about 2½ hours from Betioky on a reasonable dirt road. Ejeda to Ampanihy takes about five hours by truck on a very bad, rocky road. All along this road you should see Mahafaly tombs.

AMPANIHY The name means 'the place of bats', but it is now the place of the goats. The weaving of mohair carpets was a thriving business in the 1970s and 1980s but the careless cross-breeding of the angora goats reduced the quality of the wool until the industry collapsed. In 1994 Frenchman Eric Mallet built a new carpet factory and trained local women to work the looms. The wool, however, was imported from France and New Zealand. Thanks to EU funding, 1999 saw the first pure-bred angora goats born in Ampanihy for decades and the industry seems set for a good future. These rugs are very beautiful, incorporating traditional Mahafaly motifs. Only natural colours and vegetable dyes are used. Visit Le Tapis Malagache (m *032 07 767 16;* e *erictapismohair@hotmail.com*) for the best rugs. The cost in 2006 was around 100,000Ar. Weavers can make rugs according to your specifications, provided you order a few days ahead.

🏠 **Where to stay** Hôtel Angora provides comfortable accommodation, and camping is allowed in the garden.

AMPANIHY TO AMBOVOMBE After Ampanihy you enter Antandroy country and will understand why their name means 'people of the thorns' (Androy means 'land of the thorns'). The road deteriorates (if you thought that possible) as you make your way to Tranoroa (the name means 'two houses') in about five hours. This is one of the main weaving towns in the south. Another five hours and you approach Beloha on an improving road (much favoured by tortoises, which thrive in the area since it is fady to eat them) and with tombs all around.

If you stop in Beloha, visit the Catholic church with its beautiful stained glass made by a local craftsman. This is also the departure point for the coastal village of Lavanono.

Between Beloha and Tsiombe is the most interesting stretch of the entire journey. There are baobabs, tortoises and tombs about 33km before Tsiombe. Two roads lead from this village to Faux Cap (Betanty) and Cap Sainte Marie.

If you are travelling by *taxi-brousse* or 4x4, you might want to stop overnight in Tsiombe where there is a decent hotel/restaurant with a small bar and dining area.

🏠 **Paradis du Sud** (4 bungalows & 4 rooms) ⟍
92 727 28. A collection of rooms & bungalows
located on the main road near the church.
Communal bathroom. Some rooms have mosquito
nets. They can prepare meals on request, & the
food is delicious. €

Just beyond Tsiombe are some interesting tombs. Then it is 67km to Ambovombe. The next place you come to is **Ambondro**, the main centre for weaving in the region. Though much of the cloth is now being made in surrounding villages and brought into the town to sell, you can still purchase woven cloth directly from the makers. Resident Peace Corps volunteer Joe Block also recommends, 'If you are passing through on a Saturday, stop and check out the impressive zebu market.' You are now not far from Ambovombe and the main tourist beat.

AMBOVOMBE TO AMBOASARY AND TAOLAGNARO Meaning 'place of many wells', Ambovombe is a bustling town in the heart of Androy country. It holds a colourful Monday market and hosts the annual Androy music festival, which showcases a wonderful mix of local and regional musicians. It is a free, three-day event held around the end of October.

At this point many travellers prefer to press on to Taolagnaro but there are several hotel-restaurants located on the main street if you decide to stay the night.

 🏠 **L'Oasis** (8 rooms) ↘ 92 700 16. A favourite among travellers; clean, bright atmosphere. Rooms with communal balcony facing the street & good Malagasy food. No running water; communal shower & toilet. Electricity outlets. €€

🏠 **Ezaka Magnevarova** (formerly the Relais des Androy) (13 rooms) Basic rooms, located on the main street in town. No running water; communal

bathroom. Small restaurant. €

🏠 **Jo's Hôtel-Restaurant** (4 rooms & 2 bungalows) ↘ 92 704 75; m 032 07 989 72. The first hotel you come to as you approach Ambovombe from the west. Bungalows have showers; rooms have shared facilities. Friendly staff. Restaurant often packed in the evenings with locals; serves traditional Malagasy fare. No running water. €

About 35km from Ambovombe is Ambosoary, the town that marks the turn-off to Berenty. If you plan to drop in to Berenty, thus saving the very high transfer fee from Taolagnaro, think again. Transport from Taolagnaro is part of the package and you may not be admitted on your own (although with your own car this is less of a problem). From Amboasary to Taolagnaro takes less than two hours on a paved road.

AMBOASARY This thriving town with a busy marketplace makes a worthwhile stop if you are visiting Lake Anony or Amboasary Sud.

Where to stay/eat

🏠 **Discovery Hotel** (11 bungalows) Quietly tucked away from the town centre, on the south side.

Café/restaurant. Some of the bungalows are en suite. €€€

There are lots of small *hotely*s along the main stretch of road through town where you can eat a quick lunch.

THE FAR SOUTH

Adventurous travellers are increasingly seeking out the extreme southwest which is, as yet, relatively untouched by tourism. The coastal village of Lavanono has been recommended by several tough travellers, and the whole area is worth investigating.

This is a good area to see humpback whales; between September and November they can be observed quite close to shore with their calves.

LAVANONO The 'road' to this lovely place runs from Beloha via Tranovaho. Access is difficult without your own 4x4, but worth the effort.

Where to stay

 🏠 **Chez Gigi** Rupert Parker writes: 'Gigi is from Réunion but all profits are ploughed back into the village. It's a very beautiful spot: nicely constructed,

right by the sea with good surfing close by. The bungalows are simple but cosy & food is good — lobster is a mainstay. Prices are reasonable'.

CAP SAINTE MARIE Cap Sainte Marie is the southernmost tip of Madagascar and is as spectacular as its neighbours, with high sandstone cliffs and dwarf plants resembling a rock garden. Some years ago Andrew Cook walked here from Lavanono (a distance of 30km which took him two days). The Cape can also be accessed by 4x4. Note that since Cap Sainte Marie is a reserve, a permit must be purchased, and this is best arranged in Tana. Bill Love, who drove this route in 2003, has this comment: 'I should mention that the heaviest occurrence of radiated tortoises was between Lavanona and Cap Sainte Marie – we counted 110 just on the coastal road in about two hours of driving. On the drive out to the lighthouse at Cap Sainte Marie, we literally had to move them off the two-track dirt road many times. The "road" was so narrow in places where the prickly pear cactus had grown up that we frequently had to back up hundreds of feet to find places wide enough to open the 4x4's doors, get out, and shove torts into "holes" in the wall of cactus. The cactus was scraping the car mirrors often as we drove; a man on an open ox-cart would get flayed alive unless he sat in the exact centre of his cart.'

FAUX CAP I made my first visit to this dramatic, lonely place in 1997, and then predicted that it would soon be developed for tourism. This hasn't happened yet, but with the recent improvement of the road it has become more accessible so it is only a question of time.

Faux Cap is a small community, isolated from the outside world not only by the poor roads, but by wild seas and a treacherous coral reef. The huge, shifting sand dunes are littered with fragments of *Aepyornis* shell. It is an extraordinary place which is worth making a considerable effort to visit.

Getting there and away The starting point for a trip to Faux Cap is Tsiombe. Ask around for ongoing transport. With your own 4x4 the 30km journey should take about 3½ hours. If you decide to hike, be prepared to carry all that you need. There is a good chance that you will catch a lift, however. The village at Faux Cap is called **Betanty**.

Where to stay/eat

⌂ **Libertalia** (5 bungalows) Contact through Xavier & Henriette Chabanis (☎ 92 211 13; e madalibertalia@yahoo.fr). Solar-powered bungalows. 'Beautiful locale, stone buildings, good food, cold beer, & a wind that didn't stop' (B&S Cushman). *Excursions to Cap Ste Marie 140,000Ar; canoe/kayak rental 14,000Ar/hr.* €€

⌂ **Hôtel Cactus** (18 bungalows). Nina French, who arrived by bicycle comments: 'Bungalows in different stages of disrepair. But the food is great, especially lobster. Portions are enormous!' Basic; no running water or electricity but beautifully located & run by the very friendly Marie Zela. €

FROM CAP SAINTE MARIE TO ITAMPOLO

The following account was sent by intrepid Madexplorers John and Valerie Middleton. 'It is possible to follow this very southerly route in a 4x4, for those with an adventurous mind and good navigational skills, all within a long day. A stay at Lavanono is to be recommended as apart from the situation and friendly villagers it involves a spectacular descent from the plateau. Once back on the plateau we set a GPS course for the Erea Gorge of the Menarandra River, this keeping us between three and eight kilometres from the sea. A confusion of dead-end tracks and a sparse population plus having to remove 100+ football-sized reticulated tortoises from the road slowed us considerably. The dry riverbed of the Menarandra is rather like crossing a desert and the track on the far side not obvious. From the gorge the route continues with equal interest via Bevoalava west, Soadona and the Linta River and finally to Itampolo.'

TAOLAGNARO (FORT DAUPHIN)

HISTORY The remains of two forts can still be seen in or near this town on the extreme southeast tip of Madagascar: Fort Flacourt built in 1643; and another that dates from 1504 – thus making it the oldest building in the country – which was erected by shipwrecked Portuguese sailors. This ill-fated group of 80 reluctant colonists stayed about 15 years before falling foul of the local tribes. The survivors of the massacre fled to the surrounding countryside where disease and hostile natives finished them off.

A French expedition, organised in 1642 by the Société Française de l'Orient and led by Sieur Pronis, had instructions to 'found colonies and commerce in Madagascar and to take possession of it in the name of His Most Christian Majesty'. An early settlement at the Bay of Sainte Luce was soon abandoned in favour of a healthier peninsula to the south, and a fort was built and named after the Dauphin (later Louis XIV) in 1643. At first the Antanosy were quite keen on the commerce part of the deal but were less enthusiastic about losing their land. The heavily defended fort survived only by use of force and with many casualties on both sides. The French finally abandoned the place in 1674, but their 30-year occupation formed one of the foundations of the later claim to the island as a French colony. During this period the first published work on Madagascar was written by Pronis's successor, Etienne de Flacourt. His *Histoire de la Grande Île de Madagascar* brought the island's amazing flora and fauna to the attention of European naturalists, and is still used as a valuable historical source book.

TAOLAGNARO (FORT DAUPHIN) TODAY This laidback coastal town is one of the most beautifully located of all popular destinations in Madagascar. Built on a small peninsula, it is bordered on three sides by beaches and breakers and backed by high green mountains which dwindle into spiny forest to the west. One eye-catching feature of the bay is the shipwrecks. A romantic imagination associates these with pirates or wreckers of a bygone era. In fact they are 'all unfortunate insurance scams with boats that should have been out of use years ago'. Pity!

Most people (myself included) still use the French name, Fort Dauphin, but to be consistent with the rest of the book I shall stick to Taolagnaro in the text.

Taolagnaro is experiencing an unprecedented influx of new residents. The rising tourist trade, the QMM/Rio Tinto mining activities, and new government initiatives identifying Taolagnaro as a key region for growth have all played their part. Road improvements and new businesses, as well as refurbishments of older buildings, are changing the face of the town. As a consequence, prices here are rising faster than in any other part of the country.

Telephone code The area code for Taolagnaro is 92.

☞ *WARNING!* There have been incidences of muggings and sexual assault on some Taolagnaro beaches. Shipwreck Bay is risky, especially in the early morning or at dusk. Libanona beach and the Baie des Galions are usually safe and relatively hassle-free.

GETTING THERE AND AWAY

By road The overland route from Tana (bypassing Toliara) is reportedly best done with the companies Sonatra or Tata which operate three times a week from the

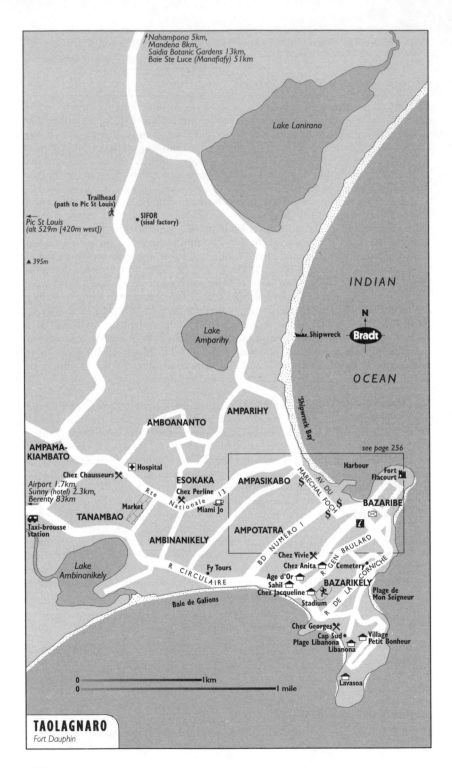

Nahampona 5km,
Mandena 8km,
Saidia Botanic Gardens 13km,
Baie Ste Luce (Manafiafy) 51km

Lake Lanirano

Trailhead
(path to Pic St Louis)

Pic St Louis
(alt 529m [420m west])

SIFOR
(sisal factory)

▲ 395m

INDIAN

N

Shipwreck **Bradt**

Lake
Amparihy

OCEAN

'Shipwreck Bay'

AMPARIHY

AMBOANANTO

AMPAMA-
KIAMBATO

see page 256

Harbour

Fort
Flacourt

Hospital

Chez Chausseurs

ESOKAKA

AMPASIKABO

BAZARIBE

Airport 1.7km,
Sunny (hotel) 2.3km,
Berenty 83km

Chez Perline

Rte Nationale 13

Miami Jo

Market

TANAMBAO

AMPOTATRA

Taxi-brousse
station

AMBINANIKELY

Lake
Ambinanikely

R CIRCULAIRE

Fy Tours

Chez Vivie

Chez Anita Cemetery

Age d'Or
Sahil

BAZARIKELY

Chez Jacqueline
Stadium

Plage de
Mon Seigneur

Baie de Galions

Chez Georges

Cap Sud
Plage Libanona
Libanona

Village
Petit Bonheur

0 ————————— 1km
0 ————————————— 1 mile

Lavasoa

TAOLAGNARO
Fort Dauphin

taxi-brousse station on the far side of Lake Anosy. These buses go via Ihosy, Betroka and Ambovombe. You should book your seat as far in advance as possible. For the journey overland from Toliara, see page 249.

By air There are flights to Taolagnaro from Tana and Toliara every day (but check the latest Air Mad schedule). The current price (one way) is 315,000Ar. Sit on the right for the best views of Taolagnaro's mountains and bays. Flights are usually heavily booked. Airport transfers from the de Heaulme hotels are expensive. Take a taxi (fixed rate) for the 4km ride into town.

WHERE TO STAY The town's available hotels are often stretched to full capacity, so book ahead if possible.

Top end €€€€€

⌂ **Sunny Hotel** (25 rooms) 1km beyond airport; ☎ 92 902 14; e sunnygarden@wanadoo.mg. One of the few upper-range hotels not owned by the de Heaulmes. New in 2006; comfortable. Swimming pool; internet facilities.

Upper range €€€€

⌂ **Libanona Beach View** m 033 12 510 46; e libanonabeachview@fortnet.net. Suites & self-catering units. Under construction at time of writing but due to open by late 2007. Aims to be the best accommodation in town, with stunning views of Libanona beach & to Pic St Louis; spacious rooms with phone, cable TV & fridge. English-speaking staff. All guests have access to kitchen facilities; some rooms with private kitchenette. B/fast inc.

⌂ **Hôtels Le Dauphin** & **Croix du Sud** (53 rooms & 4 bungalows) ☎ 92 212 38; m 033 11 300 28. This hotel & annexe belong to M Jean de Heaulme, the owner of Berenty Reserve. You are expected to stay here if you want to visit Berenty. Meals are taken in the Dauphin which has a lovely garden. They are building a 3rd hotel: **Le Galion** (opening 2007).

⌂ **Hôtel Lavasoa** (5 bungalows) ☎/f 92 211 75; e info@lavasoa.mg; www.lavasoa.com. Bungalows have en-suite bathroom & balcony overlooking Libanona beach. Owners Anne & Eric Marmorat go out of their way to look after their guests. A small breakfast bar also overlooks the beach. Offers excursions to hard-to-reach places such as Lokaro (where Lavasoa has built basic bungalows near the lagoon). 4x4 rental with driver (€100/day).

Mid range €€€

⌂ **Soavy Hotel** (15 rooms & 6 bungalows) Ampasikabo; ☎ 92 213 59; m 032 40 657 46; e deriazi@soavy.com; www.soavy.com. Rooms & bungalows of various price/standard. Best rooms have hot water, electricity & mozzie nets. Their restaurant **La Vanille** has good pizzas at reasonable prices.

⌂ **Hôtel Village Petit Bonheur** (5 bungalows) ☎ 92 212 60; e villagepetitbonheur@fortnet.net. Simple, comfortable dbl bungalows. Good restaurant with Malagasy dishes & great views. Organises day trips to Lokaro, Manantantely waterfalls, Pic St Louis & Andohahela National Park. English-speaking staff.

⌂ **Motel Gina** (14 bungalows & 2 rooms) ☎ 92 212 66; m 033 14 511 34; f 92 217 24; e motelgina2005@yahoo.fr. Run by the Aubert family. Attractive bungalows & rooms around a tranquil, manicured garden. Various standards. Friendly, knowledgeable staff. A wide variety of excursions & vehicle/bike hire. Credit cards accepted.

⌂ **Hôtel Nepenthes** (7 bungalows) Ampasikabo; m 033 12 531 13. Sgl & dbl bungalows & restaurant in quiet, spacious grounds. Conference room. Can supply guides & transport for day trips to Lokaro/Evatraha by private boat.

⌂ **Hôtel Panorama** (4 bungalows) ☎ 92 216 56; m 033 12 516 04; e panorama@fortnet.net. En-suite bungalows with balcony overlooking Shipwreck Bay. Often full. **La Terrasse** restaurant next door.

⌂ **Tournesol** (8 rooms) ☎ 92 216 71; m 033 12 513 16. One of the 1st hotels you pass coming into town. Twin & dbl rooms with TV. Nice communal garden; stunning views of Pic St Louis. Resident guide Narcisse can organise just about any excursion in the area.

⌂ **Gina Village** (10 bungalows) m 033 11 429 92; e ginavillage@yahoo.fr. Unconnected with Motel Gina opposite. Dbl & twin bungalows with en-suite bathrooms, hot showers & mosquito nets.

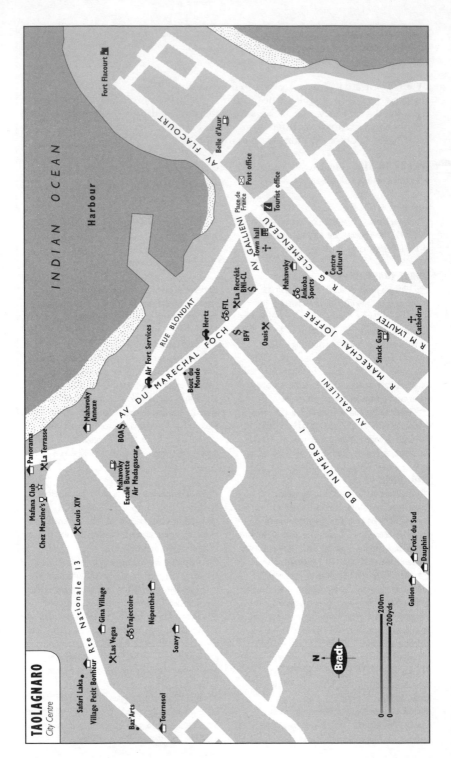

TAOLAGNARO
City Centre

INDIAN OCEAN

Harbour

Fort Flacourt

AV FLACOURT

Belle d'Azur

Post office

Place de France

Tourist office

AV GALLIENI

Town hall

R G CLEMENCEAU

Centre Culturel

Mahavoky

La Recréat

BNI-CL

Ankoba Sports

FTL

Hertz

AV DU MARECHAL FOCH

BFV

Oasis

Bout du Monde

Air Fort Services

RUE BLONDIAT

Mahavoky Annexe

Panorama

La Terrasse

Mafana Club

Chez Martine's

Louis XIV

Rte Nationale 13

Safari Laka

Village Petit Bonheur

Baz'Arts

Tournesol

Las Vegas

Gina Village

Trajectoire

Népenthès

Soavy

Mahavoky

Escale Buvette

Air Madagascar

BOA

R MARECHAL JOFFRE

R M LYAUTEY

Snack Gasy

Cathedral

AV GALLIENI

BD NUMERO I

Croix du Sud

Dauphin

Galion

200m

200yds

N

Bradt

256

Chez Anita (8 rooms & 6 bungalows) ⚏ 92 213 22; m 032 04 655 90; e anitahotel@fortnet.net. Bungalows nestled in a quiet garden tucked away from the main road. Hot water & mosquito nets. The

Budget €€

Sahil Hotel (7 rooms) Bazarikely; ⚏ 92 216 04. A modest, clean hotel; 2nd floor panoramic view of Baie de Galions. Dbl rooms with en-suite bathroom, hot water & phone. Friendly, attentive staff. Restaurant open all day (but no alcohol). Mozzie nets.
Mahavoky Annexe (9 rooms) ⚏ 92 213 97. Centrally located. Most rooms have a balcony with dramatic views of the shipwrecks in the bay.

Penny-pincher €

Hôtel Chez Jacqueline (6 rooms) Ampasimasay; ⚏ 92 217 68. Popular with budget travellers. Basic en-suite rooms. Malagasy dishes can be ordered in advance.

restaurant is ideally located for a quiet lunch/dinner on a shaded terrace. Kelsey Lynd 'highly recommends the chai (Indian) tea. It is homemade & by far the best in town.

Cheaper rooms facing road. Friendly manager & staff. Restaurant serves tasty food at fair prices.
Hôtel Mahavoky (12 rooms) Bazaribe; m 032 07 990 79. Recently renovated; gaining popularity with budget travellers. Inexpensive, large dbl & twin rooms with communal (outside) hot showers & toilet. Games room with table tennis, pool, table football & even multigym! Restaurant; tasty food, bargain prices.

Age d'Or (2 rooms) Bazarikely. A small, colourful backpacker hotel run by Krishna Hasimboto. Basic en-suite rooms; currently renovating 4 more. Bring your own mosquito net. Rooms may also be rented by the month for 300,000Ar.

✕ WHERE TO EAT Restaurants in Taolagnaro offer a wonderful mix of Malagasy dishes and international cuisine, with an emphasis on freshly caught seafood. Lobster, ocean fish, oysters, crab and shrimp are a must if you are staying in town. The following restaurants are recommended by former resident Mei-Ling McNamara and other *vazaha* living in the town.

✕ Le Dauphin Restaurant A lovely indoor/outdoor restaurant at Hôtel Le Dauphin. A wide selection of consistently good fare; impeccable service. The seafood is usually excellent. Try the selection of fresh fruit sorbets, which change according to the season. Live traditional music Fri/Sat eve.
✕ Restaurant Las Vegas Opposite Motel Gina. Friendly restaurant serving pizza, seafood & a good selection of Malagasy dishes. Order a fresh fruit juice on the outdoor terrace & watch the bustling street action below. ⊕ Mon–Sun all day.
✕ Gina Restaurant At Motel Gina. The food is excellent, though not cheap. A new annex serves delicious pizzas. Highly recommended.
✕ Tournesol This hotel/restaurant has been recently renovated to expand its indoor dining capacity. Usually quite empty but don't let that dissuade you; the soups & salads are very good; the *beignets des crevettes* recommended.
✕ Chez Georges (Le Local) A lovely restaurant with stunning sunset views over Libanona Bay. The stuffed crab is delicious & the daily catch of white fish fresh each morning. George is happy to cater to larger groups who would like to pre-order seafood. Service can be slow, so it is recommended that you

order, go for a swim, then come back after an hour for a delicious meal.
✕ La Recréat A lovely outdoor café/restaurant. A great place to come if you want to sit back & people-watch. Generous portions of seafood & zebu brochettes at a great price.
✕ La Terrasse Overlooking Shipwreck Bay. A good menu & a full bar, with a wide selection of spirits. The dishes offer a nice change from the usual fare. Within easy walking distance of the clubs & bars.
✕ Mahavoky Annexe Nice views of the harbour. Friendly staff & the chef can cook a wide range of dishes, inc fresh fish & seafood. 'The *gratin au fruit de mer* is by far the best I have ever eaten. Don't miss it!' (Jennifer Talbot).
✕ Chez Perline Specialises in seafood dishes such as lobster & crab. The curried shrimp with sauce comes highly recommended. Cheap & cheerful.
✕ Les Chausseurs The 1st restaurant as you approach town into the Tanambao market. 'Fairly quick service with efficient, knowledgeable staff' (Lauren Dean). Well-equipped for larger groups too, but order in advance.
✕ Oasis A newish restaurant, popular among the locals, offering Malagasy *plats du jour*. There is also a

selection of *vazaha* dishes inc cheeseburgers, which (according to a Peace Corps volunteer) 'are the best (& only!) burgers you can get in town. The first place I come to when I arrive in Fort Dauphin!'

✗ **Chez Vivie** Bazarikely. A family-run restaurant serving Malagasy dishes at bargain prices. The portions are not large, but the food is tasty & the service amenable. Popular with locals.

✗ **Louis XIV Pub & Restaurant** (formerly Calypso Bar). Under new ownership. The recent changes involve a new menu, live music evenings & more outdoor pub-style seating. 'This was our favourite hangout. A really nice place to have a THB or a small bite. The owner has a great taste in music so it's a great place to chill' (G Venema & J de Bekker).

Snack bars

🍴 **Mahavoky Escale Buvette** Recently renovated (the former building was sliding gently down the hill!), this family-run *hotely* is a lively local place for drinks & brochettes. 'Claude & his wife Mamanina are always hospitable & friendly for those who want to get to know the locals better' (Mark Fenn).

🍴 **Snack Gasy** Bazarikely. This *hotely* comes recommended. 'If you want to try authentic Malagasy food with a nice family atmosphere, this is a great place to go. Dishes are a bargain. Vegetarian-friendly too!' (Lauren Dean).

🍴 **Belle d'Azur** Tucked away in Bazaribe behind the mosque, this snack bar/restaurant serves up good salads & spring rolls. A nice place to come & relax on a sunny outdoor terrace, away from the bustle of town.

🍴 **Epi d'Or** Bazaribe. A bakery-cum-café with a wide selection of cakes, pastries, desserts & sundries. 'The *café espresso* is the real thing, & the homemade chocolate ice cream is the best you'll find in town. You'll pay for it, but it's worth every penny!' (Kelsey Lynd).

🍴 **Miami Jo** Esokaka. This small but popular Malagasy & Chinese cuisine *hotely* is great for a quick, cheap meal. A massive choice & the *sambos* are great to tuck into whilst waiting for your main to arrive.

🍴 **Madame du Coq's** Right in the heart of Tanambao, the market area, this place is great any time of day for a quick snack. The Malagasy doughnuts are always fresh. Nice cheap pasta & salad dishes for 200Ar/scoop. Shows the latest Malagasy music videos & always busy.

Bars There are a number of bars dotted along the main road in town that serve a limited selection of rums and THB beer. These are great places to go to experience the local flavour of Taolagnaro, or before you head out to one of the nightclubs.

🍸 **Tranobongo Chez Martine's** A great bar for a few cheap drinks before heading to the disco. Also great for *tsaky-tsaky* (Malagasy for 'snack food'). The chicken on offer is always fresh & tasty.

🍸 **Las Vegas** At the restaurant of the same name. They have a good selection of flavoured rums & the staff are friendly & attentive. Pricier than many of the bars, but does have its own toilet — a rare find in Taolagnaro! Good music & often cabaret at the w/end.

NIGHTLIFE

☆ **Mafana Club** e mafanaclub@wanadoo.mg; www.mafanaclub.mg. Formerly the Panorama Disco, this nightspot is under new management & has received an eagerly awaited renovation. It is fast becoming the most decadent & popular club in Taolagnaro. With an outdoor deck overlooking Shipwreck Bay & luxurious décor & seating inside, the club suits all tastes. Music is a mix of Malagasy & Western. Full bar, snacks, pool table, lounge &

dance floor. ⊕ Wed–Sun 17.00–04.00. Entry 10,000Ar men; women free.

☆ **Gina Nightclub** This dance club is very popular with the locals & can be a great night out if you are with a group. Every Fri/Sat night DJs play Malagasy music to a lively packed crowd. Outdoor bar serves beer & spirits. Be warned: sex workers are notoriously aggressive here. ⊕ 21.00–04.00. Entry 1,000–2,000Ar.

SHOPPING Taolagnaro has some distinctive local crafts. Most typical are the heavy (and expensive) silver bracelets worn traditionally by men. Also on offer are the handmade shoes and handbags woven from the natural fibres of the raffia palm.

There are a few souvenir shops in town, such as **Au Bout du Monde** boutique and **La Baz'Arts** on the main road. There is also a Malagasy-Italian artisanal co-operative, which sells handmade items such as sisal handbags, carved wooden sculptures and raffia lampshades (often at half the cost of the retail shops). The proceeds go directly to women's groups and disabled people who are working to support themselves through these crafts. It is located on the road below the Mafana Club, near Shipwreck Bay.

TOURIST OFFICE AND TOUR OPERATORS

▨ Fort Dauphin Tourist Office Rue Realy Abel; m 032 02 846 34; e rollandee2000@yahoo.fr; www.fort-dauphin.com. Very helpful staff who can arrange excursions with tour operators in town. Informative placards covering all the main tourist sites in the region.
Safari Laka ✎ 92 212 66; m 032 02 329 96; e safarilakatours@yahoo.fr; www.safarilaka.com. Run by Patrick Aubert at Motel Gina, they offer guides for local excursions & adventure trips, ranging from mountain biking to trekking & canoeing. Some unique destinations include the Bay of Italy, the primary rainforest of Enato & Ste Luce, in addition to places

such as Pic St Louis, Nahampoana & Evatraha/Lokaro.
Fy Tours m 032 04 212 04; f 92 211 71; e fytour1@yahoo.fr. Located near the Baie des Singes by the Ankoba Beach Club entrance. The owner, Olivier Ranaivo, says he can organise 10-day excursions for tourists to all the main sites in the southeast. 'They can organise just about any tour you could imagine & we have found them to be highly competitive price-wise' (BM). *Day trips & camping excursions to Andohahela National Park start at 180,000Ar pp inc car, fuel, permit, guide & lunch. Fy also rent out 4x4 vehicles (with driver) for €60/day plus fuel.*

VEHICLE HIRE

🚗 Hertz – Fort Dauphin m 032 05 416 75. Run by the de Heaulme family. Located next to the Jovenna petrol station in the main part of town. Car rental.
🚗 Air Fort Services ✎ 92 212 24; e air.fort@wanadoo.mg; www.airfortservices.com. The main tour

operator in the region. They hire out vehicles (from cars to buses, but not bicycles) & even small planes, as well as offering a variety of tours. This company owns the private reserve of Nahampoana. They also do flight reservations.

Bicycle hire

🚲 Trajectoire ✎/f 92 212 06; m 032 07 601 22; e trajectoire.evolution@fortnet.net; www.trajectoire.it. Located next to Motel Gina, they can organise adventure tours stretching from Toliara to Taolagnaro, inc a motorbike tour of Le Grand Sud (inc Bay of Italy). They also have local guides & transport available for day excursions to Lokaro/Evatraha with private boat. *Motorbike & quad bike rental €60/day, €382/week, €1,481/month (deposit: €500 for all rentals).*

🚲 FTL Madagascar m 032 07 930 03; e alain.ftlfd@yahoo.fr; www.ftl.mu. Opposite the BFV Bank & next door to La Recréât restaurant (& with the same proprietor) is a motorbike & bicycle hire business. *Motorbikes €40–60/day; bicycles €5–15/day.*
🚲 Cap Sud m 032 42 560 14. Run by owner Eric Chevalier, offering hourly, daily & weekly rental of motorbikes. Located at Chez Georges restaurant. *€30/day, €147/week.*

WATERSPORTS

▲ Base Nautique Vinanibe ✎ 92 211 32; www.perso.wanadoo.fr/madafunboard/. Situated 8km from Taolagnaro in Ambinambibe, on the shores of Lake Vinanibe, this club offers windsurfing & water skiing, paddleboats & sun lounges with a view over the lake. Accommodation & restaurant.
▲ Ankoba Sports ✎ 92 215 15; m 033 12 514 17; e ankoba@fortnet.net; www.ankoba.com. The main office is near the BNI bank, & the beach bar is at Baie des Galions. They offer excursions to

Lokaro/Evatraha (130,000Ar/day) & can also organise whale-watching & fishing trips around Taolagnaro. 'They hire everything that you could need for a water-based holiday, from a surfboard (5,000Ar/hr, 20,000Ar/day) to a motorboat (260,000–350,000Ar/day inc fuel & skipper) & at their beach location they have a wonderful tree-fringed hideaway with direct beach access. There they serve cold drinks, hire windsurfers, snorkelling & diving gear etc. This beach near Ankoba, south to

Ambinanibe, is popular with tourists as you can usually avoid the shell necklace sellers, it is clean & the water is shallow for safe frolicking' (BM).

Surfing With some of the most superb coastline of the Indian Ocean, the south of Madagascar offers fantastic and, as yet, relatively unexplored surfing opportunities. Some of the best places to surf are in the Bay of Monseigneur, on the other side from Libanona beach, and in the Baie des Galions, near Ankoba beach (you can also hire an instructor and rent surfboards here for 20,000/day).

WHAT TO SEE AND DO

In and around town Taolagnaro offers a choice of beach or mountain. The best easy-to-reach beach is **Libanona**, with excellent swimming (but beware the strong current), snorkelling and tide-pools. The pools to the left of the beach (as you face the sea) seem to be the best. Look out for a bizarre, frilly sea-hare, anemones and other extraordinary invertebrates, as well as beautiful little fish. There is also the swimming at the Ankoba Surf Club, in the Baie des Galions, which is shallower and is excellent for watersports.

Pic St Louis The mountain that dominates the town, is a rewarding climb up a good path and offers nice views. The hike can be demanding, and the trail is not always clearly marked, so if you are not up for an adventure by scaling several peaks, it is recommended that you take a local guide. The trail starts opposite SIFOR, the sisal factory about 3km along the road to Lake Lanirano. It takes 1½–2hrs to get to the summit, so allow at least a half day to get up there and back – or better still take a picnic. The view from the top is spectacular: on a clear day you can see as far as Baie Sainte Luce.

The Libanona Ecology Centre (*www.libanonaecology.org*) This was started by a group of local ecologists as a regional training centre on environmental sciences and conservation in 1996, helped by a generous grant from the Andrew Lees Trust. It is one of the most beautiful sites in Madagascar. The centre has prepared high school graduates from the south to fill jobs in conservation and rural development programmes in southern Madagascar.

Mark Fenn, one of the founders, says: 'If you are interested in visiting a creative technical training programme for the Malagasy, stop by. The LEC is always open to visitors and the students welcome the opportunity to practice their English language skills. If you have any skills that you would like to share, or would like to volunteer, the LEC welcomes any support that it can get as it further develops as a university.'

Cultures and conservation (e *culturesconservation@yahoo.fr*; *www.culturesconservationmada.org*) The C&C programme helps local communities to conserve and manage their natural resources and sacred sites. To date, 17 unique natural areas across the south have been identified. One goal is to develop ecotourism in these areas. For a list of the areas involved, email or visit the website.

Day trips There are numerous places to visit as a day trip in this beautiful part of Madagascar. If you haven't a car you will probably need to join an organised tour or rent a taxi, though the energetic could reach most places by hired bike.

Portuguese Fort/Ile aux Portuguais The tour to the old fort involves a pirogue ride up the River Vinanibe, about 6km from Taolagnaro, and then a short walk to the sturdy-looking stone fortress (the walls are 1m thick) set in zebu-grazed parkland.

This is the oldest building in Madagascar, and worth a visit for the beautiful surroundings. Despite its name it pre-dates the Portuguese and is probably of Swahili origin, dating from the 14th century.

La Domaine de la Cascade, Manantantely (m *032 07 678 23. Entry 10,000Ar. Rooms 30,000Ar; tent 6,000Ar*) Meaning 'place of honey', this tranquil park contains tree nurseries, fruit plantations, an apiary, a natural waterfall, rooms and campsites. Located about 8km west of Taolagnaro, on the way to Amboasary, this is a great place to take a picnic, hike, or swim in the waterfall pools.

Nahampoana Resereve (*Entry 34,000Ar inc guide*) This is an easily accessible zoo-cum-reserve owned by Air Fort Services (see page 259). The 67ha park is just 7km (15mins) from Taolagnaro, on the way to Sainte Luce. It provides the usual tame lemurs (not all local species), reptiles (again, some of the chameleon species do not really belong here) and regional vegetation. This is the ideal lemur-fix for those on a tight budget. 'This is always a big hit and I try to set aside five hours for a visit. Although it is an artificial setup (botanical garden) the lemurs are in top condition and very, very charming' (M Burger, tour leader). *There are eight rooms with en-suite bathrooms for 70,000Ar.*

Further afield
Baie Sainte Luce (Manafiafy) About 65km northeast of Taolagnaro is the beautiful and historically interesting bay where the French colonists of 1638 first landed. There is a superb beach and a protected area of humid coastal forest here, owned by M de Heaulme, and also some bungalows (usual de Heaulme price). It is possible to reach Manafiafy by *taxi-brousse* but most people will opt for an organised tour run by Air Fort Services, among others.

Evatraha This is a very attractive coastal village to the north of Taolagnaro, situated on the mouth of a small river just south of Lokaro. Day trips here, by boat, can be organised through many tour operators, or a longer stay through the operator Tour Laka, run by Fy. *There are two en-suite double bungalows for 10,000Ar (negotiable with the guardian).*

Evatraha is accessible by bicycle but Nina French reports that the last 15km off the main road have some long stretches of deep sand.

☞ **WARNING!** There have been assaults on the beach between Taolagnaro and Evatraha. It is inadvisable to walk there without a Malagasy guide or at the very least being in a group.

Lokaro The isolated Bay of Lokaro is perhaps the most beautiful spot on the southeast coast. Most visitors see Lokaro only as part of a day's excursion, but there is a strong case for spending more time there, which is no problem if you stay at Evatraha or Lokaro (camping or bungalows). There is no public transport, but Evatraha can be reached from Taolagnaro either by pirogue (a peaceful sail downriver), by road in a sturdy 4x4 or mountain bike, or on foot – a three-hour (10km) walk along the beach running north from Taolagnaro. You can rent 4x4 vehicles in Taolagnaro (journey time around two hours). From Evatraha, it is an hour's walk through hills and forest to the beach at Lokaro.

'By far the best way by to reach Lokaro is to stroll up on the spectacularly long beach that heads out north of Taolagnaro. It's an awesome stretch of fine white sand with enormous breakers crashing down every few seconds. As for campsites, there are some of the most mind-bendingly beautiful spots I've ever visited that would be just perfect to pitch a tent. Or try getting a pirogue there and then walking back – the silent sail down the meandering river through the forest to Evatraha is not to be missed. It makes you feel as though you're in a Conrad novel set in southern Madagascar' (Alasdair Harris).

 Where to stay

⌂ Camp Pirate (3 bungalows) Run by Hôtel Lavasoa (see page 255), the 'camp' consists of very simple bungalows with mosquito nets. Communal toilet/shower. An open-air restaurant serves fresh seafood. Lavasoa can take you via the inland waterways on their Zodiac & the campsite is fully equipped & very peaceful – perfect for those who don't want the bother of bringing tents & equipment from Taolagnaro. There are also kayaks for clients to use if they would like to explore on their own. *Transport (round-trip) € 45pp for 2 people, € 35pp for 3 or more; rooms € 20.*

THE WILDLIFE RESERVES

The southeast of Madagascar gives the best opportunity in all of Madagascar for wildlife-viewing to suit all budgets and all levels of energy. Whilst **Berenty** is rightly world famous, adventurous visitors should give equal consideration to **Andohahela National Park**, whilst those on a tight budget can consider the **Mandena Conservation Zone** or the newly-established community project of **Ifotaka.**

BERENTY PRIVATE RESERVE This is the key destination of most package tours and most visitors love it here. The combination of tame lemurs, comfortable accommodation and the tranquillity of the forest trails makes this *the* Madagascar memory for many people. The danger is that Berenty is already becoming overcrowded, and too many groups bring problems. Fortunately, there is only a limited amount of accommodation, so if you can arrange to spend a night or two you will at least have the reserve to yourself in the magic hours of dawn and dusk.

Visits to the reserve must be organised through Hôtel Dauphin (Taolagnaro) or Hôtel Capricorne (Toliara). *Accommodation is half-board: € 69 dbl inc a meal.*

The road to Berenty The reserve lies some 89km to the west of Taolagnaro, amid a vast sisal plantation, and the drive there is part of the experience. For the first half of the journey the skyline is rugged green mountains, often backed by menacing grey clouds or obscured by rain. Traveller's trees (*Ravenala*) dot the landscape, and near **Ranopiso** is a grove of the very rare triangle palm, *Neodypsis decaryi*. (To see an example close up, wait until you arrive in Berenty; there is one near the entrance gate.)

Your first stop will be a visit to some **pitcher plants**, *Nepenthes madagascariensis*, whose nearest relatives are in Asia, and you may stop at an **Anosy tomb**. While driving look out for what look like clusters of missiles lurking in the forest. These Antanosy cenotaphs commemorate those buried in a communal tomb or where the body could not be recovered.

Shortly after Ranopiso, and the turn-off to Andohahela National Park, there is a dramatic change in the scenery: within a few kilometres the hills flatten and disappear, the clouds clear, and the bizarre fingers of *Didierea* and *Alluaudia* appear on the skyline, interspersed with the bulky trunks of baobabs. You are entering the spiny forest, making the transition from the Eastern Domain to the Southern Domain. If you are on a Berenty tour your guide will identify some of the flora. If on your own, turn to page 41.

The exhilaration of driving through the spiny forest is dampened by the sight of all the **charcoal sellers** waiting by their sacks of ex-*Alluaudia*. These marvellous

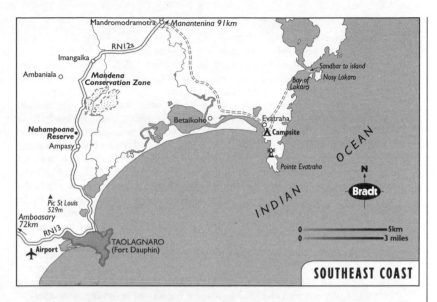

trees are being cut down at an alarming rate by people who have no other means of support. While condemning the practice, give uneasy thought to the fact that your sumptuous meals in Berenty will be cooked on stoves fuelled with locally produced charcoal. And that it is city-dwellers who consume the most charcoal in Madagascar: on average two sacks a month.

One enterprising community sells **woodcarvings** of subjects that are always hard to find in Madagascar: the local fauna. These are carved from a lightweight Burseraceae wood known locally as *daro*. For a dollar or so you can buy primitive but delightful lemurs, tortoises and chameleons.

If you pass through the village of **Ankaraneno** (25km from Taolagnaro) on a Thursday, do stop for the **zebu market** – fascinating.

SISAL

This crop was introduced to Madagascar in the inter-war years, with the first exports taking place in 1922 when 42 tons were sent to France. By 1938, 2,537 tons were exported and 3,500ha of sisal were planted in the Toliara and Taolagnaro region. By 1950 production reached 3,080 tons. In 1952 a synthetic substitute was developed in the US and the market dropped. The French government stepped in with subsidies and bought 10,000 tons.

The Toliara plantations were closed in 1958 leaving only the de Heaulme plantations in Taolagnaro. In 1960 these covered 16,000ha and, by the mid-1990s, 30,000ha of endemic spiny forest (that's about 100 square miles!) had been cleared to make way for the crop, with plantations under the ownership of six different companies. Workers earn 32,000Ar per month (1999 figure). There is no sick pay or pension provision. The de Heaulme plantation alone employs 15,000 people who cut 300,000 leaves per day.

And here's something to think about: in the late 1990s there was a resurgence of demand for sisal, with exports reaching 5,000 tons in the year 2005, putting more spiny forest at risk. Why? Because we 'green' consumers in the EU are demanding biodegradable packaging. And what is the best biodegradable substance? Sisal!

When I first started leading trips to Madagascar in the 1980s we always visited Berenty. It was one reliable success in an island of mishaps. So once a year I would make the drive from Taolagnaro (Fort Dauphin) and stop at a tiny settlement beside the road to see the Tomb of Ranonda. The village was a scattering of stick and mud huts, seeming barely large enough to house one person, let alone a whole family. It was like every other village along that road except for one thing: the collection of wooden carvings commemorating the dead. Unlike their more famous neighbours, the Mahafaly, the Antanosy people rarely use figurative carvings or paintings in their memorials. They prefer to mark the burial place with a cluster of concrete cenotaphs lurking like missiles in the thorn scrub. So this was a rarity, but what set it apart from any other tomb I've seen was the exquisite craftsmanship. We even know the sculptor's name: Fiasia. Ranonda herself was evidently a religious young woman – she holds a bible and a cross – but much livelier is the man losing a leg to a crocodile and an expertly carved boatload of people, their expressions tranquil except for the helmsman who poles his overloaded canoe to its end: the vessel sank and all on board were drowned. His face shows some anxiety as he looks round, perhaps at the oncoming waves.

The boat-people were the most famous but my favourite was a group of three zebu. These animals, destined to be sacrificed to the ancestors, are usually portrayed in a stylised form with an exaggeratedly large hump. So it was with the two bulls but among them was a cow and her calf. Here the sculptor has moved away from symbolism and used his chisels with real affection for his subject. Like all southerners, he will have lived with cattle all his life, and his knowledge is revealed in the way the cow's head is turned as she licks her suckling calf. The youngster responds by flicking its tail across her muzzle. Towering above them was their protector – a wooden herdsman.

For seven years I stopped my bus-load of tourists and showed them the carvings. The first year the children were too shy to approach us but peeped, bright-eyed, from the

Amboasary, which also has a terrific market, is the last town before the bridge across the River Mandrare and the turn-off to Berenty. The rutted red road takes you past acres of sisal and some lonely looking baobabs, to the entrance of the reserve.

The reserve The name means 'big eel' but Berenty is famous for its population of ring-tailed lemurs and sifakas. Henri de Heaulme and now his son Jean have made this one of the best-studied 260ha of forest in Madagascar. Although in the arid south, its location along the River Mandrare ensures a well-watered habitat (gallery or riverine forest) for the large variety of animals that live there. The forest is divided into two sections: **Malaza** (the section near the tourist bungalows) and **Ankoba** to its northwest.

The joy of Berenty is the selection of broad forest trails that allow safe wandering on your own, including nocturnal jaunts. Remember, many creatures are active only at night and are easy to spot with a torch/flashlight; also the eyes of moths and spiders shine red or white, and all sorts of other arthropods and reptiles can be seen easily. A dusk visit (with a guide) to the reserve's area of spiny forest is a must: you'll observe mouse lemurs, but just seeing those weird, giant trees in silhouette and hearing the silence is a magical experience.

Next day get up at dawn; you can do your best birdwatching, see the sifakas opening their arms to the sun, and enjoy the coolness of the forest before going in to breakfast.

Berenty wildlife: an overview Lemurs are what most people come here for, and seeing the following species is guaranteed: brown lemur, ring-tailed lemur

dark doorways of their huts. As years passed they became bolder and eventually tried the 'bonbon?' question but without much hope. Tourists didn't linger, and no-one thought of giving anything back to the village whose beautiful memorial provided so much pleasure. And these children were starving. Literally. I'm haunted by a photo I took of a sombre little girl with matted reddish hair, about six years old, carrying her little brother whose distended stomach and stick-like arms and legs show the classic signs of malnutrition. I used to fantasise about somehow persuading the Peace Corps, or similar NGO, to set up a health clinic at the village which would be funded from the income generated by tourists visiting the tomb. But I did nothing.

In 1989 I stopped as usual and led my group to the tomb. Where the carved cattle used to stand under the watchful eye of their guard, only the herdsman remained. The cow and her calf, and the two bulls, had been ripped away leaving only the jagged remains of their wooded plinth. In their place was a row of fresh zebu skulls, their horns sprouting fungi as they decomposed in the humid air. I asked our driver what had happened. 'A tourist stole it.' The skulls were from the cattle slaughtered by this impoverished village to calm the ancestors' rage at this desecration.

Buses no longer stop at the village. There's no point. The tomb is surrounded by a high fence of sharpened stakes. To take a photograph, tourists must pay € 5. 'Not worth it', they mutter after peering though the fence with binoculars. 'Not worth it' I agree. The carvings have deteriorated, the wood has darkened and split, and lichen blotches the formerly smooth features of the boat-people. Somewhere, in a private collection of 'primitive art', the cow still licks her calf. Their wood retains its original grey smoothness, denied its destiny to grow old and return to the earth. And I ache for that village and its loss. Which is worst, its loss of trust or the loss of something that was not art but the tangible soul of an ancestor?

and sifaka. The lemurs here have not been hunted for 70 years, so they trust people. They were fed bananas by tourists in the 1980s and 1990s, but this is no longer allowed. Disappointed that an outstretched hand no longer offers food, they will try to sneak into your cabin to find it for themselves. **Ring-tailed lemurs** (*Lemur catta*) have an air of swaggering arrogance, are as at home on the ground as in trees, and are highly photogenic with their grey, black and white markings and waving striped tails. These fluffy tails play an important part in communication and act as benign weapons against neighbouring troops which might have designs on their territory. Male ring-tailed lemurs indulge in 'stink fights' when they scent their tails with the musk secreted from wrist and anal glands and wave them in their neighbours' faces. The opponent retreats or else waits his turn and then waves back. They also rub their genital glands on the trunks of trees and males score the bark with their wrist-spur to scent-mark their territory.

There are approximately 500 ring-tailed lemurs in Berenty, and the population has stayed remarkably stable considering that only about a quarter of the babies survive to adulthood. The females, which are wholly dominant over the males, are receptive to mating for only a week or so in April or May, so there is plenty of competition amongst the males for this once-a-year treat (April is also the best time to observe 'stink-fighting'). The young are born in September and at first cling to their mother's belly, later climbing onto her back and riding jockey-style. Ring-tails eat flowers, fruit and insects – and the occasional chameleon.

Attractive though the ring-tails are, no lemur can compete with the **Verreaux's sifaka** for soft-toy cuddliness, with its creamy white fur, brown cap, and black face.

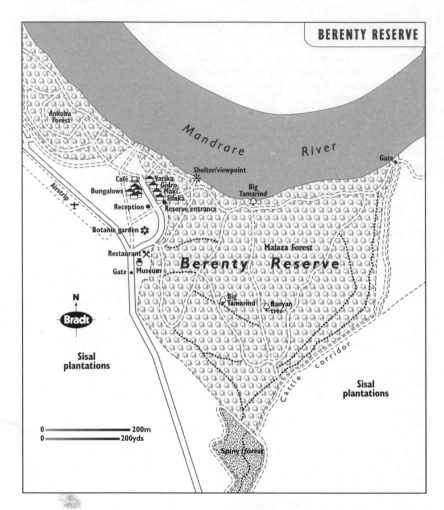

Sisal plantations

Sifakas belong to the same lemur family as indri (seen in Andasibe). The species here is *Propithecus verreauxi* and there are about 300 of them in the reserve. Unlike the ring-tails, they rarely come down to the ground, but when they do the length of their legs in comparison with their short arms necessitates a comical form of locomotion: they stand upright and jump with their feet together like competitors in a sack race. The best places to see them do this are on the trail to the left at the river and across the road by the aeroplane hangar near the restaurant and museum. Sifaka troop boundaries do not change, so your guide will know where to find the animals. The young are born in July. Like the ring-tails, sifakas make a speciality of sunbathing – spreading their arms to the morning rays from the top of their trees. They feed primarily on leaves and tamarind fruit.

The **red-fronted brown lemurs** (*Eulemur rufus*) were introduced from the west and are now well established and almost as tame as the ring-tails. These are the only sexually dimorphic lemurs in Berenty – in other words you can tell the males from the females by their colour: males have a fluffy orange cap while females have greyish heads and bodies that are a more chestnut brown than males'. Both sexes have long, black noses and white 'eyebrows'.

Berenty happens to be the perfect place to observe one of the unique aspects of lemur behaviour: female dominance. Ring-tail and sifaka males are always submissive to females, while brown lemurs are much less so. Alison Jolly, who has written so absorbingly about Berenty in her book *Lords and Lemurs* (see page 462) says 'I have seen a male brown lemur at Berenty throw a female out of a tree, which scandalised me as a ring-tail watcher.' Dr Jolly adds: 'Female dominance is very odd among primates and other mammals. Of around 400 primate species, only the 70 plus species of lemur tend toward female dominance as a group. No monkeys or apes show the 100% full-time chivalry of many lemur males. I call it chivalry rather than wimpishness, because males fight and wound each other, and could certainly fight females if they chose – but it is built-in that they don't confront females. There are half a dozen scientific theories about why female dominance and male submission evolved to be so widespread in lemurs. None of them is quite convincing so it remains an evolutionary mystery.'

There are other lemurs which, being nocturnal, are harder to spot although the **white-footed sportive lemur** can be seen peering out of its hollow tree nest during the day. Grey mouse lemurs (*Microcebus murinus*) may be glimpsed in the beam of a flashlight, especially in the spiny forest area – a popular destination for night walks.

Apart from lemurs there are other striking mammals. **Fruit bats** or flying foxes live in noisy groups on 'bat trees' in one part of the forest. You are not permitted to approach closely but you will still have a satisfying view of these appealing animals.

Birdwatching is rewarding in Berenty, and even better in Bealoka (place of much shade) beyond the sisal factory. Nearly 100 species have been recorded. You are likely to see several families unique to Madagascar, including the hook-billed vanga, and two handsome species of couas – the crested coua and the giant coua – which have dramatic blue face-markings. The cuckoo-like coucal is common, as are grey-headed lovebirds and the beautiful Madagascar paradise flycatcher with its long tail feathers. The males come in two colour morphs: chestnut brown, and black and white. Two-thirds of Berenty's paradise flycatchers are black and white. If you visit from mid-October to May you will see a variety of migrant birds from southeast Africa: broad-billed roller, Malagasy lesser cuckoo and lots of waders (sanderlings, greenshank, sandpiper, white-throated plover).

Then there are the **reptiles**. Although Berenty's chameleons are somewhat drab (two species are found here: *Furcifer verrucosus*, or warty chameleon, and *Furcifer lateralis*, often called jewel chameleon but in Berenty most un-gem-like), they are plentiful. There is also a good chance of seeing Dumeril's boa (a huge but placid snake). In captivity there is a sulky-looking crocodile (its companion escaped after its enclosure was damaged in a cyclone) and some happy radiated and spider tortoises.

THE BALD LEMURS OF BERENTY

Alison Jolly

Some ring-tailed lemurs in troops near Berenty cafeteria go nearly bald during the dry season, but grow their fur back in the wet season. This is not a contagious disease or anything to do with tourism. It is the result of feeding on *Leucaena*, a toxic introduced tree. If you see a team of veterinarians among the tourists, ask them for the latest information! And if you see workmen taking out trees, the *Leucaena* is being removed. Meanwhile lemurs in the rest of the forest away from the *Leucaena* areas are as furry as ever.

Finally, don't forget the **insects**. One of my favourite activities in Berenty is visiting the 'cockroach tree,' a large tamarind on the left of the main trail to the river. This is pockmarked with small holes, and if you visit at night and shine your torch into the holes, you will see pairs of antennae waving at you. These belong to Madagascar giant hissing cockroaches. If you are able to catch one of these 5–8cm insects it will give a loud, indignant hiss. (I have kept them as pets in England; they brought me endless enjoyment!) Another equally entertaining insect is the ant lion (see box on page 51). Look for their conical holes on the sandy paths, then find an ant as a drop-in gift.

Berenty has been welcoming tourists longer than any other place in Madagascar, and all who fall in love with it will want to do what they can to preserve it and its inhabitants. As long as visitors continue to behave responsibly they will be allowed to wander in the forest unaccompanied – a real treat for those who value solitude and the time to sit quietly and observe this unique piece of nature. However, don't miss out on the tours with the excellent English-speaking guides, who will greatly increase your knowledge and understanding. Their fee is paid by the reserve but a tip is appropriate.

Where to stay/eat There are 12 bungalows (comfortable with double bed and fairly reliable hot water) and six older buildings with pairs of twin rooms. Accommodation is also available in Ankoba. Generators are switched off at 22.00, after which there is no electricity. Without the electric fans it can get very hot. Rooms are screened, but in the older bungalows you should burn a mosquito coil (provided).

There is a snack bar near the bungalows where breakfast is served, and the bar/restaurant (near the museum) offers fixed-menu meals, and cool outdoor seats for your pre-dinner drink. Near the restaurant is quite a good souvenir shop.

An efficient and reasonable laundry service is available – ask at reception.

Excursions Tourists staying more than a day should take the two excursions offered. The area of **spiny forest** here is superb (though hot) and may be your only chance to see mature *Alluaudia* trees. Some tower over 15m – an extraordinary sight. A visit to the **sisal factory** may sound boring but is, in fact, fascinating – and, for some, disturbing. On the natural-history front, this used to be one of the best places in Madagascar to see and photograph the enormous *Nephila* spiders on their golden webs. On my last visit I was horrified to find that my beloved spiders had been cleared away; however, I have faith that *Nephila* persistence will overcome this temporary setback.

Museum of the Androy This is undoubtedly the best ethnological museum in Madagascar, and if your interest in the region extends beyond the wildlife, you should allow at least an hour here. Several of the rooms are given over to an explanation (in English and French) of the traditional practices of the Antandroy people, illustrated by excellent photos. There are some beautiful examples of handicrafts and a small but interesting natural history section including a complete *Aepyornis* egg. This museum should be seen in conjunction with the replica Antandroy 'village' near the botanical garden, where you can step inside a small house, very similar to those you pass on the road to Berenty.

All credit to M de Heaulme for celebrating the lives of the human inhabitants of the region in this way. Don't miss this opportunity to learn more about the 'people of the thorns'.

MANDENA CONSERVATION ZONE This reserve was established by QMM (see box on page 270) to protect 230ha of rare littoral forest in the region that is the centre of their controversial ilmenite (titanium ore) mining project. The conservation area includes 160ha of the least degraded fragments of forest and 60ha of wetlands. Twenty-two species of flora are endemic to this region, with about 200 species of large trees. Littoral forest is similar to coastal rainforest, but with a 2–3% difference. In 2001 a troop of collared brown lemurs (*Eulemur collaris*) were relocated to Mandena from a small, threatened area of forest outside the conservation zone.

I have visited Mandena twice and absolutely love it! It is completely different from the Berenty experience, has been thoughtfully conceived to give tourists as much variety as possible, and the local Antanosy people are involved. At present this is primarily a botanical experience. The six species of lemur in the Mandena area are still shy, but no doubt will become habituated in time, but you'll see plenty of birds and reptiles. There is a standard circuit which takes three to four hours and includes level paths (the walking is easy) and a boat trip which takes you down a waterway fringed with pandanus palms (six species in Mandena). Then it's a walk back along another forest trail to the visitor centre and tree nursery.

Mandena now has legal protected status as part of The Durban Vision and is mainly managed by local communes.

Visiting Mandena The main hotels and tour operators in Taolagnaro run day trips, but independent travellers can contact Manon Vincelette at QMM or Philo Jamba, an excellent QMM naturalist guide (m *033 12 815 04*). The reserve is about 10km from Taolagnaro (a beautiful drive) so within cycling distance. Bikes can be hired in town. A taxi costs around 50,000Ar for the round-trip. There is a campsite just outside the boundary of the reserve, and in this area you can walk around unguided, so are free to look for wildlife at your own pace. There is also a restaurant where you can eat lunch. The fee to visit the reserve is 10,000Ar (includes a boat trip). There are currently no additional fees for the guides but tips are appreciated. Tent rental is 2,000Ar.

If you cycle there, take the *second* entrance to the right (near a sign) and then keep bearing right all the way to the visitor centre. Ignore the first entrance (at the bottom of a hill) which is also signposted, as this will take you to the foresters' camp.

LAKE ANONY About 12km south of Amboasary is a brackish lagoon, Lake Anony. There are flamingoes here and a large number of other wading birds in a lunar landscape.

Valerie Middleton writes: 'The region around this lake is beautiful and a paradise both for birdwatchers and botanists. We stayed in the Village des Mineraux Lodge situated above the small fishing village of Andranobory. This excellent establishment is adapted for research purposes but if no work is being carried out other travellers may also stay. Pre-booking needs to be made through a travel agent in Antananarivo. Access is through the massive sisal plantations and is signposted from the main road.'

ANDOHAHELA NATIONAL PARK This national park (pronounced andoowahela) opened to tourists in 1998, and is a model of its kind. Much thought and sensitivity has gone into the blend of low-key tourist facilities and the involvement of local people, and all who are interested in how Madagascar is starting to solve its environmental problems should try to pay it a visit.

The reserve spans rainforest and spiny forest, and thus is of major importance and interest. A third component is the east-west transition forest, which is the last place the triangle palm can be found. These three distinct zones, or 'parcels' (from the French *parcelle*, meaning 'plot of land') make Andohahela unique in its biodiversity.

Andohahela Interpretation Centre (Centre d'Interpretation Andohahela) Even if you are not able to visit Andohahela itself, do spend some time in this beautifully organised centre. It is a green building on the left-hand side of the road as you leave Taolagnaro. The centre was set up with the help of the Peace Corps and the WWF, both for tourists and – more importantly – the local people. Through clear exhibits, labelled in English, French and Malagasy, it emphasises the importance of the forest and water to future generations of Malagasy, and explains the use of various medicinal plants. Local initiatives include the introduction of fuel-efficient cooking stoves that burn sisal leaves. Wind power is also being investigated. Schools are being built in the area, with the education of the next generation on the importance of preserving the environment as a priority. The Interpretation Centre is now under new ownership, with two rooms available for overnight stays. *Dbl 25,000Ar; camping permitted.*

Visiting Andohahela At the time of writing a visit to most areas of the national park requires the use of a 4x4 vehicle and full camping gear (all can be provided by tour operators). Fit and properly equipped hikers or cyclists can make it independently, however. From the Interpretation Centre to Tsimelahy is 5km on the main road plus a further 8km from the junction. Cyclists will find the route to Mangatsiaka easier – 13km on the road and 4km on level dirt road.

development. Transition, though, is not easy – spiralling inflation as new money comes into the region also leaves many behind.'

By creating Mandena, and two other conservation areas, QMM has given up tens of millions of dollars in lost revenue, but it is a high-profile opportunity for a company with a poor public image to redeem itself. Since 1987 QMM has run Social and Environmental Impact Assessment Studies and concluded that the mining could proceed. The integrity of this study has been questioned by people who doubt that Rio Tinto can ever do an objective environmental study, but an hour spent with Johny Rabenantoandro, the project's chief botanist, persuaded me. It was the way his eyes sparkled when he told me about his greatest find. "I found a little *brookesia* chameleon" he said. 'It was so small, hiding in the leaves by the path. It was like finding a piece of gold!' and he clasped his hands together in delight at the memory. This sort of enthusiasm cannot be bought.

Rio Tinto have pledged to leave any region where they start mining with an environment richer than when they began. Madagascar is their flagship: the project where they can say their policy is already in place. A Biodiversity Committee of experts has been recruited from Kew Garden, Missouri Botanical Gardens, Bird Life International and Fauna and Flora International to advise and monitor the changes they bring.

While generally supportive of the project, the WWF's regional representative in Madagascar, Jean-Paul Paddack, is concerned that there will be water pollution from the new port and an increase in social problems such as HIV/AIDS caused by internal migrations. The demand for charcoal for fuel will also be massive.

Time will tell. 'I see it as a gamble' says Alison Jolly. 'If it goes wrong, with uncontrolled immigration and feeble governance, of course the forests will disappear even faster, and people suffer even more. If it goes right, there is a real chance of saving some of the Malagasy natural habitat, in a place where people grow richer, rather than poorer year by year – and so far it is going right.'

Greta Venema and Joeri de Bekker report: 'We organised the trip through Safari Laka and combined both Tsimelahy and Mangatsiaka, a full day trip. If you leave Taolagnaro around 07.00, you can be back before 19.00. It takes a 4x4 about 1½–2hrs to reach Tsimelahy. There is an 8km bike trail between the two parcels, but we drove around by car. Campgrounds are still very primitive; you have to take everything with you. The track between Tsimelahy and Ihazofotsy is supposed to be very rough (too rough for a 4x4).'

Local tour operators offer packages to Andohahela. And they can provide permits; these can also be obtained from ANGAP in Taolagnaro or from the park office. Guide fees are 7,000Ar per group.

The national park

Malio (Parcel 1 – rainforest) The rainforest area has a trail system and campsites. It has lagged behind the other two parcels because most tourists have visited a rainforest reserve (Andasibe or Ranomafana) by the time they reach Taolagnaro. But this is part of its appeal – there will be no crowds. The area has all the rainforest requisites: waterfalls, orchids and lemurs (*Eulemur fulvus*). It is also popular with birders who come here looking for the rare red-tailed newtonia. To get there (dry season only) take the paved road out of Taolagnaro for approximately 15km, turn north on a dirt road before the town of Manambaro and go 6km to the nice little village of Malio. Independent travellers can buy a permit at the ANGAP office in Taolagnaro and reach the trailhead by taxi.

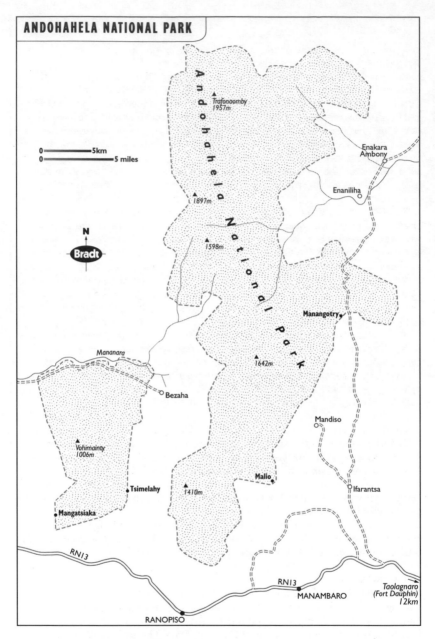

ANDOHAHELA NATIONAL PARK

Andohahela National Park

Trafonaomby
1957m

Enakara
Ambony

Enaniliha

0 ——— 5km
0 ——— 5 miles

1897m

N
Bradt

1598m

Manangotry

Mananara

1642m

Bezaha

Mandiso

Vohimainty
1006m

Malio

Tsimelahy

1410m

Ifarantsa

Mangatsiaka

RN13

RN13
MANAMBARO

Taolagnaro
(Fort Dauphin)
12km

RANOPISO

Ihazofotsy and Mangatsiaka (Parcel 2 – spiny forest) Visitors should remember that spiny forest is very hot and often shadeless, so camping/walking here can be quite arduous. That said, for the committed adventurer this is a wonderful area for wildlife, birding and botany. Even if you were to see no animals, the chance to walk through untouched spiny forest – the real Madagascar – gives you a glimpse of how extraordinary this land must have seemed to the first Europeans.

Apart from the fascinating trees and plants unique to this region, you should see sifakas (this is one of the areas where you can observe them leaping onto the spiny trunks of *Didierea* trees without apparent harm), small mammals such as tenrecs (if you're lucky) and plenty of birds endemic to the south, such as running coua and sickle-billed vanga; also many reptiles. Equally you may see nothing! Remember that this is not Berenty; the wildlife tends to be shy, and is inactive during the heat of the day. Be patient.

Of the two spiny forest parcels, Mangatsiaka is the easiest to visit, being only 6km off the main Taolagnaro–Amboasary-Sud road, so ideal for self-sufficient independent travellers. There is a well-laid-out trail system and a good campsite. Ihazofotsy is more popular with groups because you need a 4x4 to tackle the two-hour access track. Camping is permitted near the village and there is a good trail system through the superb *Alluaudia* trees. An added bonus is the view from a huge domed rock, which is crawling with *Oplurus* iguanas.

Tsimelahy (Parcel 3 – transition forest) I loved this place! Apart from reptiles (lizards and snakes), we saw little wildlife, but the scenery and plants are utterly wonderful! This region is the only area in which the triangle palm is found; it says something for the rest of the botany that seeing this was *not* the highlight of our stay. The campsite for Tsimelahy is within a stone's throw of a large deep pool, fed by a waterfall, and fringed with elephant-ear plants. You can slip into the cool water from the smooth rocks and swim to your heart's content.

Tsimelahy is clearly marked on the road to Amboasary, and is 8km from the main road to the trailhead. The rocky dirt road is pretty tough on cars, so it is recommended that you hire a knowledgeable driver. You can take a 4x4 to within a few kilometres of the campsite, then you have a marvellous walk. Once at Tsimelahy, you will be assigned a certified ANGAP guide (some speak English). A choice of two trails run along both shores of River Tarantatsa, affording super views of white-flowered *Pachypodium lameri*, and green forest. My favourite plant was the 'celebrity tree' (*lazar* in Malagasy, genus *Cyphostemma*). It seems to start as a tree, then change its mind and become a true liana (it belongs to this family), draping its droopy top over neighbouring plants. Young Malagasy seeking popularity or success will ask the *mpanandro* (soothsayer) to ask the tree for help.

Another highlight for us was the visit to the little village of Tsimelahy. This is an inspiring example of how a newly established protected area can involve and benefit the local people. There are well-made handicrafts for sale and you will be treated to a rousing song about the forest and its animals from the children in the tiny schoolroom.

IFOTAKA COMMUNITY FOREST (ICF) This admirable project began in 2001, following a government initiative encouraging communities to manage their own natural resources. The local Tandroy people allow woodcutting for fuel, building and cattle grazing in some parts of the protected area, while preserving sacred and environmentally important areas for ecotourism. All the characteristic animals of the south (including Verreaux's sifakas and ring-tailed lemurs) can be seen here at a fraction of the cost of Berenty, while visitors have the happy knowledge that their fees go directly to the local community.

Owen Beaton, who has worked in Ifotaka since 2001, says: 'Ifotaka is not for the fainthearted; it is usually very hot and dry, and the living conditions are quite basic. But for the adventurous visitor who prefers to see lemurs in the wild and wants a real taste of Tandroy village life, Ifotaka is an unforgettable experience.'

Getting there ICF is to the north of Amboasary, 80km from Taolagnaro. *Taxi-brousses* leave Amboasary between noon and 17.00. If you start from Taolagnaro you should leave before 08.00, in order to make the connection in Amboasary. *Taxi-brousses* return to Amboasary between 17.30 and 19.00.

 **Where to stay/eat** There are eight wooden bungalows built by the Tandroy Conservation Trust with the community of Ifotaka. No electricity or running water. There is also a campsite. For food you should either be self-sufficient, or organise meals with one of the local families such as Mme Memena who can either cook with ingredients that you bring or prepare local food for you (10,000Ar). *Bungalows 10,000Ar; tent hire 5,000Ar; camping 3,000Ar.*

Trekking from Ifotaka A variety of treks can be organised, costing from 5,000Ar for a visit to the forest to 12,000Ar for an overnight camping trip. Porters are also available for 4,000Ar.

Tana to Toamasina

Since the early days of the Merina kingdom, there has been a link from the country's main port to its capital. The route between the two cities will have been established during the expansionist days of King Radama I, when dignitaries were carried by palanquin and goods were transported on the heads of porters. It gained greater importance after the arrival of teachers from the London Missionary Society, the first Europeans to have a significant influence on Madagascar. They arrived in Tamatave bearing not only the word of God, but technology in the form of printing presses. The track up the escarpment was narrow, difficult and slippery in the rainy season (most of the year) but the royal government refused to build a proper road, fearing this would facilitate an invasion from outside (in fact the French invasion took place by the much easier route from Mahajanga). The first road was built by the French, but maintenance was never a high priority, especially after independence, partly to reduce competition with the state-owned railway. The collapse of the economy in the Second Republic meant that there was no money at all for maintenance and the road became at times almost impassable. However in the 1990s the road was rehabilitated to a high standard with aid from Switzerland and China.

These days many visitors take Route Nationale 2 from the capital. Most are heading for Andasibe but some continue to the coast. The route description here is aimed at those travelling in a private vehicle or by bicycle, but of course *taxi-brousse* travellers may choose to break their trip at any of the stops along the way. My thanks to Ony Rakotoarivelo for her research on this route. Note: 'PK' numbers are kilometre marker posts (*Points Kilométriques*).

☞ ***WARNING!*** RN2 is notorious for its reckless drivers and high death toll. Keep alert, especially if on a bicycle. Even if you've never suffered from motion sickness, take precautions on this trip. The macho drivers and winding road are a challenge to any stomach.

RN2: FROM TANA TO MORAMANGA

After the hectic atmosphere of Tana, the journey to Moramanga offers first-time visitors to Madagascar a gentle introduction to rural life. Rice fields, *hotely*s and roadside stalls selling seasonal fruits line the route, and it is a fine opportunity to observe activities that make up the daily routine of the vast majority of Malagasy people living outside the major cities.

The 20km of road to **Ambohimangakely** is surrounded by rice fields which, in the early morning, will be filled with local people pursuing the all-important business of supplying their families with rice: digging paddies, sowing rice, transplanting the mature plants, weeding and eventually harvesting (depending on the season of your visit).

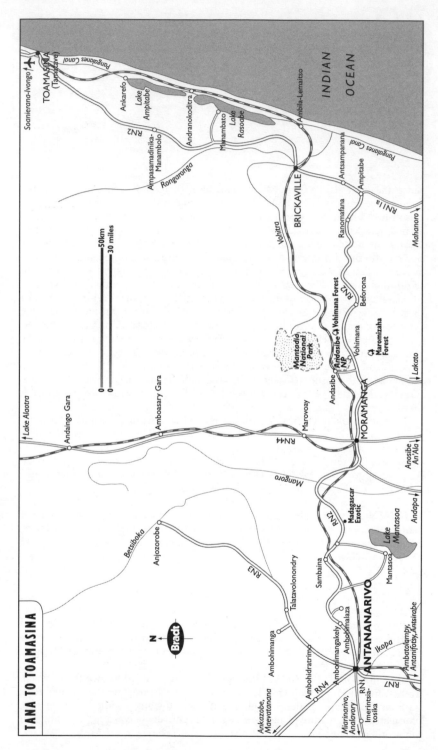

TANA TO TOAMASINA

Soanierana-Ivongo
TOAMASINA
(Tamatave)

Pangalanes Canal

Ankarefo
Lake Ampitabe
Andranokoditra
RN2
Ampasamadinika-Manambolo
Rongaronga
Manambato
Lake Rasoabe
Ambila-Lemaitso

INDIAN OCEAN

Antsampanana
Ampitabe
Pangalanes Canal
BRICKAVILLE
Ranomafana
RN11a
Mahanoro
Vohitra
Vohimana Forest
Beforona
RN2
Vohimana
Maromizaha Forest
Mantadia National Park
Andasibe NP
Andasibe
Lakato
MORAMANGA
Marovoay
RN44
Amboasary Gara
Andaingo Gara
Lake Alaotra
Anosibe An'Ala
Mangoro
Andapa
RN2
Madagascar Exotic
Betsiboka
Anjozorobe
Lake Mantasoa
Mantasoa
Sambaina
Talatavolonondry
RN3
Ambohimanga
Ambohidratrimo
RN4
Ambohimangakely
Ambohimalaza
ANTANANARIVO
Ikopa
Ambatolampy, Antanifotsy, Antsirabe
RN7
RN1
Imerintsia-tosika
Miarinarivo, Analavory
Ankazobe, Maevatanana

N

Bradt

50km
30 miles
0
0

The following 20km of well-maintained road take you through the town of **Ambohimalaza**, steeped in history and tradition (see page 178). By contrast, some 20km later, the road travels past an icon of modern Madagascar. **Sambaina** is home to the first factory of the now-famous Tiko empire, owned by President Ravalomanana.

Manjakandriana is the last major town before you descend from the *hauts plateaux*. Here the flat, straight stretches of road give way to a long series of steep, winding sections and hairpin bends as you head towards the plain below and the small town of **Ambodiamontana**. This descent offers fine views of the forest clinging to the precipitous slopes of the mountains to your left, and a good vantage point from which to survey the next phase of your journey across the flat plains towards Moramanga. If you can take your eyes off the scenery, look out for enterprising locals transporting goods in oil drums balanced on tiny carts down the hair-raisingly steep stretches of road. To your left, water plunges down the flank of a nearby mountain, powering the nearby hydroelectric station across the valley from Ambodiamontana.

As the mountains of the *hauts plateaux* recede into the distance behind you, the road to Moramanga takes you through numerous small villages and stretches of thinly populated countryside, the occasional charcoal seller popping up by the side of the road.

SAMBAINA This small village 40km from Tana gives an opportunity to stop for a good breakfast. The early morning weather is likely to be misty and cold.

✗ **Pizza Nino** (PK 42) ☏ 42 621 01. Serving European/Malagasy food & pizza. ☉ 06.30–18.30.

MANJAKANDRIANA (PK 48) This largish town 48km from Tana has a good choice of *hotelys* so is an alternative breakfast stop if you have made a pre-dawn start from Tana. The small **Manja Motel** on the left has basic rooms.

The town also has a BOA bank, a hospital, a pharmacy and petrol station.

Carrying on down the road, you reach PK 62 where there's an excuse for another stop.

Mandraka Park is on the left side of the road. This is a Malagasy-run collection of wooden bungalows offering accommodation, picnic tables, prepared meals (grilled dishes a speciality) and hikes in the neighbouring forest.

MADAGASCAR EXOTIC (☏ 22 321 01. ☉ daily 07.00–17.00. Entry 10,000Ar; guide 2,000Ar) Formerly known as Mandraka Reptile Farm, this place is well signposted at Marozevo (PK 72) on the right side of the road. It is owned by one of Madagascar's prominent naturalists, André Pereyras. The centre provides the opportunity to see and photograph some of the island's most extraordinary reptiles and invertebrates – and they are truly extraordinary: chameleons by the score (which are accustomed to being handled), leaf-tailed geckos, invertebrates, crocodiles and some mammals.

However, all this comes at a price: many of the animals are kept in crowded and stressful conditions, and although the main purpose of the centre is the breeding (for export) of various butterflies and moths, the demand for reptiles for the pet trade is also satisfied, probably through illegal collecting from the wild.

Adjacent to the 'farm' is a patch of forest with Verreaux's sifakas and common brown lemurs. It's an additional 3,000Ar for the guide to take you there.

About 2km beyond the farm is the village of **Ambodiamontana** where you can have a meal in one of the nice and typically Malagasy *hotelys* along the roadside. Rabbit is a speciality here.

Rupert Parker

We were travelling back from a *famadihana* in Ambatondrozaka to Moramanga early one morning and decided to stop halfway at a small *hotely* for breakfast. My Malagasy friends decided to order chicken and rice, but I was feeling a bit queasy and asked if they could do me 'oeuf sur le plat' – fried egg – this sounded like the safest bet. But, this being Madagascar, they asked for money in advance to buy the egg. We sat and waited for our food and eventually coffee was served; we also saw a girl going out and returning with an egg. Soon the chicken and rice arrived but there was nothing for me. We asked what the problem was and they said they had no oil and needed to buy some before they could start the cooking. I produced a few more Malagasy francs and my friends tucked into their food.

After 20 minutes, by now very hungry, still no fried egg. I enquired what was going on. A very worried man emerged from the kitchen and beckoned for us to enter the dark, smoke-filled space at the back. He explained that the problem was that they had bought an egg without a yolk and he wanted us to see it in case we didn't believe him. This was news indeed, so we all crammed inside to behold this Malagasy marvel – a world first perhaps. Of course the truth was somewhat more mundane: as we peered into the pan there was a sticky yellow mess. They'd broken the yolk, or maybe stirred the egg, and created a perfect omelette. It was delicious, but obvious that they'd never fried an egg before.

The moral is don't take anything for granted in Madagascar.

MORAMANGA

Moramanga means, prosaically, 'cheap mangoes'. It is being transformed by the new Ambatovy Nickel Project, run by the Canadian company Dynatec, so information here will soon be out of date. Moramanga is the stopping point for public transport travelling between Tana and Toamasina, which means heavy traffic on the main road day and night. Hotels with rooms facing the street are very noisy. On the plus side you can always find an open restaurant.

TELEPHONE CODE The area code for Moramanga is 56.

⌂ WHERE TO STAY

⌂ **Emeraude** (24 rooms) ☎ 56 821 57; f 56 822 35. Centrally located, with a good range of rooms at different prices, some en suite. €€

⌂ **Hôtel Espace Diamant** (12 rooms) ☎ 56 823 76; m 033 14 989 50. Opposite the church. Comfortable clean rooms, some with shared facilities, some en suite. All rooms have a small veranda. Good value. €€

⌂ **Hôtel Restaurant Nadia** (12 rooms) Central;

☎ 56 822 43. Sgl, dbl & twin rooms with facilities & hot water. W/end disco. €€

⌂ **Hôtel Restaurant Fihavanana** (12 rooms) m 033 12 591 23/032 46 097 39. On the right-hand side as you enter town from Tana, near the Jovenna Station. Sgl, dbl & twin rooms, some en suite. €–€€

⌂ **Hôtel Maitso an'Ala** (5 rooms) Very simple dbl & twin rooms. €

✗ WHERE TO EAT

✗ **Restaurant au Coq d'Or** ☎/f 56 820 45; side road in front of Emeraude Hotel. Renowned for its frog legs! Chinese, Malagasy & European menu. Great for pastries; a favourite stopping place for tour groups. ⊕ 08.00–20.00; Sun 08.30–15.00.

✗ **Restaurant Sirène Doré** RN 2, Toamasina end. Very good food in a more upscale (by local standards) setting. Chinese & European menu. Also sells a wide range of baked goods. *Closes around 21.00.*

✕ **Jovenna Station** RN2, Tana end. The Jovenna service station on the Tana end of town has a surprisingly good restaurant with reasonable prices. Basic motel-style rooms for rent behind the station.

INTERNET There are at least four internet places in town. All are on RN2, mostly clustered round the Emeraude hotel.

WHAT TO SEE AND DO Turn left on entering the town and drive for about 800m to have a quick look at the mausoleum for the people who died during the uprising in 1947, and then the Museum of Gendarmerie (⊕ *w/ends 09.00–11.00 & 14.00–17.00; on w/days ask permission to visit at the gatehouse*). 'Surely the most comprehensive collection in Madagascar, not only police, but cultural, with excellent original exhibits. A must!' (K&L Gillespie). There is a small entrance fee. 'The curator and guide speaks good English. There are displays of transport, guns, cannons (one a gift from George IV to Radama I in 1817), police uniforms and even an intriguing array of confiscated murder weapons!' (D&K).

HEADING NORTH OR SOUTH

Moramanga lies at a crossroads. To the north is the road to Lake Alaotra and to the south is a rough but interesting road to Anosibe an' Ala. Onno Heuvel took this route on his mountain bike and reports: 'The road is very bad, and climbs up all the way to the Chutes de Mort, a large waterfall 53km south of Moramanga. This makes it tough to arrive there in one day, but otherwise this is a great mountain bike trip. There is also a 4x4 *taxi-brousse* that goes to Anosibe an' Ala.'

Continuing east you reach Andasibe (Périnet) in about half an hour (see page 282).

LAKE ALAOTRA

This is the largest lake in Madagascar and looks wonderful on the map; one imagines it surrounded by overhanging forest. Sadly, forest has made way for rice, and this is one of the most abused and degraded areas in Madagascar. Half a million people now live around the lake, and deforestation has silted it up so that its maximum dry-season depth is only 60cm. Introduction of exotic fish has

NATURALIST'S PROMISED LAND

Joseph-Philibert Commerson has provided the best-known quote on Madagascar:

C'est à Madagascar que je puis annoncer aux naturalistes qu'est la véritable terre promise pour eux. C'est là que la nature semble s'être retirée dans un sanctuaire particulier pour y travailler sur d'autres modèles que ceux auxquels elle s'est asservie ailleurs. Les formes les plus insolites et les plus merveilleuses s'y rencontrent à chaque pas.

Here in Madagascar I have truly found the naturalist's promised land. Nature seems to have retreated into a private sanctuary, to work on models unlike any she has created elsewhere. At every step one encounters the most strange and marvellous forms.

Commerson was a doctor who travelled with Bougainville on a world expedition in 1766, arriving at Mauritius in 1768. He studied the natural history of that island, then in 1770 journeyed on to Madagascar where he stayed for three or four months in the Fort Dauphin region. His famous description of 'nature's sanctuary' was in a 1771 letter, written from Madagascar, to his old tutor in Paris.

Tana to Toamasina **LAKE ALAOTRA**

10

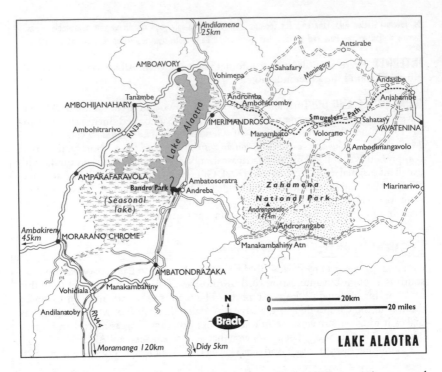

Map labels:
Andilamena 25km
Antsirabe
AMBOAVORY
Sahafary
Vohimena
Andasibe
Tanambe
Andromba
Ambohitromby
Anjahambe
AMBOHIJANAHARY
IMERIMANDROSO
Smugglers' Path
Sahatavy
VAVATENINA
Ambohitrarivo
RN3a
Manambato
Volorano
Ambodimangavolo
AMPARAFARAVOLA
Ambatosoratra
Zahamena
Miarinarivo
Bandro Park
Andreba
National Park
(Seasonal lake)
Andrangovalo 1474m
Ambakireny 45km
MORARANO CHROME
Androrangabe
Manakambahiny Atn
AMBATONDRAZAKA
Vohidiala
Manakambahiny
N
0   20km
0   20 miles
Andilanatoby
RN44
Bradt
Moramanga 120km
Didy 5km

LAKE ALAOTRA

done further damage. However, all is not lost. Since 1997 an environmental campaign led by Durrell Wildlife Conservation Trust has led to strong local support to ban marsh-burning and lemur-hunting and introduce larger net mesh sizes and a closed season for fishing. Local people recognised the role the marshes play in maintaining local hydrology, providing a spawning ground for fish and weaving materials for Alaotra's renowned basketry, an important source of income for women.

In 2006 the entire area, including watershed, rice fields, marshes and lake, was given protected status as part of The Durban Vision, and an ecotourism project developed to give tourists a chance to see one of Madagascar's most endangered species: the Lac Alaotra gentle lemur (see box opposite). Annual monitoring has shown that lemur populations have stabilised and that fish catches are on the increase. Alaotra provides a great example of conservation providing benefits for biodiversity and for local livelihoods and deserves some foreign visitors to support these local efforts.

GETTING THERE AND AWAY The dirt road (RN44) from Moramanga has been improved and, though still rough, is no longer the challenge of former years. A *taxi-brousse* from Tana to Ambatondrazaka takes around six hours, or less than four hours from Moramanga.

AMBATONDRAZAKA AND NEARBY VILLAGES This is the main town of the area, and a good centre for excursions. A tour of the lake by road will take a full day and takes you through village after village where rice, cattle, fishing and geese – along with tomatoes and onions – are the mainstays of rural life. The village **Imerimandroso** gives good views over the lake and nearby **Vohitsoa** is famed for its delicate baskets and mats woven with papyrus from the Alaotra marshes. And having got this far

Pascal Girod

Andreba is a small village at the edge of Lake Alaotra, and is the best place to see the Lac Alaotra gentle lemur (*Hapalemur alaotrensis*), or *bandro*, which is endemic to this region. This is also a great spot to observe the aquatic birds of Madagascar. Bandro Park comprises an area of papyrus bordering the lake. This has been set up as a protected area by the local community with support from Durrell Wildlife Conservation Trust and can be visited by pirogue. The best time to visit is from March to June, when the water level is highest. Since the end of 2006 the entire lake and marshes of Alaotra have been given protected area status as part of the Madagascar system of protected areas (SAPM). Local people are still permitted to fish and use the marsh products sustainably while also protecting some sensitive areas for the lemurs and water birds.

Madagascar Wildlife Conservation (MWC) has initiated a community-based project in Andreba with the goal of establishing nature tourism in the village. Income will be used for the village to finance micro projects such as the construction of public toilets, or wells for clean drinking water.

Camp Bandro is well signposted. It is a simple but beautiful tourist facility with a typical Shianaka house for accommodation (two rooms; 10,000Ar each), a kitchen, and simple showers/toilet. There's no restaurant in Andreba, but there's a little market and two *épiceries*, and for a small payment a cook will buy food and prepare a meal.

A pirogue tour on the lake and into the Bandro Park costs 10,000Ar/boat (2 people) and takes 1½–2hrs. The park fee is 10,000Ar. You will have to get up early as the *bandro* is best seen at dawn. But to experience daybreak on Lake Alaotra is well worth it.

Andreba currently has no electricity and no running water; perhaps by the end of 2007. Reservations can be made by email (e *reservation@mwc-info.net*). For more information visit www.mwc-info.net.

you really should pay a visit to the new **Bandro Park** near Andreba and enjoy an early-morning pirogue ride on the lake.

🏠 Where to stay/eat

🏠 **Hôtel Max-Irene** 📞 54 813 86. Near the train station in Ambatondrazaka, with some en-suite rooms. Friendly & clean. €–€€

🏠 **Hôtel Voahirana** Ambatondrazaka. Most rooms have mosquito nets; no en-suite facilities but hot water available. €

✕ **A la Bonne Ruche** Recommended.

THE SMUGGLERS' PATH A steady trickle of adventurers come to Lake Alaotra in order to hike the Smugglers' Path from Lake Alaotra to the east coast. I haven't done this myself and don't intend to – the feedback I've received has been quite negative. It's very tough, very steep, and not particularly rewarding (lots of deforestation).

The route takes four to five days, beginning in Andromba. The trail passes through Ambohitromby, Manambato, then various small villages before ending in Anjahambe.

From there there are *taxi-brousses* to Vavatenina, and thence to the east coast.

ANDREBA AND BANDRO PARK The main reason to come to Lake Alaotra these days is to visit the new Bandro Park at Andreba and to support this new ecotourism project. To get there take a *taxi-brousse* from Ambatondrazaka (about 45 mins; 2,000Ar).

Before reaching Andasibe, it is nice to have a stop at a small village called **Ambolomborona** at PK 124 to visit Hôtel Juema, a very simple traditional *hotely* on the right-hand side of the road. They can serve you *soupe Chinoise*, but if you plan to have lunch there you must give them time to prepare the food. Use the time to watch them making bamboo furniture.

About 1km before the Andasibe turn-off is the long (5½km) track to a new hotel which offers enough nature to be an alternative to Andasibe for those with their own transport (bicycle or car).

Eulophiella Lodge (10 bungalows) ☎ 22 242 30; m 032 07 567 82. Named after an endemic white orchid that only grows in the bases of pandanus plants. Malagasy-owned. Well-spaced A-frame bungalows in cleared forest with nice walking paths between. En-suite bathrooms, but only screened from the bedroom by a curtain. Mosquito nets. The dining hall & meeting room is huge — cavernous, even — with good food. The restaurant terrace faces a rainforest-covered slope containing the hotel's private reserve. The birding here is excellent & there's several lemurs: diademed sifakas, red-bellied lemurs & even indri. At night there are mouse, dwarf & woolly lemurs. Guided walks are 13,000–15,000Ar pp, depending on group size; night walks 7,000–9,000Ar. €€€€

ANDASIBE-MANTADIA NATIONAL PARK/ASSOCIATION MITSINJO

In the late 1990s the long-established reserve generally known by its colonial name of Périnet (but officially Analamazaotra) was combined with Mantadia 20km to the north to form Andasibe-Mantadia National Park. Because of its proximity to Tana and its exceptional fauna, this is now one of Madagascar's most popular reserves, receiving up to 300 visitors a day. These two areas of moist montane forest (altitude: 930–1,049m) are home to a variety of lemurs, birds, reptiles and invertebrates which can be seen by any reasonably fit visitor. The experience is enhanced by the quality of the local guides. If you visit only one national park in Madagascar it should be this or its neighbour, Association Mitsinjo. The latter is a newish, NGO-run reserve encompassing the Analamazaotra forest. It offers all the same wildlife as the national park but at a lower price, making it perfect for independent travellers. Visitors have been confused by the proximity of the two entrances: the national park is on the right as you approach from RN2 and Mitsinjo just beyond this, on the left.

Although the vast majority of visitors spend one or two nights here it is possible to visit Andasibe as a day trip from Tana. 'Hire a car with driver for €29 (and €40 for petrol). Leave at 06.00, arrive at 09.00, walk for two hours, you will see the indri and then return to your hotel in Tana' (Joyce Wouters).

☞ **WARNING!** In the winter months of May to August it can feel very cold in Andasibe, especially when it rains (as it does at that time of year). Hotels without heaters can be quite an ordeal. At any time of year bring warm clothing and adequate waterproofs.

ANDASIBE VILLAGE Derek Antonio Serra writes: 'If you'd like to spend a few days living in the midst of a typical Malagasy village, then book into Hôtel Orchidée in Andasibe. Sitting on the balcony, one has a unique opportunity to observe daily village life – people rushing off to market twice daily, cute kids playing in the streets, disputes between neighbours – it's all there. Bear in mind that there is no bank to exchange money, no internet access and – believe it or not – not one taxi in Andasibe. You have to walk everywhere, including a couple of kilometres to the

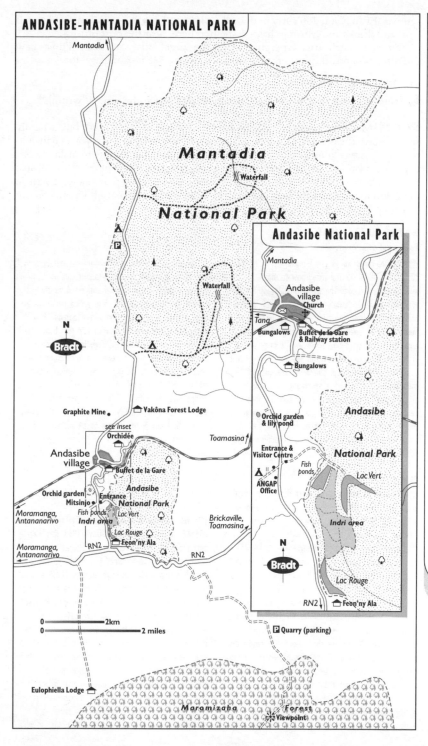

ANDASIBE-MANTADIA NATIONAL PARK

Mantadia

Mantadia

National Park

Waterfall

Waterfall

N

Bradt

Graphite Mine

Vakôna Forest Lodge

see inset

Orchidée

Andasibe village

Buffet de la Gare

Toamasina

Orchid garden

Mitsinjo

Entrance

Fish ponds

Lac Vert

Andasibe

National Park

Brickaville, Toamasina

Indri area

Lac Rouge

Feon'ny Ala

Moramanga, Antananarivo

Moramanga, Antananarivo

RN2

RN2

0 _____ 2km

0 _____ 2 miles

P Quarry (parking)

Eulophiella Lodge

Maromizaha *Forest*

Viewpoint

Andasibe National Park

Mantadia

Andasibe village   Church

Tana

Bungalows

Buffet de la Gare & Railway station

Bungalows

Andasibe

Orchid garden & lily pond

Entrance & Visitor Centre

National Park

ANGAP Office

Fish ponds

Lac Vert

Indri area

N

Bradt

Lac Rouge

RN2

Feon'ny Ala

10

reserve.' Even if you don't stay in the village it is well worth a visit. Small shops sell fruit and drinks and Mitsinjo has a craft shop here, near the post office.

You can watch bats emerging from the post office at dusk. Three new interpretation boards give information about them. See box on page 466.

GETTING THERE AND AWAY
By train No passenger trains are running on this line at the time of writing.

By road MadaBus goes to Andasibe for €9, leaving Tana at 07.00, but it hardly seems worth the cost for a three-hour trip, especially since it drops you at Mitsinjo reserve, at least a kilometre from the nearest hotel (and just too late to make it a day trip). Regular *taxi-brousses* leave from Tana's eastern *taxi-brousse* station. Most people take one to Moramanga (a regular stop, 5,000Ar) and a then a local vehicle the 25km to the Andasibe turn-off from RN2 or to the village itself where you can be dropped off at the hotel of your choice.

WHERE TO STAY/EAT
Top end €€€€€
🏠 **Vakôna Forest Lodge** (24 bungalows) ✆ 22 624 80; f 22 230 70; e izouard@bow.dts.mg; www.hotel-vakona.com. The name is Malagasy for the pandanus plant. Andasibe's only luxury hotel, located just over 1km from the park. The main building is thoughtfully designed with an octagonal reception area, bar & lounge-dining room with a huge log-fire in the middle (very welcome in the cold season). The upper storey has a shop. Bungalows are quiet & comfortable. There's also a swimming pool. The management is efficient & courteous, & the food delicious. Vakôna deserves longer than the normal couple of days so you can relax, enjoy the pool & some horseriding as well as the usual lemur-viewing. The hotel has its own little 'reserve' where former pet lemurs live in relative freedom. In past editions I have been unreasonably sniffy about this place, so let me say that I'm now a total convert & as thrilled as anyone to have a black-&-white ruffed lemur dangle from a branch to eat my preferred banana, & to photograph a brown lemur with her tiny baby. Not to mention the adorable (though lonely) diademed sifaka. Let's face it – no one will know your superb photo of one of Madagascar's rarest lemurs was taken here! To reach Vakôna from Andasibe, cross the bridge into the village, & fork left then follow the signs. If you don't have your own vehicle it's easiest to use MadaBus & prearrange to be picked up by the hotel's vehicle (but quite expensive). If you haven't much luggage, it's a pleasant 2km walk.

Mid range €€€
🏠 **Eulophiella Lodge** (for contact details, see page 282). Over 5km off RN2 so you need your own car if you are to use this as accommodation when visiting Andasibe.

🏠 **Hôtel Feon' ny Ala** (30 bungalows) ✆ 56 832 02. On the right side of the road coming from RN2. Most bungalows en suite but 7 with shared facilities for only 14,400Ar. The name means 'voice of the forest'. This is a popular place in a prime location overlooking the river adjacent to the reserve (close enough to hear the indri call, hence the name). Orchid garden & resident chameleons. But reportedly becoming quite shabby & the lack of heaters in the cold winter months is a problem, as is the noise: some people complain that the only 'voice of the forest' is the nocturnal snores of the guests in nearby bungalows. Bring earplugs! The Chinese owners, M & Mme Sum Chuk Lan, are, however, very helpful. The restaurant is reasonable. Camping for 4,000Ar.

🏠 **Hôtel Buffet de la Gare** (15 bungalows) ✆ 56 832 08. Next to the station. Until 1993 this was the only place to stay in Andasibe & its list of distinguished guests includes Prince Philip, Gerald Durrell & David Attenborough. Built in 1938 it must once have been appropriate for its role of housing the great & the good who wished to visit Périnet, but rooms in the main hotel have deteriorated beyond habitability (although drivers are sometimes put up here). The more recently built bungalows are fine; there are 8 in a lovely meadow close to the forest, each with 3–4 beds, hot water & fireplace – what joy! Less comfortable, but perfectly adequate, are 7 chalet-type bungalows. The dining-room is truly elegant – fresh flowers on the tables & a marvellous rosewood bar, though the service is very,

very slow. But do take at least a beer here to see one of Andasibe's celebrated sights: the *Phelsuma* gecko which stuck to the new paintwork near the door; the enthusiastic workman simply applied another coat of paint over its little body, & there it remains!

Budget €€

⌂ **Hôtel Orchidée** ✆ 56 832 05. In Andasibe village, away from the main tourist infrastructure. Basic rooms with shared bathrooms & hot water. Very good value. Owner speaks English. The only sit-down restaurant in the village has very good soups. Order in advance to avoid a long wait.

⛺ **Camping** You can camp at the entrance to the park (no running water) or on the lawn at Hôtel Feon' ny Ala where there's access to flush toilets and a hot shower.

🍴 **WHERE TO EAT** Most people eat at their hotel but Alex Holroyd-Smith recommends **Halal**, just off the main road (RN2). 'I borrowed the park office bike to get there! It's a great little restaurant, especially for early breakfasts.'

The small restaurant by the park entrance serves fairly expensive food, offers good views over the clearing and great birdwatching! It closes at 17.00.

PERMITS AND GUIDES You can get your permit from ANGAP in Tana, or at the park entrance.

The Andasibe guides are among the best in Madagascar and an example to the rest of the country for knowledge, enthusiasm and an awareness of what tourists want. The Association des Guides Andasibe (AGA) ensures that standards are maintained. All the guides know where to find indri and other lemurs and many are expert birders. A board in the park office displays their names, photos, specialist subjects and languages spoken. There are set routes taking various amounts of time and priced accordingly. The shortest, Indri 1, is 1–2hrs (4,000Ar), Indri 2 is 3–5hrs (8,000Ar). A 4–5hr visit to Mantadia costs 20,000Ar. On top of the fee guides expect a tip.

VISITOR CENTRE The visitor centre is terrific! Excellent explanations of animal behaviour and the whole ecology of this montane rainforest. There are also some nice souvenirs such as T-shirts and a good snack bar outside, as well as a rather splendid toilet.

ANDASIBE NATIONAL PARK (PÉRINET) This 810ha reserve protects the largest of the lemurs, *Indri indri*. Standing about a metre high, with a barely visible tail, black-and-white markings and a surprised teddy-bear face, the indri looks more like a gone-wrong panda than a lemur. The long back legs are immensely powerful, and an indri can propel itself 10m, executing a turn in mid-air, to hug a new tree and gaze down benevolently at its observers. And you will be an observer: everyone now sees indris in this reserve, and most also hear them. For it is the voice that makes this lemur extra special: whilst other lemurs grunt or swear, the indri sings. It is an eerie, wailing sound somewhere between the song of a whale and a police siren, and it carries for up to 3km as troops call to each other across the forest. The indris are fairly punctual with their song, but if they oversleep the guides now encourage them with taped calls (I have mixed feelings about the ethics of this, but it certainly works). They also generally call shortly before dusk, but during the middle of the day they take a long siesta in the canopy so you are unlikely to see them.

Indri are monogamous, living in small family groups of up to five animals, and give birth in June every two years. In Malagasy the indri is called *babakoto* which means 'father of Koto'. It is *fady* to kill an indri, the legend being that the boy Koto climbed a tree in the forest to collect wild honey, and was severely stung by the bees. Losing his hold, he fell, but was caught by an indri which carried him on its back to safety.

There are 11 species of lemur altogether in Andasibe (including aye-aye), although you will not see them all. In addition to indri, you may find the troop of grey bamboo lemurs which are diurnal and sometimes seen near the concrete bridge at Lac Vert, common brown lemurs and perhaps a sleeping avahi (woolly lemur) curled up in the fork of a tree. Diademed sifakas and black-and-white ruffed lemurs have been translocated here from Mantadia.

Lemurs are only some of the creatures to be found in Andasibe. There are tenrecs, beautiful and varied insects and spiders, as well as reptiles. Sadly the latter are becoming very scarce, as the illegal reptile trade takes its toll. In the old days boys would bring some spectacular Parson's chameleons (bright green and half a metre long) to the trees by the entrance. Now even this artificial display has gone, although if you're lucky your guide will leave you while he 'looks' for a chameleon. However, snakes are still quite common, including some handsome boas.

This is also a great place for birdwatching. Specials to look out for include the velvet asity, blue coua and nuthatch vanga.

Leeches can be an unpleasant aspect of the reserve if you've pushed through vegetation and it's been raining recently. Tuck your trousers into your socks and apply insect repellent. If a leech gets through your defences a handy supply of salt will persuade it to let go.

The trails in Andasibe have been carefully constructed, but nevertheless, there is quite a steep ascent (up steps) to the plateau where the indri are found, and to follow these animals you may have to scramble a bit. You may find this difficult if your walking is impaired.

Night walks are not allowed in the national park itself (but see *Association Mitsinjo*), though it's worth going on a guided nocturnal stroll along the road for the frogs and chameleons which are easier to see at night. One memorable time our group disturbed a streaked tenrec that fell/jumped into the lake. When the little animal reached the far shore in safety our cheers will have woken every sleeping indri for miles!

MANTADIA NATIONAL PARK While Andasibe (Périnet/Analamazaotra) is for almost everyone, Mantadia, 20km to the north, is for the enthusiast. The trails are rugged but the rewards are exceptional. Mantadia varies more in altitude (between 800m and 1,260m) than the more popular reserve and consequently harbours different species. What makes it so special is that, in contrast to Andasibe, it comprises virtually untouched primary forest. There are 10,000ha with just a few constructed trails – visitors must be prepared to work for their wildlife – but this is a naturalist's goldmine with many seldom-seen species of mammals, reptiles and birds.

The forest is bisected by the road, with the three trails on the eastern side. Here you may see the beautiful golden-coloured diademed sifaka (*simpona*) and some indri (curiously much darker in colour than in Andasibe). Both these lemur species are getting easier to see as they become habituated to humans. This section of Mantadia has some good, but steep, trails with gorgeous views across the forest and super birdwatching possibilities, including specials such as the scaly ground-roller, pitta-like ground-roller and red-breasted coua.

There are two main trail areas: the northern Tsokoko circuit at 14km is the toughest and best for wildlife, and a couple of trails to the south. One is an easy two-hour trail which leads up through the forest to a waterfall and lake (Cascade and Lac Sacré). Bring your swimsuit for a cooling dip in the pool beneath the waterfall. The alternative is the longer Rianasoa circuit.

To do justice to Mantadia you should spend the whole day there, bringing a picnic, and leave the hotel at dawn. You will need your own transport and, of course, a guide. If you stay until dusk you will find a nocturnal walk up to the waterfall very rewarding. Best of all is to camp overnight.

ASSOCIATION MITSINJO (✆ *56 832 33;* e *mitsinjo@hotmail.com.* ⊕ *07.00–17.00 & 18.30–21.30. Prices (inc guide): 2–3hrs 15,000Ar, 4–5hrs 25,000Ar, night walk 12,000Ar)* This local NGO is promoting reforestation and other conservation measures while offering the same attractions as the national park. There are seven groups of indri here, but only one group is habituated. The entrance is roughly opposite that of the national park. Here you'll find Mitsinjo's office and visitor centre. They also operate in the bird reserve of Torotorofotsy and run a handicrafts shop in Andasibe village. Tourist revenue is used to finance conservation and development activities in order to achieve sustainable use of natural resources by local communities. Mitsinjo works with 400 households in the region, providing mosquito nets and water purifying kits in addition to their work with HIV/AIDS and family planning. They have their own tree nursery where 6,000 seedlings are being raised to provide the 30 endemic species that will re-establish corridors between blocks of forest now isolated from each other due to slash-and-burn agriculture.

I was thrilled by my visit here in 2005, not only for what I saw (my first ever mossy leaf-tailed gecko, *Uroplatus sikorae*) but the enthusiasm of the guide and the work the Association is doing. Chris Howles agrees: 'We look back at the 4½-hour trek we did as one of the highlights of the holiday. Our guide spoke good English and had a very good knowledge of all the local flora and fauna. He worked hard to find everything for us, including of course a family of indri. They came really close to us and we stayed with them for about 45mins, stopping when our necks started to ache from all that looking up in the trees!'

This is a rewarding place for night walks, especially since these are not permitted in the national park. Derek Schuurman reports: 'The recently described (2005)

Goodman's mouse lemur is readily seen. Your chances of seeing reptiles such as Parson's chameleons and Uroplatus geckos are better here and, being able to walk around inside the rainforest at night as opposed to scouring secondary growth along the road, you are bound to see a lot more in terms of frogs and other nocturnal creatures.'

MAD'ARBRES (✆ *22 417 54;* m *032 40 300 59/033 12 343 17;* e *madarbres@yahoo.fr; www.madarbres.com. Prices: half day 50,000Ar, full day 80,000Ar*) This company offering canopy tours (April to November) operates from the same office as Mitsinjo. Only small groups are taken at a time so book in advance if possible.

TOROTOROFOTSY

In the old days this marsh 11km west of Andasibe was an important part of any birding trip. But it was unprotected and difficult to reach so was removed from tour operators' itineraries. Now it's back, thanks to Mitsinjo and the Ramsar Convention of Wetlands; Torotorofotsy was declared a Ramsar Site in 2005.

MAROMIZAHA

In the 1990s this forested but unprotected area provided some excellent hiking, distant lemur viewing, and an impressive variety of weevils, some wearing little yellow tutus. Then the loggers arrived, and in a few years there was nothing to see except cleared hillsides. Now Maromizaha is being rehabilitated as a protected area. It is still a beautiful walk and the sound of the chainsaws has been silenced. It will take a few years for the lemurs to return, but I see no reason why the weevils should stay away! Enquire at the Andasibe park office.

VOHIMANA

This forest reserve, a few kilometres east of Andasibe, is protected through a partnership with local villagers and an NGO, Man And The Environment (www.mate.mg). They are working towards reducing the local community's dependence on slash-and-burn farming. Clearly this is a project worth supporting, but Vohimana is much more than that – it provides arguably the best 'herping' experience in the area. Anyone with a serious interest in Madagascar's reptiles and frogs should plan a visit here. The reserve is roughly the same size as Andasibe but it includes rainforest of a great range of elevations (700–1,080m) and is known for its frog diversity (over 80 species) and various chameleons not found in Andasibe, including *Calumma galleus*, which has a spectacularly long nasal extension. If you're still in doubt, here's Derek Schuurman who visited in 2006: 'An unforgettable night-walk highlight was one tree which contained so many chameleons on the outer leaves and small branches that it looked like a Christmas tree with live decorations.'

GETTING THERE The entrance to Vohimana is off RN2, on the left, shortly after the turn-off to Andasibe, near the village of Ambavaniasy, between PK 148 and 149. The walk to the reserve takes about 45mins, the latter part along the railway line.

WHERE TO STAY At present there are three simple bungalows and a dormitory with eight beds. However, by the time you read this, a large house with four en-suite rooms will have been completed. There's an electric socket in the dining room so camera batteries can be recharged. Accommodation and meals should be prebooked, either through a tour operator or by contacting MATE (e *mail@mate.mg*).

WHAT TO SEE AND DO You can divide your time between seeing what MATE is doing to help Madagascar's environmental crisis, such as visiting the tree nursery (like at Mitsinjo, these saplings will be used to establish a forest corridor linking isolated areas of forest), the distillery – which demonstrates that revenue can be earned from the leaves of trees without having to cut them down – or searching for wildlife.

Circuits vary from 2.5km (the Flying Fox Trail) to a 12km trip to seek out indri. Derek and Toky hiked a 7.2km trail 'which took us past the researchers' village and through cultivated fields into beautiful rainforest. At lower elevations, pandanus were especially abundant while from the highest viewpoints, you can take in spectacular vistas of the rainforest. Besides encountering three groups of diademed sifakas, a highlight was finding a few *Mantella pulchra* frogs. It is also a good site for the even-more-beautiful *Mantella baroni*.

'Olivier Behra of MATE took us on another walk to a fascinating tunnel which was part of the old railway built in 1905. This is a roosting site for four species of bat, and is one of a handful of known sites for two endemic species, Peters's sheath-tailed bat (*Emballonura atrata*) and Malagasy mouse-eared bat (*Myotis goudoti*).'

MATE is a non-profit organisation so all tourist income is ploughed back into the project.

BEFORONA

Christina Dodwell recommends a visit to the agro-ecology project here: 'Their guided tour shows how they tackle erosion on the mountain slopes using vetiver grass, and their terraces of fish ponds and rice fields have an ingenious bamboo pipe water supply, each pond flowing to another lower down the slope. The centre is run by a local farmers' co-operative and a representative is happy to explain to you about their conservation and development work. The tour takes an hour. It is free but donations are greatly appreciated. All proceeds go to the co-operative. They have a cheerful little canteen, and dormitories (max 25 people) for study groups and overnight visitors. These cost 3,000Ar or 6,000Ar full board. Reserve in advance by contacting Mparany (e *HBP@chemonics.mg with copy to nyrapa@yahoo.fr*).'

FROM ANDASIBE TO TOAMASINA

The start of the journey from Andasibe down to Toamasina is lovely, taking you through lush, mist-enshrouded rainforest which includes Maromizaha and Vohimana. Derek Schuurman drove this route in 2006: 'All these sites are part of an extensive rainforest area which includes Vohimana, Mantadia and the even-larger but as yet unprotected Vohidrazona. The plan is to link separated blocks with corridors of rainforest, hence the establishment of various tree nurseries.

'The rainforest is eventually replaced by eucalyptus woods, which after some 40km give way to *savoka* (secondary growth) dotted with *Ravenala* trees, and then *bozaka* (the short, tough grassland which replaces *savoka* once the same plot of land has been burnt too severely or frequently).

'Of all the regions in Madagascar, the east has arguably suffered most from deforestation and in the 15-odd years I have been travelling to the island, I have never undertaken a road journey through landscape so depressing. It was during this road stint that the severity of Madagascar's environmental crisis hit me head-on, like a freight train.

'In time, an increasing population requires more space. There is competition coupled with tradition. Forests have been – and continue to be – torched and felled apace. Places we visitors admired for their achingly beautiful scenery as little as a decade ago aren't looking so picturesque now.'

That said, Derek and I agree that the efforts of conservation groups and the active help of the current government do offer real hope for the future.

The first town of interest is Ambodiaviavy (PK 173). Ony writes:

'While driving down the road I was attracted by the nice garden with flowers and green grass on the left side at where you can see a waterfall called Andriampotsimbato. So I stopped and talked to a young man called Lezoma who has built a chalet with a garden for the people passing by. He charges visitors a small fee to picnic here.'

Plan to stop in **Bedary** (PK 203) just to taste the delicious Malagasy food prepared by Mme Evelyne, the owner of the small blue wooden restaurant called **Elegance**.

The next place worth stopping at is **Ranomafana** (PK 205) – a name encountered often in Madagascar since it simply means 'hot water'. Ony continues: 'The village has a natural hot spring which is not exploited since it is considered by the local people to be sacred, and is used instead for asking blessings from the ancestors. The turn-off is just beyond the village before the bridge. Then you take the slippery, muddy path on the right and cross the river on foot during the dry season. When I went there I spoke to a local couple who had been childless for seven years; after asking for blessing in this place they had a baby. I was told that meat or eggs can be cooked in this hot spring. If you have time to visit, it is better to ask the local people to guide you there.'

There is a post office in this village, and a few *hotelys*. Restaurant **La Girolle** serves inexpensive Malagasy food. They also have three very simple rooms and one small bungalow.

If you are looking for somewhere to eat, **Manambonitra** (PK 215) has a few *hotelys* along the road and a fruit stall. Restaurant **Ami d'Or** has a nice view from its veranda and is open every day.

ANTSAPANANA The last town before Brickaville, and of new importance now the road to Vatomandry has been improved (it lies at the junction). This is where you look for a *taxi-brousse* going south.

The town is brimming with stalls offering a huge variety of fruit and vegetables. Good for reprovisioning and photography. If you want to dally longer there is the basic **Hôtel Espérance** – a good name for a town that only got a piped water supply in 2006! Stuart Cassie recommends the restaurant **Fantasia** (yes, in your dreams …): 'It's recently opened, clean, simple and inexpensive. Run by a couple of young women friends, both university graduates from Tana: Viviane and Loulou; Viviane speaks English.'

If you are heading west towards Tana you are now about 1½ hours' drive from Andasibe.

BRICKAVILLE After almost 225km of smooth roads and wide open spaces, the potholes, noise and industry of Brickaville can come as a bit of a shock. However fruit, vegetables and friendly *hotelys* can be found there in abundance allowing ample opportunity for reprovisioning and refreshment before heading on towards Toamasina across an enormous, ageing (but sturdy) iron bridge over the Rongaronga River.

This is one of those Malagasy towns which has resisted changing its name, despite the efforts of mapmakers. Everyone, Malagasy included, knows it as

MANGOSTEENS IN BRICKAVILLE

Derek Schuurman

As a teenager in the 1970s, I read in an encyclopedia that of all the world's known edible fruits, the one regarded as tastiest is the mangosteen (*Garcinia mangostana*). Mangosteen trees can attain a height of 25m, are strictly tropical and the species is of Mollucan origin. The outside of the edible fruit – which is roughly the size of a small orange – is a deep reddish-purple when ripe. Its fragrant white flesh, separated into segments, is quite sweet and creamy, slightly citrusy with a touch of peach flavour thrown in. In Asia, it is appropriately referred to as the 'queen of fruits'. There's also apparently a tale about Queen Victoria offering a cash reward to anyone who could deliver to her the fabled fruit. (When you taste one as I did after a 25-year wait, you'll quickly understand why she offered a reward – and why mangosteen is so highly rated.)

The problem for those of us living outside tropical countries is that obtaining fresh mangosteens is virtually impossible: it is hardly, if ever, sold fresh in western countries. Importing them without fumigation or irradiation is illegal because of fears that they may harbour the Asian fruit fly which could devastate fruit crops.

For the next 25 years, whenever I was in the tropics, I sometimes wondered about whether I would ever get to see a mangosteen. And then in late November 2006, while driving from Andasibe-Mantadia to Manambato, we were stopped at a roadblock just outside Brickaville. Suddenly, some Betsimisaraka kids appoached the stationary car, offering small plastic bagfuls of round, hard-shelled, deep maroon fruit. I looked at them, looked again and wondered aloud: 'good grief – is this mangosteen?' They were indeed, and for the equivalent of 20p we bought a bag of them. So if you are in Madagascar in November, and happen to be in the hot eastern coastal plains, your chances of finding the world's tastiest fruit, are very good indeed.

Brickaville, but its official name is Ampasimanolotra. It lies 134km south of Toamasina.

The town is the centre of sugarcane and citrus production and has a few hotels, but few people would stay intentionally.

🏠 Where to stay

🏠 **Hôtel Bricka Cool** (7 bungalows) Dbl bungalows, some of which are en suite. Perhaps the best of a poor lot. €–€€

🏠 **Hôtel Restaurant Mevasoa** (3 bungalows) Malagasy food served. €

🏠 **Hôtel des Amis** 'You wouldn't put your worst enemies there' (Rupert Parker). But it's cheap. Bathroom & toilet outside. €

✕ **Retaurant Florida** Near the railway station; Malagasy food.

AMBILA-LEMAITSO This is a seaside/canalside resort town, where you can happily get stuck for a day or so. But now the trains are not running it is quite hard to reach by public transport. Best to get off at Brickaville and walk to Ambila along the railway line. It takes 3–4 hours.

From Ambila you can walk north for 2–3 hours to lake Ampitabe (Ankanin'ny Nofy); see page 296.

🏠 Where to stay/eat

🏠 **Hôtel Relais Malaky** ☎ 56 260 13/22 644 68. Probably the best hotel, in a good situation close to the station & overlooking the ocean. However, it has no running water (a problem in all of Ambila). Very friendly owner; good food. A range of bungalows & rooms, some en suite. Canoe rental 2,000Ar/hr. €€€€

Ambila Beach About 3km from the station, overlooking the Pangalanes Canal. Very nice bungalows, some with cooking facilities, but dodgy water supply. Pool under construction. €€€€

 Le Nirvana m 030 55 852 69. An efficient, French-run hotel near the ferry. €€€

 Le Tropicana Nice new wooden bungalows (dbl & 4-person) near the station. Bucket shower; shared toilet. Friendly Malagasy owners. Order food in advance to avoid long wait. €

MANAMBATO

This is a picturesque lakeside resort, about 20km northeast of Brickaville, 7km from RN2. The turn-off is between PK 260 and 261 on a road which is muddy and slippery after rain. Lake Rasoabe is part of the Pangalanes Canal system, and Manambato is popular with weekenders from Tana and their children (the bathing is much safer than in the ocean). It is also an access town for boat trips to Ankanin'ny Nofy and Lake Ampitabe. A few hotels face the lake and there are wide beaches of white sand. An advantage of Manambato over Ankanin'ny Nofy is that it can be reached by car, although there are also boats from Toamasina. The disadvantage is that there is no public transport there; you need to take a taxi or go on foot from Ambila.

WHERE TO STAY/EAT

 Chez Luigi ☎ 56 720 20. Very comfortable bungalows, rooms & excellent restaurant. Rooms for up to 5 people; en suite. Popular so book in advance for w/ends & holidays. €€€

 Hôtel Rasoa Beach (10 bungaows) ☎ 56 720 18; m 032 02 361 87; f 56 720 19; e rasoab@dts.mg. Dbl & 4-person bungalows & a 'Tarzan' hut on stilts! The more expensive ones have lake views. Good food; half-board only. €€€

 Acacias ☎ 56 720 35/22 404 29; f 22 404 29. Dbl, twin & family bungalows. Meals served. €€€

 Au Bon Coin Zanatany At the entrance to the village. Malagasy-run chalets for budget travellers. Shared facilities. Very good food. €€

 Hôtel Hibiscus (4 bungalows) Lac Rasoabe. Simple bungalows with shared facilities. Malagasy food. €

Beyond Brickaville, a few glimpses of the ocean and Pangalanes lakes convinces you that you've reached the coast, beyond which it's a relatively uneventful 94km to Toamasina through degraded forest and palm plantations.

11

South of Toamasina

This chapter covers the increasingly visited Pangalanes Lake resorts to the south of Toamasina. It touches on the little-visited (but surely that's part of the attraction) towns that may be accessed via the Pangalanes Canal, before rejoining the good road which joins the two seaside towns of Manakara and Mananjary, and continues to the pleasant town of Farafangana. After Vangaindrano the road/track becomes unpredictable, although a trickle of adventurous travellers manage to reach Taolagnaro (Fort Dauphin).

The Pangalanes region is a stronghold of the Betsimisaraka, the second-largest ethnic group in Madagascar. Perhaps because of the isolation imposed by lack of transport, there have been fewer mixed marriages here so the culture has remained remarkably pure.

PANGALANES

This series of lakes was linked by artificial canals in French colonial times for commercial use, a quiet inland water being preferable to an often stormy sea. Over the years the canals became choked with vegetation and no longer passable, but they are gradually being cleared so that in future there may once again be an unbroken waterway stretching 665km from Toamasina to Vangaindrano (see box on page 295). Currently 430km are, in theory, navigable, and some tour operators offer one- to four-day trips down the canal. Surprisingly, I have never heard of anyone taking their own kayak or canoe down the canals; it must certainly be an option.

The quiet waters of the canal and lakes are much used by local fishermen for transporting their goods in pirogues and for fishing. The canal and ocean are separated by about a kilometre of dense bush, so it is not easy to go from one to the other.

In recent years Pangalanes has been developed for tourism, with lakeside bungalows and private nature reserves competing with the traditional ocean resorts for custom. The tourist centre is **Lake Ampitabe** which has broad beaches of dazzlingly white sand, clean water for swimming, and a private nature reserve with several introduced species of lemur.

GETTING THERE AND AWAY Each hotel provides its own transport for booked-in guests, and a service is also provided by La Maison de Sainte-Marie, which shares

DISTANCES IN KILOMETRES			
Toamasina–Vatomandry	189km	Mananjary–Manakara	152km
Vatomandry–Mahanoro	70km	Manakara–Farafangana	109km
Mahanoro–Nosy Varika	91km	Farafangana–Vangaindrano	75km
Nosy Varika–Mananjary	109km		

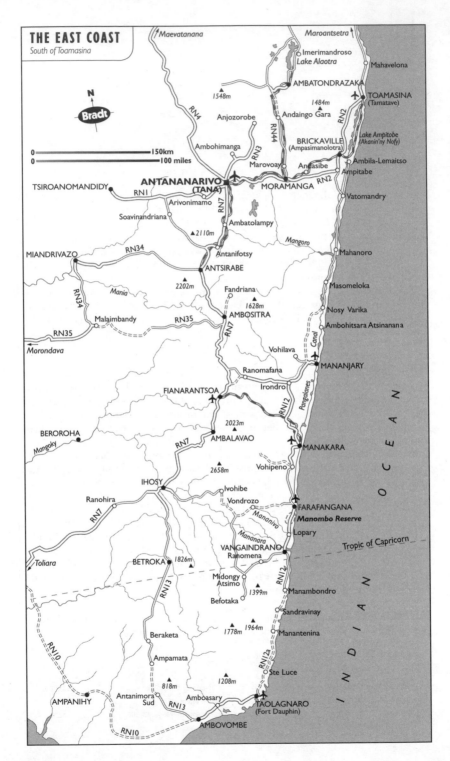

THE EAST COAST
South of Toamasina

Bradt

N

0 ———— 150km
0 ———— 100 miles

Maevatanana

Maroantsetra

Imerimandroso
Lake Alaotra

Mahavelona

AMBATONDRAZAKA

▲ 1548m

TOAMASINA
(Tamatave)

Anjozorobe

Andaingo Gara

▲ 1484m

RN4

Ambohimanga

Marovoay

BRICKAVILLE
(Ampasimanolotra)

RN3

RN44

Lake Ampitobe
(Akanin'ny Nofy)

Ambila-Lemaitso

ANTANANARIVO
(TANA)

Andasibe

Ampitabe

TSIROANOMANDIDY

RN1

Arivonimamo

MORAMANGA

RN2

RN7

Vatomandry

Soavinandriana

Ambatolampy

▲ 2110m

Mangoro

Mahanoro

MIANDRIVAZO

RN34

Antanifotsy

ANTSIRABE

Masomeloka

Mania

▲ 2202m

Fandriana

Nosy Varika

RN34

▲ 1628m

Ambohitsara Atsinanana

Malaimbandy

RN35

AMBOSITRA

RN7

RN35

Vohilava

Canal

Morondava

Ranomafana

MANANJARY

FIANARANTSOA

Irondro

Pangalanes

RN12

BEROROHA

▲ 2023m

Mangoky

AMBALAVAO

RN7

MANAKARA

▲ 2658m

Vohipeno

IHOSY

Ivohibe

Ranohira

Vondrozo

FARAFANGANA

RN7

Mananivo

Manombo Reserve

Lopary

Mananara

VANGAINDRANO

Tropic of Capricorn

Toliara

Ranomena

BETROKA

▲ 1826m

Midongy
Atsimo

RN13

▲ 1399m

Manambondro

Befotaka

Sandravinay

▲ 1778m ▲ 1964m

Manantenina

Beraketa

RN10

Ampamata

▲ 818m

▲ 1208m

RN12a

Ste Luce

Antanimora
Sud

Amboasary

TAOLAGNARO
(Fort Dauphin)

RN13

AMPANIHY

RN10

AMBOVOMBE

I N D I A N   O C E A N

Colin Palmer

The Canal des Pangalanes was created in colonial times to provide a safe means of transport along the east coast. The shore is surf-beaten and the few harbours are shallow and dangerous. The inland water passage provided a safe alternative and around the turn of the century regular ferry services were in operation. The canal interconnected the natural rivers and lagoons, where necessary cutting through the low-lying coastal plain. At intervals it crosses rivers which flow to the sea, providing access for fishermen and ensuring that the level is stable.

The waterways fell into disuse, but in the 1980s a grand project to rehabilitate them was carried out. Silted canals were dredged, new warehouses built and a fleet of modern tug barge units purchased to operate a cargo service. That may once have worked, but now the warehouses and quaysides are empty and the tug barge units lie in a jumble in the harbour at Toamasina.

Meanwhile, local people make good use of the waterways. Mechanised ferries run from Toamasina and every house along the way seems to have a wooden pirogue. The communities face the water and for many people it is the only reliable means of transport, especially in the wet season. It is also a vital source of livelihood and the stakes of fish traps almost fill the channels, while fields of cassava line the banks. Piles of dried fish, wood and charcoal stand in heaps awaiting collection by the returning ferries. Coming from the town, they are overflowing with people competing for space with beer crates, bicycles, sacks of food and all the other paraphernalia of life.

To travel on the Pangalanes is a joy – well, mostly. Start at Toamasina and you get the worst bit over and done with quickly. Boats leave from the bleak Port Fluvial, with its empty warehouses and discarded tug barges. The first, manmade, cut of the canal runs south from the town, past the oil refinery. The air is thick with the smell of hydrocarbons and greasy black outfalls show all too clearly the source of the grey slime that coats the water hyacinth – seemingly the only thing capable of growing. But persevere and soon you start to pass family canoes tied to the bank and the slender, deeply loaded ferry boats pushed by struggling outboard motors. As the water starts to clear, the vegetation recolonises the riverbank and the pervasive odour of industrialisation slips away.

The artificial straightness of the first sections gives way to twisting channels and the wider expanses of lagoons and lakes – a world where communities of thatched wooden houses cluster around small landing places, grey rectangles in a canvas of green and blue, delineated here and there by the stark white of sandy beaches.

Those planning an exploration of the Pangalanes in their own canoe should buy maps no 6 and no 8 of the 1:500,000 series published by FTM (see page 172). French sea charts also show the canal.

an office in Tana with MadaBus (📞 *24 265 02;* 📱 *032 04 887 09;* ✉ *cap-sainte-marie@wanadoo.mg*). Reaching the lodges at Ankanin'ny Nofy on Lake Ampitabe from RN2 involves a drive to Manambato, at the edge of Lake Rasoabe (see page 292), followed by a 45-minute boat journey along Pangalanes.

You can also take a motor launch from the Port Fluvial in Toamasina. The ride takes 1½ hours and is most enjoyable, giving a good flavour of the lakes and connecting canal, and the activities of the local people. It's nice to see the speedboats slow down to a crawl when they pass the laden pirogues, to avoid capsizing them in the wash.

A do-it-yourself option is to walk from Ambila-Lemaitso (2–3 hours).

This isolated lake is accessible (for tourists) only by boat so is beautifully quiet and peaceful. There are white, sandy beaches, a delightful little reserve, and the Lac aux Nepenthes where there are literally thousands of (insect-eating) pitcher plants. There is also the opportunity to offset your carbon emissions in a local and realistic way by planting a tree at the admirable Vohibola reserve.

 WHERE TO STAY There are three sets of beach bungalows at Ankanin'ny Nofy, which means 'house of dreams'. Phone the agencies in Tana or Toamasina (details below) for latest prices and availability. Quoted prices usually include a double bungalow, plus transfers and meals.

🏠 **Bush House** (11 bungalows & 2 rooms) Book through Boogie Pilgrim (40 Av de l'Indépendance, Tana; ❞ 22 258 78; f 22 625 56; e bushhouse@simicro.mg; www.boogiepilgrim-madagascar.com). German-run, comfortable, beautiful location. Bush House has been highly praised by readers: 'Definitely the best night of the trip. The food, the accommodation & the people were all exceptional.' €€€€

🏠 **Le Palmarium** m 033 14 847 34; e hotelpalmarium@yahoo.fr. Large bungalows with en-suite bathrooms & hot water. Electric sockets. Large restaurant & bar; good food. A stay here is considerably enlivened by Philibert the tame vasa parrot & a pair of extremely cheeky brown lemurs. €€€€
🏠 **Hôtel Pangalanes** (12 bungalows) ❞ 53 334 03/321 77. Dbl, twin & family bungalows. €€€

PALMARIUM RESERVE The hotel of the same name is adjacent to this private reserve that has existed for a while under different ownership. The 50ha of littoral forest protects a wide variety of palms, hence its name. It has broad, well-maintained trails on flat terrain and absurdly tame lemurs. The manager, Sylvain, is an excellent guide, 'doing far more than simply pointing things out; he brings the forest alive. In addition to several species of lemur – some native, some introduced from other regions – that will happily eat from your hand, there are orchids, chameleons, frogs, birds, colourful green lynx spiders and interesting plants including the only endemic Malagasy cactus, which grows as a bizarre epiphyte, and both the island's species of pitcher plants' (Derek Schuurman).

Guided walks cost 10,000Ar.

VOHIBOLA This is a new project run by MATE (Man And The Environment; www.mate.mg) which is being developed for tourism. It is 45 minutes south of Ankanin'ny Nofy by boat. Project co-ordinator Barbara Mathevon writes: 'Vohibola is one of the two largest remaining fragments of littoral forest in Madagascar. The site is in an interesting area in the middle of lakes, the Canal des Pangalanes and the Indian Ocean. The forest is delimited at the

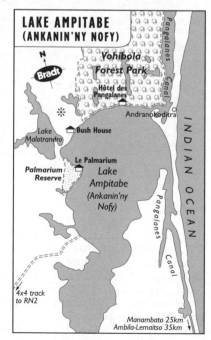

LAKE AMPITABE
(ANKANIN'NY NOFY)

Yohibola Forest Park
Hôtel des Pangalanes
Andranokoditra
Lake Malotrandro
Bush House
Le Palmarium
Palmarium Reserve
Lake Ampitabe (Ankanin'ny Nofy)
Pangalanes Canal
INDIAN OCEAN
4x4 track to RN2
Manambato 25km
Ambila-Lemaitso 35km

north by Tampina and in the south by Andranokoditra, both fishing villages located on a narrow sandbank.'

Derek Schuurman visited the project in 2006 and adds: 'Among the flora of this littoral forest are a number of critically endangered trees, notably *Humbertiodendron saboureaui*, which had not been seen for 50 years and was thought extinct. In Vohibola, several dozen mature trees were found, so the species was effectively rediscovered. It exists nowhere else. Vohibola has an extensive tree nursery and during our visit each of us was given the opportunity to plant an indigenous tree – a truly gratifying experience and a wonderful way of literally putting something back.'

There are two interesting and contrasting circuits, the Discovery Trail and the Wetlands Trail, and other activities are planned such as canoeing and mountain biking. Like Vohimana, the other reserve run by MATE (see page 288), this is a super place for independent travellers who want to see what the people of Madagascar are doing to solve their environmental problems.

THE SOUTHEAST COAST

Formerly, for most people a visit to this region began with Mananjary, which is linked to the highlands by both air and road, or Manakara with its rail service from Fianar. However, the road from RN2 to Vatomandry – once almost impassable – has been improved and the number of independent travellers taking this rewarding route is bound to increase.

VATOMANDRY The name means 'sleeping rocks' from two flat, black rocks close to the shore. This was an important town in its time, growing from a small settlement on the east bank of the River Sandramanongy to the administrative centre of the Hova government in the pre-colonial 19th century. At this time, Vatomandry was a prosperous port and merchandise was carried by porters to the capital along the paths of the eastern forest. Another claim to fame is that Vatomandry is the birthplace of former President Ratsiraka.

Present-day Vatomandry marks the end of the navigable part of the Pangalanes Canal, so is likely to become an increasingly popular resort.

Getting there and away The journey by car from RN2 on the improved road takes less than an hour. (In the old days it could take up to three days!)

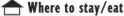 **Where to stay/eat**

⌂ **Espace Zazah Robert** Ambilakely; 🕿 53 821 03. Located on the northern outskirts. 'The owner also runs a transport business which is nearby. Look out for trucks with his name on if lost. A simple motel-style establishment fairly recently built. Rooms are clean with en-suite facilities but no mosquito nets. Bring your own towel. Some rooms have AC. Bar, but no restaurant when we were there, but you order from a menu & they bring it in from nearby. Fair choice of both *gasy* & *vazaha*. Open-sided eating/drinking area. They provided coils to deter the *biby kely*' (Stuart Cassie). €€–€€€

MAHANORO The name means 'who makes happy' but whether Mahanoro will have this effect on all visitors is debatable. The town is to the north of the Mangoro River, so most of the places of interest are watery (although there is said to be a Merina fortress here). The impressive Chutes de la Sahatsio are 18km to the north. There is accommodation too: a hotel with bungalows.

NOSY VARIKA The name means 'lemur island' but I think you'd be lucky to see any *varika* (brown lemurs) here now.

Sally Crook

Sambatra means 'blessed' or 'happy' in Malagasy, and it is the word used for the circumcision ceremonies which are performed in much of Madagascar. The Antambahoaka, probably the smallest tribe in Madagascar, live around Mananjary on the east coast, and young boys and their families from the surrounding villages congregate every seven years for a communal circumcision ceremony there. They become 'blessed', though the actual deed of removal of the penis foreskin is now performed at a different time, usually in the hygienic conditions of a hospital.

In October 1986, the week-long celebrations commenced at a leisurely pace and culminated (after a Thursday of inactivity due to the *fady* nature of this day) on a Friday. Women collected reeds and wove mats in preparation for the big day, and later men carved and painted wooden birds, three of which were fixed on the roof of each *trano be* (literally 'big house'), facing east. This in itself caused much excitement and some unwished-for precipitous descents from the sloped, thatched roofs, while the men continued to beat their oval wooden or hide shields with sticks wielded like swords. Similar activity, drumming and chanting continued below, and the women chanted as they stepped from side to side in their dance. A boy standing astride a barrel on a wheeled cart, brandishing shield and stick gave the most fiery display, encouraging the crowds around.

The fathers of boys to be circumcised wore long colourful robes, gathered at the neck. The *trano be* in which the people drink and talk for days, should not be entered by foreign females, and even the Malagasy women must wear their hair in the traditional style – the many plaits on each side of the centre parting being drawn to a cluster at each side of the neck.

In the afternoon of the Wednesday, women shuffled around the *trano be* in an anticlockwise direction, chanting and holding aloft the white-braided and tasselled red ceremonial caps of their young sons. At the front and back of the procession, the rolled mats woven especially for the occasion were held aloft. After several circuits of the house, the crowds proceeded to the beach where, apparently spontaneously, the women's cries were periodically renewed.

The most interesting excursion in the area is to the Chutes de la Sakaleona, a waterfall which plunges 200m, but this requires an expedition of several days.

AMBOHITSARA This isolated village 60km north of Mananjary is only accessible by boat, yet there is an upmarket hotel here. Apart from the opportunity to relax on and around the Pangalanes Canal, one of Madagascar's most enigmatic sights is here: a stone elephant. No one seems to know the origin of this or how it came to be in Ambohitsara.

 Where to stay

Auberge Ambohitsara m 032 072 67 21 or (Tana) 22 267 21. A set of very pleasant bungalows overlooking the Canal. Owned & run by German-born Mme Manambelona who also organises tours in the area.

MANANJARY AND MANAKARA

These two pleasant seaside towns have good communications with the rest of Madagascar and are gaining popularity among discerning travellers, especially now the railway from the highlands to the coast has been rehabilitated.

The excitement spilt over into a kind of fighting between men with green pointed sticks cut from the mid ribs of palm fronds, and soon the fathers of the circumcision candidates were being routed and chased back into town as the green sticks were hurled at their retreating backs. The apparent terror with which men fled from these harmless weapons indicates a far greater symbolic significance than their physical power.

As Thursday became Friday at midnight, sacred water was collected from the wide River Mananjary where it enters the sea. In the morning gloom nine zebu were sacrificed – one for each clan – by the cutting of the jugular vein after prayers. Some escapees caused excitement before the animals could be bound and lain on their sides with a piece of wood between the teeth. At the first sight of blood, little boys rushed forward to collect it in buckets or in bamboo pipes, just as their 'cousins' in Toraja, Sulawesi, do to this day.

Dancing, music and the women's chant of 'eeee-ay' changed to processions and a chorus of 'aaa-ooh' as crowds converged once again on the beach. The young boys, in red-and-white smocks and wearing their tasselled caps, were carried on their fathers' shoulders. The mind-dulling chant continued as the separate clans were herded along like sheep by men with sticks, following the man with the sacred water held in a small pot on his head, protected by a movable 'hedge' of four poles carried by other robed men.

That night, the boys, bearing white marks on their faces to indicate their clan, were carried on the shoulders of adults around the *trano be*. Each was passed through the west door of the house, and, wearing a string around the waist, was sat upon the severed head of a fine male zebu for a while in the presence of the clan leader, adorned with colourful striped cloth and a fez. The virility of the animal was thus conferred on the boy, and, as he passed through the east door he became a man.

These tiny men were almost dropping with exhaustion as they were paraded once again near the house, the northern end of which had been cordoned off and was guarded from trespass throughout the ceremonial days. The joy of their mothers was vocal and infectious as if they were relieved to have their sons now accepted as adults.

GETTING THERE AND AWAY Mananjary is usually reached by road from Ranomafana, and Manakara is the end (or beginning) of the railway journey from Fianarantsoa (see page 205). The road between the two towns is surfaced and in good condition and the journey by *taxi-brousse* takes only four hours.

MANANJARY Formerly a rather sleepy little town, Mananjary is going to have a surge of popularity in October 2007, when the mass **circumcision ceremony**, *sambatra*, for which the town is famed, takes place (see above).

The town is accessible by good road and *taxi-brousse* from Ranomafana, and currently has a twice-monthly Air Mad flight from Tana.

Telephone code The area code for Mananjary is 72

🏠 Where to stay

🏠 **Vahily Lodge** (formerly Le Plantation) m 032 024 68 22/032 439 64 93. A resort hotel on the edge of town near the airport. Swimming pool, classy (but not overpriced) restaurant. Bungalows are richly furnished. The hotel also runs a spice business; tours of the plantation can be arranged. 👑

🏠 **Jardin de la Mer** (7 bungalows) ☎ 72 092 70. A set of beach bungalows (sgl & twin). En-suite hot showers & toilet. Swimming pool. Restaurant. €€€

⌂ **Sorafahotel** (9 rooms, 5 bungalows) Bd Maritime; ✆ 72 092 01. Pleasant beach bungalows, some with verandas, & sgl & dbl rooms. Swimming pool, very good open-air restaurant facing the beach; pizza a speciality. Occasional evening disco. Tours of the Pangalanes Canal. €€€

⌂ **Yvonna Bungalows** ✆ 032 020 49 93. Good-value simple bungalows located on the other side of the canal, near the college. Cold water (but buckets of hot water provided on request). The Malagasy owners are very friendly & helpful & can provide delicious meals on request. €€

⌂ **Chez Stenny** (2 rooms & 3 bungalows) ✆ 72 942 66. A small, friendly guesthouse. Cold water only. €

⌂ **Hotel Ideal** Next to the cathedral. Cold water only. €

⌂ **Hotel des Bons Amis** Near JIRAMA. Cold water only. €

✖ **Where to eat** In addition to the hotel restaurants, Mananjary has a few independent restaurants recommended here by Peace Corps Volunteer Sheena Jones.

✖ **Route des Epices** The best restaurant in town. On R25, just before the cathedral. English spoken, birding tours offered.

✖ **Le Grillion** A friendly restaurant near the cathedral. Good food at reasonable prices.

Nightlife
Palace Nightclub A lively disco on the far side of town.

Internet Note there is currently no internet in Mananjary.

Money There are two banks where you can use your Visa card to withdraw money. They are not able to exchange foreign currency, however.

What to see and do Mananary's weekend fish market, held at the mouth of the river (*embouchure*), is well worth a visit. 'All the fishermen are selling their daily catches from their canoes, which are parked up on the shore. Like all markets in Madagascar, there's a lot of action. In addition to the fish-selling, the ladies wash their clothes there and lay them out to dry on the beach while their children play in the water.' (Sheena Jones)

MANAKARA This town at the end of the line is experiencing a surge of popularity. 'The Allée des Filaos running between ex-colonial buildings and the ocean makes the waterfront a very attractive part of town. The new town and station are across the river bridge and of no interest. *Pousse-pousses* provide the best local transport' (Andrea Jarman). The *taxi-brousse* station is some way from the centre of town; take a *pousse-pousse* if your bags are heavy.

You should not swim in Manakara because of dangerous currents and sharks. But the sea is infinitely rewarding anyway: 'We absolutely fell in love with the beach (except for trash piles and human excrement). The combination of the offshore reef, the breakers, the wide sand strip, the grass and other foliage, then the first line of pine trees gave the place a park-like atmosphere. The breakers alone proved fascinating, partly because of the endless interplay between the incoming and outgoing surf' (John Robertson).

Telephone code The area code for Manakara is 72.

⌂ Where to stay/eat
⌂ **Parthenay Club** ✆ 72 216 63. A club for the locals with some tourist bungalows. Some en suite, others share very clean bathrooms. Peaceful. & recommended. €€–€€€

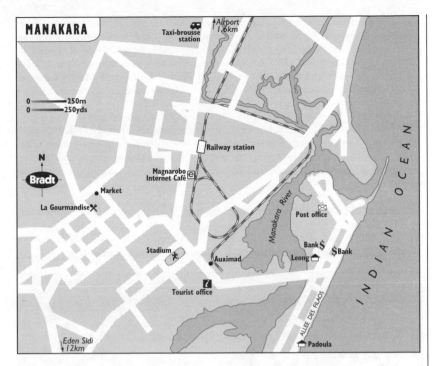

MANAKARA

Taxi-brousse station

Airport 1.6km

0 ——— 250m
0 ——— 250yds

N

Bradt

Railway station

Magnarobo Internet Café

Market

La Gourmandise

INDIAN OCEAN

Manakara River

Post office

Bank

Bank

Stadium

Auximad

Leong

Tourist office

ALLEE DES FILAOS

Eden Sidi 12km

Padoula

🏠 **Delices d'Orient Annexe** Near the Parthenay Club. New dbl bungalows overlooking the canal. €€

🏠 **Leong Hotel** In the town centre. Budget rooms. €€

🏠 **Padoula Chambres d'Hôtes** Lot IB 132, Manakara Be; ✆ 72 216 23. According to 2 readers, this once-praised budget hotel seems to have fallen on hard times & is no longer highly recommended. Simple dbl rooms by the sea; also a campsite with use of shower. €€

🏠 **Eden Sidi Hotel** If you're heading south, this is a nice set of bungalows 12km from Manakara. €€

🏠 **Hôtel Restaurant Delices d'Orient** (6 rooms) Just opposite the market. Now seems to be the budget hotel of choice. Spacious en-suite rooms with fans & nets. Simple but clean. 'The food is marvellous! They serve the best & biggest langoustes in all of Madagascar!' (Kim Loohuis). €

✕ **Restaurant La Gourmandise** On the left side of the market. 'Highly recommended! Great food & cakes & homemade guava juice. Also better-priced than restaurants closer to hotels opposite the market' (Nina French).

✕ **Chez Clo** Another restaurant/*salon de thé* near the market; good food.

MANAKARA TO FIANARANTSOA BY TRAIN This is the most interesting – and, let's face it, the only – train ride in Madagascar, and now that it has been privatised it's pretty reliable, although the old engines do find it a struggle to go uphill so the train towards Fianar sometimes runs late.

The train leaves on Wednesday, Thursday and Sunday at 07.00, and you can pre-book your seat: first class 24,000Ar, second class 16,000Ar. There is little difference in comfort, but first class is slightly less crowded. The journey takes ten hours.

CONTINUING SOUTH

VOHIPENO Situated some 45km south of Manakara, this small town is the centre of the Antaimoro tribe who reportedly came from Arabia about 600 years ago, bringing the first script to Madagascar. Their Islamic history is shown by their clothing (turban and fez, as well as Arab-style robes). They are the inheritors of the 'great writings', *sorabe*, written in Malagasy using Arabic script. *Sorabe* continues to be written, still in Arabic, still on *Antaimoro* paper. The scribes who practise this art are known as *katibo* and the writing and their knowledge of it give them a special power. The writing itself ranges from accounts of historical events to astrology, and the books are considered sacred.

FARAFANGANA On the map this appears to be a seaside resort, but its position near the mouth of a river means that the beach and ocean are not easily accessible. The town is a prosperous commercial centre, with well-stocked shops and a busy market. It is also the last place that you can change foreign currency if travelling south.

Telephone code The area code for Farafangana is 73 – but phones rarely work here!

Getting there and away Air Mad's Twin Otter service no longer covers Farafangana but I've heard that the new airline ATTR has replaced it.

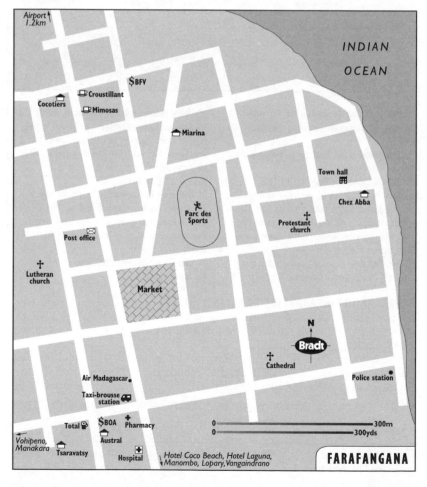

Marko Petravic

My alarm clock went off at a quarter to four in the morning. I quickly got up and cycled the half mile or so to the Antaimoro fishermen's village at the northern end of Farafangana, with a half-moon lighting the way. The village was fast asleep but soon one of the fishermen, with whom I had arranged to go sea-fishing, appeared. He quietly took my bicycle, pulled it into his little wooden house and fastened it to the wall behind the bed. The other members of the family were still sleeping but a cock was already beginning to crow.

With an oar each in hand, we set off to the nearby river where the pirogues lie on the sandy beach. We waded through the warm water to reach the long sandy bank that separates river from ocean. There we were joined by another two fishermen and we all clambered into a larger, wider pirogue, shaped more like a banana in order to better tackle the waves. I thought we would have more difficulty getting over the violent waves that break onto the beach, but our departure was timed perfectly and we were past them in no time. Away from the coast the waves move more slowly and do not break, so there is little danger of being turned over. We paddled away from the coast, where lone fishermen in small boats were casting their nets. Every so often we saw a fish coming to the surface and the fishermen, instead of exclaiming 'trondro!' ('fish'), said 'laoka!' which means 'food to accompany rice'!

About half a mile out to sea we came across our first float. It was pulled aboard followed by the net. The net had been left for two days, as the fishermen normally go out on alternate days – weather-permitting, of course. The net was 50m long, with a heavy stone to anchor it to the seabed. We checked five or six nets that morning. One contained a kind of flat fish, whose wings were cut off and tied to the net as bait before it was put back in the water. Another contained three small, toothless sharks, brown and white in colour.

At first I didn't feel seasick, but by the end the smell of the sea, the fish and the constant rising and falling of our small vessel on the large waves combined to make me ill. The fishermen said they were not sick – even on their first ever outing – saying they were 'already used to it'. They meant they already had the sea in their blood, since their forefathers were all fishermen. They had no idea where Europe, America, Japan and so on lie, and they were fascinated when I pointed out the general direction of these places.

Our arrival on the beach was as perfect as the departure: beautifully executed despite the large waves. We all happily jumped out of the narrow boat in which we had been sitting or crouching for almost fours hours. Others on the beach expressed surprise at the sight of a white fisherman!

On the way back across the river it began to rain heavily, but it was actually an incredibly pleasant feeling; you don't mind getting wet when it's warm and you feel at one with nature and the locals.

A *taxi-brousse* from Tana to Farafangana takes about 24 hours, but most people will come here via Ranomafana (one day's drive) or Manakara. Farafangana is only two or three hours away on a good road.

Where to stay/eat

🏠 **Coco Beach** Beachside bungalows on the southern outskirts of town, just beyond the lighthouse.

🏠 **Laguna** More bungalows about 4km south of Farafangana.

South of Toamasina **CONTINUING SOUTH**

11

Hôtel Les Cocotiers ➤ 73 911 87/88. Near the post office. An upmarket hotel with en-suite bathrooms & hot water. Good restaurant. €€€

Chez Abba ➤ 73 911 85. Seafront bungalow with simple bucket showers.

Miarina The rooms are all called after different shades of red! Now primarily a restaurant but it still has some rooms. Good food & parking.

Tsaravatsy Hotel ➤ 73 910 36. Popular with Malagasy; good restaurant (Malagasy & Chinese specialities). Cold water; shared facilities. €

Austral Hotel ➤ 73 912 77; f 73 912 57; e austral@netclub.mg.

Le Croustillant bakery Good selection of breads & croissants opposite Les Cocotiers.

Les Mimosas Salon de Thé Opposite Les Cocotiers. Lots of imported goodies available (at a price).

WEST TO IHOSY (MAYBE!)

If you are seriously adventurous, the road to Ihosy is now said to be passable, in the dry season, by 4x4 or motorbike. You can do the first section (to **Vohitranambo**) by *taxi-brousse*, and the next 50km (to **Vondrozo**) has been improved, so may now have public transport. You can continue by car as far as the **Vevembe** region at which point the passable road ends and jungle has taken over. You will probably need a guide to help you reach the next stretch of passable road at **Ivohibe** because of the numerous trails that have been created by the locals. If you make it to Ivohibe you're home and dry – there are *taxi-brousses* to Ihosy. But beware: the area is said to be infested with *dahalo* (cattle rustlers).

In contrast, the road to Vangaindrano is good and it takes only about an hour to cover the 70km by *taxi-brousse*.

MANOMBO RESERVE

This special reserve, 25km south of Farafangana, is being considered for upgrade to national park status. It protects an area of littoral forest and is home to four or five species of lemur, including habituated black-and-white ruffed lemurs and the rare white-collared brown lemur (*Eulemur albocollaris*) which is hard to see elsewhere.

There is no accommodation but visitors can camp at the ANGAP station on the main road, 9km from the forest.

LOPARY

This is a small village near the Mananivo River and recommended by Philip Thomas for its Saturday market. 'This is a typical rural market, selling agricultural produce and artisinal products used in the rural economy, as well as a range of woven basketware, mats etc. It draws in people from many nearby villages as well as people from Farafangano and Vangaindrano.'

VANGAINDRANO

This has the atmosphere of a frontier town; few tourists come here which gives it a certain appeal. Marko Petrovic knows the town well and reports: 'Vangaindrano itself is not a particularly interesting place, but as it is only 12km from the sea it is worth making this trip along a road which has been beautifully repaired because Madagascar's minister in charge of roads comes from that area. The road runs parallel with the enormous River Mananara, which flows past Vangaindrano. It is interesting to watch the fishermen who live by the sea going out into the 10ft waves in their narrow wooden pirogues. I swam there many times enjoying the amazing power of the waves, but was always careful not to go too far out because currents can very quickly take you in the direction of Australia! Sharks, too, are a possible danger although I never saw any. The beach is beautifully sandy but beware of rocks under the water.'

Where to stay/eat The best hotel is the **Tropic** 'built in time for the eclipse in 2002 in the hope that tourists would flock to Vangaindrano – which they didn't. It is quite a grand building, situated in a fairly central part of Vangaindrano called Ampasy, and I found the cost of a night in the large suite on the top floor pretty cheap' (MP). There are several small hotels, including the **Antsika** which is about 500m from the town centre on the left-hand side as you enter town from the north. Until 2002 the best-quality hotel was probably the new **Shell Motel** (named for its petrol station rather than bivalves) which is to the north of the town.

FROM VANGAINDRANO TO TAOLAGNARO (FORT DAUPHIN) The road to Taolagnaro has been improved recently and it's now possible to drive there from Vangaindrano, a distance of 230km.

Marko Petrovic, who had previously spent four exhausting days getting to Taolagnaro by motorbike, reports the latest developments (2006): 'It is just about possible by car except that at **Befasy**, on the river Sandra, you must get the ferry to take you along the river as far as the sea where you can then follow the tracks of the lobster merchants. The ferries are all supposed to work but they do break down from time to time and you can end up paying 100,000Ar to people who will row you across. Apparently the ferry on the river Sandra is currently being renovated while on Lake Masianaka a new one is being introduced that can carry two trucks at once.

'The road from Vangaindrano to Midongy is OK as far as **Ranomena**, but is horrendous thereafter; it recently took a missionary 12 hours to cover the 52km. (It would have taken him ten hours on foot!)'

With the amount of road improvement currently taking place in Madagascar, it's entirely possible that this route will be achievable by *taxi-brousse* by the time you read this.

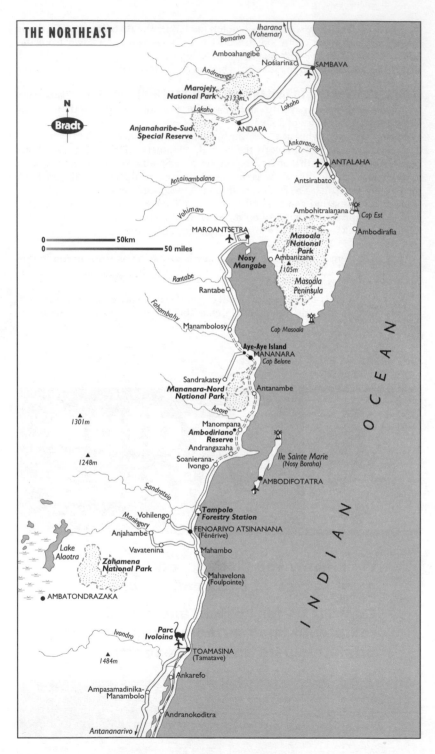

THE NORTHEAST

Bradt

N

Iharana
(Vohemar)
Bemarivo
Amboahangibe
Nosiarina   SAMBAVA
Andraranga
Marojejy
National Park   2133m
Lokoho   ANDAPA   Lokoho
Anjanaharibe-Sud
Special Reserve   Ankavanana

ANTALAHA
Antsirabato

Antainambalana   Ambohitralanana   Cap Est
Vohimaro   Ambodirafia
MAROANTSETRA   Masoala
                     National
                     Park
0   50km   Ambanizana
0   50 miles
Nosy   1105m
Mangabe
Rantabe   Masoala
Peninsula
Rantabe

Fahambahy
Manambolosy   Cap Masoala

Aye-Aye Island
MANANARA
Cap Belone
Sandrakatsy
Mananara-Nord   Antanambe
National Park
Anove
1301m   Manompana
Ambodiriano
Reserve
Andrangazaha
1248m   Soanierana-   Ile Sainte Marie
Ivongo   (Nosy Boraha)
Sandratsio
AMBODIFOTATRA
Maningory Vohilengo
Anjahambe   Tampolo
Vavatenina   Forestry Station
FENOARIVO ATSINANANA
Lake   (Fénérive)
Alaotra   Mahambo
Zahamena
National Park   Mahavelona
(Foulpointe)
AMBATONDRAZAKA

Parc
Ivondro   Ivoloina
1484m   TOAMASINA
(Tamatave)
Ankarefo
Ampasamadinika-
Manambolo
Andranokoditra
Antananarivo

INDIAN OCEAN

12

Toamasina and the Northeast

Punished by its weather (rain, cyclones), eastern Madagascar is notoriously challenging to travellers. In July 1817 James Hastie wrote in his diary: 'If this is the good season for travelling this country, I assert it is impossible to proceed in the bad.' With this in mind you should avoid the wettest months of February and March, and remember that June to August can be very damp as well. The driest months are September to November, with December and January worth the risk. April and May are fairly safe apart from the possibility of cyclones. The east coast has other problems: sharks and dangerous currents. So although there are beautiful beaches, swimming is safe only in protected areas.

Despite – or perhaps because of – these drawbacks, the northeast is perhaps Madagascar's most rewarding region for independent travellers. It is not yet on the itinerary for many groups, yet has a few beautifully situated upmarket hotels for that once-in-a-lifetime holiday, and wonderful exploratory possibilities for the intrepid backpacker. Much of Madagascar's unique flora and fauna is concentrated in the eastern rainforests and any serious naturalist will want to pay a visit. Other attractions are the rugged mountain scenery with rivers tumbling down to the Indian Ocean, the friendly people, abundant fruit and seafood, and access to the lovely island of Nosy Boraha (Ile Sainte Marie). The chief products of the east are coffee, vanilla, bananas, coconuts, cloves and lychees.

BACKGROUND INFORMATION

HISTORY This region has an interesting history dominated by European pirates and slave traders. While powerful kingdoms were being forged in other parts of the country, the east coast remained divided among numerous small clans. It was not until the 18th century that one ruler, Ratsimilaho, unified the region. The half-caste son of Thomas White, an English pirate, and briefly educated in Britain, Ratsimilaho responded to the attempt by Chief Ramanano to take over all the east coast ports. His successful revolt was furthered by his judiciously marrying an important princess; by his death in 1754 he ruled an area stretching from the Masoala Peninsula to Mananjary.

The result of this liaison of various tribes was the Betsimisaraka, now the second-largest ethnic group in Madagascar. Some (in the area of Maroantsetra) practise second burial, although with less ritual than the Merina and Betsileo.

DISTANCES IN KILOMETRES			
Toamasina–Mahambo	90km	Iharana–Sambava	153km
Toamasina–Soanierana-Ivongo	163km	Sambava–Antalaha	89km
Toamasina–Mahavelona	61km	Sambava–Andapa	119km

GETTING AROUND Although the map shows roads of some sort running almost the full length of the east coast, this is deceptive. Rain and cyclones regularly destroy bridges so it is impossible to know in advance whether a selected route will be usable, even in the 'dry' season. The rain-saturated forests drain into the Indian Ocean in numerous rivers, many of which can be crossed only by ferry. And there is not enough traffic to ensure a regular service. For those with limited time, therefore, the only practical way to get to the less accessible towns is by air. There are regular planes to Nosy Boraha (Ile Sainte Marie), and flights between Toamasina (Tamatave) and Antsiranana (Diego Suarez). Planes go several days a week from Toamasina to Maroantsetra, Antalaha and Sambava.

For the truly adventurous it is possible to work your way down (or up) the coast providing you have plenty of time and are prepared to walk.

TOAMASINA (TAMATAVE)

HISTORY As in all the east coast ports, Toamasina (pronounced too*ama*sin) began as a pirate community. In the late 18th century its harbour attracted the French, who already had a foothold in Ile Sainte Marie, and Napoleon I sent his agent Sylvain Roux to establish a trading post there. In 1811, Sir Robert Farquhar, governor of the newly British island of Mauritius, sent a small naval squadron to take the port of Toamasina. This was not simply an extension of the usual British-French antagonism, but an effort to stamp out slavery at its source, Madagascar being the main supplier to the Indian Ocean. The slave trade had been abolished by the British parliament in 1807. The attack was successful, and Sylvain Roux was exiled. During subsequent years, trade between Mauritius and Madagascar built Toamasina into a major port. In 1845, after a royal edict subjecting European traders to the harsh Malagasy laws, French and British warships bombarded Toamasina, but a landing was repelled leaving 20 dead. During the 1883–85 war the French occupied Toamasina but Malagasy troops successfully defended the fort of Farafaty just outside the town.

Theories on the origin of the name Toamasina vary, but one is that King Radama I tasted the seawater here and remarked '*Toa masina*' – 'It's salty'.

TOAMASINA TODAY Toamasina (still popularly known as Tamatave) has always had an air of shabby elegance with some fine palm-lined boulevards and once-impressive colonial houses. Every few years it's hit by a cyclone, and spends some time in a new state of shabbiness before rebuilding. As you'd expect, it's a spirited, bustling city with a good variety of bars, snack bars and restaurants. Not many tourists stay here for any length of time, which is a shame; there is plenty to see and do. For instance the wonderful Parc Ivoloina (see page 316) provides one of the most accessible and delightful natural history experiences in Madagascar.

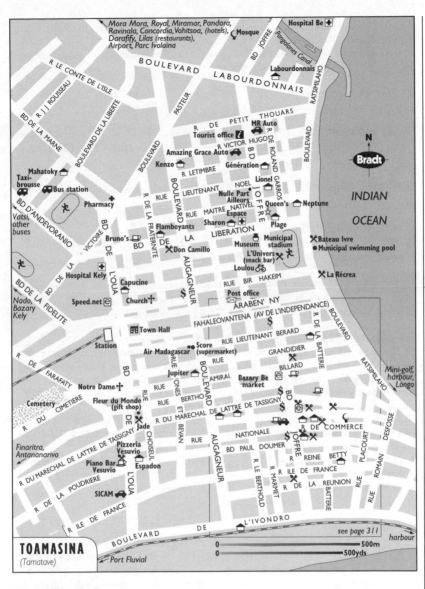

TOAMASINA
(Tamatave)

TELEPHONE CODE The area code for Toamasina is 53.

GETTING THERE AND AWAY

By road Route Nationale 2 (RN2) is one of the country's best roads (see *Chapter 10*) and is the fastest and cheapest way of reaching Toamasina from Tana. MadaBus (see page 174) runs from Tana to Toamasina on Monday, Wednesday and Friday, returning on Tuesday, Thursday and Saturday The 2006 cost was €19. Cheaper vehicles run twice a day, morning or night, and take from six to 12 hours. There is a wide choice: bus (auto-car), minibus and Peugeot station wagon.

Try to book your seat at least a day in advance at the *taxi-brousse* departure point, Fasan'ny Karana, on the road to the airport in Tana.

By air There are daily flights between Tana and Toamasina. A taxi from the airport into town costs 7,000Ar.

In Toamasina the Air Madagascar office is open weekdays 07.30–16.30 (closed for lunch 11.00–14.00); Saturday, open 08.00–11.00.

By rail The once-famous train from Tana to Toamasina sadly no longer takes passengers. For the time being, at least, it is for freight only.

By sea and river Toamasina is one of the starting – or finishing – points for a trip down the Pangalanes Canal. Most boats leave from Toamasina's Port Fluvial at the southwest edge of the town (separate from the harbour).

GETTING AROUND Any taxi ride in the town should cost 2,000Ar. There is an abundance of *pousse-pousses*.

TOURIST INFORMATION
ORTT (Tourist Office) Rue Victor Hugo; ☎ 53 310 92; m 030 40 247 78; e officetouristmv@yahoo.fr. Near Hôtel Génération. ⊕ Mon–Fri 08.00–11.30 & 14.30–17.00; Sat 08.00–12.00.

WHERE TO STAY
I am greatly indebted to Toamasina resident Kim Radford for her insider's information on hotels and restaurants in the town. Kim runs the charity HELP which welcomes visitors (see box on page 308).

Top end and Upper range €€€€€ & €€€€
Hôtel Sharon (35 rooms & 2 suites) Bd de la Libération; ☎ 53 304 20 to 26; f 53 331 29; e sharonhotel@blueline.mg; www.sharon-hotel.com. The nicest hotel in Tamatave following recent renovations; popular with businesspeople. Rooms have AC, minibar, safe, TV & Internet (can be pricey). There is a beauty salon (inc massage), sauna, gym & a nice pool. Good Italian/European restaurant **La Rose des Vents** & an excellent pizzeria. Visa accepted.
Le Neptune (47 rooms) 35 Bd Ratsimilaho; ☎ 53 322 26; f 53 324 26; e neptune@ wanadoo.mg; www.hotel-neptune-tamatave.com. Once the poshest hotel in town. A lovely seafront setting, but rooms lack character. Pool, good food & nice bar. Casino & disco daily except Sun. Credit cards accepted.
Hôtel Le Toamasina (22 rooms & 2 suites) 13 Rue de la Colonne; ☎ 53 335 49; f 53 336 12; e letoamasinahotel@wanadoo.mg; www.3dmadagascar.com/hotel-toamasina/. Comfortable rooms with TV, safe, telephone, minibar & some have AC. Reasonable food. €€€€

Mid range €€€
Hôtel Longo (24 rooms) Rue Amiral Pierre; ☎ 53 339 54; f 53 344 13; e longohotel@yahoo.fr. New hotel near the port entrance, behind Bonnet & Fils (store). Comfortable, clean rooms with TV, en-suite toilet & shower. Chinese/European restaurant open daily; reportedly very good.
Hôtel Le Joffre (20 rooms) 18 Bd Joffre; ☎ 53 323 90; f 53 332 94; e hotel.joffre@wanadoo.mg; www.tamatave-hotel-joffre.com. An atmospheric old hotel with all facilities & good restaurant (closed Sun, except b/fast). Rooms & studios have AC & en-suite bath/shower with 'a seemingly endless supply of hot water'. Some small single rooms, but these are usually reserved for guides & regulars. Credit cards accepted.
Villa Vohitsoa (2 rooms) Rte d'Ivoloina; ☎/f 53 349 00; m 032 40 100 60; e villa_vohitsoa@ wanadoo.mg. New guesthouse run by a German/Swiss couple. Very close to airport & within walking distance of beach & several restaurants. B/fast on request.
Labourdonnais (5 rooms) Bd Labourdonnais; ☎ 53 350 67; f 53 343 43. New hotel, 1 block from the beach. Comfortable rooms with AC, TV, fridge, safe & balcony. Secure parking. Good restaurant with charming décor; Creole specialities (owner is from Réunion). Restaurant closed Sun.
Royal Hotel (15 rooms) Rte d'Ivoloina; ☎ 53 311 15/312 81. A clean but rather characterless concrete high-rise on a busy street halfway

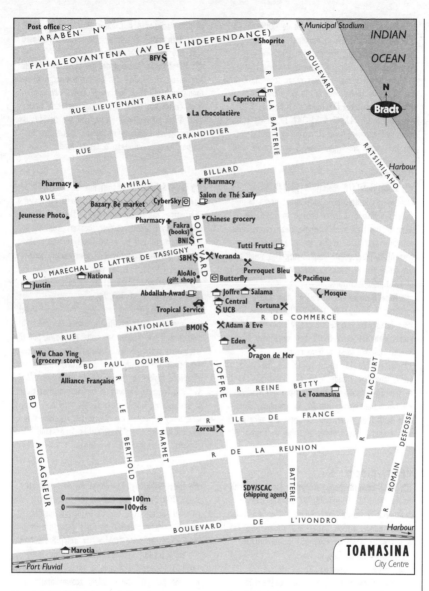

TOAMASINA
City Centre

between the airport & town centre. Large rooms with AC & TV; mostly en suite; some with fridge. The popular snack bar **Super Goût** is right outside.

🏠 **Hôtel Génération** (30 rooms) 129 Bd Joffre; 🔧 53 321 05; **f** 53 328 34; **e** generationhotel@ wanadoo.mg; www.hotel-generation.com. A nice hotel with large, pleasant rooms. Restaurant serves good food with several vegetarian options. Same owner has bungalows & a restaurant in Foulpointe (transfers available).

🏠 **Central Hotel** (12 rooms) 16 Bd Joffre; 🔧 53 340 86; **f** 53 341 19; **e** central_hotel_mada@ yahoo.fr; www.central-hotel-tamatave.com. Lots of stairs, but attractive rooms with AC, TV, telephone, safe & mosquito nets. Same ownership as Veranda restaurant. Visa accepted.

🏠 **Hôtel les Flamboyants** (36 rooms) Bd de la Libération; 🔧/**f** 53 323 50. An older hotel with decent-sized rooms that are en suite with TV & mosquito net; some with AC. Good value. Bar & restaurant (closed Sun, except b/fast).

Espadon Hotel (36 rooms) Bd de l'OUA; ☎ 53 303 86; f 53 303 87; e espadon-hotel@wanadoo.mg. The Espadon (meaning 'swordfish') is a concrete high-rise building mostly used by businesspeople. Rooms range from basic with fan to family rooms with AC, TV & minibar.

Hôtel Capricorne (21 rooms) 33 Rue de la Batterie; ☎ 53 347 40; f 53 347 39. Newly renovated; excellent value. Unassuming street front, but the rooms are large, clean & comfortable with

Budget €€

Lionel Hotel (18 rooms) ☎ 53 348 04. Conveniently located on a side street north of Queen's nightclub (but far enough to avoid the worst of the loud music). Simple, clean rooms with mosquito nets. Some rooms are en suite & a few have AC & TV (7,000Ar supplement). This small hotel has fallen out of favour locally owing to the number of prostitutes it attracts.

Hôtel National (15 rooms) 13 Rue Lattre de Tassigny; ☎ 53 322 90. Centrally located, one block from *bazary be* (market). Recently renovated. All rooms with hot water & the best ones with AC. Rooms available for long-term rent.

Hôtel Nado (15 rooms) opposite Eglise Sacré Cœur, Tanambao V Sud; ☎ 53 333 11; f 53 333 14; e sedo@wanadoo.mg. Not far from bus station. Pleasant rooms, some with AC, TV, telephone & en-suite bath (hot water). The cheapest are very small with shared facilities. Meals available with advance notice.

Penny-pincher €

Hôtel Eden (8 rooms) Bd Joffre (opposite BMOI Bank); m 032 40 247 78/032 04 628 82. Appropriately situated near Adam & Eve Snack Bar. A good budget option. Basic, clean rooms have fan & hot water; some en suite with balcony. Under same ownership as Calypso Tours (www.calypstour.freesurf.fr).

Hôtel Capucine (13 rooms) Rue Guynemer; m 032 04 517 27. Basic clean rooms with fan; some are en suite with hot water. Small restaurant.

Beach hotels and bungalows

Hôtel Miramar (20 bungalows) Bd Ratsimilaho, Salazamay; ☎ 53 332 15; f 53 330 13; e miramar-hotel-tmv@netcourrier.com; www.miramar-hotel-tamatave.com. Comfortable chalets & bungalows in a good location (to the north, near the beach; convenient for the airport). Chalets (with

en-suite facilities & hot water. Most have AC & TV; some with fridge & balcony. The restaurant (closed Sun) also recently refurbished.

Hôtel Kenzo/Auberge des Iles (4 rooms) 35 Bd Augagneur; ☎ 53 349 10. Modest, but large en-suite rooms with AC, TV & hot water. Some way from the town centre but there is a cheap cybercafé next door & it's conveniently located for the *taxi-brousse* station. Above **Le Kenzo** restaurant, specialising in *soupe Chinoise*, European & Creole food.

Hôtel Salama (20 rooms) Rue Lt Hubert; ☎ 53 307 50. Central location but the rooms are basic & uninspiring: 'rather damp & dingy'. The 5-times-daily call to prayer broadcast over speakers from the nearby mosque can be heard loudly in the rooms. Small snack bar. There is a 5-room annexe near the town hall (☎ 53 333 36) with secure parking.

Hôtel Plage (45 rooms) Bd de la Libération; ☎ 53 320 90; f 53 307 24; e hotel_plage@simicro.mg. Near the Lionel Hotel, this is in the heart of what becomes the red light district at night. Rooms are quite run-down, but the location is central & within easy walking distance of the beach. The nightly disco is murder.

Hôtel Jupiter (8 rooms) 21 Bd Augagneur; ☎ 53 321 01. Concrete building in business district close to the market. Simple clean rooms with hot water & fans. Bring a mozzie net. Restaurant specialises in *soupe Chinoise* & Malagasy dishes. Stone Club nightclub next door (⊕ Fri–Sun).

Hôtel Mahatoky (14 rooms) Bd de la Liberté; ☎ 53 300 21. Located behind the main bus terminal (across from Magro). Basic, but ideally located for a late arrival or early departure by bus. Some rooms en suite (cold water only). Restaurant.

Hôtel Justin (16 rooms) Rue Lattre de Tassigny; m 033 14 458 54. A humble establishment popular with the Malagasy; good budget accommodation in a fairly central location. Rooms are en suite (cold water only). Bring your own mozzie net & avoid rooms near the street.

fan) & bungalows (with AC) available. Newly renovated restaurant. Pool open to the public. Credit cards not accepted. €€€–€€€€

La Ravinala (9 rooms) Bd Ratsimilaho; ☎ 53 308 83; e vdbdtruong@belgacom.net. On the beach about 200m north of Hôtel Miramar. Rooms with fans, mostly en suite with hot water; nicely decorated with bamboo. Quiet & peaceful. Good restaurant serving European & Malagasy food & pizza (closed Wed eve). Friendly Vietnamese/Belgian owners; recommended. €€€

🏠 **Daraffy** (20 bungalows) Ampanalana (north end of town); ➋ 53 326 18. Seafront location between the airport & Miramar Hotel. 3 types of en-suite bungalows from cement (dbl with fan & hot water) to traditional *falafa* (family; cold water). Small playground for children. Nice staff. Restaurant very popular with resident foreigners (closed Tue eve); halal menu. Named after a legendary giant (see box on page 383). €€–€€€

🏠 **Concordia** (14 units in 9 bungalows) Rte de l'Aéroport; ➋/f 53 317 42; e chanpowoo@ wanadoo.mg; http://takelaka.dts.mg/concordia/. The closest hotel to airport (within walking distance) on the road towards town. Pleasant bungalows/units in an attractive setting; en-suite facilities with hot water, fan & TV. Restaurant with Chinese, French & Malagasy specialities (closed Sun). €€

🏠 **Marotia Hotel** (20 bungalows) Bd de l'Ivondro; ➋ 53 350 74. 'A little off the road that the trucks take to the port.' Not a very nice part of town (take a taxi after dark) & a bit far from restaurants & the town centre, but nice clean bungalows in the quiet setting of a palm grove by the ocean (although separated by an unattractive fence). All en suite; some with hot water. Popular with the Peace Corps crowd. Snack bar only; meals available with advance notice. The less impressive **Marotia Annex** is near the bus terminal behind the Eglise Sacré Cœur. €€

🏠 **Finaritra Bungalows** (9 bungalows) Mangarano II; ➋ 53 339 79; m 033 11 907 07/032 40 122 74. Pleasant en-suite bungalows with hot water, fan & mosquito net. Far from town centre & beach, but close to university & main road to Tana. Snack bar. Secure parking. Airport transfers. €–€€

✗ WHERE TO EAT Toamasina is known for its many restaurants. One speciality is *soupe Chinoise*, which can be a meal in itself. Most restaurants open at 19.00. This list is loosely ordered as one would encounter these restaurants if driving from the airport towards the centre of town. Several of the hotel/bungalow establishments also have excellent restaurants worth trying.

✗ **Lilas** Rte d'Ivoloina; ➋ 53 324 12. A very small but clean & pleasant little family-run Chinese restaurant, which adjoins their general store. Short walk from the Concordia. Tasty Chinese dishes & soups at good prices. ⏰ 07.30–13.00 & 15.30–19.30; closed Mon.

✗ **Mora Mora** (formerly **Eurasie**) Bd Labourdonnais; m 032 02 775 99. Located on the road that becomes Route d'Ivoloina, but not far from centre of town. Good food with a diverse menu featuring French & Malagasy dishes, as well as crêpe specialities. Nice décor with TV & bar. ⏰ 11.00–14.30 & 18.00–24.00; closed Tue.

✗ **L'Univers** Bd Joffre. Incorporated into the stadium on its west side. Serves grillades & simple plates. Hallal food. The only non-stop restaurant in town. ⏰ 24hrs daily.

✗ **Don Camillo** Bd de la Libération (across from Hôtel les Flamboyants); m 032 07 668 10. Italian food & bar. Eat in, take away or delivery. The pizza gets great reviews from local expats. ⏰ Tue–Sat 10.00–21.00; Sun/Mon 17.00–21.00.

✗ **Bateau Ivre** Bd Ratsimilaho; ➋ 53 302 94; e batoivre@wanadoo.mg; www.hotel-restaurant-tamatave.com. Adjoins the old municipal swimming pool on the east side of the stadium. A beachfront bar & restaurant with character. Owners have done a very nice job of fixing up the old municipal pool complex, so you can go there to swim & eat. Moderately priced European food, with seafood a speciality. Live music in the evenings (piano & singer). Boutique on premises. ⏰ daily 09.00–23.30.

✗ **La Récrea** Bd Ratsimilaho; m 032 04 610 71; e jnp@wanadoo.mg. Pleasant setting on the beach. Good food & a nice place to stop for a drink. Live music some weekends. Bar, billiards & boutique with T-shirts & handmade souvenirs. ⏰ daily 10.00–23.00.

✗ **Veranda** Bd Joffre; ➋ 53 334 35. One block north of Hôtel Joffre, in an old Creole house with a nicely decorated interior – popular & full of character. Under same ownership as Central Hotel. European, Malagasy & Chinese food. ⏰ 07.30–14.00 & 19.00–22.00; closed Sun.

✗ **Perroquet Bleu** 11 Rue Aviateur Goulette; m 032 02 672 88. An open-air bar & small restaurant which is a local hangout. Pizza & Italian food. ⏰ daily 08.00–21.00 or later.

✗ **La Pacifique** 22 Rue G Clemenceau; ➋ 53 322 23. Chinese restaurant serving very good meals at reasonable prices. ⏰ 11.00–13.30 & 18.00–21.30 (restaurant); 07.30–13.30 & 18.00–21.30 (soupe Chinoise); both closed Mon.

✘ **Restaurant Fortuna** Rue de la Batterie; ☎ 53 338 28. A very good Chinese restaurant (but slow service). Next door, under the same management, is a *soupe Chinoise* which serves the eponymous soup & noodle specialities. If you don't eat pork, this is one of the few *soupes Chinoises* in town that will do a chicken stock base (on request). ⊕ *11.00–13.30 & 18.00–21.30 (restaurant), 07.15–11.00 & 17.00–20.30 (soupe Chinoise); both closed Mon.*
✘ **Jade** 44 Rue Lattre de Tassigny; ☎ 53 335 65. Chinese restaurant with excellent food, including vegetarian options. Reasonably priced lunch specials; AC. ⊕ *11.00–13.30 & 18.00–21.30; closed Sun.*

✘ **Pizzeria Vesuvio** Bd de l'OUA; ☎ 53 935 19. For years considered the best pizza in town. Also serves Creole food. Eat in, take away & delivery. ⊕ *11.30–14.00 & 17.30–21.30; closed Wed lunch.*
✘ **Dragon de Mer** 8 Rue Paul Doumer; m 032 02 883 75. Chinese restaurant in an area with lots of parked trucks. Very good Chinese food at reasonable prices. ⊕ *08.00–13.00 & 18.00–21.00; closed Tue.*
✘ **Zoreal** 11 Bd Joffre (north of BMOI bank); ☎ 53 332 36. A local hangout with 2 billiard tables, darts & bar. French & Creole food, plus excellent pizzas. ⊕ *Tue/Thu/Fri/Sat 11.00–14.30 & daily 17.30–24.00.*

Snack bars

🍴 **Bruno's Salon de Thé** Bd de la Libération. Down from Hôtel Les Flamboyants which is under same ownership. Best bakery in town, but get there early for morning pastries. Great coffee; also serves ice cream. ⊕ *daily (inc holidays) 08.00–12.00 & 15.00–19.00 or later if busy.*
🍴 **Salon de Thé Saïfy Fils** 30 Bd Joffre; ☎ 53 928 80. Average pastries, but decent coffee & fruit juices in season. B/fast & other savouries available. Great place for people-watching, although sometimes plagued with vendors. ⊕ *06.30–12.00 & 15.30–18.30; closed Sun afternoon.*
🍴 **Tutti Frutti Glacier** Known locally as 'Le Glacier'. Serves ice cream, pastries, b/fast & light meals. Excellent natural fruit juice. ⊕ *07.00–12.00 & 15.00–19.00; closed Mon.*

🍴 **Adam & Eve Snack Bar** 13 Rue Nationale; ☎ 53 334 56; e adameve33456@yahoo.fr. A long-time *vazaha* favourite with good prices, strong, hot coffee & delicious samosas (*sambo*). Particularly good value for b/fast. 'We took to starting each day with one of their delectable banana milkshakes' (D&K). Always busy; slow service. ⊕ *08.00–20.30; closed Sun.*
🍴 **Abdallah-Awad** Off Bd Joffre. Look for a small foodstuffs shop & head to the back. Coconut & coffee ice creams highly recommended by local expats. ⊕ *08.00–12.00 & 14.30–18.30; closed Sun.*
🍴 **Piano Bar Vesuvio** Bd de l'OUA (next to Pizzeria Vesuvio). Newly opened 'piano bar' (karaoke) serving snacks & light meals. ⊕ *07.00–24.00; closed Sun.*

INTERNET There are many internet facilities in Toamasina, especially around Bd Joffre and the *bazary be*.

🌐 **CyberSky** Bd Joffre; ☎ 53 940 29; e cyberskytmm@yahoo.fr. ⊕ *daily 09.00–19.30; price 25Ar/min.*
🌐 **Speed.Net** Bd de l'OUA; ☎ 53 916 03; m 033 11 908 80/032 40 750 86; e speedcomputertamatave@yahoo.fr.

⊕ *07.30–19.30; closed Sun; price 15Ar/min.*
🌐 **Butterfly** Bd Joffre (near Hôtel Joffre); ☎ 53 317 04; e bnc@wanadoo.mg; www.chez.com/bnc/. Smart cybercafé with AC, 5 computers & facility to connect laptops. ⊕ *08.30–12.00 & 14.30–18.00; closed Sun; price 30Ar/min.*

MONEY There are two offices, one at the BFV Bank on the corner of Avenue de l'Indépendance and Boulevard Joffre, and the other on Boulevard Augangeur.

SHOPPING

Score Av de l'Indépendance. The largest supermarket in town; located east of the Air Mad office. It stocks mostly European & local brands, including some T-shirts. Decent deli & bakery. ⊕ *Mon–Fri 08.30–13.00 & 14.30–19.00; Sat 08.30–19.00; Sun 08.30–12.30.*
Shoprite Av de l'Indépendance. Supermarket located

near the beach. It carries mainly South African & local products. ⊕ *Mon–Thu 08.30–13.00 & 14.30–19.00; Fri/Sat 08.30–19.00; Sun 09.00–13.00.*
La Chocolatière Bd Joffre. For a chocolate fix, or to buy locally made candy gifts, look for the Robert's chocolate shop next to Clementy clothing store – down from the defunct Ritz cinema.

Librairie GM Fakra 29 Bd Joffre; ☎ 53 321 30. This mainly French bookshop has a decent selection of postcards & some coffee-table photo books & CDs of Malagasy music. ⊕ Mon–Fri 08.00–12.00 & 14.30–18.00; Sat 08.00–12.00.

AloAlo 25 Bd Joffre (next to Courts). Interesting selection of handicrafts, different from that found elsewhere. ⊕ 08.30–12.00 & 14.30–18.00; closed Sun.

Fleur du Monde 16 Bd de l'OUA. Unique, upscale souvenirs & some imported items. Worth a visit if you're at this end of town. Look for the blue shopfront with large white flowers near Notre Dame church. ⊕ 08.30–12.00 & 14.30–17.00; closed Sun.

Nulle Part Ailleurs 69 Bd Joffre; ☎ 53 325 06. Roughly opposite Hôtel Génération. Probably the most diverse collection of quality Malagasy gifts in Toamasina: everything from T-shirts & baskets to items made from semi-precious stone. Good selection of handbags. Visa accepted. A second shop is located on the side street next to Courts (opposite Hôtel Joffre); it sells mainly clothing. ⊕ Mon–Fri 08.30–12.00 & 14.30–17.45; Sat 08.30–12.00. Annexe ⊕ Mon–Fri 08.15–12.00 & 14.30–17.45; Sat 08.15–12.00 & 15.00–17.45.

Bazary be ('big market') In typical Malagasy logic, the big market in Toamasina is actually much smaller than the small market – bazary kely. Toamasina is known for its baskets & other woven items; the bazary be is a great place to find such souvenirs. Pause for a fresh coconut on the north side. After drinking the juice, have the coconut cracked open so that you can enjoy the flesh. The vendor will make you a nifty scoop from the shell. T-shirts & CDs are available at shops surrounding the market. **Jeunesse Photo** on the west side has an excellent selection of postcards.

CAR HIRE Renting a car in Toamasina is more expensive than in Tana. Most of the car rental businesses here cannot accommodate walk-in requests. Be sure to contact them in advance. Alternatively ask at your hotel reception (staff usually know someone willing to hire out a private vehicle) or stop a decent-looking taxi and negotiate. You'll be obliged to accept the driver's services, but that isn't necessarily a bad thing since they know the area. The bulletin board at Score supermarket frequently displays vehicles for hire too.

🚗 **Amazing Grace** Villa Rabary, Rue Victor Hugo; ☎ 53 301 52; f 53 339 58; e gracetours@wanadoo.mg.

🚗 **MR Auto** Bd Joffre (near Hôtel Génération); ☎ 53 308 70; m 033 11 049 91. Recommended by an expat who frequently uses this business; reasonable rates.

🚗 **SICAM** Bd de l'OUA (near Espadon Hotel); ☎ 53 321 04; f 53 334 55; e sicam@sicam.mg or sicam.tamatave@simicro.mg. Hertz representative; must arrange in advance.

🚗 **Tropical Service** 23 Bd Joffre; ☎ 53 336 79; f 53 334 80; e tropicalservice@wanao.mg; www.croisiere-madagascar.com. Travel agent across from Hôtel Joffre; extensive details on website under 'location de voiture'. The same travel agent handles reservations for Indian Ocean cruises via Toamasina, as well as the fast boat to Ile Sainte Marie.

BICYCLE HIRE

🚲 **Loulou Location Velos** Bd Joffre; m 032 04 414 83. Good, reliable bicycles. ⊕ daily; prices 8,000Ar/day, 5,000Ar/half-day, 2,000Ar/hr.

NIGHTLIFE

☆ **Pandora Station** Near the Hôtel Miramar. 'An interesting nightclub. Fun place to go dancing without hassles from night ladies (for men). Safe place for women to dance unhassled as well. Used to serve meals but they seem to be moving away from that. Simple snacks served: omelettes, sandwiches, hamburgers etc. Décor is imaginative' (Charlie Welch). Closed Mon.

☆ **Queen's Club** Bd Joffre (near Hôtel Plage & Hôtel Sharon).

Other nightclubs in town are at **Le Neptune** and **Stone Club** at Hôtel Jupiter.

WHAT TO SEE AND DO

Alliance Française (13 Bd Paul Doumer; ☎ 53 334 94; e aftamve@wanadoo.mg) Housed in a charming Creole house built in 1885, the Alliance Française frequently sponsors cultural events such as photo and art exhibits, film nights and concerts (including traditional Malagasy music). Programme of events displayed on the Alliance veranda and around town.

Regional Museum (Musée Régional de l'Université de Toamasina) (*Bd de la Libération, at intersection with Bd Joffre.* ⊕ *08.00–12.00 & 14.30–17.00 Mon–Fri; entrance free*) Don't plan on making a day of it, but if you have some time to kill this small regional museum is a decent filler. The entrance is opposite the fuel station near Hôtel Sharon. Calling itself a museum of ethnology, history and archaeology, there are exhibits from around the island relating to traditional village life, religious beliefs, musical instruments etc. Signboards include text in English.

La Place de Benemy Kim Loohuis recommends this botanical garden 'where you find big, 500-year-old trees. People play pétangue here. Very tranquil and a good place to meet the real Malagasy.

Mini-golf (⊕ *08.00–21.00 daily except Sun. Games 1,000/500Ar adult/child*) 18-hole course at the end of Rue de Commerce, down from the port entrance opposite Bonnet et Fils. 'Sounds corny but is nicely laid out and kept up with bar and grillade restaurant' (CW). Great if you're looking for something completely different to do.

Swimming pool (Piscine Municipale) (⊕ *09.00–17.00 daily. Entrance 1,500/2,000Ar child/adult*) Already mentioned along with its Bateau Ivre restaurant. A nice place for a dip if you are not staying at the Neptune, Miramar or Sharon. Eat poolside or in the restaurant.

Horseback riding (❭ *53 342 93;* f *53 324 25*) For those who have ever harboured romantic notions of riding a horse down a tropical beach, here's your chance. The equestrian centre is located off the main airport road, just before the street to the Hôtel Miramar (coming from town). The sandy road is marked by two signboards ('Domaine des Haras: Masteva'). Contact in advance.

PARC IVOLOINA

This began life in 1898 as a rather grand botanical garden but is now a conservation centre and zoo. It is funded by the Madagascar Fauna Group, a consortium of some 30 zoos from around the world with a special interest in Madagascar. It supports Ivoloina and the reserve of Betampona. See their excellent website (www.savethelemur.org).

A visit here is hugely rewarding, both for what you see and what the MFG is doing in terms of educating the local population about conservation. First the lemurs: in total there are 13 species here, including a female aye-aye. Free-ranging lemurs include black-and-white ruffed lemurs, white-fronted brown lemurs, red-bellied lemurs and crowned lemurs. These offer great photo opportunities, as well as the pleasure of seeing 'zoo animals' living in freedom. There are also reptiles (tortoises, chameleons and boas), tenrecs, vasa parrots and tomato frogs which are unique to the Maroantsetra area.

You can explore the forest around the zoo on a network of seven forest and lakeside trails of varying levels of difficulty, which include wildlife interpretation boards, two waterfalls, a small pool and a viewpoint overlooking the park and the surrounding countryside to the Indian Ocean. An abundance of birds, reptiles and lemurs can be seen from the trails. No guide is needed.

In the zoo itself there is a botanical tour, with labelled native trees, and a guide-booklet in French and English. There's a snack bar (which also sells souvenirs) and you can even go on a pirogue trip on the lake!

Do visit the education centre. Grants from the American Embassy and other donors enabled this building to be carefully designed with excellent displays and explanations of the importance of conservation in the area. In addition the centre runs a teacher-training project and a teachers' manual for environmental education. Children from the local primary school come here on Saturdays to learn about conservation, and two more Saturday Schools have recently been built, one at Ambodirafia (near Betampona Reserve) and the other at Ambodiriano. 'We have also just finished construction of a brand new Ivoloina Conservation Training Centre that will be able to receive a hundred trainees at a time for courses ranging from reforestation techniques and sustainable agriculture to teacher training and veterinary techniques. We're still trying to find funding but in addition to the actual meeting room we have also built a laboratory/computer lab/mini-library. People are making donations of equipment little by little so the idea is to provide resources that aren't available in local schools or universities (the university here in Tamatave doesn't have access to a single microscope at the moment!).'

Then there's the agro-forestry model station, which is on the Station Road just before the zoo entrance. The purpose of this is to teach sustainable agriculture techniques to Malagasy cultivators, but it is a worthwhile visit for tourists who are interested in eastern Madagascar's commercial agricultural products and fruits, as well as bee-keeping, and more. It's an easy place to see a wide variety of cultivated plants in a short period of time while strolling along a peaceful winding path. It includes everything from intensive rice-cultivation techniques to vanilla and lychees, and a new medicinal garden.

Ivoloina encapsulates the best of conservation in Madagascar. Don't miss it!

GETTING THERE Ivoloina is 12km north of Toamasina. It is possible to get there by *taxi-brousse*, although to the village only. From here there is a 4km track to the park, but those on foot can take the 2km shortcut (turn left off the track 60m past the small bridge and welcome arch). The easiest way is to take a taxi or transport arranged through one of the hotels in town. Alternatively hire a bicycle in Toamasina (see page 315).

The park is open 09.00–17.00 daily; the entrance fee is 10,000Ar (4,000Ar for children). Guided tours run on the first Saturday of each month. The leisurely one-hour pirogue trip on the lake costs 2,000Ar. The best time to visit is late afternoon when the lemurs, including the aye-aye, are anticipating feeding time. If you are particularly keen to see the aye-aye, contact the MFG office (✆ 53 308 42) on the Route d'Ivoloina just north of the Royal Hotel.

The ideal way to see the park and its animals is by camping overnight (with your own tent and food; no facilities except three sheltered tent pitches and long-drop toilet). However, Ivoloina is on the airport side of town so if you are stuck in Toamasina for a few hours between planes there is still time for a short visit.

THE ROUTE NORTH

The road is tarred and in good condition as far as Soanierana-Ivongo. Beyond that it is usually passable (just) as far as Maroantsetra. Then you have to take to the air or journey on foot across the neck of the road-free Masoala Peninsula. An increasing number of good-quality seaside hotels are being built along the coast.

MAHAVELONA (FOULPOINTE) The town of Mahavelona is unremarkable, but
nearby is an interesting old circular fortress with mighty walls faced with an iron-
hard mixture of sand, shells and eggs. There are some old British cannons marked
'GR'. This fortress was built in the early 19th century by the Merina governor of
the town, Rafaralahy, shortly after the Merina conquest of the east coast. The entry
fee is 3,000Ar and guided tours are available (in French).

This is becoming a popular beach resort, with the Malagasy as well as *vazaha*,
and there's a growing number of places to stay.

 Where to stay/eat

🏠 **Hôtel Manda Beach** ℡ 57 220 00;
e mandabeach@moov.mg; www.mandabeach-
hotel.com. By far the best hotel in the area, located
on the Toamasina side of town. Bungalows & safe
swimming. €€€€

🏠 **Mangabe Hotel** Double bungalows. €€€
🏠 **Au Gentil Pêcheur** Next door to Manda Beach.
Less expensive bungalows & excellent food. €€
✗ **Le Foulpointe** This restaurant is receiving rave
reviews.

MAHAMBO A lovely beach resort with safe swimming (but nasty sandflies, called
moka fohy in Malagasy).

 Where to stay/eat

🏠 **Hôtel Dola** (20 bungalows) ℡ 57 331 01;
e hoteldola_madagascar@voila.fr;
http://hoteldola.site.voila.fr. 'About a zillion
unattractive, tiny, windowless bungalows, but the place
does look well-kept. Most of his business comes from
meetings & seminars' (CW). €€–€€€
🏠 **La Pirogue** ℡ 57 301 71; www.pirogue-hotel.com.
A pleasant set of bungalows, reasonably priced. Very
nicely decorated with all sorts of artisinal products,
giant geodes & even whale bones. Good food. €€

🏠 **Hôtel Le Récif** (10 bungalows) ℡ 57 300 50;
f 57 301 32. 'The restaurant is really excellent. The
French couple who run it serve wonderful
French/European cuisine' (C Welch). €€
🏠 **Hôtel Restaurant Ylang-Ylang** ℡ 57 331 00/300
08; e mamitina@wanadoo.mg. A very nice
bungalow complex, owned & run by a Chinese family
from Fenoarivo. Bungalows for up to 6 people; all
with hot water. Restaurant has good cheap food.
€–€€

HEADING WEST Between Mahambo and Fenoarivo Atsinanana is a road leading
inland to Vavatenina, where there is basic accommodation in bungalows, and on to
Anjahambe. This town marks the beginning (or end) of the Smugglers' Path to
Lake Alaotra (see page 281).

FENOARIVO ATSINANANA (FÉNÉRIVE) Beyond Mahambo is the former capital of the Betsimisaraka Empire. There is a clove factory in town which distils the essence of cloves, cinnamon and green peppers for the perfume industry. They are not geared up for tourist visits but will show you round if you ask.

There are several basic hotels, including **Belle Rose Bungalows** on the road leading to the hospital, and an excellent Chinese bakery. Dolphins can sometimes be seen swimming offshore.

VOHILENGO From Fenoarivo a road leads west to Vohilengo. This makes a pleasant diversion for those with their own transport, especially during the lychee season. 'We arrived at the start of a six-week lychee bonanza. Along the road to Vohilengo were pre-arranged pick-up points where the pickers would bring their two 10kg panniers. Vohilengo is a small village, perfumed with the scent of cloves laid out to dry; the local *hotely* sells coffee at amazingly cheap prices' (Clare Hermans).

TAMPOLO FORESTRY STATION About 10km north of Fenoarivo is this small forestry station. It is managed by the agricultural branch of the university, and partly supported by the Lemur Conservation Foundation in the USA. They have recently opened a nice little interpretive museum within the grounds. There are paths into the coastal forest that can be taken with guides. It's a good opportunity to see some of Madagascar's most endangered flora: the littoral (coastal) forest.

SOANIERANA-IVONGO Known more familiarly as 'S-Ivongo', this little town is one of the starting points for the boat ride to Ile Sainte Marie. It is also the end of the tarred road.

Where to stay/eat

🏠 **Relais Sainte Marie** Nice bungalows. €

🏠 **Hôtel Espece** Basic bungalows. The best budget option. Near the boat departure point for Ile Sainte

Marie. Well run by Emile, friendly, with excellent food. €

CONTINUING NORTH (IF YOU DARE!)

From Soanierana-Ivongo the road is unreliable, to say the least. As fast as bridges are repaired they wash away again. You may have a fairly smooth *taxi-brousse* ride with ferries taking you across the rivers, or you may end up walking for hours and wading rivers or finding a pirogue to take you across. You should get local advice before setting out, especially if you have a lot of luggage to carry or are on a tight schedule.

ANDRANGAZAHA There is just one reason to stop at this little place midway between S-Ivongo and Manompana: Madame Zakia. 'Madame runs the best place north of Tamatave. All vehicles going north stop there to eat. Why? Because Madame feeds the drivers for free, passengers pay. Her food is excellent, bungalows clean with mozzie nets, away from the noise and bustle of town in the bush where you can wait for a lift in quiet comfort.'

MANOMPANA For many years this village (pronounced man*oom*pe) was the departure point for Nosy Boraha (Ile Sainte Marie). There is no scheduled service now, but you can find a private boat to take you over. Beware of pirogues, however, which are too small to cross the reef safely.

The village has plenty of charm: 'I loved the place! Even two days sitting outside the epi-bar waiting for transport were a pleasure. The owner and his wife are kind and hospitable, and village life was fascinating' (FRB).

Duncan Murrell

In 2003 I was awarded a Winston Churchill Travelling Fellowship to go on a kayaking trip which would make a significant contribution to my work as an environmental educator, writer and photographer. I chose to begin a circumnavigation of Madagascar which has over 3,000 miles of coastline, and hundreds of unexplored islets, particularly off the northwest coast. I wanted to contribute to a greater awareness of the unique and diverse marine habitats of a country that is much better known for its terrestrial treasures. I have had a long association with humpback whales in southeast Alaska, and Madagascar would also give me the opportunity to experience those magnificent animals in a completely different setting.

I started my epic journey at Tamatave at the beginning of September so that I could encounter the migrating whales from Ile Sainte Marie up into Antongil Bay. Unfortunately my careful planning came undone on the very first day of the trip because I hadn't reckoned on the power of the surf generated by the thousands of miles of open ocean extending all of the way down to Antarctica. On my first landing on a very exposed and steep beach north of Tamatave my kayak was swamped by the pounding waves and had it not been for the timely arrival of a local young man I would have lost everything. This unexpected early calamity had served to bring me into immediate contact with the generosity and hospitality of the Malagasy people. My shivering saviour would accept no reward for his heroics and over the next few days I was visited by many local people who brought me water and plenty of good cheer. I learnt my first Malagasy expression, '*tsara be*' (very good), and that became the regular mantra as we toasted Madagascar with endless cups of tea and fits of laughter. That really set the tone for future encounters with isolated coastal communities where the inhabitants were always so surprised to see a waterborne *vazaha* landing on their beaches. They would scrutinise my gear with endless curiosity but I never felt for one moment that anything would be stolen, as indeed was the case until I reached larger towns.

The volatile ocean continued to slow my progress towards my first tropical rendezvous with humpbacks and was responsible for inflicting more injuries in addition to the ones that I had sustained on the first day, and which had since become badly infected. I was exploring Nosy Atafana, a group of three beautiful islands protected by a coral reef, and one of four marine parks on the east coast. I was struck by a mighty wave while standing on a massive breakwater of a rock that was being pounded by the incoming swells. It was a sledgehammer blow that dashed me against the rocks and gashed my foot wide open. My next destination was a doctor in Mananara and my first course of antibiotics.

Around Manompana there is good surfing and swimming, and a small reserve run by ADEFA (Association de Défense de la Forêt d'Ambodiriano), who have an office in the village. As well as guiding you in the reserve, they will take you on a tour of the village, showing a number of interesting things: the baker's oven, coffee being dried on mats, vanilla pods drying in glass Coca-Cola bottles, sea cucumbers drying on mats before being shipped over to Japan to end up in sushi. You also see how they make their very bitter local drink, *betsabetsa*, which is made in a week using sugarcane juice and has about the same alcohol percentage as wine.

Where to stay/eat

Chez Wen-Ki's (5 bungalows) Far end of town; spacious beachfront bungalows with a bucket shower (cold water). Secluded. Laundry service. Mountain bikes for hire. 'The meals were superb, the bungalows

The true benefits of having my own water transportation were realised when I was able to paddle along the Masoala Peninsula and up into several of its rivers. Snorkelling in the protected waters of Tompolo gave me a glimpse of the fantastic marine biodiversity that had vanished from a lot of the degraded coastal areas that I had paddled through. It was usual to be up at the crack of dawn and see legions of silhouetted figures armed with sticks poking and prodding the coral in search of octopuses or any other marine morsels to fill their baskets. Much of the coral that I had paddled past was dead, perhaps as a result of rising sea temperatures but undoubtedly aggravated by the daily abrasion of feet and sticks.

The coastline between Tompolo and Antalavia is the wildest stretch along the peninsula and is adorned with some of the most curious rocks that I have ever seen. Each smooth boulder appears to be crowned with a set of broken teeth. Farther down the peninsula the Isava River afforded me the deepest penetration into the forest although I was never that far from the small homesteads that are creeping up the rivers. This was the immersion that I was looking for; I was alone and tuned in to every nuance of life around me. Unfortunately I was oblivious to the fact that by wandering up and down the river barefoot I was opening the door to the next, and by far the worst affliction of my trip. What was most likely a parasitic schistosome worm had entered the back of my ankle and started a swelling process that inflated my foot like a balloon. It was excruciatingly painful if I stood upright for more than five to ten minutes. Ironically the gash on my other foot had only just healed.

I had to press onwards towards the outer coast and another tussle with the vagaries of the Indian Ocean; my goal, Antalaha and my next course of antibiotics. On the way someone pointed out that the suspicious looking black spots on my toes were in fact the egg repositories of a parasitic flea. I acknowledged his experience and invited him to scrape the eggs out for me.

The ocean was calming somewhat with the onset of the austral summer but as soon as even moderate swells encounter the submerged reefs they create waves that rise up in an instant and come crashing down with explosive force. It was a marine minefield that called for the greatest vigilance. I had to negotiate narrow passages through the reefs with waves funnelling into them from every quarter. It was gripping stuff but all I could think of was getting over to the relatively placid waters of the west coast. My ocean journey ended in Antalaha for this chapter of my kayaking adventure in Madagascar and my kayak awaits me in Diego Suarez for the next leg, which I hope will be less memorable in some respects.

Duncan Murrell is available for school and public lectures (e dunksmurrell@yahoo.com).

delightful, & M Wen Ki the most enchanting & courteous gentleman imaginable' (FRB). €

🏠 **Chez Lou Lou** (6 bungalows) Central; beachfront A-frame bungalows, very clean, good toilets, good seafood. €

🏠 **Mahle Hotel** On Mahle Point, 1km from the village. 'Run by an incredibly friendly brother-&-sister team, the punch coco was the best we tried!' (A Willis). The food is also excellent. This is a very beautiful, oceanfront place with good diving & a lovely nearby forest. €

12

AMBODIRIANO RESERVE This was set up by two school teachers from Réunion in the mid 1990s, and is now run by the local community, ADEFA. The small (65ha) reserve incorporates three dramatic waterfalls, above which shelters have been set up for picnics or overnight camping. If you have your own tent it's worth spending the night in order to search for chameleons (always easier by torchlight) and to get the best dawn birdwatching. You may also see lemurs.

TOAMASINA TO MAROANTSETRA BY MOUNTAIN BIKE

Kailas Narendran & Katie Fillion

The section 'Continuing north (if you dare!)' in this guide was simply too inviting to pass up, and left us spending the most incredible seven days of our lives making the trek from Tamatave to Maroantsetra by mountain bike in June 2005. The trip gave us the opportunity to experience the essence of Madagascar on an intimate level, leaving us with a wealth of stories and memories.

The first 150km of the journey were on flat paved road, with lush scenery and almost no vehicular traffic. We got our first, well-deserved night's rest to the sounds of the ocean crashing onto the beach at Fénérive. After Soanirana-Ivongo we embarked on the first of what seemed like an infinite number of river-crossings. Whatever road and bridge infrastructure once existed along RN5 is now replaced by 4x4 tracks and guys with dugout canoes.

The hard-packed dirt road turned to sand, making the going very slow. As night fell we found a brushy spot off the side of the road (in a swamp, incidentally) and pitched our tents. The hum of mosquitoes, tropical rain, rustle of exotic plants, calls of wildlife and exhaustion from long days of riding with inadequate food is a recipe for sleep like no other!

The following day we understood why the east coast has two seasons: the rainy one and the season in which it rains. I'm not sure which one it was, but it rained almost constantly. The hotel in Antanabe provided us with a welcome opportunity to get some real food and clean up the bikes.

We started Day 3 with an air of great confidence. We only had to go about 40–50km. The scenery was astounding and the trail was perfect bike-touring terrain. Unfortunately the '30km to Mananara' answer never changed, even after hours of riding. Pretty soon the sun was starting to set and the road was just getting worse, with sections of unridable boulder fields covered with slippery red mud. We hadn't seen a hotel and didn't know where we were on the map. In the darkness we waded through mud, finally arriving at a village where we discovered we still had about 15km to go.

As the bad news started to sink in, the rain began to pour and the bugs came out. Luckily we ran into a gentleman (M Jacki) who invited us to stay with his family. We were saturated and completely covered in thick Madagascar mud. He pulled our bikes into his hut, gathered some rainwater for us to wash with, and provided us with a delicious dinner. The rain on the tin roof lulled our exhausted bodies and minds to sleep. Given the stresses of the day, I'd have to say that was the most relaxing night of my life.

We woke to the family hanging around outside the hut and spent the morning exchanging stories about home in broken French. We had a hard time explaining that Katie worked with the small flies that were eating their fruit, modifying their DNA.

Back on the improved road, we were in Mananara within three hours. After Mananara, the road got increasingly better. We spent one night on a deserted beach. The riding was relaxing, the scenery was awesome, and we had enough local know-how to choose our meals and eat on a regular basis.

As we approached the civilization of Maroantsetra, the traffic increased (but never more than a car every ten minutes or so) and we started to see lots more pedestrians and cyclists. On arrival at Hotel Coco Beach we met the first Americans of our trip, and spoke the most English we had spoken since our pedals started turning.

Kailas and Katie may be contacted at kailas@gmail.com.

The road north can be an adventure in itself: 'Intending to set out on foot one morning I found myself in the back of a vehicle bound for a nearby village and was subsequently transferred to a lorry. The experience of watching happy and unconcerned Malagasy cutting down saplings to reinforce bridges, diving into the river to retrieve bits of erstwhile bridge and unloading/reloading the lorry to get it safely across – then repeating the process just a few kilometres on – together with negotiation of the near impossible "road" in between, will stay with me forever! I suspect too that images of the astounded *vazaha* may stay with those with whom I shared this journey!' It took FRB nine hours to reach Antanambe.

Bill French notes that this stretch is tough-going for cyclists, especially the part north of Antanambe, the worst part being around Ivontaka (see also the box on opposite).

ANTANAMBE Some 35km north of Manompana, on the edge of the UNESCO biosphere project, is this pretty little town with one of the east coast's nicest hotels.

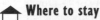

Where to stay

🏠 **Chez Grandin** This lodge, run by Alain & Céline Grandin, is deservedly popular. Despite its remote location it verges on the luxury, with gas cooking, filtered running water, pressure showers & flushing toilets with soft paper; comfortable beds with mozzie nets. There is a great restaurant with Creole & French cooking & fresh fish daily. The Grandins arrange tours to Mananara-Nord & diving/fishing excursions to a vast reef 1km away. There is no way to contact Alain & Céline in advance, but it's worth taking pot luck & simply turning up. €€€

🏠 **Hôtel Vahibe** This is probably the only budget accommodation in the area. The hotel is next to the ferry some 2km north of Antanambe. The owner speaks some English. €

The stretch of road from Anatanambe to Mananara is still in a dreadful state. Many travellers do it on foot rather than braving a *taxi-brousse*. Here's part of a 1998 report from Rupert Parker who did the trip in a 4x4. 'The road is the worst I've ever experienced but also the most spectacular. It hugs the coast climbing up and down through virgin forest right down to the sea, affording stunning glimpses of cliffs and deserted bays if you can divert your attention from holding on for dear life. It took us four hours to do the 40km. There are ferries, broken-down bridges and huge boulders haphazardly scattered over steep inclines. Definitely Mission Impossible, but because of that the forest is largely uncleared and it's one of the most beautiful areas in Madagascar.'

SAHASOA Continuing north for another 20km or so, you reach this village which is the gateway to Mananara-Nord – the UNESCO Biosphere Reserve. The **Hôtel du Centre** has a cheap bungalow for just 3,000Ar. Mosquito net supplied but otherwise very basic. The ANGAP office for Mananara-Nord is situated at the southern end of Sahasoa village.

MANANARA-NORD NATIONAL PARK Mananara-Nord Biosphere Reserve covers an area of 140,000ha, with a variety of ecosystems including tropical humid forest, sandy coastal plains with littoral vegetation, river vegetation, mangrove formations, marshlands and coral reefs. Occasional tourists visit its marine reserve that protects, among other things, dugongs. At the centre of this is a small island, **Nosy Antafana**, where bats can be seen in great numbers. Until fairly recently this was a great place for snorkelling but the coral is now, sadly, dead. ANGAP can help with boats; the trip takes two hours each way and will cost around 270,000Ar (per boat).

Very few people visit the forest, which is a two-hour hike from Sahasoa. 'We spent a very long, sweaty day hiking in the forest. Apart from a party of 11 Dutch birders who had visited two weeks before us, there had apparently only been ten other visitors to the terrestrial part of the park in the whole of the previous 12 months. So it was with great ceremony that we were given the visitor book to sign at the ANGAP office' (D&K).

FROM SAHASOA TO MANANARA Ongoing transport becomes increasingly scarce, but if you get stuck, **Seranambe**, which lies roughly half way, has the **Capital** hotel with a basic bungalow for 4,000Ar.

MANANARA This friendly small village 127km north of Soanierana-Ivongo sees few visitors despite the fact that it is the only place in Madagascar where one can be pretty much assured of seeing an aye-aye in the wild. There is a lively market and the ocean for relaxation. About 3km south of the village is a secluded bay, protected by a reef, with safe swimming.

Getting there and away Mananara used to be served by Air Mad but this service has been discontinued so the village is truly isolated. See page 326 for ways of reaching Maroantsetra.

By road The account by FRB of her journey by road from Soanierana-Ivongo illustrates the joys and perils of this route. 'The *taxi-brousse* ride from Mananara back to Tamatave was a delight – even though it was a 26-hour delight of which only three hours were spent asleep!'

On foot See page 325.

By sea If you don't want to subject your body to this sort of torture, the only way to reach Mananara is by speedboat from Maroantsetra.

 Where to stay

⌂ **Hôtel Aye-Aye** On the beachfront opposite the airport. Pleasant en-suite bungalows, enlivened by free-range bamboo & brown lemurs. French-run (Carine & Max). 'I can recommend the kind services of the new management. The food is great & they offered a lot of services free of charge' (Wybe Rood). Tours to Aye-Aye Island can usually be arranged from here. €€

⌂ **Chez Roger** (6 bungalows) If visiting Aye-Aye Island is your main reason for coming to Mananara you should stay here, since M Roger owns the island & will deal with all the arrangements, not just for this visit but for other places of interest in the area. Good accommodation & restaurant. En-suite bathrooms (hot shower facilities). €

🏠 **Ton-Ton Galet** A friendly, modest set of bungalows located near the hospital. Good meals & convivial atmosphere. 'I quite liked the close proximity of pigs & assorted poultry!' (FRB). €

Communication Mananara has recently been added to Madacom's network coverage area, so mobile phones work fine. There are currently no facilities for internet access.

AYE-AYE ISLAND This is *the* reason most people come to Mananara. The privately-owned island of about 10ha has a few resident aye-ayes as well as white-fronted brown lemurs. The natural habitat for aye-ayes is high in the rain-forest canopy, which is why they are so hard to see in Nosy Mangabe, but they are partial to coconuts and coconut palms are found in abundance on Aye-Aye Island. When I visited the island in 2005 we immediately found a pair of aye-ayes just beginning their breakfast of coconuts a couple of metres above our heads. Now, in all my visits to Madagascar this was the first wild aye-aye I'd seen, so I was ecstatic! And lucky. Daniel and Kelly failed to find any aye-ayes during their evening visit; but fortunately they had chosen to camp, and were woken in the small hours by their guide who had located the animals. And Wybe Rood wonders if the animal really exists! 'Went to Aye-Aye Island and didn't see any. After having spent almost two years in all in Madagascar since 1999, having been to Nosy Mangabe and Aye-Aye Island, I am now convinced this creature is a fabrication!'

Botanically the island is interesting; not only are there coconuts, but bananas, pineapples, jackfruits, papayas, vanilla, coffee, cloves and maize are all cultivated there.

Visits to Aye-Aye Island are arranged at the hotel Chez Roger, and cost €8 per person.

MANANARA TO MAROANTSETRA To continue the journey north is an adventure, but that's part of the attraction. It is possible (just) by road and also by sea. Since the mid 1990s, readers have recounted their experiences using both forms of transport, most ending in extreme hardship with some near-deaths. As the road continues to deteriorate, the trek on foot is at least safe, if hard work.

Getting there and away
By road In 2005 Jeremy Sabel reported: 'This 114km journey took 14 hrs in a 4x4 *taxi-brousse*. Again the 'road' was terrible and the passengers were packed in like sardines, and two suffered from motion sickness. *Taxi-brousses* leave when there are sufficient passengers (roughly once every two days).'

By boat It is worth enquiring at the port of Mananara if there are any cargo boats heading north as they regularly ply the route. Alternatively you can take the ANGAP boat (expensive!) to Antafana island and then onwards to Antanambe.

On foot/by bicycle Dylan Lossie did it (from Maroantsetra) in 2006 with the help of tour operator Ortour (*www.ortour.com*). 'We had five porters, a cook and two guides. The first 20km from Maroantretra we went by *taxi-brousse* but the vehicle completely collapsed after 18km and we had to leave the poor driver and his destroyed vehicle behind. We walked 2km to the first village, **Voloina**, where lunch was prepared for us. Then another 12km to **Rantabe**, where we camped on a beach.' After that, Dylan's journey was a combination of walking, bicycle and *taxi-*

brousse for the final leg from **Manambolosy** to Mananara. 'Not an easy ride! It took more than two hours for just 20km. All along the way between Maroantsetra to Mananara, bridges were collapsed, or just about to. The roads are in a terrible state. Nevertheless, the area is beautiful and I would not have missed it!'

MAROANTSETRA AND THE MASOALA PENINSULA

Despite difficulty of access and dodgy weather, this is perhaps the leading destination for ecotourists who want to see Madagascar's most important natural habitat in terms of biodiversity – the eastern rainforest, exemplified by Nosy Mangabe and the Masoala Peninsula.

These places require fitness and fortitude but the rewards for nature-lovers are great. Fitness is needed for the hills and mud which are an aspect of all the reserves, and fortitude because this is the wettest place in Madagascar, with the annual rainfall exceeding 5,000mm. The driest months tend to be November and December.

MAROANTSETRA Nestled at the far end of the Antongil Bay, Maroantsetra is Madagascar at its most authentic. Well away from the usual tourist circuits, it is a prosperous, friendly little town, with enough comfortable hotels to make a visit a pleasure for both packaged and independent travellers.

☞ *WARNING!* There is no ATM here and Visa cards are not accepted anywhere. MasterCard is accepted at the only bank, as are travellers' cheques and foreign currency, but the exchange rate is very poor. Try to bring sufficient Ariary for your stay.

At the time of writing the Maroantsetra bridge is collapsed and replaced by a ferry.

Getting there and away

By air Most people fly. Consequently flights tend to be booked well in advance. Currently there are flights every day but Wednesday and Sunday, but check latest schedules/availability with Air Mad (www.airmadagascar.mg). The airport is 8km from town.

By land You can come on foot (and occasional vehicle) from Mananara (see page 325) or hike to/from Antalaha (see page 332).

By sea There are regular cargo boats (*boutres*) between Toamasina and Maroantsetra. They will stop *en route* at Ile Sainte Marie if requested. The cost is approximately 20,000Ar to Ile Sainte Marie (10hrs) and 30,000Ar to Toamasina (18hrs). Beware of stopovers and choppy seas. 'For added value, boat journeys in late August and September may give you a glimpse of humpback whales (we were fortunate!) outside the usual whale-watching scenario' (J Sabel).

Where to stay

🏠 **Relais du Masoala** (15 bungalows) ☏ 22 349 93 (Tana); e relais@simicro.mg; www.relaismasoala.com. Spacious, palm-thatched bungalows set in 7ha of gardens & coconut groves overlooking Antongil Bay. A super place, American-owned & very comfortable. There is a swimming pool & the food is very good. Runs tours to Nosy Mangabe (with optional camping overnight), birdwatching on the Masoala Peninsula, pirogue excursions upriver, whale-watching etc. The guide Julien (brother of Maurice & Patrice of Andasibe) is a fount of knowledge & takes guests on night walks & other excursions here. He even knows where to find aye-ayes in the Maroantsetra area. €€€€

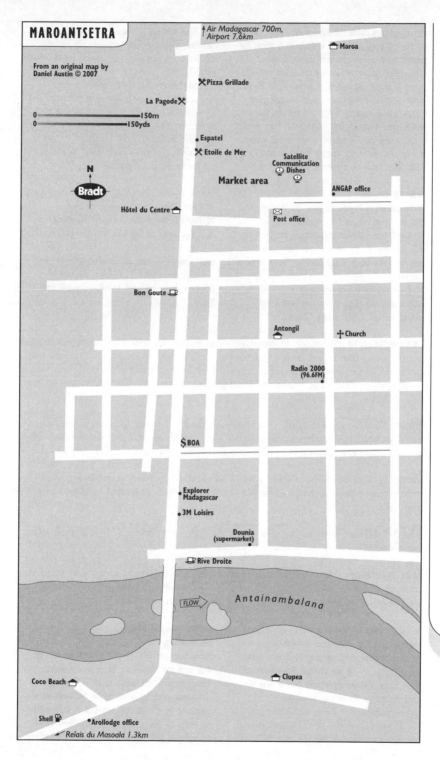

MAROANTSETRA

From an original map by
Daniel Austin © 2007

0 ——————— 150m
0 ——————— 150yds

N

Bradt

Air Madagascar 700m,
Airport 7.6km

Maroa

Pizza Grillade

La Pagode

Espatel

Etoile de Mer

Satellite
Communication
Dishes

Market area

ANGAP office

Hôtel du Centre

Post office

Bon Goute

Antongil

Church

Radio 2000
(96.6FM)

$ BOA

Explorer
Madagascar

3M Loisirs

Dounia
(supermarket)

Rive Droite

FLOW

Antainambalana

Coco Beach

Clupea

Shell

Arollodge office

Relais du Masoala 1.3km

🏠 **Motel Coco Beach** (10 bungalows) ➘ 57 720 06. The dbl bungalows vary in facilities & price. The simplest have an en-suite cold shower & shared toilet, others also have en-suite toilet (but still cold water) & at the top end there is hot water. Meals in the spacious dining-room are of variable quality & slow service even by Malagasy standards. Laundry service good & cheap. One attraction of Coco Beach is the striped tenrecs running about in the garden at night. For excursions contact Rakoto Vazaha (see Maroa Tour under *Tour operators*). €€–€€€

🏠 **Hôtel Antongil** (8 rooms) ➘ 17 (via post office switchboard). Rooms have wide (shared) balconies, showers & shared toilets. Fan supplied but no mozzie nets. €

🏠 **Hôtel Maroa** Nice quiet bungalows with mosquito nets & en-suite bathrooms. Restaurant, but the food was indifferent when I ate there & the service very slow. €

🏠 **Hôtel du Centre** ➘ 57 721 31; e tsimanova@yahoo.fr. Across from the market; inexpensive rooms & bungalows. €

✖ Where to eat

✖ **Restaurant La Pagode** Opposite the market. Good food but open only in the evenings.

✖ **Rive Droite** Open-air restaurant & bar built out over the river. To the right as you come into town from the Coco Beach. 'Good food, but flies can be a nuisance.'

✖ **Baguette d'Or** A Chinese restaurant behind the market, near the Hôtel Maroa. Excellent & huge seafood; chicken & beef *soupe Chinoise*.

✖ **Pizza Grillade** An inexpensive *hotely*.

✖ **Etoile de Mer** A simple Chinese restaurant.

🍽 **Restaurant au Bon Goût** A Muslim-run *salon de thé*. 'We found it very good for breakfast. They sell bread, croissants, pain au chocalat, cakes etc. Time your visit for around 10.00 when the fresh croissants have just been baked & are still hot!' (D&K)

Communication 'Although Maroantsetra has electricity and telephones, there is at present no place to get online. However, cellphone coverage has recently been extended to this town. **Espatel** (opposite La Pagode) is the place to go to make a phone call or send a fax, and if the town gets an internet connection it will be here first' (D&K).

Money Maroantsetra has only one bank: the Bank of Africa. Unlike the other main banks in Madagascar, they do not handle Visa withdrawals, only MasterCard. This has led many unprepared travellers into financial difficulties.

Shopping Dounia Supermarket is well stocked with items suitable for taking as provisions on trips to Masoala or Nosy Mangabe such as tinned food and cartons of drinks.

ANGAP office Address BP 86, Maroantsetra, telephone 111 (via post office switchboard).

Tour operators Here, more than anywhere else in Madagascar, you need the services of a local tour operator to secure a boat to Nosy Mangabe or Masoala, as well as other excursions which are difficult to do on your own.

3M Loisirs Owned & run by Christian Calvet. This one-stop outfitters will provide everything you need for an expedition: tents, sleeping bags, quad bikes, snorkelling gear — & the excellent English-speaking guide, Emile. Such comprehensive service does not come cheap, but the quality is assured.

Explorer Madagascar — Bureau des Guides ➘ 57 721 49; m 033 14 471 20; e f-f@wanadoo.mg. Silke Rother reports that they offer trips to Masoala

& Nosy Mangabe, boat hire, trekking, & whale- & bird-watching.

Maroa Tour m 033 12 057 19/032 43 482 09. Run from the Motel Coco Beach by the indefatigable **Rakoto Vazaha**, who seems to be able to organise just about anything in the region. 'We were very impressed by the phenomenon that is Rakoto Vazaha. He seems to live in a perpetual whirlwind of arranging & planning — as far from the traditional

Malagasy *mora mora* ethic as one could be – as he goes about organising everything for his clients. He speaks excellent English & will arrange a complete package (boats, guides, permits, accommodation etc) according to your budget & needs' (D&K).

Adrien Bemirhary On the main street; ❧ 57 721 42; m 032 02 039 10. Speedboat owner. 'He is a tough negotiator & seems to control the market (his business card states: Président du Groupement des Opérateurs Touristiques de Maroantsetra). Best to form a group before meeting him.'

Relais de Masoala The hotel has been organising trips to Masoala & other hard-to-reach places longer than anyone. They are not cheap, but you can be assured of the quality of the boat, the camping equipment & the site chosen for your stay.

Paul Harimala Clememt ❧ 53 339 12; m 033 02 259 43; f 53 313 50; e laly_son@yahoo.fr. An experienced guide who is reportedly keen to organise tours that allow tourists to experience & contribute to social aspects of the region. Speaks several languages including English & some Japanese.

LOCAL EXCURSIONS Sil Westra did a full-day tour organised by Rakoto Vazaha. 'This was excellent and I really recommend it! You can see lots of things in a short time. You can see kingfishers and Parson's chameleons on the banks of the river while you try to balance yourself inside the ever-unstable pirogue. You can taste local sugar cane wine *betsabetsa* in a traditional small village where you will constantly be surrounded by curious children. You can hike through the rural countryside and be pulled across the river on a raft. You can experience the petrol-saving driving techniques of the taxi drivers by rolling to a standstill with the engine shut off before the massive acceleration starts again. A farmer will show you around his vanilla plantation and explain how cinnamon is grown and harvested. And you can have a look at the huge endemic tomato frog in people's backyards.' It's good to hear of a tour that involves local people in this way.

Andranofotsy and Navana It is worth taking a pirogue trip up the Andranofotsy River to the village of the same name. The vegetation and river-life viewed on the way are fascinating, and the relatively unspoilt village is delightful.

Equally worthwhile is a visit to Navana. Follow the coast east along a beach backed by thickets, through waterways clogged with flowering water hyacinths and past plenty of forest. You need to cross a lot of water on a pirogue, a regular local service. It takes an hour through little canals and costs very little.

NOSY MANGABE In fine weather the island of Nosy Mangabe is superb. This Special Reserve has beautiful sandy coves, marvellous trees with huge buttress roots and also strangler figs. And it's bursting with wildlife including, of course, its famous aye-ayes which were released here in the 1960s to prevent what was then thought to be their imminent extinction. If aye-ayes are what you're after, there's little point in coming here just for the day (they are nocturnal) but there is plenty to see on a day visit, including the weird and wonderful leaf-tailed gecko, *Uroplatus fimbriatus*, green-backed mantella frogs, white-fronted brown lemurs and black-and-white ruffed lemurs.

Leo Barasi spent six days on the island: 'I don't regret on any of it. OK we didn't manage to see any aye-aye, but the rest of the wildlife and the scenery more than made up for it. I loved the leaf-tailed geckos, particularly at night when they took on a completely new appearance. Lots of chameleons, including *Brookesia*, some very nice boas and several other attractive snakes. The black-and-white ruffed lemurs could be heard from all points of the island and sounded like dying pigs. Best of all, though, were the dolphins and sea turtles that we saw swimming around the bay on our last day – fantastic!'

Daniel and Kelly stayed five days (also no aye-ayes): 'On the second day there we decided to follow the circuit to the summit. Our guide assured us that the round-trip would take no more than four hours, but we encountered so much wildlife along the route that we had not even reached the summit in this time! It seemed that every few paces we were pausing to examine another frog or gecko.'

You can see from the above that though it's famous for its aye-ayes very few people see them on Nosy Mangabe even during a prolonged visit. However, Simon Jackson got lucky: 'We were fortunate enough to have the island to ourselves for two days in perfect weather at the beginning of December. Our guide, Armand, feared (mistakenly) that he had lost face on the first evening, having presented himself as Mr Aye-Aye, then had us sit on a log in the middle of the forest for an hour in the pitch black waiting in vain for the animals to betray their presence by dropping partially consumed fruit on our heads.

'The next morning at 05.30, just after dawn, he woke us in our tent in a state of high excitement. Determined to make amends, he had risen in the dark to follow some cries. He dragged us off the path up a steep slope, our hearts racing from the rapid transition from deep sleep to violent exercise, and there at eye-level, not five metres away, were two aye-ayes making more aye-ayes while a rejected suitor slunk off. The female was grasping a vertical bamboo stem while the smaller male hung on doggedly below/behind her. They seemed bemused but unfazed by our presence, and were still blissfully conjoined when we left them 20 minutes later.'

As you leave Nosy Mangabe, ask your boatman to take you to see the old (17th-century) Dutch inscriptions carved on rocks at the Plage des Hollandais. Fascinating! And there is also a recent shipwreck.

Practicalities There is no accommodation on the island – you must camp in the thatched shelters which cost 5,000Ar per night (not including tent hire). The trails are well-made and walking, though strenuous, is not difficult. In rain, though, the paths are slippery and it's pretty unpleasant. And it rains often.

Two-day permits cost 15,000Ar, payable at the park headquarters on the island. Full details of permit prices on page 75.

Getting there and away Boats and a guide can be arranged at the Masoala park headquarters next to the Bureau des Guides in Maroantsetra. The boat trip from Maroantsetra takes 30 minutes. Or arrange a visit through Rakoto Vazaha at Motel Coco Beach.

THE MASOALA PENINSULA The peninsula (pronounced mash*wahl*) is one of the largest and most diverse areas of virgin rainforest in Madagascar, and probably harbours the greatest number of unclassified species. The peninsula's importance was recognised by the French back in 1927 when they created a small reserve there, but independent Madagascar was swift to remove the protection in 1964. However, 230,000ha has now been set aside as a national park.

Visitors should be warned that logging and clearance for agriculture still persists outside the national park and maps of the peninsula tend to be deceptively green. That said, there are still large expanses of virgin forest along with stunning beaches of golden sand dotted with eroded rocks. Some parts of the peninsula, seen on a sunny day, can arguably be described as the most beautiful in Madagascar.

The wildlife is equally stunning. You will need to work for it, but nevertheless the opportunity to see red ruffed lemur in its only habitat, helmet and Bernier's vangas, scaly ground-roller and other rare endemic birds plus a host of reptiles and invertebrates is not to be missed.

Switzerland's Zoo Zürich has established a link with Masoala and are financing some development projects to encourage conservation of the peninsula (see box on page 334). Their Masoala Kely exhibit – an 11,000m² indoor replica rainforest – is well worth visiting (*www.zoo.ch/masoala/*).

How to visit Masoala National Park Masoala can be reached only by boat, which takes 1½–2 hours from Maroantsetra. For independent travellers, finding a safe but affordable boat is the main difficulty. The trip, which can cost as much as 120,000Ar per person, should be made as early in the morning as possible. The sea gets rough in the afternoon and, apart from the seasickness, the trip takes twice as long. It is said to be possible to get a local cargo boat to Ambanizana, Andranobe and Lohatrozona, but they don't run every day.

If you are staying in one of the Masoala lodges the boat transfer will be part of the arrangement, otherwise you will need to make arrangements through one of Maroantsetra's tour operators.

A three-day park permit costs 20,000Ar for three days. Full details of permit prices on page 75.

🏠 **Where to stay** While camping is still popular and gives instant access to the rainforest, there are three lodges that allow a more comfortable stay and are in or near Tampolo, arguably the most beautiful beach in Madagascar. The orange-gold sand is backed by the dark green of the rainforest; fresh water runs down from the hillsides into the sea, and comet orchids shine like stars against the dark eroded rocks. All can be booked in town through the Relais de Masoala or Rakoto Vazaha.

🏠 **Masoala Forest Lodge** (5 'African safari' tents) 📞 22 261 14; e mea@wanadoo.mg or in Switzerland through Let's Go Tours (📞 +41 52624 1077; e info@letsgo.ch); www.masoalaforestlodge.com. Contact via Rokoto Vazaha at Motel Coco Beach, or in Tana at Madagascar Expedition Agency. A new (2005), upmarket South African/Swiss-owned tented camp in Tampolo. Furnished tents under thatched shelters on hard-wood decks; toilets & bathrooms (hot water!) are in separate huts. Excursions include trips by kayak to explore rivers & stretches of coast, as well as snorkelling in the marine reserve. Forest trails provide excellent bird & wildlife viewing; some traditional forest settlements can also be visited. It is cheaper to book in Maroantsetra but you risk it being full. €€€€€–💰

🏠 **Tampolodge** www.masoalamadagascar.com. Contact via Explorer Madagascar in Maroantsetra. Owned by Italian Giuseppe la Marca, this is a collection of rustic huts in a superb location at Tampolo. Basic accommodation, excellent food. €€€€

🏠 **Arollodge** (8 bungalows) 📱 033 12 902 77; e masoala@free.fr; http://arollodge.free.fr/home.htm. Office in Maroantsetra near Motel Coco Beach. Owner: Olivier Fournajoux. The palm-thatched huts, 2 of which are en suite, are set back from the beach so the setting is not as nice as Tampolodge, but the accommodation is more comfortable, though still very simple: cold water, & electricity for 3hrs each evening. Solar oven. Fresh bread & cakes from the lodge's own baker in high season. In low season meals must be ordered in advance & paid for whether eaten or not (because of the difficulty of buying fresh food in this remote area). Olivier also sells a Masoala/Nosy Mangabe package & can organise treks across the peninsula. *Transfers* € 145–181 (up to 4 people). €€€

CAP EST The most easterly point of Madagascar, Cap Est is gradually opening up to adventurous travellers. It can be accessed via boat and on foot from Maroantsetra or, more easily, from Antalaha. Depending on the state of the road, it takes about three hours to reach the town nearest to the cape, **Ambodirafia**, by *taxi-brousse*. There are two river crossings by ferry.

The littoral forest inland from Cap Est is part of Masoala National Park and an excellent place to see the carnivorous Masoala pitcher plant. Cap Est is also the closest access point on the coast to the impressive Bevontsira Waterfall, two to three days' walk inland towards Maroantsetra. Avoid hiking during periods of high rainfall because river crossings may be a problem.

Where to stay

🏠 **La Résidence du Cap** A former upmarket hotel at Cap Est, now run by a Frenchman named Sam. It was almost totally destroyed by the cyclones in 2004 but is still open for business. €€

🏠 **Hôtel du Voyageur** (16 bungalows) A straightforward setup of huts with beds, mosquito nets & buckets for washing. No electricity. €

FROM MAROANTSETRA TO ANTALAHA THE ADVENTUROUS WAY ANGAP now offer three hikes from Maroantsetra:

- Maroantsetra–Antalaha (4 days)
- Maroantsetra–Cap Est (6 days)
- Maroantsetra–Andapa (8 days)

Although it is possible to do the first two of these alone, you are advised to find a guide if only to avoid being hassled continuously by locals wanting to guide you. You will need the relevant FTM map: *No 4 Antalaha*.

Maroantsetra to Antalaha: across the neck of the peninsula I have heard mixed reports of this four- or five-day hike. The distance is 152km, and in the heat it is very strenuous. Considering that you are mainly passing through secondary forest and cultivated areas, it doesn't attract me much. However, many people want to do it, and will be faced with the choice of going it alone or hiring a guide and porters. This is the route:

Day 1 Maroantsetra to Mahalevona, the village beyond Navana, which is described under *Excursions*, page 329. A pleasant 5km walk.

Day 2 Mahalevona to Ankovona. The track climbs into the mountains and there are rivers to cross.

Day 3 Ankovona to Ampokafo. A long trek to Ampokafo which marks the halfway point. Very hilly and very beautiful, with lots of streams and orchids. The village has a small shop.

Day 4 Ampokafo to Analampontsy. Less wild, but still orchids along the way. Most villages *en route* have shops.

Day 5 Analampontsy to Antalaha. You emerge onto the road at the village of Marofinaritra, about 30km from Antalaha. From here you can get a *taxi-brousse* to Antalaha.

Via Cap Est A more scenic (but equally tough) route to Antalaha from Maroantsetra is via Cap Est. You can hire tents and a guide for this trip from 3M Loisirs in Maroantsetra. Here are accounts by two recent (2005) travellers:

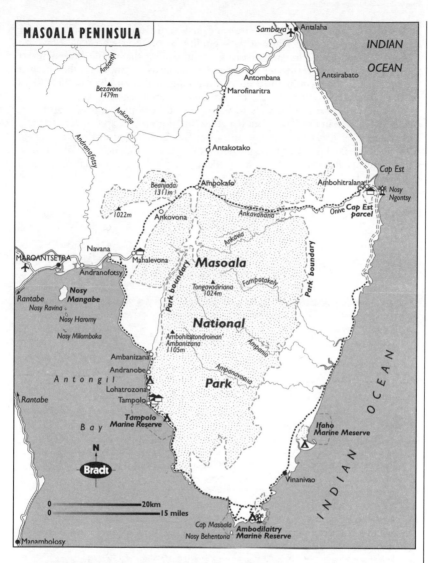

INDIAN

OCEAN

Sambava · Antalaha

Antombana

Marofinaritra

Antsirabato

Bezavona
1479m

Antakotako

Cap Est

Beanjada
1311m

Ampokafo

Ambohitralanana

Nosy
Ngontsy

1022m

Ankovona

Ankavanana

Onive · Cap Est
parcel

Navana

Masoala

MAROANTSETRA

Mahalevona

Tongavadiriana
1024m

Fampotakely

Andranofotsy

Nosy
Mangabe

National

Nosy Ravina

Nosy Haromy

Ambohitsitondroinan'
Ambanizana
1105m

Rantabe

Nosy Milomboka

Ambanizana

Ampanavoana

Andranobe

A n t o n g i l

Lohatrozona

Tampolo

Rantabe

B a y

Tampolo
Marine Reserve

Ifaho
Marine Meserve

N

Vinanivao

Bradt

0   20km
0   15 miles

Cap Masoala

Nosy Behentona

Ambodilaitry
Marine Reserve

Manambolosy

12

'I did the Maroantsetra–Cap Est route. The first two days are the same as Maroantsetra–Antalaha (as far as Ampokafo): very muddy and hard going. The third day you turn east and climb 600m up a muddy slope into Masoala National Park. Although I went in the dry season it was raining constantly. If you don't mind leeches, slipping, falling, getting muddy and crossing rivers up to your chest, then this is the hike for you. It's definitely not the option for those who just want a stroll and I recommend taking porters (I took two at 5,000Ar each per day). Not only did they carry my bags but they cooked too. You must have camping equipment, bring food and be prepared to hike for up to eight hours per day. I really enjoyed the experience, and even got to see the elusive fossa.

'The final day of the trip is a four-hour pirogue ride down the Ankavanana River to the village of Ambohitralalana. From here it is a 5km walk to the village of Ambodirafia which is on Cap Est. Here I visited a small portion of the National

Park which is separated from the rest and just 1km from Ambodirafia. Ask for Paulin, a member of the national park guiding association who will show you *Nepenthes masoalenis* a rare insectivorous plant among the fragile littoral forest ecosystem. I also saw freshwater turtles and many birds. I camped on the beach at Ambodirafia at the recommendation of Paulin and had no problems. The 40km north to Antalaha should only take three hours' (Jeremy Sabel).

Wybe Rood reports on his walk in the reverse direction: 'I did the Cap Est to Maroantsetra trek in five days. Found a guide and porters in Cap Est; very friendly and strong. Day 1 was in a pirogue and nice; Day 2 we hiked to Bizono, crossed the river about 20 times: waist-high water, slippery rocks. Bizono is a relatively new village, created for relocated forest dwellers. They've recently opened a school there for 22 kids.

MASOALA COMES TO ZURICH

Janet Mears

A unique ecosystem project has recently come to fruition at Zoo Zürich in Switzerland and is well worth a visit. With input from the Wildlife Conservation Society, Parcs Nationaux Madagascar (ANGAP) and Parc National Masoala, Zoo Zürich is now home to the Masoala biome, some 11,000m^2 of Madagascar rainforest. The brainchild of Dr Alex Rübel, Director of Zoo Zürich, the idea was first conceived in 1992. The Masoala biome gives an impressive snapshot of the Malagasy rainforest and has really captured the natural relationships between the tropical plant and animal worlds under artificial conditions.

There are approximately a hundred different plant and tree species in the biome, with 55% of the trees being endemic to Madagascar. About 20% of the 17,000 trees, shrubs and plants in the exhibit were brought in directly from a specially established nursery in Madagascar while others were located in various botanical gardens around the world. With a temperature of 26°C and 80% humidity, there are plants in flower year-round.

About 30 species of Malagasy animals, reptiles and birds live in the biome, including a superb group of Aldabran giant tortoises, a species now extinct in Madagascar. As in the real rainforest, you need to use your ears and eyes as you wander between lush green-fringed pathways with the occasional glint of water from the streams running through to lakes. A rustling overhead gives notice that flying foxes are on the move. Then the tiniest of movements on a traveller's palm shows up a large day gecko, slowly making his way along a frond, which takes your eye to a chameleon sitting silent and stationary a few feet away. And, suddenly, a cacophony of noise from deep in the forest disturbs the whispering conversation of the viewing public as four red ruffed lemurs chase each other out onto the branches above the path. Round bright eyes staring out of dark faces, they look at us, realise we are not a threat, and then run up and down the trees, onto a fallen branch before disappearing back into the forest. Magical.

The Masoala biome has created considerable interest both in Switzerland and further afield. As well as teaching people about Madagascar, the zoo is actively encouraging the public to make donations towards the management of Masoala National Park. They use the maxim 'In Madagascar, an area of rainforest as large as the entire Masoala Hall of Zoo Zürich is destroyed every five minutes. This is not inevitable. With your help, the destruction of the rainforest can be stopped.'

Zoo Zürich is open every day of the year and is a pleasant 15-minute tram ride (no 6) from the Hauptbahnhof. Further details can be found on their websites (*www.zoo.ch* and *www.masoala.ch*) where you can also join the Friends of Masoala.

Matthew Hatchwell

One of the most fascinating episodes in the history of European presence in the Masoala region is the extraordinary story of Count Auguste de Benyowski, who established a French colony named Louisbourg on the site of modern-day Maroantsetra in 1774.

A Hungarian aristocrat by birth, Benyowski first arrived in Madagascar in 1772 at the culmination of a series of adventures that had taken him all the way across Russia to the Kamchatka Peninsula, down the Pacific coast of mainland Asia in a commandeered battleship, and finally across the Indian Ocean. Following a brief reconnoitre, Benyowski travelled on to France where he persuaded Louis XV to fund the creation of a new French colony at Maroantsetra which, he argued, could serve later as the basis for claiming Madagascar for France. Like every other early attempt to establish a permanent European settlement in Madagascar, the enterprise was a failure. Benyowski returned to France in 1776, where he met the famous American scientist and diplomat Benjamin Franklin, who inspired him to sail to the New World where he played a minor role in the American War of Independence against the British. Ten years later, he returned to Madagascar with American backing and was killed by French troops after establishing a trading station near Cap Est across the Masoala Peninsula from Maroantsetra.

All traces of Benyowski's original colony have been lost, but at least one 19th-century traveller observed finding a stone engraved with the names of some of Benyowski's fellow colonists at a second settlement which they established inland to escape the ravages of malaria. On Nosy Mangabe, many traces remain of European occupation in the 17th and 18th centuries, when first the Dutch and later the French established slave-trading stations there to supply labourers for their colonies elsewhere in the region. It is unknown which of these date from Benyowski's day, although one of the main tourist trails on the island retraces an earlier path complete with stone steps which he must have used when he established a quarantine station on the island. Many European sailors did not survive the rigours of their long sea journeys and are buried on Nosy Mangabe. One, a Dutchman named Willem Cornelisz Schouten, is famous as the navigator of the first European fleet to round the southern tip of South America, which he named after his native village in the Netherlands: Hoorn.

We know too that Nosy Mangabe was one of the first sites in Madagascar settled by humans when they first arrived some 1,500–1,700 years ago. Another historical site worth visiting on the island is an enormous boulder at the Plage des Hollandais where Dutch sailors left carved messages for each other during the 1600s. A few decades later, Antongil Bay and nearby Ile Sainte Marie became infamous to sailors as the strongholds of pirates such as Henry Avery and James Plantain. Traces of many of these eras can still be seen in the Masoala region. Others remain to be rediscovered! *Text summarised from* Masoala: The Eye of the Forest *(page 461).*

'Then the hardest day involved another 20 times of river crossing. I'd recommend to bring shoes to protect your feet from the rocks, as well as hiking boots. The forest was a bit disappointing though. Most of the time you walk through parts that have been lived in. We saw no wildlife apart from geckos. The bit from Ampokafo to Maroantsetra was very pretty and relatively easy.'

Via Masoala Sebastian Bulmer and Jamie Gibbs did a variation of the Cap Est walk from Antalaha to Maroantsetra in May 2003, following the coast down to the tip of the peninsula. Here is their report:

'*Taxi-brousse* from Antalaha to Ambodirafia, close to Cap Est. Walk from here to the southern tip of Masoala Peninsula. Seven days, including one day off for the Independence Day celebrations. One guide/porter (96,000Ar) and one porter (84,000Ar); food and accommodation are extra (rooms are about 2,000–3,000Ar per night).

'Walking at a gentle pace, staying in villages along the way, empty beaches, mangrove swamps, cleared woodland and a little rainforest towards the end as well as the scars of previous cyclones. Plenty of rivers to ford, either with log "bridges", pirogues or on foot. Independence Day at Fampotakely was quite a party, the two *vazaha* creating a serious distraction for the children on their parade! Shortly before arriving at Sahamalaza village on day five, we crossed a river with a series of large wooden posts sticking out of the water. After enquiries it was explained that this used to be a bridge capable of carrying vehicles and that up to the 1960s it was possible to drive most of the way down the east coast of the peninsula.

'On entering villages the children tended to run away screaming. It seems their mothers tell them that if they misbehave they will be taken to market and sold to the *vazaha* who will cook and eat them, so two *vazaha* arriving unannounced is a cause for concern! The braver would make a timid reappearance for a game of Grandmother's Footsteps.

'From Masoala village there is an irregular boat service to Maroantsetra, 10,000Ar per person, slow going and very heavily loaded. Visitors should ensure that they have budgeted for an additional few days whilst awaiting the boat.'

ANTALAHA AND BEYOND

ANTALAHA This prosperous, vanilla-financed town suffered devastating damage from Cyclone Gafilo in March 2004. About 80% of the town was destroyed and about 50 people killed. In true Malagasy fashion it was rebuilt and now (March 2007) Cyclone Indlala has hit the town wiping out 90% of the vanilla crop. By the time you visit it will be back to its old self, until the next time …

Getting there and away The only easy way to get to Antalaha is by plane (the Air Mad office is on the seafront), or by road from the north. The alternatives are the trek across the peninsula from Maroantsetra or via Cap Est (see page 332), or by sea. There are regular cargo boats to/from Maroantsetra and Toamasina.

 Where to stay/eat

🏠 **Hotel Palissandre** m 032 05 000 65. Run by M Brigitte Bezokiny. An upmarket hotel with comfortable rooms with fridge, minibar, safe & TV. €€€€

🏠 **Chez Momo** m 032 02 340 69; e momo@wandadoo.mg; www; www.ocean-momo.com. AC bungalows. Reduced rates for groups.

The owner is in the rosewood business. €€€€

🏠 **Vitasoa** m 032 40 765 74. A good-value hotel with hot water & mosquito nets. Good restaurant. €€

🏠 **Hôtel Chez Nanie** m 032 02 232 51. Pleasant (basic) bungalows, right next to the sea opposite the pier. The more expensive ones have AC. €€

Money and communication Antalaha has internet at the Madacom offices in the centre of town, and an ATM accepting Visa at Crédit Lyonnais Bank.

Trekking and nature

Masoala trekking A Swiss-run organisation, Projet d'Analalava, organises various treks in Masoala treks as well as Marojejy (see www.projet-analalava). They are in partnership with the tour operator PRIORI in Tana. (see page 94). Once in

Antalaha you can contact the *gérante*, Mme Olga, on m 032 04 340 27 or the guide Ilderic on m 032 07 713 64.

La Colline de Vinany private reserve Paul Goodman writes: 'Just off the main road after you cross the bridge going into town, there's a botanical wonderland with gorgeous views of the river and Indian Ocean created by Marie-Helene Kam-Hyo Zschocke, who owns the big pharmacy in town. She's established several villages in the area for recovered lepers and employs them in *pepinières*, where they propagate tree seedlings for reforestation projects in Masoala National Park. She is now hoping to open her reserve to tourism, creating more jobs (gardeners, guides) for recovered lepers and their families. I was highly impressed with her work.'

CONTINUING NORTH The road from Antalaha to Sambava is in excellent condition. The journey takes 1½ hours.

SAMBAVA

The centre of the vanilla- and coconut-growing region, and an important area for cloves and coffee production, Sambava merits a stay of a couple of days. The town is basically two very long, parallel streets, the main one being 5km from end to end. A dirt track runs close to the ocean servicing the better hotels and a few beach houses for the wealthier residents. This geography discourages exploration which is a shame because the people are friendly and easy-going, and there is plenty to see and do.

Sambava has a good beach and a dramatic sea with, at times, huge – and dangerous – waves.

TELEPHONE CODE The area code for Sambava is 88.

GETTING THERE AND AWAY Sambava has air connections with Tana, Toamasina and Antsiranana (for current schedule see www.airmadagascar.mg). The airport is not far from town: you can even walk it if you are a backpacker. The Air Mad office is open 08.00–11.00 and 14.00–19.00 weekdays.

The town is accessible by good road from Iharana (Vohemar), taking approximately two hours, but be warned: the *taxi-brousses* that ply this route are the most overloaded I have ever seen. We counted 15 people in a Renault 4! The *taxi-brousse* station is on the northwest outskirts, 30 minutes' walk from the market.

⌂ WHERE TO STAY

⌂ **Hôtel Orchidea Beach II** (2 bungalows & 8 rooms) ☏ 88 923 24; m 032 04 383 77; e orchideabeach2@wanadoo.mg. This replaced the original Orchidea Beach which was flattened by Cyclone Gafilo. It's a lovely beachfront hotel set in a beautifully planted garden, with a good restaurant (huge portions!) & bar. The 2 beachfront bungalows feel a bit exposed to curious passers-by (a track passes both the front & beachside door) but you're right on the beach so they're great for an early-morning swim. These have a fan but the 8 rooms in the hotel block have AC & balcony — & are rightly more expensive. All rooms have en-suite bathrooms with hot water. This is the best-value hotel in

Sambava, efficiently run by Marco Filossi & his Chinese wife. B/fast 4,000Ar. €€–€€€
⌂ **Hôtel Paradis** Only the top-price rooms have hot water, but all have a shower or bath & fan. It is above a disco, so be sure to ask for a second-floor room if staying on Fri or Sat. No mozzie nets, but rooms are well furnished & clean. The restaurant here is not recommended. €€–€€€
⌂ **Las Palmas** (6 bungalows, 2 rooms) ☏ 88 920 87; m 032 40 073 72; e las.palmas@laposte.net. A nicely-situated beachfront hotel with no restaurant but b/fast & drinks are available. The cheaper bungalows have fans, others have AC. Rooms have AC. They organise excursions including to a nearby

vanilla plantation & farming area as well as airport transfers. Car parking. €€€

⌂ **Hôtel Carrefour** (36 rooms) ☎ 88 920 60; f 88 923 22. Near the beach, with en-suite bathrooms, some with cold water, some hot. AC rooms also available, with TV & minibar. No restaurant but serves b/fast. €€–€€€

⌂ **Hôtel Melrose** (6 rooms) m 032 04 572 14/033 14 574 79. 3 cheaper rooms with fans, others with AC. Mozzie nets supplied. No restaurant but serves b/fast. Guarded car park. €€€

⌂ **Hôtel Cantonnais** (8 rooms) A hotel rather than beach bungalows, but in a quiet part of town & most rooms have balconies. A good range of prices & facilities, from cold shower only to en-suite toilet with cold shower & toilet with hot shower. Good value. Restaurant opens from 18.00. €–€€

⌂ **Chez l'Ambassadeur** m 032 02 113 47. Contact M Rolland or Mme Zoe. A good backpacker place. €–€€

⌂ **Hôtel la Romance de Jupiter** m 032 04 633 89. North of the *taxi-brousse* station. €

✖ **WHERE TO EAT** The **Hôtel Orchidea** probably serves the best meals in town. But for budget options try the following:

✖ **La Dynastie** 'A pleasant little Chinese-run restaurant with approximately fifty flies per table. Large menu, good food, sizeable portions; open breezy dining area with 10 tables' (D&K).

✖ **Etoile Rouge** 'Like La Dynastie but a little more opulent & without the flies!'

INTERNET

🖥 **SBS** There are 4 computers & facilities for printing, faxing, photocopying etc. *Price 2,000Ar for first 15mins, 100Ar/min thereafter.*

🖥 **BIC** An alternative charging similar rates. Closes for lunch.

MONEY The best place for changing money is at the BFV-SG bank/Western Union on the beach road. Visa accepted.

WHAT TO SEE AND DO

In and around town There is a good market which is known as *bazary kely*, not because it's small or *kely* (it isn't – and certainly not on Tuesday, market day), but because there used to be two markets and no-one thought of changing the name when they amalgamated them.

As this is one of the main vanilla-producing areas in Madagascar, a tour of the vanilla factory, Lopat, is interesting and teaches you a lot about the laborious process of preparing one of Madagascar's main exports.

The highlight for us, however, was a visit to CLUE, the Center for Learning and Understanding English. This lively place was set up by the Peace Corps and welcomes visits from tourists to help the (adult) students practise their spoken English and gain an understanding of a variety of accents. For the visitors it's an excellent chance to learn from the people of the east coast. CLUE is on the main street (you can't miss it). North of Sambava is a beautiful beach with safe swimming, and marvellous *Nephila* spiders on their golden webs between the branches of the shady trees.

Excursions further afield Many of the hotels can organise excursions, as can the tour operator **Sambava Voyages** (☎ *88 921 10; no email*). The manageress, Mme Seramila, speaks some English.

River Bemarivo A pleasant do-it-yourself excursion is up the Bemarivo, though this won't be possible at the end of the dry season – the river is very shallow. Take a *taxi-brousse* to Nosiarina, on the road north, and look for a pirogue to take you the five-hour journey upriver to Amboahangibe. 'It's a beautiful river trip. The river is wide and there are some small villages that you pass periodically. However, the land by the river has been deforested' (A Axel).

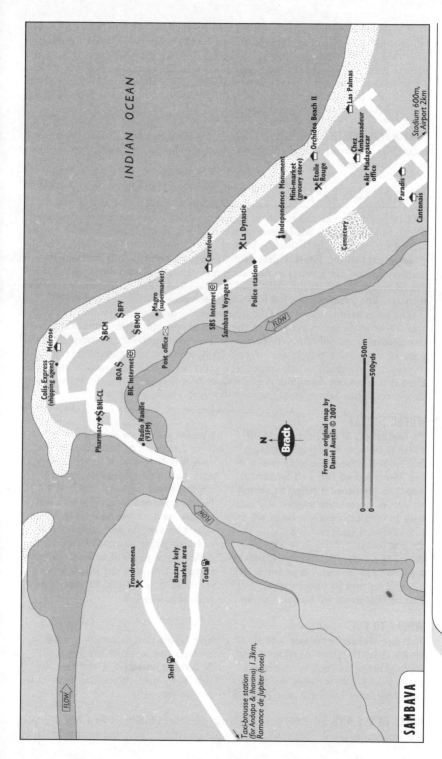

SAMBAVA

INDIAN OCEAN

Colis Express
(shipping agent)
Melrose

Pharmacy
BNI-CL

$BCM

$BFV

$BMOI

BOA$

BIC Internet

Radio Vanille
(93FM)

Post office

Magro
(supermarket)

Carrefour

La Dynastie

Independence Monument

Mini-market
(grocery store)

Etoile
Rouge
Orchidea Beach II

Las Palmas

Chez
Ambassadeur

Air Madagascar
office

Paradis

Cantonais

Cemetery

SBS Internet

Sambava Voyages

Police station

FLOW

FLOW

N

Bradt

From an original map by
Daniel Austin © 2007

0   500m
0   500yds

Trondromena

Bazary kely
market area

Total

Shell

Taxi-brousse station
(for Andapa & Iharana) 1.3km,
Romance de Jupiter (hotel)

FLOW

FLOW

Stadium 600m,
Airport 2km

It is also possible to find a cargo boat to Amboahangibe. This is quite a large village with several grocery stores and some houses with rooms. Look for the sign *'misy chambres'* ('rooms available'). These fill up with vanilla-pickers during the harvest. Anne Axel found the last room in town, at the Hôtel Fandrosoana. 'It had a captive crocodile in the yard next to the WC.' As an alternative to taking a boat back, it is a pleasant hike along the river, with some interesting above-ground coffins and groves of shady giant bamboos.

CONTINUING NORTH The road to the next town of importance, Iharana (Vohemar), is excellent and transport is no problem (about two hours). For a description of this very pleasant town see *Chapter 14*.

ANDAPA AND AREA

Andapa lies in a fertile and beautiful region, a 105km drive southwest of Sambava, where much of north Madagascar's rice is grown. This is also a major coffee-producing area. To help facilitate export, the EEC provided funding to build an all-weather road in the 1960s. It has been resurfaced subsequently and remains in good condition. The journey to Andapa is really beautiful, with the jagged peaks of the Marojejy Massif to the right, and bamboo and palm-thatch villages by the roadside. The journey takes 3–4 hours by *taxi-brousse*.

The town itself is one of my favourite in Madagascar. The relative wealth of the area shows in the goods available in the many shops, but because it sees relatively few tourists – and only the very best sort: those willing to hike up steep slopes in pouring rain – the people are exceptionally friendly and easygoing. It is also wonderfully compact, which comes as a relief after straggly Sambava, and cool. Even if you are not doing the major trek in Marojejy (which is the reason most people come here) there are numerous wonderful walks in the area.

🏠 WHERE TO STAY

🏠 **Hôtel Riziky** ☎ 88 072 31; m 032 02 007 43/032 40 214 22; e htl_riziky@wanadoo.mg. Quiet bungalows in Ambendrana, on the outskirts of town (towards Sambava). There are a few rooms at budget price (the cheapest in Andapa) but still with hot water, & very comfortable bungalows at a much higher price (the most expensive in Andapa with en-suite bathrooms, & TV). €–€€€€

🏠 **Hôtel Beanana** (10 rooms) ☎ 88 070 47; m 032 40 226 10; e http://hsbeanana@yahoo.fr; http://hotel-beanana.no-ip.com. I stayed here in 2006 & loved it! The rooms are grouped round a courtyard where you eat your breakfast, & overlook

a beautiful garden at the rear. It is quiet, the service is excellent & the breakfast delicious. The owner, M. Lo Pao, goes out of his way to help his clients. The best value for money in town. €€

🏠 **Hôtel Vatosoa** (pronounced *vats*) ☎ 88 070 78. This once-popular hotel is starting to get a little run down, but is still comfortable with en-suite rooms & hot water. The food is amazing (but a set meal & not good for vegetarians) & there is a large detailed map on the wall of the lounge which shows footpaths & tracks in the area (actually, a reproduction of the FTM 1:100,000 which can be purchased in Tana). €€

✖ WHERE TO EAT

✖ **Le Regal – Le Relais des Montagnes** ☎ 88 072 19; m 032 02 388 83; e bruno-lee.s.t@wanadoo.mg; http://regal.marojejy.com. This is the place to go if you are planning to hike in Marojejy, since the owner, Bruno Lee Sio Tsion is a 'Friend of Marojejy' &

knows as much about the mountain as anyone. He can help organise a visit. The food is good, too.

✖ **Restaurant Maroantsetra** An alternative eating place roughly opposite Hôtel Vatosoa. The service can be a bit slow.

WHAT TO SEE AND DO This is a wonderful area for wandering. At every step you see something interesting from the people or wildlife perspective (in the latter

Clare & Johan Hermans

Vanilla is the major foreign currency earner for Madagascar, which together with Réunion and the Comoros, grows 80% of the world's crop. Its cultivation in Madagascar is centred along the eastern coastal region, the main production centres being Andapa, Antalaha and Sambava.

The climbing plants are normally grown supported on 1.5m-high moisture-retaining trunks and under ideal conditions take three years to mature. When the plants bloom, during the drier months, the vines are checked on alternate days for open flowers to hand-pollinate. The pod then takes nine months to develop; each 15–20cm pod will contain tens of thousands of tiny seeds.

The pods are taken to a vanilla processing plant to begin the long process of preparing them for the commercial market. First they are plunged into a cauldron of hot water (70°C) for two minutes and are then kept hot for two days. During this time the pods change colour from green to chestnut brown. At this stage they are exposed to the sun (mornings only to avoid over-cooking) for three to four weeks.

After maturing, the pods are sorted by size; the workers sit in front of a large rack with 'pigeon-holes' for the different lengths. The bundles of sorted pods, approximately 30 to a bunch, are tied with raffia. They are checked for quality by sniffing and bending before being packed into wooden crates with 90% of the product going to the USA for use in the ice cream industry.

The vanilla used in cultivation in Madagascar is *Vanilla planifolia* which originates from Mexico. It was brought to Madagascar by the French once the secret of hand-pollination had been discovered – the flower has no natural pollinator in its foreign home. The culinary and pharmaceutical use of vanilla dates back to pre-Aztec times when it was used as a drink or as an ingredient of a lotion against fatigue for those holding public office. Similarly a native Malagasy vanilla stem can be found for sale in the market in Tana as a male invigorator.

Four different species of vanilla orchid occur naturally in Madagascar, most of them totally leafless. One species can be seen on the roadside between Sambava and Antahala resembling lengths of red-green tubing festooned over the scrub; another is to be found in the spiny forest near Berenty in the south. Most of the native species contain sap that burns the skin and their fruits contain too little vanillin to make cultivation economic.

USES FOR VANILLA PODS Although conventionally used for cooking, vanilla is also an insect repellent or the wonderful-smelling pods can be put in drawers instead of the traditional pomander to scent clothing or linen.

When cooking with vanilla you can reuse the pods for as long as you remember to retrieve them – wash and dry them after each use. Vanilla does wonders to tea or coffee (just add a pod to the teapot or coffee filter, or grind a dried pod with the coffee beans) and can be boiled with milk to make a yummy hot drink (add a dash of brandy!) or custard. If you take sugar in tea or coffee put some beans in your sugar tin and the flavour will be absorbed. Vanilla adds a subtle flavour to chicken or duck, rice or … whatever you fancy.

category butterflies, snakes and chameleons) and the scenery is consistently beautiful.

Travellers are invited to call into **Pièces Auto** in Andapa for help and advice on visiting the region (see http://travel.marojejy.com).

HIKING By using the map in the Hôtel Vatosoa you can plan a variety of day hikes. Almost any dirt road through villages would bring you the pleasures we experienced on our walk a few years ago. Here are some of the highlights: chameleons in the bushes, coffee laid out to dry on the ground, an entire school of shrieking kids surging up the hill towards us, a village elder matching his stride with ours in order to converse in French, little girls fishing with basket-nets in the irrigation channels, homemade musical instruments, smiles, laughter and stares. It helped that we had our local guide with us who could interpret the village activities. In one place we experienced the power of Malagasy oratory (*kabary*) at full throttle. The theme was communal work. The 20 or so men of the village listened respectfully as the *Président du Fokontany* exhorted them to contribute their labour towards the building of a new fence. Some young men demurred: they would rather pay the let-out fee of 500Ar. The *Président* discussed the issue with them, explaining the importance of the community working together. By the end of the discussion the young men had started stripping the leaves of a raffia palm to bind up the bamboo poles and begin fence-making.

If you explore off the beaten path, just remember the enormous power you have to change things irreversibly. Your gift or payment will certainly be received with delight and will make you feel warm inside; but will it benefit the village in the long run?

PROTECTED AREAS

Marojejy National Park and Anjanaharibe-Sud Special Reserve are two of Madagascar's most exciting wilderness areas, in what are perhaps the most remote and pristine rainforests remaining on the island.

ANJANAHARIBE-SUD SPECIAL RESERVE The Anjanaharibe-Sud Special Reserve comprises 28,624ha (recently increased from 17,194ha) of mountainous rainforest. The name, pronounced *andzanaribay*, means Place of the Great God and although only 20km southwest of Andapa, it is appropriately difficult to reach. The wildlife is not easy to see since it was hunted until recently, but repays the effort. This is the most northerly range of the indri which here occurs in a very dark form – almost black. The silky sifaka is also found here, but you are more likely to see the troops of white-fronted brown lemurs. Birders will be on the lookout for four species of ground-roller.

Even without seeing any mammals it is a most rewarding visit, with an easy-to-follow (though rugged) trail through primary forest to some hot springs. The reserve is also a vital element in the prosperity of the area. The Lokoho River, which rises in Anjanaharibe-Sud, is the only source of water for the largest irrigated rice producer in the country. For more information visit http://anjanaharibe.marojejy.com.

Visiting the reserve Ask at the Le Regal restaurant or Eric Mathieu (m *032 40 118 81*) for help with obtaining a permit and other logistics. The normal route is from the east, via Andasibe and Befingotra, along the now very poor road.

The trailhead is indicated with a rusty, barely legible WWF board: 'Piste Touristique de Ranomafana Source Thermal à 4,260m'. It used to take about an hour to reach the campsite and a further hour to the hot springs, but Paul Goodman reports that the reserve 'suffered terrible damage during Cyclones Hudah and Gafilo and there are many fallen trees.' The paths still haven't been completely cleared. Once there, your efforts are worthwhile. A few years ago John

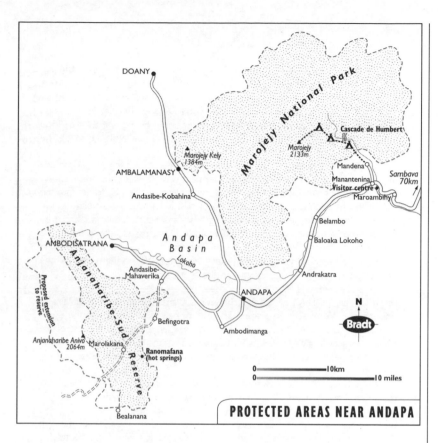

Kupiec reported: 'There are three springs. One is too hot to keep your feet in; another is shallow but it meets a stream which makes it easier to take; the third is a pool to swim in which also merged with stream water.' This reserve saw only ten visitors in 2006, so lovers of real wilderness might consider the effort worthwhile.

If you are looking for a serious challenge you can follow the route of Kathryn Goodenough, an impressivly fit geologist whom I met whizzing up Marojejy in 2006. Her account is on page 344.

MAROJEJY NATIONAL PARK This stunningly beautiful national park (sometimes spelled Marojezy) was established in 1998, and in 2007 becomes a UNESCO World Heritage Site. You need to be reasonably fit – and able to tolerate the heat – to enjoy it fully, but there are few other areas in Madagascar to compare to Marojejy for awesome splendour and the feeling of ultimate wilderness. Imposing mountains and craggy cliffs are surrounded by lush rainforests full of wildlife. Having made a return visit in 2006 after being disastrously lost there in 1976, I can echo Dylan Lossie who says: 'Marojejy is how I once imagined Madagascar as a child, long before I first went there: exotic, rugged, isolated and prehistorical!' And then there is the wildlife. This is the best place in Madagascar to see the silky sifaka, one of the five rarest primates in the world (I failed) and the helmet vanga (I succeeded). The panther chameleons are as I remember from 30 years ago – huge, and outrageously coloured – and there are leaf-tailed geckos, frogs galore, huge millipedes, wonderful spiders … and lots of leeches.

Kathryn Goodenough

We set off from the village of Ambodiasina, which is about 30km from Andapa, but 2½ hours' drive in a 4x4 over dreadful roads! We hired local guide/porters there, but none of them spoke more than a few words of French. As usual, their only English words were 'Hello' and 'I love you'! We were heading for the town of Ambalaromba, on the west side of the mountains, which is well used by local people and there are several small *hotelys* serving meat and rice along the route.

Having crossed a deep river, we climbed fairly steeply, crossing a 1,200m ridge that is largely clothed in primary forest. The path was absolutely incredible – only ever wide enough for one person, but in some places eroded up to 5m into the soil, so that the tree roots were above our heads. It was also a great place to see Malagasy life – people passed us carrying rice, chickens, bicycles, suitcases, and even driving zebu along the narrow paths. Eventually, we crossed a large river by a pirogue ferry, then followed this river downstream for a while. It was fast and furious, with many rapids. On the other side was the northern end of the Anjanaharibe mountain chain, which must be entirely inaccessible.

The path eventually left the river and ascended a ridge of more open, upland heath vegetation. This gave us superb views towards the forested mountains of Anjanaharibe. We reached a summit of 1,500m, before descending to the open, agricultural valley of Ambalaromba. This is quite a large town, with most of the houses being built of clay bricks rather than wood. I don't think they had ever seen a foreigner before, and so the whole town clustered around me as one of my colleagues talked to the mayor!

Next day we set off to walk south to another town (possibly called Ankaibe) on the western side of the Anjanaharibe mountain range, but again with the mountains separated from us by a major river. This path was much less well frequented, and we often had to clamber over logs or find a way round an obstacle. For much of the day, we were walking on hills with fairly open vegetation, affording us wonderful views of the emerald forests and sparkling waterfalls. Towards the end of the day, high on a ridge, we entered an area of primary forest, and just as we did so we saw a family of brown lemurs in the trees. From there we descended through the forest, sliding on tree roots and treacherous muddy chutes, and constantly stopping to flick off leeches! Eventually we emerged into a more populous, agricultural area with many small villages, and finally arrived at the town, on what was once the main road from Bealanana to Andapa. At Marolakana, where the road is broken because a bridge has failed, we were picked up by one of our drivers – the road is only just passable in a 4x4! To complete the trek, one could walk out to Ambodipont, on one of the main roads around Andapa.

It was an amazing trek, but would be very hard for tourists to do – you'd need a 4x4 to drop you off and pick you up, and you'd need guides who spoke both Malagasy and French/English. Food was hard to get – we should have carried more than we did. We stayed in rooms that we were kindly given in the villages, but tents would undoubtedly have been cleaner and easier!

☞ **WARNING!** Marojejy is a vulnerable area and cannot support large numbers of visitors. There is just one path to the top of the mountain which is suffering from the booted feet of tourists. The maximum number of beds is 17 (including guides and porters). Therefore the park cannot accept large groups. Because you will be expected to share a hut, a group of three or four friends is ideal.

Organising your visit My two companions and I put our arrangements into the hands of Eric Mathieu, a charming Frenchman living in Andapa with his wife Flavienne (m *032 40 118 81;* e *info@marojejy.com*). Eric and former Peace Corps volunteer Paul Atkinson created the excellent websites for the park: www.marojejy.com, http://travel.marojejy.com and www.anjanaharibe.marojejy.com. He did a great job for us, organising the guides (including the delightful Desiré Rabary), cook, porters and food – and transport from Sambava.

You can also arrange your trip through Bruno Lee at Le Regal restaurant in Andapa, or just turn up at the visitor centre mid-way between Sambava and Andapa. Coming from Sambava it's 200m before Manantenina on the left side of the road.

There are three 'camps' at different altitudes, each with its own distinctive flora and fauna. Individually they comprise four comfortable bunk beds in wooden chalets with a shared shower and flush toilet, and separate cooking/eating area. Marojejy requires advance planning. You will need proper hiking boots, and I found a hiking pole very useful. Pack a sweater or fleece for the nights (or something warmer if you are going during the coolest months), and a bandana to mop your streaming face during the very hot days. A sheet sleeping bag is useful; although sheets are in theory provided they cannot be guaranteed. Don't forget a good headlight torch, binoculars and some entertainment (such as cards) for the evenings. If you are travelling on your own you would be safer to bring a tent, unless you team up with other travellers for the four-person huts.

The best times to visit are April to May and September to December when there's less rain.

The visitor centre The personnel at the ANGAP centre are helpful and the place is well set up for visitors. It sells a series of excellent leaflets/checklists on the flora and fauna of the massif: birds, lemurs, reptiles and amphibians, and palms.

In the national park In 2006 work to construct bridges over the river on the track to Mandena was nearly finished, so the first part of the trip can now be done by vehicle. It's a lovely walk, however, taking you through rice paddies and cultivated areas. It can also be very hot. After 2.7km you arrive at the village of Mandena, a delightful place with a private school (!) full of friendly, well-behaved children. Then it's a further 2.9km to the park entrance. This is the best stretch for finding panther chameleons so keep an eye on the track-side bushes. At the park entrance there's a good map showing the trails and distances, and a chance for a rest under a shelter. A white-headed vanga was nesting in one of the trees when we were there, and once in the park we watched a noisy troop of white-fronted brown lemurs. It's 4.3km through rainforest to the first camp, Camp Mantella. This first stretch from road to camp will take four to five hours. It's quite easy but still tiring and you will be glad to see the chalets.

Camp Mantella, at 425m, is situated in the heart of superb lowland rainforest. There is a total of 17 beds here and a nice eating area. A night walk from here is particularly rewarding, revealing *Brookesia* chameleons, *Uroplatus* and many species of frog.

If you're lucky (and visiting in October/November) in less than an hour beyond Camp Mantella, you'll see a helmet vanga (*Euryceros prevostii*) on its nest. Considering this is the iconic bird species for Marojejy we could hardly believe our good fortune. We had an unobstructed view, with a shaft of sunlight illuminating the extraordinary blue bill.

Camp Marojejia (750m) is an hour from the first camp, and lies at the transition between lowland and mid-altitude rainforest. It sits opposite an amazing

12

outcrop of rock cloaked in rainforest. This peak, called Ambatotsondrona, or Leaning Rock, is one of the most spectacular views in Madagascar. To eat your breakfast watching the changing light on its flank is perfection, which is a good thing because the path beyond this camp is very, very tough. The compensation is that the areas above Camp Marojejia are the best for seeing the silky sifaka (*Propithecus candidus*), although it can still take time and luck to track them down. Although the path is very steep, it's extremely well made, with steps cut into the clay and fallen logs shaped by machete, so for the first couple of hours it's not too difficult. The final stretch is very narrow, however, with many roots to negotiate. You need strong legs and arms to haul yourself up.

Camp Simpona (1,250m) is a welcome sight. There are just eight beds here, and room for only one tent. The forest here is more stunted because of the altitude, but is still good for silky sifaka, and birds such as rufous-headed ground-roller and

LEECHES

Few classes of invertebrates elicit more disgust than leeches. Perhaps some facts about these extraordinarily well-adapted animals will give them more appeal.

Terrestrial leeches such as those found in Madagascar are small (1–2cm long) and find their warm-blooded prey by vibrations and odour. Suckers at each end enable the leech to move around in a series of loops and to attach itself to a leaf by its posterior while seeking its meal with the front end. It has sharp jaws and can quickly – and painlessly – bite through the skin and start feeding. When it has filled its digestive tract with blood the leech drops off and digests its meal. This process can take several months since leeches have pouches all along their gut to hold as much blood as possible – up to ten times their own weight. The salivary glands manufacture an anticoagulant which prevents the blood clotting during the meal or period of digestion. This is why leech wounds bleed so spectacularly. Leeches also inject an anaesthetic which is why you don't feel them biting.

Leeches are hermaphrodites but still have pretty exciting sex lives. To consummate their union they need to exchange packets of sperm. This is done either the conventional way via a leechy penis or by injection, allowing the sperm to make its way through the body tissues to find and fertilise the eggs.

Readers who are disappointed with the small size of Malagasy leeches will be interested to hear that an expedition to French Guiana in the 1970s discovered the world's largest leech: at full stretch 45cm long!

Wherever there are blood vessels there are leeches, and travellers compete for the worst leech story. Here's one from Frankie Kerridge, a researcher in the southeast rainforest: 'A highlight was my guide getting a leech on his eyeball. Mega shouting and screaming. Got it off by killing it (slowly) with a tobacco leaf.'

Reader T T Terpening had an equally gruesome experience: a leech in his nose. This he dealt with thus: 'I pushed on my left nostril with my finger and blew hard. Some blood, a little snot, and a big glossy leech flies out into the rainforest litter.' But then: 'My guide says a dab of tobacco will keep my respiratory system leech-free for the remainder of the hike. I take a scoop and plug both nostrils. Immediately I feel dizzy and sick and my nose burns. I brace myself against a tree and my head clears. My nose definitely still feels weird. Over the next minute I come to the realisation that another leech is travelling the length of my sinus. "Probably running away from the tobacco," says my guide helpfully. Within 12 hours the leech has run its course, journeying the length of my nose, then sinus to my throat where I eventually swallow it. Most of Madagascar's wildlife is found nowhere else on earth. Thank God!'

yellow-bellied sunbird-asity. The frogs in the nearby stream are diverse and abundant. A viewing platform has been built on the ridge shortly before the camp. The vista is breathtaking.

The camp is used to facilitate treks to Marojejy peak at 2,132m, a four- to five-hour climb. Not much harder than what you did the day before, but you need good weather and that's pretty rare. But Nick Garbutt was lucky and did it on a clear day: 'It's one of the most spectacular walks I've ever done – fantastic views over rainforest-clad ridges, amazing mountains and above the treeline bizarre moorland-type habitat. The view from the top is awesome and the feeling of space and wilderness is the greatest I've experienced.'

Mr Flavien's Farm A hospitable gentleman, Flavien Zandrimanana, owns the land on the opposite bank of the river facing the Marojejy Visitor Centre. You can camp there or arrange a tour of the farm. Contact him through Eric Mathieu in Andapa.

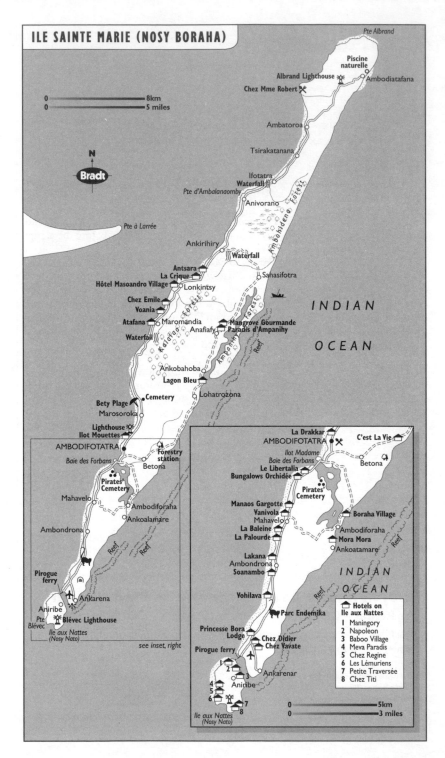

ILE SAINTE MARIE (NOSY BORAHA)

Pte Albrand

0 ———— 8km
0 ———— 5 miles

Bradt

N

Piscine
naturelle

Albrand Lighthouse
Chez Mme Robert

Ambodiatafana

Ambatoroa

Tsirakatanana

INDIAN

Ifotatra
Waterfall
Pte d'Ambalanaomby
Anivorano

Pte à Larrée

Ankirihiry

Waterfall

Antsara
La Crique
Hôtel Masoandro Village
Lonkintsy

Sahasifotra

Chez Emile
Voania

Mangrove Gourmande
Paradis d'Ampanihy

Atafana
Maromandia
Anafiafy

OCEAN

Waterfall

Ankobahoba

Lagon Bleu

Lohatrozona

Bety Plage
Cemetery

Marosoroka

Lighthouse
Ilot Mouettes

AMBODIFOTATRA
Baie des Forbans
Betona

Forestry
station

La Drakkar
AMBODIFOTATRA
Ilot Madame
Baie des Forbans

C'est La Vie

Betona

Pirates'
Cemetery

Le Libertalia
Bungalows Orchidée

Mahavelo

Ambodiforaha
Ankoalamare

Pirates'
Cemetery

Manaos Gargotte
Vanivola
Mahavelo
La Baleine
La Palourde

Boraha Village

Ambodiforaha
Mora Mora
Ankoatamare

Ambondrona

Lakana
Ambondrona
Soanambo

INDIAN
OCEAN

Pirogue
ferry

Ankarena

Aniribe
Pte
Blévec
Blévec Lighthouse

Ile aux Nattes
(Nosy Nato)

see inset, right

Vohilava

Parc Endemika

Princesse Bora
Lodge

Pirogue ferry

Chez Didier
Chez Yavate

Ankarenar

Hotels on
Ile aux Nattes
1 Maningory
2 Napoleon
3 Baboo Village
4 Meva Paradis
5 Chez Regine
6 Les Lémuriens
7 Petite Traversée
8 Chez Titi

Aniribe

Ile aux Nattes
(Nosy Nato)

0 ———— 5km
0 ———— 3 miles

348

13

Ile Sainte Marie

Here is a cliché of a tropical island with endless deserted beaches overhung by coconut palms, bays protected from sharks by coral reefs, hills covered with luxuriant vegetation, and a relative absence of unsightly tourist development. Most travellers love it: 'As soon as we saw the island from the air, we were ready to ditch our travel plans and spend the rest of our trip nestled in paradise. Everything about the island is intoxicating: the smell of cloves drying in the sun, the taste of coco rum and the warmth of the sea.' In addition to this heady, holiday atmosphere, Ile Sainte Marie is the best place in Madagascar for whale-watching.

The island, due east of Soanierana-Ivongo, is 50km long and 7km at its widest point. The only significant town is Ambodifotatra; other small villages comprise bamboo and palm huts. The island is almost universally known as Sainte Marie – few people use its Malagasy name: Nosy Boraha. Sainte Marie unfortunately – or perhaps fortunately, given the dangers of overdevelopment – has a far less settled weather pattern than its island rival, Nosy Be. Cyclones strike regularly and you can expect several days of rain and wind all year round, but interspersed with calm sunny weather. The best months for a visit seem to be June and mid-August to December, although a reader tells me she twice had perfect weather in January, and another reports that in July most days were hot and sunny, but with frequent light rain overnight or in the morning, and fairly strong winds from the south.

TELEPHONE CODE The area code for Ile Sainte Marie is 57.

BACKGROUND INFORMATION

HISTORY The origin of the Malagasy name is obscure. It means either 'island of Abraham' or 'island of Ibrahim', with probable reference to an early Semitic culture. It was named Ile Sainte Marie by European sailors when the island became the major hideout of pirates in the Indian Ocean. From the 1680s to around 1720 these pirates dominated the seas around Africa. There was a Welshman (David Williams), Englishmen (Thomas White, John Every and William Kidd) and an American (Thomas Tew) among a Madagascar pirate population which, in its heyday, numbered nearly one thousand.

Later a Frenchman, Jean-Onésime Filet ('La Bigorne'), was shipwrecked on Sainte Marie while escaping the wrath of a jealous husband in Réunion. La Bigorne turned his amorous attentions with remarkable success to Princess Bety, the daughter of King Ratsimilaho. Upon their marriage the happy couple received Nosy Boraha as a gift from the king, and the island was in turn presented to the mother country by La Bigorne (or rather, put under the protection of France by Princess Bety). Thus France gained its first piece of Madagascar in 1750.

GETTING THERE AND AWAY

By air Air Madagascar flies every day from Tana and Toamasina to Sainte Marie. Flights are heavily booked, especially in July and August, so you should try to make your reservations well in advance. Make sure your hotel reconfirms your return flight (or do it yourself at the Air Mad office in the north of Ambodifotatra).

By land/boat MadaBus (see page 174), in partnership with Cap Sainte Marie, runs a daily service from Toamasina to Soanierana-Ivongo and on by boat to Ste Marie for €27; the package price for Tana–Sainte Marie–Tana, valid for two months, is €100.

The cheapest option is to take a *taxi-brousse* north from Toamasina to Soanierana-Ivongo and catch the daily (except Sunday) motor launch to Ambodifotatra (see page 319).

GETTING AROUND THE ISLAND There is a *taxi-brousse* service, at least up the west coast. Prices are higher than on the mainland but they will sometimes pick you up at a pre-arranged time. Look out for the cheaper *taxi asaka*, yellow *taxi-brousse*. It's worth flagging down any vehicle. Most will stop and charge the standard rate.

Most hotels have bikes for rent (note: the French for mountain bike is 'VTT') for around 5,000Ar per day. They are cheaper in Ambodifotatra. You can see quite a lot of the island by bike, especially now the road has been surfaced as far as Loukintsy. Not all bikes are in good condition – remember to check the brakes!

You can hire motorbikes opposite Hôtel Soanambo, and mopeds are also available in Ambodifotatra. A motorbike typically costs 40,000Ar per day.

AMBODIFOTATRA

This town (pronounced am*boo*difoo*tar*tr) is growing; it has several boutiques and a patisserie which runs out of bread in the late morning. Market days are Tuesday and Thursday.

 WHERE TO STAY

🏠 **Hôtel Hortensia** On the main street of Ambodifotatra heading north. Clean, spacious rooms with hot water. No beach, but family rooms have sea views; dbl rooms have balconies facing the road. Good, reasonably priced restaurant. Some English spoken. Ideal for early-morning boat departures. €€

🏠 **Le Drakkar** ☎ 57 400 22. About 1km north of Ambodifotatra. Simple bamboo bungalows with cold shower. 'Grim, dirty rooms with dubious security.' But they're cheap. €

🏠 **Hôtel La Bigorne** (2 bungalows) ☎ 57 401 23. About 200m south of the Air Madagascar office in

Ambodifotatra. A good bar & restaurant with bungalows in the back garden. €

🏠 **Hôtel Zinnia** (6 bungalows) ☎ 57 400 09; f 57 400 32. Right by the harbour wall at Ambodifotatra. Double bungalows with hot water, fans & outside flush toilet. Good, neat & pleasant restaurant with excellent food & 'the best coffee on Sainte Marie.' Mountain bikes for hire. €

🏠 **Chez Alain/Manaus** (3 bungalows) Basic (homemade) bungalows with outside toilets; located between Vanilla Café & Orchidée. Clean & friendly, with terrific food. €

✖ **WHERE TO EAT**

✖ **Restaurant La Jardine** Good, inexpensive food; recommended for b/fast. Homemade hot croissants with hot chocolate & friendly people.

✖ **La Bigorne** 'A wonderful restaurant. Colonial style – very laid back. Excellent lobster.'

✖ **Bar-Restaurant Le Barachois** Across the road from the harbour, next to the ferry booking office. 'The

most comprehensive menu encountered anywhere.' Quite inexpensive & the tables on the porch are great for people-watching.

✖ **Restaurant La Banane** On the left, heading north. 'A place to meet other *vazaha*. Good food' (Kim Loohuis).

✖ **Restaurant Chez Claudine** Just across the road

from Hôtel Soanambo. 'Order at least 2hr in advance; the food is *that* fresh! Langoustes for 12,000Ar. Very small restaurant; typical Malagasy' (Kim Loohuis).

MONEY Two modern banks, open 07.30–10.30 and 13.30–15.00, have Visa cash machines. Bank of Africa even changes travellers' cheques!

INTERNET

🖼 **Cyber Corsair** Ambodifotatra. Across the street from La Banane. Only 2 computers.

🖼 **Cyber Jeunesse** About 500m before Cyber Corsair on your right if you're going north. *1,500Ar per 15mins.*

WHAT TO SEE AND DO There are some interesting sights around Ambodifotatra and the Baie des Forbans which are an easy cycle ride from most of the hotels. In the town itself there is a **Catholic church** built in 1837, which serves as a reminder that Ile Sainte Marie was owned by France from 1750. As a further reminder of French domination there is a **war monument** to a French-British skirmish in 1845.

The **Pirates' Cemetery** is just before the bay bridge to the town (when coming from the south). A signposted track, not usable at high tide, leads to the cemetery. It takes 20 minutes and although you don't need a guide, the kids that hang around there will accompany you anyway (and will demand a tip). If you manage to go alone, note that you should turn left when the path branches after crossing a stone sea wall. This is quite an impressive place, with gravestones dating from the 1830s. One has a classic skull and crossbones carved on it, but there's not many graves. There is a 2,000Ar charge to visit the cemetery.

The **town cemetery** is worth a visit too, though it lacks the story-book drama of the pirates' final resting place. The graveyard is about 6km north of Ambodifotatra, at Bety Plage on the right-hand side of the road.

SNORKELLING AND DIVING The shallows around Sainte Marie are ideal for snorkelling and diving, although the island's inshore waters are overfished by local Malagasy. Most of the coral reefs are in good condition and the water is usually clear. There are several huge table corals, some nearly two metres wide, but unfortunately a number have been broken off by fish traps.

Divers should read the box on safety (page 128); and everyone should watch out for the vicious spines of sea urchins (see pages 244–5).

🤿 **Il Balenottero Dive Centre** 🕿 57 400 36/22 450 17 (Tana); e ilbalenottero@simicro.mg; www.ilbalenottero.com. Italian-owned. A well-run & professional dive centre located in Ambodifotatra. Very good equipment, organised dive trips to wrecks & reefs. Whale-watching & swimming with whales!

🤿 **Le Lemurien Palme Dive Center** m 032 04 607 34; e lemurienpalme@aol.com; www.lemurien-palme.com. Expert diver Christina Dodwell reports: 'It's a well established outfit run by 2 ex-paramedic women who are very helpful & professional.' Their office is in Ambodifotatra.

 BEACH HOTELS

Almost all of Ile Sainte Marie's beach hotels are ranged along the west coast of the island, with only a few in the east or on Ile aux Nattes in the south. There are several factors to take into account when choosing a hotel. Are you, for example, looking for tranquil isolation, or variety and perhaps a touch of nightlife? If the latter, you'll want to stay near Ambodifotatra where there's a choice of restaurants, internet cafés, and some sightseeing. If arriving by boat you will also probably want to spend at least the first night near the town. If you are coming by air and on a tight budget you'll need to look for a hotel near the airport; the cost of airport transfers to the more isolated hotels in the north of the island is about 11,000Ar and you'll need to eat (perhaps expensive) meals there as well.

Prices below are for high season (usually September to mid-November, Christmas and school holidays). Almost all offer substantially reduced rates – up to 50% – in the low season. During the low season the best weather is November to mid-December and May to July. Unusually for Madagascar, prices are normally quoted per person, not per room.

Three of Sainte Marie's best hotels – Soanambo, Masoandro Lodge and Hôtel Orchidée Napoleon (Ile aux Nattes) – are under the management of HSM (www.hsm.mg) which makes booking online simple. Their user-friendly website also gives their latest rates.

I am grateful to Derek Antonio Serra for extensive updates.

HOTELS BETWEEN THE AIRPORT AND AMBODIFOTATRA
Luxury 🏨
🏠 **Princesse Bora Lodge** (15 bungalows) ✆ 57 040 03; m 032 07 090 48; f 57 401 47; e bora@wandadoo.mg; www.princesse-bora.com. Within walking distance of the airport, but transfers are usually by zebu-cart. Owned by François-Xavier Mayer, whose family has been on Ste Marie for over 200yrs & his partner (the architect of the hotel) Sophie de Michelis. This beautifully designed hotel is the best on the island. Everything about it is excellent: the management, the food, the location, the whale-watching trips. Many other hotels offer whale-watching, but as far as I know only François brings in a scientific element so that visitors are collecting data about the whales as well as watching them. The 6 luxury bungalows have twin beds; the others are dbl. 'Total luxury & a great opportunity to soothe the aching limbs. The best food, wine & relaxation' (Daniel Morgan). Mountain bikes for hire. Visa accepted.

Top end €€€€€
🏠 **Vanivola** (9 bungalows & 10 rooms) m 032 42 357 67; e info@vanivola.com; www.vanivola.com. Upmarket, modern French-run hotel north of Mahavelo. The vivacious wife, Favienne, speaks perfect English. Excellent facilities: pool & fancy cabaret bar/restaurant. Plush AC bungalows & various good-value rooms.
🏠 **Soanambo** (40 bungalows) ✆ 57 401 37/22 536 06 (Tana); m 033 11 414 25; e info@hsm.mg. About 3km from airport; 10km from Ambodifotatra. Rather characterless bungalows of varying size & price. Lovely garden with *Angraecum* orchids & a terrace bar/restaurant from which you can watch whales. One of the best – & longest – private beaches in Ste Marie. Swimming pool. Bicycles & motorbikes for hire. Credit cards accepted.
🏠 **Lakana** (6 bungalows) ✆ 57 040 32/032 07 090 22; f 57 401 33; e lakana@moov.mg. About 5km from the airport. Simple but very comfortable wooden bungalows, inc 4 perched along the jetty. 'Friendly staff, really personal service, snorkelling 25m from the end of jetty, excellent food, our favourite hotel of all of them – we felt so relaxed & welcome' (Katie Slocombe). Mainly French-speaking. Mountain bikes & motorbikes for hire. Visa accepted.

Upper range €€€€
🏠 **Bungalows de Vohilava** (8 bungalows) ✆ 57 040 65; mob 032 04 757 84; f 57 401 40; e vohilava@malagasy.com; www.vohilava.com. About 3km from the airport. Spacious bungalows on a tiny beach. En-suite toilet & hot shower. 'Good restaurant, bar, TV with DVDs, & loads & loads of books. At night the path towards the bungalows is lit with oil lamps; very romantic! The owners Henry & Mia are very friendly & the new patron Nico can always give you tips on what to see & do. They arrange excursions & you can hire bikes & motorbikes. They were installing ADSL when I was there so you can use the internet (200Ar/min). No fans but the 4-poster beds have nets' (Kim Loohuis).
🏠 **Le Libertalia** (7 bungalows) ✆ 57 403 03; e libertalia@wanadoo.mg; www.lelibertalia.com. French-owned & managed. English spoken. Situated about 2¹/₂km from town in a very nice setting. Impeccably furnished. There's a jetty out to a small private islet. Very popular; often fully booked when other nearby resorts are empty. Excellent food in stunning restaurant, with an ambience that belies its reasonable prices.

🏠 **Hôtel La Baleine** (8 bungalows) 📞 57 401 34. About 7km from the airport. Rustic bungalows owned by Albert Lanton. Communal bathroom with cold water. Very good food. With the proceeds of the hotel, Albert sponsors a youth football club & other local projects. The only negative point is that the beach is not particularly nice here — but who cares?

Mid range €€€
🏠 **Hôtel/Bungalows Orchidée** (10 bungalows & 4 rooms) 📞 57 400 54. Located 3km south of Ambodifotatra; 12km from the airport. Under new management & a bit characterless, but clean bungalows with hot water & AC at very reasonable price. Good beach. English spoken.

Budget €€
🏠 **Chez Vavate** (6 bungalows & 12 rooms) 📞 57 401 15. On first appearance an unprepossessing collection of local huts built on a ridge to the north of the airstrip. Don't be taken in by first impressions; the food here is wonderful (the *punch coco* also ensures that you spend your evenings in a convivial haze) & the relaxed family atmosphere makes this very popular with young travellers. It's one of the longest-established hotels in Ile Ste Marie (I stayed here on my first visit in 1984 when it had already been going for 6yrs). Each room has a mosquito net & shower, but the toilet is shared. A courtesy vehicle meets flights but otherwise you need to walk & it is quite a strenuous 1½km from the airport. Take the wide grassy track which runs parallel to the airstrip then veers to the left up a steep hill. The guide here, Amadé, is knowledgeable & friendly.
🏠 **La Palourde** (4 bungalows) 📞 57 403 07. Clean bungalows on a mediocre beach with en-suite cold shower; hot water on request. The Malagasy/Mauritian owner is a great cook, especially if meals are ordered in advance. Clean & friendly.

Penny-pincher €
🏠 **Manaos Gargotte** 📱 032 40 019 94. Traditional Malagasy bamboo bungalows built by the owner himself. Shared toilets. Good restaurant serves tasty, fresh meals. 'Communal dining at its best — we spent hours chatting about politics & Malagasy life with the friendly owners. Unfortunately little English spoken, so bring your phrase book!' (DAS).
🏠 **Chez Didier** The first place you come to (on the right) as you walk up the road from the airport. Noisy, basic, but very cheap.

HOTELS NORTH OF AMBODIFOTATRA
🏠 **Hôtel Masoandro Village** (12 bungalows) 📞 22 640 54; ✉ info@hsm.mg. About 35km from the airport, these HSM-owned luxury bungalows are built in the local style with a sea view. One of the best hotels in Ste Marie; lovely location opposite Pointe Larée (just south of La Crique) near Maromandia village. Diving & snorkelling. Excursions to Forêt d'Ampanihy & camping on Pointe Larée. Mountain bikes for hire. Good English spoken. €€€€€
🏠 **La Crique** (12 bungalows) 📞 57 902 45/57 040 77; ✉ lacrique@wanadoo.mg; www.lacrique.net. One of the longest-established hotels on the island; deservedly popular so book well ahead. 2 bungalows have private (but outside) shower/toilet; the others are en suite. One of the prettiest locations on the island, 1km north of Loukintsy; convenient for tours of the north or east. The bungalows are right on the beach, cooled by a sea breeze & 'only 100ft from bed to sea'. Snorkelling equipment available. Wonderful ambience & delicious, good-value meals. In September you can watch humpback whales cavorting offshore. Electricity 08.00–14.00 & 17.30–10.30. Mountain bikes & motorbikes for hire. Guided walks across the island & boat or hiking trips to the Petite Cascade or lighthouse. €€€€
🏠 **Hôtel Atafana** (9 bungalows) 📞 57 040 54; ✉ info@atafana.com; www.atafano.com. About 12km from Ambodifotatra; 4km south of La Crique. In a beautiful bay of its own, this resort offers good value for a great location. Good snorkelling, tasty food & whale-watching from the beach. English-speaking staff. Highly recommended for relaxation, but if you need internet & nightlife it's not for you — transport to town costs 15,000Ar each way. Scooters for hire (44,000Ar/day). €€€
🏠 **Ilot Mouettes** (4 bungalows) 📞 57 401 00; 📱 032 02 369 37. About 4km north of Ambodifotatra. Bungalows set in 24ha with private beach; they sleep 2–5 people. Meals not included. Family-run by locals Françoise & Renée; very friendly (but no English spoken). Terrific food. €€
🏠 **Chez Emilie** About 1km north of Hôtel Atafana. 'The beach & bungalows are almost as good as Atafana (but no hot water). But it is

Emilie & her food that makes it such a fantastic place to stay. Emilie is a super-charming, always-cheerful lady, & she served the best meals that we ate during our 3-week stay in Madagascar' (Øyvind Sæthre). €€

🏠 Hôtel Voania Roughly 200m from Hôtel Atafana. On a beach, raked clean daily. Next to the local village, but the newest part is private & secluded.

HOTELS IN THE EAST OF ILE SAINTE MARIE
🏠 Boraha Village (9 bungalows) ☎ 57 400 71; e boraha@wanadoo.mg; www.boraha.com. French-owned; on the east coast facing the lagoon, 30mins from the airport & only 4km east of Ambodifotatra. There are 8 dbl bungalows & 1 family one (2 rooms, shared bathroom), all facing the water. No beach, but a lovely jetty-style veranda. Specialises in deep-sea fishing. Minimum stay: 2 nights. €€€€€

🏠 Mora Mora Hotel (13 bungalows) Ambodiforaha; ☎ 57 401 14; m 032 07 090 99; f 47 400 48. 9 of the bungalows are en suite. This Italian-owned place specialises in boat trips to watch whales & watersports, inc diving. Some visitors have been disappointed that it does not have a beach & is a bit isolated. €€€€

🏠 Hôtel C'est La Vie Nord Ilampy (east coast, more or less opposite Ambodifotatra). A new, South-African-run set of bungalows with 'the best views on the island.' €€€€

No electricity, but equipped with powerful pressure lanterns. The restaurant is slightly cheaper than at Atafana's. €€

🏠 Hôtel Antsara (13 bungalows) Only 300m north of La Crique. 5 beach bungalows plus 8 more on a slope further back. Some have en-suite bathrooms. Excellent Réunionese-French hosts. Snorkelling gear available. Noisy disco, but only at w/ends. €€

🏠 Restaurant Bungalows Paradis d'Ampanihy On the river close to Anafiafy, opposite Forêt d'Ampanihy. Run by Helène, a Malagasy woman, & her family. Basic bungalows with mosquito net; some with en-suite shower. 4-course meals in a beautiful dining-room with outside tables & several tame lemurs. €€€

🏠 Hôtel Lagon Bleu On the east coast, near Marofilao, 7km from Anafiafy. A small & cosy site, but clean & peaceful. €€

🏠 La Mangrove Gourmande Restaurant & bungalows just north of Anafiafy. 'We took a pirogue trip to the peninsula whilst lunch was prepared. The beach here was deserted apart from a caretaker overseeing the land on which a resort is to be built by 2007. When we retuned to La Mangrove Gourmande we ate crabs & fish: one of the best meals in Madagascar' (James Brehaut). €

WHALE-WATCHING July to September is the best time to see humpback whales; you can watch them from the beach from any of the hotels or take a boat excursion (offered by many of the hotels and diving clubs). See box on page 356.

EXPLORING THE ISLAND The best way to explore Ile Sainte Marie is by bike (hard work), motorbike or on foot. In the low season, if you are fit and energetic, you could walk or cycle around most of the island and take your chance on places to stay. But during peak seasons most of the hotels will be full.

CROSSING FROM WEST TO EAST From Ambodifotatra or Ankirihiry the walk across the island takes about 2½ hours. Although possible to do on your own, it's easy to get lost, so many young men make a lucrative business of guiding visitors to the Indian Ocean side of the island. Many overcharge and have no information except for the route. Another starting-point for the walk across the island is Antsara. If you take a guide for the island crossing, be sure to agree on the price first.

It is well worth taking a pirogue trip to explore the coast around the northeastern peninsula with its Forêt d'Ampanihy. Most of the northern hotels run excursions there.

WATERFALL AND NATURAL POOL About 5km from La Crique, north of La Cocoteraie with its great restaurant, **Chez Mme Robert**, is a beautiful and impressive *piscine naturelle* with a waterfall, a big pool and enormous basalt rocks. The beach here is spectacularly beautiful.

Keep walking north and you'll come to a lighthouse, dating from French colonial times.

PARC ENDEMIKA (*Entry: 10,000Ar*) A very small park-cum-zoo at the village of Vohilava (south end of Sainte Marie). The owner, Arnaud, rescues animals (mainly lemurs) that are captured for sale or are kept as pets by hotels. His aim is to establish an educational centre for the island, but in the short term he has opened the zoo to visitors. There's a good guide, Prosper, who is knowledgeable about the plants and animals. 'The fun part is that with some animals (baby bamboo lemur!) you can actually go into the cage to pet it' (Kim Loohuis).

PANORAMA At the southern tip of Ile Sainte Marie there is a viewpoint where you can see Ile aux Nattes and watch the sunset. Go to Hôtel Chez Vavatte and follow the signs for 'Panorama'.

ILE AUX NATTES (NOSY NATO)

To many people this little island off the south coast of Ile Sainte Marie is even better than the main island. Being car-free it is much more peaceful. 'If I were to do the trip again, I'd split my time equally between both islands. Nosy Nato is about as fantasy-islandesque as it gets. Pristine beaches, quiet villages, hidden bungalows, excellent restaurants' (Debbie Fellner).

A pirogue transfer here from near the airport on Sainte Marie is inexpensive and will take you directly to your chosen hotel.

WHERE TO STAY
Top end and upper range

Maningory ⟍ 57 040 69; m 032 07 090 05/06; e maningoryhotel@wanadoo.mg; www.maningory.com. Well-equipped bungalows built in the local style in an idyllic location on a beautiful beach, some facing the sea. Only French spoken. 'Reef 20m into water, teeming with fish. We spent hours snorkelling' (Katie Slocombe). €€€€€

Baboo Village (14 bungalows) ⟍ 57 042 07; m 032 04 791 26; www.baboo-village.com. 'Some of the bungalows are arranged right on the water. They are large & airy, with mosquito nets & bathrooms (separate for the rooms on the water). I was

travelling alone, but never felt lonely there. The restaurant has large tables in a friendly atmosphere, so that guests can mingle. No TV, phone or anything modern (but there is a generator for power at night); hot water in buckets on request. It was heaven!' (Karen Paterson). €€€€

Meva Paradis (6 bungalows) ⟍ 57 042 08; m 032 02 207 80; e hotel@mevaparadis.com; www.mevaparadis.com. This collection of palm-thatched bungalows fronting the white-sand beach is well-named: it really is close to perfection. €€€€

Mid range €€€

Napoléon (10 A-frame huts) ⟍ 22 640 54 (Tana); m 032 07 635 71; e info@hsm.mg; www.hsm.mg. Napoléon, who died in 1986, was a charismatic character who 'ruled' – in various guises – this little island & enjoyed entertaining *vazaha*.

His place is now owned by the Soanambo group (HSM) but the simplicity befitting Ile aux Nattes has been maintained. There's a restaurant, where Napoléon's famous *poulet au coco* is still served to appreciative diners.

Budget €€

Les Lemuriens (10 A-frame huts) Comfortable huts, many with bay views & balconies, at the southern end of the island. Named after the friendly

black-&-white ruffed lemurs that live there. Very good restaurant with a pleasant atmosphere.

Duncan Murrell

Every year humpback whales migrating from their summer feeding-grounds in Antarctica arrive in the waters off Madagascar between July and September to mate, give birth and nurture their young. Humpback whales, like several other species of whale, migrate between their colder, high latitude feeding-grounds to the warmer shallow waters around tropical islands or on continental shelves. There is more food available in the nutrient-rich waters of polar regions than in tropical waters but the calves have insufficient insulating blubber to protect them from colder water. It takes 1½ months for the whales to travel the 3,000-mile journey from Antarctica during which they lose up to a third of their bodyweight. As with all of the baleen whales, the gestation period of 10–12 months is closely linked to the timing of their annual migration.

The majority of the whales end up in the relatively protected, shallow waters of Antongil Bay but many can be observed either in transit or lingering between Ile Sainte Marie and the mainland, often in very close viewing distance of the shore; this is especially true between Atafana and Antsara where the channel narrows considerably. They can also be seen passing Taolagnaro (Fort Dauphin) early and late in the season, and a few travel up the west coast and can be viewed near Anakao and Morondava.

Humpback whales are undoubtedly one of the most entertaining of whales because of their exuberant displays of breaching (jumping), lobtailing (tail-slapping) and pec-slapping (flipper-slapping). Males competing for females often indulge in forceful displays of head-lunging and slapping to create surges and explosions of water to intimidate their rivals. In their feeding-grounds they often deploy a unique feeding strategy where they herd their prey with bubbles.

But probably the behaviour that the humpback whale is most renowned for is its singing. The male produces one of the most complex songs in the animal kingdom using sounds spanning the highest and lowest frequencies audible to the human ear. These songs constantly evolve; as the season progresses new themes may be added or old ones changed. Each whale changes its song to keep in tune with other singers. As a result the song heard at the end of the season is quite different from that at the beginning. When the whales return the following year, they resume singing the version in vogue at the end of the previous season. Many whale-watching boats are now equipped with hydrophones to enable visitors to listen to this singing. The haunting songs elicit both the mystery and the majesty of these incredible animals.

Until recently the humpbacks of Madagascar were one of the least-studied and least-understood populations in the world. In the last few years researchers have been using DNA testing, satellite-tagging, photographic identification and other methods to increase our knowledge of this significant population. In 2000 Madagascar's Ministry of the Environment wholeheartedly endorsed new laws governing whale-watching to protect the whales along their migration route. Training has been provided to instruct local students and faculties from Malagasy universities in research techniques, and for local ecotourism representatives to encourage safe, enjoyable, conservation-oriented whale-watching procedures. The humpback whales are a fantastic offshore bonus for the visitor, and as with the rest of Madagascar's dwindling natural treasures there is no room for complacency.

Humpback whales have been protected since 1966 and their numbers are recovering very slowly. Before they were hunted intensively in the 19th century, humpbacks probably numbered about 150,000 worldwide; today's estimates range from 25,000 to 35,000. Increased demands on their habitat, including unregulated whale-watching, continue to threaten the likelihood that they will ever recover fully.

Destiny is a chameleon at the top of a tree:
a child simply whistles and it changes colour.
The lake did not want to create mud,
but if the water is stirred it appears.
There are many trees,
but it is the sugarcane that is sweet.
There are many grasshoppers,
but it is the *ambolo* that has beautiful colours.
There are many people,
but it is in you that my spirit reposes.

🏠 **Chez Regine** (6 bungalows) 📞 57 042 14. Quiet, basic accommodation on a beautiful beach which is excellent for swimming. Snorkelling equipment for hire. Some bungalows are en suite.

Peaceful, friendly. Excellent food. No way of pre-booking, as far as I know, so just turn up!
🏠 **Chez Titi & La Petite Traversée** are 2 small hotels on the west of the island.

✗ WHERE TO EAT

✗ **Epicerie Restaurant** North of **Zanzibar Restaurant**, about 15mins south of Chez Regine along the beach. 'This simple place provides great meals from 3,000Ar (a real bargain on Ile aux Nattes); order in advance

where possible. We also bought all the required ingredients for *punch coco* from this shop & made our own brew – beautiful!' (James Brehaut).

WHAT TO SEE AND DO The circumference of the island is 8km, and it takes at least three hours to walk round it. Don't try this at high tide – there are some tricky bits to negotiate, often past rough seas.

There is much to see during a short walking tour, including the island's unique – and amazing – orchid *Eulophiella roempleriana*, known popularly as *l'orchidée rose*. It is 2m high with deep pink flowers.

The best beach is at the north of the island: 'crystal clear, shallow water, calm tide, soft sand – absolute paradise!'

Have lunch at Hôtel Les Lemuriens and visit the lemurs, as well as getting a delicious meal. 'We walked here from Chez Regine. This stretch of beach is absolutely stunning. White sandy beaches and palm trees hanging across the clear blue water; true paradise. A small trip to the interior of the island is also recommended. About a 15-minute walk from the coast lies a magnificent unspoiled village. From Chez Regine you have to walk through knee-deep water of the rice paddies surrounding the village so it is best to go barefoot or with beach sandals' (Sil Westra).

👉 Check the Bradt website (www.bradtguides.com) for hotel updates on Ile Sainte Marie.

Ile Sainte Marie   ILE AUX NATTES (NOSY NATO)

13

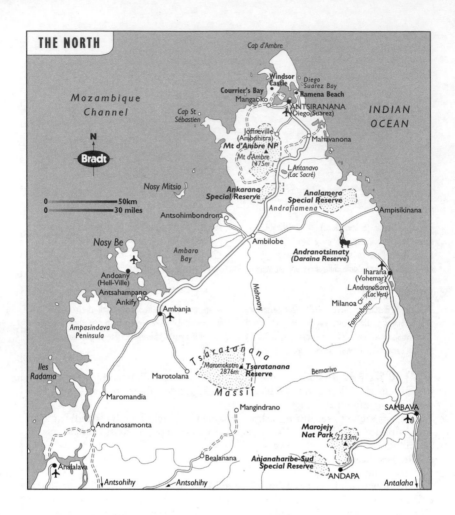

14

The North

The north of Madagascar is characterised by its variety. With the Tsaratanana massif (including Maromokotro, Madagascar's highest peak at 2,876m) bringing more rain to the Nosy Be area than is normal for the west coast, and the pocket of dry climate around Antsiranana (Diego Suarez), the weather can alter dramatically within short distances. The Antsiranana area has seven months of dry weather, with nine tenths of its 900mm annual rainfall concentrated between December and April. With changes of weather come changes of vegetation and its accompanying fauna, making this region particularly interesting to botanists and other naturalists.

This is the domain of the Antankarana people. Cut off by rugged mountains, the Antankarana were left to their own devices until the mid 1700s when they were conquered by the Sakalava; they in turn submitted to the Merina King Radama I, aided by his military adviser James Hastie, in 1823.

Roads in the area are being improved and Antsiranana is losing its isolation. Distances are long, however, so most people prefer to fly between the major towns.

ANTSIRANANA (DIEGO SUAREZ)

HISTORY Forgivingly named after two Portuguese admirals, Diego Diaz and Fernando Suarez, who arrived in 1506 and proceeded to murder and rape the inhabitants or sell them into slavery, this large town has had an eventful history with truth blending into fiction. An often-told story, probably started by Daniel Defoe, is that pirates in the 17th century founded the Republic of Libertalia here. Not true, say modern historians.

Most people still call the town Diego. The Malagasy name simply means 'port' and its strategic importance as a deep-water harbour has long been recognised. The French installed a military base here in 1885, and the town played an important role in World War II when Madagascar was under the control of the Vichy French (see box on page 366). To prevent Japanese warships and submarines making use of the magnificent harbour, and thus threatening vital sea routes, Britain and the allies captured and occupied Diego Suarez in 1942. There is a British cemetery in the town honouring those killed at this time.

DISTANCES IN KILOMETRES

Ambondromamy–Antsiranana	756km	Antsiranana–Ambanja	240km
Antsohihy–Ambanja	217km	Antsiranana–Anivorano	75km
Antsiranana–Ambilobe	138km	Antsiranana–Daraina	245km
Antsiranana–Ankarana	108km	Antsiranana–Vohemar	301km

ANTSIRANANA TODAY This is Madagascar's fifth largest town and of increasing interest to visitors for its diverse attractions and superb location. The harbour is encircled by hills with a conical 'sugarloaf' plonked in one of the bays to the east of the town. The port's isolation behind its mountain barrier and its long association with non-Malagasy races have given it an unusually cosmopolitan population and lots of colour: there are Arabs, Creoles (descendants of Europeans), Indians, Chinese and Comorans.

Almost everyone enjoys Antsiranana. Lee Miller writes: 'The area north of Place Foch is the old colonial sector, with an atmosphere of faded French occupation. Big brick colonial buildings, with street arcades topped by upper-story verandas, crumbling in disuse, abandon and neglect. Here is where you find most of the tourist activity: hotels, restaurants, and handicraft shops. It has a languid, empty feel. But walk south down Rue Lafayette, then Rue du Suffren, and the activity increases exponentially as you find yourself in the bustle of the Malagasy city centre. Lots of small stores, a big active market one block over, streets filled with people, and very few white faces. I suddenly heard again "*vazaha*" repeated in waves as I walked the streets, rather comforted to be back in the real Madagascar.'

The name 'Joffre' seems to be everywhere in and around the town. General Joseph Joffre was the military commander of the town in 1897 and later became Maréchal de France. In 1911 he took over supreme command of the French armies and was the victor of the Battle of the Marne in 1914.

If you want to relax on a beach for a few days, stay at **Ramena** (see page 365).

TELEPHONE CODE The area code for Antsiranana is 82.

GETTING THERE AND AWAY

By air There are flights from Tana (returning the same day) via Mahajanga on most days, also regular flights from/to Nosy Be. Twin Otters link Antsiranana with the east coast towns of Iharana (Vohemar), Sambava and Toamasina.

There are taxis waiting at the airport but they are expensive. A cheaper alternative is to walk 250m to the main road and wait for a *taxi-brousse*.

By road The overland route between Ambaja (nearest town to Nosy Be) and Antsiranana is scenically beautiful and on a good road. Much tougher, but possible, is the road to Iharana (Vohemar). Both routes are described later in this chapter.

GETTING AROUND Within the town, taxis should cost a flat rate of 800Ar (2006 price) but once outside the town it's much more expensive: airport 10,000Ar, Ramena Beach 40,000Ar return. You can also rent bicycles (see page 368).

WHERE TO STAY
Luxury ♔

🏠 **Hôtel la Note Bleue** (18 rooms) Rte de Ramena; m 032 07 125 48/032 07 666 26; e diegobai@hotellanotebleue.mg or hotellanotebleue@wanadoo.mg; www.diego-hotel.com or www.notebleuediegobaie.com. New; spectacular view overlooking the sugarloaf in Diego bay. Huge swimming pool, watersports, fitness centre, business centre & even a crèche; indeed, everything that goes with conventional luxury. Sgl to 4-person rooms;

honeymoon suite & ocean suite.

🏠 **Le Grand Hotel** (66 rooms) 46 Rue Colbert; ☏ 82 230 63/64; f 82 225 94; e grandhotel_diego@yahoo.fr; www.grand-hotel-diego.com. Newly opened in the centre of town, under the same ownership as Le Colbert in Tana. International-standard rooms with satellite TV & AC. The large swimming pool is open to non-residents for 10,000Ar (towel provided).

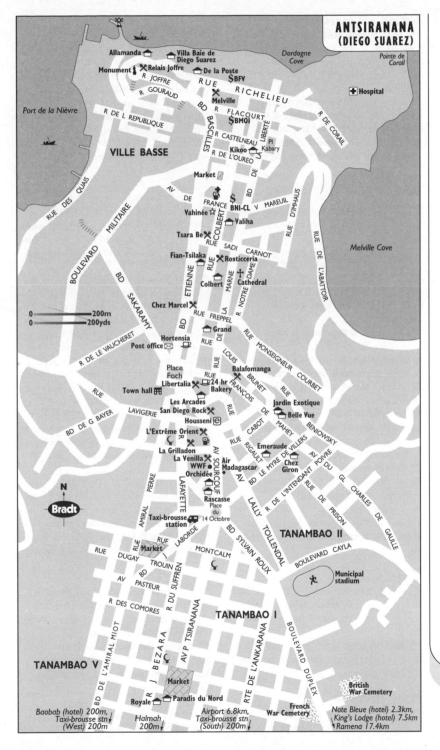

Dordogne
Cove

Pointe de
Corail

Allamanda ⌂ ⌂ Villa Baie de
Diego Suarez

Monument ⛪ ✗ Relais Joffre ⌂ De la Poste
R. JOFFRE 🕈 BFV

R. GOURAUD R U E RICHELIEU

✗ Melville

Port de la Nièvre R. DE L REPUBLIQUE R FLACOURT
🕈 BMOI

R. CASTELNEAU PI
VILLE BASSE Kikoo ⌂ Kabary

R. DE L'OUREO

Market ▨

AV. DE
FRANCE ⛪ $ BNI-CL V MAREUIL

Vahinée ☆ ⌂ Valiha

Tsara Be ✗ RUE SADI CARNOT

Fian-Tsilaka ✗ ✗ Rosticceria

RUE LA MARNE ✝ Cathedral
Colbert ⌂

Chez Marcel ✗ RUE FREPPEL

Hortensia ⌂ ⌂ Grand
Post office ✉

Place
Foch

Balafomanga
Libertalia ✗ ☐ 24 hr
Bakery

Town hall 🏛 RUE FRANCOIS

Les Arcades Jardin Exotique
San Diego Rock ✗ ⌂ Belle Vue

Housseni ©

L'Extrême Orient ✗ Emeraude

La Grilladon Chez
La Venilla ✗ Giron
WWF ● Air
Orchidée ⌂ Madagascar

Rascasse
⌂ Place
du
Taxi-brousse 🚌 14 Octobre
station

TANAMBAO II

Market ▨
RUE DUGAY MONTCALM

AV. PASTEUR

R DES COMORES TANAMBAO I

TANAMBAO V Municipal
stadium

BOULEVARD CAYLA

Market ▨

British
Royale ⌂ Paradis du Nord War Cemetery

French
War Cemetery

Baobab (hotel) 200m, Airport 6.8km, Note Bleue (hotel) 2.3km,
Taxi-brousse stn Halmah Taxi-brousse stn King's Lodge (hotel) 7.5km,
(West) 200m 200m (South) 200m Ramena 17.4km

+ Hospital

Melville Cove

Bradt

0 ▬▬▬ 200m
0 ▬▬▬ 200yds

Top end and upper range

⌂ **Hôtel Allamanda** Rue Richelieu; ☎ 82 210 33; f 82 221 80; e resa.allamanda@blueline.mg; www.hotels-diego.com. A new, luxury hotel in the centre of town. €€€€€

⌂ **Panorama** (12 bungalows) ☎ 82 225 99; e infoking@wanadoo.mg; www.kingdelapiste.de. Owned by King de la Piste. Comfortable & efficient; overlooking the sugarloaf. Good food; library. Bungalows have private shower & terrace set in spacious gardens with large swimming pool. €€€€

⌂ **King's Lodge** (8 rooms) At the foot of Montagne des Français. Owned by King de la Piste (contact details above). An excellent base for climbing Montagne des Français & seeing the rare plants there (see page 364). Well-designed, set on a gentle slope with a shaded terrace & sea view. Good restaurant. There is also a **botanical garden** here, still in preparation at the time of writing, but surely worth a visit. €€€€

Mid range €€€

⌂ **Hôtel Colbert** (27 rooms) 51 Rue Colbert; ☎ 82 232 89; f 82 232 90; e hicdiego@dts.mg. En-suite rooms with AC, safe & TV. Good restaurant, but expensive.

⌂ **Emeraude** (18 rooms) Rue Rigault (at intersection with Rue Gauche); ☎ 82 225 44; m 032 02 783 81; e contact@hotelemeraude; www.hotelemeraude-diego.com. Centrally located, comfortable, classy; some suites with large bathrooms.

⌂ **Villa La Baie de Diego Suarez** (6 rooms) 5 Rue Richelieu; m 032 40 250 59; e baiedediegosuarez@wanadoo.mg. A B&B owned by friendly French couple Rémy & Danielle. Rooms on the upper floor of their house at the far north of the city. The sitting-room, where b/fast is served, opens to a balcony with a stunning bay view. Comfortable, attractive rooms; some en suite. Rémy can arrange day excursions & airport transfers if notified. No English spoken.

⌂ **Le Jardin Exotique** (14 rooms) 9 Rue Louis Brunet (off Av Colbert); ☎ 82 219 33; e lejardinexotique@wanadoo.mg; www.lejardinexotique.net. 'Warm & welcoming service with en-suite rooms set around a pleasant patio garden.' AC in 5 rooms; some have a view over the bay.

⌂ **Hôtel la Rascasse** Rue Surcouf (opposite Air Mad); ☎ 82 223 64. A range of good-value, comfortable, spacious rooms in a convenient location. Inexpensive 1st-floor restaurant opens early & closes late. Laundry service. All rooms en suite; some with fans, others with AC & TV.

⌂ **Hôtel Restaurant Les Arcades** (8 rooms) 3 Av Tollendal (opposite the town hall); ☎ 82 231 04; e arcades@blueline.mg. In the heart of town. A typical French colonial building with courtyard, restaurant & bar. Most rooms en suite; 3 rooms with AC, others have fans. The popular restaurant serves specialities such as coconut crab curry & paella.

⌂ **Hôtel Paradis du Nord** Av Villaret Joyeuse, across from the market; ☎ 82 214 05. Sgl & dbl en-suite rooms. Good value since everything works – AC, hot water. The rooms themselves are cell-like except for no 1 which is marvellously spacious & overlooks the colourful market. Pleasant balcony dining-room (good food), laundry service & secure garage. Car & 4x4 hire.

⌂ **Hôtel de la Poste** ☎ 82 220 44. Near Clémenceau Sq, overlooking the bay. A superb location but few other redeeming features when I last visited (admittedly a few years ago; it may have improved).

⌂ **Hôtel Valiha** 41 Rue Colbert; ☎ 82 293 95; e valiha@ddt.mg. Clean rooms with AC & hot water.

Budget €€

⌂ **Hôtel Orchidée** Rue Surcouf; ☎ 82 210 65. Dbl rooms with fan or AC. Friendly, helpful, Chinese-run hotel with a small restaurant. A few cheap rooms too.

⌂ **Hôtel Fian-tsilaka** 13 Bd Etienne; ☎ 82 223 48. Dbl & family rooms, some with en-suite hot shower & AC. Good restaurant.

⌂ **Hôtel Royale** Rue Suffren (around the corner from Paradis du Nord). Cell-like rooms but clean, with fan & safe. Interior rooms are quieter. Friendly; some English spoken. Good value.

⌂ **Belle Vue (Chez Layac)** 35 Rue François de Mahy; ☎ 82 210 21. Dbl rooms, some en suite. Good value. Good place to meet other travellers.

Penny-pincher €

⌂ **Chez Yvette Giron** Villa Elise, Polygone III, Rte de la SIM; ☎ 82 220 89. This is a private house with good-value rooms. Recommended by Debbie Fellner: 'Yvette Giron's home is beautiful, safe & clean, within walking distance of downtown; she provides an excellent breakfast.'

🏠 **Kikoo Hotel** Bd de la Liberté (at intersection with Rue Castelneau). Good value.

✖ WHERE TO EAT

✖ **Balafomanga** ☎ 82 228 94. An expensive French-run restaurant; excellent food. Try the marinated zebu or *coco* shrimp.

✖ **La Venilla** Up the road from Hôtel La Rascasse, opposite the WWF office. Arguably the best restaurant in town, yet keeps its prices reasonable.

✖ **La Grilladon** Av Sourcouf (not far from the WWF office). An upmarket restaurant with a pool table & outdoor bar; excellent food. Try the fish with mushroom & aubergine.

✖ **Halmah Resto** Rue Roi Tsimiaro. Where the locals eat; always busy. Good value.

✖ **Restaurant Libertalia** Offers a few good, low-priced meals on the 1st floor. There's also a lovely garden restaurant. 'The best for a Friday night! We had a full moon, good food, great music, prostitutes dancing for their expats.'

✖ **L'Extrème Orient** A popular restaurant near Air Mad; inexpensive, good food.

✖ **La Rosticceria** Rue Colbert (north of Grand Hotel). 'A wonderful little Italian restaurant with veranda. Highly recommended for its excellent food, great atmosphere & jovial owner. Possibly the best restaurant in Madagascar' (D&K).

✖ **San Diego Rock Café** Av Tollendal; ☎ 82 219 88. An open-fronted bar & restaurant with tremendous pizzas & burgers. Great atmosphere; plays music videos.

✖ **Tsara Be** Rue Colbert (opposite Hôtel Valiha). 'It had tables spilling out onto the sidewalk, a friendly & casual atmosphere, & the food was, as the name of the restaurant says, very good' (Lee Miller).

✖ **Vahinée Bar** 'Surprisingly good food considering that it's a bit of a dive. The best soup I ate in Madagascar: 1,900Ar for an enormous bowl of tasty broth with noodles. Popular with locals wanting to watch satellite TV or enjoy live music.

✖ **Le Melville** A fancy restaurant on Rue Richelieu. 'Tables were laid with fine linen & wine glasses. Local & French menu; very European feel restaurant & bar. I ate out on the deck overlooking the bay. It couldn't have been more pleasant & removed from everything. Was this still Madagascar?' (LM)

✖ **Le Relais Joffre** Pl Joffre. It has tables arranged under the trees outdoors, with a large kiosk for a kitchen. 'A very pleasant place for a simple & inexpensive lunch. Lovely views of the port & bay, music wafting out of the kiosk' (LM).

Snacks and fast food are easy to find. The **Hortensia**, near the post office, does fast food all day. If your hotel does not serve breakfast, go to the **Boulangerie Amicale**, between La Rascasse and the cinema: excellent hot rolls and *pains au chocolat*. **La Fourandole**, on Rue Colbert, probably serves the best ice cream in town and is recommended for breakfast. The **bakery** on Rue François de Mahey, around the corner from the Libertalia, sells baguettes day and night. And ice cream. And the **Grand Hotel** has a patisserie.

NIGHTLIFE

☆ **Vahinée Bar** Rue Colbert, opposite BNI-CL bank. 'The food is adequate, the atmosphere & the staff sublime' (JG).

INTERNET Antsiranana has two Housseni.com internet cafés which are reasonably priced and usually fairly fast. The most convenient is in the Ny Havana building opposite the petrol station on Av Tollendal. About 20 terminals; 25Ar/min. 'Burns

> **HAINTENY**
>
> It is through his subjects that the sovereign reigns,
> It is the rocks that cause the stream to sing.
> It is its feathers that make the chicken large.
> The palm trees are the feet of the water
> The winds are the feet of the fire.
> The beloved is the tree of life.

14

data to disc from memory cards, but bring your own card reader. Les Arcades on Rue Colbert has a slower connection and less friendly service' (DAS).

SHOPPING Antsiranana has some high-quality souvenir shops, including two stores run by the ubiquitous Baobab Company (✆ 82 228 38; m 032 02 288 80) on Rue Colbert.

Supermarket There is a 24hr shop at the petrol station on Av Tollendal up the road from La Rascasse which stocks tinned foods, yoghurt, ice cream, fruit juice and basic necessities.

MONEY Derek A Serra reports: 'It was a nightmare to exchange travellers' cheques at BFV at the bottom of Rue Colbert. They only exchange denominations of $50 or less, take about an hour to photocopy every possible document in your possession, charge a commission and don't speak English. Only later did I find Crédit Lyonnaise off Rue Colbert that changes travellers' cheques in 5mins. BMOI strangely cashes only euros, not dollars or travellers' cheques. Avoid BOA, as the Antsiranana branch is in a constant state of chaos.' Of course all this may have changed by the time you read this. The new Grand Hotel has a small branch of BFV where good English is spoken.

WATERSPORTS A watersports centre has been established at Sakalava Bay. The turn-off is 8km from Ramena, then it's another 6km to the hotel. **Hôtel-Club de Sakalava** (*7 bungalows;* m 032 04 512 39) offers windsurfing and kitesurfing. For the latest information see their website (*www.sakalava.com*). Another very swanky hotel is being built in the same area. It will probably cost twice as much as the Sakalava.

WHAT TO SEE AND DO

British cemetery On the outskirts of town on the road that leads to the airport, the British cemetery is on a side road opposite the main Malagasy cemetery. It is well signposted. Here is a sad insight into Anglo-Malagasy history: rows of graves of the British troops killed in the battle for Diego in 1942 (see box on page 366) and the larger numbers, mainly East African and Indian soldiers serving in the British army, who died from disease during the occupation of the port. Impeccably maintained by the Commonwealth War Graves Commission, this is a peaceful and moving place.

Montagne des Français (French Mountain) The mountain gets its name from the memorial to the French and Malagasy killed during the allied invasion in 1942. Another reminder of a war about which the locals can have little understanding. There are several crosses but the main one was laboriously carried up in 1956 to emulate Jesus's journey to Calvary.

The start of the trail is just before King's Lodge hotel, 8km from Antsiranana towards Ramena Beach. At the foot of the mountain, close to the road, are some specimens of the critically endangered locally endemic baobab species, *Adansonia suarezensis* (they are the ones with smooth reddish bark; the grey-barked ones are *A. madagascariensis*).

It is a hot but rewarding climb up to the cross, with splendid views and some nearby caves. Go early in the morning for the best birdwatching (and to avoid the heat of the day). The footpath is marked with red paint about 300m along the track on the left. 'In the area of *tsingy* just before the high cliffs we spotted Sandford's brown lemurs. Many more small footpaths extend from left to right and make enjoyable walking including some which lead to the obvious large cave high above King's Lodge. Since early 2000 these cliffs and the interior of the cave have become a mecca for rock climbers where French groups have put up many bolted routes. Full details of these can be found at the King's Lodge' (V & J Middleton).

Apparently the flora and fauna are much more rewarding on the Indian Ocean side of the mountain.

RAMENA This fast-growing beach resort provides a pleasant alternative to staying in Antsiranana. Ramena is about 18km from the town centre, 45 minutes from the airport. Get there by *taxi-brousse* or by private taxi (about 40,000Ar round-trip). It's a beautiful drive around the curve of the bay, with some fine baobabs *en route*. The road down to the beach is just after the Fihary Hotel.

🏠 Where to stay/eat

🏠 **Meva Plage Hotel** (7 rooms) Meva Beach, near Ramena; m 032 04 715 22/032 04 782 42; e mevaplagehotel@blueline.mg or atyla@wanadoo.mg. Probably the best of the beach hotels, but closed in 2005, perhaps temporarily. €€€€

🏠 **Ramena Nofy** Bungalows. Very clean & quiet, with fans, 2mins from the beach. Delicious food, especially fish. €€€

🏠 **Le 5 Trop Près** (3 bungalows) m 032 07 740 60/032 07 724 63 ; e le5troppres@wanadoo.mg; www.normada.com/5TROP1/. The name is pronounced 'Saint-Tropez'. New bungalows right on the beach. Good restaurant. €€€

🏠 **Fihary Hotel** (15 chalets) ☏ 82 228 62/294 15; f 82 294 13. En-suite bathrooms, hot water & mosquito nets. Large restaurant with a terrace. €€€

🏠 **La Case en Falafy (Chez Bruno);** m 032 02 674 33. Thatched bungalows; en-suite showers (but water supply dodgy), nice swimming pool & a good open-air kitchen/bar/restaurant. Away from the beach. €€–€€€

🏠 **Badamera** Near the beach. Friendly. Wonderful food. Huts or rooms with shared bathrooms. €€

✗ **Restaurant Emeraude** 'Walk down the road to the beach from Fihary Hotel. Turn left onto the beach at the pier. This is the first restaurant you'll come to. Excellent.'

An excursion from Ramena Several readers have recommended this walk to the **Baie des Dunes** (part of the Orangea Peninsula which forms the southeastern arm of the entrance to the bay). Since part of the route passes through a military zone you will need to buy a permit from one of the sentries. ID (passport) may be needed. 'The walk is best done early in the morning or late afternoon because of the heat; also carry plenty of water. It starts from the village of Ramena. Walk along the metalled road towards the headland – straight on from the bungalows rather than down to the beach – which will take you to the military installation where you show your pass at the gatehouse. Once in the camp follow the signs to the lighthouse or dunes past the barracks then along an open stretch to the hillside and follow the contour along an obvious track. Birdlife is very good: two species of vanga (sickle-billed and Chabert's), bee-eaters and kestrels.

'The track continues past some ruined buildings and there is a signpost to the lighthouse. Carry on along the track, which can be hard going at times in the soft sand, and then the view opens up seaward. A word of caution at this point: if you leave the track to look at the view (which I can recommend as there are white-tailed tropic-birds) be careful of the cliffs. All along the walk there are numerous animal tracks, mainly land crabs but some reptiles also. Then you arrive at the Baie des Dunes; the bay itself is overlooked by an old gun emplacement. On the beach to the right of this there is a stretch of white sand gently sloping to the sea; to the left there is a remnant reef with pools, then a steep drop off into the water; excellent for snorkelling. In front of the emplacement there is a small island which is accessible from the beach.

14

John Grehan

In the days before mass air transportation, Madagascar's geographical location gave the island immense strategical importance. In World War II, British convoys to the Middle East and India sailed round the north of Madagascar, passing the great French naval base of Antsirane (now Antsiranana) at Diego Suarez. Antsirane, its harbour facilities completed in 1935, was France's most modern colonial port with a dry dock that could accommodate 28,000-ton battleships and an arsenal capable of repairing the largest of guns.

It was evident to both the Allied and Axis Powers that whoever held Diego Suarez controlled the western Indian Ocean. As the French authorities in Madagascar were firm supporters of the German-influenced Vichy Government, Britain believed that it had to occupy the island before it was handed over to her enemies. So, in the spring of 1942, Britain mounted Operation Ironclad, its first ever large-scale combined land, sea and air operation, to capture Diego Suarez as the initial step in occupying the whole island.

A force of some 13,000 troops with tanks and artillery, supported by 46 warships and transport vessels and 101 aircraft of the Fleet Air Arm, assembled to the north of Cap d'Ambre before dawn on 5 May 1942. The narrow entrance to Diego Suarez Bay was known to be powerfully defended by large-calibre artillery so the British decided to land in Courrier's Bay and march across country to take Antsirane from the landward side.

The first troops to land were Commandos, who captured the small battery that overlooked Courrier's Bay. The French and Senegalese defenders were still asleep and the position was taken with little loss of life. However, a small French force ensconced in an observation post on the summit of Windsor Castle could not be dislodged. For two days the French clung to their eyrie, despite repeated bombardments from the Royal Navy and attacks by the Fleet Air Arm and the Commandos.

With the beaches secured, the main British force landed and began its march upon Antsirane. Meanwhile, the Fleet Air Arm depth-charged and torpedoed the French warships and submarines at anchor in Diego Suarez Bay and bombed Arrachart airfield. But the defenders were now at their posts and an intense battle for possession of Diego Suarez began.

Some three miles to the south of Antsirane the French had built a strong defensive line across the isthmus of the Antsirane Peninsula. Devised by General Joffre in 1909, it comprised a trench network and an anti-tank ditch strengthened by forts and pillboxes

'The whole area is excellent for wildlife, especially the pools, and there is the potential to spend the whole day here exploring if you bring a packed lunch. Further over in the same woodland we found crowned and Sanford's brown lemurs' (A Slater & D Pollard).

EXCURSIONS FROM ANTSIRANANA

Antsiranana is the starting point for several outstanding excursions, some nearby and possible as a day trip, such as the Red Tsingy and Montagne d'Ambre. Some require several days, eg: Ankarana and Analamera. With a 4x4, or even a sturdy Renault, you can also spend a few days visiting the far north at Cap d'Ambre and Windsor Castle.

GETTING ORGANISED Many hotels in Antsiranana will be able to put you in touch with someone who will organise a tour. Perhaps more risky than using one of the established companies below, but more personal and often more enjoyable for this reason.

housing artillery and machine-guns. For two days the British forces assaulted the French line without success and with mounting losses.

The breakthrough came on the evening of 6 May when a British destroyer charged through the entrance of Diego Suarez Bay under the guns of the French batteries. The destroyer successfully landed a body of 50 Marines onto the quay. This tiny force stormed through the town, capturing the main barracks and the artillery headquarters. This disruption in their rear finally broke the defenders' resolve and when the main frontal attack was renewed the French line was overrun.

The fighting resulted in more than 1,000 casualties. The British commander submitted recommendations for more than 250 decorations, including three posthumous Victoria Crosses.

Britain's vital route to the east had been secured – but only in the nick of time. Barely three weeks after the capture of Antsirane, a Japanese submarine flotilla arrived off the coast of Madagascar. In a daring night raid the Japanese attacked the ships in Diego Suarez Bay, sinking one supply ship and severely damaging the flag ship of the British expedition, the battleship *Ramillies*.

With the island's main naval base in British hands, it was expected that the French Governor General, Armand Annet, would bow to the inevitable and relinquish control of the whole island. However, despite months of negotiations, Annet refused to surrender and Britain was forced to mount further military operations.

In September 1942, British and Commonwealth troops landed at Majunga and Tamatave. Brushing aside all attempts to stop and delay them, the Allies captured Tananarive only to find that Annet had retreated to the south of the island. But when a South African force landed at Tulear, Annet realised that he was trapped.

The French strung out surrender negotiations until one minute after midnight on 6 November – exactly six months and one day after the start of the British attack upon Diego Suarez. The significance of this was that French troops involved in a campaign lasting longer than six months were entitled to a medal and an increased state pension!

After a brief period of British Military Administration, the island was handed over to General de Gaulle's Free French movement. The key naval base of Antsirane, however, remained under British control until 1944.

John Grehan is the author of The Forgotten Invasion, *see Further Information on page 459.*

Jasmin Ravalohery m 032 04 056 62. 'Genuine, friendly, interesting & very enthusiastic.' But speaks only French.
Jean Noel has also been recommended as 'enthusiastic, has a great knowledge about the area's flora & fauna & speaks English.' Most hotels &

agencies will know where to find him.
M Titi (☏ 82 231 06; m 032 02 619 58), **M Peter** (m 032 02 997 07) & **M Finardy** (☏ 82 230 61; m 032 04 516 80). English-speaking guides recommended for Ankarana.

Tour operators
King de la Piste Bd Bazeilles; ☏/f 82 225 99; m 032 04 908 10; e infoking@wanadoo.mg; www.kingdelapiste.de This agency, run by York Pareik (German), is the best in town for trips by 4x4 (min 2 people) to hard-to-reach places such as Windsor Castle, Cap d'Ambre, Analamera & the Red Tsingy. York & his Malagasy wife Lydia also organise excursions by motorbike or mountain bike. Prices are very high (cash only; credit cards not accepted) but most people

consider it worth it for the efficient service.
Nature et Océan 5 Rue Cabot; ☏ 82 226 32. They run 4x4 vehicles to places of interest such as Montagne d'Ambre, Ankarana, Antanavo, Windsor Castle, Courrier's Bay & Ambilobe. Also run sea & fishing trips. The dependable agency **Madagascar Airtours** also has an office here.
Ecotours 14 Av Sourcouf (next to Hôtel Rascasse); m 032 40 118 14; e madagascarecotours@

yahoo.fr. 'Not only is this one of the cheapest operators, the patron has English-speaking guides. Having spent a week with me, both of them now know a great deal about Britain's involvement in Madagascar in World War II!' (John Grehan).

Zanatany Tours ✆ 82 237 88; f 82 224 44. This outfit is run by one of Madagascar's best guides to the north, Hyacinthe (Luc Hyacinthe Kotra) & his team which includes brothers Angelin & Angeluc Razafimanantsoa who are known by many visitors for their outstanding knowledge of Ankarana &

Montagne d'Ambre. They specialise in natural history tours to reserves such as Ankarana, Analamera & Daraina, providing all necessary camping equipment & 4x4s. Highly recommended.

Cap Nord Voyages 51 Rue Colbert; ✆ 82 235 06; m 032 071 88 74; e cap.nord.voyages@ wanadoo.mg; www.cap-nord-voyages.com. 'We had a great tour with them, spending 3 full days at Ankarana' (Petra van der Bij).

Evasions Sans Frontieres & Ocean Adventures Both have offices in the Grand Hotel.

Car and bicycle hire

ADA Location Bd Duplex (SICAM building); ✆ 82 224 98; e sicam.diego@simicro.mg. A Peugeot 106 costs about 60,000Ar/day inc driver.

Hôtel Paradis du Nord Sometimes has cars plus drivers.

Bicycles Rue Colbert (just north of Hôtel Colbert, before Rue Sadi Carnot, on the east side of the street). 'The young man working there was extremely helpful; the bikes were almost new (!); he even had helmets, air pumps, spare tyres, you name it. 10,000Ar/day' (G Venema & J de Bekker).

WINDSOR CASTLE AND COURRIER'S BAY A half-day drive (preferably by 4x4, but ordinary taxis can usually do it) or full-day bike excursion takes you to the fantastic rock known as Windsor Castle. This monolith (visible from Antsiranana and – better – if you arrive by ship) is steep-sided and flat-topped, so made a perfect lookout point during times of war. The views from there are superb. It was fortified by the French, occupied by the Vichy forces, and liberated by the British. A ruined staircase still runs to the top (if you can find it). There is some *tsingy* here, and many endemic succulents including a local species of pachypodium, *P. windsorii.*

To get there take the road that runs west towards Ampasindava, where you turn right (north) along a rocky road, then left towards Windsor Castle. The road continuing north is the very rough one to Cap d'Ambre. This is a hot, dry, shadeless climb. Take plenty of water and allow yourself enough time. Courrier's Bay, half an hour beyond, is an exceptionally fine beach.

CAP D'AMBRE John and Valerie Middleton sent this report for the last edition. I have had no recent feedback. 'The road is surprisingly easy; in fact the slowest bit is the first 10km from Antsiranana. It is approximately 75km to the Cap and this should take no more than seven hours with photo stops – and the views are often superb with both the Indian Ocean and Mozambique Channel at once. The obvious route via a straight road north is poor due to the tide covering the track and making it extremely muddy most of the time. The best way is via the villages of Bedarabe and Ambatonjanohavy in the east. The final tip beneath the lighthouse is an amazing wilderness of fantastic wave-eroded limestone. The lighthouse itself has a 10cm-wide crack all down one side and is currently not working. Beneath this on the landward side, several old lighthouse buildings house the friendly keeper and another family. On our return we camped beneath La Butte at the northern end of the escarpment at the opposite end of which is Windsor Castle. Our interest was to explore the not inconsiderable areas of *tsingy* and associated plants but we also found the whole plateau has excellent walking opportunities. The several large outcrops were almost all as impressive as Windsor Castle.'

LAKE ANTANAVO (LAC SACRÉ) The sacred lake is about 75km south of Antsiranana, near the small town of Anivorano. It attracts visitors more for its legends than for the reality of a not particularly scenic lake, and the possibility of seeing a crocodile. The story is that once upon a time Anivorano was situated amid semi-desert and a thirsty traveller arrived at the village asking for a drink. When his request was refused he warned the villagers that they would soon have more water than they could cope with. No sooner had he left than the earth opened, water gushed out, and the mean-minded locals and their houses were inundated. The crocodiles which now inhabit the lake are considered to be ancestors (and to wear jewellery belonging to their previous selves, so they say).

The crocodiles are sometimes fed by the villagers, so you may do best to book a tour in Antsiranana; the tour operator should know when croc-feeding day is. There are two smaller lakes nearby which the locals fish cautiously – often from the branches of a tree to avoid a surprise crocodile attack.

MONTAGNE D'AMBRE (AMBER MOUNTAIN) NATIONAL PARK

This 18,500ha national park was created in 1958, the French colonial government recognising the unique nature of the volcanic massif and its forest. The park is part of the Montagne d'Ambre Reserves Complex which also includes the Special Reserves of Ankarana, Analamera and Forêt d'Ambre. The project, initiated in 1989, was the first to involve local people in all stages of planning and management. The aims of conservation, rural development and education have largely been achieved. Ecotourism has been encouraged successfully with good information and facilities now available.

Montagne d'Ambre National Park is a splendid example of montane rainforest. The massif ranges in altitude from 850m to 1,475m and has its own micro-climate with rainfall similar to the eastern region. It is one of the most visitor-friendly of Madagascar's protected areas, with broad trails, fascinating flora and fauna, a comfortable climate and readily available information. In the dry season vehicles can drive right up to the main picnic area, giving a unique opportunity (in Madagascar) for elderly or disabled visitors to see the rainforest and its inhabitants.

The name comes not from deposits of precious amber, but from the amber-coloured resin which oozes from some of its trees and is used medicinally by the local people.

☞ **WARNING!** Antsiranana is now firmly on the itinerary of cruise ships, with Montagne d'Ambre the focus of the day's excursion. This means that a hundred or more passengers will pour into the park. Independent travellers may wish to visit the port to check if a ship is due before planning their visit.

PERMITS AND INFORMATION Permits and a very good information booklet are available at the park entrance. The ANGAP office is on the outskirts of town towards the airport. Permits are also available here. It is compulsory to take a guide.

GETTING THERE The entrance to the park is 27km south of Antsiranana, 4km from the town of Ambohitra (or Joffreville as almost everyone still calls it). *Taxi-brousses* leave from the *gare routière* at the crossroads south of the town (on the way to the airport) from approximately 06.00. The journey takes about an hour (the road is tarred) and cost 3,000Ar in 2006. Some drivers will take you up to the park for an additional payment.

 WHERE TO STAY/EAT (JOFFREVILLE)

🏠 **Le Domaine de Fontenay** (8 rooms & 1 suite) m 033 11 345 81; e contact@lefontenay-

madagascar.com; www.lefontenay-madagascar.com. One of Madagascar's best hotels in a beautifully furnished

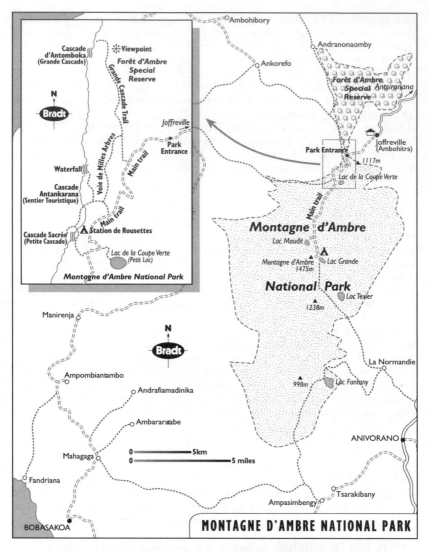

MONTAGNE D'AMBRE NATIONAL PARK

& renovated manor house. Owned & run by English-speaking Marie-Jose de Spéville & Karl-Heinz Horner. Personal attention, delicious cooking & huge rooms set in a beautiful garden. 'Rarely have we enjoyed such a warm welcome & kind hospitality' (E Cox). Extensive library. The hotel has its own small reserve which is excellent for reptiles. I saw the appropriately named blue-nosed chameleon, a *Brookesia ebenaui* (stump-tailed chameleon) & a gorgeous *Stenophis arctifasciatus* snake, which looked as though it was made of pink plastic. ♛

⌂ **Nature Lodge** (10 bungalows) m 032 07 123 06; e naturelodge@wanadoo.mg; www.naturelodge-

ambre.com. Very comfortable bungalows, with a tastefully designed bar & restaurant. Friendly, excellent food. Can also be booked through Grill du Rova in Tana (22 356 07). €€€€€

⌂ **Hôtellerie du Monastère** (8 rooms & dorms) m 032 04 795 34; e contact@gitesaintbenoit.com. This Benedictine convent has good-value rooms with en-suite bathrooms as well as dormitories with 5–7 beds. Community-style meals. Gift shop sells local crafts. B/fast inc. €€€

⌂ **Auberge Sakay-Tanay** m 032 04 281 22; e contact@sakay-tany.com; www.sakay-tany.com. Good-value accommodation but no running water. €€

Accommodation in the national park There are shelters and bunk beds in the park for visitors equipped with their own sleeping bags (bring your own food). From the wildlife point of view, staying in or near the park is far preferable to making a day trip from Antsiranana.

There is a campsite (often crowded) at the car park/picnic area (known as Station des Rousettes). It has running water, shower, toilet and barbeque facilities. Firewood is available from the warden, but bring your own food.

WEATHER The rainy season (and cyclone season) is from December to April. It is usually dry from May to August, but there is a strong wind, *varatraza*, almost every day and it can feel quite cold. The temperature in the park is, on average, 5°C cooler than in Antsiranana, it is often wet and muddy and there may be leeches. So be wary of wearing shorts and sandals however hot and dry you are at sea level. Bring rain gear, insect repellent and even a light sweater.

The most rewarding time to visit is during the warm season: September to November. There will be some rain, but most animals are active and visible, and the lemurs will have babies.

FLORA AND FAUNA Montagne d'Ambre is as exciting for its plants as for its animals. A very informative booklet, available from the visitor centre, gives details and illustrations of the species most commonly seen. All visitors are impressed by the tree-ferns and the huge, epiphytic bird's nest ferns which grow on trees. The distinctive *Pandanus* is also common and you can see Madagascar's endemic cycad. Huge strangler figs add to the spectacle.

Most visitors want to see lemurs and two diurnal species have become habituated: Sanford's brown lemur and crowned lemur. Male Sanford's lemurs have white/beige ear-tufts and side-whiskers surrounding black faces, whilst the females are more uniform in colour with no whiskers and a grey face. Crowned lemurs get their names from the triangle of black between the ears of the male; the rest of the animal is reddish brown. Females are mainly grey, with a little red tiara across the forehead. Both sexes have a lighter-coloured belly; in the female this is almost white. Young are born from September to November. There are also five species of nocturnal lemur.

Another mammal often seen is the ring-tailed mongoose – one regularly raids the rubbish bins at the picnic site. If you are really lucky you could see a fossa or its relative the falanouc.

At eye level you may spot some large chameleons, also often seen crossing the road during the drive up from Antsiranana. A good guide should be able to find some leaf-mimic *Brookesia* chameleons (some less than 2cm long) and also *Uroplatus sikorae*, perhaps the most amazingly camouflaged of all this genus of gecko. You won't find it yourself, believe me! There are other lizards like the spectacular *Paroedura* gecko, plus pill millipedes rolling into a perfect ball, many frogs, butterflies and other invertebrates.

Even non-birders will be fascinated by the numerous species here: the Madagascar crested ibis is striking enough to impress anybody, as is the Madagascar paradise flycatcher with its long, trailing tail feathers. The locally endemic Amber Mountain rock thrush is tame and ubiquitous, and the black-and-white magpie robin is often seen. The jackpot, however, is one of Madagascar's most beautiful birds: the pitta-like ground-roller.

TRAILS, WATERFALLS AND LAKES The park has 30km of paths and most of these have now been cleared and improved, so none is difficult although there are long climbs and descents.

Three waterfalls provide the focal points for day visitors. If time is short and you want to watch wildlife rather than walk far, go to the **Cascade Sacrée**. This is only about 100m along the track beyond the picnic area (Station des Rousettes) and on the way you should see lemurs, chameleons, orchids and birds galore. Take a small path on your left to the river for a possible glimpse of the white-throated rail and the Madagascar malachite kingfisher. The Cascade Sacrée is an idyllic fern-fringed grotto with waterfalls splashing into a pool.

The **Sentier Touristique** is also easy and starts near the Station des Rousettes (walk back towards the entrance, cross the bridge and turn left). The path terminates at a viewpoint above **Cascade Antankarana**: a highly photogenic spot.

The walk to the **Cascade d'Antomboka** is tougher, with some up-and-down stretches, and a steep descent to the waterfall. There is some excellent birdwatching here, some lovely tree-ferns and a good chance of seeing lemurs.

On your way back you'll pass a path on the right (left as you go towards the waterfall) marked **Voie des Mille Arbres**. It's a tough roller-coaster of a walk, but very rewarding, and eventually joins the main track. Ring-tailed mongooses are often seen along this stretch,

If you continue beyond the Cascade d'Amtomboka, the trail eventually reaches a river and the rarest of all baobab species: *Adansonia perrieri*. There are two or three in the area, and the largest stands at a truly impressive 25m or so tall with a massive girth. The stream is lovely and makes for an ideal picnic spot before tackling the arduous climb back to the main trail. This is a tough walk; you should allow 3–4 hours for the round-trip.

Other walks from Station des Rousettes include the easy climb to the viewpoint above the crater lake, **Lac de la Coupe Verte**. A full day's walk takes you to a crater lake known as **Lac Maudit**, or Matsabory Fantany, then on for another hour to **Lac Grand**. Beyond that is the highest point in the park, **Montagne d'Ambre** itself (1,475m). Unless you are a fit, fast walker it would be best to take two days on this trek and camp by Lac Grand. That way you can wait for weather conditions to allow the spectacular view.

NIGHT WALKS Night walks are hugely rewarding, even if you don't see any nocturnal lemurs. With a good guide (and I had the best: Louis-Philippe d'Arvisenet) you can see some spectacular reptiles, including several species of leaf-tailed gecko, *Uroplatus sikorae* and *U. ebenaui*. Our prize, however, was seeing the extremely localised subspecies of O'Shaughnessy's chameleon, *Calumma oshaughnessyi ambreensis*. Daniel and Kelly had an even luckier sighting: 'we were astounded to find *Uroplatus alluaudi*, an exceedingly rare, locally endemic leaf-tailed gecko. Our guide danced around, yelping and punching the air with excitement for a full five minutes!'

RED TSINGY

About an hour from Antsiranana, on a rough road leading east from the main route to Ankarana, is a spectacular area of eroded laterite known as the Red Tsingy. Although not true *tsingy*, this is an amazing sight and much more photogenic than limestone because of its varieties of colours. It's not an easy place to reach independently, but drivers *en route* to Ankarana can deviate here by prior arrangement.

ANALAMERA (ANALAMERANA) SPECIAL RESERVE

This 34,700ha reserve is in remote and virtually unexplored deciduous forest some 20km southeast of Montagne d'Ambre, and is the last refuge of the very rare

Perrier's sifaka (*Propithecus perrieri*). The reserve is open to visitors and, for the enthusiast, easily merits between two and four nights' camping. There are no facilities of any kind, so visitors must be totally self-sufficient.

To reach the reserve from Antsiranana drive 50km south on the main road, and then a further 11km on a dreadful stretch which is impassable in the rainy season. Guides and porters can be organised in the nearby village of Menagisy, but it is more sensible to arrange the visit through a tour operator in Antsiranana. In addition to Perrier's sifaka, you may also see crowned lemurs, Sanford's brown lemurs and endangered birds such as the white-breasted mesite and Van Dam's vanga.

ANKARANA SPECIAL RESERVE

About 108km south of Antsiranana is a small limestone massif, Ankarana. An 'island' of *tsingy* (limestone karst pinnacles) and forest, the massif is penetrated by numerous caves and canyons. Some of the largest caves have collapsed, forming isolated pockets of river-fed forest with their own perfectly protected flora and fauna. Dry deciduous forest grows around the periphery and into the wider canyons. The caves and their rivers are also home to crocodiles, some reportedly six metres long. The reserve is known for its many lemur species, including crowned and Sanford's brown lemurs, and also the inquisitive ring-tailed mongoose (*Galidia elegans*), but it is marvellous for birds, reptiles and insects as well. Indeed, the wow-factor is as high here as anywhere I have visited.

Ankarana (18,220ha) is rightly among the most popular western reserves, although at present it is a hiking and camping trip only. Ankarana is also The Real Thing. Old Madaphiles who've seen the new posh hotels in Antsiranana and wonder if Madagascar's gone soft, can take heart at Daniel and Kelly's experiences of a December trip, described in the box on page 376.

GETTING THERE AND AWAY With a 4x4 you can drive all the way to the main campsite, Campement Anilotra (Camp des Anglais), in the dry season. Most drivers approach from the north, turning off at Anivorano and heading for the village of Matsaborimanga. Allow five hours for this drive from Antsiranana.

By far the most interesting way to get there, however, is to hike in from RN6 – a good tarred road which runs between Ambanja and Antsiranana. The journey by *taxi-brousse* to the village of Mahamasina takes about three hours from Ambanja or 2½ hours from Antsiranana. There is an ANGAP office near the trailhead at the PK 108 milestone. It's a super walk of about 11km into the reserve; allow 2½ to 3 hours. The first part is down a wide track, then, after about 20 minutes, you turn right down a gully and cross a river. Shortly after that the trail levels out, enters some beautiful forest (you are now in one of the wide canyons). A huge *Ficus* marks the halfway point and a steep gully indicates that you are arriving at Campement Anilotra.

On the way back, if you use the same route, your guide will take you along an alternative trail to visit the bat caves – a tough scramble, but well worth it.

ORGANISED TOURS It is not easy to do Ankarana independently. You need transport and a guide anyway, so it makes sense to take an organised tour (see page 367 for recommended tour operators). Levels of organisation and comfort vary considerably, so your choice will probably depend on your budget. At the top end of the market are King de la Piste and Zanatany, who will arrange all-inclusive camping visits, but for backpackers without their own tent it's cheapest to stay outside the reserve and hike in.

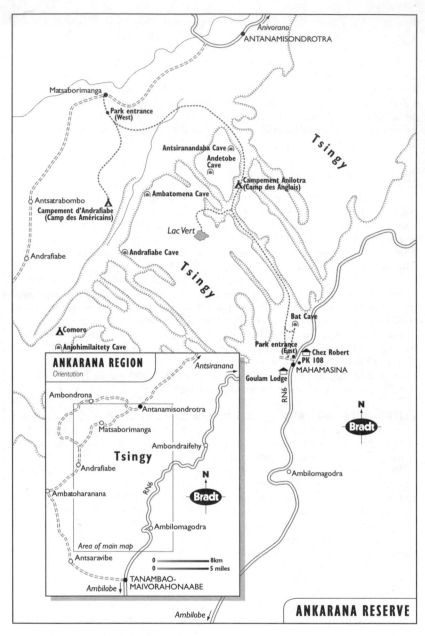

ANKARANA RESERVE

ANKARANA REGION
Orientation

Tsingy

Area of main map

0 — 8km
0 — 5 miles

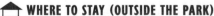

WHERE TO STAY (OUTSIDE THE PARK)

Chez Tonton (12 rooms) Ambatomitsangana (10 km off RN6). Owned by Robert Lieu Wang Tchou, & heartily recommended by Peace Corps volunteer Christi Turner, this hotel has a total of 30 beds with mosquito nets. A palm-thatch pavilion has dining & lounge space, all constructed from local materials in the local style. 'The lovely grounds are filled with local trees & plants, many fruit-bearing & many with medicinal uses, all of which Robert enthusiastically discusses & shares with his guests. Meals are prepared on a large clay stove built by Robert in his outdoor covered kitchen, & small dishes are prepared on a solar cooker. Robert's menus use local ingredients, & combine traditional Malagasy, Chinese & French cuisine.' Shared (flush) toilets but no running water. Independent travellers can catch a *taxi-brousse* from Ambilobe to Antsaravibe (only dependable May–Nov); get out at Maromena & walk 2km to Chez Tonton. €€

⌂ **Chez Robert** Basic bungalows near the entrance of the park. Good food. €
⌂ **Goulam Lodge** Simple bungalows near the entrance at Mahamasina. Outside toilet; cold water. Goulam is one of the most experienced Ankarana guides. €

PERMITS AND GUIDES A permit for Ankarana should be purchased from ANGAP in Antsiranana or Tana. A guide is compulsory. Most live in Matsaborimanga, but are available at the park office in Mahamasina where permits may also be obtained.

CAMPSITES INSIDE THE RESERVE The main campsite, formerly known as Camp des Anglais (following the Crocodile Caves Expedition), has been renamed **Campement Anilotra**. It is equipped with long-drop toilets and picnic tables. There are three separate areas, so although it tends to get crowded you can usually escape from other travellers. Note that the camp offers considerably more shade than Campement d'Andrafiabe, as well as a chance to bathe in the river running through the cave. However, as the reserve becomes more popular, so does the likelihood of finding this campsite fully occupied. The water supply is a good ten-minute walk away down a slippery slope.

The usual alternative campsite is **Campement d'Andrafiabe** (Camp des Américains), which is handy for the Andrafiabe Cave. It has a water supply and toilets, but can get very crowded and littered.

An increasingly popular camp is **Camp des Africains** (it seems to have kept its old name) which has long-drop toilets and picnic tables. Water is a problem – it's hard to get to in the dry season so you need to bring your own. There is a bat cave nearby and some small *tsingy* about half an hour's walk away, but to reach the main *tsingy* you must walk a 32km round-trip.

Camp de Fleur is about two hours from Campement Anilotra and is a good base for visiting Lac Vert and some of the best *tsingy*.

WHAT TO BRING You'll need strong shoes or boots, a daypack, a two-litre water bottle, insect repellent, torch (flashlight) for the caves plus spare batteries. And earplugs. Not just because of the snoring from other campers – the *Lepilemurs* and cicadas of Ankarana are highly vocal!

WHAT TO SEE AND DO Ankarana reminds me of J-P Commerson's famous quote: 'At every step one encounters the most strange and marvellous forms.' Everything is strange and marvellous: the animals, the birds, the plants, the landscape. 'Some of our most special memories of Madagascar are of Ankarana. Our chance fossa sighting alone was amazing. But there were so many other wildlife encounters that were out of this world – things we've never seen anywhere else in Madagascar: crocodiles, tarantulas, a metre-long earthworm, many unusual reptiles, hundreds of bats in the caves. And the *tsingy*, of course. And a very cute little snake (who kept biting my hand) which we later identified as a recently described species. And the hilarious giant snails which left broad mucus trails all over our tent and loved to eat our anti-mosquito coils … while they were burning!' (D&K).

Tsingy and lake Although found in other countries, *tsingy* is very much a Madagascar phenomenon and you won't want to leave Ankarana without seeing it. If staying at Anilotra Camp, the best *tsingy* is about two hours away, over very rugged terrain, just beyond the beautiful crater lake, Lac Vert. This is a very hot, all-day trip (start early, in the cool of the day, and bring a picnic and plenty of water) and is absolutely magnificent. Board walks have been constructed to allow safe passage over the *tsingy*, protecting the fragile rock while you admire the strange succulents such as *Pachypodiums* which seem to grow right out of the limestone.

Lac Vert is as green as its name, and if you are crazy enough you can hike down a steep, slippery slope to the water's edge. An easier alternative is Le Petit Tsingy which is found just 15 minutes from the campsite. Although smaller, there are similar plants and also lemurs.

Caves From Andrafiabe Camp you can explore the gigantic passageways of Andrafiabe Cave. 'We don't believe that even the most claustrophobic person could have problems here! This is well worth a visit with an exit halfway through into one of the spectacular canyons from where an interesting return can be made. The Crocodile Caves in the southern end of the reserve seem to be little-visited but are well worth the effort – the situation is spectacular and the passageways are huge' (V&J Middleton). 'The Crocodile Cave was easily walkable in about 30 minutes

THE TRIALS AND TRIBULATIONS OF ANKARANA

Daniel Austin & Kelly Green

This was one of our most testing reserve visits, and the suffering began as soon as we left Antsiranana. Ankarana is some 100km to the south. Hiring a car and driver for this four-day trip was not a viable option; our limited funds simply wouldn't allow for such luxuries. (We were attempting to spend half a year exploring Madagascar on the kind of budget some folk blow on a ten-day package holiday there.)

So instead we caught a *taxi-brousse* for 8,000Ar each. Sardines don't even know what 'crammed in' means – there were fully *thirty* of us in this small 15-seater minibus for the majority of the three-hour trip.

On arrival at Ankarana, the relief of having the use of our limbs again soon turned to irritation: this time by the local cicadas. These pesky insects are about 7cm long and look like a cross between a cockroach and a gigantic bluebottle. All day long a cicada's job is to sit on a tree and screech. Their shrill tones fill the forest, sounding like something between a scream and a chainsaw. We've often seen and heard solitary cicadas elsewhere, but at Ankarana there were literally thousands of them vibrating their tymbals (noise-making membranes) in unison.

But even when the calls of the cicadas subsided, there was no respite. Large, orange-brown flies – like horseflies – follow you everywhere, circling your head, buzzing constantly and occasionally diving in for a bite. Killing them is fruitless, they are merely replaced by another in seconds. And then there are the swarms of mosquitoes. Inexplicably they found Kelly's anklebones particularly tasty, biting them (through her socks) until they were red raw and infuriatingly itchy.

On top of all this we had to be particularly wary of scorpions, carefully checking inside our shoes and rucksack pockets. And there were tarantulas. And crocodiles …

But we would be lying if we said Ankarana wasn't one of our most fantastic experiences during the whole six months we were in Madagascar. All of its downsides combined don't even come close to equalling the positives; it is a magical place of stunning landscapes and fascinating creatures.

Visitors must not be put off by our experiences. We later discovered that December can be one of the most difficult times to visit this reserve.

from the entrance to the eastern end where it took a steep, rocky climb out into the sunken forest. I saw croc-tail drag marks, but no live ones. Fish and large eels were trapped in interior puddles and sections of river' (Bill Love).

Don't miss the wonderful bat caves, especially Crystal Cave. 'This is an underground fairytale land of sparkling stalagmites and stalactites. Bring a headlamp or flashlight – hiking over such delicate terrain can be tricky and dangerous. You'll feel like a mouse in the Bat Cave with its towering walls pocked with bat and swift nests. The ground crawls with cockroaches and is littered with bat carcasses' (D Fellner).

Other places of interest in the area Christi Turner, a Peace Corps volunteer, recommends the following excursions if staying at Chez Tonton.

Ambavanankarana This is a traditional Malagasy fishing village, way out on the coastal edge of Antsaravibe, approximately 15km from Chez Tonton. Pirogues and larger boats pull their catches to shore throughout the day (especially early mornings), where local people come to buy it in large quantity, many of whom then bike it or carry it around Antsaravibe to sell it at profit.

Ambatoharanana This village is the home of the Antakarana *mpanjaka*, or traditional king. The village is only 2–3km from Ambavanankarana, and at certain times of the year traditional ceremonies are held there; every five years is the *tsagatsaina*, the most celebrated of all, honouring the reign of the traditional leader.

Ampotsehy About 5km from Chez Tonton, this is the place to get a pirogue across the Mahavavy River to the southernmost *tsingy* of the area. Here there is a small covered viewpoint from where you can watch the sunset.

FROM ANTSIRANANA TO IHARANA (VOHEMAR) BY ROAD

A *taxi-brousse* from Antsiranana (Diego Suarez) to Ambilobe (on RN6) takes about three hours. After that, the trouble begins because the road is truly awful. 'It took us at least 21 hours to cover some 150km. We left Ambilobe in the early afternoon (after having been told to be ready for 06.30 that morning), travelling in what is known as a *camion Kosovo* through the night, and arrived in Vohemar around 11.00 the next day, battered, bruised and exhausted' (Sebastian Bulmer).

Sebastian does seem to have been particularly unfortunate. Ten to 12 hours is more usual for the trip. However, if you can possibly afford it, hire a private car. This is not just because it cuts the trip down to a manageable seven hours or so but it gives you the chance to visit one of the most rewarding reserves in Madagascar: Daraina (see page 378).

AMBILOBE This is a very gritty transit town, busy at all hours with traffic. It lies at an important junction linking Antsiranana in the north with Iharana (Vohemar) on the eastern coast so you may need to stop here. There are some basic hotels and, most surprisingly, a superb pizzeria which almost makes the stop worthwhile.

Getting there and away There are frequent minibuses between Ambilobe and Ambanja (9,000Ar; 2hrs), and Ambilobe and Antsiranana (9,000Ar; 3hrs). They cruise around town from early in the morning collecting customers, so pick an almost-full one if you want a reasonably quick getaway. There are also *bachés* for the very rough journey to Vohemar via Daraina.

If you're looking for 4x4 rental, one owner (m *032 02 691 10*) advertises his vehicle on hotel noticeboards for 150,000Ar per day plus fuel. We paid 240,000Ar including petrol but for a Renault 4L taxi booked in Vohemar.

🏠 Where to stay

🏠 **Hôtel National Ambilobe** ☎ 82 065 41. Probably the best place in town & clean enough. It's a modern block at the southern end of town. En-suite dbl rooms, some with AC. €€–€€€

🏠 **Noor Hotel** ☎ 82 061 95. Behind the Jovenna fuel station at the northern end of town. It's a pleasant old-fashioned place built around a courtyard with en-suite bathrooms & some AC rooms; others have a fan. €€

🏠 **Hôtel Amicale** ☎ 82 650 24 (this number is for a grocery shop under same ownership). Opposite Hôtel National. This is a last resort; if their disco doesn't wake you the 4am call to prayer of the nearby mosque will. Bring earplugs. The rooms are on the 2nd floor, off of a wide balcony. No mosquito nets (though plenty of mosquitoes). Cold water only, moderately clean, secure with window bars. €

✖ Where to eat
For provisions there's the market and a good grocery store at the front of Hôtel Amicale; on the corner of the same block is a bakery. Thanks go to Bryn Thomas for the Ambilobe update.

✖ **Restaurant Escargot** Down a side street in the middle of town.

✖ **Coco Pizza** By far the best place. It's opposite the Jovenna fuel station. They have a wood-fired oven for a range of delicious thin-crust pizzas. ⊕ 10.00–14.00 & 17.00–20.30; closed Sun eve.

DARAINA Daraina is a small town around 70km northwest of Iharana (2½hrs), or 100km (5hrs) from Ambilobe. If you are taking that road anyway, it makes the whole journey worthwhile; if you're staying in Iharana it's worth making it a day's excursion. Expect to take two to three hours to get there.

The reason to go here is to see the beautiful golden-crowned sifaka (*Propithecus tattersalli*), one of the rarest of all lemurs and listed as one of the 25 most threatened primates in the world. What makes the visit so worthwhile is that you *will* see the sifaka, and close-up (see box opposite) and this is probably the only place in Madagascar where you can have this sort of experience without crowds of other visitors sharing it with you. It's a rare privilege and worth putting up with the journey there. And do it soon – before this efficient government improves the road and brings the hordes.

Remember that sifaka tend to sleep in the heat of midday (and it's murderously hot then for humans too) so if coming from Iharana make a really early start.

A Malagasy NGO called FANAMBY is working with the local communities to preserve the forests and the sifakas. One of their aims is to establish a network of protected areas in the region (currently none of the forests where the sifakas live is protected). The region has deposits of gold and is rich in semi-precious stones. This is one of the factors causing conflict with the establishment of a park.

Bryn Thomas reports: 'The FANAMBY office is on the left just as you enter the town coming in from Iharana. They send you into the town to pick up a guide from the mayor. The fee for a guide in 2006 was 10,000Ar each.' Part of this payment goes to Daraina and part to the village of Andranotsimaty, near the sifaka forest.

'From Daraina you need to allow about three hours for a visit to the sifakas; it takes an hour to reach them. Drive west out of Daraina for 20 minutes on the main road before turning right onto a very bad track, still passable in a Renault 4L in the dry season. After 20 more minutes you'll reach the end of this track and it's then a 20-minute walk through the forest to the dry river bed which you follow until you reach the few huts of the village of Andranotsimaty. You'll start seeing sifakas and

Lee Miller

On arriving in Daraina, we check at the offices of FANAMBY, the environmental NGO that is working to save the endangered golden-crowned sifaka. They are busy in a meeting, and we are directed into town to ask for a guide. We stop at the *hotely* to share a Coca-Cola with our driver, and before we are finished a young man arrives telling us that he will guide us for 10,000Ar (in addition to the fee for the *mairie*). We accept his price and head out in the car. After about half an hour we are directed to turn off the main road onto what can only be described as a path. We have to get out of the car several times so that it will have maximum clearance to navigate the terrain. At the end of the road we set out on foot with our guide, leaving our taxi driver to wait. The forest floor soon becomes pock-marked with holes in the ground, 4–6 feet across and equally deep. We realise that these are holes dug by gold miners; and indeed we come upon a group of people panning for gold. After hiking in the heat for another half hour, our guide points to the top of a tree where we see … a sifaka! Soon enough, he motions us along further, and there is a group of eight sifakas, all far up in the trees. As we watch them, they begin to come down to us, scrambling down the trunks, and leaping from tree to tree. Their leaping is one of the most amazing things I've ever seen. They are spring-loaded. With barely a sign that it is about to leap, a sifaka will suddenly thrust with its back legs and shoot 20–30 feet horizontally to another tree, grabbing without effort to cling to that trunk. Beautiful and thrilling. They keep coming down, peering around the trees at us, until some are just 4–5 feet away, watching us with their curious brown eyes. A little baby clings to his mother's back as she approaches. As she settles in to watch us, he asserts his independence and climbs onto a nearby branch, only to leap again onto her back at the slightest sound. Later we watch as she walks on her hind legs across the forest floor, walking in a kind of dance with her baby riding along. It is *fady* to kill them in this area and so they have no fear of humans. These are among the 25 most endangered primate species in the world; yet when you reach here, their home, they are so easily viewed. It is a remarkable and delightful opportunity, well worth the discomforts of the journey.

as soon as they see you watching them they'll come down to investigate, letting you get within a few metres of them. We were told that this was because some visitors have been feeding them.

'Back in Daraina you can have lunch (chicken, rice & veg 9,500Ar for four of us) at **Hôtel Camarade**, run by a large, jolly woman.' If you need a basic room for the night, enquire here.

For more information contact Serge Rajaobelina at FANAMBY in Tana (✆/f *22 288 78;* e *fanamby@fanamby.org.mg; www.fanamby.org.mg*).

IHARANA (VOHEMAR) I made my first ever visit here in 2006 and *loved* it! Granted, there were contributory factors: good travel companions, and the need to relax in comfort after a tough four days on Mt Marojejy. Part of its charm was also the absence of other tourists (although I'm sure that will change once the road from Ambilobe has been improved). Note that everyone seems to call it Vohemar, but it's a case of writing one thing and thinking another – for consistency.

So what has the town got to offer? The sea, for one thing, with just two beachfront hotels. This is a very different ocean to the rolling waves of Sambava, where you swim at your own risk. Iharana's bay is sheltered and protected by a reef. If you potter along the tide pools at low tide you can find a wealth of sea creatures:

little fish, shells, anemones, sea urchins, and unidentified weird things. Keep walking and you'll pass a sacred tree, hung with white cloth and zebu skulls. It's a reminder that the local culture is still very much intact in this isolated place.

The town itself is nothing special. Strung out like Sambava, the final shop is a good 2km from the beach hotels. However, there is a Bank of Africa, an internet café, a pharmacy, a lively nightclub (Zanzibar) and some surprisingly good gift shops. There are also some restaurants and no doubt some cheaper hotels than those by the beach, although I never found them.

Getting there and away The easiest way to get here is to fly to Sambava then take a *taxi-brousse* for the two-hour road journey, which takes you from wet east-coast scenery to the arid landscape of the north: quite an abrupt change. The road from Antsiranana is described earlier (see page 377). There is no longer an Air Mad service here.

Where to stay/eat

La Baie d'Iharana (16 rooms) m 032 07 131 46/032 05 131 49. A new (2006) Italian-owned upmarket hotel which was completely empty when I checked it out, but will no doubt fill up if Iharana get the numbers of tourists it – & the hotel – deserves. Set in a beautiful garden with super views of the bay from comfortable AC rooms with balconies. The spacious dining room has ocean views. Easy beach access. Excursions organised. €€€€

Sol y Mar (20 rooms) ⚫ 88 063 56; e solymar-hotel.vohemar@blueline.mg; http://hotelsolymar-vohemar.ifrance.com. Very pleasant en-suite bungalows. More expensive ones with ocean views. Frogs in the toilet at no extra charge. Laid-back atmosphere; the perfect place to relax after a tough trip (see box opposite). Meals cooked by the French manager are superb. €€€

OVERLAND FROM ANTSIRANANA TO AMBANJA AND NOSY BE

RN6 has been newly surfaced, and this route is popular with travellers heading for Nosy Be – but there is plenty to see in the area so it is a shame to rush. The 240km journey from Antsiranana to Ambanja takes about four hours (but allow at least five if you have a ferry or plane to catch). Elisabeth Cox writes: 'It is a most interesting drive, with beautiful landscapes, some markets *en route*, and cocoa plantations which we would have loved to visit if we'd had time. The street markets at Anivorano and Ambondromifehy were very colourful, like all Malagasy markets. I bought some tiny red peppers the size of redcurrants. Phew – are they *hot!*'

After those small towns comes Ambilobe (see page 377). Then on to Ambanja (95km/90mins). From Ambanja to Ankify, the departure point for Nosy Be, is 18km/30mins, the last 11km on a very bad road.

AMBANJA This is a pleasant little town set amid lush scenery.

Telephone code The area code for Ambanja is 86.

Getting there and away Most people stopping at Ambanja are on their way to or from Nosy Be. If heading north, the *taxi-brousse* station is near the main market to the north of the town. Going south they leave from the small market in the far south of Ambanja.

Where to stay/eat

Hôtel Palma Nova Probably the best hotel in Ambanja; close to the town centre. Clean, en-suite rooms with AC. €€

Hôtel Patricia A perennial *vazaha* favourite. Run by M Yvon & his wife (Chinese/Malagasy) who go out of their way to be helpful. Rooms vary in quality &

Lee Miller

We are at the beachside hotel, the Sol y Mar in Vohemar, and it is our last night together. Tomorrow Bryn and I will head west, and Hilary will return to Sambava to start her flight home. It is a faded hotel of beach bungalows, with a restaurant on the veranda. At lunch we had met the manager, a Frenchman who recounted to us how he has traveled the world only to end up in this hole. Though the hotel had clearly been set up as a seaside resort, he says that 90% of the guests stay but one night (like us). The airport is no longer functioning, and there is nowhere to go from here. It is not paradise, but rather the end of the line. He warns Hilary to take out of her guidebook the mention of *coco punch*, because he doesn't have enough call for it. He can't keep anything refrigerated because he cannot count on the electricity. He can't count on supply of anything, because no one will keep a scheduled delivery. We have landed in Casablanca.

At dinner, there are a few other guests at the outdoor tables, and some at a small cabana in the sand. Inside is a large room with a bar at one end, completely empty, with tunes from the old days wafting outside, a mix of French and Motown. There is a feeling of complete languor. The manager circulates the tables, always sardonic. Could we see the wine list? It is our last night together and we want to celebrate it. No, he doesn't have a wine list; there is no call for it, just one selection of red wine. I go to use the restroom and the electricity does not work, the washbasin has no water, and there is a frog staring at me from the windowsill. About halfway through our meal, all of the electricity inevitably goes out, for the night. But the moon is out, strong enough to cast shadows. With no music you can hear the waves gently lapping on the shore 20 feet away. The palm fronds clack in the breeze. Dinner has been the best meal we've had the entire time in Madagascar, whole fresh fish from the coral reefs, grilled perfectly. We linger over the meal and ask for lemongrass tea. We'll have to wait while they go cut the lemongrass first. It is a perfect evening in a forsaken paradise, and I've grown to love this place.

price, so there is something to suit everyone. Usually shut in the afternoon (for siesta) so be prepared to wait. There is an excellent Malagasy cookbook for sale here, written by M Yvon's sister. €€

🏠 **Hôtel Bougainvilleas** Rooms have a shower & toilet. €€
🏠 **Sambirano** ➘ 86 920 60. Low-priced rooms. €

ANKIFY AREA This beautiful area of coast is being developed as a resort, and has some very good hotels. But don't expect a proper village here – there are no shops or other ways of whiling away the time as you are waiting for the ferry.

🏠 **Where to stay/eat**

🏠 **Le Baobab** m 032 07 208 87. Located about 2km northwest of the docks, nestled between rocky cliffs & a beach that overlooks Nosy Komba. Very pleasant bungalows with separate bathrooms, hot water, table fans & mosquito nets. Friendly, English-speaking manager (Nadina Yuon). Bill Love stays here regularly: 'The grounds are beautifully planted in bougainvillea, palms, ylang-ylang etc, with paved paths between cottages. The restaurant/bar is located on top of another hill, open-air under a huge thatched roof, & is very comfy & with a

great view of the bay. Crowned lemurs pass over the trees nearby, & the panther chameleons are among the most beautiful of all – greenish bodies with brilliant blue bands.' & 'some excellent birdwatching was to be had from the comfort of a sun-lounger! The food was good & there was a good selection of wine at the bar. The electricity comes on at 17.00 & goes off at 24.00' (Chris Santry). €€€€
🏠 **Hôtel la Mer** (3 bungalows, 2 rooms) m 032 04 822 61; e info@hotel-la-mer.com; www.hotel-la-

Rupert Parker

With many years' experience of travelling by *taxi-brousse* I know that they carry anything and everything – bicycles, chickens, baskets of fish all crammed in with people filled to bursting point. On New Year's Eve we were on the way to Vohemar from Sambava on the newly surfaced road. Strapped to the roof were a gaggle of geese ready for the festive pot, baskets of mangos and other fruit, as well as everybody's luggage – oh. and a large sofa. About halfway we were flagged down by the police – just the obligatory security check, I thought, and we'd be on our way soon. The driver was called in to the police hut and a few minutes later emerged with two gun-toting officers, a couple of geese, and a rather desperate-looking prisoner handcuffed to one of the policeman. He cleared the seat in front of us and the prison detail took their places. Now what happens in a crowded *taxi-brousse* when a prisoner tries to make a break for it? Do the police start shooting, and what happens if he leans over and grabs me as a hostage? I spent a very tense couple of hours mulling all this over, but of course we reached Vohemar safely and the prisoner was taken off to spend an unhappy Christmas in a Malagasy cell.

mer.com. German-run hotel near a beach for swimming, 4.5km from Ankify. Rooms are European standard with large bathrooms inc toilet & bidet. Very good food (though service often slow) with stunning views over the bay. Boat transfers to Nosy Be. €€€€

⌂ **Le Dauphin Bleu** (7 bungalows) m 032 04 667 81. Stone bungalows with hot water. B/fast served on a beach terrace. A lovely hotel a few kilometres beyond the Baobab, with a view of Nosy Komba. German-owned, with a large garden & private beach. €€€

CONTINUING SOUTH FROM AMBANJA TO MAHAJANGA For a description of this journey see *Chapter 16*.

BAYS AND INLETS ACCESSIBLE TO YACHTS

The bays below could be reached by adventurous hikers or cyclists (many are near villages) but are visited mainly by yachties (lucky devils!).

RUSSIAN BAY (HELONDRANON AMBAVATOBY) This is a beautiful and remote place opposite the Nosy Be archipelago. It provides excellent anchorages, all-round shelter and is a traditional 'hurricane hole'. The marine life in the bay itself is terrific, offering wonderful snorkelling and diving, especially on the reefs outside the entrance. There is excellent fishing too. In the right season (October to December) whales are commonly sighted in the bay. This is also one of the best spots in which to seek the very rare whale shark. The beaches are known turtle-nesting sites. The moist tropical deciduous woods there harbour abundant birdlife, reptiles and lemurs, and there is a choice of trails for day hikes.

The bay's name dates back to an incident in 1905 during the Russo-Japanese war when a Russian warship, the *Vlötny*, anchored there. The order was to attack any passing Japanese ship, but the crew took one look at life in Madagascar and realised that they did not wish to wage war nor to return to Russia. They had barely organised a mutiny before their officers gave in, having taken one look at the lovely Malagasy women. The ship was hidden in the reaches of Russian Bay and twice emerged to trade with pirate vessels in the Mozambique Channel before they ran out of fuel for the boilers. The Russians were decimated by malaria, but the survivors quickly adapted to their new home, living by fishing. The last one died in 1936. The Russians sold anything they could remove from the ship, but its remains can still be seen at low tide.

BARAMAHAMAY BAY (MAROAKA) The Baramahamay River is navigable for about 3km inland and provides a beautiful, well-sheltered anchorage with verdant hills behind sunny, white beaches. The wide bay is conspicuous as a large gap in the coastline. Yachties should approach on the north side of the bay and anchor near the villages in 8m over sand and mud. These villages are known also for their blacksmiths, who make large knives and *pangas*. One of the small villages here is known for its wild honey, and there is a pool with good drinking water.

Your chances of seeing the (very rare) resident Madagascar fish eagles here are good.

BERANGOMAINA POINT The bay inside this headland is an attractive, well-sheltered anchorage. Good visibility is needed to access the bay, however, as there are many scattered reef patches. The channel is at its deepest on the north side, where the depth exceeds 15m right up to the reef. Anchor off the beach before the village, in 10m over a mud bottom. This place is for self-sufficient travellers only; no provisions are available.

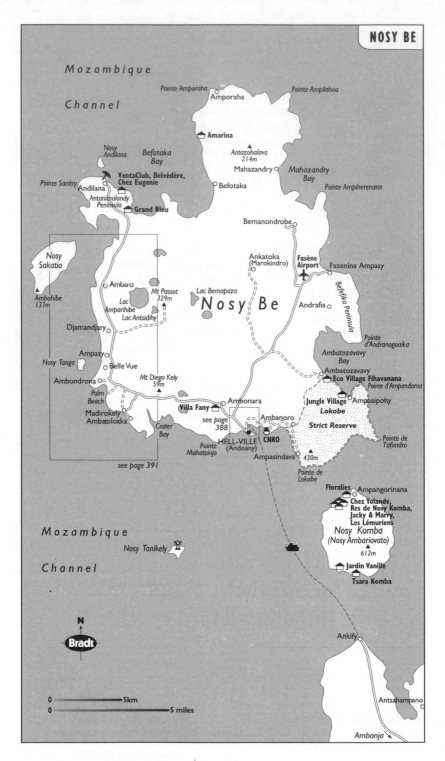

15

Nosy Be

The name means 'big island' and is pronounced *nossy bay* by the local Sakalava people, although *noos bay* is nearer the highlands pronunciation. It is blessed, in the driest months, with an almost perfect climate (sunshine with brief showers). Fertile and prosperous, with the heady scent of ylang-ylang blossoms giving it the tourist-brochure name of 'Perfumed Isle', this is the place to come for a rest – providing you can afford it. Compared with the rest of Madagascar, Nosy Be is expensive.

Nosy Be developed tourism long before mainland Madagascar, so inevitably the island seems touristy or 'commercialised' to adventurous travellers. Since the recent demise of the sugar industry, all available land is being bought up for hotel development. This, in turn, has pushed prices ever higher. That said, Nosy Be provides a taste of everything that is special to Madagascar, from good seafood to beaches, from chameleons to lemurs, so for this reason it is ideal for those with very limited time who are looking for a hassle-free holiday. It also has several options for real luxury – not always easy to find in Madagascar.

All of the accessible beaches on Nosy Be have now been taken over by hotels. None is perfect for swimming; they shelve too gradually so the water is shallow at high tide and they are a long walk out at low tide. There are sometimes the vicious sandflies known locally as *moka fohy* (see box, page 324).

TELEPHONE CODE The area code for Nosy Be is 86. Landlines seldom work, however, due to poor maintenance.

HISTORY

Nosy Be's charms were recognised as long ago as 1649 when the English colonel Robert Hunt wrote: 'I do believe, by God's blessing, that not any part of the world is more advantageous for a plantation, being every way as well for pleasure as well as profit, in my estimation.' Hunt was attempting to set up an English colony on the island, at that time known as Assada, but failed because of hostile natives and disease.

Future immigrants, both accidental and intentional, contributed to Nosy Be's racial variety. Shipwrecked Indians built a magnificent settlement several centuries ago in the southeast of the island, where the ruins can still be seen. The crew of a Russian ship that arrived during the Russo-Japanese war of 1904–5 are buried in the Hell-Ville cemetery. Other arrivals were Arabs, Comorans and – more recently – Europeans flocking to Madagascar's foremost holiday resort.

When King Radama I was completing his wars of conquest, the Boina kings took refuge in Nosy Be. First they sought protection from the Sultan of Zanzibar, who sent a warship in 1838 then, two years later, they requested help from Commander Passot who had docked his ship at Nosy Be. The Frenchman was only too happy to oblige and asked Admiral de Hell, the governor of Bourbon Island (now Réunion), to place Nosy Be under the protection of France.

The island was formally annexed in 1841.

GETTING THERE AND AWAY

BY AIR There are now direct Air Mad flights from Milan as well as Réunion, so Nosy Be may be your first taste of Madagascar. Otherwise there are daily flights to/from Tana and three times weekly to Antsiranana. Mahajanga is served only once a week (Sunday) by ATTR.

BY BOAT
From Mahajanga (m *032 02 216 86; f 62 226 86 (Mahajanga). Tickets 70,000/40,000Ar 1st/3rd class*) The *Jean-Pierre Calloc'h* leaves Mahajanga on Fridays arriving in Nosy Be the following day. It returns on Mondays. The times vary according to the tides. Although this no longer fits my earlier description of being 'more a cruise than a ferry', it is still more comfortable than many Malagasy ferries, with a first and second class lounge, a bar, a disco, televisions and airline seats. It also carries cars. This ferry is also the main supplier of fresh fruit and vegetables to Nosy Be. At the time of writing the boat was out of service due to cyclone damage.

From Ankify Nosy Be's nearest mainland town of any size is Ambanja; taxis leave from outside the Hôtel de Ville for Ankify, the departure point for Nosy Be. Speedboats to Hell-Ville leave 'hourly' (Malagasy time!) and take 30 minutes; it should cost 10,000Ar but local operators have a habit of overcharging *vazaha*. You shouldn't pay extra for your luggage, but some feel that it's easier to give in on this rather than argue the point too strenuously.

GETTING AROUND THE ISLAND

There is one well-maintained road: from the airport to Andilana via Hell-Ville. All the others are tracks, sometimes rendered impassable by cyclones. Transport (on the good road) is by *taxi-brousse* or private taxi (of which there are plenty).

BY TAXI Shared taxis are relatively inexpensive, costing a flat rate (currently 5,000Ar). Private taxis also operate on a fixed rate, but these are usually negotiable.

VEHICLE HIRE Many of the hotels rent out mountain bikes (VTT) and mopeds/motorbikes. If you hire a motorbike, check your insurance policy: many companies do not cover motorcycle accidents.

🚗 **Nosy Easy Rent** Hell-Ville; ☎ 86 063 08; m 033 11 611 00; e nosyeasy.rent@wanadoo.mg; www.nosyeasyrent.com

🚗 **Nosy Red Cars** Ambataloaka; ☎ 86 620 35; e nosyredcars@simicro.mg. Rents out self-drive Mini Mokes for 2 people.

🚗 **Moto Mada** Ambataloaka; m 032 02 680 25. Motorbike hire.

🚗 **Nosy Velo** Hell-Ville, c/o Homeopharma; ☎ 86 614 15/500 41; m 032 04 611 21; e nosyvelo@yahoo.fr; www.vtt-trekking.com. Mountain bike hire; guided bicycle excursions on Nosy Be & the mainland.

🚗 **ZigZag** ☎ 86 633 99. Bicycle & moped hire. English spoken.

TREKKING AND MOUNTAIN BIKING The following companies offer trekking or bicycling tours in Nosy Be and the mainland.

Green Adventures m 032 07 573 12/033 12 260 50; e greenadventures@hotmail.it

Evasions Sans Frontière ☎ 86 062 44 ; m 032 11 002 96; e esf.nosybe@wanadoo.mg

SAILING

▲ **Alefa** Madirokely; ☎/f 86 615 89; m 032 07 127 07; e alefa@simicro.mg. Round-island luxury sailing pirogue trips. Trips last 2–22 days, camping with cooks, tents etc provided.

▲ **Indian Ocean Charters** e info@indianoceancharters; www.indianoceancharters.com. For specialised sailing/diving holidays. South African run.

▲ **Madanautique** m 032 07 072 13; e manau@wanadoo.mg; www.madanautique.com (in French). Excellent catamarans for hire, usually for a week.

▲ **Madavoile** (also known as **Mad Planet**) ☎ 86 065 55; m 032 04 223 55 & 032 04 426 67; e mad.planet@simicro.mg; www.madavoile.com. Well-run sailing trips; efficient & helpful. Also deep-sea fishing & diving.

▲ **Tropical Adventures** Hell-Ville; m 032 04 798 80; e info@star-cat.net. The *Star Cat* catamaran.

DIVING The once-lovely coral around Nosy Be itself has sadly been destroyed, but the pristine little islands of the region offer some of the best diving in Madagascar. May to October are the recommended months. Below are just some of the many dive centres in Nosy Be.

↝ **Madagascar Dive Club** Madirokely (behind Marlin Club Hotel); ☎ 86 060 46; e madiro@simicro.mg. Member of PADI International Resort Association.
↝ **Madaplouf Bemoko** Between Djamanjary & Andilana; ☎ 86 612 69; e madaplouf@wanadoo.mg. Run by a doctor & marine biologist.
↝ **Manta Dive Club** Madirokely (near Mandira Hotel); m 032 07 207 10; e manta@wanadoo.mg.
↝ **Oceane's Dream** Ambatoloaka; ☎ 86 614 26/610 17; m 032 07 127 82; e oceaned@wanadoo.mg; www.oceanesdream.com. A long-standing & reputable operator. Organises diving trips to many of the outlying islands & even to the Comoros.

↝ **Sakatia Lodge** ☎ 86 615 14/610 91; m 032 07 126 75; e sakatialodge@netclub.mg. See Nosy Sakatia (page 398).
↝ **Aventura Diving** (Roland Fivat) Madirokely; ☎ 86 06 316; m 032 04 888 80; e info@aventura-diving.com; www.aventura-diving.com.
↝ **Tropical Diving** Hôtel Coco-Plage, Ambatoloaka; m 032 07 127 90; e tropical.diving@wanadoo.mg or tropicaldiving@simicro.mg; www.tropical-diving.com.

DEEP-SEA FISHING

↣ **Manou** Madirokely; ☎ 86 062 12; e manoufishing@simicro.mg.
↣ **Fishing World** Andilana; ☎ 86 610 80; e fishingworld@simicro.mg

↣ **Barracuda** Ambatoloaka; ☎ 86 620 66; m 032 02 629 92; e barracuda@simicro.mg
↣ **Bouana Pêche** Ambatoloaka; ☎ 86 06 304; m 032 04 94 448; e bouanapeche@wanadoo.mg

HELL-VILLE (ANDOANY)

The name comes from Admiral de Hell rather than an evocation of the state of the town. Hell-Ville is actually quite a smart little place (at least by Malagasy standards), its main street lined with boutiques and tourist shops. There is a market selling fresh fruit and vegetables (which may also be purchased from roadside stalls) and an interesting cemetery, especially if you are around on All Souls' Day (1 November).

Nosy Be **HELL-VILLE (ANDOANY)**

15

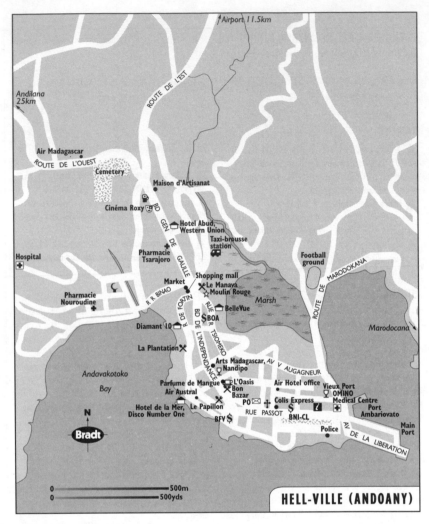

HELL-VILLE (ANDOANY)

![icon] **WHERE TO STAY** There is a good choice of inexpensive hotels in Hell-Ville. For budget travellers a night or two here while you investigate the cheaper beach hotels is almost essential. Things change so fast in Nosy Be that you are certain to find places to stay that are not listed in this chapter.

Mid range €€€

![icon] **Hôtel Diamant 10** (15 rooms) 10 La Batterie (near Hôtel de la Mer); ☎ 86 614 48; e madexof@metclub.mg. Comfortable rooms with AC.

![icon] **La Plantation** (6 rooms) m 032 07 934 45/032 400 45 08; e mdbr-plantation@hotmail.com. Small & intimate; better known as a restaurant.

![icon] **BelleVue Hotel** (15 rooms) Rue R Tsiomeko (just south of Shell station); ☎ 86 613 84; e bellevuehotel_nosybe@yahoo.fr. Hot water. Some rooms with AC; others with fan.

![icon] **Hôtel Abud** (30 rooms) ☎ 86 610 55/612 57. A 5-storey building, centrally located above Chez Abud souvenir shop. A perennial favourite with comfortable small rooms, some with en-suite toilet & balcony overlooking the street. Restaurant.

Budget €€

🏠 **Hôtel George V** (8 rooms) La Poudrière; ✆ 86 615 61; m 032 04 307 10. Low-cost rooms with fans.

🏠 **Hôtel de la Mer** (24 rooms) Bd du Docteur Manceau; ✆ 86 617 53. The once-infamous 'Hôtel de Merde' had a brief renaissance but has once again fallen on hard times. Check out the rooms before staying here. Great view from the restaurant.

✖ WHERE TO EAT

✖ **Le Manava** m 032 04 394 54. Above the Moulin Rouge Discotheque. Considered by local resident Irene Boswell to be the most reliable & best restaurant on Nosy Be. Tasty food, huge quantities & very reasonable prices.

✖ **Le Papillon** ✆ 86 615 82. On the right (as you walk towards the harbour) just before the Catholic church, where Bd de l'Indépendance becomes Rue Passot. Good food, especially pizzas.

✖ **La Plantation** m 032 07 934 45/032 400 45 08. In the Battery area behind the market.

Recommended as being 'a very nice place with sometimes delicious food, run by a European couple with long experience in catering. The meals are served outside on a typical veranda, overlooking a lively Malagasy quarter.'

🍴 **Oasis** ✆ 86 611 79. Across the road from Le Papillon. A low-priced snack bar & café on the main road, opposite BVF bank. Fresh croissants & pains au chocolat daily. Good cakes & ice cream. You can watch the world go by from the terrace while you eat.

NIGHTLIFE

☆ **Moulin Rouge** Discotheque near the market; ✆ 86 610 36. Serves pizzas during the day; disco every night. ⊕ 21.30–dawn.

☆ **Disco Number One** In a basement beneath Hôtel de la Mer. Thu & Sat.

♀ **Vieux Port** A popular place at the old port. 'Wild nights. Usually gets going around 22.00, with live music. Great salegy and reggae music.'

♀ **Bar Nandipo** ✆ 86 613 52. French-run bar in the centre of Hell-Ville (near town hall). Popular with expats. Pool table & darts. The best place for a Happy Hour cocktail.

MUSIC FESTIVAL The Donia music festival is held each Pentecost (May/June). A four-day celebration takes place in the Hell-Ville football ground southeast of town. Groups come here from Mauritius, Réunion and Seychelles, as well as all parts of Madagascar. 'I would highly recommend a visit. A great party, friendly crowd and good music. But be prepared for the basic (ie: non-existent) loo facilities' (Sebastian Bulmer). Hotels get very booked up at this time.

SHOPPING The large number of tourists visiting Nosy Be has made this one of Madagascar's main centres for souvenir production, providing a unique chance to buy direct from the makers and benefit the local people. Mind you, much of the stuff for sale in boutiques and stalls comes from Tana. Unique to Nosy Be and Nosy Komba are the carved pirogues, clay animals and Richelieu-embroidered curtains and tablecloths.

Handicraft sellers frequent the road to the port and there are some high-quality goods in Hell-Ville's many boutiques. The best shops in town are **Chez Abud**, which has the widest variety of goods, and **Arts Madagascar** which also has a good selection at reasonable prices. **Parfum des Mangue** is recommended as having a huge selection of goods and friendly, helpful sales staff. The prices are reasonable as well. It is near the Oasis snack bar.

There's an **indoor shopping 'mall'** close to the *taxi-brousse* station. This is not only a convenient shopping centre with gift and clothes shops, but also the best place in Hell-Ville for **internet** access. The connection is fast and relatively cheap.

INTERNET In the Maki Commercial Centre near the market. They can download your digital photos and burn them to a CD for 5,000Ar. *60Ar/min (min 10mins).*

MEDICAL

✚ **Espace Médicale** This well-respected organisation is located outside Helle-Ville on the road to Andilana. There is always a doctor on call.

Pharmacies There are two well-stocked pharmacies in Hell-Ville. One or other is always open as a *pharmacie de garde* for emergencies (this changes each week but the taxi drivers usually know as there are announcements on the radio). Pharmacie Tsarajoro is on the main street north of the market, almost opposite Chez Abud (↘ *86 613 82*). Pharmacie Nouroudine is in Andavakatoko not far from the small market to the west of town down the road from the main market (↘ *86 610 38*). There is also a good pharmacy, Toko, in Madirokely, near Ambatoloaka.

MONEY Credit cards are gaining acceptance in Nosy Be but only Visa; very few hotels take MasterCard. Banks and their hours are listed below, but note that they usually work only a half day before a holiday.

Banks

$ **BNI** (Crédit Lyonnaise) On the road down to the port. Often has the best exchange rates. Changes travellers' cheques & can give cash advances on Visa. ⊕ *Mon–Fri 08.00–15.30.*

$ **BOA** Rue Gallieni. Closest bank to the market. Gives cash advances on MasterCard but takes all day. Representative for Western Union. ⊕ *Mon–Fri, 07.30–11.30 & 14.30–16.30.*

$ **BFV** Close to Oasis, almost opposite the post office. Gives cash advances on Visa. Representative for Western Union. ⊕ *Mon–Fri 07.30–11.30 & 14.00–16.00.*

SUPERMARKETS, YACHT SUPPLIES AND REPAIRS

The best supermarket is said to be Big Bazar in Daresalama, near Ambatoloaka. In Hell-Ville, Shamion is recommended, but locals in the know go to Leon-Cheuk, an independent grocer opposite the market. Helpful and friendly. Mécabe, in Hell-Ville, sells spare parts for yachts and will facilitate repairs.

AIRLINE OFFICES

✈ **Air Madagascar** North Hell-Ville; ↘ 86 613 57/613 60. ⊕ *Mon–Fri 08.00–11.00 & 14.00–17.00; Sat 08.00–09.30.*

✈ **Agence Ario** Rue Passot, Hell-Ville; ↘ 86 612 40; e arionos@dts.mg. Represents Air Mauritius & Air Austral. ⊕ *Mon–Fri 08.00–12.00 & 14.00–17.00; Sat 08.00–10.00.*

 BEACH HOTELS

Most visitors prefer to stay in beach hotels located mainly along the sandy western coast. Nosy Be now competes with other tropical islands in the quality of its hotels, most of which have ocean views, swimming pools, and extras such as massage, jacuzzi and the like.

Hoteliers separate the west coast into seven zones, including Hell-Ville and Nosy Komba. For simplification I have used (mostly) the same divisions, although now there are hotel developments all down coast this is fairly arbitrary. There is also beach accommodation in the north and in other areas such as Lokobe and some of the outlying islands. These are listed under the appropriate headings.

Note that if you choose a hotel north of Djamandjary, you will not easily find transport to Ambatoloaka or Hell-Ville if you fancy a meal elsewhere or some nightlife.

All hotels do airport transfers, costing about € 10.

The price-bands are for the high season (mid-July to mid-September, and over the Christmas holiday). Low-season rates are cheaper. Below is just a sample of what is available: with the speed of change in Nosy Be it is impossible to keep up!

The following sections are ordered as encountered going north to south.

BEFOTAKA BAY Nosy Be's first four-star hotel opened in 2006 on the western part of the island's northern peninsula, about an hour's drive from the airport. Other hotels are being built in the area.

🏠 **Amarina Hotel** (37 rooms) 📞 86 92 128; m 032 07 307 47; f 86 921 29; e amarinahotel@simicro.mg or amarinahotel@blueline.mg; www.amarinahotel.com. Check out the website — if you like it, you'll like the hotel. This hotel has the works: Molton Brown toiletries, Malagasy handcrafted soap, AC, DVD player, hairdryer & fine linen. Enormous pool, open-air jacuzzi, large open-air restaurant, beach bar, watersports & dive centre. Good snorkelling from the hotel beach. Excursions & massage. Special attention to honeymooners. Reports from readers who've stayed here vary. Some say it is too isolated, so that excursions away from the resort are problematic; others feel it is a bit 'over the top' & at odds with what makes Madagascar special. But some love it for the same reason: it's a 4-star hotel with all the trappings. ♨

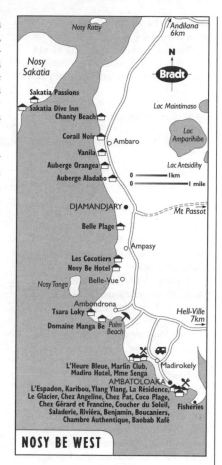

NOSY BE WEST

ANDILANA Northern Nosy Be is the most beautiful part of the island, with good beaches, though it has succumbed to development. It is 45 minutes' drive from Hell-Ville.

🏠 **VentaClub** (205 rooms) 📞 86 634 60; e andilana.booking@ventaglio.com; www.ventaclub-andilana.com. Under new management so the name may change. This is the only all-inclusive hotel in Madagascar, using the tried-and-tested Club Med format. 'They give you a green bracelet when you arrive, & this entitles you to 3 sumptuous meals a day (lunch & dinner are 5-course with heaps of fresh shellfish & fish), all drinks, snacks, watersports etc; Italian-owned & super-professional'. Remember that the rates include absolutely everything. Facilities for disabled travellers too. Must be pre-booked. ♨

🏠 **Auberge Le Grand Bleu** (10 bungalows) 📞 86 920 23; m 033 14 248 16; f 86 634 08;

e legrandbleu@dts.mg; www.legrandbleunosybe.com. French-owned; set high on a hill to the east of the road. Splendid views. No beach, but an exceptional swimming pool. 'The water just drops off & past it you get the most magnificent view over the ocean. In many years of visiting hotels & flicking through travel brochures, I've yet to see another pool as nice. Gorgeous' (Chris Howles). Boat excursions, sailing, fishing, waterskiing, sea-kayaking, quad bikes for hire. €€€€€

🏠 **Belvédère** (6 rooms) 📞 86 611 22; m 032 04 619 96. A few simple bungalows with some more comfortable rooms. Set on a hill close to the beach; lovely view. Below is the restaurant Chez

Loulou which does excellent meals & a good Sunday buffet. €€€€

🏠 **Chez Eugenie** (5 rooms) m 032 40 634 48; e chezeugenie@yahoo.fr. Chris Howles could barely contain her enthusiasm for this new place just around the corner from VentaClub: 'We stumbled upon it hot, dusty, muddy, short of cash, thirsty & hungry having walked along the coast from Le Grand Bleu. The French owner welcomed us like he'd been waiting for us most of his life! He fed us huge meals of the best poulet coco & seafood salad we had in the whole country.' Chris reports that the rooms are equally lovely & seem good value. B/fast inc. €€€€

ORANGEA A pleasant area with good, gently shelving beaches.

🏠 **Corail Noir** (9 bungalows & 15 rooms) ☎ 86 920 52/53; f 86 920 54; e corailnoir@ netclub.mg; www.corailnoir.com. 'Built & managed by a friendly & enthusiastic Italian/Malagasy couple, it is an incredibly attractive, comfortable & relaxing place to unwind. There are ground-floor rooms with little front garden, 1st floor with balcony, plus bungalows with decks out front. Spaced amongst beautiful & well-maintained grounds, with a fabulous open-air bar/restaurant & swimming pool, the whole complex sits next to the beach looking out across the sea & to Nosy Sakatia. Buildings are mostly made from stone, bamboo & palm leaves & decorated very simply in natural colours & accessories'. Boat trips, diving school, ping-pong etc. ☷

🏠 **Hôtel Vanila** (35 rooms & 6 suites) ☎ 86 921 01/02; f 86 921 05; e vanilahotel@simicro.mg; www.vanila-hotel.com. About 3km north of Dzamandzar. Very comfortable rooms with fan & private terrace. Beautiful garden. One of the better hotels in Nosy Be; very well managed; lovely swimming pool; variable food. Large – you won't get a feeling of intimacy here. Visa accepted. ☷

🏠 **Chanty Beach** (5 apts) ☎ 86 614 73; f 86 614 74; e cherz@wanadoo.mg; http://travel.to/Chanty-Beach/. 2 luxury dbl self-catering apts & 3 en-suite rooms with spacious veranda & AC. All facing a private beach. Beach restaurant. €€€€€

🏠 **Auberge Orangea** (10 bungalows & more under construction) Bemoko; ☎ 86 610 67/927 90; e orangea@wanadoo.mg; www.orangea-nosybe.com. Owned & run by an enthusiastic French-Belgian couple, this is an exceptionally attractive & relaxing place. Rooms with fans set in a beautiful garden with pool. Very good food – must be ordered in advance. ☷

🏠 **Auberge Aladabo** (8 bungalows) About 2km north of Djamandjary; ☎ 86 922 00; m 032 02 323 93. Attractive traditional bungalows on the seafront. €€€€

DJAMANDJARY Djamandjary is an ugly small town with some strange igloo-shaped cement houses. When I first came to Nosy Be in 1976 I was told that they were cyclone-proof housing provided by a relief organisation. But local resident Irene Boswell says they were built by South Africans, nostalgic for *rondavels*, as accommodation for the workers at the nearby sugar factory. Either way, the *vazaha* who introduced them did not know about Malagasy beliefs. It is essential for a house to have corners, one of which is reserved for the ancestors. The 'igloos' were quickly abandoned.

Although the beach here is uninspiring it is shaded by coconut palms, and a chain of hotels stretches down the coast as far as Ambatoloaka.

The shallow gradient of beaches from Djamandjary southwards makes low-tide swimming difficult.

AMPASY AREA

🏠 **Belle Plage Suite** (16 bungalows) ☎ 86 06 184; e hotel@belleplage.com; www.belleplage.com. Swiss-owned; established since 1995. Right on a private beach. Plain rooms & small swimming pool. €€€€€

🏠 **Les Cocotiers** (26 bungalows) ☎ 86 068 00; m 033 14 448 00; e cocotier@wanadoo.mg; http://lescocotiers.nemo.it. Italian-owned concrete bungalows on the beach facing a small island (accessible at low tide). Pleasant rooms with en-suite bathrooms & fans. Diving; bike hire. €€€€€

⌂ **Nosy Be Hotel** (2 bungalows & 36 rooms) ☎ 86 061 51/929 04; e nosy.be.hotel@ simicro.mg; www.nosybehotel.com. Architecturally

sympathetic bungalows set in a pleasant garden with pool. The outdoor restaurant has a sea view. Good range of activities inc diving, hang-gliding, quad-biking, billiards, ping-pong & massage. €€€€€

AMBONDRONA AND MADIROKELY South of Djamandjary; some prefer this area to the busier, noisier Ambatoloaka. If you don't want to eat at your hotel it's close enough to walk to Ambatoloaka and get a taxi back.

⌂ **Domaine Manga Be** Ambondrona; ☎ 86 060 88; m 032 42 092 82; e info@ domainemangabe.com; www.domainemangabe.com. Range of accommodation from rooms to apts & bungalows. €€€€€–♨.

⌂ **Tsara Loky** (6 bungalows & 6 rooms) Ambondrona; ☎ 86 610 22; Malagasy-run. Simple en-suite bungalows with fans. Rooms have shared facilities. €€€€

⌂ **L'Heure Bleue** (11 bungalows) Madirokely; ☎ 86 060 20; m 032 02 003 61; e heure.bleue@simicro.mg; www.heurebleue.com. Wooden A-frame bungalows on Madirokely beach. Swimming pool. Restaurant (open only to guests). Popular & beautifully situated with stunning views over Ambatoloaka Bay. B/fast inc if you book online. €€€€€

⌂ **Chez Madame Senga** (6 bungalows) Madirokely; m 032 40 378 01. Simple en-suite bungalows with fan. Good restaurant, well known for its local

specialities. Very good value. €€€€

⌂ **Marlin Club** (16 rooms & 6 suites) Madirokely; ☎ 86 610 70; m 032 07 127 62; f 86 614 45; e marlin.club@simcro.mg; www.marlin-club.com. Very comfortable rooms & a few bungalows (but not on the beach). As the name suggests, this is mainly a deep-sea fishing centre, but it also runs adventure trips to outlying islands such as Mitsio & Iranja. Also watersports. Good restaurant. B/fast inc. €€€€€

⌂ **Madiro Hotel** (16 rooms) Madirokely; ☎ 86 060 46; m 032 04 386 77/032 04 750 48; e contact@madirohotel.com; www.madirohotel.com. Italian-owned. A 1-storey building with adjacent rooms facing a large swimming pool in a lovely garden; some have AC, others with fans. Rather alarmingly, they have a 'body-building room'. The Manta Dive Club is here – one of the best dive centres on the island..€€€€€–♨

AMBATOLOAKA (AND DARESALAMA) Once upon a time this was a charming fishing village. Now it is full of bars and good-time girls. In an effort to clamp down on sex tourism, some of the hotels are wary about taking single men. However, this lively centre offers the best options for inexpensive places to stay in Nosy Be and is the place to be if you're looking for nightlife rather than somewhere to relax.

Top end €€€€€

⌂ **Chez Pat** (6 rooms) m 032 40 247 86/032 04 793 15; e patricia.chaponnay@wanadoo.fr. Renovated rooms on the beach. Bar & restaurant on a beautiful terrace; French dishes & pizza.

⌂ **Hôtel l'Espadon** (21 bungalows) ☎ 86 921 47/920 43; m 032 07 125 03;

e hotel.espadon@malagasy.com; www.espadon-nosy-be.com. Some bungalows face the ocean, others are set back in a very pleasant garden. Very comfortable with AC & TV. Sunday barbeque. Specialises in deep-sea fishing. Visa & MasterCard accepted.

Upper range €€€€

⌂ **Les Boucaniers** (18 bungalows) ☎ 86 620 38; m 032 02 675 20; e info@lesboucaniers.com; www.hotel-lesboucaniers.com. Not a beachfront hotel but rather on the hillside opposite Chez Gérard et Francine. Tastefully furnished bungalows, some with ocean views. Satellite TV in the bar.

⌂ **Hôtel L'Ylang Ylang** (12 rooms) ☎ 86 926 32/928 13; m 032 07 126 93; e hotel.lylang@ wanadoo.mg; www.hotel-lylangylang.com. All en suite with wall safe & minibar; some with AC. British-owned & very good value. A good location, excellent cuisine, & friendly service. Visa accepted. B/fast inc.

Chez Gérard et Francine (10 rooms) ✆ 86 061 05; m 032 07 127 93; e geretfra@simicro.mg; www.hotelgerardetfrancine.com. At the southern end of Ambatoloaka, tucked up against the cliff & set in a beautifully-maintained & peaceful garden, this delightful small hotel is ideal for families, couples or single people who want to steer clear of the local nightlife (if you're a single man you will want to make this clear). All rooms with ceiling fan & en-suite shower; 7 have verandas. Deservedly popular so often full. Visa accepted. B/fast inc.

Clair de Lune (6 bungalows) m 032 04 197 18; e lescheres@netclub.mg. At Matasabory, above Ambatoloaka. A charming & quiet small hotel set in a lovely garden. French-run (Louis & Brigitte). Single men not accepted. Own generator (handy in case of powercuts).

La Résidence Ambatoloaka (12 rooms) ✆ 86 610 91; f 86 616 43. This once-popular place is under new management but struggling to regain its former position; the restaurant is said to be very good, however. En-suite rooms with AC. Good terrace/lounge.

Hôtel Benjamin (Villa Razambe) (6 rooms) ✆ 86 060 93; m 032 02 408 13; e hotelbenjamin@simicro.mg; www.hotelbenjamin-nosybe.com. Very comfortable bungalows, each with a terrace, set in a nice garden with a swimming pool. Very good value.

Mid range €€€

Hôtel Coco Plage (11 rooms) m 032 07 769 64. About 1km south of the village.

La Riviéra (5 bungalows) Rte d'Ambatoloaka; ✆ 86 614 05/612 26. Bungalows with en-suite bathrooms, hot water & fans.

Coucher du Soleil (7 bungalows) ✆/f 86 616 20. Hotel & Restaurant; very clean, comfortable en-suite bungalows (basic showers, new toilets). Not on the beach, but sea view.

Chambre Authentique Clean bungalows with en-suite bathroom, mosquito nets & fans. Conveniently placed in the middle of the village.

AMBONARA This village to the east of Hell-Ville may lack the glamour of the sandy beaches and luxury hotels of the west, but makes up for it in isolation.

Villa Fany (8 rooms) ✆ 86 611 70; m 032 02 343 79; e villafany@villafany.com; www.villafany.com. Good-value accommodation and restaurant away from the over-development of the west coast. €€

✗ **WHERE TO EAT** Most of the main hotels have good restaurants, with L'Ylang Ylang particularly recommended. Because there are frequent powercuts, hotels without their own generators have problems keeping their food fresh. Seafood can be risky under such circumstances. You will be guaranteed a good meal at Le Manava in Hell-Ville.

✗ **Chez Angeline** ✆ 86 616 21. Before the arrival of big-time tourism in Nosy Be, this was its most popular little restaurant, famous for its seafood & poulet au coco. Worth checking out.

✗ **Baobab Kafé** Opposite Résidence Ambatoloaka. Serves snacks as well as main meals.

✗ **Le Restaurant d'Ambonara** ✆ 86 613 67; e ambonara@wanadoo.mg. A distinctive restaurant situated in an old coffee plantation.

✗ **Karibou** ✆ 86 616 47. Italian food, inc pizzas.

✗ **Soleil** A lively bar/restaurant.

✗ **La Saladerie** ✆ 86 614 52. Salads & sandwiches. Deservedly popular.

NIGHTLIFE

☆ **Le Djembe** 'The best-equipped nightclub in the whole of Mada: AC, high-tech lighting and special effects, mirrored walls … even a waterfall behind the bar' (S Edghill).

☆ **Le Jackpot** A gambling place next to the Djembe nightclub. More downmarket than Le Casino.

☆ **Le Casino** Set on a hillside like an old plantation house, diagonally opposite on the right as you leave Ambatoloaka. Fruit machines, roulette, blackjack etc. Live music Sat nights.

☆ **La Sirène** Opposite Le Djembe; if one is closed the other will be open.

☆ **Le Lion d'Or** Not far from Le Djembe. A bar frequented mainly by locals. Dancing on Sat nights.

EXCURSIONS

MONT PASSOT A popular excursion is the trip to the island's highest point, Mont Passot. *En route* there are good views of a series of deep-blue crater lakes, which are said to contain crocodiles, as well as being the home of the spirits of the Sakalava and Antakarana princes. Supposedly it is *fady* to fish there, or to smoke, wear trousers or any garment put on over the feet, or a hat, while on the lakes' shores. That said, it may be that the tourists have frightened the spirits away, since my local informant has never heard of these prohibitions. It is, in any case, difficult to get down to the water since the crater sides are very steep.

The 'road' to the peak runs from Djamandjary; hikers or bikers should make a day excursion of it and take a picnic. Those looking for solitude with a view should keep away.

LOKOBE Nosy Be's only protected area, Lokobe, is a strict nature reserve and as such is not currently open to tourists. (Plans for it to become a national park seem to have been shelved.) However, it is possible to visit the buffer zone on the northeastern side of the peninsula where permits are not required. The two little villages here, Ambatozavavy and Ampasypohy, have embraced tourism with enthusiasm and the whole area now bears little similarity to the unspoilt place I so delighted in two decades ago. However, a visit here still offers a glimpse of village life in Nosy Be and is an informative and enjoyable excursion.

Guided day trips to Lokobe are now commonplace: it takes around one hour by pirogue from Ambatozavavy to Ampasypohy. This trip is still a good option for those who cannot spend the night (see *Where to stay*). During the course of the day you are served a traditional lunch and taken on a tour of the forest (now sadly very degraded) where your guide will explain the traditional uses of various plants and point out a variety of animals. You are bound to see a grey-backed sportive lemur (*Lepilemur dorsalis*), that often spends its day dozing in the fork of a favourite tree or tangle of vines rather than in a hole. You should also see black lemurs (they are fed bananas in the forest) and probably a ground boa and chameleons (that have been placed there just in advance of your arrival). The chameleons here are the panther species (*Furcifer pardalis*) and in the breeding season (November to May) the male is bright green and the female a pinkish colour. The villagers grow vanilla and peppers, and a wide range of handicrafts can be bought direct from the makers.

Where to stay

Eco-Village Fihavanana (9 bungalows) Ambatozavavy; 86 612 36. Designed for ecotourists rather than beach fanatics. Originally Swiss-owned but now a community-run project which also trains local people in the art of hotel management. Very comfortable, spacious palm-thatched bungalows with hot showers & solar power. The manager can organise trips with local fishermen, but they also have their own Zodiac. An excellent feature is the Lokobe Nature Trail which can be walked at night so is of particular interest to those devoted to reptiles & nocturnal fauna of all kinds. €€€€€

Jungle Village 86 918 19; m 033 14 222 38/032 41 041 08; e contact@nosybe-junglevillage.net; www.junglevillage.net. A beautifully located hotel in Ampasypohy away from the crowded west coast. 2 deluxe 4-person wooden 'lodges', very nicely furnished & spacious; plus 5 bungalows & 2 rooms. €€€€€–♔

NOSY KOMBA AND NOSY TANIKELY No visit to Nosy Be is complete without an excursion to these two islands. Nosy Komba's main attraction is the black lemurs, and the marine reserve of Nosy Tanikely lures snorkellers and bird enthusiasts.

Alison Jolly

Female lemurs tend to be dominant over males. This is drastically different from our nearer relatives, the monkeys and apes, where males dominate females in the vast majority of species. In some lemur species, like the ring-tails and the white sifakas of Berenty, males virtually never challenge females. In others, like brown lemurs, it is nearer fifty-fifty, depending on the individual's character. The black lemurs of Nosy Komba are intermediate. Their females are likely to dominate males but are not certain to. If you are feeding them, the blond females are apt to be in the forefront of the scrimmage with only a few of the black males. Watch to see who grabs food from whom and – even more telling – who does not dare grab.

Female dominance also applies to sex. An unwilling female chases off a male, or even bites him. Or she may just sit down with her tail over her genitals – a perfect chastity belt. A lemur's hands can't hold another's tail, so if she puts it down, or just sits down, he is flummoxed. And in most lemur species, he would never dream of challenging her desires.

Also note the way the males rub their wet, smelly testicles and anal region on the females. Some females do not appreciate this and tell them off with a snarl. Males may also rub their bottoms on branches to scent-mark them. Then they may rub their heads on the branch in order to transfer the scent to their forehead.

You can tell a lot about a lemur's mood by where it is looking – a long hard stare is a threat, quick glances while head-flagging away is submissive. The tail, though, won't tell you much except how the animal is balanced on a branch or your shoulder. They use tails to keep track of each other, but not to signal mood.

Getting there and away All the Nosy Be hotels do excursions to Nosy Komba – usually combined with Nosy Tanikely. Most will let you do the sensible thing of taking an overnight break on Nosy Komba and rejoining the boat the following day for Nosy Tanikely. For Nosy Komba alone it is much cheaper to go by pirogue. Go to the small pirogue port (Port Ambariovato, to the east of the main port in Hell-Ville). The pirogues leave at around 11.00 each day after the morning's shopping in Hell-Ville. If you are staying on the island a 'special-service' pirogue to Nosy Be should cost 25,000–30,000Ar.

The best time to visit these two popular islands is outside the main tourist season. If you decide to fix your own trip at the harbour (rather than through your hotel) question the boat-owner carefully about what 'all-inclusive' actually means. Is snorkelling gear included? It will cover lunch but how about drinks? (Some operators charge high prices for *all* drinks, not just alcohol.) Is the Nosy Komba reserve fee included? And bananas to feed to the lemurs? It's better to know all this before you set out.

Yachties approaching from Nosy Be should wait until Nosy Vorona ('bird island' – the island with the old lighthouse) then bear 020°. Good anchorage in 3–7m over sand and mud.

Nosy Komba (Nosy Ambariovato) Once upon a time (indeed, when I first went there in 1976) Nosy Komba was an isolated island with an occasional boat service, a tiny, self-sufficient village (Ampangorinana), and a troop of semi-tame black lemurs that were held to be sacred so never hunted. Now all that has changed. Tourists arrive by the boatload from Nosy Be and from passing cruise ships which can land over a hundred people on this small island.

Komba means 'lemur' (interestingly, it is the same as the Swahili word for the bushbaby which of course is the African relative of lemurs) and it is the lemurs that bring in the visitors. During the 1980s the villagers made nothing out of these visits apart from the sale of clay animals which they glazed with the acid of spent batteries. Then they instigated a modest fee for seeing the animals and increased the variety of handicrafts. Now that Nosy Komba is on cruise-ship itineraries they have taken on the works: 'tribal dancing', face-decoration, escorted walks … anything that will earn a dollar or two.

With all the demands on your purse, it sometimes takes a bit of mental effort to see the underlying charm of Ampangorinana, but it is nevertheless a typical Malagasy community living largely on fishing and *tavy* farming (witness the horrendous deforestation of their little island; at the time of my 1976 visit it was almost completely forested with luxuriant trees) but it is the black lemurs that provide the financial support (and help prevent further degradation of their environment). The ancestor who initiated the hunting *fady* must be pleased with himself. If you want the lemurs-on-your-shoulder experience and the chance to see these engaging animals at close quarters you should definitely come here. Only the male *Eulemur macaco* is black; the females (which give birth in September) are chestnut brown with white ear-tufts.

Nosy Komba also provides an excellent opportunity for observing lemur behaviour (see box opposite) and for taking a close look at one of our relatives. Look at a lemur's hands. You will see the four flat primate fingernails (such wonderfully human hands!) and the single claw (on the hind feet, not on the hands) which is used for scratching and as an ear-pick.

En route to Lemur Park everyone in the village will try to sell you something. Since you are buying direct from the grower/maker, this is the best place to get vanilla and handicrafts (carved pirogues, clay animals and unusual and attractive Richelieu 'lace' tablecloths, curtains and bedspreads). The handicrafts here are unlike any found on the mainland, so it is worth bringing plenty of cash (small change).

One of the former glories of Nosy Komba, its coral, has sadly almost completely disappeared so snorkelling is no longer rewarding. The sea and beach near the village are polluted with human waste, but there is a good swimming beach round to the left (as you face the sea).

The best way to visit Nosy Komba is by yourself, or in a small group, avoiding the 'rush hour' (*09.30–10.30*). When there are few other tourists, it is a tranquil place, so consider staying for one or more nights. Now there is some upper-range accommodation this is a peaceful alternative to the increasingly crowded Nosy Be. Given time to explore, it is possible to find and watch lemur groups away from Lemur Park, or to take a hike up the hill for spectacular views of the whole of Nosy Be (the peak of Nosy Komba, at 630m, is higher than any point on Nosy Be), but start early before it gets too hot.

Note that drinks etc are much more expensive on Nosy Komba than Nosy Be because of the carriage costs.

BITING THE HAND THAT FEEDS IT

Alison Jolly

Be careful when feeding lemurs. They may scratch you with their fingernails in their eagerness, or give you an accidental nip while trying to get the food. Much more important: never try to catch a lemur with your hands, just let it jump on you as it wants. If you constrain it, it will react as though a hawk has grabbed it and give you a slash with its razor-sharp canines. Especially do not let children feed lemurs unless they are warned never to hold on. These are wild animals, not pets.

Where to stay Almost every month sees new hotels opening up in Nosy Komba. Backpackers on a tight budget will be more successful if they arrive on spec and check out what's available in the village.

Hôtel Tsara Komba (3 bungalows) m 033 14 823 20/032 07 440 40; e eden@wanadoo.mg; www.tsarakomba.com. Owned by the brother of Hervé, who owns Jardin Vanille, & about 2km south of this hotel. Exclusive & very beautiful bungalows overlooking a tiny beach. The high price is justified by the owners by the profits that they put back into the village: water supply, dispensary & health care, school equipment & micro-credit schemes. ♨

Jardin Vanille (8 bungalows) m 032 07 127 97; e jardinvanille@wanadoo.mg. Delightful mangrove-wood bungalows on stilts set into the hillside above the beach (62 steps up!) on the south side of the island, opposite Ankify & away from the hordes of day visitors. French-owned & firmly francophone. En-suite rooms with balcony & sea view. 'The mosquito net was the best & most user-friendly we have ever seen anywhere in the world — although there were no mozzies around to put it to the test. Only drawback: lighting too poor for bedtime reading' (Elisabeth Cox). One concrete 'honeymoon' bungalow is built out over the sea. You may see genuinely wild black lemurs here (but they are not habituated so you will need to take an excursion to Ampangorinana for a close view). Credit cards not accepted. €€€€€

Les Floralies m 032 02 200 38; e floralieskomba@wanadoo.mg. French-run (& francophone). Dbl bungalows beautifully situated at the end of the quietest beach, with en-suite cold-water shower & toilet. Bar & restaurant. B/fast inc. €€€

Chez Yolande (2 bungalows & 4 rooms) e casinca@hotmail.com; www.casinca.com. Bungalows have en-suite toilet and shower, cheaper rooms have shared facilities. Tasty, good-value meals. €€–€€€

Residence de Nosy Komba (4 rooms) Very simple accommodation, but clean & with en-suite shower in 3 rooms. €€

Jacky & Marry (2 rooms) Udi Columbus recommends this place on the northwest side of the island near Les Floralies, run by a young lady called Clair. Rooms are en suite (cold water). A nice private veranda overlooks the sea. Electricity 18.00–22.00. Very pleasant. €€

Les Lémuriens (6 bungalows) ☎ 86 921 40; e hotel-lemuriens@yahoo.fr. A long-established hotel now run by the sons of the original owner. En-suite toilet & shower plus (cheaper) shower only. €€

Nosy Tanikely Although now much visited, this is still a lovely little island. It's a marine reserve and most people come for the snorkelling which is still good, despite the hundreds of tourist boats dropping their anchors, and tourist feet stepping on the coral. In clear water you can see an amazing variety of marine life: coral, starfish, anemones, every colour and shape of fish, turtles, lobsters ...

With this new world beneath your gaze there is a real danger of forgetting the passing of time and becoming seriously sunburnt. Even the most carefully applied suncream tends to miss some areas, so wear a T-shirt and shorts.

Don't think you have finished with Nosy Tanikely when you come out of the water; at low tide it is possible to walk right round the island. During your circumambulation you will see (if you go anticlockwise): a broad beach of white sand covered in shells and bleached pieces of coral, a couple of trees full of flying foxes and – in the spring – graceful white-tailed tropic-birds flying in and out of their nests in the high cliffs. At your feet will be rock pools and some scrambling, but nothing too challenging.

Then there is the climb up to the lighthouse at the top of the island for the view.

OTHER ISLANDS IN THE NOSY BE ARCHIPELAGO

NOSY SAKATIA This rather bare island lies off the west side of Nosy Be. There are some well-run hotels here catering for divers.

🏠 **Sakatia Passions** (12 bungalows) ☎ 86 614 62; www.sakatia-passions.com. Lovely bungalows with private terraces, set amid coconut palms. Private beach. En-suite bathrooms with hot water. Deep-sea fishing & diving a speciality. B/fast inc. Airport transfer €30. €€€€€

🏠 **Sakatia Dive Inn** (6 bungalows & 5 A-frame huts) ☎ 86 615 14; m 032 07 126 75; e sakatia@wanadoo.mg. The bungalows have mosquito nets, basins & toilet; cheaper ones with shared facilities. Family-style dining. As the name implies, this place offers diving courses & excursions. €€€€

NOSY MITSIO The islands of Nosy Mitsio lies some 60 to 70km from Nosy Be and about the same distance from the mainland. This is the Maldives of Madagascar, with two exclusive (and expensive) fly-in resorts on stunningly beautiful small islands.

La Grande Mitsio The largest island is populated by local Malagasy – Antakarana and Sakalava – who survive on their denuded island through farming, cattle and goats. Overgrazing has devastated the island but some forest remains in the southern part. Huge basalt columns are a prominent feature on the northwest tip, used as an adventure playground by enterprising goats.

The island attracts yachties to its coral reefs and good anchorages. Maribe Bay provides good anchorage, protected between two hills. Manta rays can often be seen in this area.

Tsara Banjina The name means 'good to look at' and this is a small but incredibly beautiful island. The red, grey and black volcanic rocks, rising quite high at its centre, have a mass of lush, green vegetation clinging to them – from baobabs and other large trees to *Pachypodiums* and tiny 'rockery plants'. But its real glory is the pure white beaches of coarse sand, along which laps a crystal-clear green/indigo sea. Turtles and rays rest near the beaches. Divers can be kept busy for a couple of days, and there are walking trails.

Yachties can anchor off the southwest, at 6m over a sandy bottom.

 Where to stay

🏠 **L'Hôtel Tsarabanjina** (21 bungalows) ☎ 032 05 152 29; e tsarabanjina@tsarabanjina.com; www.tsarabanjina.com. This is a beautifully-designed collection of A-framed chalets constructed predominantly of natural materials & accommodating just a few people at a time. It is also a world-class scuba-diving centre; most diving takes place round Les Quatre Frères (see below) where you may see batfish,

scorpion fish, hawksbill turtles & rays, as well as colourful coral. 'Despite the exclusivity of Tsarabanjina there is a total lack of pretension as guests are encouraged to cast aside their footwear & go barefoot. It is possible to find Robinson Crusoe privacy in a little cove of bleached white sand or to swap stories with the highly-approachable staff during the evening ritual of pre-dinner cocktails at 8!' (Mark Stratton) 🏖

Nosy Ankarea Another beautiful place to spend a few luxurious days. There are some gorgeous, sun-drenched beaches and the low hills make for pleasant walking excursions. 'The island is superb. Fabulous *Pachypodiums*, flamboyants etc. Surrounded by coral reefs in an azure sea. The forest on the island is relatively undisturbed, due to numerous *fadys* and the fact that no one lives there except Marlin Club tourists. It is possible to climb up the highest hill (219m – quite steep but well worth it) to reach a plateau covered with *Pachypodiums* and lots of other weird and wonderful succulents. From here you can see all of Nosy Mitsio and the surrounding reefs' (Josephine Andrews).

Les Quatre Frères (The Four Brothers) These are four imposing lumps of silver basalt, two of which are home to hundreds of nesting seabirds, including brown

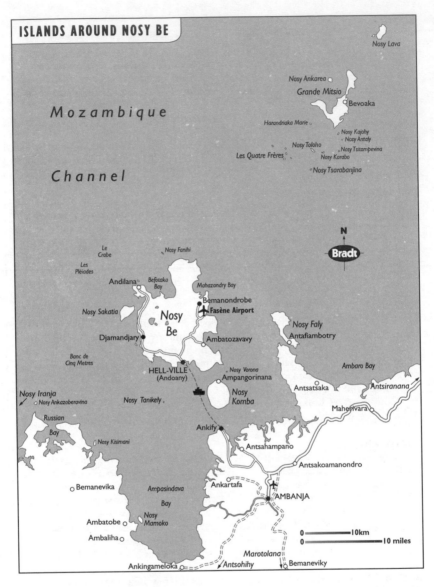

boobies, frigate birds and white-tailed tropic-birds. A pair of Madagascar fish eagles nest on one of the rocks. The sides drop vertically to about 20–30m, and divers come here because three of the boulders can be circumnavigated during one vigorous dive. Yachties can anchor to the southeast of Nosy Beangovo, roughly 100m from the mouth of a cave, at a depth of about 10m. Currents reach up to one knot. The best marine life is in the lee. There are huge caves, spectacular overhangs and rockfalls in the area.

NOSY IRANJA When I visited this island in the mid 1990s it was a beautiful and peaceful island inhabited by fisherfolk, and an important breeding reserve for hawksbill turtles. Then the luxury hotel was built, amid considerable controversy.

Initially the hotel seemed to fulfil its promise to protect the turtles. Then anxieties arose at its expansion ever closer to the nesting area and there was even a website urging visitors not to go there. But in 2006 the hotel was bought by South Africa's Legacy Hotels and Resorts International which is in the process of turning it into 'one of the most sought-after Indian Ocean destinations.' We shall see …

 Where to stay

Nosy Iranja Lodge (23 bungalows) 86 616 90; www.iranja.com. The bungalows encircle the whole island so each has a sea view. There's a restaurant, fitness centre, watersports & all the extras that you would expect in a luxury resort.

NOSY KIVINJY Otherwise known as Sugarloaf Rock, this is a great basalt boulder with 'organ-pipe' formations on one side. Not recommended for diving (poor) or anchorage (very insecure). There are strong northeast-flowing currents around the islet.

NOSY MAMOKO This little island is at the southwest end of Ampasindava Bay. Known among the yachting fraternity for its exceptional shelter in all weather, it is a lovely, tranquil spot for a few days' relaxation. Nosy Mamoko is on the itineraries of two or three operators, based in Nosy Be, who organise lengthy trips into the region. There is good fishing here and whale-watching from October to December. Good anchorage is found in the channel between the island and the mainland, in 15m over a sandy bottom.

NOSY RADAMA The Radama islands, which lie to the southwest of Nosy Be (and thus are only really accessible to yachties), compete with the Mitsios for the best diving sites in the northeast of Madagascar. They are set in a breathtaking coastline of bays backed by high mountains. Most of these high sandstone islands are steep-sided above and below water and covered with scrub, grass and trees. Sharp eroded rock formations, however, render the remaining forest rather difficult to explore. These islands are likely to become protected areas in the near future.

Nosy Kalakajoro The northernmost island, featuring dense, impenetrable forest on the south side. There are good beaches on the southern side and snorkelling is worthwhile off the southeast. Yachts should anchor 100m off the southeast side in 10–12m over good holding sand and mud, to get protection from the north-to-west winds.

Nosy Berafia (or Nosy Ovy – 'potato island') This is the largest of the group, but the environmental degradation is terrible. Nearly all the trees have been cut and goats have completed the destruction of its flora. Red soil weeps from gaping scars into the surrounding water. If you still want to visit, boats can anchor off the east side, near a protected rocky outcrop.

Nosy Valiha A small island which is privately owned, so you should not visit without permission.

15

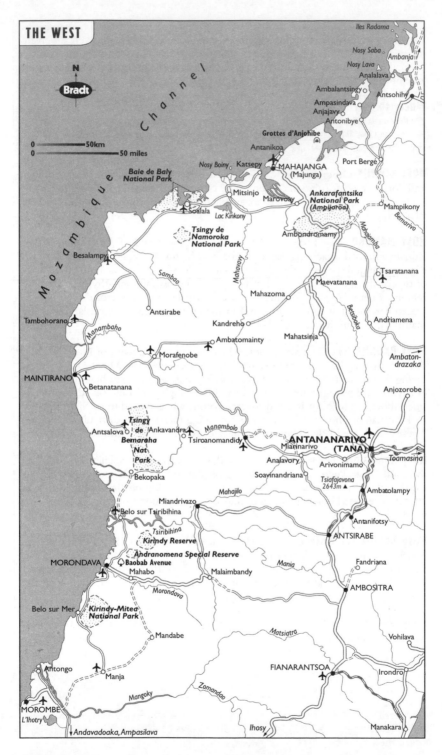

THE WEST

Iles Radama

Nosy Saba

Nosy Lava   Ambanja

                   Analalava

              Ambalantsingy   Antsohihy

              Ampasindava
              Anjajavy
                        Antonibye

         Grottes d'Anjohibe

              Antanikoa   Port Bergé

Nosy Boiny Katsepy   MAHAJANGA
                      (Majunga)   Mampikony

Baie de Baly
National Park   Mitsinjo
              Soalala   Marovoay   Ankarafantsika
          Lac Kinkony   National Park
                                       (Ampijoroa)

         Tsingy de   Ambondromamy
         Namoroka
         National Park   Bemarivo
                                                         Tsaratanana

Besalampy   Maevatanana
         Sambao   Mahazoma
                                                    Andriamena
Tambohorano   Antsirabe   Kandreho   Mahatsinja
         Manambaho   Ambaton-
                          Ambatomainty   drazaka

                     Morafenobe

MAINTIRANO   Anjozorobe
         Betanatanana

              Tsingy   Manambolo
Antsalova   de   Ankavandra   ANTANANARIVO
         Bemaraha   Tsiroanomandidy   (TANA)
         Nat   Miarinarivo   Toamasina
         Park   Analavory
         Bekopaka   Arivonimamo
                                         Tsiafajavona Ambatolampy
                     Mahajilo   Soavinandriana 2643m

         Miandrivazo   Antanifotsy
Belo sur Tsiribihina   ANTSIRABE
         Tsiribihina
         Kirindy Reserve
         Andranomena Special Reserve   Fandriana
MORONDAVA   Baobab Avenue   Mania
         Mahabo   Malaimbandy   AMBOSITRA
                     Morondava
Belo sur Mer   Kirindy-Mitea
         National Park
              Mandabe   Matsiatra   Vohilava

Antongo   Irondro
         Manja   FIANARANTSOA
              Mangoky Zomandao
MOROMBE
L'Ihotry   Ihosy   Manakara
         Andavadoaka, Ampasilava

N

Bradt

0   50km
0   50 miles

Mozambique Channel

16

The West

The west of Madagascar offers a mostly dry climate, deciduous forest (with some excellent reserves to protect it), and endless sandy beaches with little danger from sharks. It is effectively divided into two sections: the north, with its gateway town of Mahajanga, and the south with Morondava providing access. No roads directly link these two regions – the traveller is obliged to return to Tana or face the uncomfortable but adventurous journey by *boutre* – cargo boat. The lack of roads and agreeable climate makes this the ideal area for mountain bikers or walkers. Adventurous travellers will have no trouble finding a warm welcome in untouristed villages, their own deserted beach and some spectacular landscapes. This is the region to see one of Madagascar's extraordinary natural wonders: the *tsingy*. Pronounced *zing*, this is exactly the sound made when one of the limestone pinnacles is struck (they can be played like a xylophone!). It is also a word for 'sharp' in Malagasy. Limestone karst is not unique to Madagascar, but it is rare to see such dramatic forms, such an impenetrable forest of spikes and spires. The endemic succulents that struggle for a foothold in this waterless environment add to the unworldly feeling of a *tsingy* landscape. There are now three national parks showcasing *tsingy*.

Opposite major rivers the sea water along the west coast is a brick-red colour: 'like swimming in soup' as one traveller put it. This is the laterite washed into the rivers from the eroded hillsides of the highlands and discharged into the sea: Madagascar's bleeding wounds.

HISTORY

The west is the home of the Sakalava people. For a while in Malagasy history this was the largest and most powerful tribe, ruled by their own kings and queens. The Sakalava kingdom was founded by the Volamena branch of the Maroserana dynasty which emerged in the southwest during the 16th century. Early in the 17th century a Volamena prince, Andriamisara, reached the Sakalava River and gave its name to his new kingdom. His son, Andriandahifotsy (which means 'white man'), succeeded him around 1650 and, with the aid of firearms acquired from European traders, conquered the southwestern area between the Onilahy and Manambolo rivers. This region became known as the Menabe. Later kings conquered first the Boina, the area from the Manambolo to north of present-day Mahajanga, and then the northwest coast as far as Antsiranana.

By the 18th century the Sakalava Empire occupied a huge area in the west, but was divided into the Menabe in the south and the Boina in the north. The two rulers fell out, unity was abandoned, and in the 19th century the area came under the control of the Merina. The Sakalava did not take kindly to domination and sporadic guerrilla warfare continued in the Menabe area until French colonial times.

The Sakalava kingdom bore the brunt of the first serious efforts by the French to colonise the island. For some years France had laid claims (based on treaties

The son of the 'Wicked Queen' Ranavalona, King Radama II was a gentle ruler who abhorred bloodshed. He was pro-European, interested in Christianity (although never formally a Christian) and a friend of William Ellis, missionary and chronicler of 19th-century Madagascar. After Radama's death, Ellis wrote: 'I have never said that Radama was an able ruler, or a man of large views, for these he was not; but a more humane ruler never wore a crown.' With missionaries of all denominations invited back into Madagascar, intense rivalry sprang up between the Protestants sent by Britain, and the Jesuits who arrived from France. Resentment at the influence of these foreigners over the young king, and disgust at the often rash changes he instigated, boiled over in 1863, and only eight months after his coronation he was assassinated, strangled with a silken sash so that the *fady* against shedding royal blood was not infringed.

The French-British rivalry was fuelled by the violent death of the king, even to the extent that Ellis was accused of being party to the assassination. But was Radama really dead? Both Ellis and Jean Laborde believed that he had survived the strangling and had been allowed to escape by the courtiers bearing him to the countryside for burial. Uprisings, supposedly organised by the 'dead' king, supported this rumour. In a biography of King Radama II, the French historian Raymond Delval makes a strong case that the ex-monarch eventually retreated to the area of Lake Kinkony and lived out the rest of his life in this Sakalava region.

made with local princes) on parts of the north and northwest, and in 1883 two fortresses in this region were bombarded. An attack on Mahajanga followed. This was the beginning of the end of Madagascar as an independent kingdom.

THE SAKALAVA PEOPLE TODAY The modern Sakalava have relatively dark skins. The west of Madagascar received a number of African immigrants from across the Mozambique Channel and their influence shows not only in the racial characteristics of the people, but also in their language and customs. There are a number of Bantu words in their dialect, and their belief in *tromba* (spirit possession) and *dady* (royal relics cult) is of African origin.

The Sakalava do not practise second burial. The quality of their funerary art (in one small area) rivals that of the Mahafaly: birds and naked figures are a feature of Sakalava tombs, the latter frequently in erotic positions. Concepts of sexuality and rebirth are implied here. The female figures are often disproportionately large, perhaps recognising the importance of women in the Sakalava culture.

Sakalava royalty do not require elaborate tombs since kings are considered to continue their spiritual existence through a medium with healing powers, and in royal relics. See box on page 431 for an account of a meeting with the present-day royal family.

GETTING AROUND

Roads are being improved but driving from town to town in the west can still be challenging and in much of the area the roads simply aren't there. There are regular flights to the large towns and a Twin Otter serves many of the smaller ones.

MAHAJANGA (MAJUNGA)

HISTORY Ideally located for trade with East Africa, Arabia and western Asia, Mahajanga has been a major commercial port since 1745, when the Boina capital was moved here from Marovoay. One ruler of the Boina was Queen Ravahiny, a very able monarch who maintained the unity of the Boina which was threatened by rebellions in both the north and the south. It was Mahajanga which provided her with her imported riches and caught the admiration of visiting foreigners. Madagascar was at that time a major supplier of slaves to Arab traders and in return received jewels and rich fabrics. Indian merchants were active then, as today, with a variety of exotic goods. Some of these traders from the east stayed on, the Indians remaining a separate community and running small businesses. More Indians arrived during colonial times.

During the 1883–85 war Mahajanga served as the base for the military expedition to Antananarivo which consolidated the French Protectorate. Shortly thereafter the French set about enlarging Mahajanga and reclaiming swampland from the Bombetoka River delta. Much of today's extensive town is on reclaimed land.

In World War II Mahajanga was seized from the Vichy French by British forces (see boxes on page 366 and below).

MAHAJANGA TODAY Mahajanga is a hot but breezy town with a large Indian population and plenty of local colour. The province is being opened up to ecotourism, with easily accessible hotspots such as Ankarafantsika National Park and the fly-in resorts contrasting with the barely accessible region to the southwest which is being conserved as part of the president's Durban Vision.

The town has two 'centres': the Town Hall (*Hôtel de Ville*) and statue of former President Tsiranana (the commercial centre), and the streets near the famous baobab tree. Some offices, including Air Madagascar, are here. It is quite a long walk between the two – take one of the many *pousse-pousses*. There are also some smart new buses, and taxis which operate on a fixed tariff.

A wide boulevard follows the sea along the west part of town, terminating near a lighthouse. At its elbow is the Mahajanga baobab, said to be at least 700 years old with a circumference of 14m.

Telephone code The area code for Mahajanga is 62.

GETTING THERE AND AWAY
By air Air Mad flights here are very variable. Check their website (*www.airmadagascar.mg*). There are two international flights into Mahajanga from the Comoro Islands, and daily flights from Tana. There is also a weekly flight to

---

BEWARE OF THE LOCAL WILDLIFE!

John Gehan

The port of Majunga was seized by British forces from the Vichy French in September 1942. To prevent any French troops from retreating to Antananarivo, a party of British Commandos was taken up the Ikopa River to the south of Majunga in small boats.

Unfortunately, as the boats travelled up the river, they ran aground on a sandbank. The simple solution to this was for the men to climb out of the boats and drag them into the main channel – but the river was full of crocodiles!

The Commandos found that the only way they could keep the crocs at bay was by throwing hand grenades at them. The soldiers fought their way through the crocodiles and finally reached their objective, only to find that their perilous journey had been in vain. Instead of trying to retreat, all the French had simply surrendered!

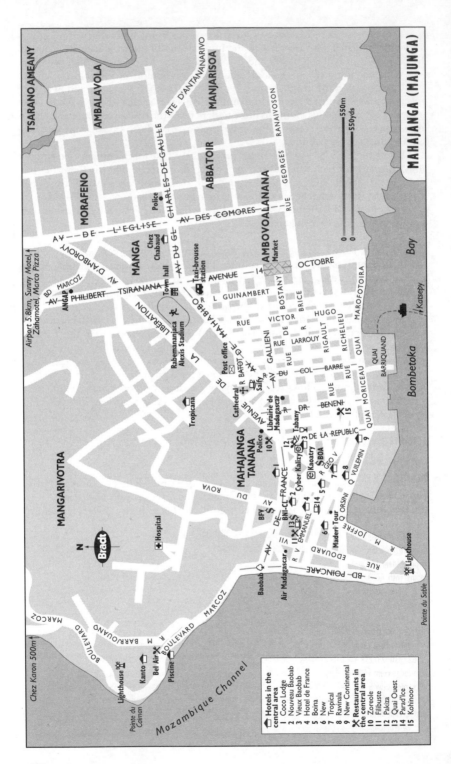

MAHAJANGA (MAJUNGA)

TSARANO AMBANY

AMBALAVOLA

MORAFENO

MANGA

MANJARISOA

ABBATOIR

AMBOVOALANANA

RTE D'ANTANANARIVO

CHARLES-DE-GAULLE

AV DES COMORES

AV — DE — L'EGLISE

AV D'AMBOROVY

Police

Chez Chabaud

AV DU GL

Market

550m
550yds

0
0

Airport 5.8km, Sunny Motel,
Zahamotel, Marco Pizza

BD MARCOZ

AV ANGAP PHILIBERT TSIRANANA

Town hall

Taxi-brousse station

AVENUE — 14 — OCTOBRE

RUE GEORGES RANAIVOSON

L GUINAMBERT

RUE VICTOR BOSTANY

RUE BRICE

HUGO

RUE DU GALLIENI

RUE LARROUY

RUE RICHELIEU

QUAI MAROFOTOIRA

QUAI BARRIQUAND

QUAI

Katsepy

Bay

Bombetoka

MANGARIVOTRA

Rabemananjaca
Alexis Stadium

Post office

LA LIBERATION

AVENUE DE

Cathedral

Tropicana

Librairie de Madagascar

Safiy

COL BARRE

RUE BENENI

DR

Tabany

AV DE LA REPUBLIC

Cyber Kalizy

Kaoatry

SBOA

QUAI MORICEAU

QUAI VUILEMIN

ORSINI

GEO

MAHAJANGA TANANA

Police

10

12

2

14

4

5

1

13

BNI-CL FRANCE

EMMANUEL

AV DE FRANCE

BFV

AV DU ROVA

RV VII

6

Maderi Tour

RUE M JOFFRE

RUE EDOUARD

BD POINCARE

Pointe du Sable

Hospital

N

Bradt

Chez Karon 500m

Lighthouse

Kanto

Bel Air

Piscine

RM BARRIQUAND

BOULEVARD MARCOZ

BOULEVARD MARCOZ

Pointe du Caiman

Baobab

Air Madagascar

Lighthouse

Mozambique Channel

Hotels in the central area
1 Coco Lodge
2 Nouveau Baobab
3 Vieux Baobab
4 Hotel de France
5 Boina
6 New
7 Tropical
8 Ravinala
9 New Continental

Restaurants in the central area
10 Zoreole
11 Filibuste
12 Pakiza
13 Quai Ouest
14 Parad'Ice
15 Kohinoor

Antananarivo–Ankarafantsika	453km	Antananarivo–Morondava	701km
Ankarafantsika–Mahajanga	108km	Miandrivazo–Morondava	286km
Antananarivo–Mahajanga	561km	Morondava–Belo-sur-Tsiribihina	106km

Antsiranana (Wednesday) and sometimes Twin Otter flights to some of the small, west-coast towns.

The airport is near the village of Amborovy, 6km northeast of the town. If you don't want to take a taxi, *taxi-brousses* pass close to the airport.

By road Mahajanga is 560km from Tana by the well-maintained RN4. It is one of the easiest routes to do by road, the journey taking about 10 hours. The buses run by **Transport Première Classe** seat only two people per row, leave on time, have careful drivers and provide a very nice packed lunch to eat in a pleasant, shady spot on the way. The 2006 price was 69,000Ar (e *firstclass@mel.wanadoo.mg; www.majunga.org*).

A cheaper, if less fancy, option is **Transpost** which runs well-maintained minibuses on this route. Book your seat at the office next door to the upper town post office in Tana or the main post office in Mahajanga. They depart daily at 07.30 except Sunday, take a similar amount of time, cost 22,000Ar and carry one person per seat (three in a row). They stop at a roadside restaurant where you can buy lunch.

Regular *taxi-brousses* leave from the eastern *gare routière* at Ambodivona. Some larger buses, called Boeing, travel at night when it is cooler.

By sea You can access Mahajanga from Nosy Be with the ferry *Jean-Pierre Calloc'h*, which sails weekly and takes 20 hours (\f *62 226 86;* m *032 02 216 86*). It is operated by Malagasy Sambo Ligne, Quai Barriquand, and leaves Mahajanga on Friday, arriving Saturday, and returns on Monday. Departure times vary according to the tides.

For the truly adventurous there the cargo boats – *boutres* – plying the west coast will take passengers (see box on page 423).

⌂ WHERE TO STAY
Top end €€€€€
⌂ **Sunny Hotel** (40 rooms & 4 suites) Rte d'Amborovy; ☎ 62 235 87/22 263 04 (Tana); f 22 290 78; e rasseta@dts.mg or rasseta@blueline.mg. Only 5mins drive from the airport; ideal for an early departure. Well-equipped rooms with AC, safe, minibar & TV. Large swimming pool, tennis courts & fitness centre. Excellent food. Excursions & car hire. The once-caged lemurs now live free in nearby trees having been released after complaints from tourists.

⌂ **La Piscine Hotel** (31 rooms) La Corniche, Bd Marcoz; ☎ 62 241 72 to 74; f 62 239 65; e piscinehotel@madatours.com. French-owned with huge swimming pool & open-air restaurant overlooking the ocean. Rooms have phone, AC, TV, minibar. Nightclub.

Upper range €€€€
⌂ **Hôtel Coco Lodge** (17 rooms) 49 Av de France; ☎ 62 230 23/238 18; f 62 226 92; e contact@coco-lodge.com; www.majunga.org. Smart, spacious en-suite rooms with AC & minibar built around a central courtyard with a lovely swimming pool. No food except b/fast.

⌂ **Le Tropicana** Oasis Gatinière, Rue Administrateur Lacaze, Mangarivotra; ☎ 62 220 69; e hotel-tropicana@tiscali.fr; www.hotel-majunga.com. Up the hill from Don Bosco school behind the cathedral. Mixed reviews: one recent traveller said the room was 'charmless, gloomy & none too clean. The pool had an oily film on it. 2 lemurs in a small cage in the garden.' It may be going through a bad patch or this person may just have been unlucky; other travellers have praised it.

ANKAFOBE FOREST

Chris Birkinshaw, Missouri Botanical Gardens, Madagascar.
Ankafobe Forest is a complex of several small and degraded forest fragments located in valleys on the Tampoketsa (high plateau savanna) of Ankazobe in central Madagascar. We selected this site because it contains much of the remaining population of one of Madagascar's most threatened trees – *Schizolaena tampoketsana*. One of the forest fragments is immediately adjacent to RN4, linking Tana and Mahajanga (around 30km northwest of Ankazobe between PK130-132). It is here that we will be building a simple chalet with educational signs and seats, and where we will be constructing a 1km trail (that will pass through savanna, valley-bottom marsh and forest) and labelling a number of the trees. Although the forest here is small it is of general interest as a living remnant of the type of forest that presumably covered much of the High Plateau. The site supports much else of interest (including three lemur species) for the bored tourist needing a short break from the journey between Tana and Mahajanga. I think many tourists will also appreciate that here we do not plan to hassle them with guides or even entry fees – rather they can just park next to the road enjoy the scenery and wander around the trail themselves. However, we are asking anyone who appreciates the project to stop at the shop in the nearby village of Firarazana (5km southeast of the site on the left) to buy a Project T-shirt. The profits from sale of the T-shirt will be used to support the various activities necessary to conserve this site.

Hôtel de France (20 rooms) 10 Rue du Maréchal Joffre; ☎ 62 237 81; f 62 223 26; e h.france@dts.mg. One of the oldest hotels in Mahajanga, conveniently located in the centre of town. En-suite rooms with AC; some with hot water. Tours organised.
New Hotel (20 rooms) 13 Rue Henri Palu; ☎ 62 221 10; f 62 293 91. En-suite (some with AC) rooms with phone, TV & hot water. Good restaurant.

Mid range €€€
New Continental Av de la République; ☎ 62 225 70; f 62 241 19. Well-run, Indian-owned in the town centre. En-suite rooms with TV, phone & AC.
Hôtel du Vieux Baobab Rue du Maréchal Joffre. AC.

Budget €€
Chez Karon (24 rooms) ☎ 62 226 94; f 62 293 44. Pleasant seaside location (at the so-called Village Touristique). Excellent food & very helpful hosts: 'Nothing was too much trouble. It was offered; we didn't ask. We felt good to have known them' (R&E Gowans). Fan or AC. Tours organised, inc hunting trips for duck, guineafowl & wild boar – probably not for readers of this guide.

Penny-pincher €
Hôtel Kanto Bd La Corniche; ☎ 62 229 78. Overlooking the sea; 2km north of town. Fans. Good restaurant. There's an annexe near the central

Zaha Motel (30 rooms) Amborovy beach; ☎ 62 225 55/237 20; f 62 237 11; e zahamotel.mjn@malagasy.com. Near the airport; 8km from Mahajanga. Rooms & bungalows. A slightly vulgar, large hotel complete with activities (tennis, volleyball etc). It offers a cool alternative to staying in Mahajanga, but you need your own transport. Good beach with blue, not red, sea. Organises excursions to Ankarafantsika.

Le Nouveau Baobab Rue du Maréchal Joffre (near Av de France). En suite with AC.
Hôtel Ravinala Quai Orsini; ☎ 62 229 68. Clean rooms with TV, phone, AC & en-suite bathroom.

Chez Chabaud (18 rooms) Near the town hall; ☎ 62 233 27; f 62 233 27; e nico@wanadoo.mg or chabaudlodge@noos.fr; http://chabaudlodge.wifeo.com. Run by Brigitte Chabaud. Most rooms en suite with AC; some cheaper with fan & shared facilities. Restaurant opposite run by Brigitte's sister, Christiane (who also runs the legendary restaurant in Katsepy). All the family speaks English.

market at the intersection of Av de la République & Rue Henri Palu.

✗ WHERE TO EAT Thanks to Peace Corps volunteers Sandra and Bobby O'Neil for the first three recommendations.

✗ **Marco Pizza** Tsaramandroso; m 032 40 032 02. Rumoured to be the best pizza restaurant in Madagascar. Owned & operated by an entrepreneurial Frenchman who personally handles all aspects of the customer's experience. Also serves homemade ice cream & cocktails. Peace Corps volunteers swear by this place!

✗ **Bel Air** Opposite La Piscine. Serves French & Malagasy dishes at fair prices but what makes this spot unique is its view of the boardwalk & ocean.

✗ **Snack le Grilladin** 32 Av Gallieni, Ampasika. An above-average Indian restaurant with an extensive menu. Tandoori & vegetarian specialities.

✗ **Kohinoor Restaurant** Rue Henri Garnier. Indian restaurant with good food & kitsch décor. One of the few places to do a vegetarian dish of the day.

✗ **Pakiza** Av de la République (near New Continental). Pizzas & excellent Indian food at reasonable prices as well as a great variety of ice creams & milkshakes; also terrific tamarind juice. 'Not

to be missed' (D&K). *Closed Tue.*

✗ **Le Zoreole** Av de la Liberation (near Av de France). 'Fabulous Creole restaurant & bar. Clean, friendly & excellent food' (HD).

✗ **La Filibuste** Between the Air Mad office & Parad'Ice. Particularly recommended for its seafood.

⊑ **Quai Ouest** Mahajanga Be; close to Hôtel de France. Posh café serving a variety of coffees, teas, fruit drinks & pastries; excellent ambience. Co-owned by a Malagasy woman & an El Salvadorean expat. Sells high-quality handicrafts.

⊑ **Salon de Thé Saify** Near the post office & cathedral. A perennial favourite for breakfast & snacks.

⊑ **Parad'Ice** Down the street from the Air Mad office (off Bd Poincaré). 'The best ice cream in Madagascar; the passion fruit ice cream is out of this world!' They also serve wonderful breakfasts.

♀ **Bar Tabany** A popular meeting-place in the west part of town, near the market.

INTERNET

e **Cyber Kalizy** Midway between Auximad office & Bank of Africa. ADSL connection.

e **NetProject** Opposite the *palais de justice* (courts).

e **Kaoatry Le Baobab** The newest cybercafé, located in the centre of town (Mahajanga Be) next to Anjary Hotel. The computers are new & the connection is usually good. Clients can order cold beverages while surfing, but more importantly they have AC! *30Ar/min.*

MAPS The Librairie de Madagascar (on Avenues de Mahabido and Gallieni) reportedly has a good selection of maps including the FTM one of the Mahajanga region.

ANGAP

ANGAP office 14 Av Philibert Tsiranana, Immeuble Jovenna; ➲ 62 226 56; e angapmjg@wanadoo.mg; www.parcs-madagascar.com.

FEELING THE PINCH

Rupert Parker

Some years ago I decided to have lunch at a beach hotel in Mahajanga and ordered crab for starters. I asked the waitress if it was a whole crab, rather than dressed crab meat served in the shell. Oh yes, she said, it was definitely the whole crab, and very fresh, caught that morning. So we ordered two of them. Imagine our disappointment when they arrived: definitely whole crabs but with the claws missing – the tastiest meat some would say. I called the waitress over and enquired about the missing appendages. She said she didn't know and would go and ask the chef. She emerged a few minutes later and said that she was very sorry but the crabs in Mahajunga were naturally like that – they did not have claws and therefore there was nothing she could do … I resisted the urge to plunge into the sea and present her with a fully intact specimen.

WHAT TO SEE AND DO

Regional tourist office (ORTM) Hôtel de France,
10 Rue du Maréchal Joffre; ☎ 62 241 81;
e eliaiagn@wanadoo.mg.
Maderi Tour Rue Jules Ferry, Mahajanga Be (BP1087,
Mahajanga); ☎ 62 023 34. This company owns the
new Antsanitia Beach Hotel (see page 415) & also
the catamaran *Komagari* which sleeps 4 in
2 cabins. Maderi Tour arranges catamaran trips
north to Nosy Be & 4x4 excursions too.

Mozea Akiba (Museum) (⊕ *Tue–Fri 09.00–11.00 & 15.00–16.00*) This museum is
situated about 4km from the centre of town, near the Plage Touristique (take a taxi
and allow half an hour to get there). It has displays showing the history of the
region, as well as an exhibition of palaeontology and ethnology. There's also photos
and descriptions of some of Mahajanga's tourist sights such as the Cirque Rouge
and Grottes d'Anjohibe. Signs are in French but some are also in English.

Fort Rova This impressive fort at Ambohitrombikely, 20km southeast of Mahajanga,
was built on the highest point in the region in 1824 by King Radama I. The entrance
has been restored, and it is worth a visit for the views and sense of history.

DAY EXCURSIONS

Cirque Rouge About 12km from Mahajanga and 2km from the airport (as the crow
flies). This is a canyon ending in an amphitheatre of red-, beige- and lilac-coloured
rock eroded into strange shapes: peaks, spires and castles. The canyon has a broad,
sandy floor decorated with chunks of lilac clay. It is a beautiful and dramatic spot
and – with its stream of fresh water running to the nearby beach – makes an idyllic
camping place. For a day visit a taxi can take you on a round-trip from Mahajanga,
or take a *taxi-brousse* from the street west of Chez Chabaud (opposite BOA bank).
This will take you to the intersection of the Zaha Motel and airport, from where
you can walk the final 6km. Give yourself at least one hour to look around. Late
afternoon is best, when the low sun sets the reds and mauves alight.

Katsepy Katsepy (pronounced kat*sep*) is a fishing village across the bay from
Mahajanga which is reached by ferry. There are two departures a day: 07.00 and
11.00 (or 14.30), returning at 09.00 and 13.00 (or 15.30). The trip takes 45 minutes
and costs 2,250Ar. Katsepy is the starting point for exploring the wildlife areas to
the southwest of Mahajanga (see page 417).

For at least three decades there has been only one reason to go to Katsepy as a day
trip: to dine at **Chez Chabaud** (m *032 07 067 34*). I still go weak at the knees
remembering my meal there in 1984, while researching the first edition of this book.
Although the pioneering Mme Chabaud has now sadly died, her daughters have
taken over the running of the place and the restaurant is reportedly as good as ever.

There is accommodation here too: seven en-suite bungalows with very
comfortable beds (20,000–52,000Ar). Christiane Chabaud can organise a variety of
tours in the area, including Analalava, on the other side of Lake Kinkony, where she
has a tented camp.

ANKARAFANTSIKA NATIONAL PARK

This is a super national park (formerly Ampijoroa Forestry Station); it's easy to get
to, thrilling to visit with abundant wildlife, and with clear, level or stepped paths
which make hiking a pleasure. With accommodation now available next to the
park, this is a 'must' for anyone with an interest in the wildlife of this region. The
130,000ha of protected area receives funding from Germany (KFW) as well as
ANGAP. Sadly, about 4,000ha went up in flames in 2006.

Ankarafantsika straddles RN4 from Mahajanga. The most-visited part of the reserve is on the southern side of the road (on your right coming from Mahajanga), with Lac Ravelobe to the north. The park stretches north all the way to the Mahajamba river.

GETTING THERE AND AWAY

From Mahajanga The reserve is 120km from Mahajanga. It takes two hours to make the journey by car, and if you are in a private vehicle it is worth stopping at Lac Amboromalandy, a reservoir which is an excellent place to see waterfowl. *Taxi-brousses* leave town early in the morning heading for Tana. Expect to pay around 25,000Ar.

Note the excellent examples of Sakalava tombs at the 16km milestone outside Mahajanga, to your left as you're driving to Ankarafantsika.

From Tana RN4 from Tana is in good condition and the journey by *taxi-brousse* will take no more than eight hours. The park is well signposted.

🏠 Where to stay

🏠 **Gîte d'Ampijoroa** (6 rooms & 7 bungalows) Book through ANGAP, 14 Rue Philibert Tsiranana, Mahajanga; ☎ 62 226 56; e angapmjg@wanadoo.mg. The rooms are fairly small, with comfortable beds with mosquito nets. Electric lighting but no power outlets. Candles supplied for power cuts & a bottle of mineral water too. Communal facilities. The en-suite bungalows are on the shores of Lake Ravelobe. Each sleeps 4. €€€–€€€€

Camping There are several options here: bring your own tent and use the sheltered tent platforms, rent an ordinary tent or go for a spot of luxury and rent a safari tent. 'These tent platforms are the best we've seen in Madagascar; they even have electric lights and sockets' (D&K). There's a kitchen for campers, and communal ablution facilities. *Pitch: 6,000Ar/tent; tent rental: 10,000Ar (standard), 23,000Ar (safari); mattress rental: 4,000Ar; use of kitchen: 20,000Ar.*

Another possibility is to stay at the Ambodimanga campsite, a local community project. Look for the sign 700m before the park entrance, on the left as you go to Mahajanga. There are two bungalows here (about 30,000Ar per night) and about 15 sheltered tent platforms for 4,000Ar with your own tent.

✖ WHERE TO EAT

Meals for guests of the *gîte* are provided at the small, simple **Restaurant La Pygargue**, run by a local women's association of the same name and close to the roadside. Fingers-crossed they are still running it – in 2007 there were plans to give the running of the restaurant to 'a more professional group'. Breakfast is 1,800–3,000Ar and main meals 3,000–7,000Ar.

PERMITS AND GUIDES

Permits are available at Ankarafantsika and cost the usual 10,000Ar for a day trip (see page 76 for prices of multi-day permits).

There are nine guides, six of whom speak English. They cost 10,000Ar for a walking tour, maximum five people per guide.

VISITORS' CENTRE

The visitors' information centre and souvenir shop are excellent, with good information on the local customs, including the *tromba* (trance) ceremony. One of these ceremonies takes place annually on New Year's Day at Lake Ravelobe.

There are several *fady* in the area, mostly pertaining to the lake (women must not wash in the lake during menstruation and nothing can be washed – or sacrificed – at the lake on a Saturday). There is also a *fady* against eating pork.

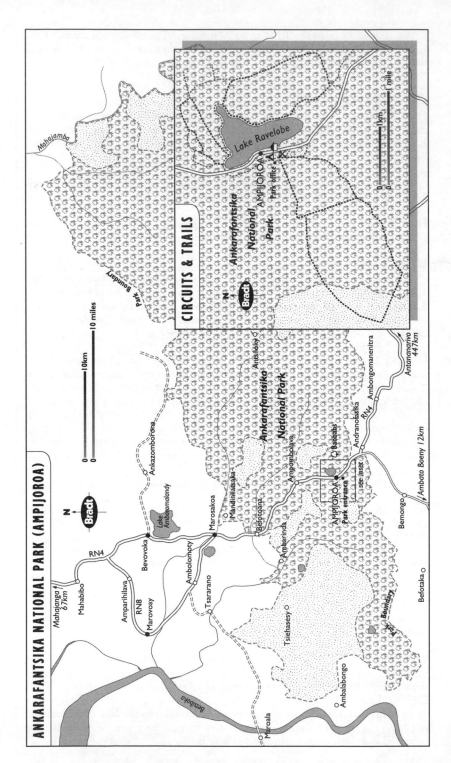

ANKARAFANTSIKA NATIONAL PARK (AMPIJOROA)

CIRCUITS & TRAILS

Lake Ravelobe

AMPIJOROA

Park office

Ankarafantsika
National
Park

Bradt

N

0   1km
0   1 mile

Mahajamba

Bounday Park

Antsiloky

Ankazomborona

Ampombolava

Ankazomborona

Andranofasika

Ambongomanenitra

RN4

Antananarivo
447km

Ambato Boeny 12km

Baobabs

AMPIJOROA
Park entrance

see inset

Bemongo

Befotaka

Andranofasika

Mandinilasaka

Befotoana

Ambarinda

Marosakoa

Ankarafantsika
National Park

Tsietsasesy

Ambalabongo

Park Boundary

Betsiboka

Maroala

Tsararano

RN8

Marovoay

Amparihilava

Mahabibo

Mahajanga
67km

RN4

Bevoyoka

Ambolonoty

Lake
Amboromalandy

N

Bradt

0   10km
0   10 miles

FLORA AND FAUNA OF ANKARAFANTSIKA This is typical dry, deciduous forest with sparse understorey and lots of lianas. In the dry winter season many of the trees have shed their leaves, but in the wet months the forest is a sea of bright greens. Conspicuous is the tree with menacing spines, *Hura crepitans,* which is actually not a native species – it was introduced from Central America. There are 129 bird species (with highlights like the Van Dam's vanga, Madagascar fish eagle and white breasted mesite), eight lemur species and reptiles galore.

Wildlife-viewing in Ankarafantsika starts as soon as you arrive. Right beside the parking area is a tree that Coquerel's sifakas use as a dormitory. They are extremely handsome animals with the usual silky white fur but with chestnut-brown arms and thighs. On your walks you may also see mongoose lemurs, western woolly lemurs and sportive lemurs if the guide shows you its tree. This is the only place in the world where you might see the golden-brown mouse lemur, *Microcebus ravelobensis,* named after Lake Ravelobe.

CIRCUITS Much has been done to maintain and upgrade the trail system in the park. There is a viewpoint, Belle Vue, on a hilltop from where there is a fantastic view over the Ankarafantsika forest. A bench has thoughtfully been put there so visitors can relax and enjoy the lemurs and birds in the trees around them.

Trails developed for visitors include:

Circuit Coquereli 1½–3hrs. Recommended for first-time visitors as an introductory walk. Good for sifakas and brown lemurs. Grading: easy.

Circuit Retendrika 2–3hrs. More focused on botany. The guides take visitors on a trail where the trees are labelled. Guides will give an account of the medicinal, magical or edible properties of the various trees and plants. It's also good for birds. Grading: moderate.

Pachypodium visit 2 hrs. Not so much a circuit as a visit to one of the park's particular attractions. Grading: medium.

Baobab Trail 1–2 hrs. To save time, you may wish to drive in the direction of Andranofasika, then take a walk near the south side of Lake Ravelobe. You traverse some raffia-dominated forest and rice paddies, cross a new hanging bridge (2003) and end up at some spectacular, very tall baobabs: *Adansonia madagascariensis.* Some scientists consider these four specimens to be a separate subspecies found nowhere else. Grading: easy.

Circuit Source de Vie 3–4 hrs. Best for visitors who wish to gain an insight into local culture and everyday life of the rural community in and around the park. Grading: moderate.

Circuit Ankarokaroka 3–4 hrs. A hike through forest and some savanna, and also to the canyon, described by one couple as 'perhaps the finest walk we did here. The canyon is an amazing multicoloured erosion feature. On this route we pretty well saw all the bird, animal and plant life that this park has to offer in daytime.' Grading: moderate.

Nocturnal walks 1½hrs. A night walk usually starts at 19.00 and is an essential part of a visit to this national park. It is the only time you will see mouse lemurs, and it's also much easier to spot chameleons at night. The most commonly seen local species is the rhinoceros chameleon. Grading: easy.

Boat trip 1–2hrs. Excursions on Lake Ravelobe. The lake is no longer considered safe for walking – or swimming – because of several crocodile attacks in recent years. Birders will find this trip very rewarding. Crocodile sightings are likely too: 'suddenly our guide jumped up. "Crocodile!" he shouted, pointing. Our hearts raced as we scanned the bank for the fearsome beast. Then we spotted it just a few feet away, basking in the sun – a baby, barely six inches long!' (D&K).

Vehicle tour Includes some 'red *tsingy*' (eroded laterite).

PROJET ANGONOKA Ankarafantsika is also home to the Angonoka Tortoise Programme operated by the Durrell Wildlife Conservation Trust (see box on page 72). This is one of Madagascar's most successful captive breeding projects. After many years of research, and much trial and error, the ploughshare tortoise – the world's rarest tortoise – is now breeding readily and is being reintroduced to the Baly Bay area – its original habitat. Almost as rare, the attractive little flat-tailed tortoise (*kapidolo*) is also being bred here.

The site has been upgraded and fortified since the theft of a large number of ploughshare tortoises in the 1990s. An exciting addition to the Durrell site is the *rere* or Madagascar big-headed/side-necked turtle, an endangered endemic freshwater turtle confined to the western lakes. Breeding success of the *rere* has been excellent, and some 150 of the captive-bred turtles have already been released into one of the lakes in the park.

Because of the extra security required to safeguard these rare animals, it is possible for tourists to glimpse them only through a chain-link fence.

NORTHEAST OF MAHAJANGA

ANJOHIBE CAVES AND BEYOND Note: *Anjohibe* means 'big cave' so this name is common in the region.

The Grottes d'Anjohibe are 82km northeast of Mahajanga and accessible only by 4x4, and only in the dry season. There are two places to visit: the caves themselves and a natural swimming pool above the Mahafanina waterfalls. The caves are full of stalactites and stalagmites (and bats), and have 2km of passages. Dan Carlsson of Project Madagascar (Sweden) excavated these caves in 1996. 'It seems as though the caves have been used for normal living but also as a place of sacrifice. We found pottery with ash, charcoal and animal bones … also several hippopotamus bones believed to be some million years old.'

Bill Love visited the caves in 2003: 'The drive took over three hours one way via very dusty, moderately bumpy roads. Sifakas seen *en route*. The ancient, rusty staircases seemed a bit creaky; they certainly can't last much longer. Flashlights a must to enjoy properly! The cave was spectacular inside.

'To reach the caves turn left at the village of **Antanamarina** (hotel Chez Marcel, 5,000Ar), from where it is another 5km. Then, to cool off, return to the village and take the road straight ahead to the waterfall and pools. There are natural pools both above and below the waterfall. To add to the excitement there may be crocodiles in the lower pool.'

John and Valerie Middleton, who explored the region in 2005, add: 'Two thirds of the way to the caves the river Mariarano is crossed next to the small, friendly village of Posima. This river is truly stunning in its beauty. It is crystal clear, about 15m across, runs over dazzling white limestone and is banked by bright white sand. We made this one of our campsites for exploration. The area is very beautiful with many cone-shaped hills often with small bits of *tsingy* on their tops and covered in savanna with palms dotted sporadically. We came across many caves in these hills, most with large passageways and beautiful formations. We also camped by the beautiful lake administered by Chez Marcel in Antanamarina. Marcel himself makes an excellent and knowledgeable guide to the region.' The Middletons go on to describe further exploration of the area. Contact Bradt Travel Guides (e *info@bradtguides.com*) for a copy.

ANTSANITIA BEACH RESORT (✆ *62 023 34 (Mahajanga);* m *032 05 196 90;* e *antsanitia@antsanitia.com; www.antsanitia.com/inauguration-hotel-antsanitia.htm. Bungalows 75,000–112,500Ar*) This new place, about an hour's drive north of Mahajanga, is getting rave reviews. 'It's in an idyllic location with an excellent and beautiful restaurant. Free use of canoe to paddle the ocean shore or up the river. Great beachcombing. Very friendly staff and delightful bungalows. The hotel works with the local community and tries to be ecologically responsible' (HD). Information from the Maderi Tour office in Mahajanga.

FLY-IN BEACH RESORTS If you look on a map of Madagascar, you'll see a glorious expanse of nothingness along the indented coastline between Mahajanga and Nosy Be. This is where three entrepreneurs have established fly-in resorts which come (in my opinion) as close to perfection as you could hope for.

Lodge des Terres Blanches (✆ *+261 320 433 820 Madagascar satellite phone;* e *lodgeterresblanches@yahoo.fr; www.lodgeterresblanches.com.* € *110 all-inclusive; transfers* € *150 by air transfer,* € *100 by boat, 2¹/₂hrs, min 6 people*) About 100km from Mahajanga and 25km south of Anjajavy. This lodge really does qualify for the cliché 'best kept secret' (at least from English-speaking tourists) since it sees far fewer visitors than Anjajavy or Marovasa-Be (see below) and no tour groups. It is owned by former bush-pilot Jacky Cauvin, the original owner of the Anjajavy plot. He provides basic, but comfortable, accommodation in six double bungalows next to a gorgeous white beach fringed with forest. Compared with the luxury lodges this is a simple, do-it-yourself resort. Electricity is by generator (but runs most of the time) and there are now power sockets for recharging cameras. Guests eat together in the lodge, and there is a bar with fridge for guests to help themselves.

If you want to go on a longer hike, or to be dropped off in a cove somewhere for the day, picnics can be arranged.

This is a popular resort for sport-fishermen, and the two boats are largely used for fishing trips. However, you can arrange to be taken to some beautiful coves along the coast, or to baobab-arrayed islands, or to an area of *tsingy*.

'The meals (not recommended for vegetarians) are a great way to practise your French: Jacky's English is impeccable, but most of his guests are francophone, and Jacky is a fantastic host and raconteur over a glass of his *rhum arrangé* after sunset, as well as being extremely knowledgeable about local Sakalava culture and Malagasy flora and fauna' (Ilya Eigenbrot).

The lodge can be booked through Madagascar Discovery in Tana (✆ *+261 20 22 351 65, www.madagascar-discovery.com*) or other tour operators.

La Maison de Marovasa-Be (✆ *+1 41 49 60 10 (France)/+870 761 291 717 Madagascar; satellite phone;* e *contactparis@marovasabe.com or marovasabe@skyfile.com; www.marovasabe.com. Room* € *150pp, suite* € *200pp; air transfers from Tana* € *300pp return, from Mahajanga* € *150 return*) Some 15–20km north of Anjajavy in Moramba Bay. The location is, perhaps, not as attractive as that of the other two lodges, and its forest has suffered from slash-and-burn agriculture (*tavy*). However, the hotel itself is beautifully thought-out and offers true luxury with a beautiful swimming pool and other amenities. The owners are also involved with Ecole du Monde (see below). Their work includes reforestation projects, and guests can contribute by planting a tree. As with all these lodges, the rates are all-inclusive and include a motorboat for exploring the area.

There are three suites and six luxury rooms, all with en-suite bathrooms and balconies. Rates are full board including wine.

Anjajavy (e *contact@anjajavy.com; www.anjajavy.com; see* Bookings *for additional contact details. Dbl per night based on a 3-night stay €190pp Dec–Mar, €245pp Apr–Nov, €270pp Christmas/New Year, min stay 5 days at Christmas, 7 days at New Year; prices about 10% cheaper for stays of 4 nights or more; honeymoon special offers apply; children aged 2–12 less than half price; prices include all meals, excursions that do not involve motor transport and a full range of sports activities)*) I don't often experience real luxury, but Anjajavy is about as good as you can get in Madagascar. And this is not just a luxury seaside hotel: in addition to its 25 villas it includes 450ha of Madagascar's dwindling dry deciduous forest. In some places this grows right on the *tsingy* limestone. This is what makes Anjajavy so special – it's the only protected area between Mahajanga and Nosy Be.

Wildlife viewing here is effortless. When I was there in late June, a troop of Coquerel's sifakas visited a fruiting tree near one of the villas promptly at 15.30 each day. Sometimes they were joined by common brown lemurs and at night our torch beam picked out the eyes of perhaps a dozen mouse lemurs (later identified as the newly described *Microcebus danfossi*, a species rather unromantically named after an industrial manufacturing company that sponsors lemur conservation projects). Sportive lemurs are also easy to spot. Then there were the birds – flocks of bright green grey-headed love-birds, sickle-billed vangas, Madagascar crested ibises, crested couas and vasa parrots, to name just a few. Reptiles are common. You may see ground boas and hognose snakes and plenty of chameleons – most common is Oustalet's chameleon, the world's largest species.

This place is also full of butterflies, with the spectacular endemic and largest Malagasy butterfly, *Atrophaneura antenor*, and in May you can see the beautiful green day-flying moth *Chrysiridia ripheus* (more commonly known by its obsolete name *Urania*), which is of particular interest because of its close resemblance to a South American species.

There's a cave, too, spectacular enough with its stalactites and stalagmites to be worth a visit, but with the addition of countless Commerson's leaf-nosed bats (see photo in the colour section). Another cave has the skulls of extinct lemur species embedded in the rocks.

Perhaps most startlingly for botanists, Anjajavy and Moramba Bay hold an unknown population of wild cycad trees. Hithero Madagascar was thought to have just one cycad species distributed only on the east coast.

Then there are the coral reefs, *tsingy*, pristine beaches and extensive mangroves … not to mention total comfort, brilliant service and superb food! Three nights is the minimum stay, five allows you to appreciate all that this amazing place has to offer. Anjajavy offers a range of land- and water-based activities. Some, such as guided forest walks in the reserve, are included in the rates. Other free activities include waterskiing, catamaran sailing, windsurfing, snorkelling and visits to the surrounding villages.

For an additional fee you can indulge in deep-sea fishing, mountain biking (a nominal charge of €10) and massages.

For a longer excursion there's the magnificent **Moramba Bay** (15km/45mins north of the lodge by boat). It costs €40 and is a must for any nature enthusiast. The bay has many small, uninhabitable limestone islands, some eroded by the sea into a *champignon* shape, and also *tsingy* limestone formations. There are also a great number of baobabs – three different species. A particularly large specimen of *Adansonia digitata* on one of the islands is considered sacred by the local Sakalava people, who once or twice a year ritually sacrifice a zebu and take the horns to the base of the tree. It is *fady* to walk anti-clockwise around the sacred baobab or to go there on a Thursday. On some of the islets, you may also see little caves – burial sites of the Sakalava people – high up and isolated because it is *fady* for pigs to walk over a Sakalava grave.

Then there are the birds. Moramba Bay is home to no fewer than four of the world's remaining hundred or so pairs of the critically endangered Madagascar fish eagle and close views of this raptor are virtually guaranteed. 'We also saw a Madagascar harrier-hawk and peregrine falcon harassing a massive colony of Madagascar black swifts. A highlight was seeing some Madagascar pratincoles, an attractive summer-breeding visitor. On our way back to the lodge, we made a quick diversion into the mangrove, where we enjoyed exceptional views of another critically endangered endemic, the Madagascar white ibis' (D Schuurman).

Ecole du Monde This NGO works with the management of Anjajavy to benefit local villages. Tour operator Derek Schuurman visited in 2006 and was favourably impressed. 'Since the hotel opened they have built four schools. A fishing school (with emphasis on marine ecology), an agricultural school and a project to send children on bursaries to secondary school in Mahajanga have all been established. I was taken to see one of the villages, Ambondro Ampasy, where windmills, sanitation blocks, a bakery and a clinic have been built. Of the village's population of 224, 64 are of school age. For a remote and virtually inaccessible village the facilities are exceptional, including a well-stocked library with television and DVD so pupils are able to watch educational films.

'The hotel lends further support to the fishing and agricultural schools through its policy of sourcing supplies locally, as far as possible. Guests are encouraged to visit the villages, observe the achievements, and contribute medicines to the clinic and educational materials to the school.

The tree nursery at the back of the lodge grows the increasingly rare *palissandre* (Madagascar rosewood) and other slow-growing endemic hardwoods, so saplings can be replanted in areas of forest degradation. Villagers are given an incentive to plant saplings, and guests may do so too. This is a wonderful way of literally giving something back' (see page 137).

Bookings Book through tour operators or the Paris headquarters (*31 Rue de Bellefond, 75009 Paris;* ☎ *+33 1 44 69 15 03;* f *+33 1 44 69 15 35;* e *lhotelparis@ prat.com*).

Getting there Anjajavy is accessible only by means of light aircraft, an 8-seater Cessna, operated by Air Hotel (they have their own little lounge in Ivato airport). Baggage allowance: 20kg. Tana–Anjajavy–Tana: Mon/Thu/Sat; Anjajavy–Nosy Be–Anjajavy: Mon/Thu. Flights leave Tana at 07.00, arriving at 08.30. Return fares: €475/300 adult/child. The flight takes 90 minutes.

Air Hotel can arrange flights for other days of the week – ask for a quote (m *032 07 228 28;* e *airhotel@wanadoo.mg*).

CONSERVATION AREAS TO THE SOUTHWEST OF MAHAJANGA

From Katsepy (see page 410) a road, of sorts, provides access to the *tsingy* and wetlands which are of great interest to anyone who loves Madagascar's diversity of landscape, plants and wildlife. Access is exceptionally difficult, however, so even adventurous travellers may prefer an organised tour.

NOSY BOENY (NOSY ANTSOHERIBORY) This is a small island, about a kilometre long, in Boina Bay, with some fascinating Antalaotra ruins dating from the 16th century (see box opposite). In its heyday the town probably supported a population of about 7,000. The ruins include several cemeteries, houses and mosques. The island is sacred to the local people so camping is prohibited. Day visits are allowed, however.

To reach the island, start from Katsepy and continue by road to the village of Boeny-Ampasy on the west side of the bay. There are some bungalows here. A 1½-hour boat journey brings you to Nosy Boeny. Patrice Kerloc (☏ *62 236 62*) can arrange trips here. If you go, bring insect repellent – there are lots of mosquitoes.

MAHAVAVY-KINKONY WETLAND COMPLEX The NGO BirdLife International is developing a programme to conserve this wetland area while encouraging ecotourism. This falls into the remit of the President's Durban Vision and received protected status in 2007. Spokesman Roger Safford says: 'All the communes are very much in favour – it will allow fishing and various other economic activities, but now controlled locally.' For birders or others interested in seeing a truly untouched part of Madagascar, it's well worth making the effort to visit. By doing so you will be supporting the Durban Vision and all it stands for.

Mitsinjo is the capital of the district but the gateway town is Namakia. The protected area covers 268,236ha, comprising marine bays (Boeny, Marambitsy), river and river delta (Mahavavy River) and lakes (Kinkony, the second largest lake of Madagascar and 22 small lakes in its vicinity). The many different ecosystems in the area include dry deciduous forest and gallery forest, savanna, marshland, lakes, mangrove and caves.

This variety of habitats leads to extraordinary biodiversity but the most striking part of it is the fauna: nine species of lemur, including crowned and Decken's sifakas and the mongoose lemur, nine species of bat (one undescribed), a host of reptiles and, of course, fish (six endemic freshwater species). But it is the birds that cause the most excitement: 143 species. And this is the only site where all of the Malagasy western waterfowl species may be seen. It's enough to make a twitcher salivate! Birders should know that July to September are the best months for seeing breeding birds.

In the Tsiombikibo Classified Forest, near Mitsinjo, are several small beautiful ponds (for example Matsaborimirafy, two hours' walk from Mitsinjo), which are the refuge of white-backed ducks and African pigmy geese.

Getting to Mitsinjo and Namakia As with so many places in the northwest, independent travellers face a challenge – though that is all part of the experience.

By sea The port of Namakia is reached in 5–6 hours by motorboat from Mahajanga but the sea is usually quite rough.

By road From Katsepy it is 3–4 hours' drive. From Katsepy to Mitsinjo the road is not bad, but thereafter it is in poor condition and closed during the rainy season. *Taxi-brousses* meet the ferry at Katsepy (around 13.00 and 20.00). They leave Mitsinjo and Namakia in the (very) small hours to be at Katsepy in time for the first ferry. Travellers can arrange with the driver to be picked up at their hotel. The cost is 5,000–6 000Ar.

Where to stay/eat
Mitsinjo

⌂ **Chez Kaloper Jean Cesar** (4 rooms) Very basic; shared facilities. Meals must be ordered in advance | or eaten at nearby *hotelys*. Camping permitted in the enclosed garden. €

'All *taxi-brousses* stop in Mitsinjo since it is the last opportunity to grab a meal until reaching Soalala (80km south). There are various *hotelys* serving Malagasy food,

Information from Jean Jacques Randriamanindry

This name, which means the 'people from the sea' was given to the Islamic traders who settled in northwest Madagascar about a thousand years ago. Racially they were a mixture of Arab, African and Malagasy, united by their Islamic faith. Their language was probably similar to Swahili with some Malagasy words. They brought trade goods from East Africa, Arabia and further afield, and settled in the west, from Maintirano north to Iharana (Vohemar) in the northeast. Here archaeological excavations have uncovered items such as Chinese porcelain and Persian glassware, some dating back to the 12th century.

The Antalaotra flourished before the arrival of the Europeans. They traded cattle, rice and slaves from Madagascar for pearls, ceramics, fabric and silver. Boeny was one of their main settlements during this period, but with the arrival of the Europeans their trading strength faded. Unable to compete with these newcomers, and threatened by the emerging power of the Sakalava Boina Kingdom, they retreated to the island of Antsoheribory. Although they continued to trade from this new base, their influence was in decline, with the Europeans dealing direct with the Sakalava. The last straw came in the late 17th and 18th centuries, when boats were built which were too large to cope with the shallow water around the island and business moved to the present-day port of Mahajanga. The Europeans, with their weapons and larger market for slaves in the Mascarene Islands and the Americas, were now dominant and the Antalaotra people became absorbed into the local populations where, some say, they remain to this day as the Malagasy Muslims of the west coast.

---

none of particular note though almost all seem to have rather delicious homemade yoghurt' (S&B O'Neil).

Namakia

⌂ **Le Cercle** This is at the former sugar factory. Comfortable & clean; a good base for exploring the area. Facilities range from basic with shared facilities to en-suite rooms. Cold water only (but no problem in this sweltering climate). Restaurant. €–€€€

⌂ **Chez Madame Zaza** A very basic hotel & restaurant. €

 Camping BirdLife International is hoping to build campsites at **Makary**, 20 minutes by car from Mitsinjo, as a base for seeing the critically endangered Sakalava rail and the birds of Lake Kinkony, and at **Ampitsopitsoka** for Bernier's teal and other birds of the delta. Also **Anjohibe** (not the Mahajanga *'grottes'*!) for the caves and bats and for forest walks to look for crowned sifakas, mongoose lemurs and forest birds.

SOALALA AND BEYOND

SOALALA Until recently very few visitors came to Soalala, though herpetologists working on the Angonoka tortoise project have been regular visitors, along with a handful of adventurous travellers. John and Valerie Middleton visited a few years ago: 'This is a fascinating port and well worth visiting. It contains several very large African baobabs and impressive *Pachypodiums*. It was previously a French fort and at least two ancient cannons can be seen on the seafront. There are also many good eating places. Across the bay is a massive French shrimp farm.' Now, that the Tsingy de Namoroka and Baie de Baly are national parks,

Soalala has gained importance as the gateway town, and facilities for visitors are opening up. My thanks to Peace Corps volunteers Sandra and Bobby O'Neill for the following information.

Getting there
By air Soalala has an airport (well, a hut with a grassy air strip) served by Twin Otter twice a week.

By road *Taxi-brousses* from Katsepy only go to Soalala twice a week. The 12-hour journey costs about 30,000Ar. A private 4x4 will cut the journey by 2–4 hours.

By sea Cargo boats that take passengers (*boutres*) make frequent trips to Soalala from Mahajanga, costing around 10,000Ar. This is not a trip for softies (see box on page 423) but at least the trip is relatively short. The *Aquamas* shrimp freighter does the trip regularly, taking 14 hours and carrying up to 60 passengers, mostly shrimp factory employees.

You may also find a pirogue (*lakana*) or motorboat (*vedette*). As the area gains popularity, the transport options will improve.

Where to stay/eat
🏠 **Chez la Mere de Nadia** m 034 01 036 79. At the time of writing work is still in progress constructing this guesthouse-cum-restaurant, but it is due to be completed in 2007. There will 2 dbl rooms & a small apartment with kitchen. The French owner, Maurice Bonafous, also provides a guide service & can organise all-in tours, thus eliminating transport problems (see below for contact details.) €–€€

Camping 'There is a patch of west-facing beachfront that offers white sand, shady coconut palms and a spectacular view of the sunset. (It is also the quietest spot in town)' (SO).

Various *hotelys* on the main road and around town serve Malagasy food. The market near the mayor's office in the town centre sells the usual variety of fresh produce including fish. Sandra adds: 'The Georgina Bar has the largest freezer in town and virtually never runs out of cold drinks or admirers to watch music videos on her colour TV.'

ANGAP There is an ANGAP office in Soalala, but it has no telephone.

Guided tours Maurice Bonafous offers a guided tour of the Baie de Baly region. The four-day excursion begins in Katsepy (or at your hotel in Mahajanga) and ends at a campsite near the *grottes* at the Tsingy de Namoroka. Transport is in a 4x4 with AC, with a couple of rest-stops on the way to Soalala. Then across the Baie de Baly by boat before heading to Namoroka. He can also arrange fishing excursions in the Baie de Baly. Bookings should be made well in advance by calling Maurice (m *034 01 036 79*) or his daughter Nadia in Mahajunga (m *033 12 179 56;* e *lakana2005@yahoo.fr*).

BAIE DE BALY NATIONAL PARK
This national park, created just a decade ago, is across the bay from Soalala, occupying the better part of the northwest peninsula and extending east across the bay to Cap Sada. It protects a variety of terrestrial and aquatic ecosystems: mangrove forests, coastal dunes, rivers, permanent lakes and dense dry semi-deciduous forests. The idyllic coastal villages surrounding the park offer visitors a glimpse into the Sakalava way of life. **Bemosary**, **Maroalika** and **Batainomby**

feature the most attractive white-sand beaches on the peninsula. Camping is permitted, although no official ANGAP camping facilities exist.

The two must-see inhabitants of the park are the *angonoka* or ploughshare tortoise (*Geochelone yniphora*), endemic to the park, and the very rare Madagascar fish eagle (*Haliaeetus vociferoides*). This eagle, known locally as *ankoay*, nests among trees bordering a lake deep within the park. Here tourists can put up tents and get the best sighting of Madagascar's largest bird of prey.

Baie de Baly also hosts a large community of migratory birds including the greater flamingo (*Phoenicopterus ruber*). Dolphins have also been known to trail the outgoing boat traffic.

GETTING THERE Transportation to and from Baie de Baly National Park can only be arranged at ANGAP's offices in Soalala and Mahajunga, or through Maurice Bonafous (m *034 01 036 79*).

TSINGY DE NAMOROKA NATIONAL PARK

Although protected since 1966, Tsingy de Namaroka only gained national park status relatively recently. It is 164km southwest of Mahajanga and 50km south of Soalala. The park offers several distinct circuits showcasing the dense sub-humid forests of the west, crocodile caves, canyons and savanna – habitats for an impressive array of wildlife. Among them are 81 species of birds, including the endangered Madagascar teal (*Anas bernieri*) and the crested ibis. The 30 species of reptile include a black-and-yellow striped nocturnal snake (a species of *Stenophis*) endemic to Namoroka, and the locally endemic side-necked (or big-headed) turtle, *Erymnochelys madagascariensis*. Then there are the five species of frog, and the lemurs: Decken's sifaka, red-fronted brown lemur and western grey bamboo lemur, not to mention three species of nocturnal lemur. And, if you're lucky, the fossa.

In addition to the wildlife there's the scenery. At Mandevy, there's a bubbling spring of clear water, and nearby baobabs cling to *tsingy*, 'giving the impression of an old man with unkempt hair'. Many of the cave networks in Namoroka are unexplored and unmapped and should be entered only with a guide.

After exploring the park, intrepid travellers can follow in the footsteps of the Middletons and continue to Vilanandro, Tondraka and beyond. For a detailed account of this trip contact Bradt (e *info@bradtguides.com*).

GETTING THERE The park cannot be accessed by public transport. You need to arrange it through the ANGAP office in Soalala, or through Maurice Bonafous (see above).

BEYOND MAHAJANGA

MAROVOAY About 50km from Mahajanga a road branches off RN4 and leads to Marovoay (12km). Formerly the residence of the Boina kings, the town's name means 'many crocodiles'. When the French attacked the Malagasy forces assembled in Marovoay in 1895 in their successful drive to conquer Madagascar, it is reported that hundreds of crocodiles emerged from the river to devour the dead and dying. Malagasy hunters have since got their revenge, and you would be lucky to see a croc these days. Colin Palmer, a self-confessed 'boat anorak', reports: 'Marovoay is just a nice place to hang out. It has warm, friendly people and a port to wander in. This was evidently quite important in French times, but is now silted up and disused by large vessels. However, local people still make use of it as a market for their produce from the delta.' **Hôtel Standard** in the main street offers good accommodation.

Rejoining RN4 you pass through **Ankarafantsika National Park** (Ampijoroa; see page 410) to meet RN6, the road to Antsiranana, at Ambondromamy. Here you have the choice of going south to Tana or north to Ambanja and Nosy Be.

THE ROUTE NORTH

THE ROAD TO ANTSOHIHY This road is gradually being improved with EU funding, but it will take a while for the tourist hordes to discover it, so make the most of this window of opportunity!

At **Ambondromamy** the road forks and you turn left onto RN6, formerly in very poor condition but perhaps improved by the time you read this. The next town, **Mampikony**, is the centre of onion production in Madagascar, even exporting them to Réunion. Accommodation is limited to the very basic **Hôtel La Mampikony** (5,000Ar) or **Les Cocotiers** (10,000Ar). 'There's a terrace by the road where we ate and watched the world go by. Everywhere there were onions: on the stalls, on lorries, loose being sorted or in sacks waiting to be transported … you have got to know your onions in Mampikony!' (SE).

The next town of importance is **Port Bergé** (Boriziny), 82km away. Here onions give way to tobacco and cotton. This is a pleasant town with at least two hotels, the **Zinnia** ('filthy, smells, rats') and **Le Monde** ('immaculate, friendly'). From Port Bergé to Antsohihy is 133km, which can normally be done in about five hours.

ANTSOHIHY Pronounced antso*ee*, this uninspiring town is a good base for exploration, and accessible by Twin Otter as well as *taxi-brousse*. It is also important for travellers, being at the crossroads of four important centres: southwest to Tana, north to **Ambanja**, northeast to **Bealanana** and southeast to **Befandriana** and **Mandritsara**. It's also possible to travel west by sea or (adventurously) by land.

Where to stay/eat

Hôtel Blaina Thatched bungalows with en-suite bathrooms. By far the best accommodation in town, so often booked up. Good restaurant but order your food well in advance – the service is very slow. €€

Vona Vatolampy Annexe (5 rooms) On the left side of Hôtel Blaina. Clean, with mosquito nets. No restaurant but you can go next door to the Blaina. €€

Hôtel de France In the upper town, by the main square. €

Hôtel La Plaisance On the opposite side of the square to Hôtel de France. 'It had fewer squashed & flying mosquitoes in the rooms than Hôtel de France. Cold shower; loos on the 2nd-floor landing. Some rooms are on the opposite side of the road. All ground-floor rooms in effect open onto the street. It also has a bar & small dance floor downstairs where there is a Friday disco' (SE). €

Getting there and away The air connection to Antsohihy no longer runs. It takes about six hours to/from **Ambanja**, a distance of 217km on a newly asphalted road. About 15km from Antohihy you turn off RN31. After the town of **Maromandia** the vegetation changes as the road climbs; scrubland gives way to tropical vegetation and cashew trees.

Sea excursions from Antsohihy Antsohihy is situated on a fjord-like arm of the sea which becomes the River Loza. There is a regular boat service to **Ananalava**, an isolated village accessible in the dry season by *taxi-brousse* but otherwise only by boat or plane (Twin Otter). There is a small hotel here, Hôtel-restaurant Malibu. 'Basic chalets right by the sea. If the owner is around the food is fantastic!' (Vicky Hopley).

Marko Petrovic

I and two Slovenian girls caught the '*taxi-brousse* of the sea' from the sailing port in Mahajanga. It wasn't hard to find one going to Morondava and we quickly settled on a price of 60,000Ar each. These sailing ships which transport goods (and people) up and down the west coast vary in size but ours was average: 15m with two masts and a 30-tonne capacity. The boats have no motor, so departure is timed to coincide with the outgoing high tide. We left in the evening and at 02.00 the sailors hoisted the sails and a strong wind blew us southwards. Everybody except the helmsman (nine sailors and 15 paying passengers) slept on the deck.

The first day the wind was strong and the big waves made us sick. The boat sailed far from the coast which at times was barely visible. The sailors have nothing to help them navigate – not even a compass – yet at every moment they know where they are relative to the coast. At night they use the stars for navigation.

The second day there was neither wind nor waves and, with no shade, the heat was terrible. We took plenty of water with us but for food we shared the rice which the other people cooked over a fire. With seasickness our appetites receded and we ate little, which wasn't a bad thing as there was no toilet on board. We stood in a queue in the bow … Once some sharks paid us a visit and circled the boat. Somebody threw them some food which disappeared frighteningly quickly. Later we were approached by a motorboat with four dead turtles. One was transferred to our boat and a sailor immediately set about cutting up the beautiful animal. Pieces of fat from the carcass were hung up on the ropes and later eaten with the rice. The awful smell accompanied us for the rest of the voyage.

That night we experienced an incredible storm. The lightning flashes turned the sea an eerie greyish-white and the rain poured. The sailors set up a large (perforated) tarpaulin over the boom and everybody squeezed underneath for shelter. We were soaked, cold, and didn't sleep much.

At the end of the third day we finally reached our first port of call: Tamborano. The sailors had spotted it from miles away, recognising it from its palm trees protruding above the horizon. The little town's harbour is reached via a river mouth – a risky business due to sand flats – so the onboard dugout canoe was sent out to guide us. When we finally set foot on dry land we swayed like drunks! This little town can only be reached by sea and air as the roads are impassable. There was no restaurant so one of the passengers we had befriended (the only French-speaker) took us to an Indian trader who kindly cooked us pasta. It was our first proper meal in four days.

The next day, thanks to a strong wind, we finally reached Maintirano, to offload our cargo of sugar and soap. It is as isolated as Tamborano due to terrible roads, but this makes the people friendly and welcoming and we really grew to like this town during our four days there.

A drunken sailor delayed the departure and the two girls decided to fly back to Tana. I, being stubborn and having enough time, decided to continue on the boat which, thanks to a very strong wind, reached Morondava in less than 24 hours. The sailors found it hilarious that I had been deserted by the girls but the drunken sailor was ashamed and avoided me!

Nosy Saba From Ananalava you may be lucky enough to find a sturdy boat to take you to this almost-perfect island for a few days. I have been here twice and doubt if any island comes closer to paradise. There is fresh water, a few fishermen's huts (abandoned in the rainy season), coconut palms, curving bays of yellow sand, a densely forested section with clouds of fruit-bats, coral, chameleons …

If arriving by yacht, the anchorage south of the eastern tip gives good shelter from the north to northwest winds. Anchor 100m off the beach over a sand shelf 1.5–4m deep. The edge of the shelf drops off steeply. Close to the shore are shallow coral patches. Further out, watch the strong tidal currents: the northwest-flowing ebb makes a rolling swell. The water is very clear and a remarkable number of large game fish can be seen even when snorkelling along the island's edge southwest of the anchorage. The coral is excellent, and scuba-diving along the drop-off is rewarding.

Nosy Lava The large island of Nosy Lava (long island) lies temptingly off Ananalava. It was formerly a maximum-security prison housing the country's most vicious murderers. In previous editions I've written 'By all accounts they lead pretty enjoyable lives: women from Ananalava are said to cross over by pirogue to fraternise with the prisoners. They've also been provided with electricity and other mod cons not available to ordinary folk. One Malagasy informant commented that "Nosy Lava is more like a holiday camp than a prison".' Another informant now tells me 'although it's no longer a prison, many of the former inmates have chosen to stay.' It could make for an interesting visit!

FROM ANTSOHIHY TO MANDRITSARA

The road is in good condition. *Taxi-brousses* leave every morning, passing through **Befandriana Nord** where there is a basic hotel (Rose de Chine) and continuing through beautiful mountain scenery to Mandritsara, the cultural centre of the Tsimihety people. The journey should take no more than five hours.

MANDRITSARA The name means 'peaceful' (literally 'lies down well'), and was reportedly bestowed on it by King Radama I during his campaigns. There are several hotels here including **Hôtel Pattes**, a nice little place with excellent food.

Mandritsara also, surprisingly, has one of the best hospitals in Madagascar: the **Baptist Missionary Hospital.** Tom Savage writes: 'The hospital is called Hopitaly Vaovao Mahafaly (HVM for short) which means "good news hospital". They are great, and people travel far and wide to get there. They also have a regular turnover of medical students on their electives from all over the world. The doctor in charge there is British: Dr David Mann.' (See box opposite for an account of the work at this hospital.)

BEALANANA

A good, paved road from Antsohihy runs northeast to Bealanana. The town is quite high, and the temperate climate with ample rainfall allows the cultivation of potatoes and a great variety of fruit. Geology students Paul Janssen and Roelf Mulder spent a while in this region. 'The road is very beautiful, climbing into the mountains to the high plateau. You cross several rivers rushing through truck-sized boulders.'

The town's electricity supply is very erratic – bear this in mind if you are dependent on electricity for recharging batteries. You may have to wait a couple of days before the power goes back on. If you are heading further inland note that Bealanana is the last place with public telephones (using only Gulfsat cards, not the common Madacom ones).

WHERE TO STAY/EAT

🏠 **La Crête** Helpful, friendly owners; very comfortable dbl rooms with en-suite bathrooms (though erratic – & cold – water). Cheaper rooms have shower but shared toilet. €

✖ **Faniry** Just 200m from La Crête. This simple *hotely* provides good meals at good prices. 'The woman who runs this *hotely* is really kind & helps you out with all sorts of things, like the laundry.'

CONTINUING INLAND Heading inland you reach **Ambatoria** in less than 1½ hours along a beautiful stretch of road. This small lively town has many shops and is the last stop for the *taxi-brousse*. It is also the last place you can buy petrol. Beyond Ambatoria you'll need a 4x4 and a guide (because there are many tracks leading away from the main road). The valley of Mangindrano is one of Madagascar's main producers of rice, so you might hitch a ride on a supply truck. There are several small rivers to ford (check the depth of the water) and it can take three hours to drive the 25km. Worth it, though. The village is at 1,100m, surrounded by mountains.

Mangindrano does not have any accommodation. Paul and Roelf were given two rooms near the hospital and a family cooked their meals.

It's possible to visit the **Massif of Tsaratanana** from here. Ask for Lefalle, who conveniently is the only person in the village to sell beer. He speaks some French, is an experienced guide and can organise porters. Paul and Roelf did a ten-day excursion for their geological research. 'After 1½ hours' walk you are already in the jungle and the mountains with their granitic peaks are really impressive. One of the great excursions you can do from here is the route to the highest mountain of Madagascar the **Maromokotro** (2,876m). We didn't do it, unfortunately; the guide said that it takes a week to reach the peak but the path is in good condition. He even told us that this peak and the surrounding ones are covered with snow in the winter.

To the northwest of Mangindrano lies the strict nature reserve of Tsaratanana, but this is not open to tourists.

MAINTIRANO AND THE MENABE REGION

This small western port is attractive for people who want to get well off the beaten track – but go soon before everyone realises the road has been improved! In former days its laid-back, friendly attitude to visitors was largely a consequence of its isolation. A reader points out that although it appears to be a seaside town on the map, 'it's as though the town has turned its back on the sea: virtually nothing in Maintirano overlooks the ocean.'

One new conservation initiative near Maintirano that is worth checking out is a WWF/Swiss-run turtle project on some islands about 25km away. Contact the director, M Geraud Leroux, for more information (m *032 04 587 67*) or visit the website (www.tortuesilesbarren.org).

GETTING THERE

By road The good news is that the new road from Tsiroanomandidy was nearly complete in late 2006 so by the time you read this it could (gasp!) be one of the best in Madagascar, making Maintirano accessible from Tana in a day. I'm a bit sad to see these last outposts of isolation in Madagascar disappearing one by one.

By air Maintirano is on Air Mad's Twin Otter route, with flights scheduled almost daily. This is likely to change once the road is finished.

WHERE TO STAY/EAT

🏠 **Hôtel Le Chalet** ✆ 65 022 52. On the edge of town opposite the shrimp factory. Clean, simple, friendly. Food inexpensive & cooked to order. AC when there's electricity, but it's sometimes off at night. Suites & cheaper chalets. €€€

Telephone code The area code for Maintirano is 65.

FROM MAINTIRANO TO MORONDAVA

A reasonable road runs from Maintirano to Antsalova, 119km away. This town, served by Air Mad's Twin Otter, is the northern entry point for the Tsingy de Bemaraha National Park. In theory there's a route through the park to Bekopaka.

TSINGY DE BEMARAHA NATIONAL PARK This national park is one of the wonders of Madagasacar and has rightly been recognised as a UNESCO World Heritage Site. I have – finally – made it there myself so can speak with first-hand enthusiasm. The scenery rivals anything in the country and it's a treasure trove for botanists. At 152,000ha it is also one of Madagascar's largest protected areas.

The awe-inspiring grey forest of rock pinnacles is matched by the care with which walkways have been constructed to allow visitors to see this place in safety. Guides proudly tell you that no-one has been injured following these challenging circuits, which all goes to show that if something looks scary enough people will take proper care. Safety harnesses and karabiners may be used (though this is not enforced). I am not always a fan of ANGAP but am amazed at what they have achieved here. Chunks of rock have been bolted to rock faces to make steps, or, where it's too steep, steel ladders and cable ropes give access to lookout points or deep, narrow canyons. One broad canyon is crossed by a swinging suspension bridge. Amid all this grey are splashes of green from the *Pachypodiums* and other succulents which find footholds in the crevices. And there's plenty of wildlife too. We emerged from the dark of a canyon to see our guide pointing excitedly at two long-eared owls perched motionless on a branch. In the forests there were troops of Decken's sifakas and red-fronted brown lemurs. And the campsites were great for chameleons and collared iguanids (*Oplurus cuvieri*). The succulent plants that survive in this harsh environment are as strange and fascinating as the animals. See box on page 430.

The River Manambolo forms the southern border of the park, cutting a spectacular gorge through the limestone. The main point of access is at **Bekopaka** on the north bank of the river. Here is the park entrance to the Petit Tsingy and the ANGAP office.

When to go Access is currently impossible in the rainy season so you need to plan a visit between April/May and November/December. The heat is a problem in the early summer (October to December) so if possible visit in the coolest months of June or July, which are also good for river travel since the water level is higher. But note that these are the least interesting months to see Kirindy, which is usually part of the package. You can't win!

Getting there In a private 4x4, Bekopaka is reached in about 10 hours from Morondava (roughly 200km) with a lunch break at Belo-sur-Tsiribihina. Reaching Bekopaka by public transport is difficult, even in the dry season, but now that the road has been improved *taxi-brousses* should run to the village rather than stopping at Ankilizato as was formerly the case. Most of the hotels and campsites can provide the necessary transport to get to the trailheads. However, if you can afford it this is one place where it really does make sense to splash out on a car and driver from Morondava. Take a look at the vehicle before agreeing on a price. These are rough roads and stories of breakdowns abound. You won't need a guide – you must anyway use the ANGAP-trained park guides.

You can also access the park from the north via Antsalova, served by Twin Otter, or down the River Manambolo.

Organised tours The hotels Les Bougainvilliers, Baobab Café, Chez Maggie (Le Masoandro) and Morondava Beach in Morondava all organise tours by 4x4 to Bemaraha.

MENABE REGION

Contacts

Projet Bemaraha ✆/f 22 627 84;
e tsingy@simicro.mg.

ANGAP ✆ 22 013 96; e bemaraha@angap.mg;
www.tsingy-madagascar.com.

🏠 **Where to stay** New lodges are being built to accommodate the wave of tourists that has taken advantage of better access. Some of these offer safari-style camping in fixed tents.

🏠 **Hôtel Relais de Tsingy** (6 bungalows) A beautifully situated set of bungalows with en-suite bathrooms, overlooking the lake. However, recent reports are that it has gone downhill in terms of service & is overpriced. €€€€
🏠 **Tsingy Lodge** (5 bungalows) m 033 11 507 56/032 40 703 98; e tsingy-lodge@yahoo.fr; www.tsingy-lodge.com. A new Malagasy-run lodge near the ANGAP office. Simple, clean bungalows. Recommended: 'Bruno used to work for ANGAP & is very knowledgeable about the local wildlife etc, & Faratiana is an excellent cook. They both speak English & I thoroughly enjoyed my 2-night stay there.' €€€€
🏠 **L'Olympe du Bemaraha** (20 bungalows) e olympedubemaraha@yahoo.fr. A new upmarket lodge (2007) on a hill overlooking the Manambolo River. E-suite bungalows with hot shower & veranda. Sleeps up to 4 people. Restaurant with bar & panoramic view. €€€€

Å **Camp Croco** Book through Mad'Caméléon (✆ 22 630 86/623 62; e madcam@wanadoo.mg). South side of the river. Safari-style tents with beds. Clean, shared toilets & showers. Bar & restaurant. Recommended. €€€
🏠 **Tanankoay** (4 bungalows & camping) m 032 02 226 62; e rj_tony@yahoo.fr. Can be booked through Les Bougainvilliers. Simple bungalows & tents on the north side of the river. Only squat toilets for campers. Organise visits to the Grand Tsingy. €€€
🏠 **Auberge de Tsingy (Chez Ibrahim)** Book at Morondava Beach (✆ 95 523 18). Good atmosphere; friendly, helpful staff. Simple dbl bungalows & shared facilities. Park tours organised. €
Å **Camping Manambolo** The main campsite is on the north shore of the river; by the park entrance. Very picturesque with groves of mango trees that provide good shade. A tent site with shared bucket showers & squat toilets. Tent rental. Snack bar with basic meals & cold drinks. €

Excursions in the park Although there are forested areas of the park with good wildlife, it is the *tsingy* that makes this place special. The park is divided broadly into Le Petit Tsingy and Le Grand Tsingy, with circuits of varying difficulty to suit all abilities. The good news is that everyone can get at least a taste of the *tsingy* (with the exception, perhaps, of the seriously overweight – there are some tight squeezes through cracks in the rocks) and the easiest circuit through the Petit Tsingy gets you among those extraordinary rock pinnacles via boardwalks and short ladders. This is the Tantely circuit and takes about two hours, or four if you combine it with some forest (Andadoany circuit). However, for the most dramatic views you need to do the difficult Ankeligoa circuit in the Petit Tsingy and also visit the even-more-dramatic Grand Tsingy, an hour's drive (25km) away. For both of these you need to be pretty fit and have no fear of heights (or at least, as one of my party expressed it: 'allow the beauty to conquer the fear').

The best circuit (Andamozavaky) in the Grand Tsingy is a full day's excursion. Try to leave as early as possible – it gets hellishly hot – and take a packed lunch and plenty of water. The *tsingy* here is amazing, with pinnacles 50m high. The circuit takes 4–6 hours, and there is a lot of climbing so you need strong arms and legs. That said, several of my group were in their late 60s and managed OK. My advice would be to bring a pair of light gardening gloves – your hands get sore hanging on to rough steel cables and handrails – and a bandana to mop your streaming face.

As a change from sweating in the *tsingy* you can take a pirogue up the Manambolo river where you have a good chance of seeing fish eagles as well as visiting a cave with stalactites and stalagmites. There's a lake adjacent to the park entrance which has a resident pair of fish eagles as well as waterfowl such as white-faced whistling ducks, Humblot's herons and purple herons.

With the time and effort needed to get to Bemaraha, you should spend at least three days here so you can experience several different circuits. These take from 1½ to 8 hours to complete, so inevitably you'll be walking in the heat of the day. Guiding rates vary according to the length of the circuit. Most run through a combination of forest areas and *tsingy*.

Note: It is *fady* in this region to point with your index finger. Guides will demonstrate how to point with your finger crooked. It takes a bit of getting used to but shows respect to the ancestors.

Permits and guides The ANGAP office is open 07.00–16.00. There is often a queue in the morning meaning that you can't get an early start. Try to arrange your trip the day before if possible. For permit prices see page 75.

Flight of Fantasy Charter flights from Morondava (either returning to Morondava or landing in Belo-sur-Tsirabihina) over the Grand Tsingy are spectacular. The flight up from Morondava takes about 35 minutes; the pilot will then fly back and forth over the best areas of *tsingy*. 'The views and spectacle are utterly amazing – massive needles of rock interspersed with pristine forest. When the pilot drops down low, it's even possible to see brilliant white Decken's sifakas sitting in the trees. I was so engrossed in taking photos I was violently sick at the end of the flight!' (Nick Garbutt). Flights are booked through the Baobab Café (see page 435) and are not always available so if this is the main purpose of your visit you may want to organise it by phone from Tana before leaving for Morondava.

BELO-SUR-TSIRIBIHINA I have been quite disparaging about this town in earlier editions, but having spent time there in 2006 I have changed my view. Where else can you find a royal family serving beer in a bar (see page 431)? Belo has several good restaurants, a lively Friday market, and is a natural stopping place *en route* to Bekopaka. It is also the town at the end of the River Tsiribihina (see *River trips*, page 446) so sees quite a few visitors. Tsiribihina means 'where one must not dive' – supposedly because of crocodiles. Be warned!

Getting there
By air Air Mad does not fly here but the airstrip serves charter flights for passengers heading for Tsingy de Bemaraha National Park.

By road Arriving from the north you have to cross the river by ferry to get to the *taxi-brousse* station for Morondava. There is no timetable and the journey takes half an hour. *Taxi-brousses* to Morondava cost 8,000Ar.

By river This is the finishing point of the Tsiribihina river descent.

🏠 Where to stay/eat
🏠 **Hôtel du Menabe** m 032 42 635 35/032 42 824 10. Opposite the Mad Zebu restaurant, this is the best hotel in town. The service is said to be poor but I enjoyed the meal I ate there. €
🏠 **Hôtel Suzanna** Budget hotel. €
🏠 **Tsiribihy Hotel** Another budget option. €
🏠 **Hanida** similar to the 2 above. €

✗ **Mad Zebu Restaurant** m 032 40 387 15/032 07 589 55. Despite its rather surprising name, this is the best restaurant in Belo. Well run by Mme Andrianasitera; popular with tour groups. Excellent food served on a breezy patio.
✗ **Restaurant Pacifique** Near the market. Good food, especially the *crevettes*.

Dr Gavin Hart

Tsingy is the Madagascar term for the razor sharp pinnacles produced by the surface erosion of limestone massifs by acidic rain. Over a prolonged period, caves have developed beneath the surface, and narrow canyons have been created by the cracking of the rock mass. There are numerous areas of *tsingy* in Madagascar but the Ankarana and Bemaraha National Parks are most readily accessible to tourists

Pandanus spp and *Dracaena* spp are encountered in *tsingy* areas and are superficially similar, with tall thin stems and long thin dark green leaves. However, *Pandanus* tend to have thicker trunks, larger leaves, spikes on the trunk and serrated edges to the leaves compared with the slender smooth leaves of *Dracaena*. *Pandanus* often features a 'tripod-effect' produced by aerial roots emerging from the lower trunk.

Pachypodium lamerei, common throughout Bemaraha, is a spiny columnar plant when young but has a pale (almost white) smooth surface and bulbous base when older. Towering trees of *P. rutenbergianum* and *P. decaryi*, a small plant with a smooth globular base, are common in Ankarana. *P. ambongense* has a very localised habitat on the tsingy of Namoroka.

Euphorbia viguieri, thick green stems up to 50cm with long whitish thorns and prominent red and green top-knots of floral parts, and numerous tree-like euphorbias with narrow green cylindrical stems, are common in both areas; whereas *E. ankarensis,* short sticks with attractive pale green cones of cyathophylls at the top, is confined to Ankarana where thousands of these plants occur. The low-growing species, *E. aureo-viridiflora, E. herman-schwarzii* and *E. neohumbertii,* and the larger species, *E. pachypodioides* and *E. tirucalli,* also occur in this area.

Commiphora spp, medium-sized trees, are common on the tsingy and are readily identified by the profuse scaling of bark, usually brown but sometimes with a greenish tinge. Eventually clumps of bark are shed to leave attractive pale-coloured plaques among the scaly bark. *Dalbergia* spp, *Cassias* (with pale green fine foliage appearing in October) and *Tamarindus indica* are huge trees common on the *tsingy*.

Adenia epigea (huge globular caudiciforms with a base up to 1m in diameter) and *A. lapiazicola* are common at Ankarana and *A. firingalavensis* occurs at Bemaraha. *A. firingalavensis* is easily identified because of the dark dull green colour of the caudex which usually tapers upwards, but is occasionally spherical. This species sometimes lacks a caudex when growing on soil, such as at Kirindy, suggesting that the harsh conditions of the *tsingy* may contribute to caudex formation as a survival mechanism.

Hildegardia erythrosiphon is a medium-sized tree with a buttressed base and masses of brilliant red flowers which are easily seen above the canopy in the deciduous forest. The bright yellow flowers with dark red or purple throat of *Uncarina* spp are also visible from a distance in the sparse forest. *U. ankaranensis* is confined to Ankarana, but *U. peltata* and *U. sakalava* are more widely distributed.

The dry deciduous forests in which the tsingy occur are characterised by very high local plant and animal endemism at the species, genera and family levels. While the adjacent grasslands are virtually sterile landscapes because of the ravages of comprehensive vegetation clearing and relentless slash-and-burn agriculture, the microenvironments on the *tsingy* have remained relatively intact and are among the most rewarding areas for plant enthusiasts visiting Madagascar.

KIRINDY This is one of the most rewarding natural areas in Madagascar and is now part of the new 125,000ha Menabe protected area. It is not to be confused with the Kirindy-Mitea National Park (page 442) south of Morondava. Until a few years ago its sole purpose was the sustainable 'harvesting' of trees, but despite this selective logging, the wildlife here is abundant. This is one of the few places where you may see the giant jumping rat and the narrow-striped mongoose, and is also the best place in Madagascar to see the fossa. You don't even have to go into the forest – they hang around the rubbish dump. But for a more exciting experience visit the park when the fossas are overcome with spring fever. Jonathan Ekstrom reports: 'They mate voraciously over four days between 5 and 20 November. The timing is pot luck but you would be guaranteed good views. There are camera teams there every year to film it!' And here's an extra nugget of information about these animals: the fossa has the largest penis bone (baculum) in relation to its size of any mammal. To put it succinctly, if it were an average-sized man, its equipment would be an impressive 16 inches long! But once you know that the fossa's lovemaking can last up to six hours, this bony support starts to make sense.

Accommodation is, at present, pretty basic but even if you normally dislike roughing it, you should try to stay a night here. Day visitors see far less than those able to observe wildlife at the optimum time of dawn and dusk, and a night-time stroll is usually an exceptional wildlife experience with nocturnal lemurs and chameleons easily seen and – if you are really lucky – a giant jumping rat.

When to go If you are seriously interested in the wildlife of Kirindy you should try to visit at the beginning of the rainy season (November to January). In addition to the fossa mating spectacle, these are the best months to see the giant jumping rat which is more active after the rain has softened the ground. This is one of the most endangered mammals in Madagascar, so it's worth choosing the optimum months for seeing it. They are seldom seen during the cold months and tend to keep out

FITAMPOHA AND A MEETING WITH ROYALTY

You don't expect to find a prince serving beer in a hot, dusty coastal town; nor to have an audience with a princess in a bar. But Belo-sur-Tsiribihina is the home of the Menabe (Sakalava) Royal Family, and even royals have to make a living, biding their time until the next *Fitampoha*.

Every eight to ten years the royal family receives empowerment from the ancestors through this ceremony of washing the sacred relics. The relics are called *dady*, and comprise bones, and perhaps fingernails and teeth. They are stored in an iron box in a sacred house, *zomba*, which you can see in the southern part of the town, protected by a high fence of sharpened staves. In the old days the *dady* would be carried into battle to ensure victory.

Over a beer, Princess 'Georgette' told me about the ceremony. Or rather she told Rija, my guide who acted as interpreter, and brought out a photo album from the last *Fitampoha* in 2004 to illustrate her story. It takes place in August, on a Friday when there's a full moon. From Thursday midnight it is forbidden to wash in the river. Reeds must be collected at midday, from a special place an hour's walk from the town. The collecting and carrying of the reeds is accompanied by singing and dancing. Descendants of nobility wash the royal clothing and hang it on the reeds to dry. Friday is the sacred day, when the relics are washed in the river.

The princess, now 70, told us she was a direct descendant of King Toera, who fought the French in the war of independence, and chose death rather than surrender. The French agreed to educate his ten-year-old son who later became King Kamamy, governor of Menabe and the father of the princess sitting with me in that hot, dark bar. 'But there are descendants all over the world'. She flashed her gold teeth. I asked when the next *Fitampoha* would be. '2008' she said, 'Or maybe 2010'. The *razana*, I gathered, do not keep to schedules.

16

Anyone who has spent time in Madagascar will realise that the Malagasy are not the most monogamous of peoples. The same is true for the island's parrots. The greater vasa parrots of Madagascar are those big black squawking things you see flying around the forest canopy. They are not the prettiest of parrots, having drab brownish-black plumage, long necks and even bald heads for some of each year. Perhaps there is a moral emerging in this story already, for vasa parrots also have one of the most exhilarating sex lives of any animal on Earth. It's the females that are dominant over the males (they're 25% bigger) and they pursue the little chaps ardently all through September and October. It's the girls that do the chasing. and they seem to know what they're doing as most females end up with four to eight mates.

You can imagine what a headache this is for the males, having to compete to fertilise the eggs of the female with all your best buddies. The male parrots have risen to the challenge, however, with some utterly unbelievable evolutionary adaptations. For a start they have a penis. Birds in general don't have penises; both sexes just have cloacal openings which are pressed together to transfer the sperm. Not so for vasa parrots: the males have evolved a penis somewhat bigger than a golf ball which they erect out of their cloaca as and when they need it. Courtship before sex takes an appropriately long time – several weeks in fact – and on the big day the female might consort with a half dozen males before settling down with one at midday in some shaded corner of the forest canopy. And of course this is not ordinary love-making, at least not for the bird world.

Sex in most bird species, like robins and sparrows, doesn't look that fun to be honest – it's all over pretty quick with a kiss of the cloacas lasting a couple of seconds, and both partners then wander off in different directions apparently pretending they don't know each other. Not so in vasa parrots: sex lasts a full two hours with the male and female locked together in passionate coitus, rather like the dog family. Tied together for two hours you

of sight when there is a full moon. However, in the warm wet season you are quite likely to see one on the road. In the glare of a strong torch or spotlight it will freeze, giving you an excellent view. Reptile viewing is excellent at this time of year. Bill Love comments: 'This is a great place to see herps up close, especially collared iguanas (*Oplurus cuvieri*) and giant hognose snakes (*Leioheterodon madagascariensis*). From December to January, the iguanas are seeking open sandy spots to lay their clutches of (on average) four jellybean-sized eggs. The hognose snakes are often eagerly waiting for them to lay, ignoring the adult lizards to find the nest by smell, unearth it with their snouts, and swallow the eggs with gusto. The lizards lay right out in the open around camp, and also along the edges of the sandy roads, and the snakes are particularly abundant in those places with little fear of people.'

However, if your interest is more general, take Jonathan Ekstrom's advice: 'Note that the weather is extremely predictable. The rains start late November or early December. Before then the forest is dry, no leaves on the trees, and birds are easy to see. Climatically September and October are the best months. November is getting hot but still OK (and remember you might get lucky with those mating fossas!). December to March is very hot and humid and the road is often impassable. January and February: terrible, terrible horseflies!'

Getting there and away Kirindy is about 65km northeast of Morondava – about two hours by poor road (in a private vehicle) or three tedious hours by *taxi-brousse*, or 1½ hours from Belo.

can see them crooning over each other, preening their partner's plumage, squawking when things get a bit rough … it's a real event. So much so that it frequently attracts onlookers: a whole crowd of parrots can turn up to watch. Sometimes things get a bit out of hand and some of her other boyfriends get a bit frisky and try jumping on top of the copulating pair, sometimes managing to disturb them and have a go themselves. However, it's all down to the female's choice as she has the beak and claws to control her diminutive boyfriends.

Well, after such persistent promiscuity, when it comes to feed the chicks you can imagine the confusion. The males have normally found several girlfriends for themselves as well, and these avian harems often mean it's not clear which chicks belong to which dad. It's the males that do all the work bringing in the food and you can see the lads (carrying fruits and seeds freshly gathered from the forest), vexing over which of their girlfriends to feed next. Once again the females don't just sit back and see what happens, they sing long and complex songs to attract their boyfriends in to feed them. Each female has her own unique song, so November in the forests of Madagascar is rather like a huge singing contest where females with chicks compete to be the best singer. And it works – females singing longer or more complex songs attract more males and get more food. The males benefit from feeding the best singing girlfriends because these are also the strongest birds with the most chicks in the nest.

Greater vasa parrots have the most complex sex life of any parrot so far studied. Scientists think most other species of parrot are probably monogamous and have the same partner their whole life – making parrots real bastions of chastity in the avian world. So vasas have broken all the rules and are pillars of promiscuity instead. That's evolution in isolation for you. Like so much of Madagascar's wildlife, if you leave some normal, decent-living animals by themselves in the middle of the Indian Ocean for a few dozen million years they are bound to come up with something bizarre.

Dr Jonathan Ekstrom did his PhD research on the greater vasa parrot in western Madagascar. He now runs The Biodiversity Consultancy in London (www.thebiodiversityconsultancy.com).

Package tours are offered by many Morondava hotels such as Les Bougainvilliers, Boabab Café, Continental and Chez Maggie.

Where to stay There are 12 bungalows, including four new ones with attached (cold) showers and shared flush toilets (40,000Ar). The remaining eight bungalows have only long-drop (smelly) toilets and communal showers (20,000Ar). Some dormitory accommodation (15,000Ar). Mosquito nets, sheets and blankets provided. Limited electricity. There is also a small restaurant (cold beer!) serving simple meals. Camping permitted for 10,000Ar.

Permits and guides The entrance fee is 15,000Ar for three days; guide 4,000Ar per hour (up to five people), 6,000Ar per hour night walk.

ANALABE This private nature reserve is owned by M Jean de Heaulme, of Berenty fame. Tourist accommodation is being built here but at the time of writing no more information is available. The reserve is 60km north of Morondava, to the west of Kirindy by the village of Beroboka. In addition to forest it contains some mangrove areas as well as marshes and lakes typical of coastal plain.

MAROFANDILIA If driving to or from Kirindy, do stop at this inspiring place. The **Boutique d'Art Sakalave** is a roadside shop 45 kilometres from Morondava on

16

the road to Kirindy. Begun as a Peace Corps project, the boutique is now a thriving independent business. The quality of the woodcarvings for sale is excellent and only wood from trees that are already dead and collected from community-managed forests is used. The prices are fair and the profits go directly to help the local community and to conserve the remaining forest. The boutique fosters a pride among the local Sakalava for their traditional craft and culture.

The famous **Baobabs Amoureaux** are near here (see page 439).

ANDRANOMENA SPECIAL RESERVE Lying 30km (one hour) northeast of Morondava, this 6,420ha reserve is now open to tourists. It protects dry deciduous forests, home to 11 species of reptile, 48 birds and seven species of lemur including Verreaux's sifakas and red-fronted brown lemurs which are readily seen by day-time visitors. A further five species may be added if you go on a night walk. The giant jumping rat is also found here. And there are several lakes with accompanying waterfowl. Circuit trails allow you to see a good variety of landscapes. Enter via Marofandilia.

Guides cost around 4,000Ar per tour. For permit prices see page 75.

The advantage of Andranomena over Kirindy is that it can be visited from Morondava as a day trip, whereas with Kirindy you really need to spend the night.

Most hotels in Morondava can arrange a tour, or enquire at ANGAP.

MORONDAVA

The Morondava area was the centre of the Sakalava kingdom and their tombs – sadly now desecrated by souvenir hunters – bear witness to their power and creativity.

This was evidently a popular stopping-place for sailors in the past and they seem to have treated the natives generously. In 1833, Captain W F W Owen wrote of Morondava: 'Five boats came alongside and stunned us by vociferating for presents and beseeching us to anchor.'

Today Morondava is the centre of a prosperous rice-growing area – and has successfully introduced ostrich farming to Madagascar! For tourists it is best-known as a seaside resort with a laid-back atmosphere. Morondava is the southern gateway to many of the attractions of the western region and is the centre for visiting the western deciduous forest, the famous baobabs, Belo-sur-Mer and the Tsingy de Bemaraha National Park.

TELEPHONE CODE The area code for Morondava is 95.

GETTING THERE AND AWAY

By road Morondava is 700km from Tana and served by a once-good road. Driving time from Tana to Morondava ranges between 12 and 17 hours depending on current road and weather conditions. The road is not bad until the 120km stretch between Miandrivazo and Malaimbandy, which can take six hours. The final stretch is also very poor but has its compensations: 'It's breathtakingly beautiful, with miles and miles of rice paddies interspersed with grand baobabs picked out by the rays of the rising sun as you make your early morning arrival' (D&K).

The *taxi-brousse* station in Morondava is about 15 minutes' walk from the beach hotels at Nosy Kely – a hot, tiring hike when carrying a backpack. Local taxis are available for about 2,000Ar. If you are driving, note that there is no diesel between Antsirabe and Morondava.

See also *Travelling between Morondava and Toliara*, page 440.

By air There is a daily service from Tana or Toliara, and the Twin Otter calls here after visiting smaller west-coast towns including Morombe.

By sea There is a ferry, or *taxi de la mer*, which runs twice a week from Morondava south to Belo-sur-Mer, taking 2½ hours. 50,000Ar each way. They have an office near the port (where the road makes a right-angle turn) or enquire at the Hatea Café (m *032 04 692 61;* e *hatea04@yahoo.fr*).

GETTING AROUND The Baobab Café rents out quad bikes and the Madabar has motorbikes for hire.

WHERE TO STAY Most hotels are clustered along the beach on the peninsula known as Nosy Kely, which has suffered some major damage from erosion. There are further hotels in the downtown area.

Upper range €€€€
Baobab Café (27 rooms) Nosy Kely; ☎ 95 520 12; f 95 521 86; e baobab@blueline.mg; www.baobabtour.mg. The hotel backs onto the river on the east side of Nosy Kely (so rooms overlooking the river can be a bit smelly at low tide). AC rooms with en-suite facilities, minibar, TV, & hot water. Good restaurant. Billiards & large swimming pool open to non-residents. Organises many tours, inc the 'Flight of Fantasy' over the *tsingy* & deep-sea fishing.
Chez Maggie (La Masoandro) (8 bungalows & 1 apartment) Nosy Kely; ☎ 95 523 47; m 032 04 341 14; e info@chezmaggie.com; www.chezmaggie.com. There's 6 spacious bungalows & 2 2-storey chalets, all

en suite with AC & hot water. Lovely garden setting, right on the beach; small pool. Excellent restaurant. Excursions inc the baobab avenue, Kirindy & the *tsingy* as well as their trademark river trips (see www.remoterivers.com). Sea transfers to Belo or Toliara & a 42ft catamaran for charter. Owned by American Gary Lemmer who likes to chat to his guests. An ideal place for lone English-speaking travellers to chill out.
Renala (13 bugalows & 6 rooms) Nosy Kely; ☎ 95 520 89. Solid wooden bungalows surrounded by landscaped gardens & grass. Most bungalows with AC, others with fans 2 dbl apts & 4 AC rooms, all en suite. The least expensive AC rooms on the peninsula.

Mid range €€€
Hôtel Les Philaos (19 rooms) Nosy Kely; ☎/f 95 520 81; m 032 05 621 02; e sica@wanadoo.mg. Apartment-style rooms, 9 with AC & small kitchen & 9 much cheaper with fans. Very nice; secluded. No restaurant but they can serve b/fast & cold drinks. Under same ownership as Hôtel Central.

Hôtel Morondava Beach (15 bungalows) ☎/f 95 523 18; m 032 04 692 28; e mbeach@blueline.mg; www.hgi-mbeach.com. A wide range of rooms at varying prices; all en suite. The cheapest have fan & cold shower; more expensive with hot water, minibar & AC, but not highly rated for

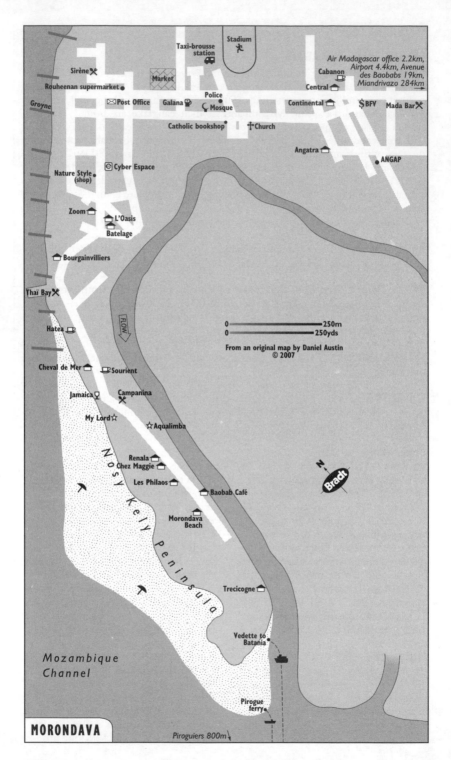

comfort, however. Very good food. Full range of excursions inc the *tsingy*.

🏠 **Les Bougainvilliers** (8 bungalows & 12 rooms) Nosy Kely; ❧ 95 521 63/921 63; e bol_nd@ yahoo.fr. Wide range of rooms/prices, all with fan/AC; some en suite with hot water. Good food. Visa accepted. Organises a variety of excursions inc the *tsingy*. Manager Francois Vahiako is the head of the Morondava Guide Association & can assist with arranging guides/tours in the area.

🏠 **Hôtel Continental** Downtown. A 3-storey hotel

with a variety of rooms, some with AC. Cheapest rooms only 10,800Ar.

🏠 **Hôtel les Piroguiers** (4 bungalows) Betania; ❧ 95 526 19; e piroguiers@yahoo.fr. Bungalows on stilts. This is one of Jim Bond's 'best discoveries in recent years' & Jim knows the area well. Betania is 'a delightful Makoa fishing village across the river, famous for its fabulously large, sunbathing pigs'. Take a *taxi-pirogue* or a *vedette*. Owned by Pascal & Bodo Boisard, involved members of the Betania community.

Budget €€

🏠 **Hôtel Le Batelage** (8 rooms) ❧ 95 527 32. A 4-storey hotel near the Oasis. En-suite rooms: 4 have fans, 4 with AC.

🏠 **Trecicogne Hôtel Restaurant** ❧ 95 520 69. En-suite rooms (hot water) with fans; some with shared facilities. Good, friendly restaurant. Tours available.

🏠 **Cheval de Mer** (6 rooms) Rooms en suite (cold water) with fan.

🏠 **Zoom Hotel** (9 rooms) ❧ 95 920 59; f 95 522 42. Up the road from the Oasis. Good value en-suite

dbl rooms with fans; 2 have AC. No restaurant, but can provide b/fast upon request.

🏠 **Hôtel L'Oasis** Rte de Batelage; ❧ 95 522 22; e vazahabe@dts.mad. Bungalows are run-down; not really recommended since Zoom (opposite) is better for the same price. But the bar & restaurant are great (see *Where to eat*).

🏠 **Hôtel Central** (8 rooms) m 032 05 621 02. On the main street. Fan, hot shower & WC. No restaurant but b/fast served.

✖ **WHERE TO EAT** Apart from the hotel restaurants, there are quite a few very good eateries in Morondava. Peace Corps volunteer Kerri Poore has added some favourites to the list below.

✖ **La Sirène** Quality seafood at a reasonable price. The name means 'mermaid'.

✖ **Le Thaï Bay** m 032 40 129 23. Restaurant & tapas bar in a lovely location.

✖ **Mada Bar** On the main street at the eastern end of town (opposite My Lord). Specialises in amazing ice cream. 'Small, relaxed & has excellent food & fresh fruit juice' (SB). 'Best pizza in Morondava' (KP). Kayaks & motorbikes for rent.

✖ **Hôtel L'Oasis** Rte de Batelage; ❧ 95 522 22. Often has live music, drums & reggae performed by the owner Jean La Rasta & local musicians. 'My tip for an evening meal. The owner was so genuinely friendly, & as a lone diner he made me feel extremely comfortable & welcomed. The food was fantastic!' (Stuart Riddle). Mountain bikes available here. See *Tour operator & guides*.

✖ **Campanina** Across the road from My Lord. 'This is by far my favourite place in town. The owners (Malagasy & Italian) are perfectly charming & the food is always good. Their 'caiprissima' is the best drink in Madagascar!' (KP).

🍺 **Hatea** Nosy Kely. A small beachfront snack bar.

🍺 **Le Cabanon** 'This is a small snack bar with the best French fries & homemade yoghurt in Morondava. It is not on the main tourist road but it is worth the trip. Local expats all take the extra walk to enjoy the food there. Turn right at the new BFV intersection if coming from the east & it is just past Jirama. Great for lunch' (KP).

🍺 **Le Sourient** Snack bar & 4x4 hire.

🍸 **Jamaica** 'A wonderful place to catch the sunset & drink the best homemade *punch coco* in Morondava' (KP).

INTERNET The most popular cybercafé is CyberEspace (🕐 *Mon–Sat 07.00–19.00; Sun 07.00–12.00*). Fast connection at 70Ar/min. Be warned: it gets *very* hot inside. You will drip onto your (French) keyboard.

NIGHTCLUBS

☆ **My Lord** Nosy Kely.

☆ **L'Aqualimba** Large open venue which hosts major

musical events from time to time.

MONEY There's a functioning ATM at the BFV bank.

ANGAP The ANGAP office (☎ *95 524 20;* m *032 05 531 26;* e *ventyodile@yahoo.fr*) is in the Ni Havana building, Andakabe.

TOUR OPERATOR AND GUIDES

Baobab Tours Located at the Baobab Café (see *Where to stay* for contact details), they offer a large selection of vehicle & boat trips, inc excursions to Kirindy, deep-sea fishing, the Tsingy de Bemaraha & flights over the *tsingy*. Prices are high, however.

Chez Maggie Vehicles & multilingual guides available; also a small boat for excursions down the coast.

Francois Vahiako Head of the Morondava Guide Association. Contact him at Les Bougainvilliers hotel.

Jean Michel Golfier Raherinirina ☎ 95 921 14; m

032 04 704 53; e hyerna2002@yahoo.fr. Recommended as an English-speaking guide/fixer.

Jean le Rasta (Rasta Jean) Recommended by several travellers as being 'efficient, reliable & charismatic'. Speaks good English & has a 4x4. Contact through Hôtel Oasis.

Yves Marohao ☎ 95 520 89; e codemena@ malagasy.com. An English-speaking guide recommended by David Bostock. Yves can organise any tour you want.

EXCURSIONS FROM MORONDAVA

Parc Menabe (☎ *95 52 417.* ⊕ *daily 07.00–17.00. Entry 5,000Ar*) Situated 12km north of Morondava, this is an ostrich farm and small zoo. It's a beautiful setting and makes a nice place to stop off from a northern excursion. They also have a designated walk along the river, and a small zoo with some caged animals as well as free-ranging lemurs. There's a good selection of ostrich products for sale.

Baobabs Morondava is the region of the splendid Grandidier's baobabs, *Adansonia grandidieri*, best seen at the **Avenue des Baobabs**. Also popular are Les Baobabs Amoureux (a pair of entwined baobab 'lovers') and there's a Sacred Baobab as well. Mountain bikes and quad bikes are available at some of the hotels and are an excellent way to see the baobabs – but beware of the heat, flies and thorns on the road. By car or taxi, the Avenue of the Baobabs is 45 minutes from Morondava. The best light for photography is just before sunset (it brings out the red hue in the bark). But since everyone knows that, it gets very crowded. Better to aim to reach there at sunrise.

The junction for **Les Baobabs Amoureux** is about 4km north of the Avenue as you continue towards Marofandilia. Turn left at the small rock indicating Mangily and you will find them about 7km from the junction.

Namahora If you arrive by air you will pass through this small town on the way to Morondava from the airport. There is a very lively Friday market and the place is of historic interest, being the site of the Sakalava defeat of the Merina back in the 19th century. The name means 'place where they were tied' (ie: the captive Merina). If you want to stay, there is a small hotel on the edge of town, nearest the airport.

Reserves north of Morondava The dry deciduous forests between the rivers Morondava and Tsiribihina are of great biological importance. Indeed, this is one of the most threatened forest types in the world and many endemic species of flora and fauna are found here.

There are three protected areas between the two rivers: Andranomena, Analabe and Kirindy. Andranomena and Analabe (page 433) can be visited as a day trip, as can Kirindy (page 430) but it is far more rewarding to stay here at least one night.

☞ *WARNING!* Sakalava tombs: although the Menabe region is famous for its tombs, some things of obvious interest to tourists should be left alone. This applies particularly to the famous erotic carvings on tombs in the area around Morondava.

These carvings are fertility symbols, and often depict figures engaged in sexual activities which the Sakalava consider *fady* to practise (eg: oral sex). Erotic carvings of this kind can nowadays be seen in cultural museums in larger towns such as Tana or Toliara, and small replicas are often carved and sold as souvenirs – erotica always has a ready market. In the early 1970s unscrupulous art dealers pillaged the tombs around Morondava, removing nearly all the erotic carvings. As a result, the Sakalava now keep secret the locations of those tombs which still have carvings. As one guide reported: 'Some of the graveyards are for the tourists, but most are secret – for the people.'

TRAVELLING BETWEEN MORONDAVA AND TOLIARA

BY SEA AND ROAD The best way to get to Belo-sur-Mer is via the Taxi Be de Mer (see page 435). Then there's a daily *taxi-brousse* (dry-season only) between Morombe and the Ifaty road north of Toliara.

BY AIR There is one northbound and one southbound flight a week, but these are sold out weeks in advance.

BELO-SUR-MER Not to be confused with Belo-sur-Tsiribihina, this Vezo village and regional ship-building centre 70km south of Morondava is growing in popularity, and with the Kirindy-Mitea National Park on its doorstep it deserves a stay of a few days.
   The village itself is a collection of small houses and huts, on the border of a small lagoon, shrouded in palm trees; each family keeps a pig which is allowed to forage at night – Belo's mobile garbage disposals.
   Offshore from Belo-sur-Mer, seven coral-fringed islands offer excellent snorkelling and scuba-diving. Little-known and seldom-visited, the reefs are in

CORAL BLEACHING

Alasdair Harris, Blue Ventures
Climate change, El Niño and the associated increases in sea surface temperatures have resulted in severe coral bleaching events in Madagascar in recent years and represent the greatest natural threat to these systems. Bleaching events are increasing in their frequency and severity and current estimates suggest it could become an annual event in the next 25–50 years. Dive operators in the tourist centres of Anakao and Ifaty have claimed almost 100% mortality of hard corals in shallow sites.
   In addition to large-scale natural threats, local populations have significant effects on the health of Madagascar's coral reefs. Poor land-use practices are one of the primary anthropogenic threats to coastal biodiversity, and large areas of forest have been destroyed by rapid expansion of slash-and-burn agricultural systems. Wide-scale burning has exacerbated soil erosion, which now affects more than 80% of Madagascar's total land area. Raised levels of siltation on coral reefs, in particular in western Madagascar, have already been widely reported, most notably on near-shore reefs close to the mouths of rivers, such as the Onilahy and Fiherenana rivers near Toliara.
   There is now a critical need for better knowledge and understanding of Madagascar's marine and coastal ecosystem processes. For example, it is essential to monitor the impacts of bleaching and the recovery rates of coral reefs, in order to incorporate resilience and resistance factors into the future selection and management of protected marine areas.

very good condition. Studies are planned in the near future and following the inventory of the marine life and coral, this area may become a protected marine reserve.

There are huge cargo vessels (*boutres*, gaffe-rigged *goelettes*) among the coconut palms at the Belo lagoon, and these are still built there using exactly the same designs as the Bretons used centuries back (see box on page 423). The lagoon presents a picturesque setting with *boutres* in all stages of construction. This is done entirely by hand, and typically takes some four to six years for the completion of one ship.

Gary Lemmer reports: 'A traditional, but slightly improved version is being constructed at the moment. It will be motorised so that when the winds aren't blowing in the right direction it will be able to run on coconut oil or other locally-produced biofuels – a first in the region, and the whole of Madagascar for that matter! It should be operational in June 2008 and will offer a picturesque but more comfortable and reliable alternative for visiting the Mozambique Channel coast.' For further details e laetiti@tsangatsanga.com.

Getting there and away

By sea Adventurers can go by pirogue, but it's easy to be overcharged for this uncomfortable trip. The normal price is 50,000–60,000Ar for a three- to four-day return trip. Under good winds it can take six to ten hours to sail to Belo from Morondava. Be prepared to camp overnight in a fishing village on the way. It's much easier to take the Taxi de la Mer, when it runs. Also the Chez Maggie hotel in Morondava has a small (7m) fibreglass motor pirogue and offers shuttles for its guests.

By land Overland by 4x4 is also an option from Morondava (approx 4hrs) or Morombe (1½ days). Once the river levels drop the road is open – typically mid-June to mid-October.

Where to stay/eat

🏠 **La Marina** (8 bungalows & 1 suite) ☎ 95 249 50; m 032 02 803 68; e lamarinabelo@yahoo.fr. €€€€

🏠 **Ecolodge du Menabe** (8 rooms) ☎ +871 763 963 816 (satellite phone); e info@menabelo.com; www.menabelo.com. A well-run hotel with 5 dbl & 3 twin rooms. There's a diving school that offers courses & (expensive) tours from Belo-sur-Mer to the fringing reefs of the islands. Restaurant serves good food but it's a fixed menu & quite expensive. €€€

🏠 **Hôtel le Dauphin** (6 bungalows) Spacious, clean bungalows, with a separate toilet/shower block. The excellent restaurant has the only (satellite) TV in town so is a magnet for locals. 'We watched the World Cup here. So did the mayor of Belo!' Bookings can be made by radio contact at 19.00 every evening from MadaBar, on the main road into Morondava. €€

🏠 **Bungalows Chez Dorothé** (7 bungalows) On the beach close to the village. Basic low-priced bungalows with shared toilet & basic shower. Friendly owners with nice but simple restaurant. Food needs to be ordered in advance. Offers a range of excursions inc transport to Morombe. €

🏠 **Chez Lova** m 032 40 192 49/032 02 217 79; e restolovabelo@yahoo.fr or rluc7177@yahoo.fr. Madame Vola speaks French, English & a little German & wins praise from more than one traveller. 'A very nice family-run business, open throughout the year. Very good food; clean, well-appointed restaurant, good music' (Gary Lemmer). Excursions to the islands 20,000Ar. €

There are now numerous other hotels open in Belo-sur-Mer, which start from about 10,000Ar. Bungalows have also been built on Nosy Andravano but although they have huge bathrooms there is no water. And they are a real eyesore.

NOSY ANDRAVANO AND OTHER ISLANDS Belo is the base for visiting a cluster of nine interesting offshore islands, the largest of which is Nosy Andravano, but there are numerous islets. Those to the north are mere sandbanks, but the islands to the south have vegetative cover. Nomadic Vezo fishermen live on the northerly islands for six months of the year. There are shark carcasses and turtle shells left to dry on the sand, and fish and shark fins are salted in troughs. Each of the islands is fringed by coral reefs, although to view the healthy coral you may have to go up to 2km off the coast. You can hire a pirogue from Belo-sur-Mer to take you around the islands. Remember to bring your own drinking water – enough food for yourself and the piroguers if you intend to camp on the islands. Eucare researcher Rob Conway warns: 'Those islands south of Nosy Andravano are infested by rats that have a remarkable ability to chew through anything.'

KIRINDY-MITEA NATIONAL PARK (also known as KIRINDY-MITE) This new and little-known national park (only 70 visitors in 2006) is adjacent to Belo and protects a great variety of habitats. It lies at the crossroads of two ecosystems: the west and the south, as well as coastal mangroves (comprising an astonishing seven tree species), dunes, lakes and beaches.

The two lakes, **Ambondro** and **Sirave**, are particularly interesting since they are *fady* to the local people so have been undisturbed for generations.

In terms of wildlife, there are most of the species of lemur that can be found in Kirindy or Andromena, and additionally ring-tails. Kirindy-Mitea marks the northern limit of their territory. Mark Fenn writes: 'The park was not open to tourists until 2006. Since then the WWF and ANGAP have begun identifying and developing trail systems. This park is a veritable kingdom of baobabs with three species and a density of these trees unparalleled elsewhere in Madagascar. The park offers a diversity of ecosystems including tropical dry forest and littoral spiny forest. The lakes near to Manahy have over 30 species of birds, many rare, and endangered waterfowl. In 2007, the park will expand to include a marine area covering the reefs around seven offshore islands. Several of the islands are underwater at high tides but two of them can be visited and plans are to develop tourism facilities on them. This is evolving into one of the more interesting parks to visit in Madagascar.'

The entrance to the park is at Manahy; the entrance fee is 10,000Ar and you must be a self-sufficient camper to stay there.

MOROMBE This small, isolated town has reinvented itself for the 21st century. In the 1996 edition of this book Chris Balance wrote: 'Morombe clearly died when the French left, but 9,000 souls remain and they spend their time walking up and down the only street very slowly, shaking hands with each other and discussing the possibility that someone might build a proper road to them someday.' After the total eclipse of 2001 I wrote: 'The citizens now walk briskly up and down the street, shaking hands, and lamenting that the tourists have gone and there is still no decent road to their town.' In 2004 Alexander Elphinstone of Blue Ventures wrote: 'Contrary to Chris Balance, I feel that Morombe is a town that rocks every night of the week. It's the only Malagasy town I visited where the locals are partying Monday through Sunday. Friendly people, for whom tourism is still a novelty. Beware the over-friendly local girls in bars; unfortunately I think Morombe is a place visited by old French men looking for such girls.'

There is still no decent road to Morombe. But it deserves a (short) visit. It's an unpretentious seaside town with a pleasant beach, active fishing village and mangroves.

Getting there and away

By road Morombe is usually accessible by *taxi-brousse* from Ifaty, north of Toliara. There are two roads north. One, that hugs the coast, is sandy and in poor condition, and the 200km journey takes about ten hours. In a private 4x4 vehicle, however, it is a worthwhile prospect because of the breathtaking scenery *en route*. 'On your left is the blue sea and white sand, and on your right is the incredible spiny forest where the Mikea people live. This is a paradise for birders, and for baobab lovers. Normally it takes eight to ten hours to drive from Ifaty to Andavadoaka or Ampasilava. It is practicable only between late June and early November. The car can get stuck in the sand forever without the help of villagers to pull you out' (Nivo Ravelojaona).

The *taxi-brousse* route (inland) is through the spiny forest, but is not nearly as beautiful. This 240km journey can take from 12 to 24 hours. Do not attempt it during the rainy season; it once took a Blue Ventures team three days! This bus leaves daily, at 06.00 from Toliara going north, and usually at 03.00 from Morombe going south. Buy a ticket the evening before and ask the driver to pass by your hotel at 03.00.

By sea Apart from the Taxi Be de la Mer from Morondava, you can enquire about cargo boats at Sisa, the shop next to Galana petrol station. Pirogues can also be arranged (bargain hard). The average price in 2006 from Morondava was 150,000Ar. And on to Ifaty for about 100,000Ar.

By air Morombe Airport can take only Twin Otters, but it is a short hop from Morondava. The Air Mad service currently runs twice a week from Toliara and Tana (via Morondava). There are no taxis at the airport and it's about a 20-minute walk into town.

⌂ Where to stay/eat

⌂ **Hôtel Baobab** (16 bungalows) Book through Tana office (📞 22 427 01). Concrete bungalows on the beach on the south side of the town, with fans or AC. Good restaurant. €€€

⌂ **Lakana Volamena** Basic rooms grouped round a central courtyard, some with bathrooms. A pleasant hotel, right on the beach just north of the Baobab with a range of room prices. Serves good food. It is of a similar standard to Baobab but with much more atmosphere. €–€€€

Other hotels include **La Croix du Sud** & **Hôtel Crabe** (in the northern part of town). These are 'simple what-you-see-is-what-you-get type places: a bed with mosquito net & something resembling a shower, for about 7,000Ar per night' (AE).

What to see and do Morombe rewards those with time to stroll. It's quite a prosperous-looking little town, with some spacious houses in the north and a bustling fishing village of wooden huts to the south. Like so many Malagasy seaside towns, it is very spread-out with no obvious centre.

If you continue south along the beach beyond Hôtel Baobab you will come to a rewarding group of mangroves where you can watch mudskippers. Behind this area are some local tombs; we did not investigate these, respecting the local *fady* against such visits.

ANDAVADOAKA AND AMPASILAVA These two villages are adjacent to each other by 'one of the best beaches in Madagascar' some 45km to the south of Morombe. Coming south from Morombe, you first reach Andavadoaka then, 5km further on, Ampasilava. The drive there is varied and very beautiful.

Andavadoaka has been described as the only coastal village in Madagascar whose setting rivals that of Taolagnaro (Fort Dauphin). The area can boast the richest marine ecosystem on the southwest coast, and has therefore become the home for many migrating fishermen, as well as a developing tourist resort. The diving is far superior to any that can be found at Anakao or Ifaty, with some sites having guaranteed sightings of potato groupers and Napoleon wrasses. Manta rays,

Karen Foerstel, Blue Ventures Conservation

The people of Madagascar's coastal villages are culturally, economically and spiritually tied to the sea. Villagers rely on marine resources for food, transport and trade, and often hold ceremonies and erect shrines thanking their ancestors for the bounty provided by the ocean. The Vezo people, located along the southwest coastal areas of Madagascar, are known as 'the people of the sea' and believe that foreigners can 'become' Vezo by learning how to sail pirogues.

With some 3,000km of submerged coral reefs, Madagascar's coastal areas are among the most biologically diverse and yet least-studied ecosystems on Earth. Species diversity of these reefs is among the highest in the Indian Ocean. However, local demand for these resources is growing as more and more villagers – particularly in the country's southwest region – are moving to the coasts, sometimes because of raids on inland villages by *malaso*, cattle rustlers. Madagascar's coast is also a growing tourist attraction. It has been estimated that at least half of all tourists arriving in Madagascar each year visit a coral reef area.

Despite the biodiversity, economic importance and vulnerability of Madagascar's coastal areas, the country's coral reefs have been neglected from a conservation perspective, primarily because they do not harbour the same endemicity – or level of species unique to Madagascar – that is seen in the terrestrial ecosystems. But the good news is the people of Madagascar are now beginning to take steps to protect the marine resources they rely upon for survival.

Andavadoaka recently created the world's first community-run protected area for octopuses. With the help of international conservation groups Blue Ventures and the Wildlife Conservation Society established a no-take zone in 2004, banning octopus fishing for several months of the year. This seasonal ban allows octopuses – a major commodity for the village and Madagascar as a whole – to reproduce in greater numbers and grow larger in size. No-take zones not only promote the long-term survival of octopus species, but local fishermen reported greater yields when the ban was lifted. Octopus catches were 13 times larger following the ban than before it was implemented.

Because of the massive increase in octopus size and number, hundreds of eager fishermen from neighbouring villages descended on Andavadoaka when the fishing restrictions were lifted at the no-take zone. The local community was not pleased. However, these neighbouring villages are now working to replicate the project. So far,

whales, sharks and turtles are seen quite regularly and phenomenal superpods of up to 500 dolphins have also been sighted in recent years. Humpback whales may be seen between June and October (as well as some stragglers outside these months), as they migrate to and from their breeding grounds to the north. The area also hosts the marine organisation Blue Ventures (www.blueventures.org) which is working closely with the local fishing communities as well as the University of Toliara's Institut Halieutique et des Sciences Marines (IHSM).

Richard Nimmo of Blue Ventures writes: 'Andavadoaka is a remote village but tremendously rewarding as a result; a very different experience to the beach resorts around Toliara like Ifaty and Anakao. It is a place where you can truly experience local culture and see the lives of fishermen unchanged for centuries. Andavadoaka is one of the largest fishing communities on the southwest coast and on a calm morning the fleet of outrigger canoes (*lakana Vezo* or *pirogues*) sailing out to fish at dawn is a magical sight.'

There are wonderful beaches as well as a rugged and striking arid landscape. 3km from Andavadoaka are magnificent, stunted Grandidier's baobabs which attract enthusiasts from all over the world.

villages in the region have created eight additional no-take zones for octopuses that they will manage with fishing restrictions that go beyond national law.

The huge increase in size and numbers of octopus also caught the attention of Madagascar's national government which in 2005 passed legislation creating seasonal no-take zones for octopuses across the country.

The success of this project is prompting local villages to pursue other conservation activities as well. More than 15 villages along the southwest coast are now joining forces to develop expanded marine protected areas that will benefit a wide variety of marine species beyond just octopuses. Andavadoaka also recently created its first children's environmental club: the Alo Alo Club. Children regularly give song and dance performances warning of the dangers of overfishing and other destructive fishing practices, and they recently broke ground on the village's first vegetable garden.

Andavadoaka's elders have begun to incorporate the success of the marine protected reserves into traditional ceremonies. Before the fishing bans of each no-take zone are lifted, village elders hold a traditional *fomba* to appease their ancestors before opening the reserve, asking permission to collaborate with the conservation groups. A village elder leads the ceremony offering small amounts of money and rum to the *doany*, the supernatural spirits of the ancestors. Everybody at the ceremony is required to taste the rum, although those not willing to drink are able to pour some over their head instead to show respect to the *doany*. The elder then reads a prayer:

'You the *doany*, live here in this sacred land. We have come here to present our collaboration with these new friends regarding putting in place a marine protected area. They bring with them rum and money for you. We accept to work with them if you permit because they want to help us to improve our fisheries. Bless them because the reserve will be good, and please protect them from any danger when travelling on your seas.'

Blue Ventures Conservation is an award-winning not-for-profit organisation dedicated to working with local communities to conserve threatened marine habitats and resources in Madagascar for the betterment of people and nature. Funded almost entirely through ecotourism revenue, Blue Ventures brings paying volunteers to project sites and trains them in scientific research, community outreach and on-the-ground conservation. For information and research updates see www.blueventures.org.

Getting there Ask in Morombe about any possible lifts. Hôtel Baobab is owned by the same family as Coco Beach in Andavadoaka, so transport is often available when supplies are sent. As Morombe is such a small town, if a lift is available most people will know – especially some of the Indian shop owners. The journey by road takes around two hours. The alternative is to take a pirogue from Morombe, which takes about five hours, and hitch a lift back, or to organise your trip in Ifaty via a pirogue (about 100,000Ar) or one of the regular supply boats. This is a particularly scenic journey.

Where to stay/eat Richard Nimmo comments: 'accommodation in Andavadoaka is limited. It is essential that visitors are aware of the impact that they make on this fragile eco-system. So minimise your water usage and try to use biodegradable products wherever possible as waste disposal is basic: showers and sinks often drain straight into the soil and water table. Buy drinks in glass bottles which will be re-used, and avoid packaged goods: there are plenty of delicious fruits and snacks for sale in the village.'

Laguna Blu Resort Ampasilava; e lagunabluresort@lagunabluresort.com; www.lagunabluresort.com (in Italian). Classy, expensive Italian-owned bungalows. Excellent facilities with quality mattresses, good food, extremely comfortable bungalows & hot running water, which for this part of the country is no mean feat. Very little English spoken. The Manta scuba-diving/snorkelling centre is based here. A team of Italian owners run the hotel & one, Sandro, is a doctor who also runs a clinic for local people. 4x4 transfers from Toliara (8hrs) €300pp; Morombe transfers also arranged. ☕

Manga Lodge ☎ +881 631 554 454 (satellite phone; only on Sun/Tue/Thu 11.00–12.00). Run by Mme Guicheteau. Just round the bay from Andavadoaka village. Bungalows right on the beach; beautiful view but quite isolated. No AC. You can walk to the mangroves for wonderful snorkelling. Food excellent & copious. €€€

Hôtel Coco Beach. Charming, friendly; Malagasy-owned. Rustic beach bungalows in one of the most beautiful settings in southern Madagascar. Excellent food served on request. Book through Hôtel Baobab in Morombe, or through Blue Ventures which is based here. €

Chez Antoine Very clean, multicoloured bungalows an the upper end of Andavadoaka. Some bungalows have en-suite bathroom (but shared toilets) others share bucket showers. The Malagasy owners are very friendly & helpful. Simple but tasty Malagasy meals served. €

MIANDRIVAZO Said to be the hottest place in Madagascar. The town lies on the banks of the Mahajilo, a tributary of the Tsiribihina, and is the starting point for the descent of that river. Supposedly the name comes from when King Radama was waiting for his messenger to return with Rasalimo, the Sakalava princess of Malaimbandy with whom he had fallen in love. He fell into a pensive mood and when asked if he was well replied '*Miandry vazo aho*' ('I am waiting for a wife').

Getting there It's a ten-hour journey from Morondava by car or *taxi-brousse*, with one infamously bad stretch of road between Miandrivazo and Malaimbandy. The first 48km out of Morondava is almost as bad. By *taxi-brousse* you'll be lucky to average 30km/h on this stretch. However, with the current pace of road improvement in Madagascar I would expect this road to have been upgraded before the next edition of this book.

Where to stay/eat

Hôtel Lakana (6 bungalows & 6 rooms) New, but reportedly (in 2006) struggling to attain an acceptable standard. Great views, fan-cooled. Rooms are cheaper than bungalows. €€

Hôtel Chez la Reine Rasalimo Concrete bungalows on a hill overlooking the river. Very friendly staff; good restaurant. Dbl & tpl rooms with mosquito nets & fans. €€

Le Coin d'Or et le Gîte de Tsiribihina A long name for a simple hotel with basic rooms. €

Le Relais de Miandrivazo On the main square. Comfortable rooms with mosquito nets. Reasonable food; good atmosphere. Intermittent water. €

Hôtel Laizama 'A simple but homely hotel (we often found ducks in the shower). Helpful management' (R Harris). €

DESCENDING THE TSIRIBIHINA RIVER This is a popular trip (see below) and can easily be set up from Miandrivazo. The guides have organised themselves into the Association Guide Piroguier Miandrivazo (AGPM) which seems very professional. Wherever you are staying, someone from AGPM will find you.

RIVER TRIPS

River trips offer an excellent way to access remote areas of Madagascar. Combining a river journey with standard overland, biking or trekking programmes can make an ideal adventure holiday. Several tour operators offer comfortable, well-catered river journeys and multi-activity itineraries suitable for all ages and interests.

The most popular are floats on the lazy western rivers: Tsiribihina, Mangoky, Manambolo and Mahavavy. These trips can be done as organised tours or independently.

TSIRIBIHINA This is a three- to five-day trip, starting in Miandrivazo, and most people love it for the wildlife seen from the boat as well as the glimpses of rural life on the riverbanks. Being the most popular river trip carries its penalties, however, as these extracts from Heather Merriam's diary demonstrate: 'The morning revealed a pristine sandbank. As there wasn't a toilet on the boat, we looked at it as a cat would a giant, clean litter box. We buried our faeces with feline expertise …

'That was the night we caught up with the other Eurotouro-laden boats, and we all camped together on a not-so-clean sandbank. Each boat had a bonfire in front and groups of villagers danced and sang for "*petit cadeaux*" around each one. The influx of tourists probably represented a new source of income for the otherwise remote village. In the morning, we had to share the litter box with at least 20 other tourists.' In the dry season Heather recommends booking as early as possible to avoid getting an oversized boat (the lighter craft are snapped up early). Large heavy vessels have to be manually pushed around the sandbars when the water is low.

MANAMBOLO The descent of the Manambolo can be arranged through the tour operator Mad'Cameleon (see page 93) or through Remote River Expeditions (see advert on page 437).

On an organised tour the trip takes three days (though five allows for some rest and sightseeing), beginning at Ankavandra. This is a spectacular trip through the untouched homeland of the Sakalava. On the third day you pass through the dramatic Manambolo gorge between towering limestone cliffs, and through the Tsingy de Bemaraha Reserve. The chances of seeing the area's special wildlife, such as Decken's sifaka and the Madagascar fish eagle, are high.

It's rare for anyone to do the Manambolo independently, but Herman Snippe and Jolijn Geels achieved it in 1999. They took a variety of *taxi-brousses* from Tana to Tsiromanomandidy and on to Belobaka. From here they hired a guide to take them on foot to Ankavandra along the Route de Riz used by rice porters. This walk took three days and was 'wonderful' although they warn of a shortage of drinking water in the dry season. Ankavandra is pretty much owned and run by a M Nouradine, who owns the only hotel and river-worthy pirogues. The trip downriver cost Herman and Jolijn about € 100 (a high price for Madagascar). The price included two piroguiers and their food. In April, after rain, the two-and-a-half-day descent of the river was thrilling and spectacularly beautiful.

MANGOKY The journey from Beroroha to Bevoay (approx 160km) runs through an isolated region in the southwest of the island, with no roads north or south of the river for more than 100km. This calm water stretch offers expansive beaches for camping and many yet-to-be-explored side canyons. The Mangoky passes through sections of dry deciduous forests which are dominated by perhaps the largest baobab forest on Earth. There are at least three species, the most predominant being the huge *Adansonia grandidieri*.

However, this is no longer the pristine experience described in the last edition of this book when Gary Lemmer wrote: 'Given the vast unexploited area along the river, its rich wildlife and the sheer beauty of the river itself, perhaps the Mangoky deserves to be designated Madagascar's first national river reserve.' Gary now reports: 'Large fires on the south side of the river in recent years are forcing local populations to move closer to the river; small villages and camps are beginning to be seen. The effects of their presence will become more and more evident in the future.'

MAHAVAVY Another 'special' from Remote River Expeditions, the Mahavavy was first explored in 1998, when the rafting team put in at Kandreho and ended in Mitsinjo. The area was extremely rich in both lemurs and birds, with large expanses of beautiful forest. Lemur-viewing was far superior to the other western rivers. 'For sheer numbers, proximity and ease of viewing, the Mahavavy was superb, mainly for Decken's and crowned sifakas (*Propithecus deckeni* and *P. coronatus*) and red-fronted brown lemurs (*Eulemur rufus*).

'The outstanding areas for these species were around the Kasijy forest and the riverine tamarind gallery forest between Bekipay and Ambinany. To give some ideas of densities in both the Kasijy area and also the forest between Bekipay and Ambinany, I can say that a short foray into the forest, moving maybe 200–300m, staying one hour, would produce five to six families of sifakas, which were remarkably unconcerned by our presence. Red-fronted brown lemurs were very numerous, especially in Kasijy. The Mahavavy is very rich in birds: the most exciting sightings of the trip were of six Madagascar fish eagles' (Conrad Hirsh).

TOUR OPERATORS Most of the main ground operators listed in *Chapter 4* organise river trips on comfortable vessels with good food, camping equipment and experienced guides.

The following are specialists in the west:

Mad'Cameleon ⟍ 22 630 86; f 22 344 20; e madcam@wanadoo.mg. Canoe trips on the Manambolo River.
Remote River Expeditions ⟍ 95 523 47; m 032 04 341 14; www.remoterivers.com. Takes small groups on all the main rivers of Madagascar & regularly pioneers new trips. In March/April 2008, this operator will be offering a multi-activity programme: Mangoky/Mikea Baobab Quest. The itinerary will combine floating the Mangoky with trekking in the seldom-visited Mikea Forest north of the river.

Appendix I

HISTORICAL CHRONOLOGY

AD 000	Approximate date for the first significant settlement of the island.
800–900	Dates of the first identifiable village sites in the north of the island. Penetration of the interior begins in the south.
1200	Establishment of Arab settlements. First mosques built.
1500	'Discovery' of Madagascar by the Portuguese Diego Dias. Unsuccessful attempts to establish permanent European bases on the island followed.
1650s	Emergence of Sakalava kingdoms.
Early 1700s	Eastern Madagascar is increasingly used as a base by pirates.
1716	Fénérive captured by Ratsimilaho. The beginnings of the Betsimisaraka confederacy.
1750	Death of Ratsimilaho.
1787	The future Andrianampoinimerina declared King of Ambohimanga.
1795/6	Andrianampoinimerina established his capital at Antananarivo.
1810–28	Reign of Radama I, Merina king.
1818	First mission school opened in Tamatave.
1820	First mission school opened in Antananarivo.
1828–61	Reign of Ranavalona I, Merina queen.
1835	Publication of the Bible in Malagasy, but profession of the Christian faith declared illegal.
1836	Most Europeans and missionaries leave the island.
1861–63	Reign of Radama II, Merina king.
1861	Missionaries re-admitted. Freedom of religion proclaimed.
1863–68	Queen Rasoherina succeeds after Radama II assassinated.
1868–83	Reign of Queen Ranavalona II.
1883	Coronation of Queen Ranavalona III.
1883–85	Franco-Malagasy War.
1895	Establishment of full French protectorate; Madagascar became a full colony the following year.
1897	Ranavalona III exiled first to Réunion and later to Algiers. Merina monarchy abolished.
1917	Death of Ranavalona III in exile.
1942	British troops occupy Madagascar.
1946	Madagascar becomes an Overseas Territory of France.
1947	Nationalist rebellion suppressed with thousands killed.
1958	Autonomy achieved within the French community.
1960	June 26. Madagascar achieves full independence with Philibert Tsiranana as president.
1972	Tsiranana dissolves parliament and hands power to General Ramanantsoa who forges links with Soviet Union.

1975	Lieutenant-Commander Didier Ratsiraka is named head of state after a coup. The country is renamed the Democratic Republic of Madagascar and Ratsiraka is elected president for a seven-year term.
1976	Ratsiraka nationalises large parts of the economy and forms the AREMA party
1986	Ratsiraka changes position and promotes a market economy.
1991	Demonstrations and strikes. Ratsiraka orders security forces to open fire on the crowds outside the presidential palace demanding his resignation. About 130 people are killed.
1992	Under pressure of demonstrations, Ratsiraka introduces democratic reforms replacing the socialist system, but is forced to resign.
1993	Albert Zafy elected president in the country's first multi-party elections. The birth of the Third Republic.
1996	Albert Zafy impeached.
1997	Didier Ratsiraka re-elected president.
2000	December. AREMA wins in most of the cities, apart from Antananarivo, in provincial elections. 70% of voters boycott the elections.
2001	May. Senate reopens after 29 years, completing the government framework provided for in the 1992 constitution.
2001	December. First round of presidential elections. Marc Ravalomanana claims the election was rigged and refuses to take part in a run-off. This leads to six months of turmoil.
2002	July. *La Crise Politique* ends and Marc Ravalomanana becomes president.
2003	At the 5th World Parks Congress in Durban, South Africa, President Ravalomanana announces his intention to triple the protected areas of Madagascar by 2008.
2006	December. Marc Ravalomanana wins a second term in office. He announces the Madagascar Action Plan (MAP).

Appendix 2

THE MALAGASY LANGUAGE

SOME BASIC RULES

Pronunciation The Malagasy alphabet is made up of 21 letters. C, Q, U, W and X are omitted. Individual letters are pronounced as follows:

a	as in 'father'
e	as in the a in 'late'
g	as in 'get'
h	almost silent
i	as ee in 'seen'
j	pronounced dz
o	oo as in 'too'
s	usually midway between sh and s but varies according to region
z	as in 'zoo'

Combinations of letters needing different pronunciations are:

ai	like y in 'my'
ao	like ow in 'cow'
eo	pronounced ay-oo

When k or g is preceded by i or y this vowel is also sounded after the consonant. For example *alika* (dog) is pronounced Aleekya, and *ary koa* (and also) is pronounced Ahreekewa.

Stressed syllables Some syllables are stressed, others almost eliminated. This causes great problems for visitors trying to pronounce place names, and unfortunately – like in English – the basic rules are frequently broken. Generally, the stress is on the penultimate syllable except in words ending in na, ka and tra when it is generally on the last syllable but two. Words ending in e stress that vowel. Occasionally a word with the same spelling changes its meaning according to the stressed syllable, but in this case it is written with an accent. For example, *tanana* means 'hand', and *tanána* means 'town'.

When a word ends in a vowel, this final syllable is pronounced so lightly it is often just a stressed last consonant. For instance the sifaka lemur is pronounced 'She-fak'. Words derived from English, like *hotely* and *banky*, are pronounced much the same as in English.

GETTING STARTED The easiest way to begin to get a grip on Malagasy is to build on your knowledge of place names (you have to learn how to pronounce these in order to get around) and to this end I have given the phonetic pronunciation in the text. As noted in the text, most place names mean something so you have only to learn these meanings and – hey presto! – you have the elements of the language! Here are some bits of place names:

A2

An-, Am-, I-	at, the place where	Manga	blue or good
Arivo	thousand	Maro	many
Be	big, plenty of	Nosy	island
Fotsy, -potsy	white	Rano, -drano	water
Kely	small	Tany, tani-	land
Kily	tamarind	Tsara	good
Mafana	hot	Tsy, Tsi	(negative)
Maha	which causes	Vato, -bato	stone
Mainti	black	Vohitra, vohi-,	hill
Maintso	green	bohi-	

In Malagasy the plural form of a noun is the same as the singular form.

VOCABULARY
Social phrases Stressed letters or phrases are underlined.

English	Malagasy	Phonetic pronunciation
Hello	Manao ahoana	Mano _own_
Hello	Salama	Sal_aam_
(north and east coast)	Mbola tsara	M'boola tsara
What news?	Inona no vaovao?	_Inan_ vowvow?
No news	Tsy misy	Tsim_ees_

These three easy-to-learn phrases of ritualised greetings establish contact with people you pass on the road or meet in their village. For extra courtesy (important in Madagascar) add *tompoko* (pronounced 'toomp'k') at the end of each phrase.

Simple phrases for 'conversation'

English	Malagasy	Phonetic pronunciation
What's your name?	Iza no anaranao?	Eeza nan_aranow?_
My name is	Ny anarako	Ny anar_akoo_
Goodbye	Veloma	Vel_oom_
See you again	Mandra pihaona	Mandra pi_oon_
I don't understand	Tsy azoko	Tsi az_ook_
I don't know	Tsy haiko	Tsi haikou
Very good	Tsara tokoa	Tsara t'k_oo_
Bad	Ratsy	Rats
Please/Excuse me	Aza fady	Aza_fad_
Thank you	Misaotra	Mis_ow_tr
Thank you very much	Misaotra betsaka	Mis_ow_tr bets_ak_
Pardon me		
(ie: may I pass)	Ombay lalana	M'_buy_ lalan
Let's go	Andao andeha	And_ow_ and_ay_
Crazy	Adaladala	Adal_adal_
Long life! (Cheers!)	Ho ela velona!	Wellavell!

If you are pestered by beggars try:

English	Malagasy	Phonetic pronunciation
I have nothing	Tsy misy	Tsim_eess_
(there is none)		
Thank you, I don't need it	Misaotra fa tsy mila	Mis_ow_tr, fa tsi meel
Go away!	Mandehana!	Man day _han_

Note: The words for yes (*eny*) and no (*tsia*) are hardly ever used in conversation. The Malagasy tend to say '*yoh*' for yes and '*ah*' for no, along with appropriate gestures.

Market phrases

English	Malagasy	Phonetic pronunciation
How much?	*Ohatrinona?*	*Ohtreen?*
Too expensive!	*Lafo be!*	*Laff be!*
No way!	*Tsy lasa!*	*Tsee lass!*

Basic needs

English	Malagasy	Phonetic pronunciation
Where is…?	*Aiza…?*	*Ize…?*
Is it far?	*Lavitra ve izany?*	*Lavtra vayzan?*
Is there any…?	*Misy ve…?*	*Mees vay…?*
I want…	*Mila … aho*	*Meel … a*
I'm looking for…	*Mitady … aho*	*M'tadi … a*
Is there a place to sleep?	*Misy toerana hatoriana ve?*	*Mees too ayran atureen vay?*
Is it ready?	*Vita ve?*	*Veeta vay?*
I would like to buy some food	*Te hividy sakafo aho*	*Tayveed sakaff wah*
I'm hungry	*Noana aho*	*Noonah*
I'm thirsty	*Mangetaheta aho*	*Mangataytah*
I'm tired	*Vizaka aho*	*Veesacar*
Please help me!	*Mba ampio aho!*	*Bampeewha!*

Useful words

English	Malagasy	Phonetic pronunciation
village	*vohitra*	*voo-itra*
house	*trano*	*tran*
food/meal	*hanina/sakafo*	*an/sakaff*
water	*rano*	*rahn*
rice	*vary*	*var*
eggs	*atody*	*atood*
chicken	*akoho*	*akoo*
bread	*mofo*	*moof*
milk	*ronono*	*roonoon*
road	*lalana*	*lalan*
town	*tanana*	*tanan*
river (large)	*ony*	*oon*
river (small)	*riaka*	*reek*
ox/cow	*omby/omby vavy*	*oomby/omb varve*
child/baby	*ankizy/zaza kely*	*ankeeze/zaza kail*
man/woman	*lehilahy/vehivavy*	*layla/vayvarve*

Appendix 3

MADAGASCAR'S MOST READILY SEEN MAMMALS Nick Garbutt

WHERE TO FIND THEM Although there are relatively few species (compared to mainland Africa), Madagascar is an exceptional place to watch mammals. Of course, everyone wants to see lemurs, but for those with time, patience and a little luck, there is far more to see besides. Listed below are the best places to try and find Madagascar's mammals. Species marked with an asterisk (*) are nocturnal.

Lemurs There have been numerous recent discoveries and descriptions of new species that have rendered established species distribution obsolete. These particularly affect some nocturnal lemurs, most notably the **mouse lemurs** (genus *Microcebus*, now contains 16 species), the **dwarf lemurs** (genus *Cheirogaleus*, now contains seven species) and the **sportive lemurs** (genus *Lepilemur*, now contains 23 species).

Included here are the most frequently seen species currently known from the major wildlife sites that most tourists visit.

Common/scientific name	Distribution/where to see
Grey mouse lemur	Western dry forests and some southern spiny forests
*Microcebus murinus**	Ampijoroa, Kirindy and Berenty
Brown mouse lemur	Some eastern rainforest areas
*Microcebus rufus**	Ranomafana National Park
Goodman's mouse lemur	Some eastern rainforest areas
*Microcebus lehilahytsara**	Ranomafana National Park
Madame Berthe's mouse lemur	Only known from Kirindy and nearby forests.
*Microcebus berthae**	Kirindy
Golden-brown mouse lemur	Forests north of Betsiboka River
*Microcebus ravelobensis**	Ampijoroa
Hairy-eared dwarf lemur	Central and northeastern lowland rainforests
*Allocebus trichotis**	Analamazaotra Reserve and Mantadia National Park
Greater dwarf lemur	Eastern rainforests
*Cheirogaleus major**	Ranomafana National Park
Furry-eared dwarf lemur	Eastern rainforests around Andasibe
*Cheirogaleus crossleyi**	Andasibe-Mantadia National Park
Fat-tailed dwarf lemur	Dry forests of the west
*Cheirogaleus medius**	Ampijoroa and Kirindy
Coquerel's dwarf lemur	Dry forests of the west
*Mirza coquereli**	Kirindy
Pale fork-marked lemur	Dry western forest
*Phaner pallescens**	Kirindy
Amber Mountain fork-marked lemur	Montagne d'Ambre, Ankarana and Analamera region of northern Madagascar
*Phaner electromontis**	Montagne d'Ambre National Park

Common/scientific name	Distribution/where to see
Weasel sportive lemur	Central eastern rainforest
Lepilemur mustelinus★	Andasibe-Mantadia National Park
Small-toothed sportive lemur	Some southern areas in eastern rainforest
Lepilemur microdon★	Ranomafana National Park
Ankarana sportive lemur	Some forests of extreme north
Lepilemur ankaranensis★	Ankarana and Montagne d'Ambre National Park
Hawk's sportive lemur	Offshore islands in northwest
Lepilemur tymerlachsoni★	Lokobe Reserve on Nosy Be
Milne-Edwards sportive lemur	Dry forests of west, north of Betsiboka River
Lepilemur edwardsi★	Ampijoroa
Red-tailed sportive lemur	Dry forests of west, south of Manambolo River
Lepilemur ruficaudatus★	Kirindy
White-footed sportive lemur	Spiny and gallery forests in south
Lepilemur leucopus★	Berenty
Eastern grey bamboo lemur	Eastern rainforest belt
Hapalemur griseus	Andasibe-Mantadia and Ranomafana National Parks
Golden bamboo lemur	Rainforests of Ranomafana and Andringitra in
Hapalemur aureus	southeast
	Ranomafana National Park
Greater bamboo lemur	Rainforests of southeast
Prolemur simus	Ranomafana National Park
Ring-tailed lemur	Spiny forests and gallery forests of south and
Lemur catta	southwest and the Andringitra Massif
	Berenty, Isalo National Park and Anja Reserve near
	Ambalavao
Mongoose lemur	Dry forests of northwest
Eulemur mongoz	Tsiombikibo Forest near Mitsinjo and Ampijoroa
Crowned lemur	Forest of extreme north
Eulemur coronatus	Ankarana, Analamera and Montagne d'Ambre
	National Park
Red-bellied lemur	Eastern rainforest belt (mid to high elevations)
Eulemur rubriventer	Ranomafana, Andasibe-Mantadia and Marojejy
	National Parks
Common brown lemur	Dry forests of northwest and central eastern
Eulemur fulvus	rainforests
	Ampijoroa and Andasibe-Mantadia National Park
Sanford's brown lemur	Forests of the far north
Eulemur sanfordi	Montagne d'Ambre National Park and Ankarana
White-fronted brown lemur	Rainforests of northeast
Eulemur albifrons	Nosy Mangabe, Marojejy and Masoala National Parks
Red-fronted brown lemur	Dry forests of west and rainforests of southeast
Eulemur rufus	Kirindy and Ranomafana National Park
Collared brown lemur	Rainforests of extreme southeast
Eulemur collaris	Andohahela National Park and Stie Luce
Black lemur	Sambirano region and offshore islands in northeast
Eulemur macaco macaco	Lokobe Reserve on Nosy Be and island of Nosy Komba
Black-and-white ruffed lemur	Eastern rainforests
Varecia variegata	Nosy Mangabe, Ranomafana and Mantadia National
	Parks
Red ruffed lemur	Rainforests of Masoala Peninsula
Varecia rubra	Andranobe, Lohatrozona and Tampolo in Masoala
	National Park

Common/scientific name	Distribution/where to see
Eastern avahi or **eastern woolly lemur** *Avahi laniger*	Throughout eastern rainforest belt Andasibe-Mantadia and Ranomafana National Parks
Western avahi or **western woolly lemur** *Avahi occidentalis*	Northwestern forests Ampijoroa
Diademed sifaka *Propithecus diadema*	Central and northeastern rainforests Mantadia National Park
Milne-Edward's sifaka *Propithecus edwardsi*	Southeastern rainforests Ranomafana National Park
Silky sifaka *Propithecus candidus*	Northeastern rainforests (at higher elevations) Marojejy National Park
Perrier's sifaka *Propithecus perrieri*	Dry forests in extreme north between Loky and Irodo rivers Analamera
Verreaux's sifaka *Propithecus verreauxi*	Dry forests of west, south of Tsiribihina River and spiny forests of south and southwest Kirindy, Berenty, Andohahela and Isalo National Parks
Coquerel's sifaka *Propithecus coquereli*	Dry forests of northwest Ampijoroa and Anjajavy
Decken's sifaka *Propithecus deckeni*	West between the Manambolo and Mahavavy Rivers Tsiombikibo Forest near Mitsinjo and Tsingy de Bemaraha National Park near Bekopaka
Crowned sifaka *Propithecus coronatus*	Dry forests between Mahavavy and Betsiboka Rivers and the Bongolava Massif Near lighthouse north of Katsepy and the forest around Anjamena on banks of Mahavavy River
Golden-crowned sifaka *Propithecus tattersalli*	Between Manambato and Loky rivers in northeast Madagascar Forests close to village of Andranotsimaty, 5km northeast of Daraina
Indri *Indri indri*	Central eastern and northeastern rainforests Andasibe-Mantadia National Park
Aye-aye *Daubentonia madagascariensis★*	Eastern rainforests and some western dry forests Aye-aye Island near Mananara and Nosy Mangabe

OTHER MAMMALS
Carnivores

Fanaloka or **striped civet** *Fossa fossana★*	Rainforest of east and north, Sambirano in northwest and dry forests of extreme north Ranomafana National Park and Ankarana
Falanouc *Eupleres goudotii★*	Eastern rainforests and dry forests of northwest and extreme north Montagne d'Ambre National Park
Fossa *Cryptoprocta ferox*	All native forests Kirindy and Ankarana
Ring-tailed mongoose *Galidia elegans*	Native forests of east, north and west Ankarana, Ranomafana and Marojejy National Parks
Narrow-striped mongoose *Mungotictis decemlineata*	Dry forests of west, south of Tsiribihina River Kirindy

Common/scientific name	Distribution/where to see

Tenrecs

Common tenrec	All native forest areas
Tenrec ecaudatus★	Ranomafana National Park, Kirindy and Ampijoroa
Greater hedgehog tenrec	Most native forest types
Setifer setosus★	Nosy Mangabe, Andasibe-Mantadia and Ranomafana National Parks
Lesser hedgehog tenrec	Dry forest of west and spiny forest and gallery forests
Echinops telfairi★	of south
	Ifaty and Berenty
Lowland streaked tenrec	Eastern rainforest areas
Hemicentetes semispinosus	Maroantsetra area, Andasibe-Mantadia, Masoala and Ranomafana National Parks

Rodents

Giant jumping rat	Western dry forest between Andranomena and
Hypogeomys antimena★	Tsiribihina Rivers
	Kirindy
Red forest rat	Eastern rainforests
Nesomys rufus	Ranomafana and Andasibe-Mantadia National Parks
Long-tailed big-footed mouse	Western forest around Ankarafantsika
Macrotarsomys ingens	Ampijoroa

Bats

Madagascar flying fox	Eastern rainforests, western dry forests and southern gallery forests
Pteropus rufus★	Berenty, Nosy Tanikely off Nosy Be
Mauritian tomb bat	Western and eastern forests
Taphozous mauritianus	Ampijoroa

A3

TRAVELLER'S TALE, 1669

'There are some birds the size of a large turkeycock which have the head made like a cat and the rest of the body like a griffin; these birds hide themselves in the thick woods, and when anyone passes under the tree where they are they let themselves fall so heavily on the head of the passengers that they stun them, and in the moment they pierce their heads with their talons, then they eat them.'

Sieur de Bois, 1669

Appendix 4

FURTHER INFORMATION Updated by Daniel Austin

BOOKS Madagascar's historical links with Britain and the current interest in its natural history and culture have produced a century of excellent books written in English. This bibliography is a selection of my favourites in each category. Note that many are out of print but may be found second-hand.

General – history, the country, the people

Allen, P M; Covell M *Historical Dictionary of Madagascar* Scarecrow, US 2005 (2nd edition). A pricey (£59) but very comprehensive dictionary of important people and events in Madagascar's political, economic, social and cultural history from early times to the present day.

Bradt, H *Madagascar* (World Bibliographical Series) Clio (UK); ABC (US) 1992. An annotated selection of nearly 400 titles on Madagascar, from the classic early works to those published in the early 1990s.

Brown, M A *History of Madagascar* D Tunnacliffe, UK 1996. The most accurate, comprehensive and readable of the histories, brought completely up to date by Britain's foremost expert on the subject.

Clifford, B *Return to Treasure Island and the Search for Captain Kidd* HarperCollins 2003. The story of Captain Kidd and the author's expedition to Madagascar to search for his ship, the *Adventure Galley*.

Covell, M *Madagascar: Politics, Economics and Society* (Marxist Regimes series) Frances Pinter, UK 1987. An interesting look at Madagascar's Marxist past.

Croft-Cooke, R *The Blood-Red Island* Staples, UK 1953. A racy and engaging account of a somewhat unconventional officer's adventures during the British Military occupation of Madagascar in 1942.

Crook, S *Distant Shores: by Traditional Canoe from Asia to Madagascar* Impact Books, UK 1990. The story of the 4,000-mile Sarimanok Expedition by outrigger canoe across the Indian Ocean from Bali to Madagascar. An interesting account of an eventful and historically important journey.

Dodwell, C *Madagascar Travels* Hodder & Stoughton, UK 1995. An account of a journey through Madagascar's most remote regions by one of Britain's leading travel writers.

Donenfeld, J Mankafy *Sakafo: Delicious Meals from Madagascar* iUniverse, USA 2007. The first English-language cookbook of Malagasy cuisine (the title means 'tasty food'). Some 70 recipes interspersed with endearing tales of the author's travels in Madagascar.

Drysdale, H *Dancing with the Dead: a Journey through Zanzibar and Madagascar* Hamish Hamilton, UK 1991. An account of Helena's journeys in search of her trading ancestor. Informative, entertaining and well written.

Ecott, T *Vanilla* Penguin, 2004. The UK and US editions are subtitled 'travels in search of the luscious substance' and 'travels in search of the ice cream orchid' respectively. Among other places, the author visits Madagascar, the world's biggest producer of this fragrant pod.

Ellis, W *Madagascar Revisited* John Murray, UK 1867. The Rev William Ellis of the London Missionary Society was one of the most observant and sympathetic of the missionary writers. His books are well worth the search for second-hand copies.

Eveleigh, M *Maverick in Madagascar* (Lonely Planet Journeys) Lonely Planet 2001. A well-written account of an exceptionally adventurous trip in the north of Madagascar.

Fox, L *Hainteny: the Traditional Poetry of Madagascar* Associated University Presses, UK & Canada 1990. Over 400 beautifully translated *hainteny* with an excellent introduction to the history and spiritual life of the Merina.

Grehan, J *The Forgotten Invasion: The Story of Britain's First Large-Scale Combined Operation, the Invasion of Madagascar 1942* Historic Military Press 2007. The first detailed account of a little-known aspect of Anglo-Malagasy history by a leading military historian.

Grunewald, O & Wolozan, D *Tsingy – Stone Forest, Madagascar* Editions Altus, France 2006. Stunning photography of Tsingy de Bemaraha. Available in UK from NHBS.

Laidler, K *Female Caligula: Ranavalona, the Mad Queen of Madagascar* John Wiley, UK 2005. The fascinating tale of Ranavalona's bizarre reign.

Lanting, F *Madagascar, a World out of Time* Robert Hale, UK 1991. A book of stunning and somewhat surreal, photos of the landscape, people and wildlife. Text by renowned Madagascar experts John Mack and Alison Jolly.

McCaughrean, G *Plundering Paradise* Oxford University Press, UK 1996. Children's fiction (but good light reading for adults too) based on the story of pirate's son Ratsimilaho. An English brother and sister get caught up in real pirate adventures.

Murphy, D *Muddling through in Madagascar* John Murray, UK 1985. An entertaining account of a journey (by foot and truck) through the highlands and south.

Rasoloson, J *Malagasy-English/English-Malagasy Dictionary and Phrasebook* Hippocrene, US 2001. Handy local language guide for travellers.

Parker Pearson, Mike & Godden, Karen *In Search of the Red Slave* Sutton Publishing, UK 2002. An archaeological team goes in search of Robert Drury. An absorbing account which reads like a whodunit, but is equally interesting as a portrait of the Tandroy people.

Sibree, J *Madagascar Before the Conquest: the Island, the Country, and the People* T Fisher Unwin, UK 1896. Sibree (with William Ellis) was the main documenter of Madagascar during the days of the London Missionary Society. He wrote many books on the island, all of which are perceptive, informative and a pleasure to read.

Spong, C *Madagascar: Rail and Mail* Indian Ocean Study Circle, 2003. Available from Keith Fitton, 50 Firlands, Weybridge, Surrey KT13 OHR. £12 plus postage. A monograph detailing the country's philately and railways.

Ethnography

Astuti, R *People of the sea: Identity and descent among the Vezo of Madagascar* Cambridge University Press, UK 1995. An academic exploration of what it means to be Vezo.

Bloch, M *From Blessing to Violence* Cambridge University Press, UK 1986. History and ideology of the circumcision ritual of the Merina people.

Haring, Lee *Verbal Arts in Madagascar: Performance in Historical Perspective* University of Pennsylvania Press, US 1992. Study of Malagasy folklore inc more than 100 translated riddles, proverbs, *hainteny* and oratories.

Lambek, M *The Weight of the Past: Living with History in Mahajanga* Palgrave Macmillan, US 2002. The author looks at the role of history in the identity of the Sakalava.

Mack, J *Madagascar: Island of the Ancestors* British Museum, UK 1986. A scholarly and informative account of the ethnography of Madagascar.

Mack, J *Malagasy Textiles* Shire Publications, UK 1989.

Powe, E L *Lore of Madagascar* Dan Aiki (530 W Johnson St, Apt 210, Madison, WI 53703), US 1994. An immense work – over 700 pages and 260 colour photos – with a price to match: $300. This is the only book to describe in detail and in a readable form all 39 ethnic groups in Madagascar.

Ruud, J *Taboo: a Study of Malagasy Customs and Beliefs* Oslo University Press/George Allen & Unwin, UK 1960. Written by a Norwegian Lutheran missionary who worked for 20 years in Madagascar. A detailed study of *fady*, *vintana* and other Malagasy beliefs. Recently reprinted in Tana.

Sharp, L A *The Possessed and the Dispossessed: Spirits, Identity and Power in a Madagascar Migrant Town* University of California Press, US 1993. Describes the daily life and the phenomenon of possession (*tromba*) in the town of Ambanja.

Sharp, L A *The Sacrificed Generation: Youth, History and the Colonized Mind in Madagascar* University of California Press, US 2002. An academic but very readable look at the role of the younger generation in Madagascar.

Wilson, P J *Freedom by a Hair's Breadth* University of Michigan, US 1993. An anthropological study of the Tsimihety people, written in a clear style and accessible to the general reader.

Natural history
Literature

Attenborough, D *Zoo Quest to Madagascar* Lutterworth, UK 1961. Still one of the best travel books ever written about Madagascar, with, of course, plenty of original wildlife observations. Out of print, but copies can be found; more readily available as part of the three-book compilation *Journeys to the Past* 1981.

Durrell, G *The Aye-aye and I* Harper Collins, UK 1992. The focal point is the collecting of aye-ayes for Jersey Zoo, written in the inimitable Durrell style with plenty of humour and travellers' tales.

Heying, H E *Antipode: Seasons with the Extraordinary Wildlife and Culture of Madagascar* St Martin's, USA 2002. Herpetologist Heather Heying recounts her experiences studying mantella frogs on Nosy Mangabe and presents her own view of the Malagasy.

Jolly, A *A World Like Our Own: Man and Nature in Madagascar* Yale University Press, 1980. The first and still the best look at the relationship between the natural history and people of the island. Highly readable.

Jolly, A *Lords and Lemurs* Houghton Mifflin, US 2004. The long-awaited sequel to *A World Like Our Own*. Alison Jolly knows Berenty better than anyone and writes about it better than anyone. This is a marvellous blend of scientific and anthropological fact in a book that reads like a novel. It's funny, engrossing and often surprising.

Pakenham, T *The Remarkable Baobab* Weidenfeld & Nicolson, UK 2004. A follow-up to *Remarkable Trees of the World* by the same author. This is the story of the baobab, six out of eight species of which live exclusively in Madagascar.

Preston-Mafham, K *Madagascar: A Natural History* Facts on File, UK & US 1991. The most enjoyable and useful book on the subject. Illustrated with superb colour photos (coffee-table format), it is as good for identifying strange invertebrates and unusual plants as in describing animal behaviour.

Quammen, D *The Song of the Dodo* Hutchinson, UK 1996. An interesting account of island biogeography and its implications for nature reserves.

Thompson, P *Madagascar: The Great Red Island* UK 2004. A self-published account of travels in Madagascar by a botanist, so of particular interest to plant-lovers. There's a useful appendix on plant names. Available from Amazon or the author, tel: 01588 672106, email: peterthompson@burwaynet.com.

Tyson, P *The Eighth Continent: Life, Death and Discovery in the Lost World of Madagascar* Perennial (HarperCollins), 2001. An American journalist's description of accompanying four scientific expeditions in Madagascar, with American, British and Malagasy scientists. This is interspersed with extensive information on Madagascar's history, archaeology and natural history.

Weinberg, S *A Fish Caught in Time* Fourth Estate, UK 1999. The fascinating tale of the 1938 discovery of a live coelacanth – a fish previously believed extinct for millions of years – off Madagascar's shores.

Wilson, J *Lemurs of the Lost World: Exploring the Forests and Crocodile Caves of Madagascar* Revised 1995 and available from the author (see page 448). An amusing and lively account of British scientific expeditions to Ankarana and subsequent travels in Madagascar.

Specialist literature and guides

Bradt, H; Schuurman, D & Garbutt, N *Madagascar Wildlife: a visitor's guide* Bradt Travel Guides (UK); Globe Pequot Press (US) 2001 (2nd edition). A photographic guide to the island's most interesting and appealing wildlife, including where best to see it.

Cribb, P & Hermans, J *Field Guide to the Orchids of Madagascar* Royal Botanic Gardens, Kew, UK 2007. Guide to Madagascar's extensive orchid flora; over 600 colour photos.

Dorr, L J *Plant Collectors in Madagascar and the Comoro Islands* Royal Botanic Gardens, Kew, UK 1997. Biographical and bibliographical information on over 1,000 individuals and groups.

Dransfield, J & Beentje, H *The Palms of Madagascar* Royal Botanic Gardens, Kew, UK 1996. A beautiful and much-needed book describing the many palm species of Madagascar.

Dransfield, J; Beentje, H; Britt, A; Ranarivelo, T & Razafitsalama, J *Field Guide to the Palms of Madagascar* Royal Botanic Gardens, Kew, UK 2006. A guide to more than 100 of the native palms with over 180 colour photo plus distribution maps for each species.

Garbutt, N *Mammals of Madagascar: A Complete Guide* A&C Black, UK 2007. This completely revised and updated guide contains photographs and distribution maps for all Malagasy mammals, including dozens of newly described species. Very comprehensive. Paperback; suitable for use as a field guide.

Glaw, F & Vences, M A *Field Guide to the Amphibians and Reptiles of Madagascar* 2007. The long-awaited 3rd edition of this thorough guide to the herpetofauna gives over 700 detailed species profiles and 1,500 colour photos. Available through NHBS.

Goodman, S & Benstead, J *The Natural History of Madagascar* Chicago University Press 2004. The most thorough and comprehensive account yet published. The island's geology, climate, human ecology and impact, marine ecosystems, plants, invertebrates, fish, amphibians, reptiles, birds, mammals and conservation written by no fewer than 281 authorities in their field. A hefty 1,709 pages with a price to match (£59.50).

Hermans, J; Hermans, C; Cribb, P; Bosser, J & Du Puy, D *Orchids of Madagascar* Royal Botanic Gardens, Kew, UK 2007. A checklist of all known Malagasy orchid species, with complete bibliography, superbly illustrated with colour photos. New edition; pricey (£75) but orchid enthusiasts will not care.

Hillerman, F E; Holst, A W *An Introduction to the Cultivated Angraecoid Orchids of Madagascar* Timber Press, US 1987. Includes a good section on climate and other plant life.

Martin, J *Masters of Disguise: A Natural History of Chameleons* Facts on File (US); Blandford (UK) 1992. Beautifully illustrated with photos by Art Wolfe; everything a chameleon aficionado could hope for.

Mittermeier, M (*et al*) *Lemurs of Madagascar* Conservation International 2006 (2nd edition). An extensively updated, illustrated field guide to all Madagascar's lemurs.

Morris, P; Hawkins, F *Birds of Madagascar: a Photographic Guide* Pica Press, UK 1999. I find this well-respected guide difficult to use in the field (too heavy, no distribution maps) but it is the authoritative text and photos provide serious birders with the details they need for reliable identification.

Rauh, W *Succulent and Xerophytic Plants of Madagascar* Strawberry Press, US 1995 & 1998. In two volumes. Expensive but detailed and comprehensive; lavishly illustrated with photos.

Rübel, A; Hatchwell, M; MacKinnon, J *Masoala: the Eye of the Forest* Theodor Gut Verlag, Switzerland 2003. A photographic book on the Masoala National Park available in English, French and German editions.

Sinclair, I & Langrand, O *Birds of the Indian Ocean Islands* Struik, South Africa 1999. The most user-friendly of the field guides to Madagascar's birds. Clear layout with a large number of excellent illustrations and distribution maps for quick reference on the trail. No photos but see next entry.

Sinclair, I; Langrand, O & Andriamialisoa *A Photographic Guide to the Birds of the Indian Ocean Islands* Struik, South Africa 2006. Similar to the above guide by the same authors, but with photos instead of illustrations and bilingual English/French text.

Where to buy books on Madagascar

Madagascar Library (Daniel Austin) www.madagascar-library.com. A detailed online catalogue of more than 900 books & articles. Photocopies of items from the library can be purchased (subject to copyright). The online bookstore (*www.madagascar-library.com/shop.html*) has more than 150 in-print book/CD titles for sale.

Discover Madagascar (Seraphine Tierney) 7 Hazledene Rd, Chiswick, London W4 3JB; ✆ 020 8995 3529; e discovermadagascar@yahoo.co.uk; www.discovermadagascar.co.uk. Seraphine puts out a catalogue of books on Madagascar which are in print but may be hard to find in conventional outlets. She also sells Malagasy music cassettes & CDs.

Mad Books (Rupert Parker) 151 Wilberforce Rd, London N4 2SX; ✆ 020 7226 4490; e Rupert@madbooks.co.uk; www.madbooks.co.uk. Rupert specialises in old & rare (out-of-print) books on Madagascar & will send out his catalogue on request. He will also search for books.

Editions Karthala (France) 22–24 Bd Arago, 75013 Paris; www.karthala.com. This French publisher specialises in Madagascar, both for new titles & reprints.

Natural History Book Service (NHBS) 2 Wills Rd, Totnes, Devon TQ9 5XN; ✆ 01803 865913; f 01803 865280; www.nhbs.com.

MAGAZINES All available internationally by subscription unless otherwise stated.

Vintsy (bimonthly; mainly in French and Malagasy but always at least one article in English) www.vintsy.mg. WWF-Madagascar's conservation magazine.

Madagascar Magazine (quarterly; in French) www.madagascarmagazine.com. Latest news in economics, commerce, culture and tourism.

New Magazine Madagascar (monthly; in French) www.newmagazine.mg. Malagasy music, fashion, art and events.

Enjeux (monthly; in French) email: enjeux@netclub.mg. Business, tourism and economic analysis.

Revue de l'Océan Indien (monthly; in French) www.madatours.com/roi/. News and features from the Madagascar region.

GOTO Madagascar Magazine (quarterly; in English and French) www.go2mada.com. Glossy tourism magazine. Not available by subscription but free copies can be picked up at their office (*5 Rue Raveloary, Isoraka, Antananarivo*); back issues online at www.goto-magazine.com.

MALAGASY PRESS

Madagascar Tribune (daily in French) www.madagascar-tribune.com
Midi Madagasikara (daily in French and Malagasy) www.midi-madagasikara.mg
L'Express (daily in French and Malagasy) www.lexpressmada.com
La Gazette de la Grande Ile (daily in French and Malagasy) www.lagazette-dgi.com
Dans les Média Demain (weekly in French) www.dmd.mg

USEFUL ADDRESSES
Conservation bodies

Association Nationale de Gestion des Aires Protégées (ANGAP) BP 1424, Antananarivo; ✆ 22 415 54/415 38; e angap@dts.mg. Contact: Mme Chantal Andrianarivo.

Marine conservation
Central

Office National de l'Environnement (Marine & Coastal Unit) BP 822, Antananarivo; ✆ 22 556 24/552 76; e one@pnae.mg. Contact: Mme Haja Razafindrainibe.

Centre National de Recherche Environnementale (CNRE) Coastal Management Unit BP 1739, Antananarivo; ✆ 22 630 27; e cnre@dts.mg. Contacts: Dr Jean Maharavo; Prof Germain Refeno. **WWF-Madagascar Marine Programme** BP 738, Antananarivo; ✆ 22 348 85;

e wwfrep@dts.mg. Contact: Dr Rémi Ratsimbazafy. **Wildlife Conservation Society (WCS)** Marine Programme BP 8500, Antananarivo; ✆ 22 528 79; e wcsmad@dts.mg. Contact: Mr Herilala Randriamahazo.

Regional

Institut Halieutique et des Sciences Marines (IHSM) BP 141, Toliara; ✆ 94 435 52; e ihsm@syfed.refer.mg. Contact: Dr Man Wai Rabevenana.

Centre National de Recherche Océanographique (CNRO) Hell-Ville, Nosy Be. Contact: The Director.

USEFUL WEBSITES
General
www.madagascar-contacts.com – information on hotels, tour operators etc.
www.airmadagascar.mg – information from Air Madagascar.
www.madonline.com – chat and general information.
www.fco.gov.uk – British Foreign Office advice on travel safety.
www.anglo-malagasysociety.co.uk – Anglo-Malagasy Society.
www.unusualdestination.com – tour specialists based in South Africa.
www.malagasyworld.org – interactive Malagasy dictionary.
https://www.cia.gov/cia/publications/factbook/geos/ma.html – CIA Factbook.
www.madagascar.gov.mg – Malagasy government.
www.tim-madagascar.net – President Marc Ravalomanana's TIM party.
www.madagascar-library-com – Detailed catalogue of books and articles on Madagascar.
www.wildmadagascar.org – Madagascar's wildlife, parks, people and history by Rhett Butler; many photos.

Natural history
www.savethelemur.com – Madagascar Fauna Group.
www.panda.org – World Wide Fund for Nature.
www.conservation.org – Conservation International.
www.parcs-madagascar.com – ANGAP/National Parks Madagascar.
www.masoala.org – Masoala National Park.
www.marojejy.com – Marojejy National Park inc Anjanaharibe-Sud Reserve.
www.wemc.org.uk – World Conservation Monitoring Centre.
www.duke.edu/web/primate – Duke University Primate Center.
www.masoala.ch – Zoo Zürich's Masoala project.
www.durrellwildlife.org – Durrell Wildlife Conservation Trust/Jersey Zoo.
www.rbgkew.org.uk/scihort/madagascar/ – Madagascar Science Team at Royal Botanic Gardens, Kew

Index

CLAIM YOUR HALF-PRICE BRADT GUIDE!

Order Form

To order your half-price copy of a Bradt guide, and to enter our prize draw to win £100 (see overleaf), please fill in the order form below, complete the questionnaire overleaf, and send it to Bradt Travel Guides by post, fax or email.

Please send me one copy of the following guide at half the UK retail price

Title	Retail price	Half price
...	...	...

Please send the following additional guides at full UK retail price

No	Title	Retail price	Total
...	...	...	...
...	...	...	...
...	...	...	...

Sub total ......
Post & packing ......
(£1 per book UK; £2 per book Europe; £3 per book rest of world)
Total ......

Name ....

Address...

Tel .... Email ....

☐ I enclose a cheque for £........ made payable to Bradt Travel Guides Ltd

☐ I would like to pay by credit card. Number: ....

Expiry date: ... / ...   3-digit security code (on reverse of card) .....

☐ Please add my name to your catalogue mailing list.

☐ I would be happy for you to use my name and comments in Bradt marketing material.

Send your order on this form, with the completed questionnaire, to:

Bradt Travel Guides/MAD9
23 High Street, Chalfont St Peter, Bucks SL9 9QE
☏ +44 (0)1753 893444   f +44 (0)1753 892333
e info@bradtguides.com   www.bradtguides.com

WIN £100 CASH!
READER QUESTIONNAIRE

**Send in your completed questionnaire for the chance to win
£100 cash in our regular draw**

All respondents may order a Bradt guide at half the UK retail price – please
complete the order form overleaf.

(Entries may be posted or faxed to us, or scanned and emailed.)

We are interested in getting feedback from our readers to help us plan future Bradt
guides. Please answer ALL the questions below and return the form to us in order
to qualify for an entry in our regular draw.

Have you used any other Bradt guides? If so, which titles? . . . .
. . . .

What other publishers' travel guides do you use regularly? . . . .
. . . .

Where did you buy this guidebook? . . . .

What was the main purpose of your trip to Madagascar (or for what other reason
did you read our guide)? eg: holiday/business/charity etc. . . . .
. . . .

What other destinations would you like to see covered by a Bradt guide?
. . . .

Would you like to receive our catalogue/newsletters?

YES / NO (If yes, please complete details on reverse)

If yes – by post or email? . . . .

Age (circle relevant category) 16–25   26–45   46–60   60+

Male/Female (delete as appropriate)

Home country . . . .

Please send us any comments about our guide to Madagascar or other Bradt Travel
Guides. . . . .
. . . .
. . . .
. . .

D0009325

vel Guides
t Peter, Bucks SL9 9QE, UK
44 f +44 (0)1753 892333
adtguides.com
ltguides.com